Thomas Campbell

THE POETICAL WORKS OF THOMAS CAMPBELL.

WITH A MEMOIR.

BOSTON:
LITTLE, BROWN, AND COMPANY.
1866.

ADVERTISEMENT.

THIS edition of Campbell's Poems is printed from the London edition of 1851. The Biographical Sketch of the Poet, and the notes which stand at the end of several of the pieces, relating to the circumstances of their composition and the success they met with, are by the Rev. W. A. Hill, who is connected with Campbell's family by marriage with his niece. It is proper to remark that the Memoir has been slightly, and the Notes considerably abridged, and that some of the notes of the London edition have been omitted.

It has not been thought advisable to reprint in this volume pieces which the Author deliberately rejected. A single exception has been made in the case of the "Dirge of Wallace," which is given in an Appendix for the sake of one energetic stanza. C.

CONTENTS.

BIOGRAPHICAL SKETCH

OF

THOMAS CAMPBELL.

* "I SIT down to take a retrospect of my life. Why should the task make me sad? Have I not many blessings and many friends? Yes! thanks to God, very many. But life, when we look back upon it, has also many painful recollections; and pain, when viewed either as past or to come, makes a deeper impression on the imagination than either the past pleasures or comforts of life that can be recalled. In the remembrance of our lives we are like unfair tradesmen, who omit a part of their debts in their balance of accounts. We resign ourselves to forget—myriads of the easy, tranquil, or even pleasing though anxious hours of our being; but for an hour of pain we make a large charge in our estimate of compared misery and happiness. I do not think that it is a fair argument to urge against individual-comparative happiness, that because most of us, if the question were put—Would you wish to spend your life over again?—would probably say—No,

* Retrospect of life, written by himself.

I thank you; I have had enough of it. This is just as if you were to ask me, after I had finished a narrative book that had much amused me — How should you like to read it over again? Why, possibly, unless the book were Robinson Crusoe, I should say — No, I cannot now read the book with the same curiosity as before. Even so it is with life. Its evils are sweetened by hope, novelty, and curiosity. How can we imagine ourselves animated by these feelings a second time, if we were to enter on a second existence? But why, it may be asked, if the retrospect of life be in the least sad, should I set down to the task of noting its memoranda? Why, unimportant as I am, I know that some account of me will be written. Dr. Beattie has even volunteered to be my biographer. He is likely to survive me by fifteen years, and a better biographer I could not find, except that he would be too laudatory. I know not, however, what business Dr. Beattie may have on his hands at the time when it may please God to call me away, and to leave my friend to grope his way through letters collected from my correspondents, or through confused memoranda of my own writing, would be but a sorry bequest to my best of friends.

"I shall leave to you, therefore, my dear niece,* a series of the recollections of my life, as distinctly connected as I can make them, and he and you, after my death, may make what use of them you think most proper.

"I was born, as our family Bible states (for this is none of my own recollection), in Glasgow on the 27th of July, 1777, at 7 o'clock in the

* Mary Campbell, now Mrs. W. Alfred Hill.

morning. The house which my father and his family inhabited then, and for fourteen years afterwards, was in the High Street of Glasgow, a little above, and on the opposite side of the Havannah Street, but was pulled down to open a new street crossing the High Street between the new grammar-school and the road east of the Gallowgate, so that the house and room in which I was born is not now an earthly locality, but a place in the empty air, emblematic, perhaps, of my future memory.

"I have uncommonly early recollections of life; I remember, that is to say, I seem to remember, many circumstances which I was told had occurred when I could not have been quite three years old.

"In very early years I was boarded, during the summer, in the country near Glasgow, at Pollock Shaws, in the humble house of a stocking-weaver, John Stewart, whose wife Janet was as kind to me as my own mother could be.

"During the winter, in those infantine years, I returned to my father's house, and my youngest sister taught me reading. My reading, of course, was principally in the Bible, and I contracted a liking for the Old Testament which has never left me. The recollection of this period makes an exception to the general retrospect of my life, making me *somewhat* sad. I was then the happiest of young human animals, at least, during the months which I spent under the roof of John and Janet Stewart. It is true I slept on a bed of chaff, and my fare, as may be supposed, was not sumptuous, but life was young within me. Pollock Shaws was at that time rural and delightful. The stocking-weaver's house was on a flat piece of ground, half circularly inclosed by a small running stream, called by the Scotch, a 'burn. On one side above it were ascending fields which terminated in trees along the high road to Glasgow. I remember no picture by Claude that ever threw me into such dreams of delight as this landscape. I remember leaping over the tallest yellow weeds with ecstasy. I remember seeing beautiful weed-flowers on the opposite side of the burn which I could not approach to pull, and wishing in my very soul to get at them, still I could not cross the burn. There were trouts, too, in the stream, and what a glorious event was the catching a trout. I was happy, however. Once only in my life perfectly happy.

"At eight years old I went to the grammar-school of Glasgow, where, among seventy other boys, I was the pupil of David Alison. He was a severe disciplinarian of the old school, and might be compared to Gil Blas's master, '*who was the most expert flogger in all Oviedo.*' But I was one of his pet scholars, and he told my father that he often spared me, when he ought to have whipt me, because I looked so innocent. He was a noble-looking man. At the periodical examinations by the magistrates, he looked a prince in comparison even with the Provost with his golden chain. And he

> "'Was kind, or if severe in aught,
> The love he bore to learning was in fault.'

" So that he was popular even among his whippees. I was so early devoted to poetry, that at ten years old, when our master interpreted to us the first Eclogue of Virgil, I was literally thrilled by its beauty. Already we had read bits of Ovid, but *he* never affected me half so much as the apostrophe of Tityrus to his cottage, from which he had been driven:—

> "'En unquam patrios longo post tempore fines
> Pauperis et tuguri congestum cespite culmen
> Post aliquot, mea regna videns, mirabor aristas.'

"David Alison was, I believe, a very good teacher of Latin, and he attended more to prosody than his predecessors are said to have done. At the same time the whole mode of tuition was barbarous and inefficient. Some seventy boys in each of the four classes were confined in their class rooms, for two hours at a stretch, three times in a day. Out of the seventy, I believe that scarcely seven acquired, during four years, more Latin than a boy of ordinary capacity might have been taught, by proper management, in one year. There was a general and pretty noisy murmur in the room. When the seven who could say their lessons had been heard, they were, instead of being set at liberty, confined till the sixty-three dunces were examined in divisions, and whipped in a geometrical scale of descent, and loud were the screeches of those who suffered from the leathern thong. I understand that there is now a fifth class, and a rector in the grammar-school of Glasgow;—that it has even a professor of elocution attached to it, and that great improvement has taken place.

"In my thirteenth year, I went to the University of Glasgow, and put on the red gown. The joy of the occasion made me unable to eat my breakfast. I am told that race-horses, on the morning of the day when they know they are to be brought to the race, are so agitated that they refuse their oats. Whether it was presentiment, or the mere castle-building of my vanity, I had even then a day-dream that I should be one day Lord Rector of the University. In my own lifetime, Lord Jeffrey and myself have been the only two Rectors who were educated at Glasgow.

"The Professor of Latin in Glasgow University at that time was William Richardson, somewhat known among our little known poets, and author of a tragedy called 'The Indians.' He was a gentlemanlike man, though rather mincing and fribbling in his gait and manner, and a thorough-paced Tory slave, in what he called his principles,—a mere creature of the Duke of Montrose. Yet he was a very fair teacher, and I ought to remember him with gratitude, for he encouraged and gave me the distinction of a prize for my earliest attempts in poetical translation."

Here the MS., contained in Campbell's handwriting, which is believed to have been writen in 1842, breaks off, and recommences at another part of his biography.

The editor requests the reader, *in limine*, to glance for a moment at the history of the Poet's family, which may be traced for many generations.

From documentary evidence and records of the presbytery of Inverary, it appears that this "branch of the Campbell's" were long settled in that part of the Argyle frontier, which lies between Lochawe and Lochfyne, bordered by the ducal territory of Inverary.

Archibald, Lord and Knight of Lochawe, was grandson of Sir Neil, chief of the clan, and a contemporary of King Robert Bruce.

This Archibald died A. D. 1360, leaving issue three sons, Tavis, ancestor of Dunardrie, and Iver, from whom sprang the *Campbells of Kirnan*, the distinctive name of Iver's descendants, who, during the lapse of many generations, became identified with the place as lairds and heritors of Kirnan; a race who could show their descent as far back as Gilèspic-le-Camile, first Norman lord of Lochawe. The poet's grandfather, Archibald Campbell, was the last of the name who resided on the family estate. When past his prime, he contracted marriage with Margaret Stuart, daughter of Stuart of Ascog, in the island of Bute, then the widow of John M'Arthur of Milton.

From this union sprung three sons, Robert, Archibald, and Alexander. On the decease of the father, who died in the Canongate of Edinburgh, Robert Campbell, the eldest son, appears to have taken possession of the family estate at Kirnan; but, after a time, through the exercise of lavish Highland hospitality, a love of military display, and the expenses incidental to a large establishment, liabilities were incurred. The estate was sold, and became annexed to the estate of Milton, the proprietor of which was John M'Arthur, his half-brother, son of Mrs. Campbell by her first marriage. Robert died in London, after a chequered career, as a political writer, under the Walpole administration. Archibald, the next brother, was a D.D. of Edinburgh, and after officiating as a Presbyterian minister in Jamaica for some years, finally settled abroad in the State of Virginia, in America, where he and his family became people of high repute and importance; and in after time his grandson, Frederick Campbell, through failure of intermediate heirs, succeeded, under an entail executed in 1763, to the estates of Whitebarony, in Peebleshire, Ascog in Bute, and Kilfinnan and Kirnan in Argyleshire. The youngest brother, Alexander Campbell (father of the poet), was born in 1710, and was educated with a view to commerce. In the early part of his life he resided at Falmouth, in Virginia, where, after making a fair start, he entered into copartnership with Daniel Campbell, and in his company returned to Scotland, and commenced business in the Virginian trade, at Glasgow, under the firm of "Alexander and Daniel Campbell." For nearly forty years success crowned the exertions of the firm; it rapidly advanced in commercial importance, and bid fair to distance the first houses in the trade.

The differences which had long subsisted between Great Britain, the mother country, and her American colonies, and which in the year 1775 ripened into open war, and at last resulted in the declaration of independence on the part of the States, had, for some time before the actual outbreak, operated strongly against the mercantile interest; but the baneful effect of the unnatural contest was most severely felt in the northern ports particularly in Glasgow. There, firms of vast resources and credit, one by one gave way, under the united pressure of stagnation in trade, and what is so well understood on change, by the term tightness of the money market. Campbell & Co. suffered severely; and at length as the cloud still hung dark over their future prospects, the partners resolved on a dissolution, and general wind-up.

The resolution, having been deliberately determined upon, was carried out with a firmness worthy of imitation and a better fate; and at length, every claim and liability having been first liquidated, the firm ceased to exist.

Mr. A. Campbell retired into privacy with a shattered income, yet competent to enable him to maintain his family in comfort and respectability, and obtain for them a liberal education; and to this important object all the remaining energies of a matured and cultivated intellect were directed. It was fortunate that the care of a numerous family restrained him from brooding over his losses, that a something sufficiently powerful as to engage his mind still existed; he had always been used to an active life, and the dangerous tendencies of want of occupation and overwhelming misfortunes can be far better imagined than described. Mr. Campbell at this period was sixty-five years of age, strong, hale, and hearty, and, aided by the consolation of religion, even resigned to his fate; his family circle consisted of a wife and ten children, the eldest of whom had not then completed her nineteenth year; labouring then with the sad memory of the past, and the doubtful prospect of his own and his children's future welfare, for ten years he spared no pains to perform his duty as a father, and complete to the full that social contract, which should ever be felt an imperative and mutual duty upon parent and offspring.

Thus the autumn of life glided onwards, but soon came winter, stern and rugged, for a fresh misfortune befell him,—an adverse judgment in a chancery suit: now his cup of misery was filled to overflowing, and in drinking it to the dregs the old man's heart was crushed; by little and little the fearful reality became too apparent that the costs and legal expenses entailed by the failure of the cause would leave but a wretched pittance for the support of his family; gradually he became unequal to mental exertion,—an iron constitution carried him on for some years, yet he could scarcely be said to live, and at length he breathed his last at Edinburgh, in the month of March, 1801, falling to the earth as a shock of corn fully ripe, having reached the patriarchal age of ninety-one years, and dying respected and beloved by all who knew him.

Thomas Campbell, as before mentioned, was born at Glasgow the 27th of July, 1777, being the eighth son, and the youngest of eleven children. His appearance in life was made two years after his father's retirement from business, and blighted as were family prospects through undeserved misfortunes, yet both Mr. and Mrs. Campbell found comfort and solace in their youngest boy. One by one the elder ones went forth to seek their fortunes in the world; and as the number round the domestic hearth lessened, the last comer seemed almost as of right to be entitled to a warmer corner, and if possible to a more jealous affection. His form has been described as fragile and his constitution delicate, with a pale expressive countenance, and a gentleness of manner which gained insensibly on the beholder. Very early his parents expressed the belief that genius sparkled in his eye, and consequently they lost no opportunity of improving by care and cultivation their discovery. Mrs. Margaret Campbell, his mother, had a strong taste for music, and from her he imbibed a fondness for the ballad poetry of Scotland, which never abandoned him; that lady, even in the wane of life, loved to sing the favourite melodies of her youth, and thus, her last born, from his cradle became skilled in sweet sounds and the power of flowing numbers.

Until his eighth year he was grounded in his "rudiments" at home, when (as mentioned in his own reminiscences) he was confided to the care of David Alison, who appears to have been a ripe scholar and a skilful tutor; under his eye Campbell showed "he was no vulgar boy;" the learned scholiast's experience and insight into character enabled him to see the course to be adopted; he fathomed the child's sensitive disposition; "he saw he was alive to praise, and readily daunted even by a look of sternness,"—the fruits of cultivation soon followed: he succeeded in obtaining the post of honour at the head of his little class,—all parties were pleased,—the master commended his pupil,—the prizes, taken home, commended him to his parents; and the feeling of having done his duty and deserved commendation, to some extent, even then, brought its own reward.

Each day increased his ardour and strengthened his exertions, but this precocity produced physical debility; his constitution, naturally delicate, suffered under study and sedentary habits, a serious illness followed, from which he recovered so tardily that change of scene and total vacuity from every thing like mental toil was deemed imperatively necessary. Accordingly a spot (supposed to be the place already alluded to under the name of Pollock Shaws) was selected, where he was left to roam in green fields, taste the pure country air, and pick flowers. In a very few weeks the change worked wonders, and on his return home he seemed altogether another creature; his countenance was radiant with health and beauty, and to the latest period of his life, he was wont to refer with pleasure to the happiness he then enjoyed.

These halcyon days of freedom and tranquillity brought, in addition to renewed health, other advantages. Nature, viewed in all her loveliness, under a summer sun, aroused his mind to beauties previously unknown; from this moment he awoke to poetry, and his very first attempt at verse was written upon the beauties of nature, in a "Poem on the Seasons."

> "Oh joyful spring, thy cheerful days prolong
> (The feathered songsters thus begin the song)
> Lo! smiling May doth now return at last,
> But ah! she runs along *too fast.*
> The sultry June arrives, May's pleasure 's short;
> Yet July yields some fruit for cool resort.
> Blest Autumn comes, arrayed in golden grain,
> And bounteously rewards the labouring swain," &c.

On returning to the grammar-school in September, he recommenced study with readiness, and made such rapid progress that, before he had completed his twelfth year, he had read through various Greek and Latin authors and poets, and could recite at length many of their most brilliant passages.

Now appeared the first dawn of that enthusiasm which strongly developed itself in after years on the subject of Greek poetry; he exhibited so much feeling to be well thought of in this department of literature, that it has been remarked by his intimate friends that Campbell's ambition was not so much to be esteemed a genuine poet as a ripe Greek scholar; and so skilful was he in Greek translations rendered into English verse, that, prior to the close of his scholastic career, he had not only gained popularity among his companions, encomiums oftentimes repeated from his master, but several prizes at the public examination of the School by the Chief Magistrate.*

The University of Glasgow differs from Oxford and Cambridge, particularly in this respect that it has, from the time of its foundation (shortly before the Reformation), received students at a very early age, and thus it happened that Campbell commenced his preparation for college life before he had completed his thirteenth year. With the prospect of matriculation at hand, for months previous to the actual commencement of the October session he was engaged in a reperusal of his "old books," feeling a laudable desire to be prepared for "a fair start" with the freshmen of his year. Mr. Alison prophesied distinction, his family expected great things, and he determined to aim high, and realize, if possible, their fondest hopes. This may seem far-fetched in speaking of a mere child, yet it will be remembered that his mind was cast in no ordinary mould, and his zeal much heightened by early successes.

In the October term of 1791 commenced his novitiate at college, and here the effect of judicious training at school quickly manifested itself. Before many months had elapsed he had gained a position in the Latin, Greek, and Logic classes, and, before he had completed his fourteenth year, had gained from the college authorities a prize for English and Latin verse, and a still more substantial mark of approbation, a bursary or exhibition on Archbishop Leighton's foundation. This boon was not awarded without reference to merit and ability, or upon the ground of the known straitened

* See specimens of translations from Anacreon at the age of twelve years, "Beattie's Life and Letters of Campbell," vol. i. p. 36.

circumstances of his parents, but was fairly won after an examination before the whole faculty in construing and Latin writing, and after competition with a fellow student by several years his senior. The result of the first session was satisfactory, yet in after years he often confessed that he was much more inclined to sport than to study, and it would seem that what he accomplished was not always the result of patient application to books, but rather of that natural facility which enabled him to see clearer than many of his fellow undergraduates, who trusted solely to unwearied attention for the chance of distinction. There can be no question that the colour of the remainder of his college career took its brightest tinge from the first essay, though he himself, with pleasing modesty, speaks in the following terms of his academical career:—"*Some* of my biographers have, in their friendly zeal, exaggerated my triumphs at the University. It is not true that I carried away all the prizes, for I was idle in some of the classes, and being obliged by my necessities to give elementary instruction to younger lads, my powers of attention were exhausted in teaching when I ought to have been learning." Yet the facts are in his favour; the repeated prizes awarded (many of them now in existence) speak for themselves, and show that he was not, in the ordinary acceptation of the word, idle; probably he placed his standard so high, that, failing in his own judgment to reach it, this induced dispraise and the self-imputation of idleness.

At this period his first ballad, entitled "Morven and Fillan," was printed for distribution and circulation amongst his friends and fellow-students: it comprised one hundred and forty lines, many of them both spirited and original. The following are the first four :—

"Loud breathed afar the angry sprite
That rode upon the storm of night,
And loud the waves were heard to roar,
That lashed on Morven's rocky shore."

Campbell's second year at the University (Sessions 1792 and 1793) was marked by fresh indications of progress. Professor Jardine, Lecturer in the Logic class, awarded him the eighth prize for the best composition on various subjects, the third prize in the Greek class for exemplary conduct, and further paid him the compliment of appointing him examiner of the exercises sent in by the members of the Logic class; but the crowning honour of the year was reserved for the last day of the session, the 1st of May, when his "Poem on Description" carried away the palm against a host of competitors. This production marks the progress he had made in versification since the previous autumn, and is entitled "A Description of the Distribution of Prizes in the Common Hall of the University of Glasgow, on the 1st of May, 1793,"—his motto was taken from Pope.

"Nor fame I slight, nor for her favour call,
She comes unlooked for, if she comes at all."

For some weeks after the commencement of the vacation, Campbell "tried his hand" at the law, and with a view of adopting it as a profession, was accommodated with a desk and seat in the office of his relative, Mr. Alexander Campbell, writer to the Signet of Glasgow. Here, according to the approved fashion and custom of that day (happily, now in a great measure exploded), he commenced the study of jurisprudence,—not by learning principles, but groping in the dark at the practice of the profession by transcribing "drafts, deeds, abbreviating pleadings," and the like drudgery.

This mysterious method of penetrating the arcana of an honourable and scientific calling, operated so prejudicially that before autumn he gave up all thoughts of advancing his fortunes by the avenue of the law, and, therefore, relinquishing his seat in the office, directed his mind to more congenial pursuits—poetry, classical reading, and preparation for the ensuing college term.

Among the miscellaneous pieces struck off in the course of the autumn was a *brochure* suggested by the enormities of the French Revolution—the subject being the cruelties inflicted on the ill-fated Marie Antoinette, Queen of France. This effusion excited the sympathy of many who read it, and was deemed worth insertion in the "Poet's Corner" of the leading journal of Glasgow.

In the course of his third year at the University (1793–4), in addition to a debating society into which Campbell had been previously enrolled, whereat he was a popular orator, and to which belonged nearly all his principal contemporaries, there was another, called the "Discursive," of which he himself has thus written: "There was, moreover, a debating society, called the Discursive, composed almost entirely of boys as young as myself, and I was infatuated enough to become a leader in this spouting club. It is true, that we had promising spirits among us, and, in particular, could boast of Gregory Watt, son of the immortal Watt, a youth unparalleled in his early talent for eloquence. With melodious elocution, great acuteness in argument, and rich unfailing fluency of diction, he seemed born to become a great orator, and I have no doubt would have shone in Parliament, had he not been carried off by consumption in his five-and-twentieth year. He was literally the most beautiful youth I ever saw. When he was only twenty-two, an eminent English artist (Howard, I think) made his head the model of a picture of Adam. But though we had this splendid stripling, and other members that were not untalented, we had no head among us old and judicious enough to make the society a proper *palæstra* for our mental powers, and it degenerated into a place of general quizzing and eccentricity."

In the spring of 1794, Campbell, in consideration of good conduct, obtained a few days' leave of absence from his "Alma Mater," and visited Edinburgh to witness the trial of Joseph Gerrald and others (the Scottish Reformers) charged with the crime of sedition. To him, all the proceedings were novel: it was his first visit to the Parliament House, and the scene he there beheld made so powerful an impression upon his mind, that the lapse of years could not efface its vivid recollection. Various circumstances conspired to produce this: intense political excitement reigned at the time, crowds thronged the court, the bearing of the prisoners was touching; Gerrald's demeanour, in particular, was very bold and determined; his appeal to the court and jury was eloquent; and when the case terminated with the conviction of the accused and their sentence to transportation, he left the court all glowing in the cause of freedom, and full of sympathy with those he deemed oppressed. With feelings wrought to the highest pitch, he returned to college a graver, if not a wiser, youth—determined to devote all his powers to the pursuit of learning, in order to aid the better in the emancipation of his family from their impoverished condition. Hitherto he had been one of "the gayest of the gay," in vacation-time, and had joined, with that ardour which is usually the companion of sanguine temperaments, in the sports and amusements of youth. Now, these were at once and for ever laid aside,—his characteristic wit and sprightliness for a time seemed gone, and, in their place, appeared the gravity and subdued bearing of "a reverend senior." He read with avidity the newspapers, and particularly the journals supposed to have a liberal bias; in fact many of the works he greedily perused had been previously unheard of and unknown to him. At the debating society, he commented in glowing language upon the "animus" which pervaded the political trials of the day, pased severe strictures on the corrupt state of modern legislation, sighed over the departed glories of Athens and Sparta, and, in private, appeared as though he had sustained some severe personal wrong which he could not forgive without some manifestation of feeling or retaliation. Raillery in plenty he met with; yet this he bore with the heroism of a martyr; and it was, at last, Time alone that healed the wound, and enabled him to dismount from his stilts and recover his composure.

At the termination of the third session, he came in again for honours. In the Moral Philosophy class he received a prize for his poetical essay on the Origin of Evil. In the Greek class he gained the first prize for the best translation of passages from the Clouds of Aristophanes. In reference to these pleasing incidents he has left the following:—"Professor Young pronounced my version, in his opinion, the best essay that had ever been given in by any student at the University." This was no small praise to a boy of fifteen, from John Young, who, with the exception of Miller, was the ablest man in the college.

One day, shortly before the close of this session, while Professor Arthur, of the Moral Philosophy Chair, was showing the University to an English gentleman, who had come into the class-room, the poet says,—"I happened to be standing unobserved behind him, and could hear distinctly the conversation that passed between them. 'And is there any one among your students,' inquired the stranger, 'who shows a talent for poetry?' 'Yes,' said the Professor, 'there is one, Campbell, who shows a very promising talent.' Little knew the Professor that I was listening to this question and answer. In explanation of this 'talent,' I had written in Arthur's class a verse essay on the Origin of Evil, for which I afterwards received the prize, and which gave me a local celebrity throughout all Glasgow, from the High Church down to the bottom of the Salt-market! It was even talked of, as I am credibly informed, by the students over their oysters at Lucky M'Alpine's, in the Trongate!"

At this period, in addition to Campbell's labours on his own account, were added those of tuition; for thus early he was employed, on the recommendation of some of the college authorities, as private tutor to several of his fellow-students.

From the period of gaining the last-mentioned prizes may be dated constantly increasing manifestations of esteem and good-will from the " Professors " and his fellow-students. By the latter his talents had been already appreciated. Now the high opinion entertained by them was more openly acknowledged; his opinion was asked on difficult and abstruse readings, his style of composition imitated, and *envy*, if she existed at all in the breasts of any of his contemporaries, seemed disarmed of her string; his sympathies were heart and soul with his companions, and there was lavished upon him all the warmth and affection of generous hearts unscathed by misfortunes, in no degree hardened by contact with the world.

At this time he believed (and he luxuriated in the thought) that all difficulties could be surmounted by industry and perseverance; and strong in this reliance he directed his mind to the study of the Old Testament in the original Hebrew, and to the works of the best commentators and writers on ecclesiastical history, experiencing then a desire to make the Church his future calling. One of the first results of this theological train of thought was his well-known " Hymn on the Advent of Christ," which may be found in most compilations of sacred poetry. Yet at this time he was fully alive to the low ebb of his family fortunes; that Kirnan, " the home of his forefathers," was " roofless and wild; " and further, that without interest, preferment in the clerical profession might be very tardy in rewarding labours, though undertaken with the purest motives. This, and no foolish vacillation or love for change, compelled him to watch events, and endeavour to strike out a path not merely congenial to his wishes, but capable of affording a sufficiency for the supply of his necessary wants.

About this time he went so far as to attend certain medical lectures, but unfortunately being too hastily introduced into the operating room, and there witnessing a succession of "casualties," amputations, and the thousand other "ills that flesh is heir to," he contracted so strong a repugnance to surgical "operations," that he could not bring his mind to renew his visits either to the demonstrator's apartment, or the wards of the hospital.

In the session of 1794 and 1795 (his fourth year at college), honours still attended him, yet his brightest hours were haunted by the knowledge that his father's slender income had become still more limited by the failure of the chancery suit. Young as Campbell was, he determined to make some effort to smooth the declining days of his venerable sire. He therefore eagerly sought for something which might aid in this labour of love; and through the patronage of the College Professors, willingly exercised, he became tutor to the children of Mrs. Campbell, of Sunipol, in the Hebrides (a distant relative), from the month of May to the ensuing October, when it was arranged that he should return home, and resume his academic studies.

Preliminaries having been settled he started (on the 18th of May, 1795) with his friend and class-fellow the late Rev. Joseph Finlayson, D. D.) who was about to pass the vacation in the same mode as himself. The young travellers took the road to Inverary, and after a journey full of incident, the wild shores of Mull broke upon their sight. At first Campbell acutely felt the loneliness of his situation, but soon became reconciled, for the country, though bleak and wild, was peculiarly romantic, and nourished the poetry in his soul.

In the autumn he returned to Glasgow, with a mind enlarged by the realization of objects at that time little visited. Staffa and Icolmkill, and the venerable ruins of Iona, these and other wonders filled his mind with sensations hitherto unknown. The return journey occupied himself and friend (Finlayson), four days, and was performed in bad weather. Between Oban and Lochawe Side the travellers were benighted, and losing their way, were forced to bivouac for the night on the lee-side of a bare wall, without any other covering than their Highland plaids.

In Campbell's fifth and last session at College (1795 and 1796) it was his good fortune, in addition to the pecuniary emolument realized by tuition, to gain two prize poems, one for the Choephoræ of Æschylus, and the other for a Chorus in the Medea of Euripides. Among his pupils at this time was one of the present Lords of Session, Lord Cuninghame, of whom the poet has left the following reminiscence: — "After my return from Mull, I supported myself during the winter by private tuition. Among other scholars, I had a youth named Cuninghame, who is now Lord Cuninghame, in the Justiciary Court of Edinburgh. Grave as he is now, he was, when I taught him Xenophon and Lucian, a fine, laughing, open-hearted boy, and so near my own age, that we were rather like playfellows than preceptor and pupil. Sometimes, indeed, I used to belabour him — jocosely alleging my sacred duty as a tutor—but I seldom succeeded in suppressing his risibility."

During his last year at College, Campbell's

mind largely expanded, and in after years he referred with especial pleasure to the benefit he derived from the lectures of Professor Miller on the Roman Law, and his explanations of Heineccius.

At length, academic studies completed, days gilded by success and honours, the future broke in upon him dark and stern, and, compelled to act with promptitude, he entered General Napier's family as tutor to the present Sir William Napier, of Milliken, Argyleshire, where he continued until the end of March, 1797, when he re-visited Glasgow, carrying with him the respect and esteem of all with whom he had become acquainted. The General himself felt so strong an interest in his welfare that he expended much time and trouble to smooth the way for his going to the bar; but the want of the necessary pecuniary advances from his *protégé's* friends rendered his efforts abortive.

The disappointment occasioned by blighted hope was acutely felt; the apathy of family connections, who might have materially aided his onward progress, was "gall and wormwood;" many of his connections warmly applauded his talents, but any thing further than barren praise seemed quite foreign to their views; the effect of hope deferred was in this case truly to make the heart sick; a raging fever supervened; youth, however, befriended him—he slowly recovered, and happily his sufferings were productive of this beneficial result—they engendered calmness and resignation, and he was enabled at length to gaze upon the future, barren and cheerless as it was, with a steady eye. The next effort to better himself was a journey to Edinburgh, where he obtained an introduction to Dr. Robert Anderson, who, at first sight, pleased with his appearance and conversation, recognized a kindred spirit, soothed and cherished him, and in a few days recommended him as a young gentleman of great promise to Mr. Mundell, deceased, the publisher, who at once employed him to compile an abridgment of Bryan Edwards's West Indies; this he gladly accepted, and when the task was completed, other literary work was provided, yet the remuneration for this compilatory writing was so scanty as to do little more than provide the bare necessaries of life, and this compelled Campbell, against his inclination, to recommence teaching, and then he found his recommendations to Professor Dalzell of essential service, through whose assistance he obtained pupils, by whom he was remunerated upon a liberal scale.

In this way, for some time, he made a comfortable livelihood, but at last, as his pupils finished their course of study, he took no pains to recruit the vacancies in his class, but directed his mind (for he would be an author) to original composition. The subject he at length fixed upon was, "The Pleasures of Hope," a theme suggested in part at least by Rogers's "Pleasures of Memory," and in part, while melancholy and lonely on the wild shores of Mull, by his friend Mr. Hamilton Paul.

In writing of these early days, Campbell says, "And now I lived in the Scottish metropolis by instructing pupils in Greek and Latin. In this vocation I made a comfortable livelihood, as long as I was industrious. But 'The Pleasures of Hope' came over me. I took long walks about Arthur's Seat, conning over my own (as I thought them) magnificent lines; and as my 'Pleasures of Hope' got on, my pupils fell off. I was not friendless, nor quite solitary at this period in Edinburgh. My aunt, Mrs. Campbell, and her beautiful daughter Margaret—so beautiful that she was commonly called Mary, Queen of Scots—used to receive me kindly of an evening, whenever I called; and it was to them—and with no small encouragement—that I first recited my poem when it was finished."—"I had other friends also whose attachment was a solace to my life. Before I became known as an author, I was intimate with Francis Jeffrey, and with Thomas Brown, afterwards the successor of Dugald Stewart in the Moral Philosophy Chair of Edinburgh. I was also acquainted with Dr. Anderson, author of 'The Lives of the British Poets.'"

For a short time Campbell was absent from the Scottish metropolis, on a visit to Glasgow; on his return, having shown "The Pleasures of Hope" to some confidential friends, they suggested its immediate publication. But how? This was the question. At first it was proposed to publish by subscription, and the patronage of his own and the sister University of Edinburgh was promised; yet, after calculation of the probable expenses of printing and publishing, it seemed doubtful if the author would reap much substantial reward, and consequently he was advised to sell to the booksellers the copyright of his work.

With this in view, Dr. Anderson waited upon Mr. Mundell, (the only publisher with whom Campbell had, up to this time, realized any profitable connection,) and entered with him upon the merits of the Poem; and after the matter had been well weighed, considered, and reconsidered,

Mr. Mundell offered for the copyright, *Sixty Pounds*, which the author was fain to accept.

Some time before the work actually appeared, it was announced "in the press;" and both subject and author afforded matter for speculation and conversation in the literary world. Some parties had already seen the manuscript, or parts of it, and these all spoke in favour of the production, so that the writer found his circle of acquaintance daily extending. On the 27th of April, 1799, "The Pleasures of Hope" appeared for the first time, its author being at that time just twenty-one years and nine months old. It fully equalled the expectations previously formed of it; the topics worked out in realizing the subject were the very matters at the time before the public,—the great Revolution in France—the Partition of Poland—the question of the Abolition of Negro Slavery—all these the writer had by a plastic hand made completely his own. Few generous minds failed to experience delight on reading Campbell's glowing language and rich imagery.

Madame de Staël was one of the foremost of the eminent literary characters of the day, who expressed her admiration of this poem. Some time afterwards, she told Campbell that she had been so captivated with the episode (Conrad and Ellenore), that she could read it twenty times over without lessening the effect which the first perusal had awakened in her mind.* The addition

"*Stockholm, ce* 5 *Janvier*, 1813.

"Á M. THOMAS CAMPBELL.

"Pendant les dix années que m'ayent séparé de l'Angleterre, Monsieur, le Pöeme anglais qui m'a causé le plus d' émotion—la pöeme qui ne me quittait jamais—et que je relisai sans cesse pour adoucir mes chagrins par l'élévation de

of "The Pleasures of Hope" to British poesy soon became widely known, and few were the political réunions, on the liberal side at least, where some quotations were not made, from language which marked a generous heart and an ardent love of liberty.

Every line in this work is now as "familiar in our mouths as household words," yet it can be comprehended with what eagerness such strains as the following must have been caught up, and reëchoed throughout the length and breadth of the land:—

"Departed spirits of the mighty dead,
Ye that at Marathon and Leuctra bled,
Friends of the world! restore your swords to man,
Fight in his sacred cause, and lead the van."

In a second edition (which was speedily followed by several others) new passages were felicitously introduced, particularly one descriptive of the dissolution of the body, and the flight of the soul to its original source; these served to cement the more closely the fabric already erected. Some smaller poems, the "Harper," "Gilderoy," and others, meeting with a favourable reception from the public, inspired their author with fresh courage and energy.

Various shadowy castles now floated through the poet's brain, but the bent of his inclination, in the spring of the year 1800, led him to celebrate the achievements of Scotia's mighty dead, in her struggles for independence and liberty; the work

l'âme, c'est Les Plaisirs de l'Esperance. L'épisode d'Ellenore surtout, allait tellement à mon cœur que je pourrais la relire vingt fois, sans en affaiblir l'impression. . . . .
BARONNE DE STAEL, *Holstein.*"

was to have been called the "Queen of the North," and to enable him to collect *matériel*, he proposed making a personal visit to the Continent, for it was men as well as their writings he would converse with. Having arranged preliminaries, and being armed with letters of introduction to gentlemen eminent in various departments, he set sail for Leith, bound for Hamburg, on the 1st of June, 1800 (being accompanied to the vessel by Mr. Richardson, and his old pupil Mr. Cuninghame). After a protracted voyage of several days, he reached the port of Hamburg in safety, where he was received by the British residents with great kindness. In some instances fame had already preceded him ; in other cases his letters of introduction obtained all he desired. To his new friends he frankly stated the object of his visit, and acting upon their suggestions, he remained in the port of disembarcation for some time, in order to gain a more accurate knowledge of German, and a greater facility in its dialogue, than he had previously attained. At this period the fever of politics ran high both at home and abroad, and Campbell, dissuaded from prosecuting his original plan of visiting Gottingen, Jena, and Weimar, yielded to the counsel of those who advised him, on the expiration of his sojourn at Hamburg, to proceed to Ratisbon, place himself under the protection of the venerable President of the Scotch College (Arbuthnot), and there in freedom from interruption, having enjoyed facility for study, afterwards in security sail down the Danube to Vienna. After a stay of some nine or ten weeks, Campbell set out for Ratisbon, where he arrived three days only before it was taken by the French; happily for him he gained a sanctuary in time, and was, on his arrival, most kindly received by his compatriots—the monks of the Benedictine College, from whose walls he beheld sights of horror which nothing could obliterate from his recollection. His first introduction to the miseries of war was in company with his new acquaintances; from their hospice he beheld a charge of Klennan's cavalry upon the French under Grenier—he saw the fire given and returned, and heard distinctly the sound of the French *pas-de-charge* collecting the lines to attack in close column, then a park of artillery opened just beneath the walls of the monastery, and several drivers there stationed to convey the wounded in spring wagons, were killed in his sight. Campbell thus referred to the sad scene:—"This formed the most important epoch of my life in point of impressions, but these impressions of seeing numbers of men strewed dead on the field, or what was worse, seeing them in the act of dying, were so horrible to my memory, that I studied to banish them. At times, when I have been fevered and ill, I have awoke from nightmare, dreaming about these dreadful images."

Campbell was detained in Ratisbon longer than he anticipated, and these scenes of strife and bloodshed were by no means conducive to quiet and steady reading; his mind also was harassed by uncertainty concerning the future; great difficulty existed in keeping up a communication with Great Britain; two armies were present in the country; there was a probability of long protracted war. These things produced no small depression of spirits. Some absurb rumours also were afloat, that his visit to the Continent (made at such a crisis) was for a political purpose—in other words, he was suspected of being a spy: thus his state of suspense was increased by the fear that, even if war ceased, and the French dragoons were withdrawn, he might be detained a prisoner. These things, in combination, served to excite him and to induce great discomfort. At length, after many days of doubt, during which he was "cabined" within the walls of Ratisbon (though it seems he did avail himself of an armistice, and penetrate as far as Munich), he obtained his passports, and, in the month of November, *viâ* Leipsic, returned to Hamburg, whence he proceeded to Altona, and passed the winter in study and retirement. To the reading of Kant's Philosophy many successive weeks were devoted, varied, for the sake of relaxation, by the perusal of the works of Schiller, Wieland, and Bürger, and occasional pedestrian excursions into the neighbouring country. Here he composed or revised for publication fourteen small pieces, which appeared successively in the "Morning Chronicle;" of these, only four have been preserved amongst his printed poems. As the winter drew to a close, and while in actual correspondence with a friend, touching a grand tour through Hungary and Turkey, the real state of matters on the Continent appeared. In a moment the crisis came. Great Britain, fearing a strong coalition against her, took measures to prevent it; and, on the 12th of March, her fleet appeared in the Sound, ready for any demonstration. This arrival produced great excitement amongst the English residents at Altona, and was increased materially by the fact of the town being situate on the Danish shore. It required no prophet or herald to warn foreigners that Altona was no place of safety for them. Campbell himself convinced of the necessity of retiring from the scene, prepared to follow the example of such of the British subjects as were able to leave, and, accordingly, he secured a passage for Leith in a vessel called the Royal George. When the ship raised anchors and dropped down the river, she became an object of intense interest to many bystanders: some mourned that they had no homes to flee to; others felt deep uncertainty touching the events of a single day—whether famine, incarceration, or death. At the mouth of the Elbe, the Royal George was detained several days by adverse winds; and when, at last, they became favourable, much to the disappointment of the passengers, signal was given by the convoy to sail for Yarmouth Roads, instead of Leith, for the reason that most of the ships convoyed were English.

After a wearisome passage, and a narrow escape from a Danish privateer, who chased the ship almost into port, Campbell arrived at Yarmouth, and proceeded in the mail to London, where he was most cordially welcomed by Mr. Perry, of the "Morning Chronicle," who declared, warmly, "I will be your friend; I will be all that you could wish me to be!" And nobly did he fulfil his promise: he took his *protégé* by the hand, encouraged him, and circulated the news of his arrival; so that, in a few days, under the patronage of Lord Holland, he was at once introduced to some of the most eminent literary characters of the time.

On the poet's first *début* into London life, and within a fortnight after his arrival from the Continent, intelligence reached him, through Dr. Anderson, of the death of his father. This event, for a time, destroyed the will and the power of enjoying the brilliant society into which he had been received, and actuated by feelings of sympathy and affection, he promptly proceeded to Edinburgh to console and comfort his mother. He performed the journey by sea; and during the voyage, one of his fellow passengers, a lady, informed him "that the author of the 'Pleasures of Hope' had been arrested in London for high treason and sent to the Tower." Amazed at the suggestion of his treason, no sooner had he seen his mother, and comforted her to the best of his ability, than he found some enemy had been at work—there was truth in the alleged rumor of his treasonable practices. Desirous to refute the calumny as speedily as possible, on the day succeeding his arrival, he waited upon the sheriff of Edinburgh, who at once expressed regret at his presence, saying, "There is a warrant out against you for high treason. It seems that you have been conspiring with General Moreau in Austria, and with the Irish at Hamburg to get a French army landed in Ireland, but I know there is a general unwillingness among those in power to punish your error, so take my advice and do not press yourself on my notice." Campbell urged upon the sheriff the absurdity of his (a mere boy) conspiring against the British Empire, and demanded proofs, when it was urged, "Oh, you attended Jacobin clubs at Hamburg, and came over thence in the same vessel with Donovan, who commanded a regiment of the rebels at Vinegar Hill;" to this it was answered that he (Campbell) had never heard of Jacobin clubs at Hamburg, and as to the rebel Donovan he did not know of his being a fellow passenger, until he saw him on deck. On further examination, and reading the contents of papers found in the poet's trunk, which had been seized on its way from Yarmouth to Edinburgh, the sheriff began to see the groundlessness of the charge, and when he had read a copy of the "Mariners of England," found amongst the supposed treasonable papers, he said, "This comes of trusting to a Hamburg spy," and observing that the evening was cold and wet, he insisted upon Campbell remaining and partaking with him a bottle of wine, after which he dismissed him in high good humour. And thus, with a character honourably cleared, the young poet was restored to the good opinion of many who had been foolishly credulous in his guilt.

Campbell, on entering upon family prospects, found cause for great solicitude, yet he did not shrink from what he considered his duty to provide house and home for his mother and sisters; and with this praiseworthy object in view, he undertook some heavy literary task-works, the proceeds whereof he devoted entirely to their use.

In the autumn of this year (1801), Lord Minto, who had then recently returned from the Court of Vienna, where he had resided as British Envoy Extraordinary, invited him on a visit to Minto Castle. The invitation was accepted, and the result of the visit was so agreeable to both parties, that Campbell consented to take up his quarters for the ensuing season at his Lordship's mansion in Hanover Square.

On his arrival in the metropolis, all faces seemed to smile upon him. Cards of invitation from persons of the highest distinction were left for him, the world greeted him with its most seductive smile. Lords Minto and Holland vied with each other in their fostering care, and, as by the wave of a fairy wand, he was received into the best and most intellectual society of the whole world.

The season was passed in one continual whirl of excitement and gayety. His happiest moments were those which he passed in quiet conversation with Telford, Mrs. Siddons, and the Kembles, of whose notice and friendship he was most justly proud.

At length tired of dust, spangle, and the gayety of fashionable life, he hailed with delight the termination of the fashionable year, and the prospect of repose. He had been solicited to spend the summer at Minto, and, after some hesitation, accepted this renewed offer of hospitality, and in due course proceeded northwards with his lordship; but on reaching Newcastle, tidings arrived that the scarlet fever had appeared at the castle. This induced a postponement of the visit, and the poet betook himself to Edinburgh, where he passed some time in Alison Square, with his mother and sisters, occupied in preparing for press the poems of Lochiel and Hohenlinden (which soon afterwards appeared, dedicated to Mr. Alison, Prebendary of Salisbury). The autumn was chiefly spent at Minto, during which period he was engaged in revising the proofs of a new edition of his poems, writing articles in prose for booksellers (a labour, as he himself said, little superior to compilation, and more connected with profit than reputation), editing an edition of Greek tragedies, collecting materials for a continuation of Hume and Smollett's England, and thus the winter passed away.

In the month of February, 1802, he proceeded to Liverpool, and after a *détour* through the Staffordshire potteries (under the escort of Mr. Stevenson), he proceeded to London on a visit to his stanch friend, Mr. Thomas Telford, the celebrated engineer, who at that time occupied a suite of apartments at the Salopian Hotel, in Charing Cross, and felt much anxiety on behalf of his young friend, wishing to bind him to a sort of compact to act as he and Mr. Alison might suggest, not because he had any fear of his success in the literary world, but because he knew that he was but partially acquainted with business rules and habits, upon which human happiness and worldly success so greatly depend.

The *locale* of Charing Cross was uncongenial to Campbell's taste; the noise, dust, and crowd, made him sigh for a quiet, rural home; and his remarks and letters to his friends at the time, manifest that the gayeties of a London life were very far from consonant to his feelings. He complained of being unable to fix himself to any thing, having one eternal round of invitations to occupy him, having entered "a style of life which neither suited purse nor health, not one day free of headaches, nor one night of tolerable rest."

In the month of June, the first quarto edition of "The Pleasures of Hope," with illustrations, and accompanied by several new pieces of poetry, appeared, and was so eagerly sought after that, added to the incense of praise he received, his spirits became so elevated and buoyed up by faith in his old creed, that industry and perseverance could surmount all difficulties, he made up his mind to get married, and take a partner for life. He had long cherished feelings of regard for his cousin, Matilda Sinclair, daughter of Mr. Robert Sinclair, for many years a wealthy merchant, and first magistrate of Greenock, but who at this time, through severe losses, had contracted his sphere, and transferred his counting-house to Trinity Square, City, and his family to Park Street, Westminster. Here Campbell was allowed the *entrée*, and soon the old attachment ripened on both sides into an ardent flame. The young lady's hand was in due course solicited; he became an accepted suitor; a something was said about ways and means, for Mr. Sinclair candidly confessed he was unable to give any dowry. All difficulties, however, were made light of, scruples vanished, and the young couple were united in Hymen's bonds at St. Margaret's, Westminster, on the 10th of September, 1802, in the presence of Mr. Sinclair's family, and a party of friends.

At the expiration of the honeymoon, the bride and bridegroom returned to London, and took up their residence in apartments in Pimlico, which had been furnished and prepared for them by Mr. Sinclair.

For many months life seemed more and more sunny; literary employment poured in upon him, and he was honoured by the offer of the Regent's Chair in the Russian University of Wilna. His friends, the Lords Minto and Holland, and Mr. Dugald Stewart, thought this a favourable opportunity for his advancement, but Campbell, though at first relishing the proposition, and even going so far as to have an interview on the subject with the Russian minister, on second thoughts, and hearing stipulations, felt that he could not abandon liberal opinions cherished from early youth, and inculcate views totally foreign to them, without much mental torture and sacrifice of independence; therefore he respectfully declined the distinction: besides, in a pecuniary point of view, his prospects looked well; many of his articles appeared in the leading periodicals of the day, and though oftentimes anonymous, yet they afforded the means of living respectably, and thus he worked away on biographical notices of poets, statesmen, and philosophy, classics, and matters of general interest; not being idle, as many supposed, but working secretly, and oftentimes, from an over-fastidiousness, erasing in a moment the labours of an entire day.

On the 1st of July the poet became a father; the child was christened Thomas Telford, and his birth called forth feelings and language beautifully expressive of delight and tender affection. Soon after this event, his health and spirits suffered much through an awkward *contretemps* with Mr. Doig, the Scotch bookseller. The difficulty, however, was settled through friendly interference, yet the traces of harass and vexation remained behind, and change and country air was advised. After consultations with medical and other friends, Sydenham was selected as his future residence; and to this place, at Michaelmas (1804), the family removed, and were received with open arms by many of the principal residents in the neighbourhood; this became a sort of oasis in the desert,—here, to use Campbell's own language, "I contrived to support my mother, my wife, and children; life became tolerable to me, and even agreeable. I had always my town friends to come and partake of my humble fare of a Sunday; and among my neighbours, I had an elegant society among whom I counted sincere friends."

Yet with this domestic comfort, he had his moments of anxiety, especially as he was called upon to sustain alone the burden of supporting his mother and sisters. Up to this period he had shared the produce of his brain, his only farm, with his family; he had allowed his mother an annuity of 70*l.*, but now his eldest brother, resident in America, wrote to say, that the remittances he had for sometime made for his mother, must for the future cease on account of his own slender means. Who can feel surprise at a young man, thus situated, becoming nervous and agitated touching the future? Two establishments to provide for, provisions dear, war prices prevailing in every department,—to use Campbell's own words—"I had never known in earnest the fear of poverty before, but now it came upon me like a ruthless fiend. If I were sentenced to live my life over again, and had the power of supplicating adversity to spare me, I would say, oh! adversity take any other shape. To meet these pressing demands I obtained literary engagements both in prose and poetry, but a malady came over me which put all poetry, and even imaginative prose, out of the question. My anxiety to wake in the morning, in order to be at my literary labours, kept me awake all night, and from less to more I became a victim to the disease called coma vigil." At this time he received a "stab in the dark," in the shape of an anonymous letter from Glasgow, written in a female hand, purporting to emanate from a society called the "Glasgow Female Society," which upbraided him in bitter terms for neglect of a near relative, leaving that relative, as it declared, to poverty and distress. Possibly, it may be said, he was over-sensitive; yet it was hard, after great exertion and sacrifices, that his conduct should be totally misrepresented, and reproaches be heaped upon him. Time, however, healed them, and during the autumn we find him translating foreign correspondence, contributing to the "Philosophical Magazine," the "Star" newspaper,—attending daily in London,—subject at times to occasional fits of depression and fear, yet not without his sunny moments,—he had hopes of advancement, and was encouraged by persons of influence to believe that he would not be overlooked by a liberal ministry.

About this time the first idea of the "Specimens of the British Poets," suggested itself to his mind,—a work which it has been well said "established him on our library shelves as a prose writer, and is the test of his unrhymed, not unpoetical works."* He wrote to Sir Walter Scott on the subject, stating his plan, and proposing to divide both labour and profit. Sir Walter was highly pleased, and left him authority to arrange the details; but for a time the matter was broken off by a difference about terms with the booksellers.

In the month of June, 1805, his second son Alison was born. In the same year his circumstances were rendered more easy by a pension of 200*l.* per annum, conferred upon him by the Crown. Touching this mark of royal consideration, he left the following:—

"My pension was given to me under Charles Fox's administration. So many of my friends in power expressed a desire to see that favour conferred upon me, that I could never discover the precise individual to whom I was indebted for it. Lord Minto's interest I knew was not wanting; but I hope I may say, without ingratitude to

* This Work forms seven volumes in small 8vo. 1819.

others, that I believe Charles Fox and Lord Holland would have bestowed the boon without any other intervention." The use Campbell made of this addition to his income, was this—the one half he reserved for his own necessities, the other he generously divided between his mother and sisters.

Before the close of the year, the late Francis Horner, M. P., one of the poet's earliest friends, proposed to him to publish a new edition of his best poetical works by subscription, and volunteered his services in filling up the list. In writing shortly after he had obtained the poet's sanction, he said, "Very little exertion has been made, but we have got above 200*l.*, of which 60*l.* are from Oxford. I shall be very much disappointed if we do not put into the poet's purse more than 1000*l.*" The result was as anticipated, and with an easy mind and resources recruited, he went on his way rejoicing.

In the spring of 1806, Campbell met Mr. Fox at Lord Holland's at dinner; both were pleased with each other, and at parting, the premier said, "Mr. Campbell, you must come and see me at Saint Anne's Hill, and there we shall talk more about these matters," (referring to the heroic characters in Virgil, often much criticized as monotonous). Fox said privately in the ear of his nephew (Lord Holland), "I like Campbell, he is so right about Virgil;" and there can be no question that the poet was singularly happy at all times in his classical allusions, as Sidney Smith once said, after listening to some of his remarks, "What a vast field of literature that young man's mind has rolled over."

The poem of "Gertrude of Wyoming," which

had for some time divided Campbell's thoughts with other literary cares, was completed in the early part of 1809, and in March was shown to Mr. Alison and Lord Jeffrey, and was pronounced by them worthy of the writer's talent and acquired fame.

Lord Jeffrey, in writing to Campbell, said, "There is great beauty, and great tenderness and fancy in the work, and I am sure it will be very popular. The latter part is exquisitely pathetic, and the whole touched with those soft and skyish tints of purity and truth which fall like enchantment on all minds that can make any thing of such matters."

The public hailed with delight this new volume. Yet Campbell's joy was in a moment overcast and for a time destroyed by the sickening and death, by scarlet fever, of his son Alison, the child of many a fondly cherished hope; for some time his heart seemed crushed; the event sunk deep, and was never, even in after years, referred to without perceptible emotion; for weeks he was incapable of consecutive thought; and it was at last only through the kind sympathy of Mr. Alison that he became tranquillized and able to resume his duties, and at last set down to prepare a course of lectures for delivery at the Royal Institution.

At the commencement of the year 1812, the poet's mother died at Edinburgh, at the age of seventy-six. Mac Arthur Stewart, Campbell's highland cousin, insisted upon defraying the entire cost of her funeral, which was attended by more than two hundred people.

In the months of April and May, Campbell's Lectures on Poetry were delivered at the Royal Institution. They went off with great *éclat*, and obtained for him increased popularity, and a large sum of money. Shortly afterwards he was presented to the Princess of Wales by Lady Charlotte Campbell, and subsequently received an invitation to a grand ball given by Her Royal Highness at Blackheath, where he had the honour of dancing a reel with Royalty.

Society exerted its claims upon Campbell very much during this period. Madame de Staël, in the spring of 1813, visited England, and the poet had the gratification of meeting her frequently. In writing to a friend at this time, and referring to the Lectures then recently read at the Royal Institution, he says, "I spent a day or two with Madame de Staël this spring, and read her my lectures—one of them against her own doctrines, in poetry. She battled hard with me, but was very good-natured and complimentary. Every now and then, she said, 'When you publish your lectures, they will make a great impression over all Europe; I know nothing in English but Burke's writings so striking.' This she said before Lord Harrowby and a large party; and if her praise was flattery, she at least committed herself."

During Campbell's residence at Ratisbon he had been kindly received by General Moreau, and presented to his young and beautiful wife. This lady, in 1813, visited London. In one of his letters, he says, "I have dined with Madame Moreau; she did me the honour of talking almost exclusively to me. I sate between Madame de Staël and the lovely 'widow.'" In another letter he says, "I have spent a pleasant day at Lord Holland's; we had the Marquis of Buckingham, Sergeant Best, (Lord Winford,) Major Stanhope, Sir James Mackintosh, and a *swan* at dinner.

Lord Byron came in the evening. It was one of the best parties I ever saw."

After a dinner party at Holland House, Lord Byron, in writing of the poet, at this time, said, "Campbell looks well, seems pleased, and dresses to sprucery; a blue coat becomes him, so does a new wig,—he really looked as if Apollo had sent him a birth-day suit, or a wedding garment. He was lively and witty. We were standing in the ante-saloon, when Lord H. brought out of the other room a vessel of some composition similar to that used in Catholic churches, and seeing us, he exclaimed, 'Here is some incense for you!' Campbell answered, 'Carry it to Lord Byron, he is used to it.'"

About this time Lawrence took a sketch of Campbell. The gifted knight caused the head to be engraved at a cost of 40*l*., and having written his autograph on the proofs, presented them to the poet.

In the early part of March, in this year, he visited Madame de Staël, which procured him the acquaintance of many distinguished strangers.

At the peace of 1814, on the fall of Napoleon, the capture of Paris, and the restoration of the Bourbons, in common with many others, Campbell was seized with a desire to visit Paris. Mrs. Siddons, John Kemble, the Baroness de Staël, had pressed him to join them, and on the 25th of August he embarked for Dieppe, where he spent a week, and then proceeded to Rouen, where he rested two days, having been received with great kindness by Professor Vitalis, and subsequently elected member of the Royal Academy of that place.

In announcing his arrival at Paris, Campbell

says, "You may imagine with what feelings I caught the first sight of Paris, and passed under Montmartre, the scene of the last battle between the French and allies. It was evening when we entered Paris. Next morning I met Mrs. Siddons, walked about with her, and then visited the Louvre together. Oh! how that immortal youth, Apollo, in all his splendour, majesty, and divinity, flashed upon us from the end of the gallery! What a torrent of ideas, classically associated with this godlike form, rushed upon me at this moment! My heart palpitated, my eyes filled with tears—I was dumb with emotion.

"Here are a hundred other splendid statues,—the Venus—the Menander—the Pericles—Cato and Portia, the father and daughter in an attitude of melting tenderness."

He remained nearly two months in Paris and having in that time contracted many friendships, which animated his studies, and ripened his tastes, (Baron Cuvier and the elder Schlegel amongst the number), he embarked at Calais, and after narrowly escaping shipwreck from the ignorance of the person in charge of the vessel, who was neither captain nor seaman, and who ran the ship within a few hundred yards of the Shakespeare cliff, to the terror of the passengers, one of whom was washed overboard and drowned, he arrived at Dover, and thence proceeded to Sydenham.

On the 25th of March, 1815, a welcome accession of fortune befell him by the death of Mac Arthur Stewart, of Ascog, in whose will he was left one of the specific legatees; the amount realized, after paying legacy duty and other expenses, was 4498*l.* 10*s.* (the interest of which is still enjoyed by the poet's son). It is said that Mr. Mac

Arthur Stewart, the testator, when giving instructions for his settlement, observed that. "*The poet ought to have a legacy, because he had been so kind as to give his mother sixty pounds yearly out of his pension.*" It will be out of place here to say much on the relationship between Mr. Stewart and the poet's family, but it was the deliberate opinion of many distinguished counsel, that if Campbell's elder brother had been aware of the law which rendered aliens to the crown of Great Britain incapable of inheriting entailed estates, or of holding land within the United Kingdom, and had made up his title as the nearest heir of tailzie, on the death of Mac Arthur Stewart, or before Mr. Campbell Stewart, his successor, obtained his act of naturalization, he might have been the proprietor of the old family estates, which were afterwards sold by the American heir for 78,000*l.*

The poet was now required at Edinburgh to look after this new acquisition, and on his arrival, after years of absence, was warmly greeted by many old friends, and by Lord Gillies, and Lord Alloway, two of Mr. Mac Arthur Stewart's executors. On leaving Edinburgh, he journeyed to Kinniel, the residence of Mr. and Mrs. Dugald Stewart, where he spent some "happy days;" thence he made a tour amongst his relatives in and near Glasgow.

During the years 1816 and 1817, he was occupied in preparing for the press Specimens of the British Poets, which, preceded by an Essay on Poetry, was published by Mr. Murray.

On the occasion of the lamented death of the Princess Charlotte, he wrote a monody, which was recited by Mrs. Bartley, at Drury Lane

Theatre, for the benefit of the performers who, through this national calamity, had suffered severely.

In 1818, Mr. Roscoe, on the part of the Royal Institution of Liverpool, concluded an arrangement with him for the delivery of twelve lectures on the poetry of Greece, for 150 guineas guaranteed, and the subscriptions above that sum, and in due course these lectures were delivered and listened to with a delight and enthusiasm long remembered by many who had the gratification of hearing them. The subscriptions increased the sum of 150 guineas to upwards of 340*l*., and he received 100*l*. more for repeating them at Birmingham on his way home to London.

In 1820, Campbell, who had long wished to revisit Germany, was enabled to do so. On the 24th of May, he concluded an agreement with Mr. Colburn, the publisher, for the editorship of the "New Monthly," for three years certain, from the first of January ensuing, at 500*l*. per annum. This settled, he embarked for Holland, arrived at the port of Rotterdam, thence proceeded up the Rhine, and took up his quarters at Bonn, where he was most warmly received by the Schlegels, Professor Arndt, and other professors of the University; thence he made excursions into various districts bordering the Rhine, and after a sojourn of some weeks, revisited Ratisbon, and his old asylum, the Scotch College, and then by the Danube proceeded to Vienna, from which place, after an agreeable sojourn of some months, he returned to Bonn, thence to England, and arrived in London on the 24th of November, and immediately commenced arrangements for his editorial duties. He soon organized a staff, and with a full conviction of the arduous undertaking in hand, he lent to it all his energies, and soon the "New Monthly" exhibited fresh spirit and power, and for the ten years following, during which he continued editor, was inferior to none of the magazines in public favour and estimation.

Having bidden farewell to Sydenham, which he often said was the "greenest spot in memory's waste," he settled down permanently in London, projecting new efforts in the cause of literature.

Now another domestic calamity befell him, an affliction which embittered many days, which otherwise, humanly speaking, would have been joyous and tranquil; his only son was pronounced, either from hereditary taint or accident at school, incapable of prosecuting his studies with advantage; every thing was done that affection could devise, struggles were made, sacrifices gladly undergone, no pecuniary expense spared. It was only after many alarms that Campbell could be brought to believe that the symptoms manifested, were any thing more than the effects of temper, or mere physical derangement.

In November, 1824, while his mind was still on the rack, alternating between hope and fear concerning his son's malady, appeared the poem of "Theodric." Considerable popularity was anticipated for it, which its author, however, did not live to see realized. While the work was in the press, in writing to his sister, he says, "I am sorry there should be any great expectation excited about the poem, which is not of a nature to gratify such expectation. It is truly a *domestic* and private story. I know very well what will be its fate; there will be an outcry and regret that there is nothing grand or romantic in it, and that it is too humble and familiar. But I am prepared for this; and I also know that when it recovers from the first buzz of such criticism, it will attain a steady popularity."

The founding of the University of London is the next feature of Campbell's life which deserves notice; the idea, as is well known, entirely originated with him, and its realization he ever felt a source of satisfaction; he looked upon the event, as he chose to say, as "the only important one in his life's little history."

From the occasion of his visit to the Universities of Bonn, Heidelberg, and Vienna, this subject had occupied most of his thoughts, and from time to time, as opportunity served, he mentioned the subject to his friends. At length his plans became matured, and he was enabled, at a public meeting summoned for that purpose, to set forth his scheme in a manner which exhibited not only its feasibility, but at once won over the entire audience to coöperation and an unanimous determination to carry out his suggestions.

After the matter had progressed, and his views been explained, we find him (in a letter dated April 30th, 1825,) thus referring to the subject:—"I have had a double quick time of employment since I saw you. In addition to the business of the magazine, I have had that of the University in a formidable shape. Brougham, who must have popularity among Dissenters, propounded the matter to them. The delegates of almost all the dissenting bodies in London came to a conference at his summons. At the first meeting it was decided that there should be *Theological* chairs, partly Church of England, and partly Presbyterian. I had instructed all friends of the University to resist any attempt to make us a Theological body; but Brougham, Hume, and John Smith, came away from the first meeting saying, 'We think with you, that the introduction of divinity will be mischievous; but we must yield to the Dissenters, with Irving at their head. We must have a *Theological* College.' I immediately waited on the Church of England men, who had already subscribed to the number of a hundred, and said to them, 'You see our paction is broken. I induced you to subscribe on the faith, that no ecclesiastical interest, English or Scotch, should predominate in our scheme; but the Dissenters are rushing in. What do you say?' They—that is, the Church of England friends of the scheme—concerted that I should go commissioned from them, to say at the conference, that either the Church of England must predominate, or else there must be no Church influence. I went with this commission; I debated the matter with the Dissenters. Brougham, Hume, and John Smith, who had before deserted me, changed sides, and came over to me. Irving, and his party stoutly opposed me; but I succeeded at last in gaining a complete victory. . . . The Dissenters themselves, I must say, behaved with extreme candour: they would not even suffer me to conclude my reply to Mr. Irving; but exclaimed, 'Enough, enough. We are convinced, and concede the point, that the University shall be without religious rivalship.' The scene concluded amicably: Lord Althorp appeared on the part of the Church, and coincided in the decision.

"A directory of the association for the scheme of the University is to meet in my house on Monday, and every thing promises well. You cannot conceive what anxiety I have undergone, whilst I imagined that the whole beautiful project was likely to be reduced to a mere Dissenters' University. But I have no more reason to be dissatisfied with the Dissenters than with the hundred Church of England Subscribers, whose interests I have done my best to support. *I regard this as an eventful day in my life.*"

A few days afterwards he thus writes:—

"You will not grudge postage, to be told the agreeable news that Brougham and Hume have reported their having had a conference with the Chancellor of the Exchequer and Lord Liverpool; and that they expressed themselves not unfavourable to the plan of a great College in London. Of course, as ministers had not been asked to pledge themselves to support us, but only to give us a general idea of their disposition, we could only get what we sought, a general answer, but that being so favourable, is much. I was glad also to hear that both Mr. Robinson and Lord Liverpool approved highly of no rival theological chairs having been agreed upon. Mr. Robinson even differed from Mr. Hume, when the latter said, 'Of course getting a charter is not to be thought of.' 'I beg your pardon,' said Mr. Robinson, 'I think it might be thought of; and it is by no means an impossible supposition.'

"A copy of my scheme of education, but much mutilated and abridged, is submitted to their inspection. I mean, however, to transmit to them my scheme in an entire shape, and to publish it afterwards as a pamphlet. In the mean time, I must for a while retire and leave this business to other hands, now that it seems *safe* from any mischief which hitherto threatened it. I send you this intelligence because it is an *event to me*, or at least a step in a promised event, which will be, perhaps, *the only* important one in my life's little history."

Subsequently he wrote: — "I rejoice to find the wisest Churchmen and the wisest Dissenters decidedly agreeing on this point, that we ought in this scheme religiously to avoid all chance of *religious controversy.* Mr. Irving said, that learning and science were the natural enemies of religion; but if he said so, I paid him home for it very well. He came and shook hands with me at the conclusion."

From this time, comparatively, all was plain sailing; difficulties were mastered, and the project daily advanced in popularity. Campbell's scheme of education was founded on the basis of the plans resorted to both in British and Foreign Universities, adapting the leading features of each to the advance of knowledge and the growing necessities of the age. In order to leave no system unnoticed, he determined to visit the University of Berlin, and ascertain whether its system and *curriculum* of education could with advantage be adopted in the London University. With this in view, on the 10th of September, he embarked for Germany, and in eighty hours arrived in safety at Hamburg. On the 21st, he wrote from Berlin, "I have just been through the University. I have taken the dimensions of its rooms, and got some books which give an account of its institutions. I have also given my letter of introduction to the librarian (Dr. Spiker), who has given me the liberty of getting out any books I may wish for. I told you, in my letter from Hamburg, that I should go to Leipsic; but I was soon after informed that Berlin is a place much preferable for my object, and superadds other *agrémens*." He afterwards remarked—"I have got every piece of information respecting the University, and every book that I wished for. The librarian of the University in particular, Dr. Spiker, has sent me every book to my lodgings that I wanted to consult." . . . "I should have felt many inconveniences in many instances, had I not fortunately met with a couple of my countrymen, who are studying medicine here, although they have actually entered the London College of Surgeons.—These young men make me feel very old, for they pay me such attention that I think I must appear in their eyes as venerable as Nestor! They regulate their business for the day so as to keep themselves at my service—as they share it whenever they can be useful; so that I have no trouble but to eat and drink and go about to see sights. From anybody such attention would excite a kindly feeling; but from young men of most respectable attainments and gentlemanlike manners, it is even flattering. I am not suffered to carry my own cloak or umbrella, nor to bring any thing for myself that I want; and they offered even to write out a translation of some difficult German which I have had to get through to the amount of sixty very large-sized and small-printed quarto pages. As they are in very good circumstances, the offer was perfectly gratuitous; but I thought it would be unfair to allow them to sacrifice so much time from their own proper studies. Finally, my devoted friends have taken out their places for Hamburg, in order to be present at the dinner to be given me, whether it shall prove public or private." *

* These gentlemen were Mr. William Coulson of London, and Mr. E. J. Spry of Truro.

In the early part of the year 1826, Campbell received a communication from Glasgow, to the effect that it was desired he should become Lord Rector for the year ensuing, and adding that he "had a strong party among the students of Glasgow, who, if he accepted their invitation, would insure his election." After much hesitation, in consequence of domestic afflictions, he consented to allow himself to be put forward as a candidate. He was duly elected, by an immense majority, on the unanimous vote of the four nations. The fact was formally notified by Dr. Macfarlane, the Principal of the College, on the 15th of November, 1826.

Campbell greatly enjoyed this sun-burst of popular favour—not the less so because he knew that some of the professors had set up, in opposition to him, Mr. Canning and Sir Thomas Brisbane, and, actuated by feelings of political distrust, had exerted their utmost influence to secure the first-named gentleman's election. In consequence of Campbell's delicate state of health, his installation as Lord Rector did not take place until the 12th of April, when he delivered his inaugural address to an overflowing assembly of professors, students, and citizens, amongst whom, though divided in political sentiments, there seemed, at the time, to exist but one feeling of gratification. On the 13th of April, he wrote, "I delivered my inaugural speech yesterday with complete success; the enthusiasm was immense. I dined afterwards with the professors in the Faculty. . . . . I find the rectorship will be no sinecure. I have sat four hours examining accounts, and hearing explanations from the Faculty, with Sir John Connel, the Dean of Faculty, my co-examiner and visitor, to whom the professors are anxious to render their accounts."

As Lord Rector of the University of Glasgow, Campbell exerted himself largely for the benefit of his constituents: the lectures, the funds, the library, the examinations, were inquired into; alterations made; grievances redressed; and no pains were deemed too great to render assistance to the commissioners then acting under a commission of inquiry on the affairs of the College. On the 14th of November, Campbell was reëlected Lord Rector for the year 1828, without one dissentient voice. During his second year of office, his wife, Mrs. Campbell, died. She expired on the 10th of May, and on the 15th of the same month the poet thus writes: " . . . I am alone; and I feel that I shall need to be some time alone—prostrated in heart before that Great Being who can alone forgive my errors; and in addressing whom, alone, I can frame resolutions in my heart to make my remaining life as pure as nature's infirmities may permit a soul to be, that believes in His existence, and goodness and mercy. . . ." As the poignancy of his grief subsided, we trace him in communication with Lord Aberdeen on the Commission of Inquiry, and doing his utmost to preserve the privileges of his students; and so grateful were " his boys," as he loved to call them, that, in addition to a handsome present of silver plate made to him, they resolved to strain every nerve to reëlect him for the third time,—an honour, the highest that could be conferred. No such instance of the kind had happened for a century previously. This honour, however, was not to be gained without a struggle: Sir Walter Scott became his competitor—put forward, as supposed, by the Vice-Rector. Campbell, however, was re-elected for the year 1829; and, during this year, by his exertions, permanent advantages were conceded to the objects of his care—not the least of these being a free access, at all reasonable times, to the Museum and College Library.

The year 1830 was chiefly memorable to Campbell from the death of his friend, Sir Thomas Lawrence,—his declining the editorship of the "New Monthly Magazine,"—and active exertions made for the Poles, in whose behalf, in the year following, he organized "the Association of the Friends of Poland."

During the years 1831-2, he became editor of the "Metropolitan Magazine."

In the month of July, 1832, Campbell was invited to come forward as a candidate for the representation of a Scotch constituency in the House of Commons; but, after giving the subject full deliberation, he declined the honour (though his return seems to have been almost certain); and the grounds of his refusal seem to have rested on the multiplicity of engagements, among which the Polish Association seemed paramount. The amount of labour he underwent, and the money he spent on behalf of this oppressed people, exceeded far what either his social or pecuniary position justified.

In 1834, Campbell revisited Paris, where he was eagerly welcomed by many of the exiles from Poland. Thence he proceeded to Algiers, whence the letters were written which appeared in the pages of the "New Monthly Magazine." He returned to Great Britain in 1835 *viâ* Paris, where he was presented to the late ex-King Louis Philippe, and thence, by way of Scotland, staying at Edinburgh and Brougham Hall on the road, he arrived in London.

During the following years, he was engaged in a variety of subjects, which brought him money rather than fame; among these, the Life of Mrs. Siddons and the Life of Petrarch, and lent his name editorially to some reprints. But the "oil was now seen to burn lower and lower in the lamp, and the social wit waxed faint, or moved perplexedly among old recollections, where it had formerly struck out bright creations. It was a sorrowful thing to see him gliding about like a shadow,—to hear that his health compelled him to retreat more and more from the world he had once so adorned." On the 26th June, 1838, he was presented at Court by the late Duke of Argyle, at the first levee after her Majesty's accession, the queen having previously accepted from him the present of his poems, and afterwards sent him her picture. The effect of the crowd and detention for about two hours among at least a thousand persons, brought on a fever, which, however, was overcome under medicine and repose.

In the winter of 1840, Campbell took, on lease, a house,—No. 8, Victoria Square, Pimlico,—where he proposed to spend the autumn of his days. Having now arrived at the age of sixty-three, and experienced during preceding years the misery of repeated changes of abode, and the discomfort of a solitary life, he determined upon realizing a long-cherished wish—to adopt a favorite niece (Mary Campbell) whom he had affectionately noticed from her infancy—the youngest daughter of his brother, Alexander Campbell, late of Glasgow, deceased. After obtaining her mother's consent, he wrote thus: "She need not come to

London till the middle of May, and then, in my new house, she shall be as welcome as the flowers of that month. It will be an amusement to me to instruct her mind whenever she chooses. But assure her, from me, that she need not fear being set to learn more than she really wishes; and she must not greet at parting from her mother, for I will send her back on a visit to you as often as she likes."

In 1842, appeared "The Pilgrim of Glencoe," accompanied by a number of minor pieces; but the chief poem added nothing to his reputation, and its reception was not by any means cheering: the smaller productions were welcomed kindly as ever. Yet he was greatly disappointed. He had heard it said, a new poem by him was like a bill at sight. Now he began to realize the truth that old age was fast creeping upon him. Occasionally sunny days brightened his decline. He became restless, and somewhat careless in dress; he began to indulge much in change of scene; Dinan, on the Continent, Cheltenham, in England, and other places, were all tried, one after the other; and at last he determined to dispose of the lease of his house in London and become a denizen of Boulogne-sur-Mer, calculating that he would live there in greater seclusion and at a cheaper cost than in England.

One of the chief indications of decay was an unfounded dread of poverty. After the first blush of life had passed, he had been far more happy in his pecuniary circumstances than most poets or literary men could boast; for at this time, (1842), and for many years previously, his income was little less than 1100*l.* per annum—the interest on the legacy of 4500*l.* from the Ascog estates produced 200*l.*; his pension 200*l.*; the profits of his works, between 600*l.* and 700*l*; and, in 1843, on the death of his surviving sister, he received a sum of 800*l.*, the greater part of which, however, he sunk in an annuity, receiving for his "investment" only one pecuniary payment.

In June, 1843, a farewell party (as it turned out) was given to all his friends then in town, and in the month following he left his home never to return to it, except for a few days in order to dispose, at all hazards, of his lease in the house. On the 15th of July, he arrived at Boulogne, and was, by the kind assistance of Mr. Hamilton, the British consul, soon located with his niece at the Hôtel de Bourgogne, a quiet and well-regulated hotel, in the upper town. Here, after a month's residence, he took a house in the Haute Ville,—5, Rue Petit St. Jéan. For some months he seemed contented and benefited by the change of air and scene, but the house lay high and exposed, and in November, when the cold weather set in, a feeling of indolence and torpor seemed (as he expressed it) to grow upon him; but this evidenced not merely the effect of the change of season, but the progress of disease—an affection of the liver; yet, now and then, though expressing a belief that the lease of life had almost expired, he would rally—be himself again—and tell his plans for the future. Though in seclusion and retirement, he purposed to show to the world he was not idle, and so he made efforts and strove until wearied nature told the plain but trying truth that his days were numbered. At times, when the weather was inviting, attended by his affectionate niece, he would walk a little way down the hill leading from the Haute Ville to the Bas Ville.

His favourite haunt about mid-day was the ramparts upon which his house abutted, but, at last, when winter set in chill and rigorous, he was fain to retire to his easy chair and a warm corner in his library. Here, in writing a work, entitled "Lectures on Classical Geography," intended to have been dedicated to his niece,—in reading the journals of the day,—in listening to some of his old favourite pieces of music,—the long evenings passed onwards. The new year arrived, but opened upon the sick man with little of a hopeful character. He was oppressed by a constant sensation of cold. He now began to drop all correspondence, and to decline seeing any of the many kind friends who called to proffer their services. As spring came on, and the weather grew gradually more mild and settled, he revived for a few weeks; but this was succeeded by a perceptible, though gradual, decay of strength. Towards the end of May, he became entirely confined to his bed, and the English physician (Dr. Allatt), who had been constant in his attendance, held out no hopes of ultimate recovery.

About three weeks prior to his death, he expressed a conviction that he would never again leave his bed alive; his niece endeavoured to cheer his spirits and to infuse hope, that if God so willed it, with care, he might live for many years; to this he answered, "For your sake I had wished I might live for some years longer, for you are now the only tie I have to this world; indeed, you are the dearest object I have on earth." To which Miss Campbell replied, "Oh! that is a *poetical flight.*" He replied, "Nay, my dear, it is a *prosaic truth!*"

Every exertion that affectionate tenderness, or

woman's love, could devise, was lavished upon him; he was generally alive to all that passed; and though his sufferings at times were acute, no expressions of impatience ever escaped his lips.

About ten days before his dissolution, Dr. Beattie came from England to visit his old friend, and on his part zealously aided Miss Campbell in her labour of love, exerting to the utmost all his well-known professional skill and kindly sympathies, in striving to soothe the poet's dying pillow. As opportunity served, and the attention of the sufferer could be aroused, passages from the Scriptures, particularly from the Gospels and Epistles, were read, and his attention directed to the assurance of hope to the faithful believer through the Saviour's atonement. On several occasions he expressed to his niece a vivid sense of the beauty and sublimity of the Bible, particularly the Old Testament, and shed tears over the glowing language and poetic imagery of the sweet Psalmist of Israel.

On the 12th of June he became at times insensible, but towards evening rallied a little, and, addressing his niece, who was standing over his couch, said, "Come, let us sing praises to Christ;" then pointing to the bed-side, he added, "sit here." Miss Campbell said, "Shall I pray for you?" "Oh! yes," he replied, "let us pray for one another."

During the two following days he continued almost entirely in a state of stupor, occasionally naming friends long absent, and making observations, which from their total irrelevancy to all that was passing in his room, showed that his mind was no longer under his own control.

On the 15th instant, at a quarter past four in

the afternoon, he expired without the slightest perceptible struggle; indeed the sudden change of his countenance was the first indication that the spirit of the Bard of Hope had fled.

When the arrangements, required by the laws of France in cases of death, had been completed with the Commissaire de Police and his officials, the body was laid for several days in the drawing-room, crowned with a wreath of laurel, during which period it was visited by many strangers, English and French, and many acquaintances and friends of the deceased, all anxious to testify their kindly sympathies and take a last look at him who had so often cheered and elevated their hearts. After this manifestation of affection to his memory, the corpse was consigned to a coffin of lead, and having been duly sealed with the town seal of Boulogne, was deposited in an outer coffin of wood, upon the lid of which was inscribed, on a brass plate the following inscription:—

THOMAS CAMPBELL, LL.D.,
AUTHOR OF THE "PLEASURES OF HOPE,"
DIED JUNE XV., MDCCCXLIV.
AGED 67.

On the 27th of June, the body was embarked at midnight for London, and on its arrival in the metropolis was conveyed to the undertaker's house—thence to a chapel near the Jerusalem Chamber, Westminster Abbey, in which it remained until the 3d of July, the day of the funeral; a day well remembered by the many who witnessed the solemn ceremonial,—men of all gradations of rank, (not omitting the head of his clan, the Duke of Argyle, and the premier, the late lamented Sir Robert Peel); they all vied with each other in paying a last tribute of respect to the merits of this admired genius.

Since Campbell's decease, a full-length statue, by Mr. W. C. Marshall, has been finished, and is proposed to be erected in Poets' Corner, Westminster Abbey.

We close this short sketch of the career of this gifted individual, by a few quotations from his own words at the age of sixty-one, recorded in *Reminiscences of the Poet by Members of his Family.* He spoke frequently, if led to it, of his feelings while writing his poems. When he wrote the "Pleasures of Hope," fame, he said, was every thing in the world to him: if any one had foretold to him *then*, how indifferent he would be *now* to fame and public opinion, he would have scouted the idea. He said he hoped he really did feel, with regard to his posthumous fame, that he left it, as well as all else about himself, to the mercy of God. "I believe when I am gone, justice will be done to me in this way—that I was a pure writer. It is an inexpressible comfort, at my time of life, to be able to look back and feel that I have not written one line against religion or virtue."

Another time, speaking of the insignificance which in one sense posthumous fame must have, he said, "When I think of the existence which shall commence when the stone is laid above my head,—when I think of the momentous realities of that time, and of the awfulness of the account I shall have to give of myself, how CAN literary fame appear to me but as—nothing. Who will think of it then? If, at death, we enter on a new state of eternity, of what interest beyond his present life can a man's literary fame be to him? Of none—when he thinks most solemnly about it."—

"Farewell! if 'tis the muse's boast to crown
With deathless fame, and virtue meets renown;
While yonder orbs their measured dance pursue,
The wise shall praise, the good shall copy YOU."

PLEASURES OF HOPE.

PART THE FIRST.

ANALYSIS OF PART I.

The Poem opens with a comparison between the beauty of remote objects in a landscape, and those ideal scenes of felicity which the imagination delights to contemplate—the influence of anticipation upon the other passions is next delineated—an allusion is made to the well-known fiction in Pagan tradition, that, when all the guardian deities of mankind abandoned the world, Hope alone was left behind—the consolations of this passion in situations of danger and distress—the seaman on his watch—the soldier marching into battle—allusion to the interesting adventures of Byron.

The inspiration of Hope, as it actuates the efforts of genius, whether in the department of science, or of taste—domestic felicity, how intimately connected with views of future happiness—picture of a mother watching her infant when asleep—pictures of the prisoner, the maniac, and the wanderer.

From the consolations of individual misery a transition is made to prospects of political improvement in the future state of society—the wide field that is yet open for the progress of humanizing arts among uncivilized nations—from these views of amelioration of society, and the extension of liberty and truth over despotic and barbarous countries, by a melancholy contrast of ideas, we are led to reflect upon the hard fate of a brave people recently conspicuous in their struggles for independence—description of the capture of Warsaw, of the last contest of the oppressors and the oppressed, and the massacre of the Polish patriots at the bridge of Prague—apostrophe to the self-interested enemies of human improvement—the wrongs of Africa—the barbarous policy of Europeans in India—prophecy in the Hindoo mythology of the expected descent of the Deity to redress the miseries of their race, and to take vengeance on the violators of justice and mercy.

PLEASURES OF HOPE.

PART I.

At summer eve, when Heaven's ethereal bow
Spans with bright arch the glittering hills below,
Why to yon mountain turns the musing eye,
Whose sunbright summit mingles with the sky?
Why do those cliffs of shadowy tint appear
More sweet than all the landscape smiling near?—
'Tis distance lends enchantment to the view,
And robes the mountain in its azure hue.
Thus, with delight, we linger to survey
The promised joys of life's unmeasured way;
Thus, from afar, each dim-discover'd scene
More pleasing seems than all the past hath been,
And every form, that Fancy can repair
From dark oblivion, glows divinely there.
What potent spirit guides the raptured eye
To pierce the shades of dim futurity?
Can Wisdom lend, with all her heavenly power,
The pledge of Joy's anticipated hour?
Ah, no! she darkly sees the fate of man—
Her dim horizon bounded to a span;
Or, if she hold an image to the view,
'Tis Nature pictured too severely true.

With thee, sweet HOPE! resides the heavenly light,
That pours remotest rapture on the sight:
Thine is the charm of life's bewilder'd way,
That calls each slumbering passion into play.
Waked by thy touch, I see the sister band,
On tiptoe watching, start at thy command,
And fly where'er thy mandate bids them steer,
To Pleasure's path or Glory's bright career.
Primeval HOPE, the Aönian Muses say,
When Man and Nature mourn'd their first decay;
When every form of death, and every woe,
Shot from malignant stars to earth below;
When Murder bared her arm, and rampant War
Yoked the red dragons of her iron car;
When Peace and Mercy, banish'd from the plain,
Sprung on the viewless winds to Heaven again;
All, all forsook the friendless, guilty mind,
But HOPE, the charmer, linger'd still behind.
Thus, while Elijah's burning wheels prepare
From Carmel's heights to sweep the fields of air
The prophet's mantle, ere his flight began,
Dropt on the world—a sacred gift to man.
Auspicious HOPE! in thy sweet garden grow
Wreaths for each toil, a charm for every woe;
Won by their sweets, in Nature's languid hour,
The way-worn pilgrim seeks thy summer bower
There, as the wild bee murmurs on the wing,
What peaceful dreams thy handmaid spirits bring!

What viewless forms th' Æolian organ play,
And sweep the furrow'd lines of anxious thought away.

Angel of life! thy glittering wings explore
Earth's loneliest bounds, and Ocean's wildest shore!
Lo! to the wintry winds the pilot yields
His bark careering o'er unfathom'd fields;
Now on Atlantic waves he rides afar,
Where Andes, giant of the western star,
With meteor-standard to the winds unfurl'd,
Looks from his throne of clouds o'er half the world!

Now far he sweeps, where scarce a summer smiles,
On Behring's rocks, or Greenland's naked isles:
Cold on his midnight watch the breezes blow,
From wastes that slumber in eternal snow;
And waft, across the waves' tumultuous roar,
The wolf's long howl from Oonalaska's shore.

Poor child of danger, nursling of the storm,
Sad are the woes that wreck thy manly form!
Rocks, waves, and winds, the shatter'd bark delay;
Thy heart is sad, thy home is far away.

But Hope can here her moonlight vigils keep,
And sing to charm the spirit of the deep:
Swift as yon streamer lights the starry pole,
Her visions warm the watchman's pensive soul;
His native hills that rise in happier climes,
The grot that heard his song of other times,

His cottage home, his bark of slender sail,
His glassy lake, and broomwood-blossom'd vale,
Rush on his thought; he sweeps before the wind,
Treads the loved shore he sigh'd to leave behind;
Meets at each step a friend's familiar face,
And flies at last to Helen's long embrace;
Wipes from her cheek the rapture-speaking tear!
And clasps, with many a sigh, his children dear!
While, long neglected, but at length caress'd,
His faithful dog salutes the smiling guest,
Points to the master's eyes (where'er they roam)
His wistful face, and whines a welcome home.
  Friend of the brave! in peril's darkest hour,
Intrepid Virtue looks to thee for power;
To thee the heart its trembling homage yields,
On stormy floods, and carnage-cover'd fields,
When front to front the banner'd hosts combine,
Halt ere they close, and form the dreadful line.
When all is still on Death's devoted soil,
The march-worn soldier mingles for the toil!
As rings his glittering tube, he lifts on high
The dauntless brow and spirit-speaking eye,
Hails in his heart the triumph yet to come,
And hears thy stormy music in the drum!
  And such thy strength-inspiring aid that bore
The hardy Byron to his native shore—
In horrid climes, where Chiloe's tempests sweep
Tumultuous murmurs o'er the troubled deep,
'Twas his to mourn Misfortune's rudest shock,
Scourged by the winds, and cradled on the rock,

To wake each joyless morn and search again
The famish'd haunts of solitary men;
Whose race, unyielding as their native storm,
Know not a trace of Nature but the form;
Yet, at thy call, the hardy tar pursued,
Pale, but intrepid, sad, but unsubdued,
Pierced the deep woods, and hailing from afar
The moon's pale planet and the northern star,
Paused at each dreary cry, unheard before,
Hyænas in the wild, and mermaids on the shore;
Till, led by thee o'er many a cliff sublime,
He found a warmer world, a milder clime,
A home to rest, a shelter to defend,
Peace and repose, a Briton and a friend!
Congenial HOPE! thy passion-kindling power,
How bright, how strong, in youth's untroubled hour!
On yon proud height, with Genius hand in hand,
I see thee 'light and wave thy golden wand.
"Go, child of Heaven! (thy winged words proclaim)
'Tis thine to search the boundless fields of fame!
Lo! Newton, priest of Nature, shines afar,
Scans the wide world, and numbers every star!
Wilt thou, with him, mysterious rites apply,
And watch the shrine with wonder-beaming eye
Yes, thou shalt mark, with magic art profound,
The speed of light, the circling march of sound:
With Franklin grasp the lightning's fiery wing,
Or yield the lyre of Heaven another string.

"The Swedish sage admires, in yonder bowers,
His winged insects, and his rosy flowers;
Calls from their woodland haunts the savage train,
With sounding horn, and counts them on the plain—
So once, at Heaven's command, the wanderers came
To Eden's shade, and heard their various name.
"Far from the world, in yon sequester'd clime,
Slow pass the sons of Wisdom, more sublime;
Calm as the fields of Heaven, his sapient eye
The loved Athenian lifts to realms on high,
Admiring Plato, on his spotless page,
Stamps the bright dictates of the Father sage:
'Shall Nature bound to Earth's diurnal span
The fire of God, th' immortal soul of man?'
"Turn, child of Heaven, thy rapture-lighten'd eye
To Wisdom's walks, the sacred Nine are nigh:
Hark! from bright spires that gild the Delphian height,
From streams that wander in eternal light,
Ranged on their hill, Harmonia's daughters swell
The mingling tones of horn, and harp, and shell;
Deep from his vaults the Loxian murmurs flow,
And Pythia's awful organ peals below.
"Beloved of Heaven! the smiling Muse shall shed
Her moonlight halo on thy beauteous head;

Shall swell thy heart to rapture unconfined,
And breathe a holy madness o'er thy mind.
I see thee roam her guardian power beneath,
And talk with spirits on the midnight heath;
Enquire of guilty wanderers whence they came,
And ask each blood-stain'd form his earthly name;
Then weave in rapid verse the deeds they tell,
And read the trembling world the tales of hell.
"When Venus, throned in clouds of rosy hue,
Flings from her golden urn the vesper dew,
And bids fond man her glimmering noon employ
Sacred to love, and walks of tender joy;
A milder mood the goddess shall recall,
And soft as dew thy tones of music fall;
While Beauty's deeply-pictured smiles impart
A pang more dear than pleasure to the heart—
Warm as thy sighs shall flow the Lesbian strain,
And plead in Beauty's ear, nor plead in vain.
"Or wilt thou Orphean hymns more sacred deem,
And steep thy song in Mercy's mellow stream;
To pensive drops the radiant eye beguile—
For Beauty's tears are lovelier than her smile;—
On Nature's throbbing anguish pour relief,
And teach impassioned souls the joy of grief?
"Yes; to thy tongue shall seraph words be given,
And power on earth to plead the cause of Heaven;
The proud, the cold untroubled heart of stone,
That never mused on sorrow but its own,

Unlocks a generous store at thy command,
Like Horeb's rocks beneath the prophet's hand.
The living lumber of his kindred earth,
Charm'd into soul, receives a second birth,
Feels thy dread power another heart afford,
Whose passion-touch'd harmonious strings accord
True as the circling spheres to Nature's plan;
And man, the brother, lives the friend of man.
"Bright as the pillar rose at Heaven's command,
When Israel march'd along the desert land,
Blazed through the night on lonely wilds afar,
And told the path—a never-setting star:
So, heavenly Genius, in thy course divine,
Hope is thy star, her light is ever thine."
Propitious Power! when rankling cares annoy
The sacred home of Hymenean joy;
When doom'd to Poverty's sequester'd dell,
The wedded pair of love and virtue dwell,
Unpitied by the world, unknown to fame,
Their woes, their wishes, and their hearts the same—
Oh, there, prophetic Hope! thy smile bestow,
And chase the pangs that worth should never know—
There, as the parent deals his scanty store
To friendless babes, and weeps to give no more,
Tell, that his manly race shall yet assuage
Their father's wrongs, and shield his latter age.

What though for him no Hybla sweets distil,
Nor bloomy vines wave purple on the hill;
Tell, that when silent years have pass'd away,
That when his eye grows dim, his tresses gray,
These busy hands a lovelier cot shall build,
And deck with fairer flowers his little field,
And call from Heaven propitious dews to breathe
Arcadian beauty on the barren heath;
Tell, that while Love's spontaneous smile endears
The days of peace, the sabbath of his years,
Health shall prolong to many a festive hour
The social pleasures of his humble bower.

Lo! at the couch where infant beauty sleeps,
Her silent watch the mournful mother keeps;
She, while the lovely babe unconscious lies,
Smiles on her slumbering child with pensive eyes,
And weaves a song of melancholy joy—
"Sleep, image of thy father, sleep, my boy;
No lingering hour of sorrow shall be thine;
No sigh that rends thy father's heart and mine;
Bright as his manly sire the son shall be
In form and soul; but, ah! more blest than he!
Thy fame, thy worth, thy filial love at last,
Shall soothe his aching heart for all the past—
With many a smile my solitude repay,
And chase the world's ungenerous scorn away.

"And say, when summon'd from the world and thee,
I lay my head beneath the willow tree,

Wilt *thou*, sweet mourner! at my stone appear,
And soothe my parted spirit lingering near?
Oh, wilt thou come at evening hour to shed
The tears of Memory o'er my narrow bed;
With aching temples on thy hand reclined,
Muse on the last farewell I leave behind,
Breathe a deep sigh to winds that murmur low
And think on all my love, and all my woe?"
So speaks affection, ere the infant eye
Can look regard, or brighten in reply;
But when the cherub lip hath learnt to claim
A mother's ear by that endearing name;
Soon as the playful innocent can prove
A tear of pity, or a smile of love,
Or cons his murmuring task beneath her care,
Or lisps with holy look his evening prayer,
Or gazing, mutely pensive, sits to hear
The mournful ballad warbled in his ear;
How fondly looks admiring Hope the while,
At every artless tear, and every smile;
How glows the joyous parent to descry
A guileless bosom, true to sympathy!
Where is the troubled heart consign'd to share
Tumultuous toils, or solitary care,
Unblest by visionary thoughts that stray
To count the joys of Fortune's better day!
Lo, nature, life, and liberty relume
The dim-eyed tenant of the dungeon gloom,
A long-lost friend, or hapless child restored,
Smiles at his blazing hearth and social board;

Warm from his heart the tears of rapture flow,
And virtue triumphs o'er remember'd woe.
 Chide not his peace, proud Reason; nor destroy
The shadowy forms of uncreated joy,
That urge the lingering tide of life, and pour
Spontaneous slumber on his midnight hour.
Hark! the wild maniac sings, to chide the gale
That wafts so slow her lover's distant sail;
She, sad spectatress, on the wintry shore,
Watch'd the rude surge his shroudless corse that bore,
Knew the pale form, and, shrieking in amaze,
Clasp'd her cold hands, and fix'd her maddening gaze:
Poor widow'd wretch! 'twas there she wept in vain,
Till Memory fled her agonizing brain;—
But Mercy gave, to charm the sense of woe,
Ideal peace, that truth could ne'er bestow;
Warm on her heart the joys of Fancy beam,
And aimless Hope delights her darkest dream.
 Oft when yon moon has climb'd the midnight sky,
And the lone sea-bird wakes its wildest cry,
Piled on the steep, her blazing fagots burn
To hail the bark that never can return;
And still she waits, but scarce forbears to weep
That constant love can linger on the deep.

And, mark the wretch, whose wanderings never knew
The world's regard, that soothes, though half untrue;
Whose erring heart the lash of sorrow bore,
But found not pity when it err'd no more.
Yon friendless man, at whose dejected eye
Th' unfeeling proud one looks—and passes by,
Condemn'd on Penury's barren path to roam,
Scorn'd by the world, and left without a home—
Even he, at evening, should he chance to stray
Down by the hamlet's hawthorn-scented way,
Where, round the cot's romantic glade, are seen
The blossom'd bean-field, and the sloping green,
Leans o'er its humble gate, and thinks the while—
Oh! that for me some home like this would smile,
Some hamlet shade, to yield my sickly form
Health in the breeze, and shelter in the storm!
There should my hand no stinted boon assign
To wretched hearts with sorrow such as mine!—
That generous wish can soothe unpitied care,
And HOPE half mingles with the poor man's prayer.

HOPE! when I mourn, with sympathizing mind,
The wrongs of fate, the woes of human kind,
Thy blissful omens bid my spirit see
The boundless fields of rapture yet to be;
I watch the wheels of Nature's mazy plan,
And learn the future by the past of man.

Come, bright Improvement! on the car of Time,
And rule the spacious world from clime to clime;
Thy handmaid arts shall every wild explore,
Trace every wave, and culture every shore.
On Erie's banks, where tigers steal along,
And the dread Indian chants a dismal song,
Where human fiends on midnight errands walk,
And bathe in brains the murderous tomahawk,
There shall the flocks on thymy pasture stray,
And shepherds dance at Summer's opening day;
Each wandering genius of the lonely glen
Shall start to view the glittering haunts of men,
And silent watch, on woodland heights around,
The village curfew as it tolls profound.
In Libyan groves, where damned rites are done,
That bathe the rocks in blood, and veil the sun,
Truth shall arrest the murderous arm profane,
Wild Obi flies—the veil is rent in twain.
Where barbarous hordes on Scythian mountains roam,
Truth, Mercy, Freedom, yet shall find a home;
Where'er degraded Nature bleeds and pines,
From Guinea's coast to Sibir's dreary mines,
Truth shall pervade th' unfathom'd darkness there,
And light the dreadful features of despair.—
Hark! the stern captive spurns his heavy load,
And asks the image back that Heaven bestow'd!
Fierce in his eye the fire of valour burns,
And, as the slave departs, the man returns.

Oh! sacred Truth! thy triumph ceased a while,
And Hope, thy sister, ceased with thee to smile,
When leagued Oppression pour'd to Northern wars
Her whisker'd pandoors and her fierce hussars,
Waved her dread standard to the breeze of morn,
Peal'd her loud drum, and twang'd her trumpet horn;
Tumultuous horror brooded o'er her van,
Presaging wrath to Poland—and to man!
Warsaw's last champion from her height survey'd,
Wide o'er the fields, a waste of ruin laid,—
Oh! Heaven! he cried, my bleeding country save!—
Is there no hand on high to shield the brave?
Yet, though destruction sweep those lovely plains,
Rise, fellow-men! our country yet remains!
By that dread name, we wave the sword on high!
And swear for her to live!—with her to die!
He said, and on the rampart-heights array'd
His trusty warriors, few, but undismay'd;
Firm-paced and slow, a horrid front they form,
Still as the breeze, but dreadful as the storm;
Low murmuring sounds along their banners fly,
Revenge, or death,—the watch-word and reply;
Then peal'd the notes, omnipotent to charm,
And the loud tocsin toll'd their last alarm!—
In vain, alas! in vain, ye gallant few!
From rank to rank your volley'd thunder flew:—

Oh, bloodiest picture in the book of Time,
Sarmatia fell, unwept, without a crime;
Found not a generous friend, a pitying foe,
Strength in her arms, nor mercy in her woe!
Dropp'd from her nerveless grasp the shatter'd spear,
Closed her bright eye, and curb'd her high career;—
HOPE, for a season, bade the world farewell,
And Freedom shriek'd—as KOSCIUSKO fell!
The sun went down, nor ceased the carnage there,
Tumultuous Murder shook the midnight air—
On Prague's proud arch the fires of ruin glow,
His blood-dyed waters murmuring far below;
The storm prevails, the rampart yields a way,
Bursts the wild cry of horror and dismay!
Hark, as the smouldering piles with thunder fall,
A thousand shrieks for hopeless mercy call!
Earth shook—red meteors flash'd along the sky,
And conscious Nature shudder'd at the cry!
Oh! righteous Heaven; ere Freedom found a grave,
Why slept the sword, omnipotent to save?
Where was thine arm, O Vengeance! where thy rod,
That smote the foes of Zion and of God;
That crush'd proud Ammon, when his iron car
Was yoked in wrath, and thunder'd from afar?

Where was the storm that slumber'd till the host
Of blood-stain'd Pharaoh left their trembling coast;
Then bade the deep in wild commotion flow,
And heaved an ocean on their march below?
 Departed spirits of the mighty dead!
Ye that at Marathon and Leuctra bled!
Friends of the world! restore your swords to man,
Fight in his sacred cause, and lead the van!
Yet for Sarmatia's tears of blood atone,
And make her arm puissant as your own!
Oh! once again to Freedom's cause return
The patriot TELL—the BRUCE OF BANNOCKBURN!
 Yes! thy proud lords, unpitied land! shall see
That man hath yet a soul—and dare be free!
A little while, along thy saddening plains,
The starless night of Desolation reigns;
Truth shall restore the light by Nature given,
And, like Prometheus, bring the fire of Heaven!
Prone to the dust Oppression shall be hurl'd,
Her name, her nature, wither'd from the world!
 Ye that the rising morn invidious mark,
And hate the light—because your deeds are dark;
Ye that expanding truth invidious view,
And think, or wish, the song of HOPE untrue;
Perhaps your little hands presume to span
The march of Genius and the powers of man;
Perhaps ye watch, at Pride's unhallow'd shrine,
Her victims, newly slain, and thus divine:—

" Here shall thy triumph, Genius, cease, and here
Truth, Science, Virtue, close your short career."
  Tyrants! in vain ye trace the wizard ring;
In vain ye limit Mind's unwearied spring:
What! can ye lull the winged winds asleep,
Arrest the rolling world, or chain the deep?
No!—the wild wave contemns your sceptred
    hand:
It roll'd not back when Canute gave command!
  Man! can thy doom no brighter soul allow?
Still must thou live a blot on Nature's brow?
Shall war's polluted banner ne'er be furl'd?
Shall crimes and tyrants cease but with the
    world?
What! are thy triumphs, sacred Truth, belied?
Why then hath Plato lived—or Sidney died?
  Ye fond adorers of departed fame,
Who warm at Scipio's worth, or Tully's name!
Ye that, in fancied vision, can admire
The sword of Brutus, and the Theban lyre!
Rapt in historic ardour, who adore
Each classic haunt, and well-remember'd shore,
Where Valour tuned, amidst her chosen throng,
The Thracian trumpet, and the Spartan song;
Or, wandering thence, behold the later charms
Of England's glory, and Helvetia's arms!
See Roman fire in Hampden's bosom swell,
And fate and freedom in the shaft of Tell!
Say, ye fond zealots to the worth of yore,
Hath Valour left the world—to live no more?

No more shall Brutus bid a tyrant die,
And sternly smile with vengeance in his eye?
Hampden no more, when suffering Freedom calls,
Encounter Fate, and triumph as he falls?
Nor Tell disclose, through peril and alarm,
The might that slumbers in a peasant's arm?
Yes! in that generous cause, for ever strong,
The patriot's virtue and the poet's song,
Still, as the tide of ages rolls away,
Shall charm the world, unconscious of decay.
Yes! there are hearts, prophetic HOPE may trust,
That slumber yet in uncreated dust,
Ordain'd to fire th' adoring sons of earth,
With every charm of wisdom and of worth;
Ordain'd to light, with intellectual day,
The mazy wheels of nature as they play,
Or, warm with Fancy's energy, to glow,
And rival all but Shakspeare's name below.
And say, supernal Powers! who deeply scan
Heaven's dark decrees, unfathom'd yet by man,
When shall the world call down, to cleanse her shame,
That embryo spirit, yet without a name,—
That friend of Nature, whose avenging hands
Shall burst the Libyan's adamantine bands?
Who, sternly marking on his native soil
The blood, the tears, the anguish, and the toil,
Shall bid each righteous heart exult, to see
Peace to the slave, and vengeance on the free!

Yet, yet, degraded men! th' expected day
That breaks your bitter cup, is far away;
Trade, wealth, and fashion, ask you still to bleed,
And holy men give Scripture for the deed;
Scourged, and debased, no Briton stoops to save
A wretch, a coward; yes, because a slave!—
Eternal Nature! when thy giant hand
Had heaved the floods, and fix'd the trembling land,
When life sprang startling at thy plastic call,
Endless her forms, and man the lord of all!
Say, was that lordly form inspired by thee,
To wear eternal chains and bow the knee?
Was man ordain'd the slave of man to toil,
Yoked with the brutes, and fetter'd to the soil;
Weigh'd in a tyrant's balance with his gold?
No!—Nature stamp'd us in a heavenly mould!
She bade no wretch his thankless labour urge,
Nor, trembling, take the pittance and the scourge!
No homeless Libyan, on the stormy deep,
To call upon his country's name, and weep!—
Lo! once in triumph, on his boundless plain,
The quiver'd chief of Congo loved to reign;
With fires proportion'd to his native sky,
Strength in his arm, and lightning in his eye;
Scour'd with wild feet his sun-illumined zone,
The spear, the lion, and the woods, his own!
Or led the combat, bold without a plan,
An artless savage, but a fearless man!

The plunderer came!—alas! no glory smiles
For Congo's chief, on yonder Indian Isles;
For ever fall'n! no son of Nature now,
With Freedom charter'd on his manly brow!
Faint, bleeding, bound, he weeps the night away,
And when the sea-wind wafts the dewless day,
Starts, with a bursting heart, for evermore
To curse the sun that lights their guilty shore!
The shrill horn blew; at that alarum knell
His guardian angel took a last farewell!
That funeral dirge to darkness hath resign'd
The fiery grandeur of a generous mind!
Poor fetter'd man! I hear thee whispering low
Unhallow'd vows to Guilt, the child of Woe,
Friendless thy heart; and canst thou harbour there
A wish but death—a passion but despair?
The widow'd Indian, when her lord expires,
Mounts the dread pile, and braves the funeral fires!
So falls the heart at Thraldom's bitter sigh!
So Virtue dies, the spouse of Liberty!
But not to Libya's barren climes alone,
To Chili, or the wild Siberian zone,
Belong the wretched heart and haggard eye,
Degraded worth, and poor misfortune's sigh!—
Ye orient realms, where Ganges' waters run!
Prolific fields! dominions of the sun!
How long your tribes have trembled and obey'd!
How long was Timour's iron sceptre sway'd,

Whose marshall'd hosts, the lions of the plain,
From Scythia's northern mountains to the main,
Raged o'er your plunder'd shrines and altars bare,
With blazing torch and gory scymetar,—
Stunn'd with the cries of death each gentle gale,
And bathed in blood the verdure of the vale!
Yet could no pangs the immortal spirit tame,
When Brama's children perish'd for his name;
The martyr smiled beneath avenging power,
And braved the tyrant in his torturing hour!
 When Europe sought your subject realms to gain,
And stretch'd her giant sceptre o'er the main,
Taught her proud barks the winding way to shape,
And braved the stormy Spirit of the Cape;
Children of Brama! then was Mercy nigh
To wash the stain of blood's eternal dye?
Did Peace descend, to triumph and to save,
When freeborn Britons cross'd the Indian wave?
Ah, no!—to more than Rome's ambition true,
The Nurse of Freedom gave it not to you!
She the bold route of Europe's guilt began,
And, in the march of nations, led the van!
 Rich in the gems of India's gaudy zone,
And plunder piled from kingdoms not their own,
Degenerate trade! thy minions could despise
The heart-born anguish of a thousand cries;
Could lock, with impious hands, their teeming store,
While famish'd nations died along the shore:

Could mock the groans of fellow-men, and bear
The curse of kingdoms peopled with despair;
Could stamp disgrace on man's polluted name,
And barter, with their gold, eternal shame!
But hark! as bow'd to earth the Bramin kneels,
From heavenly climes propitious thunder peals!
Of India's fate her guardian spirits tell,
Prophetic murmurs breathing on the shell,
And solemn sounds that awe the listening mind,
Roll on the azure paths of every wind.
"Foes of mankind! (her guardian spirits say,)
Revolving ages bring the bitter day,
When Heaven's unerring arm shall fall on you,
And blood for blood these Indian plains bedew;
Nine times have Brama's wheels of lightning hurl'd
His awful presence o'er the alarmed world;
Nine times hath Guilt, through all his giant frame,
Convulsive trembled, as the Mighty came;
Nine times hath suffering Mercy spared in vain—
But Heaven shall burst her starry gates again!
He comes! dread Brama shakes the sunless sky
With murmuring wrath, and thunders from on high,
Heaven's fiery horse, beneath his warrior form,
Paws the light clouds, and gallops on the storm!
Wide waves his flickering sword; his bright arms glow
Like summer suns and light the world below!

Earth, and her trembling isles in Ocean's bed,
Are shook; and Nature rocks beneath his tread!
"To pour redress on India's injured realm,
The oppressor to dethrone, the proud to whelm;
To chase destruction from her plunder'd shore
With arts and arms that triumph'd once before,
The tenth Avatar comes! at Heaven's command
Shall Seriswattee wave her hallow'd wand!
And Camdeo bright, and Ganesa sublime,
Shall bless with joy their own propitious clime!—
Come, Heavenly Powers! primeval peace restore!
Love!—Mercy!—Wisdom!—rule for evermore!"

PLEASURES OF HOPE.

PART THE SECOND.

ANALYSIS OF PART II.

Apostrophe to the power of Love—its intimate connection with generous and social Sensibility—allusion to that beautiful passage in the beginning of the Book of Genesis, which represents the happiness of Paradise itself incomplete, till love was superadded to its other blessings—the dreams of future felicity which a lively imagination is apt to cherish, when Hope is animated by refined attachment—this disposition to combine, in one imaginary scene of residence, all that is pleasing in our estimate of happiness, compared to the skill of the great artist who personified perfect beauty, in the picture of Venus, by an assemblage of the most beautiful features he could find—a summer and winter evening described, as they may be supposed to arise in the mind of one who wishes, with enthusiasm, for the union of friendship and retirement.

Hope and Imagination inseparable agents—even in those contemplative moments when our imagination wanders beyond the boundaries of this world, our minds are not unattended with an impression that we shall some day have a wider and more distinct prospect of the universe, instead of the partial glimpse we now enjoy.

The last and most sublime influence of Hope is the concluding topic of the poem—the predominance of a belief in a future state over the terrors attendant on dissolution—the baneful influence of that sceptical philosophy which bars us from such comforts—allusion to the fate of a suicide—episode of Conrad and Ellenore—conclusion.

PLEASURES OF HOPE.

PART II.

In joyous youth, what soul hath never known
Thought, feeling, taste, harmonious to its own?
Who hath not paused while Beauty's pensive
eye
Ask'd from his heart the homage of a sigh?
Who hath not own'd, with rapture-smitten frame,
The power of grace, the magic of a name?
There be, perhaps, who barren hearts avow,
Cold as the rocks on Torneo's hoary brow;
There be, whose loveless wisdom never fail'd
In self-adoring pride securely mail'd:—
But, triumph not, ye peace-enamour'd few
Fire, Nature, Genius, never dwelt with yo
For you no fancy consecrates the scene
Where rapture utter'd vows, and wept betw
'Tis yours, unmoved, to sever and to meet;
No pledge is sacred, and no home is sweet!
Who that would ask a heart to dulness wed
The waveless calm, the slumber of the dead?
No; the wild bliss of Nature needs alloy,
And fear and sorrow fan the fire of joy!
And say, without our hopes, without our fears,
Without the home that plighted love endears,

Without the smile from partial beauty won,
Oh! what were man?—a world without a sun.
  Till Hymen brought his love-delighted hour,
There dwelt no joy in Eden's rosy bower!
In vain the viewless seraph lingering there,
At starry midnight charm'd the silent air;
In vain the wild-bird caroll'd on the steep,
To hail the sun, slow wheeling from the deep;
In vain, to soothe the solitary shade,
Aërial notes in mingling measure play'd;
The summer wind that shook the spangled tree,
The whispering wave, the murmur of the bee;—
Still slowly pass'd the melancholy day,
And still the stranger wist not where to stray.
The world was sad!—the garden was a wild!
And man, the hermit, sigh'd—till woman smiled!
  True, the sad power to generous hearts may [bring
Delirious anguish on his fiery wing;
Barr'd from delight by Fate's untimely hand,
By wealthless lot, or pitiless command:
Or doom'd to gaze on beauties that adorn
The smile of triumph or the frown of scorn;
While Memory watches o'er the sad review
Of joys that faded like the morning dew;
Peace may depart—and life and nature seem
A barren path, a wildness, and a dream!
  But can the noble mind for ever brood,
The willing victim of a weary mood,
On heartless cares that squander life away,
And cloud young Genius brightening into day?—

Shame to the coward thought that e'er betray'd
The noon of manhood to a myrtle shade!—
If Hope's creative spirit cannot raise
One trophy sacred to thy future days,
Scorn the dull crowd that haunt the gloomy
shrine,
Of hopeless love to murmur and repine!
But, should a sigh of milder mood express
Thy heart-warm wishes, true to happiness,
Should Heaven's fair harbinger delight to pour
Her blissful visions on thy pensive hour,
No tear to blot thy memory's pictured page,
No fears but such as fancy can assuage; [miss
Though thy wild heart some hapless hour may
The peaceful tenor of unvaried bliss,
(For love pursues an ever-devious race,
True to the winding lineaments of grace;)
Yet still may Hope her talisman employ
To snatch from Heaven anticipated joy,
And all her kindred energies impart
That burn the brightest in the purest heart.
When first the Rhodian's mimic art array'd
The queen of Beauty in her Cyprian shade,
The happy master mingled on his piece
Each look that charm'd him in the fair of Greece.
To faultless Nature true, he stole a grace
From every finer form and sweeter face;
And as he sojourn'd on the Ægean isles,
Woo'd all their love, and treasured all their
smiles;

Then glow'd the tints, pure, precious, and refined,
And mortal charms seem'd heavenly when combined!
Love on the picture smiled! Expression pour'd
Her mingling spirit there—and Greece adored!
So thy fair hand, enamour'd Fancy! gleans
The treasured pictures of a thousand scenes;
Thy pencil traces on the lover's thought
Some cottage-home, from towns and toil remote,
Where love and lore may claim alternate hours,
With Peace embosom'd in Idalian bowers!
Remote from busy Life's bewilder'd way,
O'er all his heart shall Taste and Beauty sway!
Free on the sunny slope, or winding shore,
With hermit steps to wander and adore!
There shall he love, when genial morn appears,
Like pensive Beauty smiling in her tears,
To watch the brightening roses of the sky,
And muse on Nature with a poet's eye!—
And when the sun's last splendour lights the deep,
The woods and waves, and murmuring winds asleep,
When fairy harps th' Hesperian planet hail,
And the lone cuckoo sighs along the vale,
His path shall be where streamy mountains swell
Their shadowy grandeur o'er the narrow dell,
Where mouldering piles and forests intervene,
Mingling with darker tints the living green;
No circling hills his ravish'd eye to bound,
Heaven, Earth, and Ocean, blazing all around.

The moon is up—the watch-tower dimly burns—
And down the vale his sober step returns;
But pauses oft, as winding rocks convey
The still sweet fall of music far away;
And oft he lingers from his home awhile
To watch the dying notes!—and start, and smile!
Let Winter come! let polar spirits sweep
The darkening world, and tempest-troubled deep!
Though boundless snows the wither'd heath deform,
And the dim sun scarce wanders through the storm,
Yet shall the smile of social love repay,
With mental light, the melancholy day!
And, when its short and sullen noon is o'er,
The ice-chain'd waters slumbering on the shore,
How bright the fagots in his little hall
Blaze on the hearth, and warm the pictured wall!
How blest he names, in Love's familiar tone,
The kind fair friend, by nature mark'd his own;
And, in the waveless mirror of his mind,
Views the fleet years of pleasure left behind,
Since when her empire o'er his heart began!
Since first he call'd her his before the holy man!
Trim the gay taper in his rustic dome,
And light the wintry paradise of home;
And let the half-uncurtain'd window hail
Some way-worn man benighted in the vale!
Now, while the moaning night-wind rages high,
As sweep the shot-stars down the troubled sky,

While fiery hosts in Heaven's wide circle play,
And bathe in lurid light the milky-way,
Safe from the storm, the meteor, and the shower
Some pleasing page shall charm the solemn hour—
With pathos shall command, with wit beguile,
A generous tear of anguish or a smile—
Thy woes, Arion! and thy simple tale,
O'er all the heart shall triumph and prevail!
Charm'd as they read the verse too sadly true,
How gallant Albert, and his weary crew,
Heaved all their guns, their foundering bark to save,
And toil'd—and shriek'd—and perish'd on the wave!
Yes, at the dead of night, by Lonna's steep,
The seaman's cry was heard along the deep;
There on his funeral waters, dark and wild,
The dying father bless'd his darling child!
Oh! Mercy, shield her innocence, he cried,
Spent on the prayer his bursting heart, and died!
Or they will learn how generous worth sublimes
The robber Moor, and pleads for all his crimes!
How poor Amelia kiss'd, with many a tear,
His hand, blood-stain'd, but ever, ever dear!
Hung on the tortured bosom of her lord,
And wept and pray'd perdition from his sword!
Nor sought in vain! at that heart-piercing cry
The strings of Nature crack'd with agony!
He, with delirious laugh, the dagger hurl'd,
And burst the ties that bound him to the world!

Turn from his dying words, that smite with steel
The shuddering thoughts, or wind them on the wheel—
Turn to the gentler melodies that suit
Thalia's harp, or Pan's Arcadian lute;
Or, down the stream of Truth's historic page,
From clime to clime descend, from age to age!
   Yet there, perhaps, may darker scenes obtrude
Than Fancy fashions in her wildest mood;
There shall he pause with horrent brow, to rate
What millions died—that Cæsar might be great!
Or learn the fate that bleeding thousands bore,
March'd by their Charles to Dneiper's swampy shore;
Faint in his wounds, and shivering in the blast,
The Swedish soldier sunk—and groan'd his last!
File after file the stormy showers benumb,
Freeze every standard-sheet, and hush the drum!
Horseman and horse confess'd the bitter pang,
And arms and warriors fell with hollow clang!
Yet, ere he sunk in Nature's last repose,
Ere life's warm torrent to the fountain froze,
The dying man to Sweden turn'd his eye,
Thought of his home, and closed it with a sigh!
Imperial Pride look'd sullen on his plight,
And Charles beheld—nor shudder'd at the sight!
   Above, below, in Ocean, Earth, and Sky,
Thy fairy worlds, Imagination, lie,
And Hope attends, companion of the way,
Thy dream by night, thy visions of the day!

In yonder pensile orb, and every sphere
That gems the starry girdle of the year;
In those unmeasured worlds, she bids thee tell,
Pure from their God, created millions dwell,
Whose names and natures, unreveal'd below,
We yet shall learn, and wonder as we know;
For, as Iona's saint, a giant form,
Throned on her towers, conversing with the storm,
(When o'er each Runic altar, weed-entwined,
The vesper clock tolls mournful to the wind,)
Counts every wave-worn isle, and mountain hoar,
From Kilda to the green Ierne's shore;
So, when thy pure and renovated mind
This perishable dust hath left behind,
Thy seraph eye shall count the starry train,
Like distant isles embosom'd in the main;
Rapt to the shrine where motion first began,
And light and life in mingling torrent ran;
From whence each bright rotundity was hurl'd,
The throne of God;—the centre of the world!
  Oh! vainly wise, the moral Muse hath sung
That suasive Hope hath but a Siren tongue!
True; she may sport with life's untutor'd day,
Nor heed the solace of its last decay,
The guileless heart her happy mansion spurn,
And part, like Ajut—never to return!
  But yet, methinks, when Wisdom shall assuage
The grief and passions of our greener age,
Though dull the close of life, and far away
Each flower that hail'd the dawning of the day;

Yet o'er her lovely hopes, that once were dear,
The time-taught spirit, pensive, not severe,
With milder griefs her aged eye shall fill,
And weep their falsehood, though she loves them
still!
Thus, with forgiving tears, and reconciled,
The king of Judah mourn'd his rebel child!
Musing on days, when yet the guiltless boy
Smiled on his sire, and fill'd his heart with joy!
My Absalom! the voice of Nature cried,
Oh! that for thee thy father could have died!
For bloody was the deed, and rashly done,
That slew my Absalom!—my son!—my son!
Unfading HOPE! when life's last embers burn,
When soul to soul, and dust to dust return!
Heaven to thy charge resigns the awful hour!
Oh! then, thy kingdom comes! Immortal Power!
What though each spark of earth-born rapture
fly
The quivering lip, pale cheek, and closing eye!
Bright to the soul thy seraph hands convey
The morning dream of life's eternal day—
Then, then, the triumph and the trance begin,
And all the phœnix spirit burns within!
Oh! deep-enchanting prelude to repose,
The dawn of bliss, the twilight of our woes!
Yet half I hear the panting spirit sigh,
It is a dread and awful thing to die!
Mysterious worlds, untravell'd by the sun!
Where Time's far-wandering tide has never run,

From your unfathom'd shades, and viewless
spheres,
A warning comes, unheard by other ears.
'Tis Heaven's commanding trumpet, long and
loud,
Like Sinai's thunder, pealing from the cloud!
While Nature hears, with terror-mingled trust,
The shock that hurls her fabric to the dust;
And, like the trembling Hebrew, when he trod
The roaring waves, and call'd upon his God,
With mortal terrors clouds immortal bliss,
And shrieks, and hovers o'er the dark abyss!
Daughter of Faith, awake, arise, illume
The dread unknown, the chaos of the tomb;
Melt, and dispel, ye spectre-doubts, that roll
Cimmerian darkness o'er the parting soul!
Fly, like the moon-eyed herald of Dismay,
Chased on his night-steed by the star of day!
The strife is o'er—the pangs of Nature close,
And life's last rapture triumphs o'er her woes.
Hark! as the spirit eyes, with eagle gaze,
The noon of Heaven undazzled by the blaze,
On heavenly winds that waft her to the sky,
Float the sweet tones of star-born melody;
Wild as that hallow'd anthem sent to hail
Bethlehem's shepherds in the lonely vale,
When Jordan hush'd his waves, and midnight still
Watch'd on the holy towers of Zion hill!
Soul of the just! companion of the dead!
Where is thy home, and whither art thou fled?

Back to its heavenly source thy being goes,
Swift as the comet wheels to whence he rose;
Doom'd on his airy path a while to burn,
And doom'd, like thee, to travel, and return.—
Hark! from the world's exploding centre driven,
With sounds that shook the firmament of Heaven,
Careers the fiery giant, fast and far,
On bickering wheels, and adamantine car;
From planet whirl'd to planet more remote,
He visits realms beyond the reach of thought;
But wheeling homeward, when his course is run,
Curbs the red yoke, and mingles with the sun!
So hath the traveller of earth unfurl'd
Her trembling wings, emerging from the world;
And o'er the path by mortal never trod,
Sprung to her source, the bosom of her God!
  Oh! lives there, Heaven, beneath thy dread expanse,
One hopeless, dark idolater of Chance,
Content to feed, with pleasures unrefined,
The lukewarm passions of a lowly mind;
Who, mouldering earthward, 'reft of every trust,
In joyless union wedded to the dust,
Could all his parting energy dismiss,
And call this barren world sufficient bliss?—
There live, alas! of heaven-directed mien,
Of cultured soul, and sapient eye serene,
Who hail thee, Man! the pilgrim of a day,
Spouse of the worm, and brother of the clay,
Frail as the leaf in Autumn's yellow bower,
Dust in the wind, or dew upon the flower;

A friendless slave, a child w'thout a sire,
Whose mortal life and momentary fire,
Light to the grave his chance-created form,
As ocean-wrecks illuminate the storm;
And, when the gun's tremendous flash is o'er,
To night and silence sink for evermore!—
Are these the pompous tidings ye proclaim,
Lights of the world, and demi-gods of Fame?
Is this your triumph—this your proud applause,
Children of Truth, and champions of her cause
For this hath Science search'd, on weary wing,
By shore and sea—each mute and living thing!
Launch'd with Iberia's pilot from the steep,
To worlds unknown, and isles beyond the deep?
Or round the cope her living chariot driven,
And wheel'd in triumph through the signs of Heaven.
Oh! star-eyed Science, hast thou wander'd there,
To waft us home the message of despair?
Then bind the palm, thy sage's brow to suit,
Of blasted leaf, and death-distilling fruit!
Ah me! the laurell'd wreath that Murder rears,
Blood-nursed, and water'd by the widow's tears,
Seems not so foul, so tainted, and so dread,
As waves the night-shade round the sceptic head.
What is the bigot's torch, the tyrant's chain?
I smile on death, if Heavenward Hope remain;
But, if the warring winds of Nature's strife
Be all the faithless charter of my life,

If Chance awaked, inexorable power,
This frail and feverish being of an hour;
Doom'd o'er the world's precarious scene to sweep,
Swift as the tempest travels on the deep,
To know Delight but by her parting smile,
And toil, and wish, and weep a little while;
Then melt, ye elements, that form'd in vain
This troubled pulse, and visionary brain!
Fade, ye wild flowers, memorials of my doom,
And sink, ye stars, that light me to the tomb!
Truth, ever lovely,—since the world began,
The foe of tyrants, and the friend of man,—
How can thy words from balmy slumber start
Reposing Virtue, pillow'd on the heart!
Yet, if thy voice the note of thunder roll'd,
And that were true which Nature never told,
Let Wisdom smile not on her conquer'd field;
No rapture dawns, no treasure is reveal'd!
Oh! let her read, nor loudly, nor elate,
The doom that bars us from a better fate;
But, sad as angels for the good man's sin,
Weep to record, and blush to give it in!
  And well may Doubt, the mother of Dismay,
Pause at her martyr's tomb, and read the lay.
Down by the wilds of yon deserted vale,
It darkly hints a melancholy tale!
There as the homeless madman sits alone,
In hollow winds he hears a spirit moan!
And there, they say, a wizard orgie crowds,
When the Moon lights her watch-tower in the clouds.

Poor lost Alonzo! Fate's neglected child!
Mild be the doom of Heaven—as thou wert mild!
For oh! thy heart in holy mould was cast,
And all thy deeds were blameless, but the last.
Poor lost Alonzo! still I seem to hear
The clod that struck thy hollow-sounding bier!
When Friendship paid, in speechless sorrow drown'd,
Thy midnight rites, but not on hallow'd ground!
Cease, every joy, to glimmer on my mind,
But leave—oh! leave the light of HOPE behind!
What though my winged hours of bliss have been,
Like angel-visits, few and far between,
Her musing mood shall every pang appease,
And charm—when pleasures lose the power to please!
Yes; let each rapture, dear to Nature, flee:
Close not the light of Fortune's stormy sea—
Mirth, Music, Friendship, Love's propitious smile,
Chase every care, and charm a little while,
Ecstatic throbs the fluttering heart employ,
And all her strings are harmonized to joy!—
But why so short is Love's delighted hour?
Why fades the dew on Beauty's sweetest flower?
Why can no hymned charm of music heal
The sleepless woes impassion'd spirits feel?
Can Fancy's fairy hands no veil create,
To hide the sad realities of fate?—
No! not the quaint remark, the sapient rule,
Nor all the pride of Wisdom's worldly school,

Have power to soothe, unaided and alone,
The heart that vibrates to a feeling tone!
When stepdame Nature every bliss recalls,
Fleet as the meteor o'er the desert falls;
When, 'reft of all, yon widow'd sire appears
A lonely hermit in the vale of years;
Say, can the world one joyous thought bestow
To Friendship, weeping at the couch of Woe?
No! but a brighter soothes the last adieu,—
Souls of impassion'd mould, she speaks to you!
Weep not, she says, at Nature's transient pain,
Congenial spirits part to meet again!
What plaintive sobs thy filial spirit drew,
What sorrow choked thy long and last adieu!
Daughter of Conrad? when he heard his knell,
And bade his country and his child farewell
Doom'd the long isles of Sidney-cove to see,
The martyr of his crimes, but true to thee?
Thrice the sad father tore thee from his heart,
And thrice return'd, to bless thee, and to part;
Thrice from his trembling lips he murmur'd low
The plaint that own'd unutterable woe;
Till Faith, prevailing o'er his sullen doom,
As bursts the morn on night's unfathom'd gloom,
Lured his dim eye to deathless hopes sublime,
Beyond the realms of Nature and of Time!
"And weep not thus," he cried, "young Ellenore,
My bosom bleeds, but soon shall bleed no more!

Short shall this half-extinguish'd spirit burn,
And soon these limbs to kindred dust return!
But not, my child, with life's precarious fire,
The immortal ties of Nature shall expire;
These shall resist the triumph of decay,
When time is o'er, and worlds have pass'd away!
Cold in the dust this perish'd heart may lie,
But that which warm'd it once shall never die!
That spark unburied in its mortal frame,
With living light, eternal, and the same,
Shall beam on Joy's interminable years,
Unveil'd by darkness—unassuaged by tears!
"Yet, on the barren shore and stormy deep,
One tedious watch is Conrad doom'd to weep;
But when I gain the home without a friend,
And press the uneasy couch where none attend,
This last embrace, still cherish'd in my heart,
Shall calm the struggling spirit ere it part!
Thy darling form shall seem to hover nigh,
And hush the groan of life's last agony!
"Farewell! when strangers lift thy father's bier,
And place my nameless stone without a tear;
When each returning pledge hath told my child
That Conrad's tomb is on the desert piled;
And when the dream of troubled Fancy sees
Its lonely rank grass waving in the breeze;
Who then will soothe thy grief, when mine is o'er?
Who will protect thee, helpless Ellenore?
Shall secret scenes thy filial sorrows hide,
Scorn'd by the world, to factious guilt allied?

Ah! no; methinks the generous and the good
Will woo thee from the shades of solitude!
O'er friendless grief Compassion shall awake,
And smile on innocence, for Mercy's sake!"
  Inspiring thought of rapture yet to be,
The tears of Love were hopeless, but for thee?
If in that frame no deathless spirit dwell,
If that faint murmur be the last farewell,
If Fate unite the faithful but to part,
Why is their memory sacred to the heart?
Why does the brother of my childhood seem
Restored a while in every pleasing dream?
Why do I joy the lonely spot to view,
By artless friendship bless'd when life was new?
  Eternal HOPE! when yonder spheres sublime
Peal'd their first notes to sound the march of Time,
Thy joyous youth began—but not to fade.—
When all the sister planets have decay'd;
When wrapt in fire the realms of ether glow,
And Heaven's last thunder shakes the world below;
Thou, undismay'd, shalt o'er the ruins smile,
And light thy torch at Nature's funeral pile.

"The Pleasures of Hope" has now passed through nearly one hundred editions, been translated into all the chief continental languages, for many years been in use in school and college as a model for imitation, and is now familiar in the mouths of our millions as "household words;" so that panegyric or criticism may be here considered quite out of place.

No first production by any poet was ever more enthusiastically received, nor did any poem ever bring its author so large a pecuniary recompense: true it is the copyright was originally sold for the small sum of 50*l.*, to the firm of Mundell & Co., the publishers of Edinburgh; yet these gentlemen, acting in a most praiseworthy spirit, presented its author with 25*l.* upon the appearance of every edition of one thousand copies; and indeed, to their credit be it recorded, after publication of the sixth edition, they allowed him to print one on his own account, by subscription; this, of itself, produced 600*l.* Unhappily, some misunderstanding afterwards arose, which caused the discontinuance of these douceurs; yet on the whole first seven editions Campbell received for his 1100 lines no less a sum than 900*l.*

The work itself, besides having the rare merit in that age of metrical accuracy, great strength combined with natural simplicity of style and peculiar sweetness, had this further advantage in its favour, that the subjects interwoven with it were the very matters at the time peculiarly before the eye of the public; the great revolution in France, the partition of Poland, the abolition of negro slavery, all stood out in bold relief; and by the judicious way in which they were handled, became, as it were, the property of the writer, and awoke a responsive echo in the bosoms of tens of thousands.

"'The Pleasures of Hope' appeared exactly when I was twenty-one years and nine months old. It gave me a general acquaintance in Edinburgh. Dr. Gregory, Henry Mackenzie, the author of the 'Man of Feeling;' Dugald Stewart, the Rev. Archibald Alison, the 'Man of Taste,' and Thomas

Telford, the engineer, became my immediate patrons."—*Note from Campbell's Autobiography.*

Campbell's acquaintance in Edinburgh, as he observes, was now general; and, to the list of distinguished friends already mentioned, were now added the names of Gillies, Henry Erskine, and Laing, the historian. There were many young men of talent, nevertheless, to whom he was still unknown, unless by the growing reputation of his Poem. Walter Scott and he were already acquainted; but to introduce him to the *élite* of his own private circle, Scott invited him to dinner. On his arrival at the hour appointed, Campbell met a strong muster of Mr. Scott's friends, among whom he was rather surprised to find himself a stranger. No introduction took place; but the subjects of conversation and the ability with which they were discussed, showed clearly that the guests, among whom he sat at table, were men of genius and talent. Great harmony prevailed; and where Scott presided, the conversation was sure to be edifying as well as pleasant. At length, when the cloth was removed and the loyal toasts were disposed of, Scott stood up, and, with a handsome and complimentary notice of the new poem, proposed a bumper to the "Author of the Pleasures of Hope." "The poem," he added, "is in the hands of all our friends; and the poet," pointing to a young gentleman on his right, "I have now the high honour of introducing to you as my guest."

The toast was received with enthusiasm. The eyes of the company were fixed on the young poet, and, although taken by surprise, he acknowledged the compliment with so much good taste and feeling, that after hearing him speak, no one felt surprised that so young a man had written "The Pleasures of Hope."

THEODRIC:

A DOMESTIC TALE.

4

THEODRIC.

'TWAS sunset, and the Ranz des Vaches was sung,
And lights were o'er th' Helvetian mountains flung,
That gave the glacier tops their richest glow,
And tinged the lakes like molten gold below;
Warmth flush'd the wonted regions of the storm,
Where, Phœnix-like, you saw the eagle's form
That high in Heaven's vermilion wheel'd and soar'd,
Woods nearer frown'd, and cataracts dash'd and roar'd
From heights browsed by the bounding bouquetin;
Herds tinkling roam'd the long-drawn vales between,
And hamlets glitter'd white, and gardens flourish'd green:
'Twas transport to inhale the bright sweet air!
The mountain-bee was revelling in its glare,
And roving with his minstrelsy across
The scented wild weeds, and enamell'd moss.
Earth's features so harmoniously were link'd,
She seem'd one great glad form, with life instinct,
That felt Heaven's ardent breath, and smiled below
Its flush of love, with consentaneous glow.
A Gothic church was near; the spot around
Was beautiful, ev'n though sepulchral ground;

For there nor yew nor cypress spread their gloom,
But roses blossom'd by each rustic tomb.
Amidst them one of spotless marble shone—
A maiden's grave—and 'twas inscribed thereon,
That young and loved she died whose dust was there: [fair!
"Yes," said my comrade, "young she died, and
Grace form'd her, and the soul of gladness play'd
Once in the blue eyes of that mountain-maid:
Her fingers witch'd the chords they pass'd along,
And her lips seem'd to kiss the soul in song:
Yet woo'd, and worshipp'd as she was, till few
Aspired to hope, 'twas sadly, strangely true,
That heart, the martyr of its fondness, burn'd
And died of love that could not be return'd.
Her father dwelt where yonder Castle shines
O'er clustering trees and terrace-mantling vines:
As gay as ever, the laburnum's pride
Waves o'er each walk where she was wont to glide,—
And still the garden whence she graced her brow,
As lovely blooms, though trode by strangers now.
How oft, from yonder window o'er the lake,
Her song of wild Helvetian swell and shake
Has made the rudest fisher bend his ear,
And rest enchanted on his oar to hear!
Thus bright, accomplish'd, spirited, and bland,
Well-born, and wealthy for that simple land,
Why had no gallant native youth the art
To win so warm—so exquisite a heart?

She, 'midst these rocks inspired with feelings strong
By mountain-freedom—music—fancy—song,
Herself descended from the brave in arms,
And conscious of romance-inspiring charms,
Dreamt of Heroic beings; hoped to find
Some extant spirit of chivalric kind;
And scorning wealth, look'd cold ev'n on the claim
Of manly worth, that lack'd the wreath of fame.
  Her younger brother, sixteen summers old,
And much her likeness both in mind and mould,
Had gone, poor boy! in soldiership to shine,
And bore an Austrian banner on the Rhine.
'Twas when, alas! our Empire's evil star
Shed all the plagues, without the pride of war;
When patriots bled, and bitterer anguish cross'd
Our brave, to die in battles foully lost.
The youth wrote home the rout of many a day;
Yet still he said, and still with truth could say,
One corps had ever made a valiant stand,—
The corps in which he served,—THEODRIC's band.
His fame, forgotten chief! is now gone by,
Eclipsed by brighter orbs in Glory's sky;
Yet once it shone, and veterans, when they show
Our fields of battle twenty years ago,
Will tell you feats his small brigade perform'd,
In charges nobly faced and trenches storm'd.
Time was, when songs were chanted to his fame,
And soldiers loved the march that bore his name
The zeal of martial hearts was at his call,
And that Helvetian's, UDOLPH's, most of all.

'Twas touching, when the storm of war blew wild,
To see a blooming boy,—almost a child,—
Spur fearless at his leader's words and signs,
Brave death in reconnoitring hostile lines,
And speed each task, and tell each message clear,
In scenes where war-train'd men were stunn'd with fear.
THEODRIC praised him, and they wept for joy
In yonder house,—when letters from the boy
Thank'd Heaven for life, and more, to use his phrase,
Than twenty lives—his own Commander's praise.
Then follow'd glowing pages, blazoning forth
The fancied image of his leader's worth,
With such hyperbolés of youthful style
As made his parents dry their tears and smile:
But differently far his words impress'd
A wondering sister's well-believing breast;—
She caught th' illusion, bless'd THEODRIC's name,
And wildly magnified his worth and fame;
Rejoicing life's reality contain'd
One, heretofore, her fancy had but feign'd,
Whose love could make her proud!—and time and chance
To passion raised that day-dream of Romance.
Once, when with hasty charge of horse and man
Our arrière-guard had check'd the Gallic van,
THEODRIC, visiting the outposts, found
His UDOLPH wounded, weltering on the ground:

Sore crush'd,—half-swooning, half-upraised he lay,
And bent his brow, fair boy! and grasp'd the clay.
His fate moved ev'n the common soldier's ruth—
Theodric succour'd him; nor left the youth
To vulgar hands, but brought him to his tent,
And lent what aid a brother would have lent.
  Meanwhile, to save his kindred half the smart
The war-gazette's dread blood-roll might impart,
He wrote th' event to them; and soon could tell
Of pains assuaged and symptoms auguring well;
And last of all, prognosticating cure,
Enclosed the leech's vouching signature.
  Their answers, on whose pages you might note
That tears had fall'n, whilst trembling fingers wrote,
Gave boundless thanks for benefits conferr'd,
Of which the boy, in secret, sent them word,
Whose memory Time, they said, would never blot;
But which the giver had himself forgot.
  In time, the stripling, vigorous and heal'd,
Resumed his barb and banner in the field,
And bore himself right soldier-like, till now
The third campaign had manlier bronzed his brow,
When peace, though but a scanty pause for breath,—
A curtain-drop between the acts of death,—
A check in frantic war's unfinish'd game,
Yet dearly bought, and direly welcome, came.
The camp broke up, and Udolph left his chief
As with a son's or younger brother's grief:

But journeying home, how rapt his spirits rose!
How light his footsteps crush'd St. Gothard's
snows; [horn,
How dear seem'd ev'n the waste and wild Shreck-
Though wrapt in clouds, and frowning as in scorn
Upon a downward world of pastoral charms;
Where, by the very smell of dairy-farms,
And fragrance from the mountain-herbage blown,
Blindfold his native hills he could have known!
His coming down yon lake,—his boat in view
Of windows where love's fluttering kerchief
flew,— [burst,—
The arms spread out for him—the tears that
('Twas JULIA'S, 'twas his sister's, met him first:)
Their pride to see war's medal at his breast,
And all their rapture's greeting, may be guess'd.
Ere long, his bosom triumph'd to unfold
A gift he meant their gayest room to hold,—
The picture of a friend in warlike dress;
And who it was he first bade JULIA guess.
'Yes,' she replied, ''twas he methought in sleep,
When you were wounded, told me not to weep.'
The painting long in that sweet mansion drew
Regards its living semblance little knew.
Meanwhile THEODRIC, who had years before
Learnt England's tongue, and loved her classic
lore,
A glad enthusiast now explored the land,
Where Nature, Freedom, Art, smile hand in
hand;

Her women fair; her men robust for toil;
Her vigorous souls, high-cultured as her soil;
Her towns, where civic independence flings
The gauntlet down to senates, courts, and kings;
Her works of art, resembling magic's powers;
Her mighty fleets, and learning's beauteous bowers,—
These he had visited, with wonder's smile,
And scarce endured to quit so fair an isle.
But how our fates from unmomentous things
May rise, like rivers out of little springs!
A trivial chance postponed his parting day,
And public tidings caused, in that delay,
An English Jubilee. 'Twas a glorious sight!
At eve stupendous London, clad in light,
Pour'd out triumphant multitudes to gaze;
Youth, age, wealth, penury, smiling in the blaze;
Th' illumined atmosphere was warm and bland,
And Beauty's groups, the fairest of the land,
Conspicuous, as in some wide festive room,
In open chariots pass'd with pearl and plume.
Amidst them he remark'd a lovelier mien
Than e'er his thoughts had shaped, or eyes had seen;
The throng detain'd her till he rein'd his steed,
And, ere the beauty pass'd, had time to read
The motto and the arms her carriage bore.
Led by that clue, he left not England's shore
Till he had known her; and to know her well
Prolong'd, exalted, bound, enchantment's spell;

For with affections warm, intense, refined,
She mix'd such calm and holy strength of mind,
That, like Heaven's image in the smiling brook,
Celestial peace was pictured in her look.
Hers was the brow, in trials unperplex'd,
That cheer'd the sad, and tranquillized the vex'd;
She studied not the meanest to eclipse,
And yet the wisest listen'd to her lips;
She sang not, knew not Music's magic skill,
But yet her voice had tones that sway'd the will.
He sought—he won her—and resolved to make
His future home in England for her sake.
Yet, ere they wedded, matters of concern
To CÆSAR's Court commanded his return,
A season's space,—and on his Alpine way,—
He reach'd those bowers, that rang with joy that day:
The boy was half beside himself,—the sire,
All frankness, honour, and Helvetian fire,
Of speedy parting would not hear him speak;
And tears bedew'd and brighten'd JULIA's cheek.
Thus, loth to wound their hospitable pride,
A month he promised with them to abide;
As blithe he trod the mountain-sward as they,
And felt his joy make ev'n the young more gay.
How jocund was their breakfast-parlour, fann'd
By yon blue water's breath,—their walks how bland!
Fair JULIA seem'd her brother's soften'd sprite—
A gem reflecting Nature's purest light,—

And with her graceful wit there was inwrought
A wildly sweet unworldliness of thought,
That almost child-like to his kindness drew,
And twin with UDOLPH in his friendship grew.
But did his thoughts to love one moment range?—
No! he who had loved CONSTANCE could not
change!
Besides, till grief betray'd her undesign'd,
Th' unlikely thought could scarcely reach his mind,
That eyes so young on years like his should beam
Unwoo'd devotion back for pure esteem.
True she sang to his very soul, and brought
Those trains before him of luxuriant thought,
Which only Music's heaven-born art can bring,
To sweep across the mind with angel wing.
Once, as he smiled amidst that waking trance,
She paus'd o'ercome, he thought it might be
chance,
And, when his first suspicions dimly stole,
Rebuked them back like phantoms from his soul.
But when he saw his caution gave her pain,
And kindness brought suspense's rack again,
Faith, honour, friendship, bound him to unmask
Truths which her timid fondness fear'd to ask.
And yet with gracefully ingenuous power
Her spirit met th' explanatory hour;—
Ev'n conscious beauty brighten'd in her eyes,
That told she knew their love no vulgar prize;
And pride like that of one more woman-grown,
Enlarg'd her mien, enrich'd her voice's tone.

'Twas then she struck the keys, and music made
That mock'd all skill her hand had e'er display'd
Inspired and warbling, rapt from things around,
She look'd the very Muse of magic sound,
Painting in sound the forms of joy and woe,
Until the mind's eye saw them melt and glow.
Her closing strain composed and calm she play'd,
And sang no words to give its pathos aid;
But grief seem'd lingering in its lengthen'd swell,
And like so many tears the trickling touches fell.
Of CONSTANCE then she heard THEODRIC speak,
And steadfast smoothness still possess'd her cheek.
But when he told her how he oft had plann'd
Of old a journey to their mountain-land,
That might have brought him hither years before,
'Ah! then,' she cried, 'you knew not England's shore!
And had you come,—and wherefore did you not?'
'Yes,' he replied, 'it would have changed our lot!'
Then burst her tears through pride's restraining bands,
And with her handkerchief, and both her hands,
She hid her voice and wept.—Contrition stung
THEODRIC for the tears his words had wrung.
'But no,' she cried, 'unsay not what you 've said,
Nor grudge one prop on which my pride is stay'd;
To think I could have merited your faith
Shall be my solace even unto death!'
'JULIA,' THEODRIC said, with purposed look
Of firmness, 'my reply deserved rebuke;

But by your pure and sacred peace of mind,
And by the dignity of womankind,
Swear that when I am gone you 'll do your best
To chase this dream of fondness from your breast.'
  Th' abrupt appeal electrified her thought;—
She look'd to Heav'n as if its aid she sought,
Dried hastily the tear-drops from her cheek,
And signified the vow she could not speak.
  Ere long he communed with her mother mild:
'Alas!' she said, 'I warn'd—conjured my child,
And grieved for this affection from the first,
But like fatality it has been nursed;
For when her fill'd eyes on your picture fix'd,
And when your name in all she spoke was mix'd,
'Twas hard to chide an over-grateful mind!
Then each attempt a likelier choice to find
Made only fresh-rejected suitors grieve,
And UDOLPH'S pride—perhaps her own—believe
That, could she meet, she might enchant ev'n you.
You came.—I augur'd the event, 'tis true,
But how was UDOLPH'S mother to exclude
The guest that claim'd our boundless gratitude?
And that unconscious you had cast a spell
On JULIA'S peace, my pride refused to tell:
Yet in my child's illusion I have seen,
Believe me well, how blameless you have been:
Nor can it cancel, howsoe'er it end,
Our debt of friendship to our boy's best friend.'
At night he parted with the aged pair;
At early morn rose JULIA to prepare

The last repast her hands for him should make:
And UDOLPH to convoy him o'er the lake.
The parting was to her such bitter grief,
That of her own accord she made it brief;
But, lingering at her window, long survey'd
His boat's last glimpses melting into shade.
  THEODRIC sped to Austria, and achieved
His journey's object. Much was he relieved
When UDOLPH'S letters told that JULIA'S mind
Had borne his loss, firm, tranquil, and resign'd.
He took the Rhenish route to England, high
Elate with hopes, fulfill'd their ecstasy,
And interchanged with CONSTANCE'S own breath
The sweet eternal vows that bound their faith.
  To paint that being to a grovelling mind
Were like portraying pictures to the blind.
'Twas needful ev'n infectiously to feel
Her temper's fond and firm and gladsome zeal,
To share existence with her, and to gain
Sparks from her love's electrifying chain
Of that pure pride, which, lessening to her breast
Life's ills, gave all its joys a treble zest,
Before the mind completely understood
That mighty truth—how happy are the good!
  Ev'n when her light forsook him, it bequeathed
Ennobling sorrow; and her memory breathed
A sweetness that survived her living days,
As odorous scents outlast the censer's blaze.
  Or, if a trouble dimm'd their golden joy,
'Twas outward dross, and not infused alloy:

Their home knew but affection's looks and speech—
A little Heaven, above dissension's reach.
But 'midst her kindred there was strife and gall;
Save one congenial sister, they were all
Such foils to her bright intellect and grace,
As if she had engross'd the virtue of her race.
Her nature strove th' unnatural feuds to heal,
Her wisdom made the weak to her appeal;
And, though the wounds she cured were soon unclosed,
Unwearied still her kindness interposed.
Oft on those errands though she went in vain,
And home, a blank without her, gave him pain,
He bore her absence for its pious end.—
But public grief his spirit came to bend;
For war laid waste his native land once more,
And German honour bled at every pore.
Oh! were he there, he thought, to rally back
One broken band, or perish in the wrack!
Nor think that CONSTANCE sought to move and melt
His purpose: like herself she spoke and felt:—
'Your fame is mine, and I will bear all woe
Except its loss!—but with you let me go
To arm you for, to embrace you from, the fight;
Harm will not reach me—hazards will delight!'
He knew those hazards better; one campaign
In England he conjured her to remain,
And she express'd assent, although her heart
In secret had resolved *they* should not part.

How oft the wisest on misfortune's shelves
Are wreck'd by errors most unlike themselves?
That little fault, *that* fraud of love's romance,
That plan's concealment, wrought their whole
mischance.
He knew it not preparing to embark,
But felt extinct his comfort's latest spark,
When, 'midst those number'd days, she made repair
Again to kindred worthless of her care.
'Tis true she said the tidings she would write
Would make her absence on his heart sit light;
But, haplessly, reveal'd not yet her plan,
And left him in his home a lonely man. [past:
Thus damp'd in thoughts, he mused upon the
'Twas long since he had heard from Udolph last,
And deep misgivings on his spirit fell
That all with Udolph's household was not well.
'Twas that too true prophetic mood of fear
That augurs griefs inevitably near,
Yet makes them not less startling to the mind
When come. Least look'd-for then of human kind
His Udolph ('twas, he thought at first, his sprite,)
With mournful joy that morn surprised his sight.
How changed was Udolph! Scarce Theodric
durst
Inquire his tidings,—he reveal'd the worst.
'At first,' he said, 'as Julia bade me tell,
She bore her fate high-mindedly and well,
Resolved from common eyes her grief to hide,
And from the world's compassion saved our pride;

But still her health gave way to secret woe,
And long she pined—for broken hearts die slow!
Her reason went, but came returning, like
The warning of her death-hour—soon to strike;
And all for which she now, poor sufferer! sighs,
Is once to see THEODRIC ere she dies.
Why should I come to tell you this caprice?
Forgive me! for my mind has lost its peace.
I blame myself, and ne'er shall cease to blame,
That my insane ambition for the name
Of brother to THEODRIC, founded all
Those high-built hopes that crush'd her by their fall.
I made her slight her mother's counsel sage,
But now my parents droop with grief and age:
And, though my sister's eyes mean no rebuke,
They overwhelm me with their dying look.
The journey 's long, but you are full of ruth;
And she who shares your heart, and knows its truth,
Has faith in your affection, far above
The fear of a poor dying object's love.'—
'She has, my UDOLPH,' he replied, ''tis true;
And oft we talk of JULIA—oft of you.'
Their converse came abruptly to a close;
For scarce could each his troubled looks compose,
When visitants, to CONSTANCE near akin,
(In all but traits of soul,) were usher'd in,
They brought not her, nor 'midst their kindred band
The sister who alone, like her, was bland;

But said—and smiled to see it gave him pain—
That CONSTANCE would a fortnight yet remain.
Vex'd by their tidings, and the haughty view
They cast on UDOLPH as the youth withdrew,
THEODRIC blamed his CONSTANCE'S intent.—
The demons went, and left him as they went
To read, when they were gone beyond recall,
A note from her loved hand explaining all.
She said, that with their house she only staid
That parting peace might with them all be made;
But pray'd for leave to share his foreign life,
And shun all future chance of kindred strife.
He wrote with speed, his soul's consent to say:
The letter miss'd her on her homeward way.
In six hours CONSTANCE was within his arms:
Moved, flush'd, unlike her wonted calm of charms,
And breathless—with uplifted hands outspread—
Burst into tears upon his neck, and said,—
'I knew that those who brought your message laugh'd,
With poison of their own to point the shaft;
And this my own kind sister thought, yet loth
Confess'd she fear'd 'twas true you had been wroth.
But here you are, and smile on me: my pain
Is gone, and CONSTANCE is herself again.'
His ecstasy, it may be guess'd, was much:
Yet pain's extreme and pleasure's seem'd to touch.
What pride! embracing beauty's perfect mould;
What terror! lest his few rash words mistold

Had agonized her pulse to fever's heat:
But calm'd again so soon it healthful beat,
And such sweet tones were in her voice's sound,
Composed herself, she breathed composure round.
Fair being! with what sympathetic grace
She heard, bewail'd, and pleaded JULIA's case;
Implored he would her dying wish attend,
'And go,' she said, 'to-morrow with your friend;
I'll wait for your return on England's shore,
And then we'll cross the deep, and part no more.'
To-morrow both his soul's compassion drew
To JULIA's call, and CONSTANCE urged anew
That not to heed her now would be to bind
A load of pain for life upon his mind.
He went with UDOLPH—from his CONSTANCE went—
Stifling, alas! a dark presentiment
Some ailment lurk'd, ev'n whilst she smiled, to mock
His fears of harm from yester-morning's shock.
Meanwhile a faithful page he singled out,
To watch at home, and follow straight his route,
If aught of threaten'd change her health should show.
—With UDOLPH then he reach'd the house of woe.
That winter's eve, how darkly Nature's brow
Scowl'd on the scenes it lights so lovely now!
The tempest, raging o'er the realms of ice,
Shook fragments from the rifted precipice;
And, whilst their falling echoed to the wind,
The wolf's long howl in dismal discord join'd.

While white yon water's foam was raised in clouds
That whirl'd like spirits wailing in their shrouds:
Without was Nature's elemental din—
And beauty died, and friendship wept, within!
Sweet JULIA, though her fate was finish'd half,
Still knew him—smiled on him with feeble laugh—
And bless'd him, till she drew her latest sigh!
But lo! while UDOLPH'S bursts of agony,
And age's tremulous wailings, round him rose,
What accents pierced him deeper yet than those!
'Twas tidings, by his English messenger,
Of CONSTANCE—brief and terrible they were.
She still was living when the page set out
From home, but whether now was left in doubt.
Poor JULIA! saw he then thy death's relief—
Stunn'd into stupor more than wrung with grief?
It was not strange; for in the human breast
Two master-passions cannot coexist,
And that alarm which now usurp'd his brain
Shut out not only peace, but other pain.
'Twas fancying CONSTANCE underneath the shroud
That cover'd JULIA made him first weep loud,
And tear himself away from them that wept.
Fast hurrying homeward, night nor day he slept,
Till, launch'd at sea, he dreamt that his soul's saint
Clung to him on a bridge of ice, pale, faint,
O'er cataracts of blood. Awake, he bless'd
The shore; nor hope left utterly his breast,
Till reaching home, terrific omen! there
The straw-laid street preluded his despair—

The servant's look—the table that reveal'd
His letter sent to CONSTANCE last, still seal'd—
Though speech and hearing left him, told too clear
That he had now to suffer—not to fear.
He felt as if he ne'er should cease to feel—
A wretch live-broken on misfortune's wheel:
Her death's cause—he might make his peace with
Heaven,
Absolved from guilt, but never self-forgiven.
The ocean has its ebbings—so has grief;
'Twas vent to anguish, if 'twas not relief,
To lay his brow ev'n on her death-cold cheek.
Then first he heard her one kind sister speak:
She bade him, in the name of Heaven, forbear
With self-reproach to deepen his despair:
''Twas blame,' she said, 'I shudder to relate,
But none of yours, that caused our darling's fate;
Her mother (must I call her such?) foresaw,
Should CONSTANCE leave the land, she would
withdraw
Our House's charm against the world's neglect—
The only gem that drew it some respect.
Hence, when you went, she came and vainly spoke
To change her purpose—grew incensed, and broke
With execrations from her kneeling child.
Start not! your angel from her knee rose mild,
Fear'd that she should not long the scene outlive,
Yet bade ev'n you th' unnatural one forgive.
Till then her ailment had been slight, or none;
But fast she droop'd, and fatal pains came on:

Foreseeing their event, she dictated [said—
And sign'd these words for you.' The letter
'THEODRIC, this is destiny above
Our power to baffle; bear it then, my love!
Rave not to learn the usage I have borne,
For one true sister left me not forlorn;
And though you 're absent in another land,
Sent from me by my own well-meant command,
Your soul, I know, as firm is knit to mine
As these clasp'd hands in blessing you now join:
Shape not imagined horrors in my fate—
Ev'n now my sufferings are not very great;
And when your grief's first transports shall subside,
I call upon your strength of soul and pride
To pay my memory, if 'tis worth the debt,
Love's glorying tribute—not forlorn regret:
I charge my name with power to conjure up
Reflection's balmy, not its bitter cup.
My pardoning angel, at the gates of Heaven,
Shall look not more regard than you have given
To me; and our life's union has been clad
In smiles of bliss as sweet as life e'er had.
Shall gloom be from such bright remembrance cast?
Shall bitterness outflow from sweetness past?
No! imaged in the sanctuary of your breast,
There let me smile, amidst high thoughts at rest;
And let contentment on your spirit shine,
As if its peace were still a part of mine:
For if you war not proudly with your pain,
For you I shall have worse than lived in vain.

But I conjure your manliness to bear
My loss with noble spirit—not despair;
I ask you by our love to promise this,
And kiss these words, where I have left a kiss,—
The latest from my living lips for yours.'—
Words that will solace him while life endures:
For though his spirit from affliction's surge
Could ne'er to life, as life had been, emerge,
Yet still that mind whose harmony elate
Rang sweetness, even beneath the crush of fate,—
That mind in whose regard all things were placed
In views that soften'd them, or lights that graced,
That soul's example could not but dispense
A portion of its own bless'd influence;
Invoking him to peace and that self-sway
Which Fortune cannot give, nor take away:
And though he mourn'd her long, 'twas with such woe
As if her spirit watch'd him still below."

THIS appears to have originated on the occasion of the poet's visit to Germany in 1820, though the idea remained in embryo until 1824.

In July of that year, Campbell, for the first time, announced to a friend this work in the following terms:—"I have a new poem—'Theodric'—a very domestic story, finished in about five hundred lines, common heroic rhyme, so-so, I think. I am rather in good heart about it, though not over sanguine." In writing to his sister, he says: "I am sorry there should be any great expectation excited about the poem, which is not of a nature to gratify such expectation. It is truly a *domestic* and private story. I know very well what will be its fate: there will be an outcry and regret that there is nothing grand or romantic in the poem, and that it is too humble and familiar. But I am prepared for this; and I also know that when it recovers from the first buzz of such criticism, it will attain a steady popularity."

"Theodric" appeared in the month of November, and was received with a coldness which deeply wounded Campbell's sensitiveness, nor did he live to see it attain the popularity he anticipated. It has well been said that "a popular author has no rival so formidable as his former self, and no comparison to sustain half so dangerous as that which is always made between the average merit of his new work and the remembered beauties of his old ones."

"Theodric" is in every way a "domestic story," and has been described by the Edinburgh Review of January, 1825, as an attempt at a very difficult kind of poetry, and one in which the most complete success can hardly ever be so splendid and striking as to make amends for the difficulty. "It is entitled 'A domestic story,'—and it is so—turning upon few incidents—embracing few characters—dealing in no marvels and no terrors—displaying no stormy passions—without complication of plot, or hurry of action—with no atrocities to shudder at, or feats of noble daring to stir the spirits of the ambitious,—it passes quietly on through the shaded paths of private life, conversing with gentle natures and patient sufferings, and unfolding, with serene pity and sober triumph, the pangs which are fated at times to wring the breast of innocence and generosity, and the courage and comfort which generosity and innocence can never fail to bestow. The taste and the feeling which led to the selection of such topics could not but impress their character on the style in which they are treated. It is distinguished accordingly by a fine and tender finish both of thought and of diction; by a chastened elegance of words and images; a mild dignity and tempered pathos in the sentiments, and a general tone of simplicity and directness in the conduct of the story, which, joined to its great brevity, tends at first perhaps to disguise both the richness and the force of the genius required for its production. But though not calculated to strike at once on the dull pallid ear of an idle and occupied world, it is of all others, perhaps, the kind of poetry best fitted to win on our softer hours, and to sink deep into vacant bosoms, unlocking all the sources of fond recollection, and leading us gently on through the mazes of deep and engrossing meditation, and thus ministering to a deeper enchantment and more lasting delight than can ever be inspired by the louder and more importunate strains of more ambitious authors.

"There are, no doubt, peculiar, and perhaps insuperable, difficulties in the management of themes so delicate, and requiring so fine and so restrained a hand: nor are we prepared to say that Mr. Campbell has on this occasion entirely escaped them. There are passages that are somewhat *fade*, there are expressions that are trivial; but the prevailing character is sweetness and beauty, and it prevails over all that is opposed to it."

In judging of this poem, it should not be concealed that it was written during intense anxiety touching the malady which at that time threatened his only surviving child, and though "Theodric" has failed to add another wreath to Campbell's laurels, yet it must be conceded there do shine in it brilliant flashes of genius which relieve its hasty transitions and the simplicity of the subject.

TRANSLATIONS.

[The following are a few only of Campbell's Translations from the Greek; they were written at the age of sixteen, during his collegiate career, and their beauty and elegance went far to win for him the notice and friendship of the Professors.]

MARTIAL ELEGY.

FROM THE GREEK OF TYRTÆUS.

How glorious fall the valiant, sword in hand,
In front of battle for their native land!
But oh! what ills await the wretch that yields,
A recreant outcast from his country's fields!
The mother whom he loves shall quit her home,
An aged father at his side shall roam;
His little ones shall weeping with him go,
And a young wife participate his woe;
While scorn'd and scowl'd upon by every face,
They pine for food, and beg from place to place.

Stain of his breed! dishonouring manhood's form,
All ills shall cleave to him:—Affliction's storm
Shall blind him wandering in the vale of years,
Till, lost to all but ignominious fears,

He shall not blush to leave a recreant's name,
And children, like himself, inured to shame.

But we will combat for our fathers' land,
And we will drain the life-blood where we stand,
To save our children:—fight ye side by side,
And serried close, ye men of youthful pride,
Disdaining fear, and deeming light the cost
Of life itself in glorious battle lost.

Leave not our sires to stem the unequal fight,
Whose limbs are nerved no more with buoyant
might;
Nor, lagging backward, let the younger breast
Permit the man of age (a sight unbless'd)
To welter in the combat's foremost thrust,
His hoary head dishevell'd in the dust,
And venerable bosom bleeding bare.

But youth's fair form, though fallen, is ever fair,
And beautiful in death the boy appears,
The hero boy, that dies in blooming years:
In man's regret he lives, and woman's tears,
More sacred than in life, and lovelier far,
For having perish'd in the front of war.

SONG OF HYBRIAS THE CRETAN.

My wealth 's a burly spear and brand,
And a right good shield of hides untann'd,
  Which on my arm I buckle:
With these I plough, I reap, I sow,
With these I make the sweet vintage flow,
  And all around me truckle.

But your wights that take no pride to wield
A massy spear and well-made shield,
  Nor joy to draw the sword:
Oh, I bring those heartless, hapless drones,
Down in a trice on their marrow-bones,
  To call me King and Lord.

FRAGMENT.

FROM THE GREEK OF ALCMAN.

The mountain summits sleep: glens, cliffs, and caves
  Are silent—all the black earth's reptile brood—
  The bees—the wild beasts of the mountain wood:
In depths beneath the dark red ocean's waves
  Its monsters rest, whilst wrapt in bower and spray
  Each bird is hush'd that stretch'd its pinions to the day.

SPECIMENS OF TRANSLATIONS FROM MEDEA.

Σκαιοὺς δὲ λέγων, κουδέν τι σοφοὺς
Τοὺς πρόσθε βροτοὺς οὐκ ἂν ἁμαρτοις.
Medea, v. 194, p. 33, Glasg. edit.

TELL me, ye bards, whose skill sublime
First charm'd the ear of youthful Time,
With numbers wrapt in heavenly fire,
Who bade delighted Echo swell
The trembling transports of the lyre,
The murmur of the shell—
Why to the burst of Joy alone
Accords sweet Music's soothing tone?
Why can no bard, with magic strain,
In slumbers steep the heart of pain?
While varied tones obey your sweep,
The mild, the plaintive, and the deep,
Bends not despairing Grief to hear
Your golden lute, with ravish'd ear?
Has all your art no power to bind
The fiercer pangs that shake the mind,
And lull the wrath at whose command
Murder bares her gory hand?
When flush'd with joy, the rosy throng
Weave the light dance, ye swell the song!
Cease, ye vain warblers! cease to charm!
The breast with other raptures warm!
Cease! till your hand with magic strain
In slumbers steep the heart of pain!

SPEECH OF THE CHORUS,

IN THE SAME TRAGEDY,

TO DISSUADE MEDEA FROM HER PURPOSE OF PUTTING HER CHILDREN TO DEATH, AND FLYING FOR PROTECTION TO ATHENS.

O HAGGARD queen! to Athens dost thou guide
Thy glowing chariot, steep'd in kindred gore;
Or seek to hide thy foul infanticide
Where Peace and Mercy dwell for evermore?

The land where Truth, pure, precious, and sublime,
Woos the deep silence of sequester'd bowers,
And warriors, matchless since the first of time,
Rear their bright banners o'er unconquer'd towers!

Where joyous youth, to Music's mellow strain,
Twines in the dance with nymphs for ever fair,
While Spring eternal on the lilied plain,
Waves amber radiance through the fields of air!

The tuneful Nine (so sacred legends tell)
First waked their heavenly lyre these scenes [among
Still in your greenwood bowers they love to dwell;
Still in your vales they swell the choral song!

But there the tuneful, chaste, Pierian fair,
The guardian nymphs of green Parnassus, now
Sprung from Harmonia, while her graceful hair
Waved in high auburn o'er her polish'd brow!

ANTISTROPHE I.

Where silent vales, and glades of green array,
The murmuring wreaths of cool Cephisus lave,
There, as the muse hath sung, at noon of day,
The Queen of Beauty bow'd to taste the wave;

And bless'd the stream, and breathed across the land [bowers;
The soft sweet gale that fans yon summer
And there the sister Loves, a smiling band,
Crown'd with the fragrant wreaths of rosy flowers!

"And go," she cries, "in yonder valleys rove,
With Beauty's torch the solemn scenes illume;
Wake in each eye the radiant light of Love,
Breathe on each cheek young Passion's tender bloom!

Entwine, with myrtle chains, your soft controul,
To sway the hearts of Freedom's darling kind!
With glowing charms enrapture Wisdom's soul,
And mould to grace ethereal Virtue's mind."

STROPHE II.

The land where Heaven's own hallowed waters play, [good,
Where friendship binds the generous and the
Say, shall it hail thee from thy frantic way,
Unholy woman! with thy hands embrued

In thine own children's gore! Oh! ere they bleed,
  Let Nature's voice thy ruthless heart appall!
Pause at the bold, irrevocable deed—
  The mother strikes—the guiltless babes shall
    fall!

Think what remorse thy maddening thoughts shall
    sting,
  When dying pangs their gentle bosoms tear!
Where shalt thou sink, when lingering echoes ring
  The screams of horror in thy tortured ear?

No! let thy bosom melt to Pity's cry,—
  In dust we kneel—by sacred Heaven implore—
O! stop thy lifted arm, ere yet they die,
  Nor dip thy horrid hands in infant gore!

ANTISTROPHE II.

Say, how shalt thou that barbarous soul assume,
  Undamp'd by horror at the daring plan?
Hast thou a heart to work thy children's doom?
  Or hands to finish what thy wrath began?

When o'er each babe you look a last adieu,
  And gaze on Innocence that smiles asleep,
Shall no fond feeling beat to Nature true,
  Charm thee to pensive thought—and bid thee
    weep?

When the young suppliants clasp their parent dear,
Heave the deep sob, and pour the artless prayer—
Ay! thou shalt melt;—and many a heart-shed tear
Gush o'er the harden'd features of despair!

Nature shall throb in every tender string,—
Thy trembling heart the ruffian's task deny;—
Thy horror-smitten hands afar shall fling
The blade, undrench'd in blood's eternal dye.

CHORUS.

Hallow'd Earth! with indignation
Mark, oh mark, the murderous deed!
Radiant eye of wide creation,
Watch th' accurs'd infanticide!

Yet, ere Colchia's rugged daughter
Perpetrate the dire design,
And consign to kindred slaughter
Children of thy golden line!

Shall mortal hand, with murder gory,
Cause immortal blood to flow?
Sun of Heaven!—array'd in glory
Rise, forbid, avert the blow!

6

In the vales of placid gladness
  Let no rueful maniac range;
Chase afar the fiend of Madness,
  Wrest the dagger from Revenge!

Say, hast thou, with kind protection,
  Rear'd thy smiling race in vain;
Fostering Nature's fond affection,
  Tender cares, and pleasing pain?

Hast thou, on the troubled ocean,
  Braved the tempest loud and strong,
Where the waves, in wild commotion,
  Roar Cyanean rocks among?

Didst thou roam the paths of danger,
  Hymenean joys to prove?
Spare, O sanguinary stranger,
  Pledges of thy sacred love!

Ask not Heaven's commiseration,
  After thou hast done the deed;
Mercy, pardon, expiation,
  Perish when thy victims bleed.

O'CONNOR'S CHILD;

OR,

"THE FLOWER OF LOVE LIES BLEEDING."

I.

OH! once the harp of Innisfail
Was strung full high to notes of gladness;
But yet it often told a tale
Of more prevailing sadness.
Sad was the note, and wild its fall,
As winds that moan at night forlorn
Along the isles of Fion-Gall,
When, for O'Connor's child to mourn,
The harper told, how lone, how far
From any mansion's twinkling star,
From any path of social men,
Or voice, but from the fox's den,
The lady in the desert dwelt;
And yet no wrongs, nor fears she felt:
Say, why should dwell in place so wild,
O'Connor's pale and lovely child?

II.

Sweet lady! she no more inspires
Green Erin's hearts with beauty's power,

As, in the palace of her sires,
She bloom'd a peerless flower.
Gone from her hand and bosom, gone,
The royal broche, the jewell'd ring,
That o'er her dazzling whiteness shone,
Like dews on lilies of the spring.
Yet why, though fall'n her brother's kerne,
Beneath De Bourgo's battle stern,
While yet in Leinster unexplored,
Her friends survive the English sword;
Why lingers she from Erin's host,
So far on Galway's shipwreck'd coast;
Why wanders she a huntress wild—
O'Connor's pale and lovely child?

III.

And fix'd on empty space, why burn
Her eyes with momentary wildness;
And wherefore do they then return
To more than woman's mildness?
Dishevell'd are her raven locks;
On Connocht Moran's name she calls;
And oft amidst the lonely rocks
She sings sweet madrigals.
Placed 'midst the foxglove and the moss,
Behold a parted warrior's cross!
That is the spot where, evermore,
The lady, at her shieling door,
Enjoys that, in communion sweet,
The living and the dead can meet,

For, lo! to love-lorn fantasy,
The hero of her heart is nigh.

IV.

Bright as the bow that spans the storm,
In Erin's yellow vesture clad,
A son of light—a lovely form,
He comes and makes her glad;
Now on the grass-green turf he sits,
His tassell'd horn beside him laid;
Now o'er the hills in chase he flits,
The hunter and the deer a shade!
Sweet mourner! these are shadows vain
That cross the twilight of her brain;
Yet she will tell you, she is blest,
Of Connocht Moran's tomb possess'd,
More richly than in Aghrim's bower,
When bards high praised her beauty's power,
And kneeling pages offer'd up
The mórat in a golden cup.

V.

"A hero's bride! this desert bower,
It ill befits thy gentle breeding:
And wherefore dost thou love this flower
To call—'My love lies bleeding?'"
"This purple flower my tears have nursed;
A hero's blood supplied its bloom:
I love it, for it was the first
That grew on Connocht Moran's tomb.

Oh! hearken, stranger, to my voice!
This desert mansion is my choice!
And blest, though fatal, be the star
That led me to its wilds afar:
For here these pathless mountains free
Gave shelter to my love and me;
And every rock and every stone
Bore witness that he was my own.

VI.

O'Connor's child, I was the bud
Of Erin's royal tree of glory;
But woe to them that wrapt in blood
The tissue of my story!
Still as I clasp my burning brain,
A death-scene rushes on my sight;
It rises o'er and o'er again,
The bloody feud—the fatal night,
When chafing Connocht Moran's scorn,
They call'd my hero basely born;
And bade him choose a meaner bride
Than from O'Connor's house of pride.
Their tribe, they said, their high degree,
Was sung in Tara's psaltery;
Witness their Eath's victorious brand,
And Cathal of the bloody hand;
Glory (they said) and power and honour
Were in the mansion of O'Connor:
But he, my loved one, bore in field
A humbler crest, a meaner shield.

VII.

Ah, brothers! what did it avail,
That fiercely and triumphantly
Ye fought the English of the Pale,
And stemm'd De Bourgo's chivalry!
And what was it to love and me,
That barons by your standard rode;
Or beal-fires for your jubilee
Upon a hundred mountains glow'd?
What though the lords of tower and dome
From Shannon to the North-sea foam,—
Thought ye your iron hands of pride
Could break the knot that love had tied?
No:—let the eagle change his plume,
The leaf its hue, the flower its bloom;
But ties around this heart were spun,
That could not, would not, be undone!

VIII.

At bleating of the wild watch-fold
Thus sang my love—'Oh, come with me:
Our bark is on the lake, behold
Our steeds are fasten'd to the tree.
Come far from Castle-Connor's clans:—
Come with thy belted forestere,
And I, beside the lake of swans,
Shall hunt for thee the fallow-deer;
And build thy hut, and bring thee home
The wild-fowl and the honey-comb;

And berries from the wood provide,
And play my clarshech by thy side.
Then come, my love!'—How could I stay?
Our nimble stag-hounds track'd the way,
And I pursued, by moonless skies,
The light of Connocht Moran's eyes.

IX.

And fast and far, before the star
Of day-spring, rush'd we through the glade,
And saw at dawn the lofty bawn
Of Castle-Connor fade.
Sweet was to us the hermitage
Of this unplough'd, untrodden shore;
Like birds all joyous from the cage,
For man's neglect we loved it more,
And well he knew, my huntsman dear,
To search the game with hawk and spear;
While I, his evening food to dress,
Would sing to him in happiness.
But, oh, that midnight of despair!
When I was doom'd to rend my hair:
The night, to me, of shrieking sorrow!
The night, to him, that had no morrow!

X.

When all was hush'd at even tide,
I heard the baying of their beagle:
Be hush'd! my Connocht Moran cried,
'Tis but the screaming of the eagle.

Alas! 'twas not the eyrie's sound;
Their bloody bands had track'd us out;
Up-listening starts our couchant hound—
And, hark! again, that nearer shout
Brings faster on the murderers.
Spare—spare him—Brazil—Desmond fierce!
In vain—no voice the adder charms;
Their weapons cross'd my sheltering arms:
Another's sword has laid him low—
Another's and another's;
And every hand that dealt the blow—
Ah me! it was a brother's!
Yes, when his moanings died away,
Their iron hands had dug the clay,
And o'er his burial turf they trod,
And I beheld—oh God! oh God!—
His life-blood oozing from the sod.

XI.

Warm in his death-wounds sepulchred,
Alas! my warrior's spirit brave
Nor mass nor ulla-lulla heard,
Lamenting, soothe his grave.
Dragg'd to their hated mansion back,
How long in thraldom's grasp I lay
I know not, for my soul was black,
And knew no change of night or day.
One night of horror round me grew;
Or if I saw, or felt, or knew,
'Twas but when those grim visages,

The angry brothers of my race,
Glared on each eye-ball's aching throb,
And check'd my bosom's power to sob,
Or when my heart with pulses drear
Beat like a death-watch to my ear.

XII.

But Heaven, at last, my soul's eclipse
Did with a vision bright inspire;
I woke and felt upon my lips
A prophetess's fire.
Thrice in the east a war-drum beat,
I heard the Saxon's trumpet sound,
And ranged, as to the judgment-seat,
My guilty, trembling brothers round.
Clad in the helm and shield they came;
For now De Bourgo's sword and flame
Had ravaged Ulster's boundaries,
And lighted up the midnight skies.
The standard of O'Connor's sway
Was in the turret where I lay;
That standard, with so dire a look,
As ghastly shone the moon and pale,
I gave,—that every bosom shook
Beneath its iron mail.

XIII.

And go! (I cried) the combat seek,
Ye hearts that unappalled bore
The anguish of a sister's shriek,

Go!—and return no more!
For sooner guilt the ordeal brand
Shall grasp unhurt, than ye shall hold
The banner with victorious hand,
Beneath a sister's curse unroll'd.
O stranger! by my country's loss!
And by my love! and by the cross!
I swear I never could have spoke
The curse that sever'd nature's yoke,
But that a spirit o'er me stood,
And fired me with the wrathful mood
And frenzy to my heart was given,
To speak the malison of heaven.

XIV.

They would have cross'd themselves, all mute;
They would have pray'd to burst the spell;
But at the stamping of my foot
Each hand down powerless fell!
And go to Athunree! (I cried)
High lift the banner of your pride!
But know that where its sheet unrolls,
The weight of blood is on your souls!
Go where the havoc of your kerne
Shall float as high as mountain fern!
Men shall no more your mansion know;
The nettles on your hearth shall grow!
Dead, as the green oblivious flood
That mantles by your walls, shall be
The glory of O'Connor's blood!

Away! away to Athunree!
Where, downward when the sun shall fall,
The raven's wing shall be your pall!
And not a vassal shall unlace
The vizor from your dying face!

XV.

A bolt that overhung our dome
Suspended till my curse was given,
Soon as it pass'd these lips of foam,
Peal'd in the blood-red heaven.
Dire was the look that o'er their backs
The angry parting brothers threw:
But now, behold! like cataracts,
Come down the hills in view
O'Connor's plumed partisans;
Thrice ten Kilnagorvian clans
Were marching to their doom:
A sudden storm their plumage toss'd,
A flash of lightning o'er them cross'd,
And all again was gloom!

XVI.

Stranger! I fled the home of grief,
At Connocht Moran's tomb to fall;
I found the helmet of my chief,
His bow still hanging on our wall,
And took it down, and vow'd to rove
This desert place a huntress bold;
Nor would I change my buried love

For any heart of living mould.
No! for I am a hero's child;
I'll hunt my quarry in the wild;
And still my home this mansion make,
Of all unheeded and unheeding,
And cherish, for my warrior's sake—
'The flower of love lies bleeding.'"

THIS small piece was suggested by Campbell seeing a flower in his own garden at Sydenham, called "Love lies bleeding;" to this circumstance we owe the touching narrative of O'Connor's Child, composed in December, 1809, and published in the spring of the following year. It has been considered by many good judges as the most highly finished of all Campbell's minor pieces.

LOCHIEL'S WARNING.

WIZARD—LOCHIEL.

WIZARD.

LOCHIEL, Lochiel! beware of the day
When the lowlands shall meet thee in battle array!
For a field of the dead rushes red on my sight,
And the clans of Culloden are scatter'd in fight.
They rally, they bleed, for their kingdom and crown;
Woe, woe to the riders that trample them down!
Proud Cumberland prances, insulting the slain,
And their hoof-beaten bosoms are trod to the plain.
But hark! through the fast-flashing lightning of war,
What steed to the desert flies frantic and far?
'Tis thine, oh Glenullin! whose bride shall await,
Like a love-lighted watch-fire, all night at the gate.
A steed comes at morning: no rider is there;
But its bridle is red with the sign of despair.
Weep, Albin! to death and captivity led!
Oh weep, but thy tears cannot number the dead:
For a merciless sword on Culloden shall wave,
Culloden! that reeks with the blood of the brave.

LOCHIEL.

Go, preach to the coward, thou death-telling seer!
Or, if gory Culloden so dreadful appear,
Draw, dotard, around thy old wavering sight
This mantle, to cover the phantoms of fright.

WIZARD.

Ha! laugh'st thou, Lochiel, my vision to scorn?
Proud bird of the mountain, thy plume shall be
Say, rush'd the bold eagle exultingly forth, [torn!
From his home, in the dark rolling clouds of the
north?
Lo! the death-shot of foemen outspeeding, he rode
Companionless, bearing destruction abroad;
But down let him stoop from his havoc on high!
Ah! home let him speed,—for the spoiler is nigh.
Why flames the far summit? Why shoot to the
blast
Those embers, like stars from the firmament cast?
'Tis the fire-shower of ruin, all dreadfully driven
From his eyrie, that beacons the darkness of
heaven.
Oh, crested Lochiel! the peerless in might,
Whose banners arise on the battlements' height,
Heaven's fire is around thee, to blast and to burn;
Return to thy dwelling! all lonely return!
For the blackness of ashes shall mark where it
stood, [brood.
And a wild mother scream o'er her famishing

LOCHIEL.

False Wizard, avaunt! I have marshall'd my clan,
Their swords are a thousand, their bosoms are one!
They are true to the last of their blood and their
 breath,
And like reapers descend to the harvest of death.
Then welcome be Cumberland's steed to the shock!
Let him dash his proud foam like a wave on the
 rock!
But woe to his kindred, and woe to his cause,
When Albin her claymore indignantly draws;
When her bonneted chieftains to victory crowd,
Clanronald the dauntless, and Moray the proud,
All plaided and plumed in their tartan array——

WIZARD.

——Lochiel, Lochiel! beware of the day;
For, dark and despairing, my sight I may seal,
But man cannot cover what God would reveal;
'Tis the sunset of life gives me mystical lore,
And coming events cast their shadows before.
I tell thee, Culloden's dread echoes shall ring
With the bloodhounds that bark for thy fugitive
 king.
Lo! anointed by Heaven with the vials of wrath,
Behold, where he flies on his desolate path!
Now in darkness and billows, he sweeps from my
 sight:
Rise, rise! ye wild tempests, and cover his flight!

'Tis finish'd. Their thunders are hush'd on the
Culloden is lost, and my country deplores. [moors:
But where is the iron-bound prisoner? Where?
For the red eye of battle is shut in despair.
Say, mounts he the ocean-wave, banish'd, forlorn,
Like a limb from his country cast bleeding and torn?
Ah no! for a darker departure is near;
The war-drum is muffled, and black is the bier;
His death-bell is tolling: oh! mercy, dispel
Yon sight, that it freezes my spirit to tell!
Life flutters convulsed in his quivering limbs,
And his blood-streaming nostril in agony swims.
Accursed be the fagots, that blaze at his feet,
Where his heart shall be thrown, ere it ceases to
beat,
With the smoke of its ashes to poison the gale——

LOCHIEL.

——Down, soothless insulter! I trust not the tale:
For never shall Albin a destiny meet,
So black with dishonour, so foul with retreat.
Tho' my perishing ranks should be strew'd in their
gore,
Like ocean-weeds heap'd on the surf-beaten shore,
Lochiel, untainted by flight or by chains,
While the kindling of life in his bosom remains,
Shall victor exult, or in death be laid low,
With his back to the field, and his feet to the foe!
And leaving in battle no blot on his name, [fame.
Look proudly to Heaven from the death-bed of

YE MARINERS OF ENGLAND:

A NAVAL ODE.

I.

Ye Mariners of England!
That guard our native seas;
Whose flag has braved, a thousand years,
The battle and the breeze!
Your glorious standard launch again
To match another foe!
And sweep through the deep,
While the stormy winds do blow;
While the battle rages loud and long,
And the stormy winds do blow.

II.

The spirits of your fathers
Shall start from every wave!—
For the deck it was their field of fame,
And Ocean was their grave:
Where Blake and mighty Nelson fell,
Your manly hearts shall glow,
As ye sweep through the deep,
While the stormy winds do blow,
While the battle rages loud and long,
And the stormy winds do blow.

III.

Britannia needs no bulwarks,
No towers along the steep;
Her march is o'er the mountain-waves,
Her home is on the deep.
With thunders from her native oak,
She quells the floods below,—
As they roar on the shore,
When the stormy winds do blow:
When the battle rages loud and long,
And the stormy winds do blow.

IV.

The meteor flag of England
Shall yet terrific burn;
Till danger's troubled night depart,
And the star of peace return.
Then, then, ye ocean-warriors!
Our song and feast shall flow
To the fame of your name,
When the storm has ceased to blow;
When the fiery fight is heard no more,
And the storm has ceased to blow.

1800.

This naval ode was written at Altona, in the winter of 1800, when the poet was twenty-three years of age; it appeared first in the *Morning Chronicle* with the following title, "Alteration of the old ballad 'Ye Gentlemen of England,' composed on the prospect of a Russian war," and signed, "Amator Patriæ." At this time the South Eastern and Southern coasts of England were first fortified with martello towers as a defence against foreign invasion; to this fact reference is elegantly made in the lines

"Britannia needs no bulwarks,
No towers along the steep."

The subject was first suggested by hearing the air of the old ballad before mentioned played at the house of a friend in Scotland; and when the rumour of war with Russia became a general topic of conversation among the British at Altona, it aroused Campbell's patriotism, and hence the result in verse.

BATTLE OF THE BALTIC.

I.

Of Nelson and the North,
Sing the glorious day's renown,
When to battle fierce came forth
All the might of Denmark's crown,
And her arms along the deep proudly shone;
By each gun the lighted brand,
In a bold determined hand,
And the Prince of all the land
Led them on.—

II.

Like leviathans afloat,
Lay their bulwarks on the brine;
While the sign of battle flew
On the lofty British line:
It was ten of April morn by the chime:
As they drifted on their path,
There was silence deep as death;
And the boldest held his breath,
For a time.—

III.

But the might of England flush'd
To anticipate the scene;
And her van the fleeter rush'd
O'er the deadly space between.
'Hearts of oak!' our captain cried; when each gun
From its adamantine lips
Spread a death-shade round the ships,
Like the hurricane eclipse
Of the sun.

IV.

Again! again! again!
And the havoc did not slack,
Till a feeble cheer the Dane
To our cheering sent us back;—
Their shots along the deep slowly boom:—
Then ceased—and all is wail,
As they strike the shatter'd sail;
Or, in conflagration pale,
Light the gloom.—

V.

Out spoke the victor then,
As he hail'd them o'er the wave;
'Ye are brothers! ye are men!
And we conquer but to save:—

So peace instead of death let us bring;
But yield, proud foe, thy fleet,
With the crews, at England's feet,
And make submission meet
To our King.'—

VI.

Then Denmark bless'd our chief,
That he gave her wounds repose;
And the sounds of joy and grief
From her people wildly rose,
As death withdrew his shades from the day.
While the sun look'd smiling bright
O'er a wide and woful sight,
Where the fires of funeral light
Died away.

VII.

Now joy, Old England, raise!
For the tidings of thy might,
By the festal cities' blaze,
Whilst the wine-cup shines in light;
And yet amidst that joy and uproar,
Let us think of them that sleep,
Full many a fathom deep,
By thy wild and stormy steep,
Elsinore!

VIII.

Brave hearts! to Britain's pride
Once so faithful and so true,
On the deck of fame that died;—
With the gallant good Riou;[1]
Soft sigh the winds of Heaven o'er their grave!
While the billow mournful rolls,
And the mermaid's song condoles,
Singing glory to the souls
Of the brave!

1805.

[1] Captain Riou, justly entitled the gallant and the good by Lord Nelson, when he wrote home his despatches.

HOHENLINDEN.

On Linden, when the sun was low,
All bloodless lay the untrodden snow,
And dark as winter was the flow
Of Iser, rolling rapidly.

But Linden saw another sight,
When the drum beat, at dead of night,
Commanding fires of death to light
The darkness of her scenery.

By torch and trumpet fast array'd,
Each horseman drew his battle-blade,
And furious every charger neigh'd,
To join the dreadful revelry.

Then shook the hills with thunder riven,
Then rush'd the steed to battle driven,
And louder than the bolts of heaven,
Far flash'd the red artillery.

But redder yet that light shall glow
On Linden's hills of stainèd snow,
And bloodier yet the torrent flow
Of Iser, rolling rapidly.

'Tis morn, but scarce yon level sun
Can pierce the war-clouds, rolling dun,
Where furious Frank, and fiery Hun,
Shout in their sulphurous canopy.

The combat deepens. On, ye brave,
Who rush to glory, or the grave!
Wave, Munich! all thy banners wave,
And charge with all thy chivalry!

Few, few, shall part where many meet!
The snow shall be their winding-sheet,
And every turf beneath their feet
Shall be a soldier's sepulchre.

1802.

THIS poem was composed in the year 1802, and printed anonymously with "Lochiel," being dedicated to the Rev. A. Alison. It has been described as "the only representation of a modern battle which possesses either interest or sublimity."

Washington Irving, in a "Biographical Sketch of Campbell," appended to "The Poetry and History of Wyoming, containing Campbell's 'Gertrude,'" speaks of this piece and Lochiel, as "Exquisite gems, sufficient of themselves to establish his title to the sacred name of poet;" and Sir Walter Scott, during a visit of the same gifted individual to Abbotsford, made the following observation—"And there 's that glorious little poem too of 'Hohenlinden;' after he had written it he did not seem to think much of it, but considered some of it d—d drum and trumpet lines. I got him to recite it to me, and I believe that the delight I felt and expressed had an effect in inducing him to print it.

"The fact is," added he, "Campbell is in a manner a bugbear to himself. The brightness of his early success is a detriment to all his further efforts. *He is afraid of the shadow that his own fame casts before him.*"

GLENARA.

O HEARD ye yon pibroch sound sad in the gale,
Where a band cometh slowly with weeping and
wail?
'Tis the chief of Glenara laments for his dear;
And her sire, and the people, are call'd to her bier.

Glenara came first with the mourners and shroud;
Her kinsmen they follow'd, but mourn'd not aloud:
Their plaids all their bosoms were folded around;
They march'd all in silence,—they look'd on the
ground.

In silence they reach'd over mountain and moor,
To a heath, where the oak-tree grew lonely and
hoar:
"Now here let us place the gray stone of her cairn:
Why speak ye no word!"—said Glenara the stern.

"And tell me, I charge you! ye clan of my spouse,
Why fold ye your mantles, why cloud ye your
brows?"
So spake the rude chieftain:—no answer is made,
But each mantle unfolding, a dagger display'd.

"I dreamt of my lady, I dreamt of her shroud,"
Cried a voice from the kinsmen, all wrathful and
loud:
"And empty that shroud and that coffin did seem:
Glenara! Glenara! now read me my dream!"

O! pale grew the cheek of that chieftain, I ween,
When the shroud was unclosed, and no lady was
seen;
When a voice from the kinsmen spoke louder in
scorn,
'Twas the youth who had loved the fair Ellen of
Lorn:

"I dreamt of my lady, I dreamt of her grief,
I dreamt that her lord was a barbarous chief:
On a rock of the ocean fair Ellen did seem;
Glenara! Glenara! now read me my dream!"

In dust, low the traitor has knelt to the ground,
And the desert reveal'd where his lady was
found;
From a rock of the ocean that beauty is borne—
Now joy to the house of fair Ellen of Lorn!

This poem of "Glenara," written in the year 1797, at the age of nineteen, was suggested by the following tradition:—"Maclean, of Duart, having determined to get rid of his wife, 'Ellen of Lorn,' had her treacherously conveyed to a rock in the sea, where she was left to perish by the rising tide. He then announced to her kinsmen 'his sudden bereavement,' and exhorted them to join in his grief. In the mean time the lady was accidentally rescued from the certain death that awaited her, and restored to her father. Her husband, little suspecting what had happened, was suffered to go through the solemn mockery of a funeral. At last, when the bier rested at the 'gray stone of her cairn,' on examination of the coffin by her kinsmen, it was found to contain stones, rubbish, &c., whereupon Maclean was instantly sacrificed by the Clan Dougal and thrown into the ready-made grave."

This wild and romantic story has been rendered immortal by the late Joanna Baillie, in "*The Family Legend.*"

EXILE OF ERIN.

THERE came to the beach a poor Exile of Erin,
The dew on his thin robe was heavy and chill;
For his country he sigh'd, when at twilight repairing
To wander alone by the wind-beaten hill:
But the day-star attracted his eye's sad devotion,
For it rose o'er his own native isle of the ocean,
Where once, in the fire of his youthful emotion,
He sang the bold anthem of Erin go bragh.

Sad is my fate! said the heart-broken stranger;
The wild deer and wolf to a covert can flee,
But I have no refuge from famine and danger,
A home and a country remain not to me.
Never again, in the green sunny bowers,
Where my forefathers lived, shall I spend the sweet hours,
Or cover my harp with the wild woven flowers,
And strike to the numbers of Erin go bragh!

Erin, my country! though sad and forsaken,
In dreams I revisit thy sea-beaten shore;

But, alas! in a far foreign land I awaken,
And sigh for the friends who can meet me no more!
Oh cruel fate! wilt thou never replace me
In a mansion of peace—where no perils can chase me?
Never again shall my brothers embrace me?
They died to defend me or live to deplore!

Where is my cabin-door, fast by the wild wood?
Sisters and sire! did ye weep for its fall?
Where is the mother that look'd on my childhood;
And where is the bosom friend dearer than all?
Oh! my sad heart! long abandoned by pleasure,
Why did it dote on a fast-fading treasure?
Tears, like the rain-drop, may fall without measure,
But rapture and beauty they cannot recall.

Yet all its sad recollections suppressing,
One dying wish my lone bosom can draw;
Erin! an exile bequeaths thee his blessing!
Land of my forefathers! Erin go bragh!
Buried and cold, when my heart stills her motion,
Green be thy fields,—sweetest isle of the ocean!
And thy harp-striking bards sing aloud with devotion,—
Erin mavournin—Erin go bragh![1]

1800.

[1] Ireland my darling, Ireland for ever.

"While tarrying at Hamburg, I made acquaintance with some of the refugee Irishmen who had been concerned in the rebellion of 1798. Among these was Anthony Mac Cann, an honest, excellent man, who is still, I believe, alive, at least I left him in prosperous circumstances at Altona a few years ago. [Mac Cann is since dead; Campbell and he met last in the autumn of 1825.] When I first knew him he was in a situation much the reverse; but Anthony commanded respect, whether he was rich or poor. It was in consequence of meeting him one evening on the banks of the Elbe, lonely and pensive at the thoughts of his situation, that I wrote the 'Exile of Erin.' . . .

LORD ULLIN'S DAUGHTER.

A CHIEFTAIN, to the Highlands bound,
  Cries, "Boatman, do not tarry!
And I'll give thee a silver pound,
  To row us o'er the ferry."—

"Now who be ye, would cross Lochgyle,
  This dark and stormy water?"
"O, I'm the chief of Ulva's isle,
  And this Lord Ullin's daughter.—

And fast before her father's men
  Three days we've fled together,
For should he find us in the glen,
  My blood would stain the heather.

His horsemen hard behind us ride;
  Should they our steps discover,
Then who will cheer my bonny bride
  When they have slain her lover?"—

Out spoke the hardy Highland wight,
  "I'll go, my chief—I'm ready:—

It is not for your silver bright;
  But for your winsome lady:

And by my word! the bonny bird
  In danger shall not tarry:
So though the waves are raging white,
  I'll row you o'er the ferry."—

By this the storm grew loud apace,
  The water-wraith was shrieking;
And in the scowl of heaven each face
  Grew dark as they were speaking.

But still as wilder blew the wind,
  And as the night grew drearer,
Adown the glen rode armed men,
  Their trampling sounded nearer.

"O haste thee, haste!" the lady cries,
  "Though tempests round us gather;
I'll meet the raging of the skies,
  But not an angry father."—

The boat has left a stormy land,
  A stormy sea before her,—
When, oh! too strong for human hand,
  The tempest gathered o'er her.—

And still they row'd amidst the roar
  Of waters fast prevailing:

Lord Uullin reach'd that fatal shore,
  His wrath was changed to wailing.—

For sore dismay'd, through storm and shade,
  His child he did discover:—
One lovely hand she stretch'd for aid,
  And one was round her lover.

"Come back! come back!" he cried in grief,
  "Across this stormy water:
And I'll forgive your Highland chief,
  My daughter!—oh my daughter!"—

'Twas vain:—the loud waves lash'd the shore,
  Return or aid preventing:—
The waters wild went o'er his child,
  And he was left lamenting.

1804.

ODE TO THE MEMORY OF BURNS.

Soul of the Poet! wheresoe'er,
Reclaim'd from earth, thy genius plume
Her wings of immortality:
Suspend thy harp in happier sphere,
And with thine influence illume
The gladness of our jubilee.

And fly like fiends from secret spell,
Discord and Strife, at Burns's name,
Exorcised by his memory;
For he was chief of bards that swell
The heart with songs of social flame,
And high delicious revelry.

And Love's own strain to him was given,
To warble all its ecstasies
With Pythian words unsought, unwill'd,—
Love, the surviving gift of Heaven,
The choicest sweet of Paradise,
In life's else bitter cup distill'd.

Who that has melted o'er his lay
To Mary's soul, in Heaven above,

But pictured sees, in fancy strong,
The landscape and the livelong day
That smiled upon their mutual love?—
Who that has felt forgets the song?

Nor skill'd one flame alone to fan:
His country's high-soul'd peasantry
What patriot-pride he taught!—how much
To weigh the inborn worth of man!
And rustic life and poverty
Grow beautiful beneath his touch.

Him, in his clay-built cot, the Muse
Entranced, and show'd him all the forms,
Of fairy-light and wizard gloom,
(That only gifted Poet views,)
The Genii of the floods and storms,
And martial shades from Glory's tomb.

On Bannock-field what thoughts arouse
The swain whom BURNS's song inspires!
Beat not his Caledonian veins,
As o'er the heroic turf he ploughs,
With all the spirit of his sires,
And all their scorn of death and chains?

And see the Scottish exile, tann'd
By many a far and foreign clime,
Bend o'er his home-born verse, and weep
In memory of his native land,

With love that scorns the lapse of time,
And ties that stretch beyond the deep.

Encamp'd by Indian rivers wild,
The soldier resting on his arms,
In BURNS'S carol sweet recalls
The scenes that bless'd him when a child,
And glows and gladdens at the charms
Of Scotia's woods and waterfalls.

O deem not, 'midst this worldly strife,
An idle art the Poet brings:
Let high Philosophy control,
And sages calm the stream of life,
'Tis he refines its fountain-springs,
The nobler passions of the soul.

It is the muse that consecrates
The native banner of the brave,
Unfurling, at the trumpet's breath,
Rose, thistle, harp; 'tis she elates
To sweep the field or ride the wave,
A sunburst in the storm of death.

And thou, young hero, when thy pall
Is cross'd with mournful sword and plume,
When public grief begins to fade,
And only tears of kindred fall,
Who but the bard shall dress thy tomb,
And greet with fame thy gallant shade?

Such was the soldier—BURNS, forgive
That sorrows of mine own intrude
In strains to thy great memory due.
In verse like thine, oh! could he live,
The friend I mourn'd—the brave—the good—
Edward that died at Waterloo![1]

Farewell, high chief of Scottish song!
That couldst alternately impart
Wisdom and rapture in thy page,
And brand each vice with satire strong,
Whose lines are mottoes of the heart,
Whose truths electrify the sage.

Farewell! and ne'er may Envy dare
To wring one baleful poison drop
From the crush'd laurels of thy bust:
But while the lark sings sweet in air,
Still may the grateful pilgrim stop,
To bless the spot that holds thy dust.

1815.

1 Major Edward Hodge, of the 7th Hussars, who fell at the head of his squadron in the attack of the Polish Lancers.

LINES

WRITTEN ON VISITING A SCENE IN ARGYLESHIRE.

At the silence of twilight's contemplative hour,
I have mused in a sorrowful mood,
On the wind-shaken weeds that embosom the bower
Where the home of my forefathers stood.
All ruin'd and wild is their roofless abode,
And lonely the dark raven's sheltering tree :
And travell'd by few is the grass-cover'd road,
Where the hunter of deer and the warrior trode,
To his hills that encircle the sea.

Yet wandering, I found on my ruinous walk,
By the dial-stone aged and green,
One rose of the wilderness left on its stalk,
To mark where a garden had been.
Like a brotherless hermit, the last of its race,
All wild in the silence of nature, it drew,
From each wandering sunbeam, a lonely embrace,
For the night-weed and thorn overshadow'd the place,
Where the flower of my forefathers grew.

Sweet bud of the wilderness! emblem of all
That remains in this desolate heart!
The fabric of bliss to its centre may fall,
But patience shall never depart!
Though the wilds of enchantment, all vernal and bright,
In the days of delusion by fancy combined
With the vanishing phantoms of love and delight,
Abandon my soul, like a dream of the night,
And leave but a desert behind.

Be hush'd, my dark spirit! for wisdom condemns
When the faint and the feeble deplore;
Be strong as the rock of the ocean that stems
A thousand wild waves on the shore!
Through the perils of chance, and the scowl of disdain,
May thy front be unalter'd, thy courage elate!
Yea! even the name I have worshipp'd in vain
Shall awake not the sigh of remembrance again:
To bear is to conquer our fate.

1800.

THE sceue visited was the ruin of "Kirnan;" situate in the vale of Glassary, about a mile and a half from the ancient manse of Kilmichael. His grandfather, Archibald Campbell, had been the last occupant; and he, when somewhat beyond the flower of youth, contracted marriage with Margaret, daughter of Stuart the laird of Ascog, in the island of Bute, widow of John Mac Arthur, of Milton, whose lands abutted upon the Kirnan estate. Upon Mr. A. Campbell's decease, Robert, his eldest son, appears to have inherited the family mansion, and in process of time to have disposed of it to John Mac Arthur, his half-brother, in order to liquidate debts incurred by profuse Highland hospitality, a love of military display, and a numerous train of retainers.

Mr. Mac Arthur, on the completion of his purchase, still continued to reside at Milton, the new property being incorporated with the old. The house at Kirnan gradually fell out of repair, became uninhabitable, and finally lay ruinous and deserted; a melancholy subject for contemplation to a stranger, but doubly so to one who saw in the "roofless abode" an evident picture of the decayed prosperity of his own family.

THE SOLDIER'S DREAM.

OUR bugles sang truce—for the night-cloud had lower'd, [sky;
And the sentinel stars set their watch in the
And thousands had sunk on the ground overpower'd,
The weary to sleep, and the wounded to die.

When reposing that night on my pallet of straw,
By the wolf-scaring fagot that guarded the slain;
At the dead of the night a sweet vision I saw,
And thrice ere the morning I dreamt it again.

Methought from the battle-field's dreadful array,
Far, far I had roam'd on a desolate track:
'Twas Autumn,—and sunshine arose on the way
To the home of my fathers, that welcomed me back.

I flew to the pleasant fields traversed so oft
In life's morning march, when my bosom was young;

I heard my own mountain-goats bleating aloft,
    And knew the sweet strain that the corn-
        reapers sung.

Then pledged we the wine-cup, and fondly I
        swore,
    From my home and my weeping friends never
        to part;
My little ones kiss'd me a thousand times o'er,
    And my wife sobb'd aloud in her fulness of
        heart.

Stay, stay with us,—rest, thou art weary and
        worn;
    And fain was their war-broken soldier to
        stay;—
But sorrow return'd with the dawning of morn,
    And the voice in my dreaming ear melted away.

TO THE RAINBOW.

TRIUMPHAL arch, that fill'st the sky
  When storms prepare to part,
I ask not proud Philosophy
  To teach me what thou art—

Still seem, as to my childhood's sight,
  A midway station given
For happy spirits to alight
  Betwixt the earth and heaven.

Can all that Optics teach, unfold
  Thy form to please me so,
As when I dreamt of gems and gold
  Hid in thy radiant bow?

When Science from Creation's face
  Enchantment's veil withdraws,
What lovely visions yield their place
  To cold material laws!

And yet, fair bow, no fabling dreams,
But words of the Most High,
Have told why first thy robe of beams
Was woven in the sky.

When o'er the green undeluged earth
Heaven's covenant thou didst shine,
How came the world's gray fathers forth
To watch thy sacred sign!

And when its yellow lustre smiled
O'er mountains yet untrod,
Each mother held aloft her child
To bless the bow of God.

Methinks, thy jubilee to keep,
The first-made anthem rang
On earth deliver'd from the deep,
And the first poet sang.

Nor ever shall the Muse's eye
Unraptured greet thy beam;
Theme of primeval prophecy,
Be still the prophet's theme!

The earth to thee her incense yields,
The lark thy welcome sings,
When glittering in the freshen'd fields
The snowy mushroom springs.

How glorious is thy girdle, cast
  O'er mountain, tower, and town,
Or mirror'd in the ocean vast,
  A thousand fathoms down!

As fresh in yon horizon dark,
  As young thy beauties seem,
As when the eagle from the ark
  First sported in thy beam:

For, faithful to its sacred page,
  Heaven still rebuilds thy span,
Nor lets the type grow pale with age
  That first spoke peace to man.

1819.

THE LAST MAN.

All worldly shapes shall melt in gloom,
  The Sun himself must die,
Before this mortal shall assume
  Its Immortality!
I saw a vision in my sleep,
That gave my spirit strength to sweep
  Adown the gulf of Time!
I saw the last of human mould
That shall Creation's death behold,
  As Adam saw her prime!

The Sun's eye had a sickly glare,
  The Earth with age was wan,
The skeletons of nations were
  Around that lonely man!
Some had expired in fight,—the brands
Still rusted in their bony hands
  In plague and famine some!
Earth's cities had no sound nor tread;
And ships were drifting with the dead
  To shores where all was dumb!

Yet, prophet-like, that lone one stood,
  With dauntless words and high,
That shook the sere leaves from the wood
  As if a storm pass'd by,

Saying, We are twins in death, proud Sun!
Thy face is cold, thy race is run,
'Tis Mercy bids thee go;
For thou ten thousand thousand years
Hast seen the tide of human tears,
That shall no longer flow.

What though beneath thee man put forth
His pomp, his pride, his skill;
And arts that made fire, flood, and earth,
The vassals of his will?—
Yet mourn I not thy parted sway,
Thou dim discrowned king of day;
For all those trophied arts
And triumphs that beneath thee sprang,
Heal'd not a passion or a pang
Entail'd on human hearts.

Go, let oblivion's curtain fall
Upon the stage of men,
Nor with thy rising beams recall
Life's tragedy again:
Its piteous pageants bring not back,
Nor waken flesh, upon the rack
Of pain anew to writhe;
Stretch'd in disease's shapes abhorr'd,
Or mown in battle by the sword,
Like grass beneath the scythe.

Ev'n I am weary in yon skies
To watch thy fading fire;

Test of all sumless agonies,
  Behold not me expire.
My lips that speak thy dirge of death—
Their rounded gasp and gurgling breath
  To see thou shalt not boast.
The eclipse of Nature spreads my pall,
The majesty of Darkness shall
  Receive my parting ghost!

This spirit shall return to Him
  Who gave its heavenly spark;
Yet think not, Sun, it shall be dim
  When thou thyself art dark!
No! it shall live again, and shine
In bliss unknown to beams of thine,
  By him recall'd to breath,
Who captive led captivity,
Who robb'd the grave of Victory,—
  And took the sting from Death!

Go, Sun, while Mercy holds me up
  On Nature's awful waste
To drink this last and bitter cup
  Of grief that man shall taste—
Go, tell the night that hides thy face,
Thou saw'st the last of Adam's race,
  On Earth's sepulchral clod,
The darkening universe defy
To quench his Immortality,
  Or shake his trust in God!

1823.

A DREAM.

WELL may sleep present us fictions,
  Since our waking moments teem
With such fanciful convictions
  As make life itself a dream.—
Half our daylight faith 's a fable ;
  Sleep disports with shadows too,
Seeming in their turn as stable
  As the world we wake to view.
Ne'er by day did Reason's mint
Give my thoughts a clearer print
Of assured reality,
Than was left by Phantasy
Stamp'd and colour'd on my sprite,
In a dream of yesternight.

In a bark, methought, lone steering,
  I was cast on Ocean's strife ;
This, 'twas whisper'd in my hearing,
    Meant the sea of life.
Sad regrets from past existence
  Came like gales of chilling breath;

Shadow'd in the forward distance
  Lay the land of Death.
Now seeming more, now less remote,
On that dim-seen shore, methought,
I beheld two hands a space
Slow unshroud a spectre's face;
And my flesh's hair upstood,—
'Twas mine own similitude.—

But my soul revived at seeing
  Ocean, like an emerald spark,
Kindle, while an air-dropt being
  Smiling steer'd my bark
Heaven-like—yet he look'd as human
  As supernal beauty can,
More compassionate than woman,
  Lordly more than man.
And as some sweet clarion's breath
Stirs the soldier's scorn of death—
So his accents bade me brook
The spectre's eyes of icy look,
Till it shut them—turn'd its head,
Like a beaten foe, and fled.

"Types not this." I said, "fair spirit!
  That my death hour is not come?
Say, what days shall I inherit?—
  Tell my soul their sum."
"No," he said, "yon phantom's aspect,

Trust me would appall thee worse,
Held in clearly measured prospect:—
Ask not for a curse!
Make not, for I overhear
Thine unspoken thoughts as clear
As thy mortal ear could catch
The close-brought tickings of a watch—
Make not the untold request
That 's now revolving in thy breast.

'Tis to live again, remeasuring
Youth's years, like a scene rehearsed,
In thy second life-time treasuring
Knowledge from the first.
Hast thou felt, poor self-deceiver!
Life's career so void of pain,
As to wish its fitful fever
New begun again?
Could experience, ten times thine,
Pain from Being disentwine—
Threads by Fate together spun?
Could thy flight Heaven's lightning shun?
No, nor could thy foresight's glance
'Scape the myriad shafts of Chance.

Wouldst thou bear again Love's trouble—
Friendship's death-dissever'd ties;
Toil to grasp or miss the bubble
Of Ambition's prize?

Say thy life's new guided action
  Flow'd from Virtue's fairest springs—
Still would Envy and Detraction
  Double not their stings?
Worth itself is but a charter
To be mankind's distinguish'd martyr."
—I caught the moral, and cried, "Hail!
Spirit! let us onward sail
Envying, fearing, hating none—
Guardian Spirit, steer me on!"

1824.

VALEDICTORY STANZAS

TO

J. P. KEMBLE, Esq.

COMPOSED FOR A PUBLIC MEETING, HELD JUNE, 1817.

Pride of the British stage,
  A long and last adieu!
Whose image brought th' heroic age
  Revived to Fancy's view.
Like fields refresh'd with dewy light
  When the sun smiles his last,
Thy parting presence makes more bright
  Our memory of the past;
And memory conjures feelings up
  That wine or music need not swell,
As high we lift the festal cup
  To Kemble—fare thee well!

His was the spell o'er hearts
  Which only Acting lends,—
The youngest of the sister Arts,
  Where all their beauty blends:
For ill can Poetry express
  Full many a tone of thought sublime,

And Painting, mute and motionless,
  Steals but a glance of time.
But by the mighty actor brought,
  Illusion's perfect triumphs come,—
Verse ceases to be airy thought,
  And Sculpture to be dumb.

Time may again revive,
  But ne'er eclipse the charm,
When Cato spoke in him alive,
  Or Hotspur kindled warm.
What soul was not resign'd entire
  To the deep sorrows of the Moor,—
What English heart was not on fire
  With him at Agincourt?
And yet a majesty possess'd
  His transport's most impetuous tone,
And to each passion of the breast
  The Graces gave their zone.

High were the task—too high,
  Ye conscious bosoms here!
In words to paint your memory
  Of Kemble and of Lear;
But who forgets that white discrowned head,
  Those bursts of Reason's half-extinguish'd glare,
Those tears upon Cordelia's bosom shed,
  In doubt more touching than despair,
    If 'twas reality he felt?

Had Shakspeare's self amidst you been,
Friends, he had seen you melt,
And triumph'd to have seen!

And there was many an hour
Of blended kindred fame,
When Siddons's auxiliar power
And sister magic came.
Together at the Muse's side
The tragic paragons had grown—
They were the children of her pride,
The columns of her throne,
And undivided favour ran
From heart to heart in their applause,
Save for the gallantry of man
In lovelier woman's cause.

Fair as some classic dome,
Robust and richly graced,
Your KEMBLE's spirit was the home
Of genius and of taste;
Taste, like the silent dial's power,
That, when supernal light is given,
Can measure inspiration's hour,
And tell its height in heaven.
At once ennobled and correct,
His mind survey'd the tragic page,
And what the actor could effect,
The scholar could presage.

These were his traits of worth :
  And must we lose them now !
And shall the scene no more shew forth
  His sternly-pleasing brow !
Alas, the moral brings a tear !—
  'Tis all a transient hour below ;
And we that would detain thee here,
  Ourselves as fleetly go !
Yet shall our latest age
  This parting scene review :
Pride of the British stage,
  A long and last adieu !

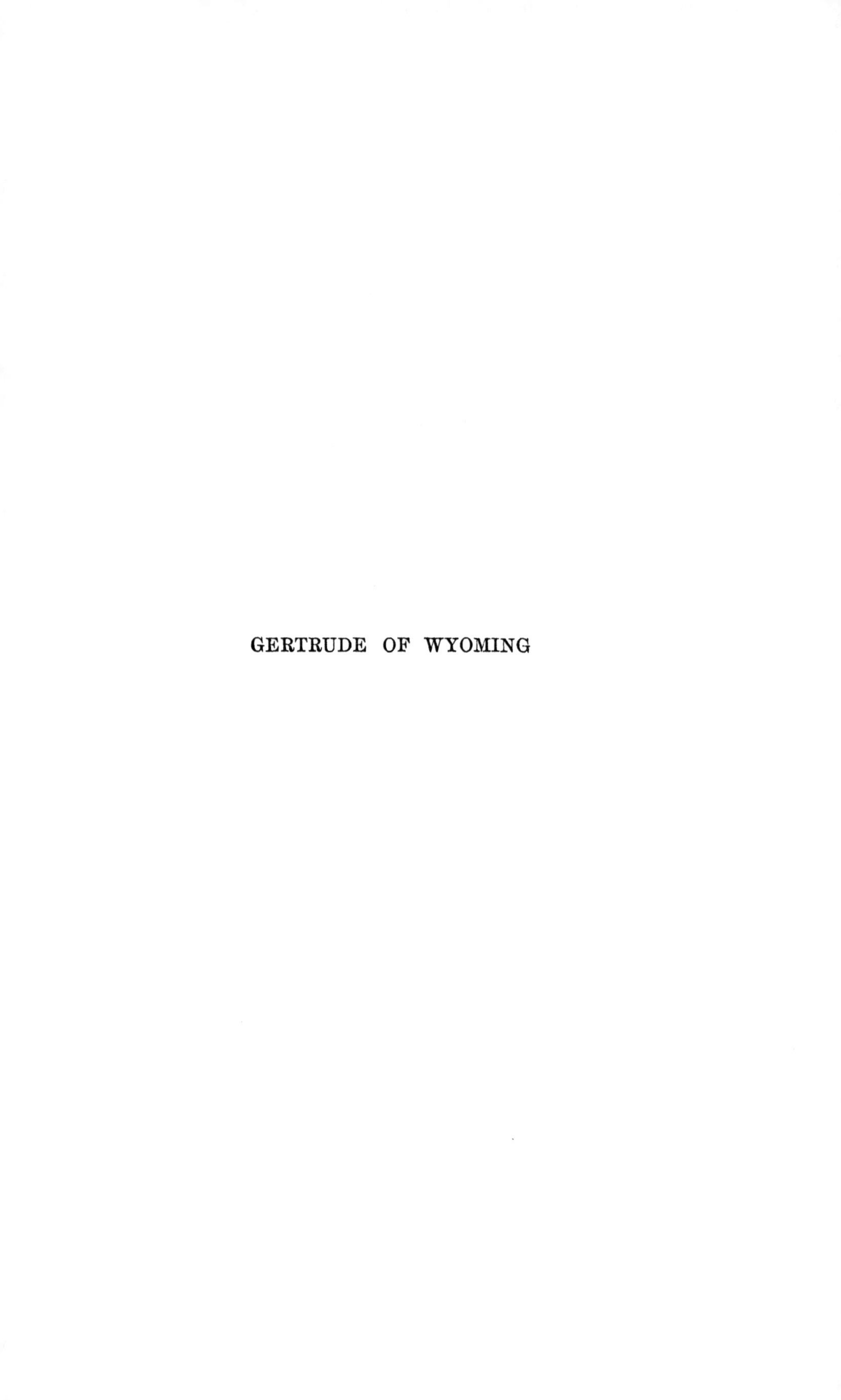

GERTRUDE OF WYOMING

ADVERTISEMENT.

Most of the popular histories of England, as well as of the American war, give an authentic account of the desolation of Wyoming, in Pennsylvania, which took place in 1778, by an incursion of the Indians. The Scenery and Incidents of the following Poem are connected with that event. The testimonies of historians and travellers concur in describing the infant colony as one of the happiest spots of human existence, for the hospitable and innocent manners of the inhabitants, the beauty of the country, and the luxuriant fertility of the soil and climate. In an evil hour, the junction of European with Indian arms converted this terrestrial paradise into a frightful waste. Mr. Isaac Weld informs us, that the ruins of many of the villages, perforated with balls, and bearing marks of conflagration, were still preserved by the recent inhabitants, when he travelled through America in 1796.

GERTRUDE OF WYOMING.

PART I.

I.

On Susquehanna's side, fair Wyoming!
Although the wild-flower on thy ruin'd wall,
And roofless homes, a sad remembrance bring
Of what thy gentle people did befall;
Yet thou wert once the loveliest land of all
That see the Atlantic wave their morn restore.
Sweet land! may I thy lost delights recall,
And paint thy Gertrude in her bowers of yore,
Whose beauty was the love of Pennsylvania's shore!

II.

Delightful Wyoming! beneath thy skies,
The happy shepherd swains had nought to do
But feed their flocks on green declivities,
Or skim perchance thy lake with light canoe,
From morn till evening's sweeter pastime grew,
With timbrel, when beneath the forest brown,
Thy lovely maidens would the dance renew;
And aye those sunny mountains half-way down
Would echo flagelet from some romantic town.

III.

Then, where of Indian hills the daylight takes
His leave, how might you the flamingo see
Disporting like a meteor on the lakes—
And playful squirrel on his nut-grown tree:
And every sound of life was full of glee,
From merry mock-bird's song, or hum of men;
While hearkening, fearing nought their revelry,
The wild deer arch'd his neck from glades, and then,
Unhunted, sought his woods and wilderness again.

IV.

And scarce had Wyoming of war or crime
Heard, but in transatlantic story rung,
For here the exile met from every clime,
And spoke in friendship every distant tongue:
Men from the blood of warring Europe sprung
Were but divided by the running brook;
And happy where no Rhenish trumpet sung,
On plains no sieging mine's volcano shook,
The blue-eyed German changed his sword to pruning-hook.

V.

Nor far some Andalusian saraband
Would sound to many a native roundelay—
But who is he that yet a dearer land
Remembers, over hills and far away?

Green Albin![1] what though he no more survey
Thy ships at anchor on the quiet shore,
Thy pellochs[2] rolling from the mountain bay,
Thy lone sepulchral cairn upon the moor,
And distant isles that hear the loud Corbrechtan[3]
roar!

VI.

Alas! poor Caledonia's mountaineer,
That want's stern edict e'er, and feudal grief,
Had forced him from a home he loved so dear!
Yet found he here a home and glad relief,
And plied the beverage from his own fair sheaf,
That fired his Highland blood with mickle glee:
And England sent her men, of men the chief,
Who taught those sires of Empire yet to be,
To plant the tree of life,—to plant fair Freedom's
tree!

VII.

Here was not mingled in the city's pomp
Of life's extremes the grandeur and the gloom;
Judgment awoke not here her dismal tromp,
Nor seal'd in blood a fellow creature's doom,
Nor mourn'd the captive in a living tomb.
One venerable man, beloved of all,
Sufficed, where innocence was yet in bloom,
To sway the strife, that seldom might befall:
And Albert was their judge, in patriarchal hall.

1 Scotland.
2 The Gaelic appellation for the porpoise.
3 The great whirlpool of the western Hebrides.

VIII.

How reverend was the look, serenely aged,
He bore, this gentle Pennsylvanian sire,
Where all but kindly fervours were assuaged,
Undimm'd by weakness' shade, or turbid ire!
And though, amidst the calm of thought entire,
Some high and haughty features might betray
A soul impetuous once, 'twas earthly fire
That fled composure's intellectual ray,
As Ætna's fires grow dim before the rising day.

IX.

I boast no song in magic wonders rife,
But yet, oh Nature! is there nought to prize,
Familiar in thy bosom scenes of life?
And dwells in daylight truth's salubrious skies
No form with which the soul may sympathize?—
Young, innocent, on whose sweet forehead mild
The parted ringlet shone in simplest guise,
An inmate in the home of Albert smiled,
Or bless'd his noonday walk—she was his only child.

X.

The rose of England bloom'd on Gertrude's cheek—
What though these shades had seen her birth, her sire
A Briton's independence taught to seek
Far western worlds; and there his household fire
The light of social love did long inspire,

And many a halcyon day he lived to see
Unbroken but by one misfortune dire,
When fate had reft his mutual heart—but she
Was gone—and Gertrude climb'd a widow'd
father's knee.

XI.

A loved bequest,—and I may half impart—
To them that feel the strong paternal tie,
How like a new existence to his heart
That living flower uprose beneath his eye,
Dear as she was from cherub infancy,
From hours when she would round his garden
play,
To time when, as the ripening years went by,
Her lovely mind could culture well repay,
And more engaging grew, from pleasing day to
day.

XII.

I may not paint those thousand infant charms:
(Unconscious fascination, undesign'd!)
The orison repeated in his arms,
For God to bless her sire and all mankind;
The book, the bosom on his knee reclined,
Or how sweet fairy-lore he heard her con,
(The playmate ere the teacher of her mind:)
All uncompanion'd else her heart had gone
Till now, in Gertrude's eyes, their ninth blue
summer shone.

XIII.

And summer was the tide, and sweet the hour,
When sire and daughter saw, with fleet descent,
An Indian from his bark approach their bower,
Of buskin'd limb, and swarthy lineament;
The red wild feathers on his brow were blent,
And bracelets bound the arm that help'd to light
A boy, who seem'd, as he beside him went,
Of Christian vesture, and complexion bright,
Led by his dusky guide, like morning brought by
night.

XIV.

Yet pensive seem'd the boy for one so young—
The dimple from his polish'd cheek had fled;
When, leaning on his forest-bow unstrung,
Th' Oneyda warrior to the planter said,
And laid his hand upon the stripling's head,
" Peace be to thee! my words this belt approve;
The paths of peace my steps have hither led:
This little nursling, take him to thy love,
And shield the bird unfledged, since gone the
parent dove.

XV.

Christian! I am the foeman of thy foe;
Our wampum league thy brethren did embrace:
Upon the Michigan, three moons ago,
We launch'd our pirogues for the bison chase,
And with the Hurons planted for a space,

With true and faithful hands, the olive-stalk ;
But snakes are in the bosoms of their race,
And though they held with us a friendly talk,
The hollow peace-tree fell beneath their tomahawk !

XVI.

It was encamping on the lake's far port,
A cry of Areouski[1] broke our sleep,
Where storm'd an ambush'd foe thy nation's fort,
And rapid, rapid whoops came o'er the deep ;
But long thy country's war-sign on the steep
Appear'd through ghastly intervals of light,
And deathfully their thunders seem'd to sweep,
Till utter darkness swallow'd up the sight,
As if a shower of blood had quench'd the fiery fight !

XVII.

It slept—it rose again—on high their tower
Sprung upwards like a torch to light the skies,
Then down again it rain'd an ember shower,
And louder lamentations heard we rise :
As when the evil Manitou that dries
Th' Ohio woods, consumes them in his ire,
In vain the desolated panther flies,
And howls amidst his wilderness of fire :
Alas ! too late, we reach'd and smote those Hurons dire !

[1] The Indian God of War.

XVIII.

But as the fox beneath the nobler hound,
So died their warriors by our battle-brand;
And from the tree we, with her child, unbound
A lonely mother of the Christian land:—
Her lord—the captain of the British band—
Amidst the slaughter of his soldiers lay.
Scarce knew the widow our delivering hand;
Upon her child she sobb'd, and swoon'd away,
Or shriek'd unto the God to whom the Christians
pray.

XIX.

Our virgins fed her with their kindly bowls
Of fever-balm and sweet sagamité:
But she was journeying to the land of souls,
And lifted up her dying head to pray
That we should bid an ancient friend convey
Her orphan to his home of England's shore;
And take, she said, this token far away,
To one that will remember us of yore,
When he beholds the ring that Waldegrave's Julia
wore.

XX.

And I, the eagle of my tribe, have rush'd
With this lorn dove."—A sage's self-command
Had quell'd the tears from Albert's heart that
gush'd;
But yet his cheek—his agitated hand—
That shower'd upon the stranger of the land

No common boon, in grief but ill beguiled
A soul that was not wont to be unmann'd ;
" And stay," he cried, " dear pilgrim of the wild,
Preserver of my old, my boon companion's child!

XXI.

Child of a race whose name my bosom warms,
On earth's remotest bounds how welcome here!
Whose mother oft, a child, has fill'd these arms,
Young as thyself, and innocently dear,
Whose grandsire was my early life's compeer.
Ah, happiest home of England's happy clime!
How beautiful ev'n now thy scenes appear,
As in the noon and sunshine of my prime!
How gone like yesterday these thrice ten years
of time!

XXII.

And Julia! when thou wert like Gertrude now,
Can I forget thee, favourite child of yore?
Or thought I, in thy father's house, when thou
Wert lightest-hearted on his festive floor,
And first of all his hospitable door
To meet and kiss me at my journey's end?
But where was I when Waldegrave was no more?
And thou didst pale thy gentle head extend
In woes, that ev'n the tribe of deserts was thy
friend!"

XXIII.

He said—and strain'd unto his heart the boy;—
Far differently, the mute Oneyda took

His calumet of peace and cup of joy;
As monumental bronze unchanged his look;
A soul that pity touch'd, but never shook;
Train'd from his tree-rock'd cradle to his bier
The fierce extreme of good and ill to brook
Impassive—fearing but the shame of fear—
A stoic of the woods—a man without a tear.

XXIV.

Yet deem not goodness on the savage stock
Of Outalissi's heart disdain'd to grow;
As lives the oak unwither'd on the rock
By storms above, and barrenness below;
He scorn'd his own, who felt another's woe:
And ere the wolf-skin on his back he flung,
Or laced his mocasins, in act to go,
A song of parting to the boy he sung,
Who slept on Albert's couch, nor heard his friendly tongue.

XXV.

"Sleep, wearied one! and in the dreaming land
Shouldst thou to-morrow with thy mother meet,
Oh! tell her spirit that the white man's hand
Hath pluck'd the thorns of sorrow from thy feet;
While I in lonely wilderness shall greet
Thy little foot-prints—or by traces know
The fountain, where at noon I thought it sweet
To feed thee with the quarry of my bow,
And pour'd the lotus-horn, or slew the mountain roe.

XXVI.

Adieu! sweet scion of the rising sun!
But should affliction's storms thy blossom mock,
Then come again—my own adopted one!
And I will graft thee on a noble stock:
The crocodile, the condor of the rock,
Shall be the pastime of thy sylvan wars;
And I will teach thee in the battle's shock,
To pay with Huron blood thy father's scars,
And gratulate his soul rejoicing in the stars!"

XXVII.

So finish'd he the rhyme (howe'er uncouth)
That true to nature's fervid feelings ran;
(And song is but the eloquence of truth:)
Then forth uprose that lone way-faring man;
But dauntless he, nor chart, nor journey's plan
In woods required, whose trained eye was keen,
As eagle of the wilderness, to scan
His path by mountain, swamp, or deep ravine,
Or ken far friendly huts on good savannas green.

XXVIII.

Old Albert saw him from the valley's side—
His pirogue launch'd—his pilgrimage begun—
Far, like the red-bird's wing he seem'd to glide;
Then dived, and vanish'd in the woodlands dun.

Oft, to that spot by tender memory won,
Would Albert climb the promontory's height,
If but a dim sail glimmer'd in the sun;
But never more to bless his longing sight,
Was Outalissi hail'd, with bark and plumage
bright.

GERTRUDE OF WYOMING.

PART II.

I

A VALLEY from the river shore withdrawn
Was Albert's home, two quiet woods between,
Whose lofty verdure overlook'd his lawn;
And waters to their resting-place serene
Came freshening, and reflecting all the scene:
(A mirror in the depth of flowery shelves;)
So sweet a spot of earth, you might (I ween)
Have guess'd some congregation of the elves,
To sport by summer moons, had shaped it for themselves.

II.

Yet wanted not the eye far scope to muse,
Nor vistas open'd by the wandering stream;
Both where at evening Alleghany views,
Through ridges burning in her western beam,
Lake after lake interminably gleam:
And past those settlers' haunts the eye might roam
Where earth's unliving silence all would seem;
Save where on rocks the beaver built his dome,
Or buffalo remote low'd far from human home.

III.

But silent not that adverse eastern path,
Which saw Aurora's hills th' horizon crown:
There was the river heard, in bed of wrath,
(A precipice of foam from mountains brown,)
Like tumults heard from some far distant town;
But softening in approach he left his gloom,
And murmur'd pleasantly, and laid him down
To kiss those easy curving banks of bloom,
That lent the windward air an exquisite perfume.

IV.

It seem'd as if those scenes sweet influence had
On Gertrude's soul, and kindness like their own
Inspired those eyes affectionate and glad,
That seem'd to love whate'er they look'd upon;
Whether with Hebe's mirth her features shone,
Or if a shade more pleasing them o'ercast,
(As if for heavenly musing meant alone;)
Yet so becomingly th' expression past,
That each succeeding look was lovelier than the
last.

V.

Nor guess I, was that Pennsylvanian home,
With all its picturesque and balmy grace,
And fields that were a luxury to roam,
Lost on the soul that look'd from such a face!
Enthusiast of the woods! when years apace

Had bound thy lovely waist with woman's zone,
The sunrise path, at morn, I see thee trace
To hills with high magnolia overgrown,
And joy to breathe the groves, romantic and alone.

VI.

The sunrise drew her thoughts to Europe forth,
That thus apostrophized its viewless scene :
" Land of my father's love, my mother's birth !
The home of kindred I have never seen !
We know not other—oceans are between :
Yet say, far friendly hearts ! from whence we came,
Of us does oft remembrance intervene ?
My mother sure—my sire a thought may claim ;—
But Gertrude is to you an unregarded name.

VII.

And yet, loved England ! when thy name I trace
In many a pilgrim's tale and poet's song,
How can I choose but wish for one embrace
Of them, the dear unknown, to whom belong
My mother's looks,—perhaps her likeness strong ?
Oh, parent ! with what reverential awe,
From features of thy own related throng,
An image of thy face my soul could draw !
And see thee once again whom I too shortly saw ! "

VIII.

Yet deem not Gertrude sigh'd for foreign joy ;
To soothe a father's couch her only care,

And keep his reverend head from all annoy:
For this, methinks, her homeward steps repair,
Soon as the morning wreath had bound her hair;
While yet the wild deer trod in spangling dew,
While boatmen caroll'd to the fresh-blown air,
And woods a horizontal shadow threw,
And early fox appear'd in momentary view.

IX.

Apart there was a deep untrodden grot,
Where oft the reading hours sweet Gertrude wore;
Tradition had not named its lonely spot;
But here (methinks) might India's sons explore
Their fathers' dust, or lift, perchance of yore,
Their voice to the great Spirit:—rocks sublime
To human art a sportive semblance bore,
And yellow lichens colour'd all the clime,
Like moonlight battlements, and towers decay'd
by time.

X.

But high in amphitheatre above,
Gay-tinted woods their massy foliage threw;
Breathed but an air of heaven, and all the grove
As if instinct with living spirit grew,
Rolling its verdant gulfs of every hue;
And now suspended was the pleasing din,
Now from a murmur faint it swell'd anew,
Like the first note of organ heard within
Cathedral aisles,—ere yet its symphony begin.

XI.

It was in this lone valley she would charm
The lingering noon, where flowers a couch had strown;
Her cheek reclining, and her snowy arm
On hillock by the pine-tree half o'ergrown;
And aye that volume on her lap is thrown,
Which every heart of human mould endears;
With Shakspeare's self she speaks and smiles alone,
And no intruding visitation fears,
To shame the unconscious laugh, or stop her sweetest tears.

XII.

And nought within the grove was heard or seen
But stock-doves plaining through its gloom profound,
Or winglet of the fairy humming-bird,
Like atoms of the rainbow fluttering round;
When, lo! there enter'd to its inmost ground
A youth, the stranger of a distant land;
He was, to weet, for eastern mountains bound;
But late th' equator suns his cheek had tann'd,
And California's gales his roving bosom fann'd.

XIII.

A steed, whose rein hung loosely o'er his arm,
He led dismounted; ere his leisure pace,

Amid the brown leaves, could her ear alarm,
Close he had come, and worshipp'd for a space
Those downcast features:—she her lovely face
Uplift on one, whose lineaments and frame
Wore youth and manhood's intermingled grace:
Iberian seem'd his boot—his robe the same,
And well the Spanish plume his lofty looks be-
came.

XIV.

For Albert's home he sought—her finger fair
Has pointed where the father's mansion stood.
Returning from the copse he soon was there;
And soon has Gertrude hied from dark green
wood;
Nor joyless, by the converse, understood
Between the man of age and pilgrim young,
That gay congeniality of mood,
And early liking from acquaintance sprung;
Full fluently conversed their guest in England's
tongue.

XV.

And well could he his pilgrimage of taste
Unfold,—and much they loved his fervid strain,
While he each fair variety retraced
Of climes, and manners, o'er the eastern main.
Now happy Switzer's hills—romantic Spain,—
Gay lilied fields of France,—or, more refined,
The soft Ausonia's monumental reign;
Nor less each rural image he design'd
Than all the city's pomp and home of human kind.

XVI.

Anon some wilder portraiture he draws;
Of Nature's savage glories he would speak,—
The loneliness of earth that overawes,—
Where, resting by some tomb of old Cacique,
The lama-driver on Peruvia's peak
Nor living voice nor motion marks around;
But storks that to the boundless forest shriek,
Or wild-cane arch high flung o'er gulf profound,
That fluctuates when the storms of El Dorado
sound.

XVII.

Pleased with his guest, the good man still would
ply
Each earnest question, and his converse court;
But Gertrude, as she eyed him, knew not why
A strange and troubling wonder stopt her short.
"In England thou hast been,—and, by report,
An orphan's name (quoth Albert) may'st have
known.
Sad tale!—when latest fell our frontier fort,—
One innocent—one soldier's child—alone
Was spared, and brought to me, who loved him as
my own.

XVIII.

Young Henry Waldegrave! three delightful years
These very walls his infant sports did see,
But most I loved him when his parting tears
Alternately bedew'd my child and me:

His sorest parting, Gertrude, was from thee;
Nor half its grief his little heart could hold;
By kindred he was sent for o'er the sea,
They tore him from us when but twelve years old,
And scarcely for his loss have I been yet consoled!"

XIX.

His face the wanderer hid—but could not hide
A tear, a smile, upon his cheek that dwell;
"And speak! mysterious stranger! (Gertrude cried)
It is!—it is!—I knew—I knew him well!
'Tis Waldegrave's self, of Waldegrave come to tell!"
A burst of joy the father's lips declare!
But Gertrude speechless on his bosom fell;
At once his open arms embraced the pair,
Was never group more blest in this wide world of care.

XX.

"And will ye pardon then (replied the youth)
Your Waldegrave's feigned name, and false attire?
I durst not in the neighbourhood, in truth,
The very fortunes of your house inquire;
Lest one that knew me might some tidings dire
Impart, and I my weakness all betray,
For had I lost my Gertrude and my sire,
I meant but o'er your tombs to weep a day,
Unknown I meant to weep, unknown to pass away.

XXI.

But here ye live, ye bloom,—in each dear face,
The changing hand of time I may not blame;
For there, it hath but shed more reverend grace,
And here, of beauty perfected the frame:
And well I know your hearts are still the same—
They could not change—ye look the very way,
As when an orphan first to you I came.
And have ye heard of my poor guide I pray?
Nay, wherefore weep ye, friends, on such a joyous
day?"

XXII.

"And art thou here? or is it but a dream?
And wilt thou, Waldegrave, wilt thou, leave us
more?"—
"No, never! thou that yet dost lovelier seem
Than aught on earth—than ev'n thyself of
yore—
I will not part thee from thy father's shore;
But we shall cherish him with mutual arms,
And hand in hand again the path explore
Which every ray of young remembrance warms,
While thou shalt be my own, with all thy truth
and charms!"

XXIII.

At morn, as if beneath a galaxy
Of over-arching groves in blossoms white,
Where all was odorous scent and harmony,

And gladness to the heart, nerve, ear, and sight:
There, if, O gentle Love! I read aright
The utterance that seal'd thy sacred bond,
'Twas listening to these accents of delight,
She hid upon his breast those eyes, beyond
Expression's power to paint, all languishingly fond—

XXIV.

" Flower of my life, so lovely and so lone!
Whom I would rather in this desert meet,
Scorning, and scorn'd by fortune's power, than own
Her pomp and splendours lavish'd at my feet!
Turn not from me thy breath more exquisite
Than odours cast on heaven's own shrine—to please—
Give me thy love, than luxury more sweet,
And more than all the wealth that loads the breeze,
When Coromandel's ships return from Indian seas."

XXV.

Then would that home admit them—happier far
Than grandeur's most magnificent saloon,
While, here and there, a solitary star
Flush'd in the darkening firmament of June;
And silence brought the soul-felt hour, full soon,
Ineffable, which I may not portray;
For never did the hymenean moon
A paradise of hearts more sacred sway,
In all that slept beneath her soft voluptuous ray.

GERTRUDE OF WYOMING.

PART III.

I.

O Love! in such a wilderness as this,
Where transport and security entwine,
Here is the empire of thy perfect bliss,
And here thou art a god indeed divine.
Here shall no forms abridge, no hours confine,
The views, the walks, that boundless joy inspire!
Roll on, ye days of raptured influence, shine!
Nor, blind with ecstasy's celestial fire,
Shall love behold the spark of earth-born time
    expire.

II.

Three little moons, how short! amidst the grove
And pastoral savannas they consume!
While she, beside her buskin'd youth to rove,
Delights, in fancifully wild costume,
Her lovely brow to shade with Indian plume;
And forth in hunter-seeming vest they fare;
But not to chase the deer in forest gloom,
'Tis but the breath of heaven—the blessed air—
And interchange of hearts unknown, unseen to
    share.

III.

What though the sportive dog oft round them note,
Or fawn, or wild bird bursting on the wing;
Yet who, in Love's own presence, would devote
To death those gentle throats that wake the spring,
Or writhing from the brook its victim bring?
No!—nor let fear one little warbler rouse;
But, fed by Gertrude's hand, still let them sing,
Acquaintance of her path, amidst the boughs,
That shade ev'n now her love, and witness'd first
her vows.

IV.

Now labyrinths, which but themselves can pierce,
Methinks, conduct them to some pleasant ground,
Where welcome hills shut out the universe,
And pines their lawny walk encompass round;
There, if a pause delicious converse found,
'Twas but when o'er each heart th' idea stole,
(Perchance a while in joy's oblivion drown'd)
That come what may, while life's glad pulses
roll,
Indissolubly thus should soul be knit to soul.

V.

And in the visions of romantic youth,
What years of endless bliss are yet to flow!
But mortal pleasure, what art thou in truth?
The torrent's smoothness, ere it dash below!
And must I change my song? and must I show,

Sweet Wyoming! the day when thou wert doom'd,
Guiltless, to mourn thy loveliest bowers laid low!
When where of yesterday a garden bloom'd,
Death overspread his pall, and blackening ashes
gloom'd!

VI.

Sad was the year, by proud oppression driven,
When Transatlantic Liberty arose,
Not in the sunshine and the smile of heaven,
But wrapt in whirlwinds, and begirt with woes,
Amidst the strife of fratricidal foes;
Her birth-star was the light of burning plains;[1]
Her baptism is the weight of blood that flows
From kindred hearts—the blood of British veins—
And famine tracks her steps, and pestilential pains.

VII.

Yet, ere the storm of death had raged remote,
Or siege unseen in heaven reflects its beams,
Who now each dreadful circumstance shall note,
That fills pale Gertrude's thoughts, and nightly
dreams!
Dismal to her the forge of battle gleams
Portentous light! and music's voice is dumb;
Save where the fife its shrill reveillé screams,
Or midnight streets reëcho to the drum,
That speaks of maddening strife, and bloodstain'd
fields to come.

1 Alluding to the miseries that attended the American civil war.

VIII.

It was in truth a momentary pang;
Yet how comprising myriad shapes of woe!
First when in Gertrude's ear the summons rang,
A husband to the battle doom'd to go!
"Nay meet not thou (she cried) thy kindred foe!
But peaceful let us seek fair England's strand!"
"Ah, Gertrude, thy beloved heart, I know,
Would feel like mine the stigmatizing brand!
Could I forsake the cause of Freedom's holy band!

IX.

But shame—but flight—a recreant's name to prove,
To hide in exile ignominious fears;
Say, ev'n if this I brook'd, the public love
Thy father's bosom to his home endears:
And how could I his few remaining years,
My Gertrude, sever from so dear a child?"
So, day by day, her boding heart he cheers:
At last that heart to hope is half beguiled,
And, pale through tears suppress'd, the mournful beauty smiled.

X.

Night came,—and in their lighted bower, full late,
The joy of converse had endured—when, hark!
Abrupt and loud, a summons shook their gate;
And heedless of the dog's obstrep'rous bark,

A form had rush'd amidst them from the dark,
And spread his arms,—and fell upon the floor:
Of aged strength his limbs retain'd the mark;
But desolate he look'd, and famish'd poor,
As ever shipwreck'd wretch lone left on desert
shore.

XI.

Uprisen, each wondering brow is knit and
arch'd:
A spirit from the dead they deem him first:
To speak he tries; but quivering, pale, and
parch'd,
From lips, as by some powerless dream accursed,
Emotions unintelligible burst;
And long his filmed eye is red and dim:
At length the pity-proffer'd cup his thirst
Had half assuaged, and nerved his shuddering
limb,
When Albert's hand he grasp'd;—but Albert
knew not him—

XII.

"And hast thou then forgot," (he cried forlorn,
And eyed the group with half indignant air,)
" O! hast thou, Christian chief, forgot the morn
When I with thee the cup of peace did share?
Then stately was this head, and dark this hair,
That now is white as Appalachia's snow;
But, if the weight of fifteen years' despair,

And age hath bow'd me, and the torturing foe,
Bring me my boy—and he will his deliverer
know!"

XIII.

It was not long, with eyes and heart of flame,
Ere Henry to his loved Oneyda flew;
"Bless thee my guide!"—but backward, as he
came,
The chief his old bewilder'd head withdrew.
And grasp'd his arm, and look'd and look'd him
through.
'Twas strange—nor could the group a smile con-
trol—
The long, the doubtful scrutiny to view:
At last delight o'er all his features stole,
"It is—my own," he cried, and clasp'd him to his
soul.

XIV.

"Yes! thou recall'st my pride of years, for then
The bowstring of my spirit was not slack,
When, spite of woods, and floods, and ambush'd
men,
I bore thee like the quiver on my back,
Fleet as the whirlwind hurries on the rack;
Nor foeman then, nor cougar's crouch I fear'd,[1]
For I was strong as mountain cataract:

[1] Cougar, the American tiger.

And dost thou not remember how we cheer'd,
Upon the last hill-top, when white men's huts
appear'd?

XV.

Then welcome be my death-song, and my death!
Since I have seen thee, and again embraced."
And longer had he spent his toil-worn breath;
But with affectionate and eager haste,
Was every arm outstretch'd around their guest,
To welcome and to bless his aged head.
Soon was the hospitable banquet placed;
And Gertrude's lovely hands a balsam shed
On wounds with fever'd joy that more profusely
bled.

XVI.

"But this is not a time,"—he started up,
And smote his breast with woe-denouncing hand—
"This is no time to fill the joyous cup,
The Mammoth comes,—the foe,—the Monster
Brandt,—
With all his howling desolating band;—
These eyes have seen their blade and burning pine
Awake at once, and silence half your land.
Red is the cup they drink; but not with wine:
Awake, and watch to-night, or see no morning
shine!

XVII.

Scorning to wield the hatchet for his bribe,
Gainst Brandt himself I went to battle forth:

Accursed Brandt! he left of all my tribe
Nor man, nor child, nor thing of living birth:
No! not the dog that watch'd my household
hearth,
Escaped that night of blood, upon our plains!
All perish'd!—I alone am left on earth!
To whom nor relative nor blood remains,
No!—not a kindred drop that runs in human
veins!

XVIII.

But go!—and rouse your warriors, for, if right
These old bewilder'd eyes could guess, by signs
Of striped and starred banners, on yon height
Of eastern cedars, o'er the creek of pines—
Some fort embattled by your country shines:
Deep roars th' innavigable gulf below
Its squared rock, and palisaded lines.
Go! seek the light its warlike beacons show;
Whilst I in ambush wait, for vengeance, and the
foe!"

XIX.

Scarce had he utter'd—when Heaven's verge
extreme
Reverberates the bomb's decending star,—
And sounds that mingled laugh,—and shout,—
and scream,—
To freeze the blood, in one discordant jar,
Rung to the pealing thunderbolts of war.
Whoop after whoop with rack the ear assail'd;
As if unearthly fiends had burst their bar;

While rapidly the marksman's shot prevail'd:
And aye, as if for death, some lonely trumpet
wail'd.

XX.

Then look'd they to the hills, where fire o'erhung
The bandit groups, in one Vesuvian glare;
Or swept, far seen, the tower, whose clock
unrung
Told legible that midnight of despair.
She faints,—she falters not,—th' heroic fair,—
As he the sword and plume in haste array'd.
One short embrace—he clasp'd his dearest care—
But hark! what nearer war-drum shakes the
glade?
Joy, joy! Columbia's friends are trampling through
the shade!

XXI.

Then came of every race the mingled swarm,
Far rung the groves and gleam'd the midnight
grass,
With flambeau, javelin, and naked arm;
As warriors wheel'd their culverins of brass,
Sprung from the woods, a bold athletic mass,
Whom virtue fires, and liberty combines:
And first the wild Moravian yagers pass,
His plumed host the dark Iberian joins—
And Scotia's sword beneath the Highland thistle
shines.

XXII.

And in the buskin'd hunters of the deer,
To Albert's home, with shout and cymbal
throng:—
Roused by their warlike pomp, and mirth, and
cheer,
Old Outalissi woke his battle-song,
And, beating with his war-club cadence strong,
Tells how his deep-stung indignation smarts,
Of them that wrapt his house in flames, ere long,
To whet a dagger on their stony hearts,
And smile avenged ere yet his eagle spirit parts.—

XXIII.

Calm, opposite the Christian father rose,
Pale on his venerable brow its rays
Of martyr light the conflagration throws;
One hand upon his lovely child he lays,
And one the uncover'd crowd to silence sways;
While, though the battle flash is faster driven,—
Unaw'd, with eye unstartled by the blaze,
He for his bleeding country prays to Heaven,—
Prays that the men of blood themselves may be
forgiven.

XXIV.

Short time is now for gratulating speech:
And yet, beloved Gertrude, ere began
Thy country's flight, yon distant towers to reach,

Look'd not on thee the rudest partisan
With brow relax'd to love? And murmurs ran,
As round and round their willing ranks they drew,
From beauty's sight to shield the hostile van.
Grateful, on them a placid look she threw,
Nor wept, but as she bade her mother's grave
 adieu!

XXV.

Past was the flight, and welcome seem'd the tower,
That like a giant standard-bearer frown'd
Defiance on the roving Indian power,
Beneath, each bold and promontory mound
With embrasure emboss'd, and armour crown'd,
And arrowy frize, and wedged ravelin,
Wove like a diadem its tracery round
The lofty summit of that mountain green;
Here stood secure the group, and eyed a distant
 scene.

XXVI.

A scene of death! where fires beneath the sun,
And blended arms, and white pavilions glow;
And for the business of destruction done,
Its requiem the war-horn seem'd to blow:
There, sad spectatress of her country's woe!
The lovely Gertrude, safe from present harm,
Had laid her cheek, and clasp'd her hands of
 snow
On Waldegrave's shoulder, half within his arm
Enclosed, that felt her heart, and hush'd its wild
 alarm!

XXVII.

But short that contemplation—sad and short
The pause to bid each much-loved scene adieu!
Beneath the very shadow of the fort,
Where friendly swords were drawn, and banners flew;
Ah! who could deem that foot of Indian crew
Was near?—yet there, with lust of murd'rous deeds,
Gleam'd like a basilisk, from woods in view,
The ambush'd foeman's eye—his volley speeds,
And Albert—Albert falls! the dear old father bleeds!

XXVIII.

And tranced in giddy horror Gertrude swoon'd;
Yet, while she clasps him lifeless to her zone,
Say, burst they, borrow'd from her father's wound,
These drops?—Oh, God! the life-blood is her own!
And faltering, on her Waldegrave's bosom thrown—
"Weep not, O Love!"—she cries, "to see me bleed—
Thee, Gertrude's sad survivor, thee alone
Heaven's peace commiserate; for scarce I heed
These wounds;—yet thee to leave is death, is death indeed!

XXIX.

Clasp me a little longer on the brink
Of fate! while I can feel thy dear caress;

And when this heart hath ceased to beat—oh! think,
And let it mitigate thy woe's excess,
That thou hast been to me all tenderness,
And friend to more than human friendship just.
Oh! by that retrospect of happiness,
And by the hopes of an immortal trust,
God shall assuage thy pangs—when I am laid in dust!

XXX.

Go, Henry, go not back when I depart,
The scene thy bursting tears too deep will move,
Where my dear father took thee to his heart,
And Gertrude thought it ecstasy to rove
With thee, as with an angel, through the grove
Of peace, imagining her lot was cast
In heaven; for ours was not like earthly love.
And must this parting be our very last?
No! I shall love thee still, when death itself is past.—

XXXI.

Half could I bear, methinks, to leave this earth,—
And thee, more loved than aught beneath the sun,
If I had lived to smile but on the birth
Of one dear pledge;—but shall there then be none,
In future times—no gentle little one,
To clasp thy neck, and look, resembling me?
Yet seems it, ev'n while life's last pulses run,
A sweetness in the cup of death to be,
Lord of my bosom's love! to die beholding thee!

XXXII.

Hush'd were his Gertrude's lips! but still their
bland
And beautiful expression seem'd to melt
With love that could not die! and still his hand
She presses to the heart no more that felt.
Ah, heart! where once each fond affection dwelt,
And features yet that spoke a soul more fair.
Mute, gazing, agonizing, as he knelt,—
Of them that stood encircling his despair,
He heard some friendly words;—but knew not
what they were.

XXXIII.

For now, to mourn their judge and child, arrives
A faithful band. With solemn rites between
'Twas sung, how they were lovely in their lives,
And in their deaths had not divided been.
Touch'd by the music, and the melting scene,
Was scarce one tearless eye amidst the crowd:—
Stern warriors, resting on their swords, were seen
To veil their eyes, as pass'd each much-loved
shroud—
While woman's softer soul in woe dissolved aloud.

XXXIV.

Then mournfully the parting bugle bid
Its farewell, o'er the grave of worth and truth;
Prone to the dust, afflicted Waldegrave hid

His face on earth;—him watch'd, in gloomy ruth,
His woodland guide: but words had none to soothe
The grief that knew not consolation's name:
Casting his Indian mantle o'er the youth,
He watch'd, beneath its folds, each burst that came
Convulsive, ague-like, across his shuddering frame!

XXXV.

"And I could weep;"—th' Oneyda chief
His descant wildly thus begun:
"But that I may not stain with grief
The death-song of my father's son,
Or bow this head in woe!
For by my wrongs, and by my wrath!
To-morrow Areouski's breath,
(That fires yon heaven with storms of death,)
Shall light us to the foe:
And we shall share, my Christian boy!
The foeman's blood, the avenger's joy!

XXXVI.

But thee, my flower, whose breath was given
By milder genii o'er the deep,
The spirits of the white man's heaven
Forbid not thee to weep:—
Nor will the Christian host,
Nor will thy father's spirit grieve,
To see thee, on the battle's eve,

Lamenting, take a mournful leave
Of her who loved thee most:
She was the rainbow to thy sight!
Thy sun—thy heaven—of lost delight!

XXXVII.

To-morrow let us do or die!
But when the bolt of death is hurl'd,
Ah! whither then with thee to fly,
Shall Outalissi roam the world?
Seek we thy once-loved home?
The hand is gone that cropt its flowers:
Unheard their clock repeats its hours!
Cold is the hearth within their bowers!
And should we thither roam,
Its echoes, and its empty tread,
Would sound like voices from the dead!

XXXVIII.

Or shall we cross yon mountains blue,
Whose streams my kindred nation quaff'd,
And by my side, in battle true,
A thousand warriors drew the shaft?
Ah! there, in desolation cold,
The desert serpent dwells alone,
Where grass o'ergrows each mouldering bone,
And stones themselves to ruin grown,
Like me, are death-like old.
Then seek we not their camp,—for there—
The silence dwells of my despair!

XXXIX.

But hark, the trump !—to-morrow thou
In glory's fires shall dry thy tears ;
Ev'n from the land of shadows now
My father's awful ghost appears,
Amidst the clouds that round us roll ;
He bids my soul for battle thirst—
He bids me dry the last—the first—
The only tears that ever burst
From Outalissi's soul ;
Because I may not stain with grief
The death-song of an Indian chief!"

In 1809, "Gertrude" appeared, dedicated to Campbell's steady friend, Lord Holland. The cordial reception it received formed a bright epoch in the Poet's life. On the same day the work was published appeared also an article in the Edinburgh Review opening with a brilliant eulogium on the taste and talent of the author. "We rejoice once more," said the writer, "to see a polished and pathetic pöem in the old style of English pathos and poetry. This is of the pitch of the 'Castle of Indolence,' and the finer parts of Spenser, with more feeling in many places than the first, and more condensation and diligent finishing than the latter." Then pointing attention to the admired poetry of the day, there was added: "We have endeavoured on former occasions to do justice to the force and originality of these brilliant productions, as well as to the genius fitted for higher things of their authors; and have little doubt of being soon called upon for a renewed tribute of applause. But we cannot help saying, in the mean time, that the work before us belongs to a class which comes nearer to our conception of pure and perfect poetry. Such productions do not, indeed, strike so strong a blow as the vehement effusions of our modern Trouveurs; but they are calculated, we think, to please more deeply, and to call out more permanently those traits of nature in which the delight of poetry will be found to consist. They may not be so loudly nor so universally applauded, but their fame will probably endure longer, and they will be oftener recalled to mingle with the reveries of solitary leisure, or the consolations of real sorrow. There is a sort of poetry, no doubt, as there is a sort of flowers, which can bear the broad sun and the ruffling winds of the world: which thrive under the hands and eyes of indiscriminate multitudes, and please as much in hot and crowded saloons as in their own sheltered repositories; but the finer and the purer sorts blossom only in the shade, and never give out their sweets but to those who seek them amid the quiet and seclusion of the scenes which gave them birth. There are torrents and cascades which attract the admiration of tittering parties, and of which even the busy must turn aside to catch a transient glance; but the haunted stream steals through a still and solitary landscape, and its beauties are never revealed but to him who strays in calm contemplation, by its course, and follows its wanderings with undiminished and unimpatient admiration."

LINES

WRITTEN AT THE REQUEST OF THE HIGHLAND SOCIETY OF LONDON, WHEN MET TO COMMEMORATE THE 21ST OF MARCH, THE DAY OF VICTORY IN EGYPT.

PLEDGE to the much-loved land that gave us birth!
Invincible romantic Scotia's shore!
Pledge to the memory of her parted worth!
And first, amidst the brave, remember Moore!

And be it deem'd not wrong that name to give,
In festive hours, which prompts the patriot's sigh!
Who would not envy such as Moore to live?
And died he not as heroes wish to die?

Yes, though too soon attaining glory's goal,
To us his bright career too short was given;
Yet in a mighty cause his phœnix soul
Rose on the flames of victory to Heaven!

How oft (if beats in subjugated Spain
One patriot heart) in secret shall it mourn
For him!—How oft on far Corunna's plain
Shall British exiles weep upon his urn!

Peace to the mighty dead!—our bosom thanks
  In sprightlier strains the living may inspire!
Joy to the chiefs that lead old Scotia's ranks,
  Of Roman garb and more than Roman fire!

Triumphant be the thistle still unfurl'd,
  Dear symbol wild! on Freedom's hills it grows,
Where Fingal stemm'd the tyrants of the world,
  And Roman eagles found unconquer'd foes.

Joy to the band[1] this day on Egypt's coast,
  Whose valour tamed proud France's tricolor,
And wrench'd the banner from her bravest host,
  Baptiz'd Invincible in Austria's gore!

Joy for the day on red Vimeira's strand,
  When, bayonet to bayonet opposed,
First of Britannia's host her Highland band
  Gave but the death-shot once, and foremost closed!

Is there a son of generous England here
  Or fervid Erin?—he with us shall join,
To pray that in eternal union dear,
  The rose, the shamrock, and the thistle twine!

Types of a race who shall th' invader scorn,
  As rocks resist the billows round their shore;
Types of a race who shall to time unborn
  Their country leave unconquer'd as of yore!

1809.

1 The 42d Regiment.

STANZAS

TO THE MEMORY OF THE SPANISH PATRIOTS LATEST KILLED IN RESISTING THE REGENCY AND THE DUKE OF ANGOULEME.

BRAVE men who at the Trocadero fell—
Beside your cannons conquer'd not, though slain,
There is a victory in dying well
For Freedom,—and ye have not died in vain;
For, come what may, there shall be hearts in
Spain
To honour, ay, embrace your martyr'd lot,
Cursing the Bigot's and the Bourbon's chain,
And looking on your graves, though trophied not,
As holier hallow'd ground than priests could make
the spot!

What though your cause be baffled—freemen cast
In dungeons—dragg'd to death, or forced to flee;
Hope is not wither'd in affliction's blast—
The patriot's blood's the seed of Freedom's tree;
And short your orgies of revenge shall be,
Cowl'd demons of the Inquisitorial cell!
Earth shudders at your victory,—for ye

Are worse than common fiends from Heaven that fell,
The baser, ranker sprung, *Autochthones* of Hell!

Go to your bloody rites again—bring back
The hall of horrors and the assessor's pen,
Recording answers shriek'd upon the rack;
Smile o'er the gaspings of spine-broken men;—
Preach, perpetrate damnation in your den;—
Then let your altars, ye blasphemers! peal
With thanks to Heaven, that let you loose again,
To practise deeds with torturing fire and steel
No eye may search—no tongue may challenge or reveal!

Yet laugh not in your carnival of crime
Too proudly, ye oppressors!—Spain was free,
Her soil has felt the foot-prints, and her clime
Been winnow'd by the wings of Liberty;
And these even parting scatter as they flee
Thoughts—influences, to live in hearts unborn,
Opinions that shall wrench the prison-key
From Persecution—show her mask off-torn,
And tramp her bloated head beneath the foot of Scorn.

Glory to them that die in this great cause;
Kings, Bigots, can inflict no brand of shame,
Or shape of death, to shroud them from applause:—

No!—manglers of the martyr's earthly frame!
Your hangmen fingers cannot touch his fame!
Still in your prostrate land there shall be some
Proud hearts, the shrines of Freedom's vestal
flame.
Long trains of ill may pass unheeded, dumb,
But vengeance is behind, and justice is to come.

1823.

SONG OF THE GREEKS.

Again to the battle, Achaians!
Our hearts bid the tyrants defiance!
Our land, the first garden of Liberty's tree—
It has been, and shall yet be, the land of the
free:
For the cross of our faith is replanted,
The pale dying crescent is daunted,
And we march that the foot-prints of Mahomet's
slaves
May be wash'd out in blood from our forefathers'
graves.
Their spirits are hovering o'er us,
And the sword shall to glory restore us.

Ah! what though no succour advances,
Nor Christendom's chivalrous lances

Are stretch'd in our aid—be the combat our
own!
And we 'll perish or conquer more proudly alone;
For we 've sworn by our Country's assaulters,
By the virgins they 've dragg'd from our altars,
By our massacred patriots, our children in chains,
By our heroes of old, and their blood in our veins,
That, living, we shall be victorious,
Or that, dying, our deaths shall be glorious.

A breath of submission we breathe not;
The sword that we 've drawn we will sheathe
not!
Its scabbard is left where our martyrs are laid,
And the vengeance of ages has whetted its blade.
Earth may hide—waves engulf—fire consume us,
But they shall not to slavery doom us:
If they rule, it shall be o'er our ashes and graves;
But we 've smote them already with fire on the
waves,
And new triumphs on land are before us,
To the charge!—Heaven's banner is o'er us.

This day shall ye blush for its story,
Or brighten your lives with its glory.
Our women, oh, say, shall they shriek in despair,
Or embrace us from conquest with wreaths in
their hair?
Accursed may his memory blacken,
If a coward there be that would slacken

Till we 've trampled the turban, and shown our-
selves worth
Being sprung from and named for the godlike of
earth.
Strike home, and the world shall revere us
As heroes descended from heroes.

Old Greece lightens up with emotion
Her inlands, her isles of the Ocean ;
Fanes rebuilt and fair towns shall with jubilee ring,
And the Nine shall new-hallow their Helicon's
spring :
Our hearths shall be kindled in gladness,
That were cold and extinguish'd in sadness ;
Whilst our maidens shall dance with their white-
waving arms,
Singing joy to the brave that deliver'd their
charms,
When the blood of yon Mussulman cravens
Shall have purpled the beaks of our ravens.

ODE TO WINTER.

When first the fiery-mantled sun
His heavenly race began to run;
Round the earth and ocean blue,
His children four the Seasons flew.
First, in green apparel dancing,
  The young Spring smiled with angel grace;
Rosy Summer next advancing,
  Rush'd into her sire's embrace:—
Her bright-hair'd sire, who bade her keep
  For ever nearest to his smiles,
On Calpe's olive-shaded steep,
  On India's citron-cover'd isles:
More remote and buxom-brown,
  The Queen of vintage bow'd before his
    throne;
A rich pomegranate gemm'd her crown,
  A ripe sheaf bound her zone.
But howling Winter fled afar,
To hills that prop the polar star,
And loves on deer-borne car to ride
With barren Darkness by his side,
Round the shore where loud Lofoden
  Whirls to death the roaring whale,

Round the hall where Runic Odin
  Howls his war-song to the gale;
Save when adown the ravaged globe
  He travels on his native storm,
Deflowering Nature's grassy robe,
  And trampling on her faded form:—
Till light's returning lord assume
  The shaft that drives him to his polar field,
Of power to pierce his raven plume
  And crystal-cover'd shield.
Oh, sire of storms! whose savage ear
The Lapland drum delights to hear,
When Frenzy with her blood-shot eye
Implores thy dreadful deity,
Archangel! power of desolation!
  Fast descending as thou art,
Say, hath mortal invocation
  Spells to touch thy stony heart?
Then, sullen Winter, hear my prayer,
And gently rule the ruin'd year;
Nor chill the wanderer's bosom bare,
Nor freeze the wretch's falling tear;—
To shuddering Want's unmantled bed
Thy horror-breathing agues cease to lead,
And gently on the orphan head
Of innocence descend.—
But chiefly spare, O king of clouds!
The sailor on his airy shrouds;
When wrecks and beacons strew the steep,
And spectres walk along the deep.

Milder yet thy snowy breezes
  Pour on yonder tented shores,
Where the Rhine's broad billow freezes,
  Or the dark-brown Danube roars.
Oh, winds of Winter! list ye there
  To many a deep and dying groan;
Or start, ye demons of the midnight air,
  At shrieks and thunders louder than your own.
Alas! ev'n your unhallow'd breath
  May spare the victim fallen low;
But man will ask no truce to death,—
  No bounds to human woe.

LINES.

SPOKEN BY MRS. BARTLEY AT DRURY-LANE THEATRE, ON THE FIRST OPENING OF THE HOUSE AFTER THE DEATH OF THE PRINCESS CHARLOTTE, 1817.

Britons! although our task is but to show
The scenes and passions of fictitious woe,
Think not we come this night without a part
In that deep sorrow of the public heart,
Which like a shade hath darken'd every place,
And moisten'd with a tear the manliest face!
The bell is scarcely hush'd in Windsor's piles,
That toll'd a requiem from the solemn aisles,

For her, the royal flower, low laid in dust,
That was your fairest hope, your fondest trust.
Unconscious of the doom, we dreamt, alas!
That ev'n these walls, ere many months should
pass,
Which but return sad accents for her now,
Perhaps had witness'd her benignant brow,
Cheer'd by the voice you would have raised on
high,
In bursts of British love and loyalty.
But, Britain! now thy chief, thy people mourn,
And Claremont's home of love is left forlorn:—
There, where the happiest of the happy dwelt
The 'scutcheon glooms, and royalty hath felt
A wound that every bosom feels its own,—
The blessing of a father's heart o'erthrown—
The most beloved and most devoted bride
Torn from an agonized husband's side,
Who "long as Memory holds her seat" shall view
That speechless, more than spoken last adieu,
When the fix'd eye long look'd connubial faith,
And beam'd affection in the trance of death.
Sad was the pomp that yesternight beheld,
As with the mourner's heart the anthem swell'd;
While torch succeeding torch illumed each high
And banner'd arch of England's chivalry.
The rich plumed canopy, the gorgeous pall,
The sacred march, and sable-vested wall,—
These were not rites of inexpressive show,
But hallow'd as the types of real woe!

Daughter of England! for a nation sighs,
A nation's heart, went with thine obsequies!—
And oft shall time revert a look of grief
On thine existence, beautiful and brief.
Fair spirit! send thy blessing from above
On realms where thou art canonized by love!
Give to a father's, husband's bleeding mind,
The peace that angels lend to human kind;
To us who in thy loved remembrance feel
A sorrowing, but a soul-ennobling zeal—
A loyalty that touches all the best
And loftiest principles of England's breast!
Still may thy name speak concord from the tomb—
Still in the Muse's breath thy memory bloom!
They shall describe thy life—thy form portray;
But all the love that mourns thee swept away,
'Tis not in language or expressive arts
To paint—ye feel it, Britons, in your hearts!

LINES ON THE GRAVE OF A SUICIDE.

By strangers left upon a lonely shore,
  Unknown, unhonour'd, was the friendless dead;
For child to weep, or widow to deplore,
  There never came to his unburied head:—
  All from his dreary habitation fled.
Nor will the lantern'd fisherman at eve
  Launch on that water by the witches' tower,
Where hellebore and hemlock seem to weave
  Round its dark vaults a melancholy bower
  For spirits of the dead at night's enchanted hour.

They dread to meet thee, poor unfortunate!
  Whose crime it was, on Life's unfinish'd road,
To feel the step-dame buffetings of fate,
  And render back thy being's heavy load.
  Ah! once, perhaps, the social passions glow'd
In thy devoted bosom—and the hand
  That smote its kindred heart, might yet be prone
To deeds of mercy. Who may understand
  Thy many woes, poor suicide, unknown?—
  He who thy being gave shall judge of thee alone.

1801.

REULLURA.[1]

Star of the morn and eve,
  Reullura shone like thee,
And well for her might Aodh grieve,
  The dark-attired Culdee.
Peace to their shades! the pure Culdees
  Were Albyn's earliest priests of God,
Ere yet an island of her seas
  By foot of Saxon monk was trod,
Long ere her churchmen by bigotry
Were barr'd from wedlock's holy tie.
'Twas then that Aodh, famed afar,
  In Iona preach'd the word with power,
And Reullura, beauty's star,
  Was the partner of his bower.

But, Aodh, the roof lies low,
  And the thistle-down waves bleaching,
And the bat flits to and fro
  Where the Gaël once heard thy preaching;
And fallen is each column'd aisle
  Where the chiefs and the people knelt.

[1] Reullura, in Gaëlic, signifies "beautiful star."

'Twas near that temple's goodly pile
  That honoured of men they dwelt.
For Aodh was wise in the sacred law,
And bright Reullura's eyes oft saw
  The veil of fate uplifted.
Alas, with what visions of awe
  Her soul in that hour was gifted—
When pale in the temple and faint,
  With Aodh she stood alone
By the statue of an aged Saint!
  Fair sculptured was the stone,
It bore a crucifix;
  Fame said it once had graced
A Christain temple, which the Picts
  In the Britons' land laid waste:
The Pictish men, by St. Columb taught,
  Had hither the holy relic brought,
Reullura eyed the statue's face,
And cried, "It is, he shall come,
Even he, in this very place,
  To avenge my martyrdom.

For, woe to the Gaël people!
  Ulvfagre is on the main,
And Iona shall look from tower and steeple
  On the coming ships of the Dane;
And, dames and daughters, shall all your locks
  With the spoiler's grasp entwine?
No! some shall have shelter in caves and rocks,

And the deep sea shall be mine.
Baffled by me shall the Dane return,
And here shall his torch in the temple burn
Until that holy man shall plough
The waves from Innisfail.
His sail is on the deep e'en now,
And swells to the southern gale."

"Ah! know'st thou not, my bride,"
The holy Aodh said,
"That the Saint whose form we stand beside
Has for ages slept with the dead?"
"He liveth, he liveth," she said again,
"For the span of his life tenfold extends
Beyond the wonted years of men.
He sits by the graves of well-loved friends
That died ere thy grandsire's grandsire's birth;
The oak is decay'd with age on earth,
Whose acorn-seed had been planted by him;
And his parents remember the day of dread
When the sun on the cross look'd dim,
And the graves gave up their dead.
Yet preaching from clime to clime,
He hath roam'd the earth for ages,
And hither he shall come in time
When the wrath of the heathen rages,
In time a remnant from the sword—
Ah! but a remnant to deliver;
Yet, blest be the name of the Lord!
His martyrs shall go into bliss for ever.

Lochlin,[1] appall'd, shall put up her steel,
And thou shalt embark on the bounding keel;
Safe shall thou pass through her hundred ships,
With the Saint and a remnant of the Gaël,
And the Lord will instruct thy lips
To preach in Innisfail." [2]

The sun, now about to set,
Was burning o'er Tiree,
And no gathering cry rose yet
O'er the isles of Albyn's sea,
Whilst Reullura saw far rowers dip
Their oars beneath the sun,
And the phantom of many a Danish ship,
Where ship there yet was none.
And the shield of alarm was dumb,
Nor did their warning till midnight come,
When watch-fires burst from across the main,
From Rona, and Uist, and Skye,
To tell that the ships of the Dane
And the red-hair'd slayers were nigh.

Our islemen arose from slumbers,
And buckled on their arms;
But few, alas! were their numbers
To Lochlin's mailed swarms.
And the blade of the bloody Norse
Has fill'd the shores of the Gaël

[1] Denmark. [2] Ireland.

With many a floating corse,
  And with many a woman's wail.
They have lighted the islands with ruin's torch,
And the holy men of Iona's church
In the temple of God lay slain;
  All but Aodh, the last Culdee,
But bound with many an iron chain,
  Bound in that church was he.
And where is Aodh's bride?
  Rocks of the ocean flood!
Plunged she not from your heights in pride,
  And mock'd the men of blood?
Then Ulvfagre and his bands
  In the temple lighted their banquet up,
And the print of their blood-red hands
  Was left on the altar cup.
'Twas then that the Norseman to Aodh said,
"Tell where thy church's treasure 's laid,
Or I 'll hew thee limb from limb."
  As he spoke the bell struck three,
And every torch grew dim
  That lighted their revelry.

But the torches again burnt bright,
  And brighter than before,
When an aged man of majestic height
  Enter'd the temple door.
Hush'd was the revellers' sound,
  They were struck as mute as the dead,
And their hearts were appall'd by the very sound

Of his footsteps' measured tread.
Nor word was spoken by one beholder,
Whilst he flung his white robe back o'er his shoulder,
And stretching his arms—as eath
Unriveted Aodh's bands,
As if the gyves had been a wreath
Of willows in his hands.

All saw the stranger's similitude
To the ancient statue's form;
The Saint before his own image stood,
And grasp'd Ulvfagre's arm.
Then up rose the Danes at last to deliver
Their chief, and shouting with one accord,
They drew the shaft from its rattling quiver,
They lifted the spear and sword,
And levell'd their spears in rows.
But down went axes and spears and bows,
When the Saint with his crosier sign'd,
The archer's hand on the string was stopt,
And down, like reeds laid flat by the wind,
Their lifted weapons dropt.
The Saint then gave a signal mute,
And though Ulvfagre will'd it not,
He came and stood at the statue's foot,
Spell-riveted to the spot,
Till hands invisible shook the wall,
And the tottering image was dash'd
Down from its lofty pedestal.

On Ulvfagre's helm it crash'd—
Helmet, and skull, and flesh, and brain,
It crush'd as millstones crush the grain.
Then spoke the Saint, whilst all and each
Of the Heathen trembled round,
And the pauses amidst his speech
Were as awful as the sound:

" Go back, ye wolves! to your dens" (he cried),
"And tell the nations abroad,
How the fiercest of your herd has died,
That slaughter'd the flock of God.
Gather him bone by bone,
And take with you o'er the flood
The fragments of that avenging stone
That drank his heathen blood.
These are the spoils from Iona's sack,
The only spoils ye shall carry back;
For the hand that uplifteth spear or sword
Shall be wither'd by palsy's shock,
And I come in the name of the Lord
To deliver a remnant of his flock."

A remnant was call'd together,
A doleful remnant of the Gaël,
And the Saint in the ship that had brought him hither
Took the mourners to Innisfail.
Unscathed they left Iona's strand,
When the opal morn first flush'd the sky,

For the Norse dropt spear, and bow, and brand,
  And look'd on them silently;
Safe from their hiding-places came
Orphans and mothers, child and dame:
But, alas! when the search for Reullura spread,
  No answering voice was given,
For the sea had gone o'er her lovely head,
  And her spirit was in Heaven.

1824.

THE TURKISH LADY.

'Twas the hour when rites unholy
  Call'd each Paynim voice to prayer,
And the star that faded slowly
  Left to dews the freshen'd air.

Day her sultry fires had wasted,
  Calm and sweet the moonlight rose;
Ev'n a captive spirit tasted
  Half oblivion of his woes.

Then 'twas from an Emir's palace
  Came an Eastern lady bright:
She, in spite of tyrants jealous,
  Saw and loved an English knight.

"Tell me, captive, why in anguish
  Foes have dragg'd thee here to dwell,
Where poor Christians as they languish
  Hear no sound of Sabbath bell?"—

"'Twas on Transylvania's Bannet,
  When the Crescent shone afar,

Like a pale disastrous planet
  O'er the purple tide of war—

In that day of desolation,
  Lady, I was captive made;
Bleeding for my Christian nation
  By the walls of high Belgrade."

"Captive! could the brightest jewel
  From my turban set thee free?"
"Lady, no!—the gift were cruel,
  Ransom'd, yet if reft of thee.

Say, fair princess! would it grieve thee
  Christian climes should we behold?"—
"Nay, bold knight! I would not leave thee
  Were thy ransom paid in gold!"

Now in Heaven's blue expansion
  Rose the midnight star to view,
When to quit her father's mansion
  Thrice she wept, and bade adieu!

"Fly we then, while none discover!
  Tyrant barks, in vain ye ride!"—
Soon at Rhodes the British lover
  Clasp'd his blooming Eastern bride.

1800.

THE BRAVE ROLAND.

The brave Roland!—the brave Roland!—
False tidings reach'd the Rhenish strand
        That he had fall'n in fight;
And thy faithful bosom swoon'd with pain,
O loveliest maid of Allémayne!
        For the loss of thine own true knight.

But why so rash has she ta'en the veil,
In yon Nonnenwerder's cloisters pale?
        For her vow had scarce been sworn,
And the fatal mantle o'er her flung,
When the Drachenfels to a trumpet rung—
        'Twas her own dear warrior's horn!

Woe! woe! each heart shall bleed—shall break!
She would have hung upon his neck,
        Had he come but yester-even!
And he had clasp'd those peerless charms,
That shall never, never fill his arms,
        Or meet him but in heaven.

Yet Roland the brave—Roland the true—
He could not bid that spot adieu;
        It was dear still midst his woes;

For he loved to breathe the neighbouring air,
And to think she bless'd him in her prayer,
When the Halleluiah rose.

There 's yet one window of that pile,
Which he built above the Nun's green isle;
Thence sad and oft look'd he
(When the chant and organ sounded slow)
On the mansion of his love below,
For herself he might not see.

She died!—he sought the battle-plain;
Her image fill'd his dying brain,
When he fell and wish'd to fall:
And her name was in his latest sigh,
When Roland, the flower of chivalry,
Expired at Roncevall.

1820.

THE SPECTRE BOAT.

A BALLAD.

LIGHT rued false Ferdinand to leave a lovely
maid forlorn,
Who broke her heart and died to hide her blush-
ing cheek from scorn.
One night he dreamt he woo'd her in their wonted
bower of love,
Where the flowers sprang thick around them, and
the birds sang sweet above.

But the scene was swiftly changed into a church-
yard's dismal view,
And her lips grew black beneath his kiss, from
love's delicious hue.
What more he dreamt, he told to none ; but shud-
dering, pale, and dumb,
Look'd out upon the waves, like one that knew
his hour was come.

'Twas now the dead watch of the night—the helm
was lashed a-lee,
And the ship rode where Mount Ætna lights the
deep Levantine sea ;

When beneath its glare a boat came, row'd by a
woman in her shroud,
Who, with eyes that made our blood run cold,
stood up and spoke aloud:—

"Come, Traitor, down, for whom my ghost still
wanders unforgiven!
Come down, false Ferdinand, for whom I broke
my peace with heaven!"—
It was vain to hold the victim, for he plunged to
meet her call,
Like the bird that shrieks and flutters in the gazing
serpent's thrall.

You may guess the boldest mariner shrunk
daunted from the sight,
For the Spectre and her winding-sheet shone blue
with hideous light;
Like a fiery wheel the boat spun with the waving
of her hand,
And round they went, and down they went, as the
cock crew from the land.

1809.

THE LOVER TO HIS MISTRESS.

ON HER BIRTH-DAY.

If any white-wing'd Power above
  My joys and griefs survey,
The day when thou wert born, my love—
  He surely bless'd that day.

I laugh'd (till taught by thee) when told
  Of Beauty's magic powers,
That ripen'd life's dull ore to gold,
  And changed its weeds to flowers.

My mind had lovely shapes portray'd;
  But thought I earth had one
Could make even Fancy's visions fade
  Like stars before the sun?

I gazed, and felt upon my lips
  The unfinish'd accents hang:
One moment's bliss, one burning kiss,
  To rapture changed each pang.

And though as swift as lightning's flash
  Those tranced moments flew,
Not all the waves of time shall wash
  Their memory from my view.

But duly shall my raptured song,
  And gladly shall my eyes,
Still bless this day's return, as long
  As thou shalt see it rise.

SONG.

Oh, how hard it is to find
The one just suited to our mind;
  And if that one should be
False, unkind, or found too late,
What can we do but sigh at fate,
  And sing, Woe 's me—Woe 's me?

Love 's a boundless burning waste,
Where Bliss's stream we seldom taste,
  And still more seldom flee
Suspense's thorns, Suspicion's stings;
Yet somehow Love a something brings
  That's sweet—ev'n when we sigh 'Woe 's me!'

ADELGITHA.

THE ordeal's fatal trumpet sounded,
  And sad pale ADELGITHA came,
When forth a valiant champion bounded,
  And slew the slanderer of her fame.

She wept, deliver'd from her danger;
  But when he knelt to claim her glove—
"Seek not," she cried, "oh! gallant stranger,
  For hapless ADELGITHA'S love.

For he is in a foreign far land
Whose arms should now have set me free;
And I must wear the willow garland
  For him that's dead, or false to me."

"Nay! say not that his faith is tainted!"—
  He raised his vizor—At the sight
She fell into his arms and fainted;
  It was indeed her own true knight!

LINES

ON RECEIVING A SEAL WITH THE CAMPBELL CREST, FROM K. M—, BEFORE HER MARRIAGE.

THIS wax returns not back more fair
  Th' impression of the gift you send,
Than stamp'd upon my thoughts I bear
  The image of your worth, my friend!—

We are not friends of yesterday;—
  But poets' fancies are a little
Disposed to heat and cool, (they say,)—
  By turns impressible and brittle.

Well! should its frailty e'er condemn
  My heart to prize or please you less,
Your type is still the sealing gem,
  And *mine* the waxen brittleness.

What transcripts of my weal and woe
  This little signet yet may lock,—
What utterances to friend or foe,
  In reason's calm or passion's shock!

What scenes of life's yet curtain'd stage
May own its confidential die,
Whose stamp awaits th' unwritten page,
And feelings of futurity!—

Yet wheresoe'er my pen I lift
To date the epistolary sheet,
The blest occasion of the gift
Shall make its recollection sweet;

Sent when the star that rules your fates
Hath reach'd its influence most benign—
When every heart congratulates,
And none more cordially than mine.

So speed my song—mark'd with the crest
That erst the advent'rous Norman wore,
Who won the Lady of the West
The daughter of Macaillan Mor.

Crest of my sires! whose blood it seal'd
With glory in the strife of swords,
Ne'er may the scroll that bears it yield
Degenerate thoughts or faithless words!

Yet little might I prize the stone,
If it but typed the feudal tree
From whence, a scattered leaf, I'm blown
In Fortune's mutability.

No !—but it tells me of a heart
  Allied by friendship's living tie ;
A prize beyond the herald's art—
  Our soul-sprung consanguinity !

Kath'rine ! to many an hour of mine
  Light wings and sunshine you have lent ;
And so adieu, and still be thine
  The all-in-all of life—Content !

1817.

GILDEROY.

The last, the fatal hour is come,
  That bears my love from me :
I hear the dead note of the drum,
  I mark the gallows' tree !

The bell has toll'd ; it shakes my heart ;
  The trumpet speaks thy name ;
And must my Gilderoy depart
  To bear a death of shame ?

No bosom trembles for thy doom ;
  No mourner wipes a tear ;
The gallows' foot is all thy tomb,
  The sledge is all thy bier.

Oh, Gilderoy! bethought we then
  So soon, so sad to part,
When first in Roslin's lovely glen
  You triumph'd o'er my heart?

Your locks they glitter'd to the sheen,
  Your hunter garb was trim;
And graceful was the ribbon green
  That bound your manly limb!

Ah! little thought I to deplore
  Those limbs in fetters bound;
Or hear, upon the scaffold floor,
  The midnight hammer sound.

Ye cruel, cruel, that combined
  The guiltless to pursue;
My Gilderoy was ever kind,
  He could not injure you!

A long adieu! but where shall fly
  Thy widow all forlorn,
When every mean and cruel eye
  Regards my woe with scorn?

Yes! they will mock thy widow's tears,
  And hate thine orphan boy;
Alas! his infant beauty wears
  The form of Gilderoy.

Then will I seek the dreary mound
  That wraps thy mouldering clay,
And weep and linger on the ground,
  And sigh my heart away.

STANZAS

ON THE THREATENED INVASION.

1803.

Our bosoms we 'll bare for the glorious strife,
  And our oath is recorded on high,
To prevail in the cause that is dearer than life,
  Or crush'd in its ruins to die!
Then rise, fellow freemen, and stretch the right hand,
And swear to prevail in your dear native land!

'Tis the home we hold sacred is laid to our trust—
  God bless the green Isle of the brave!
Should a conqueror tread on our forefathers' dust,
  It would rouse the old dead from their grave!
Then rise, fellow freemen, and stretch the right hand,
And swear to prevail in your dear native land!

In a Briton's sweet home shall a spoiler abide,
Profaning its loves and its charms?
Shall a Frenchman insult the loved fair at our side?
To arms! oh, my Country, to arms!
Then rise, fellow freemen, and stretch the right hand,
And swear to prevail in your dear native land!

Shall a tyrant enslave us, my countrymen!—No!
His head to the sword shall be given—
A death-bed repentance be taught the proud foe,
And his blood be an offering to Heaven!
Then rise, fellow freemen, and stretch the right hand,
And swear to prevail in your dear native land!

THE RITTER BANN.

THE Ritter Bann from Hungary
  Came back, renown'd in arms,
But scorning jousts of chivalry,
  And love and ladies' charms.

While other knights held revels, he
  Was rapt in thoughts of gloom,
And in Vienna's hostelrie
  Slow paced his lonely room.

There enter'd one whose face he knew,—
  Whose voice, he was aware,
He oft at mass had listen'd to
  In the holy house of prayer.

'Twas the Abbot of St. James's monks,
  A fresh and fair old man:
His reverend air arrested even
  The gloomy Ritter Bann.

But seeing with him an ancient dame
  Come clad in Scotch attire,
The Ritter's colour went and came,
  And loud he spoke in ire:

"Ha! nurse of her that was my bane,
  Name not her name to me;
I wish it blotted from my brain:
  Art poor?—take alms, and flee."

"Sir Knight," the abbot interposed,
  "This case your ear demands;"
And the crone cried, with a cross enclosed
  In both her trembling hands,

"Remember, each his sentence waits;
  And he that shall rebut
Sweet Mercy's suit, on him the gates
  Of Mercy shall be shut.

You wedded, undispensed by Church,
  Your cousin Jane in Spring;—
In Autumn, when you went to search
  For churchman's pardoning,

Her house denounced your marriage-band,
  Betroth'd her to De Grey,
And the ring you put upon her hand
  Was wrench'd by force away.

Then wept your Jane upon my neck,
  Crying, 'Help me, nurse, to flee
To my Howel Bann's Glamorgan hills;'
  But word arrived—ah me!—

You were not there; and 'twas their threat,
  By foul means or by fair,
To-morrow morning was to set
  The seal on her despair.

I had a son, a sea-boy, in
  A ship at Hartland Bay,
By his aid from her cruel kin
  I bore my bird away.

To Scotland from the Devon's
  Green myrtle shores we fled;
And the Hand that sent the ravens
  To Elijah, gave us bread.

She wrote you by my son, but he
  From England sent us word
You had gone into some far countrie,
  In grief and gloom he heard.

For they that wrong'd you, to elude
  Your wrath, defamed my child;
And you—ay, blush, Sir, as you should—
  Believed, and were beguiled.

To die but at your feet, she vow'd
  To roam the world; and we
Would both have sped and begg'd our bread,
  But so it might not be.

For when the snow-storm beat our roof,
  She bore a boy, Sir Bann,
Who grew as fair your likeness' proof
  As child e'er grew like man.

'Twas smiling on that babe one morn
  While heath bloom'd on the moor,
Her beauty struck young Lord Kinghorn
  As he hunted past our door.

She shunn'd him, but he raved of Jane,
  And roused his mother's pride:
Who came to us in high disdain,—
  'And where 's the face,' she cried,

Has witch'd my boy to wish for one
  So wretched for his wife?—
Dost love thy husband? Know, my son
  Has sworn to seek his life.'

Her anger sore dismayed us,
  For our mite was wearing scant,
And, unless that dame would aid us,
  There was none to aid our want.

So I told her, weeping bitterly,
  What all our woes had been;
And, though she was a stern ladie,
  The tears stood in her een.

And she housed us both, when, cheerfully,
  My child to her had sworn,
That even if made a widow, she
  Would never wed Kinghorn."——

Here paused the nurse, and then began
  The abbot, standing by:—
"Three months ago a wounded man
  To our abbey came to die.

He heard me long, with ghastly eyes
  And hand obdurate clench'd,
Spoke of the worm that never dies,
  And the fire that is not quench'd.

At last by what this scroll attests
  He left atonement brief,
For years of anguish to the breasts
  His guilt had wrung with grief.

'There lived,' he said, 'a fair young dame
  Beneath my mother's roof;
I loved her, but against my flame
  Her purity was proof.

I feign'd repentance, friendship pure;
  That mood she did not check,
But let her husband's miniature
  Be copied from her neck,

As means to search him; my deceit
  Took care to him was borne
Nought but his picture's counterfeit,
  And Jane's reported scorn.

The treachery took: she waited wild;
  My slave came back and lied
Whate'er I wish'd; she clasp'd her child,
  And swoon'd, and all but died.

I felt her tears for years and years
  Quench not my flame, but stir;
The very hate I bore her mate
  Increased my love for her.

Fame told us of his glory, while
  Joy flush'd the face of Jane;
And while she bless'd his name, her smile
  Struck fire into my brain.

No fears could damp; I reach'd the camp,
  Sought out its champion;
And if my broad-sword fail'd at last,
  'Twas long and well laid on.

This wound 's my meed, my name 's Kinghorn,
  My foe 's the Ritter Bann.'——
The wafer to his lips was borne,
  And we shrived the dying man.

He died not till you went to fight
  The Turks at Warradein;
But I see my tale has changed you pale."—
  The abbot went for wine;

And brought a little page who pour'd
  It out, and knelt and smiled;—
The stunned knight saw himself restored
  To childhood in his child;

And stoop'd and caught him to his breast,
  Laugh'd loud and wept anon,
And with a shower of kisses press'd
  The darling little one.

"And where went Jane?"—"To a nunnery, Sir—
  Look not again so pale—
Kinghorn's old dame grew harsh to her."—
  "And has she ta'en the veil?"—

"Sit down, Sir," said the priest, "I bar
  Rash words."—They sat all three,
And the boy play'd with the knight's broad star,
  As he kept him on his knee.

"Think ere you ask her dwelling-place,"
  The abbot further said;
"Time draws a veil o'er beauty's face
  More deep than cloister's shade.

Grief may have made her what you can
  Scarce love perhaps for life."
"Hush, abbot," cried the Ritter Bann,
  "Or tell me where 's my wife."

The priest undid two doors that hid
  The inn's adjacent room,
And there a lovely woman stood,
  Tears bathed her beauty's bloom.

One moment may with bliss repay
  Unnumber'd hours of pain;
Such was the throb and mutual sob
  Of the knight embracing Jane.

1828.

SONG.

"MEN OF ENGLAND."

Men of England! who inherit
  Rights that cost your sires their blood!
Men whose undegenerate spirit
  Has been proved on field and flood:—

By the foes you 've fought uncounted,
  By the glorious deeds ye 've done,
Trophies captured—breaches mounted,
  Navies conquer'd—kingdoms won.

Yet, remember, England gathers
  Hence but fruitless wreaths of fame,
If the freedom of your fathers
  Glow not in your hearts the same.

What are monuments of bravery,
  Where no public virtues bloom?
What avail in lands of slavery,
  Trophied temples, arch, and tomb?

Pageants!—Let the world revere us
  For our people's rights and laws,
And the breasts of civic heroes
  Bared in Freedom's holy cause.

Yours are Hampden's, Russell's glory,
 Sidney's matchless shade is yours,—
Martyrs in heroic story,
 Worth a hundred Agincourts!

We 're the sons of sires that baffled
 Crown'd and mitred tyranny;—
They defied the field and scaffold
 For their birthrights—so will we!

SONG.

Drink ye to her that each loves best,
 And if you nurse a flame
That 's told but to her mutual breast,
 We will not ask her name.

Enough, while memory tranced and glad
 Paints silently the fair,
That each should dream of joys he 's had,
 Or yet may hope to share.

Yet far, far hence be jest or boast
 From hallow'd thoughts so dear;
But drink to her that each loves most,
 As she would love to hear.

THE HARPER.

On the green banks of Shannon, when Sheelah was nigh,
No blithe Irish lad was so happy as I;
No harp like my own could so cheerily play,
And wherever I went was my poor dog Tray.

When at last I was forced from my Sheelah to part,
She said, (while the sorrow was big at her heart,)
Oh! remember your Sheelah when far, far away:
And be kind, my dear Pat, to our poor dog Tray.

Poor dog! he was faithful and kind, to be sure,
And he constantly loved me, although I was poor;
When the sour-looking folks sent me heartless away,
I had always a friend in my poor dog Tray.

When the road was so dark, and the night was so cold,
And Pat and his dog were grown weary and old,
How snugly we slept in my old coat of gray,
And he lick'd me for kindness—my poor dog Tray.

Though my wallet was scant, I remember'd his
case,
Nor refused my last crust to his pitiful face;
But he died at my feet on a cold winter day,
And I play'd a sad lament for my poor dog Tray.

Where now shall I go, poor, forsaken, and blind?
Can I find one to guide me, so faithful, and kind?
To my sweet native village, so far, far away,
I can never more return with my poor dog Tray.

THE WOUNDED HUSSAR.

ALONE to the banks of the dark-rolling Danube
Fair Adelaide hied when the battle was o'er:—
"Oh whither," she cried, "hast thou wander'd,
my lover,
Or here dost thou welter and bleed on the shore?

What voice did I hear? 'twas my Henry that
sigh'd!"
All mournful she hasten'd, nor wander'd she far,
When bleeding, and low, on the heath she descried,
By the light of the moon, her poor wounded
Hussar!

From his bosom that heaved, the last torrent was
streaming,
And pale was his visage, deep mark'd with a
scar!
And dim was that eye, once expressively beaming,
That melted in love, and that kindled in war!

How smit was poor Adelaide's heart at the sight!
How bitter she wept o'er the victim of war!
"Hast thou come, my fond Love, this last sorrow-
ful night,
To cheer the lone heart of your wounded Hus-
sar!"

"Thou shalt live," she replied, "Heaven's mercy
relieving
Each anguishing wound, shall forbid me to
mourn!"—
"Ah no! the last pang of my bosom is heaving!
No light of the morn shall to Henry return!

Thou charmer of life, ever tender and true!
Ye babes of my love, that await me afar!"—
His faltering tongue scarce could murmur adieu,
When he sunk in her arms—the poor wounded
Hussar!

LOVE AND MADNESS.

AN ELEGY. WRITTEN IN 1795.

HARK! from the battlements of yonder tower[1]
The solemn bell has toll'd the midnight hour!
Roused from drear visions of distemper'd sleep,
Poor B———k wakes—in solitude to weep!

"Cease, Memory, cease (the friendless mourner cried)
To probe the bosom too severely tried!
Oh! ever cease, my pensive thoughts, to stray
Through the bright fields of Fortune's better day,
When youthful HOPE, the music of the mind,
Tuned all its charms, and E———n was kind!

Yet, can I cease, while glows this trembling frame,
In sighs to speak thy melancholy name!
I hear thy spirit wail in every storm!
In midnight shades I view thy passing form!
Pale as in that sad hour when doom'd to feel,
Deep in thy perjured heart, the bloody steel!

1 Warwick Castle.

Demons of Vengeance! ye at whose command
I grasp'd the sword with more than woman's hand.
Say ye, did Pity's trembling voice controul,
Or horror damp the purpose of my soul?
No! my wild heart sat smiling o'er the plan,
Till Hate fulfill'd what baffled love began!

Yes; let the clay-cold breast that never knew
One tender pang to generous nature true,
Half-mingling pity with the gall of scorn,
Condemn this heart, that bled in love forlorn!

And ye, proud fair, whose soul no gladness warms,
Save Rapture's homage to your conscious charms!
Delighted idols of a gaudy train,
Ill can your blunter feelings guess the pain,
When the fond, faithful heart, inspired to prove
Friendship refined, the calm delight of Love,
Feels all its tender strings with anguish torn,
And bleeds at perjured Pride's inhuman scorn.

Say, then, did pitying Heaven condemn the deed,
When Vengeance bade thee, faithless lover! bleed?
Long had I watch'd thy dark foreboding brow,
What time thy bosom scorn'd its dearest vow!
Sad, though I wept the friend, the lover changed,
Still thy cold look was scornful and estranged,

Till from thy pity, love, and shelter thrown,
I wander'd hopeless, friendless, and alone !

Oh ! righteous Heaven ! 'twas then my tortured soul
First gave to wrath unlimited controul !
Adieu the silent look ! the streaming eye !
The murmur'd plaint ! the deep heart-heaving sigh !
Long-slumbering Vengeance wakes to better deeds ;
He shrieks, he falls, the perjured lover bleeds !
Now the last laugh of agony is o'er,
And pale in blood he sleeps, to wake no more !

'Tis done ! the flame of hate no longer burns :
Nature relents, but, ah ! too late returns !
Why does my soul this gush of fondness feel ?
Trembling and faint, I drop the guilty steel !
Cold on my heart the hand of terror lies,
And shades of horror close my languid eyes !

Oh ! 'twas a deed of Murder's deepest grain !
Could B———k's soul so true to wrath remain ?
A friend long true, a once fond lover fell ?—
Where Love was foster'd could not Pity dwell ?

Unhappy youth ! while yon pale crescent glows
To watch on silent Nature's deep repose,
Thy sleepless spirit, breathing from the tomb,
Foretells my fate, and summons me to come !

Once more I see thy sheeted spectre stand,
Roll the dim eye, and wave the paly hand!

Soon may this fluttering spark of vital flame
Forsake its languid melancholy frame!
Soon may these eyes their trembling lustre close,
Welcome the dreamless night of long repose!
Soon may this woe-worn spirit seek the bourne
Where, lull'd to slumber, Grief forgets to mourn!"

PROPERLY a monody on Miss Broderick. Written at the age of nineteen, at Downie, Argyllshire, during the poet's residence as tutor to the son of Colonel Napier, now Sir William Napier, of Milliken, who resided at that time with his mother on his grandfather's estate at Downie. The monody was transmitted to London to James Thompson, Esq., of Clitheroe, Lancashire, in a letter dated September 15, 1796, of which the following is an extract:—"I believe I hinted in my last that I proposed submitting a monody, lately finished, to your inspection. The subject is the unhappy fair one, who, you may remember, was tried about twelve months ago for the murder of Errington. Some of my critical friends have blamed me for endeavouring to recommend such a woman to sympathy; but from the moment I heard Broderick's story I could not refrain from admiring her, even amid the horror of the rash deed she committed. Errington was an inhuman villain to forsake her, and he deserved his fate; not by the laws of his country, but of friendship, which he had so heinously broken through."

HALLOWED GROUND.

WHAT's hallow'd ground? Has earth a clod
Its maker meant not should be trod
By man, the image of his God
Erect and free,
Unscourged by Superstition's rod
To bow the knee?

That 's hallow'd ground—where, mourn'd and miss'd,
The lips repose our love has kiss'd:—
But where 's their memory's mansion? Is 't
Yon churchyard's bowers?
No! in ourselves their souls exist,
A part of ours.

A kiss can consecrate the ground
Where mated hearts are mutual bound:
The spot where love's first links were wound,
That ne'er are riven,
Is hallow'd down to earth's profound,
And up to Heaven!

For time makes all but true love old;
The burning thoughts that then were told
Run molten still in memory's mould;
    And will not cool,
Until the heart itself be cold
    In Lethe's pool.

What hallows ground where heroes sleep?
'Tis not the sculptured piles you heap!
In dews that heavens far distant weep
    Their turf may bloom;
Or Genii twine beneath the deep
    Their coral tomb:

But strew his ashes to the wind
Whose sword or voice has served mankind—
And is he dead, whose glorious mind
    Lifts thine on high?—
To live in hearts we leave behind,
    Is not to die.

Is 't death to fall for Freedom's right?
He 's dead alone that lacks her light!
And murder sullies in Heaven's sight
    The sword he draws:—
What can alone ennoble fight?
    A noble cause!

Give that! and welcome War to brace
Her drums! and rend Heaven's reeking space!
The colours planted face to face,
The charging cheer,
Though Death's pale horse lead on the chase,
Shall still be dear.

And place our trophies where men kneel
To Heaven! but Heaven rebukes my zeal.
The cause of Truth and human weal,
O God above!
Transfer it from the sword's appeal
To Peace and Love.

Peace, Love! the cherubim, that join
Their spread wings o'er Devotion's shrine,
Prayers sound in vain, and temples shine,
Where they are not—
The heart alone can make divine
Religion's spot.

To incantations dost thou trust,
And pompous rites in domes august?
See mouldering stones and metal's rust
Belie the vaunt,
That men can bless one pile of dust
With chime or chaunt.

The ticking wood-worm mocks thee, man!
Thy temples—creeds themselves grow wan!
But there's a dome of nobler span,
    A temple given
Thy faith, that bigots dare not ban—
    Its space is Heaven!

Its roof star-pictured Nature's ceiling,
Where trancing the rapt spirit's feeling,
And God himself to man revealing,
    The harmonious spheres
Make music, though unheard their pealing
    By mortal ears.

Fair stars! are not your beings pure?
Can sin, can death, your worlds obscure?
Else why so swell the thoughts at your
    Aspect above?
Ye must be Heavens that make us sure
    Of heavenly love!

And in your harmony sublime
I read the doom of distant time:
That man's regenerate soul from crime
    Shall yet be drawn,
And reason on his mortal clime
    Immortal dawn.

What 's hallow'd ground? 'Tis what gives birth
To sacred thoughts in souls of worth!—
Peace! Independence! Truth! go forth
Earth's compass round;
And your high priesthood shall make earth
All hallow'd ground.

SONG.

Withdraw not yet those lips and fingers,
Whose touch to mine is rapture's spell;
Life's joy for us a moment lingers,
And death seems in the word—Farewell.
The hour that bids us part and go,
It sounds not yet,—oh! no, no, no!

Time, whilst I gaze upon thy sweetness,
Flies like a courser nigh the goal;
To-morrow where shall be his fleetness,
When thou art parted from my soul?
Our hearts shalt beat, our tears shall flow,
But not together—no, no, no!

CAROLINE.

PART I.

I 'LL bid the hyacinth to blow,
  I 'll teach my grotto green to be ;
And sing my true love, all below
  The holly bower and myrtle tree.

There all his wild-wood sweets to bring,
  The sweet South wind shall wander by,
And with the music of his wing
  Delight my rustling canopy.

Come to my close and clustering bower,
  Thou spirit of a milder clime,
Fresh with the dews of fruit and flower,
  Of mountain heath, and moory thyme.

With all thy rural echoes come,
  Sweet comrade of the rosy day,
Wafting the wild bee's gentle hum,
  Or cuckoo's plaintive roundelay.

Where'er thy morning breath has play'd,
  Whatever isles of ocean fann'd,
Come to my blossom-woven shade,
  Thou wandering wind of fairy-land.

For sure from some enchanted isle,
  Where Heaven and Love their sabbath hold,
Where pure and happy spirits smile,
  Of beauty's fairest, brightest mould:

From some green Eden of the deep,
  Where Pleasure's sigh alone is heaved,
Where tears of rapture lovers weep,
  Endear'd, undoubting, undeceived:

From some sweet paradise afar,
  Thy music wanders, distant, lost—
Where Nature lights her leading star,
  And love is never, never cross'd.

Oh gentle gale of Eden bowers,
  If back thy rosy feet should roam,
To revel with the cloudless Hours
  In Nature's more propitious home,

Name to thy loved Elysian groves,
  That o'er enchanted spirits twine,
A fairer form than Cherub loves,
  And let the name be CAROLINE.

1795.

CAROLINE.

PART II.

TO THE EVENING STAR.

Gem of the crimson-colour'd Even,
Companion of retiring day,
Why at the closing gates of Heaven,
Beloved star, dost thou delay?

So fair thy pensile beauty burns,
When soft the tear of twilight flows;
So due thy plighted love returns,
To chambers brighter than the rose:

To Peace, to Pleasure, and to Love,
So kind a star thou seem'st to be,
Sure some enamour'd orb above
Descends and burns to meet with thee.

Thine is the breathing, blushing hour,
When all unheavenly passions fly,
Chased by the soul-subduing power
Of Love's delicious witchery.

O! sacred to the fall of day,
  Queen of propitious stars, appear,
And early rise, and long delay,
  When Caroline herself is here!

Shine on her chosen green resort,
  Whose trees the sunward summit crown,
And wanton flowers, that well may court
  An angel's feet to tread them down.

Shine on her sweetly-scented road,
  Thou star of evening's purple dome,
That lead'st the nightingale abroad,
  And guid'st the pilgrim to his home.

Shine where my charmer's sweeter breath
  Embalms the soft exhaling dew,
Where dying winds a sigh bequeath
  To kiss the cheek of rosy hue.

Where, winnow'd by the gentle air,
  Her silken tresses darkly flow,
And fall upon her brow so fair,
  Like shadows on the mountain snow.

Thus, ever thus, at day's decline,
  In converse sweet, to wander far,
O bring with thee my Caroline,
  And thou shalt be my Ruling Star!

1796.

THE BEECH TREE'S PETITION.

O LEAVE this barren spot to me!
Spare, woodman, spare the beechen tree!
Though bush or floweret never grow
My dark unwarming shade below;
Nor summer bud perfume the dew
Of rosy blush, or yellow hue!
Nor fruits of autumn, blossom-born,
My green and glossy leaves adorn;
Nor murmuring tribes from me derive
Th' ambrosial amber of the hive;
Yet leave this barren spot to me:
Spare, woodman, spare the beechen tree!

Thrice twenty summers I have seen
The sky grow bright, the forest green;
And many a wintry wind have stood
In bloomless, fruitless solitude,
Since childhood in my pleasant bower
First spent its sweet and sportive hour;
Since youthful lovers in my shade
Their vows of truth and rapture made;
And on my trunk's surviving frame
Carv'd many a long-forgotten name.

Oh! by the sighs of gentle sound,
First breathed upon this sacred ground;
By all that Love has whisper'd here,
Or beauty heard with ravish'd ear;
As Love's own altar honour me:
Spare, woodman, spare the beechen tree!

FIELD FLOWERS.

Ye field flowers! the gardens eclipse you, 'tis true,
Yet wildings of Nature, I dote upon you,
For ye waft me to summers of old,
When the earth teem'd around me with fairy delight,
And when daisies and buttercups gladden'd my sight,
Like treasures of silver and gold.

I love you for lulling me back into dreams
Of the blue Highland mountains and echoing streams,
And of birchen glades breathing their balm,
While the deer was seen glancing in sunshine remote,

And the deep mellow crush of the wood-pigeon's
note
Made music that sweeten'd the calm.

Not a pastoral song has a pleasanter tune
Than ye speak to my heart, little wildings of June:
Of old ruinous castles ye tell,
Where I thought it delightful your beauties to find,
When the magic of nature first breathed on my
mind,
And your blossoms were part of her spell.

Even now what affections the violet awakes;
What loved little islands, twice seen in their lakes,
Can the wild water-lily restore;
What landscapes I read in the primrose's looks,
And what pictures of pebbled and minnowy brooks,
In the vetches that tangled their shore.

Earth's cultureless buds, to my heart ye were dear,
Ere the fever of passion, or ague of fear,
Had scathed my existence's bloom;
Once I welcome you more, in life's passionless
stage,
With the visions of youth to revisit my age,
And I wish you to grow on my tomb.

SONG.

TO THE EVENING STAR.

STAR that bringest home the bee,
And sett'st the weary labourer free!
If any star shed peace, 'tis thou,
That send'st it from above,
Appearing when Heaven's breath and brow
Are sweet as hers we love.

Come to the luxuriant skies,
Whilst the landscape's odours rise,
Whilst far-off lowing herds are heard,
And songs when toil is done,
From cottages whose smoke unstirr'd
Curls yellow in the sun.

Star of love's soft interviews,
Parted lovers on thee muse;
Their remembrancer in Heaven
Of thrilling vows thou art,
Too delicious to be riven
By absence from the heart.

STANZAS TO PAINTING.

O THOU by whose expressive art
Her perfect image Nature sees
In union with the Graces start,
And sweeter by reflection please!

In whose creative hand the hues
Fresh from yon orient rainbow shine;
I bless thee, Promethèan muse!
And call thee brightest of the Nine!

Possessing more than vocal power,
Persuasive more than poet's tongue;
Whose lineage, in a raptured hour,
From Love, the Sire of Nature, sprung;

Does Hope her high possession meet?
Is joy triumphant, sorrow flown?
Sweet is the trance, the tremor sweet
When all we love is all our own.

But oh! thou pulse of pleasure dear,
Slow throbbing, cold, I feel thee part;
Lone absence plants a pang severe,
Or death inflicts a keener dart.

Then for a beam of joy to light
  In memory's sad and wakeful eye!
Or banish from the noon of night
  Her dreams of deeper agony.

Shall Song its witching cadence roll?
  Yea, even the tenderest air repeat,
That breathed when soul was knit to soul,
  And heart to heart responsive beat?

What visions rise! to charm, to melt!
  The lost, the loved, the dead are near!
Oh, hush that strain too deeply felt!
  And cease that solace too severe!

But thou, serenely silent art!
  By heaven and love wast taught to lend
A milder solace to the heart,
  The sacred image of a friend.

All is not lost! if, yet possest,
  To me that sweet memorial shine:—
If close and closer to my breast
  I hold that idol all divine.

Or, gazing through luxurious tears,
  Melt o'er the loved departed form,
Till death's cold bosom half appears
  With life, and speech, and spirit warm.

She looks! she lives! this trancèd hour,
Her bright eye seems a purer gem
Than sparkles on the throne of power,
Or glory's wealthy diadem.

Yes, Genius, yes! thy mimic aid
A treasure to my soul has given,
Where beauty's canonizèd shade
Smiles in the sainted hues of heaven,

No spectre forms of pleasure fled,
Thy softening, sweetening, tints restore;
For thou canst give us back the dead,
E'en in the loveliest looks they wore.

Then blest be Nature's guardian Muse,
Whose hand her perish'd grace redeems!
Whose tablet of a thousand hues
The mirror of creation seems.

From Love began thy high descent;
And lovers, charm'd by gifts of thine,
Shall bless thee mutely eloquent;
And call thee brightest of the Nine!

THE MAID'S REMONSTRANCE.

NEVER wedding, ever wooing,
Still a love-lorn heart pursuing,
Read you not the wrong you 're doing
  In my cheek's pale hue?
All my life with sorrow strewing,
  Wed, or cease to woo.

Rivals banish'd, bosoms plighted,
Still our days are disunited;
Now the lamp of hope is lighted,
  Now half-quench'd appears,
Damp'd, and wavering, and benighted,
  'Midst my sighs and tears.

Charms you call your dearest blessing,
Lips that thrill at your caressing,
Eyes a mutual soul confessing,
  Soon you 'll make them grow
Dim, and worthless your possessing,
  Not with age, but woe!

ABSENCE.

'Tis not the loss of love's assurance,
  It is not doubting what thou art,
But 'tis the too, too long endurance
  Of absence, that afflicts my heart.

The fondest thoughts two hearts can cherish,
  When each is lonely doom'd to weep,
Are fruits on desert isles that perish,
  Or riches buried in the deep.

What though, untouch'd by jealous madness,
  Our bosom's peace may fall to wreck;
Th' undoubting heart, that breaks with sadness,
  Is but more slowly doom'd to break.

Absence! is not the soul torn by it
  From more than light, or life, or breath?
'Tis Lethe's gloom, but not its quiet,
  The pain without the peace of death!

LINES

INSCRIBED ON THE MONUMENT LATELY FINISHED BY MR. CHANTREY,

Which has been erected by the Widow of Admiral Sir G. Campbell, K. C. B. to the memory of her Husband.

To him, whose loyal, brave, and gentle heart,
Fulfill'd the hero's and the patriot's part,—
Whose charity, like that which Paul enjoin'd,
Was warm, beneficent, and unconfined,—
This stone is rear'd: to public duty true,
The seaman's friend, the father of his crew—
Mild in reproof, sagacious in command,
He spread fraternal zeal throughout his band,
And led each arm to act, each heart to feel,
What British valour owes to Britain's weal.
These were his public virtues :—but to trace
His private life's fair purity and grace,
To paint the traits that drew affection strong
From friends, an ample and an ardent throng,
And, more, to speak his memory's grateful claim,
On her who mourns him most, and bears his name—
O'ercomes the trembling hand of widow'd grief,
O'ercomes the heart, unconscious of relief,
Save in religion's high and holy trust,
Whilst placing their memorial o'er his dust.

STANZAS

ON THE BATTLE OF NAVARINO.

Hearts of oak that have bravely deliver'd the brave, [grave,
And uplifted old Greece from the brink of the
'Twas the helpless to help, and the hopeless to save,
That your thunderbolts swept o'er the brine:
And as long as yon sun shall look down on the wave,
The light of your glory shall shine.

For the guerdon ye sought with your bloodshed and toil,
Was it slaves, or dominion, or rapine, or spoil?
No! your lofty emprise was to fetter and foil
The uprooter of Greece's domain!
When he tore the last remnant of food from her soil,
Till her famish'd sank pale as the slain!

Yet, Navarin's heroes! does Christendom breed
The base hearts that will question the fame of your deed?

Are they men?—let ineffable scorn be their meed,
And oblivion shadow their graves!—
Are they women?—to Turkish serails let them speed;
And be mothers of Mussulman slaves.

Abettors of massacre! dare ye deplore
That the death-shriek is silenced on Hellas's shore?
That the mother aghast sees her offspring no more
By the hand of Infanticide grasp'd!
And that stretch'd on yon billows distain'd by their gore
Missolonghi's assassins have gasp'd?

Prouder scene never hallow'd war's pomp to the mind,
Than when Christendom's pennons wooed social the wind,
And the flower of her brave for the combat com- [bined,
Their watch-word, humanity's vow:
Not a sea-boy that fought in that cause, but man- [kind
Owes a garland to honour his brow!

Nor grudge, by our side, that to conquer or fall
Came the hardy rude Russ, and the high-mettled Gaul:
For whose was the genius, that plann'd at its call,
Where the whirlwind of battle should roll?
All were brave! but the star of success over all
Was the light of our Codrington's soul.

That star of thy day-spring, regenerate Greek!
Dimm'd the Saracen's moon, and struck pallid his
cheek:
In its fast flushing morning thy Muses shall speak
When their lore and their lutes they reclaim:
And the first of their songs from Parnassus's
peak
Shall be "*Glory to Codrington's name!*"

1828.

LINES

ON REVISITING A SCOTTISH RIVER.

And call they this Improvement!—to have
changed,
My native Clyde, thy once romantic shore,
Where Nature's face is banish'd and estranged,
And heaven reflected in thy wave no more;
Whose banks, that sweeten'd May-day's breath
before,
Lie sere and leafless now in summer's beam,
With sooty exhalations cover'd o'er;
And for the daisied green-sward, down thy stream
Unsightly brick lanes smoke, and clanking engines
gleam.

Speak not to me of swarms the scene sustains;
One heart free tasting Nature's breath and bloom
Is worth a thousand slaves to Mammon's gains.
But whither goes that wealth, and gladdening
whom?
See, left but life enough and breathing-room
The hunger and the hope of life to feel,
Yon pale Mechanic bending o'er his loom,
And Childhood's self as at Ixion's wheel,
From morn till midnight task'd to earn its little
meal.

Is this Improvement?—where the human breed
Degenerate as they swarm and overflow,
Till Toil grows cheaper than the trodden weed,
And man competes with man, like foe with foe,
Till Death, that thins them, scarce seems public
woe?
Improvement!—smiles it in the poor man's eyes,
Or blooms it on the cheek of Labour?—No—
To gorge a few with Trade's precarious prize,
We banish rural life, and breathe unwholesome
skies.

Nor call that evil slight; God has not given
This passion to the heart of man in vain,
For Earth's green face, th' untainted air of Heaven,
And all the bliss of Nature's rustic reign.
For not alone our frame imbibes a stain
From fœtid skies; the spirit's healthy pride

Fades in their gloom—And therefore I complain,
That thou no more through pastoral scenes shouldst
glide,
My Wallace's own stream, and once romantic
Clyde!

1827.

THE "NAME UNKNOWN."[1]

IN IMITATION OF KLOPSTOCK.

PROPHETIC pencil! wilt thou trace
A faithful image of the face,
Or wilt thou write the "Name Unknown,"
Ordain'd to bless my charmèd soul,
And all my future fate control,
Unrivall'd and alone?

Delicious Idol of my thought!
Though sylph or spirit hath not taught
My boding heart thy precious name;
Yet musing on my distant fate,
To charms unseen I consecrate
A visionary flame.

[1 These lines were written in Germany.]

17

Thy rosy blush, thy meaning eye,
Thy virgin voice of melody,
  Are ever present to my heart;
Thy murmur'd vows shall yet be mine,
My thrilling hand shall meet with thine,
  And never, never part.

Then fly, my days, on rapid wing
Till Love the viewless treasure bring
  While I, like conscious Athens, own
A power in mystic silence seal'd,
A guardian angel unreveal'd,
  And bless the "Name Unknown!"

FAREWELL TO LOVE.

I HAD a heart that doted once in passion's bound-
less pain,
And though the tyrant I abjured, I could not
break his chain;
But now that Fancy's fire is quench'd, and ne'er
can burn anew,
I 've bid to Love, for all my life, adieu! adieu!
adieu!

I 've known, if ever mortal knew, the spells of
Beauty's thrall,
And if my song has told them not, my soul has
felt them all;
But Passion robs my peace no more, and Beauty's
witching sway
Is now to me a star that 's fall'n—a dream that 's
pass'd away.

Hail! welcome tide of life, when no tumultuous
billows roll,
How wondrous to myself appears this halcyon
calm of soul!

The wearied bird blown o'er the deep would
sooner quit its shore,
Than I would cross the gulf again that time has
brought me o'er.

Why say they Angels feel the flame?—Oh, spirits
of the skies!
Can love like ours, that dotes on dust, in heavenly
bosoms rise?—
Ah no! the hearts that best have felt its power,
the best can tell,
That peace on earth itself begins, when Love has
bid farewell.

1830.

LINES

ON THE CAMP HILL, NEAR HASTINGS.

In the deep blue of eve,
Ere the twinkling of stars had begun,
Or the lark took his leave
Of the skies and the sweet setting sun,

I climb'd to yon heights,
Where the Norman encamp'd him of old,
With his bowmen and knights,
And his banner all burnish'd with gold.

At the Conqueror's side
There his minstrelsy sat harp in hand,
In pavilion wide;
And they chaunted the deeds of Roland.

Still the ramparted ground
With a vision my fancy inspires,
And I hear the trump sound,
As it marshal'd our Chivalry's sires.

On each turf of that mead
Stood the captors of England's domains,
That ennobled her breed
And high-mettled the blood of her veins.

Over hauberk and helm
As the sun's setting splendour was thrown,
Thence they look'd o'er a realm—
And to-morrow beheld it their own.

[The preceding "Lines" were composed in the year 1831, and their subject (to use the poet's own words) "is a spot of ground, not far from the Castle of Hastings, on which I have ascertained, by a comparison of histories, the camp of William the Conqueror must have been placed the evening before he defeated Harold."]

LINES ON POLAND.

And have I lived to see thee sword in hand
Uprise again, immortal Polish Land!—
Whose flag brings more than chivalry to mind,
And leaves the tri-color in shade behind;
A theme for uninspired lips too strong;
That swells my heart beyond the power of song:—
Majestic men, whose deeds have dazzled faith,
Ah! yet your fate's suspense arrests my breath:
Whilst envying bosoms, bared to shot and steel,
I feel the more that fruitlessly I feel.

Poles! with what indignation I endure
Th' half-pitying servile mouths that call you poor;
Poor! is it England mocks you with her grief,
Who hates, but dares not chide, th' *Imperial Thief?*
France with her soul beneath a Bourbon's thrall,
And Germany that has no soul at all,—
States, quailing at the giant overgrown,
Whom dauntless Poland grapples with alone!
No, ye are rich in fame e'en whilst ye bleed:
We cannot aid you—*we* are poor indeed!

In Fate's defiance—in the world's great eye,
Poland has won her immortality;
The Butcher, should he reach her bosom now,
Could not tear Glory's garland from her brow;
Wreathed, filleted, the victim falls renown'd,
And all her ashes will be holy ground!

But turn, my soul, from presages so dark:
Great Poland's spirit is a deathless spark
That's fann'd by Heaven to mock the Tyrant's
rage:
She, like the eagle, will renew her age,
And fresh historic plumes of Fame put on,—
Another Athens after Marathon,—
Where eloquence shall fulmine, arts refine,
Bright as her arms that now in battle shine.
Come—should the heavenly shock my life destroy,
And shut its flood-gates with excess of joy;
Come but the day when Poland's fight is won—
And on my grave-stone shine the morrow's
sun—
The day that sees Warsaw's cathedral glow
With endless ensigns ravish'd from the foe,—
Her woman lifting their fair hands with thanks,
Her pious warriors kneeling in their ranks,
The 'scutcheon'd walls of high heraldic boast,
The odorous altars' elevated host,
The organ sounding through the aisles' long
glooms,
The mighty dead seen sculptured o'er their tombs;

(John, Europe's saviour—Poniatowski's fair
Resemblance—Kosciusko's shall be there ;)
The taper'd pomp—the hallelujah's swell,
Shall o'er the soul's devotion cast a spell,
Till visions cross the rapt enthusiast's glance,
And all the scene becomes a waking trance.
Should Fate put far—far off that glorious scene,
And gulfs of havoc interpose between,
Imagine not, ye men of every clime,
Who act, or by your sufferance share, the crime—
Your brother Abel's blood shall vainly plead
Against the "*deep damnation*" of the deed.
Germans, ye view its horror and disgrace
With cold phosphoric eyes and phlegm of face.
Is Allemagne profound in science, lore,
And minstrel art?—her shame is but the more
To doze and dream by governments oppress'd,
The spirit of a book-worm in each breast.
Well can ye mouth fair Freedom's classic line,
And talk of Constitutions o'er your wine:
But all your vows to break the tyrant's yoke
Expire in Bacchanalian song and smoke:
Heavens! can no ray of foresight pierce the leads
And mystic metaphysics of your heads,
To show the self-same grave Oppression delves
For Poland's rights is yawning for yourselves?
See, whilst the Pole, the vanguard aid of France,
Has vaulted on his barb, and couch'd the lance,
France turns from her abandon'd friends afresh,
And soothes the Bear that prowls for patriot flesh;

Buys, ignominious purchase! short repose,
With dying curses, and the groans of those
That served, and loved, and put in her their
trust.
Frenchmen! the dead accuse you from the dust—
Brows laurell'd—bosoms mark'd with many a scar
For France—that wore her Legion's noblest
star,
Cast dumb reproaches from the field of Death
On Gallic honour: and this broken faith
Has robb'd you more of Fame—the life of life—
Than twenty battles lost in glorious strife!
And what of England—is she steep'd so low
In poverty, crest-fall'n, and palsied so,
That we must sit much wroth, but timorous more,
With murder knocking at our neighbour's
door!—
Not murder mask'd and cloak'd, with hidden knife,
Whose owner owes the gallows life for life;
But *Public Murder!*—that with pomp and gaud,
And royal scorn of Justice, walks abroad
To wring more tears and blood than e'er were
wrung
By all the culprits Justice ever hung!
We read the diadem'd Assasin's vaunt,
And wince, and wish we had not hearts to pant
With useless indignation—sigh, and frown,
But have not hearts to throw the gauntlet down.
If but a doubt hung o'er the grounds of fray,
Or trivial rapine stopp'd the world's highway;

Were this some common strife of States embroil'd ;—
Britannia on the spoiler and the spoil'd
Might calmly look, and, asking time to breathe,
Still honourably wear her olive wreath.
But this is Darkness combating with Light ;
Earth's adverse Principles for empire fight ;
Oppression, that has belted half the globe,
Far as his knout could reach or dagger probe,
Holds reeking o'er our brother-freemen slain
That dagger—shakes it at us in disdain :
Talks big to Freedom's states of Poland's thrall,
And, trampling one, contemns them one and all.

My country! colours not thy once proud brow
At this affront ?—Hast thou not fleets enow
With Glory's streamer, lofty as the lark,
Gay fluttering o'er each thunder-bearing bark,
To warm the insulter's seas with barbarous blood,
And interdict his flag from Ocean's flood ?
Ev'n now far off the sea-cliff, where I sing,
I see, my Country and my Patriot King !
Your ensign glad the deep. Becalm'd and slow
A war-ship rides ; while Heaven's prismatic bow
Uprisen behind her on th' horizon's base,
Shines flushing through the tackle, shrouds, and stays,
And wraps her giant form in one majestic blaze.
My soul accepts the omen ; Fancy's eye
Has sometimes a veracious augury :

The Rainbow types Heaven's promise to my sight;
The Ship, Britannia's interposing Might!
But if there should be none to aid you, Poles,
Ye 'll but to prouder pitch wind up your souls,
Above example, pity, praise, or blame,
To sow and reap a boundless field of Fame.
Ask aïd no more from Nations that forget
Your championship—old Europe's mighty debt.
Though Poland, Lazarus-like, has burst the gloom,
She rises not a beggar from the tomb:
In Fortune's frown, on Danger's giddiest brink,
Despair and Poland's name must never link,
All ills have bounds—plague, whirlwind, fire, and flood:
Ev'n Power can spill but bounded sums of blood.
States caring not what Freedom's price may be,
May late or soon, but must at last be free;
For body-killing tyrants cannot kill
The public soul—the hereditary will
That downward, as from sire to son it goes,
By shifting bosoms more intensely glows:
Its heirloom is the heart, and slaughter'd men
Fight fiercer in their orphans o'er again.
Poland recasts—though rich in heroes old—
Her men in more and more heroic mould;
Her eagle ensign best among mankind
Becomes, and types her eagle-strength of mind:
Her praise upon my faltering lips expires;
Resume it, younger bards, and nobler lyres!

CAMPBELL'S hatred of tyranny, and his exertions in the cause of the oppressed, and particularly the unfortunate Poles, will not lightly pass away from the memory of those who so largely benefited by his labours.

During his lifetime some of the most eminent of the ancient *noblesse* of Poland expressed a grateful sense of obligation due to him. At his funeral there were not wanting sincere mourners for his loss (some of whom scattered "kindred dust" upon his coffin). After his decease, Lord Dudley Stuart, as Vice-President of the Polish Association, forwarded to Campbell's executors a tribute of condolence, from which the following passage is extracted:—

"Nor did Mr. Campbell content himself with a mere abstract feeling of sympathy for the friendless and destitute Poles. No, his purse was open to them with a liberality far more in accordance with his generous nature than with the extent of his means: and early in the year 1832, in conjunction with the Polish poet Niemciewitz and the celebrated Prince Czartoryski, he founded this Association for the purpose of diffusing and keeping alive in the public mind a lively interest for ill-fated Poland. His pathetic, eloquent, and fervid address to our countrymen, throughout the empire, as our first president, on behalf of that unfortunate country, was eminently effective and successful. By imparting a knowledge of the objects of the parent society, he conciliated much powerful support from men of all parties in the state."

A THOUGHT SUGGESTED BY THE NEW YEAR.

THE more we live, more brief appear
  Our life's succeeding stages;
A day to childhood seems a year,
  And years like passing ages.

The gladsome current of our youth,
  Ere passion yet disorders,
Steals, lingering like a river smooth
  Along its grassy borders.

But, as the care-worn cheek grows wan,
  And sorrow's shafts fly thicker,
Ye stars, that measure life to man,
  Why seem your courses quicker?

When joys have lost their bloom and breath,
  And life itself is vapid,
Why, as we reach the Falls of death,
  Feel we its tide more rapid?

It may be strange—yet who would change
  Time's course to slower speeding;
When one by one our friends have gone,
  And left our bosoms bleeding?

Heaven gives our years of fading strength
  Indemnifying fleetness ;
And those of Youth, a *seeming length,*
  Proportion'd to their sweetness.

SONG.

How delicious is the winning
Of a kiss at Love's beginning,
When two mutual hearts are sighing
For the knot there 's no untying!

Yet, remember, 'midst your wooing,
Love has bliss, but Love has ruing ;
Other smiles may make you fickle,
Tears for other charms may trickle.

Love he comes, and Love he tarries,
Just as fate or fancy carries ;
Longest stays, when sorest chidden ;
Laughs and flies, when press'd and bidden.

Bind the sea to slumber stilly,
Bind its odour to the lily,
Bind the aspen ne'er to quiver,
Then bind Love to last for ever!

Love 's a fire that needs renewal
Of fresh beauty for its fuel ;
Love's wing moults when caged and captured,
Only free, he soars enraptured.

Can you keep the bee from ranging,
Or the ringdove's neck from changing ?
No ! nor fetter'd Love from dying
In the knot there 's no untying.

MARGARET AND DORA.

MARGARET 's beauteous—Grecian arts
Ne'er drew form completer,
Yet why, in my heart of hearts,
Hold I Dora 's sweeter?

Dora's eyes of heavenly blue
Pass all painting's reach,
Ringdoves' notes are discord to
The music of her speech.

Artists! Margaret's smile receive,
And on canvas show it ;
But for perfect worship leave
Dora to her poet.

THE POWER OF RUSSIA.

So all this gallant blood has gush'd in vain!
And Poland, by the Northern Condor's beak
And talons torn, lies prostrated again.
O British patriots, that were wont to speak
Once loudly on this theme, now hush'd or meek!
O heartless men of Europe—Goth and Gaul,
Cold, adder-deaf to Poland's dying shriek;—
That saw the world's last land of heroes fall—
The brand of burning shame is on you all—all—all!

But this is not the drama's closing act!
Its tragic curtain must uprise anew.
Nations, mute accessories to the fact!
That Upas-tree of power, whose fostering dew
Was Polish blood, has yet to cast o'er you
The lengthening shadow of its head elate—
A deadly shadow, darkening Nature's hue.
To all that's hallow'd, righteous, pure and great,
Wo! wo! when they are reach'd by Russia's withering hate.

Russia, that on his throne of adamant,
Consults what nation's breast shall next be gored:
He on Polonia's Golgotha will plant
His standard fresh; and horde succeeding horde,
On patriot tomb-stones he will whet the sword,
For more stupendous slaughters of the free.
Then Europe's realms, when their best blood is pour'd,
Shall miss thee, Poland! as they bend the knee,
All—all in grief, but none in glory, likening thee.

Why smote ye not the Giant whilst he reel'd?
O fair occasion, gone for ever by!
To have lock'd his lances in their northern field,
Innocuous as the phantom chivalry
That flames and hurtles from yon boreal sky!
Now wave thy pennon, Russia, o'er the land
Once Poland; build thy bristling castles high;
Dig dungeons deep; for Poland's wrested brand
Is now a weapon new to widen thy command—

An awful width! Norwegian woods shall build
His fleets; the Swede his vassal, and the Dane;
The glebe of fifty kingdoms shall be till'd
To feed his dazzling, desolating train,
Camp'd sumless, 'twixt the Black and Baltic main:
Brute hosts, I own; but Sparta could not write,

And Rome, half-barbarous, bound Achaia's
chain:
So Russia's spirit, 'midst Sclavonic night,
Burns with a fire more dread than all your polished
light.

But Russia's limbs (so blinded statesmen speak)
Are crude, and too colossal to cohere.
O, lamentable weakness! reckoning weak
The stripling Titan, strengthening year by
year.
What implement lacks he for war's career,
That grows on earth, or in its floods and mines,
(Eighth sharer of the inhabitable sphere)
Whom Persia bows to, China ill confines,
And India's homage waits, when Albion's star
declines!

But time will teach the Russ, ev'n conquering
War
Has handmaid arts: ay, ay, the Russ will woo
All sciences that speed Bellona's car,
All murder's tactic arts, and win them too;
But never holier Muses shall imbue
His breast, that 's made of nature's basest
clay:
The sabre, knout, and dungeon's vapour blue
His laws and ethics: far from him away
Are all the lovely Nine, that breathe but Free-
dom's day.

Say, ev'n his serfs, half-humanized, should learn
Their human rights,—will Mars put out his flame
In Russian bosoms? no, he 'll bid them burn
A thousand years for nought but martial fame,
Like Romans :—yet forgive me, Roman name!
Rome could impart what Russia never can;
Proud civic rights to salve submission's shame.
Our strife is coming; but in freedom's van
The Polish eagle's fall is big with fate to man.

Proud bird of old! Mohammed's moon recoil'd
Before thy swoop: had we been timely bold,
That swoop, still free, had stunn'd the Russ, and foil'd
Earth's new oppressors, as it foil'd her old.
Now thy majestic eyes are shut and cold:
And colder still Polonia's children find
The sympathetic hands, that we outhold.
But, Poles, when we are gone, the world will mind,
Ye bore the brunt of fate, and bled for human-kind.

So hallowedly have ye fulfill'd your part,
My pride repudiates ev'n the sigh that blends
With Poland's name—name written on my heart.
My heroes, my grief-consecrated friends!
Your sorrow, in nobility, transcends

Your conqueror's joy: his cheek may blush; but shame
Can tinge not yours, though exile's tear descends;
Nor would ye change your conscience, cause, and name,
For his, with all his wealth, and all his felon fame.

Thee, Niemciewitz, whose song of stirring power
The Czar forbids to sound in Polish lands;
Thee, Czartoryski, in thy banish'd bower,
The patricide, who in thy palace stands,
May envy: proudly may Polonia's bands
Throw down their swords at Europe's feet in scorn
Saying—"Russia from the metal of these brands
Shall forge the fetters of your sons unborn;
Our setting star is your misfortunes' rising morn."

1831.

LINES

ON LEAVING A SCENE IN BAVARIA.

ADIEU the woods and waters' side,
  Imperial Danube's rich domain!
Adieu the grotto, wild and wide,
  The rocks abrupt and grassy plain!
  For pallid Autumn once again
Hath swell'd each torrent of the hill;
  Her clouds collect, her shadows sail,
  And watery winds that sweep the vale
Grow loud and louder still.

But not the storm, dethroning fast
  Yon monarch oak of massy pile;
Nor river roaring to the blast
  Around its dark and desert isle;
  Nor church-bell tolling to beguile
The cloud-born thunder passing by,
  Can sound in discord to my soul:
  Roll on, ye mighty waters, roll!
And rage, thou darken'd sky!

Thy blossoms now no longer bright;
  Thy wither'd woods no longer green;
Yet, Eldurn shore, with dark delight
  I visit thy unlovely scene!
  For many a sunset hour serene
My steps have trod thy mellow dew;
  When his green light the glowworm gave,
  When Cynthia from the distant wave
Her twilight anchor drew,

And plough'd, as with a swelling sail,
  The billowy clouds and starry sea;
Then while thy hermit nightingale
  Sang on his fragrant apple-tree,—
  Romantic, solitary, free,
The visitant of Eldurn's shore,
  On such a moonlight mountain stray'd,
  As echoed to the music made
By Druid harps of yore.

Around thy savage hills of oak,
  Around thy waters bright and blue,
No hunter's horn the silence broke,
  No dying shriek thine echo knew;
  But safe, sweet Eldurn woods, to you
The wounded wild deer ever ran,
  Whose myrtle bound their grassy cave,
  Whose very rocks a shelter gave
From blood-pursuing man.

Oh heart effusions, that arose
  From nightly wanderings cherish'd here;
To him who flies from many woes,
  Even homeless deserts can be dear!
  The last and solitary cheer
Of those that own no earthly home,
  Say—is it not, ye banish'd race,
  In such a loved and lonely place
Companionless to roam?

Yes! I have loved thy wild abode,
  Unknown, unplough'd, untrodden shore;
Where scarce the woodman finds a road,
  And scarce the fisher plies an oar;
  For man's neglect I love thee more;
That art nor avarice intrude
  To tame thy torrent's thunder-shock,
  Or prune thy vintage of the rock
Magnificently rude.

Unheeded spreads thy blossom'd bud
  Its milky bosom to the bee;
Unheeded falls along the flood
  Thy desolate and aged tree.
  Forsaken scene, how like to thee
The fate of unbefriended Worth!
  Like thine her fruit dishonour'd falls;
  Like thee in solitude she calls
A thousand treasures forth.

Oh! silent spirit of the place,
  If, lingering with the ruin'd year,
Thy hoary form and awful face
  I yet might watch and worship here!
  Thy storm were music to mine ear,
Thy wildest walk a shelter given
  Sublimer thoughts on earth to find,
  And share, with no unhallow'd mind,
The majesty of heaven.

What though the bosom friends of Fate,—
  Prosperity's unweaned brood,—
Thy consolations cannot rate,
  O self-dependent solitude!
  Yet with a spirit unsubdued,
Though darken'd by the clouds of Care,
  To worship thy congenial gloom,
  A pilgrim to the Prophet's tomb
The Friendless shall repair.

On him the world hath never smiled
  Or look'd but with accusing eye;—
All-silent goddess of the wild,
  To thee that misanthrope shall fly!
  I hear his deep soliloquy,
I mark his proud but ravaged form,
  As stern he wraps his mantle round,
  And bids, on winter's bleakest ground,
Defiance to the storm.

Peace to his banish'd heart, at last,
  In thy dominions shall descend,
And, strong as beechwood in the blast,
  His spirit shall refuse to bend;
  Enduring life without a friend,
The world and falsehood left behind,
  Thy votary shall bear elate,
  (Triumphant o'er opposing Fate,)
His dark inspired mind.

But dost thou, Folly, mock the Muse
  A wanderer's mountain walk to sing,
Who shuns a warring world, nor woos
  The vulture cover of its wing?
  Then fly, thou cowering, shivering thing,
Back to the fostering world beguiled,
  To waste in self-consuming strife
  The loveless brotherhood of life,
Reviling and reviled!

Away, thou lover of the race
  That hither chased yon weeping deer!
If Nature's all majestic face
  More pitiless than man's appear;
  Or if the wild winds seem more drear
Than man's cold charities below,
  Behold around his peopled plains,
  Where'er the social savage reigns,
Exuberance of woe!

His art and honours wouldst thou seek
  Emboss'd on grandeur's giant walls?
Or hear his moral thunders speak
  Where senates light their airy halls,
  Where man his brother man enthralls;
Or sends his whirlwind warrant forth
  To rouse the slumbering fiends of war,
  To dye the blood-warm waves afar,
And desolate the earth?

From clime to clime pursue the scene,
  And mark in all thy spacious way,
Where'er the tyrant man has been,
  There Peace, the cherub, cannot stay;
  In wilds and woodlands far away
She builds her solitary bower,
  Where only anchorites have trod,
  Or friendless men, to worship God,
Have wander'd for an hour.

In such a far forsaken vale,—
  And such, sweet Eldurn vale, is thine,—
Afflicted nature shall inhale
  Heaven-borrow'd thoughts and joys divine;
  No longer wish, no more repine
For man's neglect or woman's scorn;—
  Then wed thee to an exile's lot,
  For if the world hath loved thee not,
Its absence may be borne.

THE DEATH-BOAT OF HELIGOLAND.

CAN restlessness reach the cold sepulchred
head ?—
Ay, the quick have their sleep-walkers, so have
the dead.
There are brains, though they moulder, that dream
in the tomb,
And that maddening forehear the last trumpet of
doom,
Till their corses start sheeted to revel on earth,
Making horror more deep by the semblance of
mirth :
By the glare of new-lighted volcanoes they dance,
Or at mid-sea appall the chill'd mariner's glance.
Such, I wot, was the band of cadaverous smile
Seen ploughing the night-surge of Heligo's isle.

The foam of the Baltic had sparkled like fire,
And the red moon look'd down with an aspect of
ire ;
But her beams on a sudden grew sick-like and
gray,
And the mews that had slept clang'd and shriek'd
far away—

And the buoys and the beacons extinguish'd their
light,
As the boat of the stony-eyed dead came in sight,
High bounding from billow to billow; each form
Had its shroud like a plaid flying loose to the
storm;
With an oar in each pulseless and icy-cold hand,
Fast they plough'd by the lee-shore of Heligoland,
Such breakers as boat of the living ne'er cross'd;
Now surf-sunk for minutes again they uptoss'd;
And with livid lips shouted reply o'er the flood
To the challenging watchman that curdled his
blood—
'We are dead—we are bound from our graves
in the west,
First to Hecla, and then to ——' Unmeet was
the rest
For man's ear. The old abbey bell thunder'd its
clang,
And their eyes gleam'd with phosphorus light as
it rang:
Ere they vanish'd, they stopp'd, and gazed silently
grim,
Till the eye could define them, garb, feature, and
limb.

Now who were those roamers? of gallows or
wheel
Bore they marks, or the mangling anatomist's
steel?

No, by magistrates' chains 'mid their grave-clothes
you saw
They were felons too proud to have perish'd by
law:
But a ribbon that hung where a rope should have
been,
'Twas the badge of their faction, its hue was not
green,
Show'd them men who had trampled and tortured
and driven
To rebellion the fairest Isle breathed on by
Heaven,—
Men whose heirs would yet finish the tyrannous
task,
If the Truth and the Time had not dragg'd off
their mask.
They parted—but not till the sight might discern
A scutcheon distinct at their pinnace's stern,
Where letters emblazon'd in blood-colour'd flame,
Named their faction—I blot not my page with its
name.

1828.

SONG.

When Love came first to earth, the Spring
  Spread rose-beds to receive him,
And back he vow'd his flight he 'd wing
  To Heaven, if she should leave him.

But Spring departing, saw his faith
  Pledged to the next new comer—
He revell'd in the warmer breath
  And richer bowers of Summer.

Then sportive Autumn claim'd by rights
  An Archer for her lover,
And even in Winter's dark cold nights
  A charm he could discover.

Her routs and balls, and fireside joy,
  For this time were his reasons—
In short, Young Love 's a gallant boy,
  That likes all times and seasons.

1829.

SONG.

Earl March look'd on his dying child,
  And smit with grief to view her—
The youth, he cried, whom I exiled,
  Shall be restored to woo her.

She 's at the window many an hour
  His coming to discover:
And *he* look'd up to Ellen's bower,
  And *she* look'd on her lover—

But ah! so pale, he knew her not,
  Though her smile on him was dwelling.
And am I then forgot—forgot?—
  It broke the heart of Ellen.

In vain he weeps, in vain he sighs,
  Her cheek is cold as ashes;
Nor love's own kiss shall wake those eyes
  To lift their silken lashes.

SONG.

WHEN NAPOLEON was flying
From the field of Waterloo,
A British soldier dying
To his brother bade adieu!

"And take," he said, "this token
To the maid that owns my faith,
With the words that I have spoken
In affection's latest breath."

Sore mourn'd the brother's heart,
When the youth beside him fell;
But the trumpet warn'd to part,
And they took a sad farewell.

There was many a friend to lose him,
For that gallant soldier sigh'd;
But the maiden of his bosom
Wept when all their tears were dried.

LINES TO JULIA M——.

SENT WITH A COPY OF THE AUTHOR'S POEMS.

Since there is magic in your look
And in your voice a witching charm,
As all our hearts consenting tell,
Enchantress, smile upon my book,
And guard its lays from hate and harm
By beauty's most resistless spell.

The sunny dew-drop of thy praise,
Young day-star of the rising time,
Shall with its odoriferous morn
Refresh my sere and wither'd bays.
Smile, and I will believe my rhyme
Shall please the beautiful unborn.

Go forth, my pictured thoughts, and rise
In traits and tints of sweeter tone,
When Julia's glance is o'er ye flung;
Glow, gladden, linger in her eyes,
And catch a magic not your own,
Read by the music of her tongue.

DRINKING SONG OF MUNICH.

Sweet Iser! were thy sunny realm
  And flowery gardens mine,
Thy waters I would shade with elm
  To prop the tender vine;
My golden flagons I would fill
With rosy draughts from every hill;
  And under every myrtle bower,
My gay companions should prolong
The laugh, the revel, and the song,
  To many an idle hour.

Like rivers crimson'd with the beam
  Of yonder planet bright,
Our balmy cups should ever stream
  Profusion of delight;
No care should touch the mellow heart,
And sad or sober none depart;
  For wine can triumph over woe,
And Love and Bacchus, brother powers,
Could build in Iser's sunny bowers
  A paradise below.

LINES

ON THE DEPARTURE OF EMIGRANTS FOR NEW SOUTH WALES.

On England's shore I saw a pensive band,
With sails unfurl'd for earth's remotest strand,
Like children parting from a mother, shed
Tears for the home that could not yield them
bread;
Grief mark'd each face receding from the view,
'Twas grief to nature honourably true.
And long, poor wanderers o'er the ecliptic deep,
The song that names but home shall make you
weep:
Oft shall ye fold your flocks by stars above
In that far world, and miss the stars ye love;
Oft when its tuneless birds scream round forlorn,
Regret the lark that gladdens England's morn,
And, giving England's names to distant scenes,
Lament that earth's extension intervenes.
But cloud not yet too long, industrious train,
Your solid good with sorrow nursed in vain:
For has the heart no interest yet as bland
As that which binds us to our native land?

The deep-drawn wish, when children crown our
hearth,
To hear the cherub-chorus of their mirth,
Undamp'd by dread that want may e'er unhouse,
Or servile misery knit those smiling brows :
The pride to rear an independent shed,
And give the lips we love unborrow'd bread:
To see a world, from shadowy forests won,
In youthful beauty wedded to the sun ;
To skirt our home with harvests widely sown,
And call the blooming landscape all our own,
Our children's heritage, in prospect long.
These are the hopes, high-minded hopes and
strong,
That beckon England's wanderers o'er the brine,
To realms where foreign constellations shine ;
Where streams from undiscover'd fountains roll,
And winds shall fan them from th' Antarctic
pole.
And what though doom'd to shores so far apart
From England's home, that ev'n the homesick
heart
Quails, thinking, ere that gulf can be recross'd,
How large a space of fleeting life is lost :
Yet there, by time, their bosoms shall be changed,
And strangers once shall cease to sigh estranged,
But jocund in the year's long sunshine roam,
That yields their sickle twice its harvest-home.

There, marking o'er his farm's expanding ring
New fleeces whiten and new fruits upspring,

The gray-hair'd swain, his grandchild sporting round,
Shall walk at eve his little empire's bound,
Emblazed with ruby vintage, ripening corn,
And verdant rampart of acacian thorn,
While, mingling with the scent his pipe exhales,
The orange grove's and fig-tree's breath prevails;
Survey with pride beyond a monarch's spoil,
His honest arm's own subjugated soil;
And, summing all the blessings God has given,
Put up his patriarchal prayer to Heaven,
That, when his bones shall here repose in peace,
The scions of his love may still increase,
And o'er a land where life has ample room,
In health and plenty innocently bloom.
  Delightful land, in wildness ev'n benign,
The glorious past is ours, the future thine!
As in a cradled Hercules, we trace
The lines of empire in thine infant face.
What nations in thy wide horizon's span
Shall teem on tracts untrodden yet by man!
What spacious cities with their spires shall gleam,
Where now the panther laps a lonely stream,
And all but brute or reptile life is dumb!
Land of the free! thy kingdom is to come,
Of states, with laws from Gothic bondage burst,
And creeds by charter'd priesthoods unaccurst:
Of navies, hoisting their emblazon'd flags,
Where shipless seas now wash unbeacon'd crags

Of hosts review'd in dazzling files and squares,
Their pennon'd trumpets breathing native airs,—
For minstrels thou shalt have of native fire,
And maids to sing the songs themselves inspire:—
Our very speech, methinks, in after-time,
Shall catch th' Ionian blandness of thy clime;
And whilst the light and luxury of thy skies
Give brighter smiles to beauteous woman's eyes,
The Arts, whose soul is love, shall all spontaneous
rise.
Untrack'd in deserts lies the marble mine,
Undug the ore that 'midst thy roofs shall shine;
Unborn the hands—but born they are to be—
Fair Australasia, that shall give to thee
Proud temple-domes, with galleries winding
high,
So vast in space, so just in symmetry,
They widen to the contemplating eye,
With colonnaded aisles in long array,
And windows that enrich the flood of day
O'er tessellated pavements, pictures fair,
And nichèd statues breathing golden air.
Nor there, whilst all that 's seen bids Fancy
swell,
Shall Music's voice refuse to seal the spell;
But choral hymns shall wake enchantment round,
And organs yield their tempests of sweet sound.
Meanwhile, ere Arts triumphant reach their
goal,
How blest the years of pastoral life shall roll!

Ev'n should some wayward hour the settler's mind
Brood sad on scenes for ever left behind,
Yet not a pang that England's name imparts
Shall touch a fibre of his children's hearts;
Bound to that native land by nature's bond,
Full little shall their wishes rove beyond
Its mountains blue, and melon-skirted streams,
Since childhood loved and dreamt of in their dreams.
How many a name, to us uncouthly wild,
Shall thrill that region's patriotic child,
And bring as sweet thoughts o'er his bosom's chords
As aught that's named in song to us affords!
Dear shall that river's margin be to him,
Where sportive first he bathed his boyish limb,
Or petted birds, still brighter than their bowers,
Or twined his tame young kangaroo with flowers.
But more magnetic yet to memory
Shall be the sacred spot, still blooming nigh,
The bower of love, where first his bosom burn'd,
And smiling passion saw its smile return'd.
Go forth and prosper then, emprising band:
May He, who in the hollow of his hand
The ocean holds, and rules the whirlwind's sweep,
Assuage its wrath, and guide you on the deep!

1828.

LINES

ON REVISITING CATHCART.

Oh! scenes of my childhood, and dear to my heart,
Ye green waving woods on the margin of Cart,
How blest in the morning of life I have stray'd,
By the stream of the vale and the grass-cover'd
glade!

Then, then every rapture was young and sincere,
Ere the sunshine of bliss was bedimm'd by a tear,
And a sweeter delight every scene seem'd to lend,
That the mansion of peace was the home of a
FRIEND.

Now the scenes of my childhood and dear to my
heart,
All pensive I visit, and sigh to depart;
Their flowers seem to languish, their beauty to
cease,
For a *stranger* inhabits the mansion of peace.

But hush'd be the sigh that untimely complains,
While Friendship and all its enchantment remains,
While it blooms like the flower of a winterless
clime,
Untainted by chance, unabated by time.

THE CHERUBS.

SUGGESTED BY AN APOLOGUE IN THE WORKS OF FRANKLIN.

Two spirits reach'd this world of ours:
The lightning's locomotive powers
  Were slow to their agility:
In broad day-light they moved incog.,
Enjoying without mist or fog,
  Entire invisibility.

The one, a simple cherub lad,
Much interest in our planet had,
  Its face was so romantic;
He couldn't persuade himself that man
Was such as heavenly rumours ran,
  A being base and frantic.

The elder spirit, wise and cool,
Brought down the youth as to a school;
  But strictly on condition,
Whatever they should see or hear,
With mortals not to interfere;
  'Twas not in their commission.

They reach'd a sovereign city proud,
Whose emperor pray'd to God aloud,

With all his people kneeling,
And priests perform'd religious rites:
"Come," said the younger of the sprites,
"This shows a pious feeling."

YOUNG SPIRIT.

"Ar'n't these a decent godly race?"

OLD SPIRIT.

"The dirtiest thieves on Nature's face."

YOUNG SPIRIT.

"But hark, what cheers they 're giving
Their emperor!—And is he a thief?"

OLD SPIRIT.

"Ay, and a cut-throat too;—in brief,
THE GREATEST SCOUNDREL LIVING."

YOUNG SPIRIT.

"But say, what were they praying for,
This people and their emperor?"

OLD SPIRIT.

"Why, for God's assistance
To help their army, late sent out:
And what that army is about,
You 'll see at no great distance."

On wings outspeeding mail or post,
Our sprites o'ertook the imperial host,

In massacres it wallow'd:
A noble nation met its hordes,
But broken fell their cause and swords,
Unfortunate, though hallow'd.

They saw a late bombarded town,
Its streets still warm with blood ran down;
Still smoked each burning rafter;
And hideously, 'midst rape and sack,
The murderer's laughter answer'd back
His prey's convulsive laughter.

They saw the captive eye the dead,
With envy of his gory bed,—
Death's quick reward of bravery:
They heard the clank of chains, and then
Saw thirty thousand bleeding men
Dragg'd manacled to slavery.

"Fie! fie!" the younger heavenly spark
Exclaim'd:—"we must have miss'd our mark,
And enter'd hell's own portals:
Earth can't be stain'd with crimes so black;
Nay, sure, we've got among a pack
Of fiends, and not of mortals?"

"No," said the elder; "no such thing:
Fiends are not fools enough to wring
The necks of one another:—
They know their interests too well:

Men fight; but every devil in hell
  Lives friendly with his brother.

And I could point you out some fellows,
On this ill-fated planet Tellus,
  In royal power that revel;
Who, at the opening of the book
Of judgment, may have cause to look
  With envy at the devil."

Name but the devil, and he'll appear.
Old Satan in a trice was near,
  With smutty face and figure:
But spotless spirits of the skies
Unseen to e'en his saucer eyes,
  Could watch the fiendish nigger.

"Halloo!" he cried, "I smell a trick:
A mortal supersedes Old Nick,
  The scourge of earth appointed:
He robs me of my trade, outrants
The blasphemy of hell, and vaunts
  Himself the Lord's anointed!

Folks make a fuss about my mischief:
D——d fools; they tamely suffer this chief
  To play his pranks unbounded."
The cherubs flew; but saw from high,
At human inhumanity,
  The devil himself astounded.

1832.

SENEX'S SOLILOQUY ON HIS YOUTHFUL IDOL.

Platonic friendship at your years,
  Says Conscience, should content ye :
Nay, name not fondness to her ears,
  The darling 's scarcely twenty.

Yes, and she 'll loathe me unforgiven,
  To dote thus out of season ;
But beauty is a beam from heaven,
  That dazzles blind our reason.

I 'll challenge Plato from the skies,
  Yes, from his spheres harmonic
To look in M—y C——'s eyes,
  And try to be Platonic.

TO SIR FRANCIS BURDETT,

ON HIS SPEECH DELIVERED IN PARLIAMENT, AUGUST 7, 1832, RESPECTING THE FOREIGN POLICY OF GREAT BRITAIN.

BURDETT, enjoy thy justly foremost fame,
Through good and ill report—through calm and storm—
For forty years the pilot of reform!
But that which shall afresh entwine thy name
With patriot laurels never to be sere,
Is that thou hast come nobly forth to chide
Our slumbering statesmen for their lack of pride—
Their flattery of Oppressors, and their fear—
When Britain's lifted finger, and her frown,
Might call the nations up, and cast their tyrants down!

Invoke the scorn—Alas! too few inherit
The scorn for despots cherish'd by our sires,
That baffled Europe's persecuting fires,
And shelter'd helpless states!—Recall that spirit,
And conjure back Old England's haughty mind—
Convert the men who waver now, and pause
Between their love of self and humankind;

And move, Amphion-like, those hearts of stone—
The hearts that have been deaf to Poland's dying
groan!

Tell them, we hold the Rights of Man too dear,
To bless ourselves with lonely freedom blest;
But could we hope, with sole and selfish breast,
To breathe untroubled Freedom's atmosphere?—
Suppose we wish'd it? England could not stand
A lone oasis in the desert ground
Of Europe's slavery; from the waste around
Oppression's fiery blast and whirling sand
Would reach and scathe us? No; it may not be:
Britannia and the world conjointly must be free!

Burdett, demand why Britons send abroad
Soft greetings to th' infanticidal Czar,
The Bear on Poland's babes that wages war.
Once, we are told, a mother's shriek o'erawed
A lion, and he dropt her lifted child;
But Nicholas, whom neither God nor law,
Nor Poland's shrieking mothers, overawe,
Outholds to us his friendship's gory clutch:
Shrink, Britain—shrink, my king and country,
from the touch!

He prays to Heaven for England's king, he says—
And dares he to the God of mercy kneel,
Besmear'd with massacres from head to heel?
No; Moloch is his God—to him he prays

And if his weird-like prayers had power to bring
An influence, their power would be to curse.
His hate is baleful, but his love is worse—
A serpent's slaver deadlier than its sting!
Oh, feeble statesmen—ignominious times,
That lick the tyrant's feet, and smile upon his crimes!

1832.

ODE TO THE GERMANS.

The spirit of Britannia
Invokes, across the main,
Her sister Allemannia
To burst the Tyrant's chain:
By our kindred blood, she cries,
Rise, Allemannians, rise,
And hallow'd thrice the band
Of our kindred hearts shall be,
When your land shall be the land
Of the free—of the free!

With Freedom's lion-banner
Britannia rules the waves;
Whilst your BROAD STONE OF HONOUR [1]

[1] Ehrenbreitstein signifies, in German, "*the broad stone of honour.*"

Is still the camp of slaves.
For shame, for glory's sake,
Wake, Allemannians, wake,
And thy tyrants now that whelm
Half the world shall quail and flee,
When your realm shall be the realm
Of the free—of the free!

MARS owes to you his thunder[1]
That shakes the battle field,
Yet to break your bonds asunder
No martial bolt has peal'd.
Shall the laurell'd land of art
Wear shackles on her heart?
No! the clock ye framed to tell,
By its sound, the march of time;
Let it clang oppression's knell
O'er your clime—o'er your clime!

The press's magic letters,
That blessing ye brought forth,—
Behold! it lies in fetters
On the soil that gave it birth:
But the trumpet must be heard,
And the charger must be spurr'd;
For your father Armin's Sprite
Calls down from heaven, that ye
Shall gird you for the fight,
And be free!—and be free!

1831.

[1] Germany invented gunpowder, clock-making, and printing.

LINES

ON A PICTURE OF A GIRL IN THE ATTITUDE OF PRAYER.

By the Artist Gruse, in the possession of Lady Stepney.

WAS man e'er doom'd that beauty made
By mimic heart should haunt him;
Like Orpheus, I adore a shade,
And dote upon a phantom.

Thou maid that in my inmost thought
Art fancifully sainted,
Why liv'st thou not—why art thou nought
But canvas sweetly painted?

Whose looks seem lifted to the skies,
Too pure for love of mortals—
As if they drew angelic eyes
To greet thee at heaven's portals.

Yet loveliness has here no grace,
Abstracted or ideal—
Art ne'er but from a living face
Drew looks so seeming real.

What wert thou, maid?—thy life—thy name.
  Oblivion hides in mystery;
Though from thy face my heart could frame
  A long romantic history.

Transported to thy time I seem,
  Though dust thy coffin covers—
And hear the songs, in fancy's dream,
  Of thy devoted lovers.

How witching must have been thy breath—
  How sweet the living charmer—
Whose every semblance after death
  Can make the heart grow warmer!

Adieu, the charms that vainly move
  My soul in their possession—
That prompt my lips to speak of love,
  Yet rob them of expression.

Yet thee, dear picture, to have praised
  Was but a poet's duty;
And shame to him that ever gazed
  Impassive on thy beauty.

1830.

LINES

ON THE VIEW FROM ST. LEONARD'S.

Hail to thy face and odours, glorious Sea!
'Twere thanklessness in me to bless thee not,
Great beauteous Being! in whose breath and smile
My heart beats calmer, and my very mind
Inhales salubrious thoughts. How welcomer
Thy murmurs than the murmurs of the world!
Though like the world thou fluctuatest, thy din
To me is peace, thy restlessness repose.
Ev'n gladly I exchange yon spring-green lanes
With all the darling field-flowers in their prime,
And gardens haunted by the nightingale's
Long trills and gushing ecstasies of song,
For these wild headlands, and the sea-mew's clang—

With thee beneath my windows, pleasant Sea,
I long not to o'erlook earth's fairest glades
And green savannahs—Earth has not a plain
So boundless or so beautiful as thine;
The eagle's vision cannot take it in:
The lightning's wing, too weak to sweep its space,

Sinks half-way o'er it like a wearied bird:
It is the mirror of the stars, where all
Their hosts within the concave firmament,
Gay marching to the music of the spheres,
Can see themselves at once.
Nor on the stage
Of rural landscape are there lights and shades
Of more harmonious dance and play than thine.
How vividly this moment brightens forth,
Between gray parallel and leaden breadths,
A belt of hues that stripes thee many a league,
Flush'd like the rainbow, or the ringdove's neck,
And giving to the glancing sea-bird's wing
The semblance of a meteor.
Mighty Sea!
Cameleon-like thou changest, but there's love
In all thy change, and constant sympathy
With yonder Sky—thy Mistress; from her brow
Thou tak'st thy moods and wear'st her colours on
Thy faithful bosom; morning's milky white,
Noon's sapphire, or the saffron glow of eve;
And all thy balmier hours, fair Element,
Have such divine complexion—crisped smiles,
Luxuriant heavings and sweet whisperings,
That little is the wonder Love's own Queen
From thee of old was fabled to have sprung—
Creation's common! which no human power
Can parcel or inclose; the lordliest floods
And cataracts that the tiny hands of man
Can tame, conduct, or bound, are drops of dew

To thee that could'st subdue the Earth itself,
And brook'st commandment from the heavens [alone
For marshalling thy waves—
Yet, potent Sea!
How placidly thy moist lips speak ev'n now
Along yon sparkling shingles. Who can be
So fanciless as to feel no gratitude
That power and grandeur can be so serene,
Soothing the home-bound navy's peaceful way,
And rocking ev'n the fisher's little bark
As gently as a mother rocks her child?—

The inhabitants of other worlds behold
Our orb more lucid for thy spacious share
On earth's rotundity; and is he not
A blind worm in the dust, great Deep, the man
Who sees not or who seeing has no joy
In thy magnificence? What though thou art
Unconscious and material, thou canst reach
The inmost immaterial mind's recess,
And with thy tints and motion stir its chords
To music, like the light on Memnon's lyre!

The Spirit of the Universe in thee
Is visible; thou hast in thee the life—
The eternal, graceful, and majestic life
Of nature, and the natural human heart
Is therefore bound to thee with holy love.
Earth has her gorgeous towns; the earth-circling sea

Has spires and mansions more amusive still—
Men's volant homes that measure liquid space
On wheel or wing. The chariot of the land
With pain'd and panting steeds and clouds of dust
Has no sight-gladdening motion like these fair
Careerers with the foam beneath their bows,
Whose streaming ensigns charm the waves by day,
Whose carols and whose watch-bells cheer the night,
Moor'd as they cast the shadows of their masts
In long array, or hither flit and yond
Mysteriously with slow and crossing lights,
Like spirits on the darkness of the deep.

There is a magnet-like attraction in
These waters to the imaginative power
That links the viewless with the visible,
And pictures things unseen. To realms beyond
Yon highway of the world my fancy flies,
When by her tall and triple mast we know
Some noble voyager that has to woo
The trade-winds and to stem the ecliptic surge.
The coral groves—the shores of conch and pearl,
Where she will cast her anchor and reflect
Her cabin-window lights on warmer waves,
And under planets brighter than our own:
The nights of palmy isles, that she will see
Lit boundless by the fire-fly—all the smells

Of tropic fruits that will regale her—all
The pomp of nature, and the inspiriting
Varieties of life she has to greet,
Come swarming o'er the meditative mind.

True, to the dream of Fancy, Ocean has
His darker tints; but where 's the element
That chequers not its usefulness to man
With casual terror? Scathes not Earth sometimes
Her children with Tartarean fires, or shakes
Their shrieking cities, and, with one last clang
Of bells for their own ruin, strews them flat
As riddled ashes—silent as the grave?
Walks not Contagion on the Air itself?
I should—old Ocean's Saturnalian days
And roaring nights of revelry and sport
With wreck and human woe—be loth to sing;
For they are few, and all their ills weigh light
Against his sacred usefulness, that bids
Our pensile globe revolve in purer air.
Here Morn and Eve with blushing thanks receive
Their freshening dews, gay fluttering breezes cool
Their wings to fan the brow of fever'd climes,
And here the Spring dips down her emerald urn
For showers to glad the earth.
Old Ocean was
Infinity of ages ere we breathed
Existence—and he will be beautiful

When all the living world that sees him now
Shall roll unconscious dust around the sun.
Quelling from age to age the vital throb
In human hearts, Death shall not subjugate
The pulse that swells in *his* stupendous breast,
Or interdict his minstrelsy to sound
In thundering concert with the quiring winds;
But long as Man to parent Nature owns
Instinctive homage, and in times beyond
The power of thought to reach, bard after bard
Shall sing thy glory, BEATIFIC SEA.

1831.

Campbell, who was peculiarly impartial in judging of the merit of his own productions, more than once expressed an opinion that these lines were his ***best***, as being the most *matured.*

THE DEAD EAGLE.

WRITTEN AT ORAN.

FALL'N as he is, this king of birds still seems
Like royalty in ruins. Though his eyes
Are shut, that look undazzled on the sun,
He was the sultan of the sky, and earth
Paid tribute to his eyry. It was perch'd
Higher than human conqueror ever built
His banner'd fort. Where Atlas' top looks o'er
Zahara's desert to the equator's line:
From thence the winged despot mark'd his prey,
Above th' encampments of the Bedouins, ere
Their watchfires were extinct, or camels knelt
To take their loads, or horsemen scour'd the plain,
And there he dried his feathers in the dawn,
Whilst yet th' unwaken'd world was dark below.

There 's such a charm in natural strength and
power,
That human fancy has for ever paid
Poetic homage to the bird of Jove.
Hence, 'neath his image, Rome array'd her turms
And cohorts for the conquest of the world.
And figuring his flight, the mind is fill'd

With thoughts that mock the pride of wingless
man.
True the carr'd aeronaut can mount as high ;
But what 's the triumph of his volant art ?
A rash intrusion on the realms of air.
His helmless vehicle, a silken toy,
A bubble bursting in the thunder-cloud ;
His course has no volition, and he drifts
The passive plaything of the winds. Not such
Was this proud bird : he clove the adverse storm,
And cuff'd it with his wings. He stopp'd his
flight
As easily as the Arab reins his steed,
And stood at pleasure 'neath Heaven's zenith,
like
A lamp suspended from its azure dome,
Whilst underneath him the world's mountains lay
Like mole hills, and her streams like lucid threads.
Then downward, faster than a falling star,
He near'd the earth, until his shape distinct
Was blackly shadow'd on the sunny ground ;
And deeper terror hush'd the wilderness,
To hear his nearer whoop. Then, up again
He soar'd and wheel'd. There was an air of scorn
In all his movements, whether he threw round
His crested head to look behind him ; or
Lay vertical and sportively display'd
The inside whiteness of his wing declined,
In gyres and undulations full of grace,
An object beautifying Heaven itself.

He—reckless who was victor, and above
The hearing of their guns—saw fleets engaged
In flaming combat. It was nought to him
What carnage, Moor or Christian, strew'd their
decks.
But if his intellect had match'd his wings,
Methinks he would have scorn'd man's vaunted
power
To plough the deep ; his pinions bore him down
To Algiers the warlike, or the coral groves,
That blush beneath the green of Bona's waves ;
And traversed in an hour a wider space
Than yonder gallant ship, with all her sails
Wooing the winds, can cross from morn till eve.
His bright eyes were his compass, earth his chart,
His talons anchor'd on the stormiest cliff,
And on the very light-house rock he perch'd,
When winds churn'd white the waves.
The earthquake's self
Disturb'd not him that memorable day,
When, o'er yon table-land, where Spain had built,
Cathedrals, cannon'd forts, and palaces,
A palsy stroke of Nature shook Oran,
Turning her city to a sepulchre,
And strewing into rubbish all her homes ;
Amidst whose traceable foundations now,
Of streets and squares, the hyæna hides himself.
That hour beheld him fly as careless o'er
The stifled shrieks of thousands buried quick,
As lately when he pounced the speckled snake,

Coil'd in yon mallows and wide nettle fields
That mantle o'er the dead old Spanish town.

Strange is the imagination's dread delight
In objects link'd with danger, death and pain!
Fresh from the luxuries of polish'd life,
The echo of these wilds enchanted me;
And my heart beat with joy when first I heard
A lion's roar come down the Lybian wind,
Across yon long, wide, lonely inland lake,
Where boat ne'er sails from homeless shore to
shore.
And yet Numidia's landscape has its spots
Of pastoral pleasantness—though far between,
The village planted near the Maraboot's
Round roof has aye its feathery palm trees
Pair'd, for in solitude they bear no fruits.
Here nature's hues all harmonize—fields white
With alasum, or blue with bugloss—banks
Of glossy fennel, blent with tulips wild,
And sunflowers, like a garment prankt with gold;
Acres and miles of opal asphodel,
Where sports and couches the black-eyed gazelle.
Here, too, the air 's harmonious—deep-toned doves
Coo to the fife-like carol of the lark;
And when they cease, the holy nightingale
Winds up his long, long shakes of ecstasy,
With notes that seem but the protracted sounds
Of glassy runnels bubbling over rocks.

SONG.

To Love in my heart, I exclaim'd t'other morning,
Thou hast dwelt here too long, little lodger, take
 warning;
Thou shalt tempt me no more from my life's sober
 duty,
To go gadding, bewitch'd by the young eyes of
 beauty.
 For weary 's the wooing, ah, weary!
When an old man will have a young dearie.

The god left my heart, at its surly reflections,
But came back on pretext of some sweet recol-
 lections,
And he made me forget what I ought to remember,
That the rose-bud of June cannot bloom in
 November.
 Ah! Tom, 'tis all o'er with thy gay days—
Write psalms, and not songs for the ladies.

But time 's been so far from my wisdom enriching,
That the longer I live, beauty seems more be-
 witching;

And the only new lore my experience traces,
Is to find fresh enchantment in magical faces.
How weary is wisdom, how weary!
When one sits by a smiling young dearie!

And should she be wroth that my homage pursues her,
I will turn and retort on my lovely accuser;
Who's to blame, that my heart by your image is haunted—
It is you, the enchantress—not I, the enchanted,
Would you have me behave more discreetly,
Beauty, look not so killingly sweetly.

LINES

WRITTEN IN A BLANK LEAF OF LA PEROUSE'S VOYAGES.

Loved Voyager! his pages had a zest
More sweet than fiction to my wondering breast,
When, rapt in fancy, many a boyish day
I track'd his wanderings o'er the watery way,
Roam'd round the Aleutian isles in waking dreams,
Or pluck'd the *fleur-de-lys* by Jesso's streams—
Or gladly leap'd on that far Tartar strand,
Where Europe's anchor ne'er had bit the sand,
Where scarce a roving wild tribe cross'd the plain,
Or human voice broke nature's silent reign;
But vast and grassy deserts feed the bear,
And sweeping deer-herds dread no hunter's snare.
Such young delight his real records brought,
His truth so touch'd romantic springs of thought,
That all my after-life—his fate and fame
Entwined romance with La Perouse's name.—
Fair were his ships, expert his gallant crews,
And glorious was th' emprise of La Perouse,—
Humanely glorious! Men will weep for him,
When many a guilty martial fame is dim:
He plough'd the deep to bind no captive's chain—

Pursued no rapine—strew'd no wreck with slain;
And, save that in the deep themselves lie low,
His heroes pluck'd no wreath from human woe.
'Twas his the earth's remotest bound to scan,
Conciliating with gifts barbaric man—
Enrich the world's contemporaneous mind,
And amplify the picture of mankind.
Far on the vast Pacific—'midst those isles,
O'er which the earliest morn of Asia smiles,
He sounded and gave charts to many a shore
And gulf of Ocean new to nautic lore;
Yet he that led Discovery o'er the wave,
Still fills himself an undiscover'd grave.
He came not back,—Conjecture's cheek grew pale,
Year after year—in no propitious gale,
His lilied banner held its homeward way,
And Science sadden'd at her martyr's stay.
An age elapsed—no wreck told where or when
The chief went down with all his gallant men,
Or whether by the storm and wild sea flood
He perish'd, or by wilder men of blood—
The shuddering Fancy only guess'd his doom,
And Doubt to Sorrow gave but deeper gloom.
An age elapsed—when men were dead or gray,
Whose hearts had mourn'd him in their youthful day;
Fame traced on Mannicolo's shore at last,
The boiling surge had mounted o'er his mast.
The islemen told of some surviving men,
But Christian eyes beheld them ne'er again.

Sad bourne of all his toils—with all his band—
To sleep, wreck'd, shroudless, on a savage strand!
Yet what is all that fires a hero's scorn
Of death?—the hope to live in hearts unborn:
Life to the brave is not its fleeting breath,
But worth—foretasting fame, that follows death.
That worth had La Perouse—that meed he won;
He sleeps—his life's long stormy watch is done.
In the great deep, whose boundaries and space
He measured, Fate ordain'd his resting-place;
But bade his fame, like th' Ocean rolling o'er
His relics—visit every earthly shore.
Fair Science on that Ocean's azure robe
Still writes his name in picturing the globe,
And paints—(what fairer wreath could glory twine?)
His watery course—a world-encircling line.

1831.

TO

WILLIAM BEATTIE, M.D.,

IN REMEMBRANCE

OF LONG-SUBSISTING AND MUTUAL FRIENDSHIP,

THE POEM "GLENCOE"

AND THE OTHER PIECES THAT FOLLOW

IN THIS VOLUME,

ARE INSCRIBED

BY

THE AUTHOR.

LONDON,
December, 1842.

THE

PILGRIM OF GLENCOE.

THE PILGRIM OF GLENCOE

I RECEIVED the substance of the tradition on which this Poem is founded, in the first instance, from a friend in London, who wrote to Matthew N. Macdonald, Esq., of Edinburgh. He had the kindness to send me a circumstantial account of the tradition; and that gentleman's knowledge of the Highlands, as well as his particular acquaintance with the district of Glencoe, leave me no doubt of the incident having really happened. I have not departed from the main facts of the tradition as reported to me by Mr. Macdonald; only I have endeavoured to colour the personages of the story, and to make them as distinctive as possible.

THE sunset sheds a horizontal smile
O'er Highland frith and Hebridean isle,
While, gay with gambols of its finny shoals,
The glancing wave rejoices as it rolls
With streamer'd busses, that distinctly shine
All downward, pictured in the glassy brine;
Whose crews, with faces brightening in the sun,
Keep measure with their oars, and all in one
Strike up th' old Gaelic song.—Sweep, rowers, sweep!
The fisher's glorious spoils are in the deep.

Day sinks—but twilight owes the traveller soon,
To reach his bourne, a round unclouded moon,

Bespeaking long undarken'd hours of time ;
False hope—the Scots are steadfast—not their
clime.
A war-worn soldier from the western land
Seeks Cona's vale by Ballihoula's strand;
The vale, by eagle-haunted cliffs o'erhung,
Where Fingal fought and Ossian's harp was
strung—
Our veteran's forehead, bronzed on sultry plains,
Had stood the brunt of thirty fought campaigns ;
He well could vouch the sad romance of wars,
And count the dates of battles by his scars ;
For he had served where o'er and o'er again
Britannia's oriflamme had lit the plain
Of glory—and victorious stamp'd her name
On Oudenarde's and Blenheim's fields of fame.
Nine times in battle-field his blood had stream'd,
Yet vivid still his veteran blue eye gleam'd ;
Full well he bore his knapsack—unoppress'd,
And march'd with soldier-like erected crest :
Nor sign of ev'n loquacious age he wore,
Save when he told his life's adventures o'er ;
Some tired of these; for terms to him were
dear
Too tactical by far for vulgar ear ;
As when he talk'd of rampart and ravine,
And trenches fenced with gabion and fascine—
But when his theme possess'd him all and whole,
He scorn'd proud puzzling words and warm'd the
soul ;

Hush'd groups hung on his lips with fond surprise,
That sketch'd old scenes—like pictures to their eyes:—
The wide war-plain, with banners glowing bright,
And bayonets to the furthest stretch of sight;
The pause, more dreadful than the peal to come
From volleys blazing at the beat of drum—
Till all the field of thundering lines became
Two level and confronted sheets of flame.
Then to the charge, when Marlbro's hot pursuit
Trode France's gilded lilies underfoot;
He came and kindled—and with martial lung
Would chant the very march their trumpets sung.—

Th' old soldier hoped, ere evening's light should fail,
To reach a home, south-east of Cona's vale;
But looking at Bennevis, capp'd with snow,
He saw its mists come curling down below,
And spread white darkness o'er the sunset glow;—
Fast rolling like tempestuous Ocean's spray,
Or clouds from troops in battle's fiery day—
So dense, his quarry 'scaped the falcon's sight,
The owl alone exulted, hating light.

Benighted thus our pilgrim groped his ground,
Half 'twixt the river's and the cataract's sound.
At last a sheep-dog's bark inform'd his ear
Some human habitation might be near;

Anon sheep-bleatings rose from rock to rock,—
'Twas Luath hounding to their fold the flock.
Ere long the cock's obstreperous clarion rang,
And next, a maid's sweet voice, that spinning sang
At last amidst the green-sward (gladsome sight!)
A cottage stood, with straw-roof golden bright.

He knock'd, was welcomed in; none ask'd his name,
Nor whither he was bound nor whence he came;
But he was beckon'd to the stranger's seat,
Right side the chimney fire of blazing peat.
Blest Hospitality makes not her home
In wallèd parks and castellated dome;
She flies the city's needy greedy crowd,
And shuns still more the mansions of the proud
The balm of savage or of simple life,
A wild flower cut by culture's polish'd knife!

The house, no common sordid shieling cot,
Spoke inmates of a comfortable lot.
The Jacobite white rose festoon'd their door;
The windows sash'd and glàzed, the oaken floor,
The chimney graced with antlers of the deer,
The rafters hung with meat for winter cheer,
And all the mansion, indicated plain
Its master a superior shepherd swain.

Their supper came—the table soon was spread
With eggs and milk and cheese and barley bread.

The family were three—a father hoar,
Whose age you'd guess at seventy years or
more,
His son look'd fifty—cheerful like her lord
His comely wife presided at the board;
All three had that peculiar courteous grace
Which marks the meanest of the Highland race;
Warm hearts that burn alike in weal and woe,
As if the north-wind fann'd their bosoms' glow!
But wide unlike their souls: old Norman's eye
Was proudly savage ev'n in courtesy.
His sinewy shoulders—each, though aged and
lean,
Broad as the curl'd Herculean head between,—
His scornful lip, his eyes of yellow fire,
And nostrils that dilated quick with ire,
With ever downward-slanting shaggy brows,
Mark'd the old lion you would dread to rouse.

Norman, in truth, had led his earlier life
In raids of red revenge and feudal strife;
Religious duty in revenge he saw,
Proud Honour's right and Nature's honest law;
First in the charge and foremost in pursuit,
Long-breath'd, deep-chested, and in speed of foot
A match for stags—still fleeter when the prey
Was man, in persecution's evil day;
Cheer'd to that chase by brutal bold Dundee,
No Highland hound had lapp'd more blood than
he.

Oft had he changed the covenanter's breath
From howls of psalmody to howls of death;
And though long bound to peace, it irk'd him still
His dirk had ne'er one hated foe to kill.

Yet Norman had fierce virtues, that would mock
Cold-blooded tories of the modern stock
Who starve the breadless poor with fraud and cant;—
He slew and saved them from the pangs of want.
Nor was his solitary lawless charm
Mere dauntlessness of soul and strength of arm;
He had his moods of kindness now and then,
And feasted ev'n well-manner'd lowland men
Who blew not up his Jacobitish flame,
Nor prefaced with "pretender" Charles's name.
Fierce, but by sense and kindness not unwon,
He loved, respected ev'n, his wiser son;
And brook'd from him expostulations sage,
When all advisers else were spurn'd with rage.

Far happier times had moulded Ronald's mind,
By nature too of more sagacious kind.
His breadth of brow, and Roman shape of chin,
Squared well with the firm man that reign'd within.
Contemning strife as childishness, he stood
With neighbours on kind terms of neighbourhood,
And whilst his father's anger nought avail'd,
His rational remonstrance never fail'd.

Full skilfully he managed farm and fold,
Wrote, cipher'd, profitably bought and sold;
And, bless'd with pastoral leisure, deeply took
Delight to be inform'd, by speech or book,
Of that wide world beyond his mountain home,
Where oft his curious fancy loved to roam.
Oft while his faithful dog ran round his flock,
He read long hours when summer warm'd the rock:
Guests who could tell him aught were welcomed warm,
Ev'n pedlars' news had to his mind a charm;
That like an intellectual magnet-stone
Drew truth from judgments simpler than his own,

His soul's proud instinct sought not to enjoy
Romantic fictions, like a minstrel boy;
Truth, standing on her solid square, from youth
He worshipp'd—stern uncompromising truth.
His goddess kindlier smiled on him, to find
A votary of her light in land so blind;
She bade majestic History unroll
Broad views of public welfare to his soul,
Until he look'd on clannish feuds and foes
With scorn, as on the wars of kites and crows;
Whilst doubts assail'd him o'er and o'er again,
If men were made for kings or kings for men.
At last, to Norman's horror and dismay,
He flat denied the Stuarts' right to sway.
No blow-pipe ever whiten'd furnace fire,
Quick as these words lit up his father's ire;

Who envied even old Abraham for his faith,
Ordain'd to put his only son to death.
He started up—in such a mood of soul
The white bear bites his showman's stirring pole;
He danced too, and brought out, with snarl and
howl,
"O Dia! Dia!" and, "Dioul! Dioul!"[1]
But sense foils fury—as the blowing whale
Spouts, bleeds, and dyes the waves without
avail—
Wears out the cable's length that makes him fast,
But, worn himself, comes up harpoon'd at last—
E'en so, devoid of sense, succumbs at length
Mere strength of zeal to intellectual strength.
His son's close logic so perplex'd his pate,
Th' old hero rather shunn'd than sought debate;
Exhausting his vocabulary's store
Of oaths and nicknames, he could say no more,
But tapp'd his mull,[2] roll'd mutely in his chair,
Or only whistled Killiecrankie's air.

Witch-legends Ronald scorn'd—ghost, kelpie,
wraith,
And all the trumpery of vulgar faith;
Grave matrons ev'n were shock'd to hear him
slight
Authenticated facts of second-sight—

[1] God and the devil—a favourite ejaculation of Highland saints.

[2] Snuff-horn.

Yet never flinch'd his mockery to confound
The brutal superstition reigning round.
Reserved himself, still Ronald loved to scan
Men's natures—and he liked the old hearty man;
So did the partner of his heart and life—
Who pleased her Ronald, ne'er displeased his
wife.
His sense, 'tis true, compared with Norman's son,
Was commonplace—his tales too long outspun:
Yet Allan Campbell's sympathizing mind
Had held large intercourse with humankind;
Seen much, and gaily graphically drew
The men of every country, clime, and hue;
Nor ever stoop'd, though soldier-like his strain,
To ribaldry of mirth or oath profane.
All went harmonious till the guest began
To talk about his kindred, chief and clan,
And, with his own biography engross'd,
Mark'd not the changed demeanour of each host;
Nor how old choleric Norman's cheek became
Flush'd at the Campbell and Breadalbane name.
Assigning, heedless of impending harm,
Their steadfast silence to his story's charm,
He touch'd a subject perilous to touch—
Saying, "'Midst this well-known vale I wonder'd
much
To lose my way. In boyhood, long ago,
I roam'd, and loved each pathway of Glencoe;
Trapp'd leverets, pluck'd wild berries on its braes,
And fish'd along its banks long summer days.

But times grew stormy—bitter feuds arose,
Our clan was merciless to prostrate foes.
I never palliated my chieftain's blame,
But mourn'd the sin, and redden'd for the shame
Of that foul morn (Heaven blot it from the year!)
Whose shapes and shrieks still haunt my dreaming
ear.
What could I do? a serf—Glenlyon's page,
A soldier sworn at nineteen years of age;
T' have breathed one grieved remonstrance to our
chief,
The pit or gallows[1] would have cured my grief.
Forced, passive as the musket in my hand,
I march'd—when, feigning royalty's command,
Against the clan Macdonald, Stair's lord
Sent forth exterminating fire and sword;
And troops at midnight through the vale defiled,
Enjoin'd to slaughter woman, man, and child.
My clansmen many a year had cause to dread
The curse that day entail'd upon their head;
Glenlyon's self confess'd th' avenging spell—
I saw it light on him.
"It so befell:—
A soldier from our ranks to death was brought,
By sentence deem'd too dreadful for his fault;
All was prepared—the coffin and the cart
Stood near twelve muskets, levell'd at his heart.

1 To hang their vassals, or starve them to death in a dungeon, was a privilege of the Highland chiefs who had hereditary jurisdictions.

The chief, whose breast for ruth had still some
room,
Obtain'd reprieve a day before his doom;—
But of the awarded boon surmised no breath.
The sufferer knelt, blindfolded waiting death,—
And met it. Though Glenlyon had desired
The musketeers to watch before they fired;
If from his pocket they should see he drew
A handkerchief—their volley should ensue;
But if he held a paper in its place,
It should be hail'd the sign of pardoning grace:—
He, in a fatal moment's absent fit,
Drew forth the handkerchief, and not the writ;
Wept o'er the corpse and wrung his hands in woe,
Crying, 'Here 's thy curse again—Glencoe!
Glencoe!'"
Though thus his guest spoke feelings just and
clear,
The cabin's patriarch lent impatient ear;
Wroth that, beneath his roof, a living man
Should boast the swine-blood of the Campbell
clan;
He hasten'd to the door—call'd out his son
To follow; walk'd a space, and thus begun:—
"You have not, Ronald, at this day to learn
The oath I took beside my father's cairn,
When you were but a babe a twelvemonth born;
Sworn on my dirk—by all that 's sacred, sworn
To be revenged for blood that cries to Heaven—
Blood unforgiveable, and unforgiven:

But never power, *since then*, have I possess'd
To plant my dagger in a Campbell's breast.
Now, here 's a self-accusing partisan,
Steep'd in the slaughter of Macdonald's clan;
I scorn his civil speech and sweet-lipp'd show
Of pity—he is still our house's foe:
I 'll perjure not myself—but sacrifice
The caitiff ere to-morrow 's sun arise.
Stand! hear me—you 're my son, the deed is just;
And if I say—it must be done—it must:
A debt of honour which my clansmen crave,
Their very dead demand it from the grave."
Conjuring then their ghosts, he humbly pray'd
Their patience till the blood-debt should be paid.
But Ronald stopp'd him.—" Sir, Sir, do not dim
Your honour by a moment's angry whim;
Your soul 's too just and generous, were you cool,
To act at once th' assassin and the fool.
Bring me the men on whom revenge is due,
And I will dirk them willingly as you!
But all the real authors of that black
Old deed are gone—you cannot bring them back.
And this poor guest, 'tis palpable to judge,
In all his life ne'er bore our clan a grudge;
Dragg'd when a boy against his will to share
That massacre, he loath'd the foul affair.
Think, if your harden'd heart be conscience-proof,
To stab a stranger underneath your roof!
One who has broken bread within your gate—
Reflect—before reflection comes too late,—

Such ugly consequences there may be
As judge and jury, rope and gallows-tree.
The days of dirking snugly are gone by,
Where could you hide the body privily
When search is made for 't?"
"Plunge it in yon flood,
That Campbells crimson'd with our kindred blood."
"Ay, but the corpse may float—"
"Pshaw! dead men tell
No tales—nor will it float if leaded well.
I am determined!"—What could Ronald do?
No house within ear-reach of his halloo,
Though that would but have publish'd household shame,
He temporized with wrath he could not tame,
And said "Come in, till night put off the deed,
And ask a few more questions ere he bleed."
They enter'd; Norman with portentous air
Strode to a nook behind the stranger's chair,
And, speaking nought, sat grimly in the shade,
With dagger in his clutch beneath his plaid.
His son's own plaid, should Norman pounce his prey,
Was coil'd thick round his arm, to turn away
Or blunt the dirk. He purposed leaving free
The door, and giving Allan time to flee,
Whilst he should wrestle with, (no safe emprise,)
His father's maniac strength and giant size.
Meanwhile he could nowise communicate
The impending peril to his anxious mate;

But she, convinced no trifling matter now
Disturb'd the wonted calm of Ronald's brow,
Divined too well the cause of gloom that lower'd,
And sat with speechless terror overpower'd,
Her face was pale, so lately blithe and bland,
The stocking knitting-wire shook in her hand.
But Ronald and the guest resumed their thread
Of converse, still its theme that day of dread.
" Much," said the veteran, " much as I bemoan
That deed, when half a hundred years have flown,
Still on one circumstance I can reflect
That mitigates the dreadful retrospect.
A mother with her child before us flew,
I had the hideous mandate to pursue;
But swift of foot, outspeeding bloodier men,
I chased, o'ertook her in the winding glen,
And show'd her palpitating, where to save
Herself and infant in a secret cave;
Nor left them till I saw that they could mock
Pursuit and search within that sheltering rock."
" Heavens!" Ronald cried, in accents gladly wild,
" That woman was my mother—I the child!
Of you unknown by name she late and air [1]
Spoke, wept, and ever bless'd you in her prayer,
Ev'n to her death; describing you withal
A well-look'd florid youth, blue-eyed and tall."
They rose, exchanged embrace: the old lion then
Upstarted, metamorphosed, from his den;

[1] Scotch for late and early.

Saying, "Come and make thy home with us for life,
Heaven-sent preserver of my child and wife.
I fear thou 'rt poor, that Hanoverian thing
Rewards his soldiers ill."—"God save the king!"
With hand upon his heart old Allan said,
"I wear his uniform, I eat his bread,
And whilst I 've tooth to bite a cartridge, all
For him and Britain's fame I 'll stand or fall."
"Bravo!" cried Ronald. "I commend your zeal,"
Quoth Norman, "and I see your heart is leal;
But I have pray'd my soul may never thrive
If thou should'st leave this house of ours alive.
Nor shalt thou; in this home protract thy breath
Of easy life, nor leave it till thy death."

The following morn arose serene as glass,
And red Bennevis shone like molten brass;
While sunrise open'd flowers with gentle force,
The guest and Ronald walk'd in long discourse.
"Words fail me," Allan said, "to thank aright
Your father's kindness shown me yesternight;
Yet scarce I 'd wish my latest days to spend
A fireside fixture with the dearest friend:
Besides, I 've but a fortnight's furlough now,
To reach Macallin More,[1] beyond Lochawe.

[1] The Duke of Argyle.

I 'd fain memorialize the powers that be,
To deign remembrance of my wounds and me;
My life-long service never bore the brand
Of sentence—lash—disgrace or reprimand.
And so I 've written, though in meagre style,
A long petition to his Grace Argyle;
I mean on reaching Innerara's shore,
To leave it safe within his castle door."
" Nay," Ronald said, " the letter that you bear
Entrust it to no lying varlet's care;
But say a soldier of King George demands
Access, to leave it in the Duke's own hands.
But show me, first, the epistle to your chief,
'Tis nought, unless succinctly clear and brief;
Great men have no great patience when they read,
And long petitions spoil the cause they plead."

That day saw Ronald from the field full soon
Return; and when they all had dined at noon,
He conn'd the old man's memorial—lopp'd its length,
And gave it style, simplicity, and strength;
'Twas finish'd in an hour—and in the next
Transcribed by Allan in perspicuous text.
At evening, he and Ronald shared once more
A long and pleasant walk by Cona's shore.
" I 'd press you," quoth his host—(" I need not say
How warmly) ever more with us to stay;
But Charles intends, 'tis said, in these same parts
To try the fealty of our Highland hearts.

'Tis my belief, that he and all his line
Have—saving to be hang'd—no right divine;
From whose mad enterprise can only flow
To thousands slaughter, and to myriads woe.
Yet have they stirr'd my father's spirit sore,
He flints his pistols—whets his old claymore—
And longs as ardently to join the fray
As boy to dance who hears the bagpipe play.
Though calm one day, the next, disdaining rule,
He 'd gore your-red coat like an angry bull:
I told him, and he own'd it might be so,
Your tempers never could in concert flow.
But 'Mark,' he added, 'Ronald! from our door
Let not this guest depart forlorn and poor;
Let not your souls the niggardness evince
Of lowland pedlar, or of German prince;
He gave you life—then feed him as you 'd feed
Your very father were he cast in need.'
He gave—you 'll find it by your bed to-night,
A leathern purse of crowns, all sterling bright:
You see I do you kindness not by stealth.
My wife—no advocate of squandering wealth—
Vows that it would be parricide, or worse,
Should we neglect you—here 's a silken purse,
Some golden pieces through the network shine,
'Tis proffer'd to you from her heart and mine.
But come! no foolish delicacy, no!
We own, but cannot cancel what we owe—
This sum shall duly reach you once a year."
Poor Allan's furrow'd face and flowing tear

Confess'd sensations which he could not speak.
Old Norman bade him farewell kindly meek.

At morn, the smiling dame rejoiced to pack
With viands full the old soldier's haversack.
He fear'd not hungry grass [1] with such a load,
And Ronald saw him miles upon his road.
A march of three days brought him to Loch-fyne.
Argyle, struck with his manly look benign,
And feeling interest in the veteran's lot,
Created him a sergeant on the spot—
An invalid, to serve not—but with pay
(A mighty sum to him), twelve-pence a day.
"But have you heard not," said Macallin More,
"Charles Stuart's landed on Eriska's shore,
And Jacobites are arming?"—"What! indeed!
Arrived! then I'm no more an invalid;
My new-got halbert I must straight employ
In battle."—"As you please, old gallant boy:
Your gray hairs well might plead excuse, 'tis true,
But now's the time we want such men as you."
In brief, at Innerara Allan staid,
And join'd the banners of Argyle's brigade.
Meanwhile, the old choleric shepherd of Glencoe
Spurn'd all advice, and girt himself to go.

1 When the hospitable Highlanders load a parting guest with provisions, they tell him he will need them, as he has to go over a great deal of *hungry grass*.

What was 't to him that foes would poind their
fold,
Their lease, their very beds beneath them sold!
And firmly to his text he would have kept,
Though Ronald argued and his daughter wept.
But 'midst the impotence of tears and prayer,
Chance snatch'd them from proscription and despair.
Old Norman's blood was headward wont to mount
Too rapid from his heart's impetuous fount;
And one day, whilst the German rats he cursed,
An artery in his wise sensorium burst.
The lancet saved him: but how changed, alas,
From him who fought at Killiecrankie's pass!
Tame as a spaniel, timid as a child,
He mutter'd incoherent words and smiled;
He wept at kindness, roll'd a vacant eye,
And laugh'd full often when he meant to cry.
Poor man! whilst in this lamentable state,
Came Allan back one morning to his gate,
Hale and unburden'd by the woes of eild,
And fresh with credit from Culloden's field.
'Twas fear'd at first, the sight of him might touch
The old Macdonald's morbid mind too much;
But no! though Norman knew him and disclosed
Ev'n rallying memory, he was still composed;
Ask'd all particulars of the fatal fight,
And only heaved a sigh for Charles's flight:
Then said, with but one moment's pride of air,
It might not have been so had I been there!

Few days elasped till he reposed beneath
His gray cairn, on the wild and lonely heath;
Son, friends, and kindred of his dust took leave,
And Allan, with the crape bound round his
sleeve.

Old Allan now hung up his sergeant's sword,
And sat, a guest for life, at Ronald's board.
He waked no longer at the barrack's drum,
Yet still you 'd see, when peep of day was come,
Th' erect tall red-coat, walking pastures round,
Or delving with his spade the garden ground,
Of cheerful temper, habits strict and sage,
He reach'd, enjoy'd, a patriarchal age—
Loved to the last by the Macdonalds. Near
Their house, his stone was placed with many a
tear;
And Ronald's self, in stoic virtue brave,
Scorn'd not to weep at Allan Campbell's grave.

"THE Pilgrim of Glencoe," dedicated, with other poems, to Dr. Beattie, was first published in the year 1842. Its reception by the public was far from cheering. No longer, as of old, lavish and enthusiastic praises were heard on all sides, or favourable critiques read on every hand, but a cold apathy seemed to reign, even amongst the reviewers, upon the subject. Campbell himself felt and admitted that the merits of the production were not of the first order; yet he was annoyed and grieved at the indifference manifested.

The affair of Glencoe, and the facts of the case concerning which so much, at different times, has been said and written, are referred to in Mr. Campbell's own note, and are drawn into a narrow focus in an anonymous pamphlet entitled "*The Massacre of Glencoe: being a true Narrative of the barbarous Murther of the Glencoe-men, in the Highlands of Scotland, by way of Military Execution, on the 13th Feb.*, 1692. *London:* 1703." Though the brochure is by a concealed writer, yet it contains within itself strong evidence of authenticity. It sets out at length the Commission, under the Great Seal of Scotland, for making inquiry into the murder; the proceedings of the Parliament of Scotland upon it; the report of the commissioners upon the inquiry, as laid before the King and Parliament; together with the address of the Parliament to King William the Third for justice upon the murderers, all stated to be *faithfully extracted from the records of Parliament, and published for undeceiving those who have been imposed upon by false accounts.* From the report of the Lord Chancellor (Marquis of Tweeddale) and his fellow-commissioners, after evidence taken, subscribed at Holyrood, 20th June, 1693, it appeared that the lairds of Glencoe and Auchintriaten, and their followers, were out in the Highland rebellions of 1689 and 1690; that in July, 1691, the Earl of Breadalbane met the heads of the clans, in order to a cessation; on which occasion Alexander Macdonald, of Glencoe, was present, and with others agreed to the cessation; that at that time there arose a quarrel between the Earl and Macdonald, concerning some cows which the Earl alleged were stolen from his men by Glencoe's men; that the Earl threatened to do him a mischief. In the month of August, 1691, the King's proclamation of indemnity and pardon was published to all the Highlanders, upon condition that all who had been in arms should take the oath of allegiance, between that date and the 1st of January following. In compliance with the proclamation, Glencoe (otherwise Alexander Macdonald) went, towards the end of December, to Colonel Hill, the governor of Fort William, at Inverlochie, and desired the Colonel to administer to him the oath of allegiance, that he might obtain the benefit of the indemnity. That officer, however, not being the proper party for the purpose, but bearing no malice, sent him with a letter to Ardkinlas, to receive him as a lost sheep; and the Colonel produced Ardkinlas's answer to that letter, of the date of January the 9th, 1691, to the effect that he had endeavoured to receive the great lost sheep Glencoe, and that Glencoe had undertaken to bring in all his friends and followers, as the Privy Council should order; that Glencoe, on obtaining the Colonel's letter to Ardkinlas, hasted to Inverary with all speed, notwithstanding bad way and weather; that he presented himself before Sir Colin Campbell, sheriff-depute of Argyle, about the beginning of January, 1692, and was there three days before Ardkinlas could get thither, because of bad weather; and that Glencoe said to him that he had not come sooner, because he was hindered by the storm; that Ardkinlas declined to administer the oath of allegiance, because the last day of December, the time appointed for taking it, was past. Glencoe begged, with tears, that he might be admitted to take it, and promised to bring in all his people, within a short time, to do the like; upon which the oath of allegiance was administered, and a certificate of the fact duly forwarded to Edinburgh, and was produced before the Clerk of the Council, but *rolled and scored*, yet not so delete but that the certificate and its purport could be read. After Glencoe had taken the oath, he went home to his own house, and lived in his family some days quietly, and calling his people together, told them the course he had adopted, and desired them to live peaceably under King William's government. Six weeks afterwards, sixscore soldiers came to Glencoe, and showing the orders of Colonel Hill, were billeted in the country, and had free entertainment and lived familiarly with the people until the 13th of February, on which day, about four in the morning, a party of the soldiers having called in a friendly manner and gained access into Glencoe's house, they shot him dead, and having killed another man, and wounded another, and stripped Glencoe's wife naked, and drawn the rings off her finger with their teeth, they proceeded to other houses, killing and slaying young and old to the number of thirty-two, burning houses, barns, and goods, and carrying away as spoil above a thousand head of cattle. Some days after the slaughter was over, there arrived a messenger from Earl Breadalbane's steward to the deceased Glencoe's sons, who had escaped, and offered, if they would declare under their hands that the Earl was clear of the slaughter, they might be assured of his kindness for procuring their remission and restitution. The proceedings above stated were sought to be defended on the ground of warrant from the King to march the troops against those rebels who had not taken the benefit of the Indemnification, and to destroy them by fire and *sword*. But Secretary Stair, who sent down the royal instructions to Sir Thomas Livingstone, wrote strongly against Glencoe, saying, "My Lord Argylle tells me that Glencoe hath not taken the oath, at which I rejoice. I *entreat the thieving tribe of Glencoe may be rooted out to purpose.*" The commission gave it as their opinion upon the whole matter that it was a great wrong that Glencoe's case as to taking the oath of allegiance, the certificate thereupon, Colonel Hill's letter to Ardkinlas, and Ardkinlas's letter to Sir Colin Campbell, were not presented to the Privy Council when sent to Edinburgh, and that those who advised the not presenting thereof were in the wrong, *and seem to have had* a malicious design against Glencoe: That the obliteration of the certificate was wrong: That it was known in London, and particularly to the Master of Stair, in the month of January, 1692: That Glencoe had taken the oath of allegiance, though after the prescribed day: That there was nothing in the king's instructions to warrant the committing of the slaughter: That the slaughter was a *barbarous murder*. This report was duly laid before the Parliament, and on the question being put to the House if the execution of the Glencoe men in February, 1692, in the manner represented, was a murder or not, it was carried in the *affirmative*. Other resolutions were subsequently passed, and on the 10th of July an address upon the subject was voted to the King, which contained, amongst other things, the following passage:—"We humbly beg that, considering that the Master of Stair's excess, in his letters against the Glencoe men, has been the original cause of this unhappy business, and hath given occasion in a great measure to so extraordinary an execution by the warm directions he gives about doing it by surprise, and considering the high station and trust he is in, and that he is absent, we do therefore beg that your Majesty will give such orders about him for vindication of your Government as you in your royal wisdom shall think fit. And, likewise, considering that the actors have barbarously killed men under trust, we humbly desire your Majesty would be pleased to send the actors home, and to give orders to your advocate to prosecute them according to law." To this follows an appeal to the royal consideration on behalf of the Glencoe men who had escaped the slaughter, and were reduced to great distress by the depredations committed upon them.

It seems there never was any prosecution against any of the parties implicated in the transaction; on the contrary, by the advice of some employed about the King, several of the parties were preferred, and the whole matter hushed up, and by the influence of some persons the report above quoted was suppressed in King William's time, though his Majesty's honour required that all the facts should be published.

NAPOLEON AND THE BRITISH SAILOR.[1]

I LOVE contemplating—apart
From all his homicidal glory,
The traits that soften to our heart
Napoleon's story!

'Twas when his banners at Boulogne
Arm'd in our island every freeman,
His navy chanced to capture one
Poor British seaman.

They suffer'd him—I know not how,
Unprison'd on the shore to roam;
And aye was bent his longing brow
On England's home.

His eye, methinks, pursued the flight
Of birds to Britain half-way over;
With envy *they* could reach the white,
Dear cliffs of Dover.

1 This anecdote has been published in several public journals, both French and British. My belief in its authenticity was confirmed by an Englishman long resident at Boulogne, lately telling me, that he remembered the circumstance to have been generally talked of in the place.

A stormy midnight watch, he thought,
  Than this sojourn would have been dearer,
If but the storm his vessel brought
  To England nearer.

At last, when care had banish'd sleep,
  He saw one morning—dreaming—doating,
An empty hogshead from the deep
  Come shoreward floating;

He hid it in a cave, and wrought
  The live-long day laborious; lurking
Until he launch'd a tiny boat
  By mighty working.

Heaven help us! 'twas a thing beyond
  Description wretched; such a wherry
Perhaps ne'er ventured on a pond,
  Or cross'd a ferry.

For ploughing in the salt-sea field,
  It would have made the boldest shudder;
Untarr'd, uncompass'd, and unkeel'd,
  No sail—no rudder.

From neighb'ring woods he interlaced
  His sorry skiff with wattled willows;
And thus equipp'd he would have pass'd
  The foaming billows—

But Frenchmen caught him on the beach,
His little Argo sorely jeering:
Till tidings of him chanced to reach
Napoleon's hearing.

With folded arms Napoleon stood,
Serene alike in peace and danger;
And, in his wonted attitude,
Address'd the stranger:—

"Rash man, that would'st yon Channel pass
On twigs and staves so rudely fashion'd;
Thy heart with some sweet British lass
Must be impassion'd."

"I have no sweetheart," said the lad;
"But—absent long from one another—
Great was the longing that I had
To see my mother."

"And so thou shalt," Napoleon said,
"Ye 've both my favour fairly won;
A noble mother must have bred
So brave a son."

He gave the tar a piece of gold,
And, with a flag of truce, commanded
He should be shipp'd to England Old,
And safely landed.

Our sailor oft could scantily shift
  To find a dinner, plain and hearty;
But *never* changed the coin and gift
  Of Bonaparté.

BENLOMOND.

Hadst thou a genius on thy peak,
  What tales, white-headed Ben,
Could'st thou of ancient ages speak,
  That mock th' historian's pen!

Thy long duration makes our lives
  Seem but so many hours;
And likens, to the bees' frail hives,
  Our most stupendous towers.

Temples and towers thou 'st seen begun,
  New creeds, new conquerors' sway;
And, like their shadows in the sun,
  Hast seen them swept away.

Thy steadfast summit, heaven-allied
  (Unlike life's little span),
Looks down, a Mentor on the pride
  Of perishable man.

THE CHILD AND HIND.

I WISH I had preserved a copy of the Wiesbaden newspaper in which this anecdote of the "Child and Hind" is recorded; but I have unfortunately lost it. The story, however, is a matter of fact; it took place in 1838: every circumstance mentioned in the following ballad literally happened. I was in Wiesbaden eight months ago, and was shown the very tree under which the boy was found sleeping with a bunch of flowers in his little hand. A similar occurrence is told by tradition, of Queen Genevova's child being preserved by being suckled by a female deer, when that Princess—an early Christian—and now a Saint in the Romish calendar, was chased to the desert by her heathen enemies. The spot assigned to the traditionary event is not a hundred miles from Wiesbaden, where a chapel still stands to her memory.

I could not ascertain whether the Hind that watched my hero "Wilhelm," suckled him or not; but it was generally believed that she had no milk to give him, and that the boy must have been for two days and a half entirely without food, unless it might be grass or leaves. If this was the case, the circumstance of the Wiesbaden deer watching the child, was a still more wonderful token of instinctive fondness than that of the deer in the Genevova tradition, who was naturally anxious to be relieved of her milk.

COME, maids and matrons, to caress
Wiesbaden's gentle hind;
And, smiling, deck its glossy neck
With forest flowers entwined.

Your forest flowers are fair to show,
And landscapes to enjoy;

But fairer is your friendly doe
That watch'd the sleeping boy.

'Twas after church—on Ascension day—
When organs ceased to sound,
Wiesbaden's people crowded gay
The deer-park's pleasant ground.

There, where Elysian meadows smile,
And noble trees upshoot,
The wild thyme and the camomile
Smell sweetly at their root;

The aspen quivers nervously,
The oak stands stilly bold—
And climbing bindweed hangs on high
His bells of beaten gold.[1]

Nor stops the eye till mountains shine
That bound a spacious view,
Beyond the lordly, lovely Rhine,
In visionary blue.

There, monuments of ages dark
Awaken thoughts sublime;
Till, swifter than the steaming bark,
We mount the stream of time.

[1] There is only one kind of bindweed that is yellow, and that is the flower here mentioned, the Paniculatus Convolvulus.

The ivy there old castles shades
That speak traditions high
Of minstrels—tournaments—crusades,
And mail-clad chivalry.

Here came a twelve years' married pair—
And with them wander'd free
Seven sons and daughters, blooming fair,
A gladsome sight to see.

Their Wilhelm, little innocent,
The youngest of the seven,
Was beautiful as painters paint
The cherubim of Heaven.

By turns he gave his hand, so dear,
To parent, sister, brother;
And each, that he was safe and near,
Confided in the other.

But Wilhelm loved the field-flowers bright,
With love beyond all measure;
And cull'd them with as keen delight
As misers gather treasure.

Unnoticed, he contrived to glide
Adown a greenwood alley,
By lilies lured—that grew beside
A streamlet in the valley;

And there, where under beech and birch
The rivulet meander'd,
He stray'd, till neither shout nor search
Could track where he had wander'd.

Still louder, with increasing dread,
They call'd his darling name;
But 'twas like speaking to the dead—
An echo only came.

Hours pass'd till evening's beetle roams,
And blackbird's songs begin;
Then all went back to happy homes,
Save Wilhelm's kith and kin.

The night came on—all others slept
Their cares away till morn;
But sleepless, all night watch'd and wept
That family forlorn.

Betimes the town-crier had been sent
With loud bell, up and down;
And told th' afflicting accident
Throughout Wiesbaden's town:

The father, too, ere morning smiled,
Had all his wealth uncoffer'd;
And to the wight would bring his child,
A thousand crowns had offer'd.

Dear friends, who would have blush'd to take
That guerdon from his hand,
Soon join'd in groups—for pity's sake,
The child-exploring band.

The news reach'd Nassau's Duke: ere earth
Was gladden'd by the lark,
He sent a hundred soldiers forth
To ransack all his park.

Their side-arms glitter'd through the wood,
With bugle-horns to sound;
Would that on errand half so good
The soldier oft were found!

But though they roused up beast and bird
From many a nest and den,
No signal of success was heard
From all the hundred men.

A second morning's light expands,
Unfound the infant fair;
And Wilhelm's household wring their hands,
Abandon'd to despair.

But, haply, a poor artisan
Search'd ceaselessly, till he
Found safe asleep the little one
Beneath a beechen tree,

His hand still grasp'd a bunch of flowers;
And (true, though wondrous) near,
To sentry his reposing hours,
There stood a female deer—

Who dipp'd her horns at all that pass'd[1]
The spot where Wilhelm lay;
Till force was had to hold her fast,
And bear the boy away.

Hail! sacred love of childhood—hail!
How sweet it is to trace
Thine instinct in Creation's scale,
Ev'n 'neath the human race.

To this poor wanderer of the wild
Speech, reason were unknown—
And yet she watch'd a sleeping child
As if it were her own;

And thou, Wiesbaden's artisan,
Restorer of the boy,
Was ever welcomed mortal man
With such a burst of joy?

The father's ecstasy—the mother's
Hysteric bosom's swell;

[1] The female deer has no such antlers as the male, and sometimes no horns at all; but I have observed many with short ones suckling their fawns.

The sisters' sobs—the shout of brothers,
I have not power to tell.

The working man, with shoulders broad,
Took blithely to his wife
The thousand crowns; a pleasant load,
That made him rich for life.

And Nassau's Duke the favourite took
Into his deer-park's centre,
To share a field with other pets
Where deer-slayer cannot enter.

There, whilst thou cropp'st thy flowery food,
Each hand shall pat thee kind;
And man shall never spill thy blood—
Wiesbaden's gentle hind.

THE JILTED NYMPH.

A SONG,

TO THE SCOTCH TUNE OF "WOO'D AND MARRIED AND A'."

I 'M jilted, forsaken, outwitted;
  Yet think not I 'll whimper or brawl—
The lass is alone to be pitied
  Who ne'er has been courted at all:
Never by great or small,
Woo'd or jilted at all;
  Oh, how unhappy 's the lass
Who has never been courted at all!

My brother call'd out the dear faithless,
  In fits I was ready to fall,
Till I found a policeman who, scatheless,
  Swore them both to the peace at Guildhall;
Seized them, seconds and all—
Pistols, powder and ball;
  I wish'd him to die my devoted,
But not in a duel to sprawl.

What though at my heart he has tilted,
  What though I have met with a fall?

Better be courted and jilted,
  Than never be courted at all.
Woo'd and jilted and all,
Still I will dance at the ball;
  And waltz and quadrille
  With light heart and heel,
With proper young men, and tall.

But lately I 've met with a suitor,
  Whose heart I have gotten in thrall,
And I hope soon to tell you in future
  That I 'm woo'd, and married and all:
Woo'd and married and all,
What greater bliss can befall?
  And you all shall partake of my bridal cake,
When I 'm woo'd and married, and all.

ON GETTING HOME

THE PORTRAIT OF A FEMALE CHILD.

SIX YEARS OLD.

PAINTED BY EUGENIO LATILLA.

Type of the Cherubim above,
Come, live with me, and be my love!
Smile from my wall, dear roguish sprite,
By sunshine and by candle-light;
For both look sweetly on thy traits:
Or, were the Lady Moon to gaze,
She 'd welcome thee with lustre bland,
Like some young fay from Fairyland.
Cast in simplicity's own mould,
How canst thou be so manifold
In sportively distracting charms?
Thy lips—thine eyes—thy little arms
That wrapt thy shoulders and thy head,
In homeliest shawl of netted thread,
Brown woollen net-work; yet it seeks
Accordance with thy lovely cheeks,
And more becomes thy beauty's bloom
Than any shawl from Cashmere's loom.

Thou hast not, to adorn thee, girl,
Flower, link of gold, or gem or pearl—
I would not let a ruby speck
The peeping whiteness of thy neck:
Thou need'st no casket, witching elf,
No gawd—thy toilet is thyself;
Not ev'n a rose-bud from the bower,
Thyself a magnet—gem and flower.

My arch and playful little creature,
Thou hast a mind in every feature;
Thy brow, with its disparted locks,
Speaks language that translation mocks;
Thy lucid eyes so beam with soul,
They on the canvas seem to roll—
Instructing both my head and heart
To idolize the painter's art.
He marshals minds to Beauty's feast—
He is Humanity's high priest
Who proves, by heavenly forms on earth,
How much this world of ours is worth.
Inspire me, child, with visions fair!
For children, in Creation, are
The only things that could be given
Back, and alive—unchanged—to Heaven.

THE PARROT.

A DOMESTIC ANECDOTE.

The following incident, so strongly illustrating the power of memory and association in the lower animals, is not a fiction. I heard it many years ago in the Island of Mull, from the family to whom the bird belonged.

The deep affections of the breast,
That Heaven to living things imparts,
Are not exclusively possess'd
By human hearts.

A parrot, from the Spanish Main,
Full young, and early caged, came o'er
With bright wings, to the bleak domain
Of Mulla's shore.

To spicy groves where he had won
His plumage of resplendent hue,
His native fruits, and skies, and sun,
He bade adieu.

For these he changed the smoke of turf,
A heathery land and misty sky,
And turn'd on rocks and raging surf
His golden eye.

But, petted, in our climate cold
  He lived and chatter'd many a day:
Until with age, from green and gold
  His wings grew gray.

At last, when blind and seeming dumb,
  He scolded, laugh'd, and spoke no more,
A Spanish stranger chanced to come
  To Mulla's shore;

He hail'd the bird in Spanish speech,
  The bird in Spanish speech replied,
Flapp'd round his cage with joyous screech,
  Dropt down, and died.

SONG OF THE COLONISTS DEPARTING FOR NEW ZEALAND.

STEER, helmsman, till you steer our way,
  By stars beyond the line;
We go to found a realm, one day,
  Like England's self to shine.

CHORUS.

Cheer up—cheer up—our course we 'll keep,
  With dauntless heart and hand;
And when we 've plough'd the stormy deep,
  We 'll plough a smiling land:—

A land, where beauties importune
  The Briton to its bowers,
To sow but plenteous seeds, and prune
  Luxuriant fruits and flowers.
      Chorus.—Cheer up—cheer up, &c.

There, tracts uncheer'd by human words,
  Seclusion's wildest holds,
Shall hear the lowing of our herds,
  And tinkling of our folds.
      Chorus.—Cheer up—cheer up, &c.

Like rubies set in gold, shall blush
  Our vineyards girt with corn;
And wine, and oil, and gladness gush
  From Amalthea's horn.
      Chorus.—Cheer up—cheer up, &c.

Britannia's pride is in our hearts,
  Her blood is in our veins—
We'll girdle earth with British arts,
  Like Ariel's magic chains.

CHORUS.

Cheer up—cheer up—our course we'll keep,
  With dauntless heart and hand;
And when we've plough'd the stormy deep,
  We'll plough a smiling land.

MOONLIGHT.

THE kiss that would make a maid's cheek flush
  Wroth, as if kissing were a sin
  Amidst the Argus eyes and din
    And tell-tale glare of noon,
Brings but a murmur and a blush,
    Beneath the modest moon.

Ye days, gone—never to come back,
  When love return'd entranced me so,
  That still its pictures move and glow
    In the dark chamber of my heart;
Leave not my memory's future track—
    I will not let you part.

'Twas moonlight, when my earliest love
  First on my bosom dropt her head;
  A moment then concentrated
The bliss of years, as if the spheres
    Their course had faster driven,
And carried, Enoch-like above,
    A living man to Heaven.

'Tis by the rolling moon we measure
  The date between our nuptial night
  And that blest hour which brings to light
    The pledge of faith—the fruit of bliss;
When we impress upon the treasure
    A father's earliest kiss.

The Moon 's the Earth's enamour'd bride;
  True to him in her very changes,
  To other stars she never ranges:
    Though, cross'd by him, sometimes she dips
Her light, in short offended pride,
    And faints to an eclipse.

The fairies revel by her sheen;
  'Tis only when the Moon 's above
  The fire-fly kindles into love,
    And flashes light to show it:
The nightingale salutes her Queen
    Of Heaven, her heav'nly poet.

Then ye that love—by moonlight gloom
  Meet at my grave, and plight regard.
  Oh! could I be the Orphéan bard
    Of whom it is reported,
That nightingales sung o'er his tomb,
    Whilst lovers came and courted.

SONG ON OUR QUEEN.

SET TO MUSIC BY CHARLES NEATE, ESQ.

VICTORIA'S sceptre o'er the deep
  Has touch'd, and broken slavery's chain;
Yet, strange magician! she enslaves
  Our hearts within her own domain.

Her spirit is devout, and burns
  With thoughts averse to bigotry;
Yet she herself, the idol, turns
  Our thoughts into idolatry.

CORA LINN, OR THE FALLS OF THE CLYDE.

WRITTEN ON REVISITING IT IN 1837.

THE time I saw thee, Cora, last,
'Twas with congenial friends;
And calmer hours of pleasure past—
My memory seldom sends.

It was as sweet an Autumn day
As ever shone on Clyde,
And Lanark's orchards all the way
Put forth their golden pride;

Ev'n hedges, busk'd in bravery,
Look'd rich that sunny morn;
The scarlet hip and blackberry
So prank'd September's thorn.

In Cora's glen the calm how deep!
That trees on loftiest hill
Like statues stood, or things asleep,
All motionless and still.

The torrent spoke, as if his noise
Bade earth be quiet round,
And give his loud and lonely voice
A more commanding sound.

His foam, beneath the yellow light
Of noon, came down like one
Continuous sheet of jaspers bright,
Broad rolling by the sun.

Dear Linn! let loftier falling floods
Have prouder names than thine;
And king of all, enthroned in woods,
Let Niagara shine.

Barbarian, let him shake his coasts
With reeking thunders far,
Extended like th' array of hosts
In broad, embattled war!

His voice appalls the wilderness:
Approaching thine, we feel
A solemn, deep melodiousness,
That needs no louder peal.

More fury would but disenchant
Thy dream-inspiring din;
Be thou the Scottish Muse's haunt,
Romantic Cora Linn.

CHAUCER AND WINDSOR.

Long shalt thou flourish, Windsor! bodying forth
Chivalric times, and long shall live around
Thy Castle—the old oaks of British birth,
Whose gnarled roots, tenacious and profound,
As with a lion's talons grasp the ground.
But should thy towers in ivied ruin rot,
There 's one, thine inmate once, whose strain renown'd
Would interdict thy name to be forgot;
For Chaucer loved thy bowers and trode this very spot.
Chaucer! our Helicon's first fountain-stream,
Our morning star of song—that led the way
To welcome the long-after coming beam
Of Spenser's light and Shakspeare's perfect day.
Old England's fathers live in Chaucer's lay,
As if they ne'er had died. He group'd and drew
Their likeness with a spirit of life so gay,
That still they live and breathe in Fancy's view,
Fresh beings fraught with truth's imperishable hue.

LINES

SUGGESTED BY THE STATUE OF ARNOLD VON WINKELRIED,[1] STANZ-UNDERWALDEN.

INSPIRING and romantic Switzers' land,
Though mark'd with majesty by Nature's hand,
What charm ennobles most thy landscape's face?
Th' heroic memory of thy native race—
Who forced tyrannic hosts to bleed or flee,
And made their rocks the ramparts of the free;
Their fastnesses roll'd back th' invading tide
Of conquest, and their mountains taught them pride.
Hence they have patriot names—in fancy's eye,
Bright as their glaciers glittering in the sky;
Patriots who make the pageantries of kings
Like shadows seem and unsubstantial things.
Their guiltless glory mocks oblivion's rust,
Imperishable, for their cause was just.
Heroes of old! to whom the Nine have strung
Their lyres, and spirit-stirring anthems sung;

[1] For an account of this patriotic Swiss and his heroic death at the battle of Sempach, see Dr. Beattie's "Switzerland Illustrated," vol. ii. pp. 111–115.

Heroes of chivalry! whose banners grace
The aisles of many a consecrated place,
Confess how few of you can match in fame
The martyr Winkelried's immortal name!

TO THE UNITED STATES OF NORTH AMERICA.

United States, your banner wears
Two emblems—one of fame;
Alas, the other that it bears
Reminds us of your shame.

Your standard's constellation types
White freedom by its stars;
But what 's the meaning of the stripes?
They mean your negroes' scars.

LINES ON MY NEW CHILD-SWEETHEART.

I HOLD it a religious duty
To love and worship children's beauty;
They 've least the taint of earthly clod,
They 're freshest from the hand of God;
With heavenly looks they make us sure
The heaven that made them must be pure.
We love them not in earthly fashion,
But with a beatific passion.
I chanced to, yesterday, behold
A maiden child of beauty's mould;
'Twas near, more sacred was the scene,
The palace of our patriot Queen.
The little charmer to my view
Was sculpture brought to life anew.
Her eyes had a poetic glow,
Her pouting mouth was Cupid's bow:
And through her frock I could descry
Her neck and shoulders' symmetry.
'Twas obvious from her walk and gait
Her limbs were beautifully straight;
I stopp'd th' enchantress, and was told,
Though tall, she was but four years old.

Her guide so grave an aspect wore
I could not ask a question more ;
But follow'd her. The little one
Threw backward ever and anon
Her lovely neck, as if to say,
" I know you love me, Mister Grey ;"
For by its instinct childhood's eye
Is shrewd in physiognomy ;
They will distinguish fawning art
From sterling fondness of the heart.

And so she flirted, like a true
Good woman, till we bade adieu.
'Twas then I with regret grew wild,
Oh, beauteous, interesting child!
Why ask'd I not thy home and name?
My courage fail'd me—more 's the shame.
But where abides this jewel rare?
Oh, ye that own her, tell me where!
For sad it makes my heart and sore
To think I ne'er may meet her more.

THE LAUNCH OF A FIRST-RATE.

WRITTEN ON WITNESSING THE SPECTACLE.

England hails thee with emotion,
  Mightiest child of naval art,
Heaven resounds thy welcome! Ocean
  Takes thee smiling to his heart.

Giant oaks of bold expansion
  O'er seven hundred acres fell,
All to build thy noble mansion,
  Where our hearts of oak shall dwell.

'Midst those trees the wild deer bounded,
  Ages long ere we were born,
And our great-grandfathers sounded
  Many a jovial hunting-horn.

Oaks that living did inherit
  Grandeur from our earth and sky,
Still robust, the native spirit
  In your timbers shall not die.

Ship to shine in martial story,
  Thou shalt cleave the ocean's path
Freighted with Britannia's glory
  And the thunders of her wrath.

Foes shall crowd their sails and fly thee,
  Threat'ning havoc to their deck,
When afar they first descry thee,
  Like the coming whirlwind's speck.

Gallant bark! thy pomp and beauty
  Storm or battle ne'er shall blast,
Whilst our tars in pride and duty
  Nail thy colours to the mast.

TO A YOUNG LADY,

WHO ASKED ME TO WRITE SOMETHING ORIGINAL FOR HER ALBUM.

An original something, fair maid, you would win me
To write—but how shall I begin?
For I fear I have nothing original in me—
Excepting Original Sin.

EPISTLE, FROM ALGIERS,

TO

HORACE SMITH.

DEAR HORACE! be melted to tears,
 For I 'm melting with heat as I rhyme;
Though the name of the place is All-jeers,
 'Tis no joke to fall in with its clime.

With a shaver[1] from France who came o'er,
 To an African inn I ascend;
I am cast on a barbarous shore,
 Where a barber alone is my friend.

Do you ask me the sights and the news
 Of this wonderful city to sing?
Alas! my hotel has its mews,
 But no muse of the Helicon's spring.

1 On board the vessel from Marseilles to Algiers I met with a fellow passenger whom I supposed to be a physician from his dress and manners, and the attentions which he paid me to alleviate the sufferings of my sea-sickness. He turned out to be a perruquier and barber in Algeria—but his vocation did not lower him in my estimation—for he continued his attentions until he passed my baggage through the customs, and helped me, when half dead with exhaustion, to the best hotel.

My windows afford me the sight
  Of a people all diverse in hue;
They are black, yellow, olive, and white,
  Whilst I in my sorrow look blue.

Here are groups for the painter to take,
  Whose figures jocosely combine,—
The Arab disguised in his haik,[1]
  And the Frenchman disguised in his wine.

In his breeches of petticoat size
  You may say, as the Mussulman goes,
That his garb is a fair compromise
  'Twixt a kilt and a pair of small-clothes.

The Mooresses, shrouded in white,
  Save two holes for their eyes to give room,
Seem like corpses in sport or in spite
  That have slyly whipp'd out of their tomb.

The old Jewish dames make me sick:
  If I were the devil—I declare
Such hags should not mount a broom-stick
  In my service to ride through the air.

But hipp'd and undined as I am,
  My hippogriff's course I must rein—
For the pain of my thirst is no sham,
  Though I 'm bawling aloud for champagne.

[1] A mantle worn by the natives.

Dinner's brought; but their wines have no pith—
 They are flat as the statutes at law;
And for all that they bring me, dear Smith!
 Would a glass of brown stout they could draw!

O'er each French trashy dish as I bend,
 My heart feels a patriot's grief!
And the round tears, O England! descend
 When I think on a round of thy beef.

Yes, my soul sentimentally craves
 British beer.—Hail, Britannia, hail!
To thy flag on the foam of the waves,
 And the foam on thy flagons of ale.

Yet I own, in this hour of my drought,
 A dessert has most welcomely come;
Here are peaches that melt in the mouth,
 And grapes blue and big as a plum.

There are melons too, luscious and great,
 But the slices I eat shall be few,
For from melons incautiously eat
 Melancholic effects may ensue.

Horrid pun! you 'll exclaim; but be calm,
 Though my letter bears date, as you view,
From the land of the date-bearing palm,
 I will palm no more puns upon you.

FRAGMENT OF AN ORATORIO,

FROM THE BOOK OF JOB.

Having met my illustrious friend the Composer Neukomm, at Algiers, several years ago, I commenced this intended Oratorio at his desire, but he left the place before I proceeded farther in the poem; and it has been thus left unfinished.

Crush'd by misfortune's yoke,
Job lamentably spoke—
"My boundless curse be on
The day that I was born;
Quench'd be the star that shone
Upon my natal morn.
In the grave I long
To shroud my breast;
Where the wicked cease to wrong,
And the weary are at rest."
Then Eliphaz rebuked his wild despair:
"What Heaven ordains, 'tis meet that man should bear.
Lately, at midnight drear,
A vision shook my bones with fear;
A spirit pass'd before my face,
And yet its form I could not trace;

It stopp'd—it stood—it chill'd my blood,
The hair upon my flesh uprose
With freezing dread!
Deep silence reign'd, and, at its close,
I heard a voice that said—
'Shall mortal man be more pure and just
Than God, who made him from the dust?
Hast thou not learnt of old, how fleet
Is the triumph of the hypocrite;
How soon the wreath of joy grows wan
On the brow of the ungodly man?
By the fire of his conscience he perisheth
In an unblown flame:
The Earth demands his death,
And the Heavens reveal his shame.'"

JOB.

Is this your consolation?
Is it thus that ye condole
With the depth of my desolation,
And the anguish of my soul?
But I will not cease to wail
The bitterness of my bale.—
Man that is born of woman,
Short and evil is his hour;
He fleeth like a shadow,
He fadeth like a flower.
My days are pass'd—my hope and trust
Is but to moulder in the dust.

CHORUS.

Bow, mortal, bow, before thy God,
Nor murmur at his chastening rod;
Fragile being of earthly clay,
Think on God's eternal sway!
Hark! from the whirlwind forth
Thy Maker speaks—"Thou child of earth,
Where wert thou when I laid
Creation's corner-stone?
When the sons of God rejoicing made,
And the morning stars together sang and shone?
Hadst thou power to bid above
Heaven's constellations glow;
Or shape the forms that live and move
On Nature's face below?
Hast thou given the horse his strength and pride?
He paws the valley, with nostril wide,
He smells far off the battle;
He neighs at the trumpet's sound—
And his speed devours the ground,
As he sweeps to where the quivers rattle,
And the spear and shield shine bright,
'Midst the shouting of the captains
And the thunder of the fight.

TO MY NIECE, MARY CAMPBELL.

[The following lines were written in Mrs. Alfred Hill's album, in the early part of 1842, about twelve months after her arrival in London from Scotland, and they exhibit the gentle and affectionate feelings which ever marked Campbell's intercourse with those he loved.]

Our friendship 's not a stream to dry,
  Or stop with angry jar;
A life-long planet in our sky—
  No meteor-shooting star.

Thy playfulness and pleasant ways
  Shall cheer my wintry track,
And give my old declining days
  A second summer back!

Proud honesty protects our lot,
  No dun infests our bowers;
Wealth's golden lamps illumine not
  Brows more content than ours.

To think, too, thy remembrance fond
  May love me after death,
Gives fancied happiness beyond
  My lease of living breath.

Meanwhile thine intellects presage
  A life-time rich in truth,
And make me feel th' advance of age
  Retarded by thy youth!

Good night! propitious dreams betide
  Thy sleep—awaken gay,
And we will make to-morrow glide
  As cheerful as to-day!

APPENDIX.

THE DIRGE OF WALLACE.

When Scotland's great Regent, our warrior most dear.
The debt of his nature did pay,
'Twas Edward, the cruel, had reason to fear,
And cause to be struck with dismay.

At the window of Edward the raven did croak,
Though Scotland a widow became;
Each tie of true honor to Wallace he broke—
The raven croaked "Sorrow and shame!"

At Elderslie Castle no raven was heard,
But the soothings of honor and truth;
His spirit inspired the soul of the bard
To comfort the Love of his youth!

They lighted the tapers at dead of night,
And chanted their holiest hymn;
But her brow and her bosom were damp with affright,
Her eye was all sleepless and dim!

And the lady of Elderslie wept for her lord,
When a death-watch beat in her lonely room,
When her curtain had shook of its own accord,
And the raven had flapped at her window board,
To tell of her warrior's doom.

Now sing ye the death-song, and loudly pray
For the soul of my knight so dear!

And call me a widow, this wretched day,
  Since the warning of God is here.

For a nightmare rests on my strangled sleep;
  The lord of my bosom is doomed to die!
His valorous heart they have wounded deep,
And the blood-red tears shall his country weep
  For Wallace of Elderslie.

Yet knew not his country, that ominous hour,
  Ere the loud matin-bell was rung,
That the trumpet of death, on an English tower,
  Had the dirge of her champion sung.

When his dungeon-light looked dim and red
  On the high-born blood of a martyr slain,
No anthem was sung at *his* lowly death-bed—
No weeping was there when his bosom bled,
  And his heart was rent in twain.

When he strode o'er the wreck of each well-fought field,
  With the yellow-haired chiefs of his native land;
For his lance was not shivered on helmet or shield,
And the sword that was fit for archangel to wield
  Was light in his terrible hand.

Yet, bleeding and bound, though "the Wallace-wight"
  For his long-loved country die,
The bugle ne'er sung to a braver knight
  Than William of Elderslie!

But the day of his triumphs shall never depart;
  His head, unentombed, shall with glory be palmed;
From its blood-streaming altar his spirit shall start;
Though the raven has fed on his mouldering heart,
  A nobler was never embalmed!

NOTES.

THE PLEASURES OF HOPE.

Page 6, line 25.

And such thy strength-inspiring aid that bore
The hardy Byron to his native shore—

THE following picture of his own distress, given by BYRON in his simple and interesting narrative, justifies the description in page 5.

After relating the barbarity of the Indian cacique to his child, he proceeds thus:—"A day or two after we put to sea again, and crossed the great bay I mentioned we had been at the bottom of when we first hauled away to the westward. The land here was very low and sandy, and something like the mouth of a river which discharged itself into the sea, and which had been taken no notice of by us before, as it was so shallow that the Indians were obliged to take every thing out of their canoes, and carry them over land. We rowed up the river four or five leagues, and then took into a branch of it that ran first to the eastward, and then to the northward; here it became much narrower, and the stream excessively rapid, so that we gained but little way, though we wrought very hard. At night we landed upon its banks, and had a most uncomfortable lodging, it being a perfect swamp, and we had nothing to cover us, though it rained excessively. The Indians were little better off than we, as there was no wood here to make their wigwams; so that all they could do was to prop up the bark, which they carry in the bottom of their canoes, and shelter themselves as well as they could to the leeward of it. Knowing the difficulties they had to encounter here, they had provided themselves with some seal; but we had not a morsel to eat, after the heavy fatigues of the day, excepting a sort of root we saw the Indians make use of, which was very disagreeable to the taste. We laboured all next day against the stream, and fared as we had done the day before. The next day brought us to the carrying-place. Here was plenty of wood, but nothing to be got for sustenance. We passed this night, as we had frequently done, under a tree; but what we suffered at this time is not easy to be expressed. I had been three days at the oar without any kind of nourishment except the wretched root above mentioned. I had no shirt, for it had rotted off by bits. All my clothes consisted of a short grieko (something like a bear-skin), a piece of red cloth which had once been a waistcoat, and a ragged pair of trowsers, without shoes or stockings."

Page 7, line 14.

——a Briton and a friend!

Don Patricio Gedd, a Scotch physician in one of the Spanish settlements, hospitably relieved Byron and his wretched associates, of which the commodore speaks in the warmest terms of gratitude.

Page 7, line 30.

Or yield the lyre of Heaven another string.

The seven strings of Apollo's harp were the symbolical representation of the seven planets. Herschel, by discovering an eighth, might be said to add another string to the instrument.

Page 8, line 1.

The Swedish-sage.

Linnæus.

Page 8, line 26.

Deep from his vaults the Loxian murmurs flow.

Loxias is the name frequently given to Apollo by Greek writers: it is met with more than once in the Choephoræ of Æschylus.

Page 10, line 1.

Unlocks a generous store at thy command,
Like Horeb's rocks beneath the prophet's hand.

See Exodus, chap. xvii. 3, 5, 6.

Page 15, line 19.

Wild Obi flies—

Among the negroes of the West Indies, Obi, or Orbiah, is the name of a magical power, which is believed by them to affect the object of its malignity with dismal calamities. Such a belief must undoubtedly have been deduced from the superstitious mythology of their kinsmen on the coast of Africa. I have, therefore, personified Obi as the evil spirit of the African, although the history of the African tribes mentions the evil spirit of their religious creed by a different appellation.

Page 15, line 24.

———*Sibir's dreary mines.*

Mr. Bell of Antermony, in his Travels through Siberia, informs us that the name of the country is universally pronounced Sibir by the Russians.

Page 16, line 10.

Presaging wrath to Poland—and to man!

The history of the partition of Poland, of the massacre in the suburbs of Warsaw, and on the bridge of Prague, the triumphant entry of Suwarrow into the Polish capital, and the insult offered to human nature, by the blasphemous thanks offered up to Heaven, for victories obtained over men fighting in the sacred cause of liberty, by murderers and oppressors, are events generally known.

Page 22, line 9.

The shrill horn blew;

The negroes in the West Indies are summoned to their morning work by a shell or horn.

Page 22, line 30.

How long was Timour's iron sceptre sway'd,

To elucidate this passage, I shall subjoin a quotation from the preface to Letters from a Hindoo Rajah, a work of elegance and celebrity.

"The impostor of Mecca had established, as one of the principles of his doctrine, the merit of extending it either by persuasion, or the sword, to all parts of the earth. How steadily this injunction was adhered to by his followers, and with what success it was pursued, is well known to all who are in the least conversant in history.

"The same overwhelming torrent which had inundated the greater part of Africa, burst its way into the very heart of Europe; and, covering many kingdoms of Asia with unbounded desolation, directed its baneful course to the flourishing provinces of Hindostan. Here these fierce and hardy adventurers, whose only improvement had been in the science of destruction, who added the fury of fanaticism to the ravages of war, found the great end of their conquest opposed by objects which neither the ardour of their persevering zeal, nor savage barbarity, could surmount. Multitudes were sacrificed by the cruel hand of religious persecution, and whole countries were deluged in blood, in the vain hope, that by the destruction of a part the remainder might be persuaded, or terrified, into the profession of Mahomedism. But all these sanguinary efforts were ineffectual; and at length, being fully convinced that, though they might extirpate, they could never hope to convert, any number of the Hindoos, they relinquished the impracticable idea with which they had entered upon their career of conquest, and contented themselves with the acquirment of the civil dominion and almost universal empire of Hindostan."—*Letters from a Hindoo Rajah, by Eliza Hamilton.*

Page 23, line 15.

And braved the stormy Spirit of the Cape;

See the description of the Cape of Good Hope, translated from CAMÖENS, by MICKLE.

Page 23, line 30.

While famish'd nations died along the shore:

The following account of British conduct, and its consequences, in Bengal, will afford a sufficient idea of the fact alluded to in this passage.

After describing the monopoly of salt, betel-nut, and tobacco, the historian proceeds thus:—" Money in this current came but by drops; it could not quench the thirst of those who waited in India to receive it. An expedient, such as it was, remained to quicken its pace. The natives could live with little salt, but could not want food. Some of the agents saw themselves well situated for collecting the rice into stores; they did so. They knew the Gentoos would rather die than violate the principles of their religion by eating flesh. The alternative would therefore be between giving what they had, or dying. The inhabitants sunk;—they that cultivated the land, and saw the harvest at the disposal of others, planted in doubt—scarcity ensued. Then the monopoly was easier managed—sickness ensued. In some districts the languid living left the bodies of their numerous dead unburied."—*Short History of the English Transactions in the East Indies*, p. 145.

Page 24, line 15.

Nine times have Brama's wheels of lightning hurl'd
His awful presence o'er the alarmed world;

Among the sublime fictions of the Hindoo mythology, it is one article of belief, that the Deity Brama has descended nine times upon the world in various forms, and that he is yet to appear a tenth time, in the figure of a warrior upon a white horse, to cut off all incorrigible offenders. Avatar is the word used to express his descent.

Page 25, line 8.

Shall Seriswattee wave her hallow'd wand!
And Camdeo bright, and Ganesa sublime,

Camdeo is the God of Love in the mythology of the Hin doos. Ganesa and Seriswattee correspond to the pagan deitie Janus and Minerva.

Page 31, line 2.

The noon of manhood to a myrtle shade!

Sacred to Venus is the myrtle shade.—DRYDEN.

Page 34, line 7.

Thy woes, Arion!

Falconer, in his poem, " The Shipwreck," speaks of himsel by the name of Arion.
See Falconer's " Shipwreck," Canto III.

Page 34, line 22.

The robber Moor.

See Schiller's tragedy of the " Robbers," Scene v.

Page 35, line 11.

What millions died—that Cæsar might be great!

The carnage occasioned by the wars of Julius Cæsar has been usually estimated at two millions of men.

Page 35, line 12.

Or learn the fate that bleeding thousands bore,
March'd by their Charles to Dneiper's swampy shore;

" In this extremity," (says the biographer of Charles XII., of Sweden, speaking of his military exploits before the battle of Pultowa,) " the memorable winter of 1709, which was still more remarkable in that part of Europe than in France, destroyed numbers of his troops; for Charles resolved to brave the seasons as he had done his enemies, and ventured to make long marches during this mortal cold. It was in one of these marches that two thousand men fell down dead with cold before his eyes."

Page 36, line 7.

For, as Iona's saint,

The natives of the island of Iona have an opinion, that on certain evenings every year the tutelary saint Columba is seen on the top of the church spires counting the surrounding islands, to see that they have not been sunk by the power of witchcraft.

Page 36, line 26.

And part, like Ajut—never to return!

See the history of Ajut and Anningait, in "The Rambler."

THEODRIC.

Page 51, line 3.

That gave the glacier tops their richest glow,

THE sight of the glaciers of Switzerland, I am told, has often disappointed travellers who had perused the accounts of their splendour and sublimity given by Bourrit and other describers of Swiss scenery. Possibly Bourrit, who had spent his life in an enamoured familiarity with the beauties of Nature in Switzerland, may have leaned to the romantic side of description. One can pardon a man for a sort of idolatry of those imposing objects of Nature which heighten our ideas of the bounty of Nature or Providence, when we reflect that the glaciers—those seas of ice—are not only sublime, but useful: they are the inexhaustible reservoirs which supply the principal rivers of Europe; and their annual melting is in proportion to the summer heat which dries up those rivers and makes them need that supply.

That the picturesque grandeur of the glaciers should sometimes disappoint the traveller, will not seem surprising to any one who has been much in a mountainous country, and recollects that the beauty of Nature in such countries is not only variable, but capriciously dependent on the weather and sunshine. There are about four hundred different glaciers,* according to the computation of M. Bourrit, between Mont Blanc and the frontiers of the Tyrol. The full effect of the most lofty and picturesque of them can, of course, only be produced by the richest and warmest lights of the atmosphere; and the very heat which illuminates them must have a changing influence on many of their appearances. I imagine it is owing to this circumstance, namely, the casualty and changeableness of the appearance of some of the glaciers, that the impressions made by them on the minds of other and more transient travellers have been less enchanting than those de-

* Occupying, if taken together, a surface of 130 square leagues.

scribed by M. Bourrit. On one occasion M. Bourrit seems even to speak of a past phenomenon, and certainly one which no other spectator attests in the same terms when he says, that there once existed between the Kandel Steig and Lauterbrun, "a pasage amidst singular glaciers, sometimes resembling magical towns of ice, with pilasters, pyramids, columns, and obelisks reflecting to the sun the most brilliant hues of the finest gems."—M. Bourrit's description of the Glacier of the Rhone is quite enchanting:—"To form an idea," he says, "of this superb spectacle, figure in your mind a scaffolding of transparent ice, filling a space of two miles, rising to the clouds, and darting flashes of light like the sun. Nor were the several parts less magnificent and surprising. One might see as it were, the streets and buildings of a city, erected in the form of an amphitheatre, and embellished with pieces of water, cascades and torrents. The effects were as prodigious as the immensity and the height;—the most beautiful azure—the most splendid white—the regular appearance of a thousand pyramids of ice, are more easy to be imagined than described."—*Bourrit*, iii. 163.

Page 51, line 10.

From heights browsed by the bounding bouquetin;

Laborde, in his "Tableau de la Suisse," gives a curious account of this animal, the wild sharp cry and elastic movements of which must heighten the picturesque appearance of its haunts.—"Nature," says Laborde "has destined it to mountains covered with snow: if it is not exposed to keen cold, it becomes blind. Its agility in leaping much surpasses that of the chamois, and would appear incredible to those who have not seen it. There is not a mountain so high or steep to which it will not trust itself, provided it has room to place its feet; it can scramble along the highest wall, if its surface be rugged."

Page 51, line 17.

——enamell'd moss.

The moss of Switzerland, as well as that of the Tyrol, is remarkable for a bright smoothness, approaching to the appearance of enamel.

Page 56, line 4.

How dear seem'd ev'n the waste and wild Shreckhorn,

The Shreckhorn means, in German, the Peak of Terror.

Page 56, line 9.

Blindfold his native hills he could have known!

I have here availed myself of a striking expression of the

Emperor Napoleon respecting his recollections of Corsica, which is recorded in Las Casas's History of the Emperor's Abode at St. Helena.

O'CONNOR'S CHILD.

Page 83, line 1.

Innisfail, the ancient name of Ireland.

Page 84, line 7.

Kerne, the plural of Kern, an Irish foot-soldier. In this sense the word is used by Shakspeare. Gainsford, in his Glories of England, says, "They (the Irish) are desperate in revenge, and their kerne think no man dead *until his head be off*."

Page 84, line 26.

Shieling, a rude cabin or hut.

Page 85, line 4.

In Erin's yellow vesture clad,

Yellow, dyed from saffron, was the favourite colour of the ancient Irish. When the Irish chieftains came to make terms with Queen Elizabeth's lord-lieutenant, we are told by Sir John Davis, that they came to court in saffron-coloured uniforms.

Page 85, line 18.

Mórat, a drink made of the juice of mulberry mixed with honey.

Page 86, line 21.

Their tribe, they said, their high degree,
Was sung in Tara's psaltery;

The pride of the Irish in ancestry was so great, that one of the O'Neals being told that Barret of Castlemone had been there only 400 years, he replied—that he hated the clown as if he had come there but yesterday.

Tara was the place of assemblage and feasting of the petty princes of Ireland. Very splendid and fabulous descriptions are given by the Irish historians of the pomp and luxury of those meetings. The psaltery of Tara was the grand national register of Ireland. The grand epoch of political eminence in the early history of the Irish is the reign of their great and favourite monarch, Ollam Fodlah, who reigned, according to Keating, about 950 years before the Christian æra. Under him was instituted the great Fes at Tara, which it is pretended was a triennial convention of the states, or a parliament; the members of which were the Druids, and other learned men, who represented the people in that assembly. Very minute accounts are given by Irish annalists of the magnificence and order of these entertainments; from which, if credible, we might collect the earliest traces of heraldry that occur in history. To preserve order and regularity in the great number and variety of the members who met on such occasions, the Irish historians inform us that, when the banquet was ready to be served up, the shield-bearers of the princes, and other members of the convention, delivered in their shields and targets, which were readily distinguished by the coats of arms emblazoned upon them. These were arranged by the grand marshal and principal herald, and hung upon the walls on the right side of the table; and, upon entering the apartments, each member took his seat under his respective shield or target, without the slightest disturbance. The concluding days of the meeting, it is allowed by the Irish antiquaries, were spent in very free excess of conviviality: but the first six, they say were devoted to the examination and settlement of the annals of the kingdom. These were publicly rehearsed. When they had passed the approbation of the assembly, they were transcribed into the authentic chronicles of the nation, which was called the Register, or Psalter, of Tara.

Col. Vallancey gives a translation of an old Irish fragment, found in Trinity-college, Dublin, in which the palace of the above assembly is thus described, as it existed in the reign of Cormac:—

"In the reign of Cormac, the palace of Tara was nine hundred feet square; the diameter of the surrounding rath, seven dice or casts of a dart; it contained one hundred and fifty apartments; one hundred and fifty dormitories, or sleeping-rooms for guards, and sixty men in each; the height was twenty-seven cubits; there were one hundred and fifty common drinking horns, twelve doors, and one thousand guests daily, besides princes, orators, and men of science, engravers of gold and silver, carvers, modellers, and nobles." The Irish description of the banqueting-hall is thus translated: "Twelve stalls or divisions in each wing; sixteen attendants on each side, and two to each table; one hundred guests in all."

Page 87, line 4.

And stemm'd De Bourgo's chivalry?

The house of O'Connor had a right to boast of their victories over the English. It was a chief of the O'Connor race who gave a check to the English champion De Courcy, so famous for his personal strength, and for cleaving a helmet at one blow of his sword, in the presence of the kings of France and England, when the French champion declined the combat with him. Though ultimately conquered by the English under De Bourgo, the O'Connors had also humbled the pride of that name on a memorable occasion: viz., when Walter De Bourgo, an ancestor of that De Bourgo who won the battle of Athunree, had become so insolent as to make excessive demands upon the territories of Connaught, and to bid defiance to all the rights and properties reserved by the Irish chiefs. Eath O'Connor, a near descendant of the famous Cathal, surnamed of the Bloody hand, rose against the usurper, and defeated the English so severely, that their general died of chagrin after the battle.

Page 87, line 7.

Or beal-fires for your jubilee

The month of May is to this day called Mi Beal tiennie, *i. e.*, the month of Beal's fire, in the original language of Ireland, and hence, I believe, the name of the Beltan festival in the Highlands. These fires were lighted on the summits of mountains (the Irish antiquaries say) in honour of the sun; and are supposed, by those conjecturing gentlemen, to prove the origin of the Irish from some nation who worshipped Baal or Belus. Many hills in Ireland still retain the name of Cnoc Greine, *i. e.*, the Hill of the Sun; and on all are to be seen the ruins of druidical altars.

Page 88, line 2.

And play my clarshech by thy side.

The clarshech, or harp, the principal musical instrument of the Hibernian bards, does not appear to be of Irish origin, nor indigenous to any of the British islands.—The Britons undoubtedly were not acquainted with it during the residence of the Romans in their country, as in all their coins, on which musical instruments are represented, we see only the Roman lyre, and not the British teylin, or harp.

Page 88, line 9.

And saw at dawn the lofty bawn

Bawn, from the Teutonic Bawen—to construct and secure with branches of trees, was so called because the primitive Celtic fortifications were made by digging a ditch, throwing up a rampart, and on the latter fixing stakes, which were interlaced with boughs of trees. This word is used by Spenser; but it is inaccurately called by Mr. Todd, his annotator, an eminence.

Page 91, line 13.

To speak the malison of heaven.

If the wrath which I have ascribed to the heroine of this little piece should seem to exhibit her character as too unnaturally stripped of patriotic and domestic affections, I must beg leave to plead the authority of Corneille in the representation of a similar passion: I allude to the denunciation of Camille, in the tragedy of "Horace." When Horace, accompanied by a soldier bearing the three swords of the Curiatii, meets his sister, and invites her to congratulate him on his victory, she expresses only her grief, which he attributes at first only to her feelings for the loss of her two brothers; but when she bursts forth into reproaches against him as the murderer of her lover, the last of the Curiatii, he exclaims:

"O ciel! qui vit jamais une pareille rage!
Crois-tu donc que je sois insensible à l'outrage,
Que je souffre en mon sang ce mortel déshonneur?
Aime, aime cette mort qui fait notre bonheur;
Et préfère du moins au souvenir d'un homme
Ce que doit ta naissance aux intérêts de Rome."

At the mention of Rome, Camille breaks out into this apostrophe:

"Rome, l'unique objet de mon ressentiment!
Rome, à qui vient ton bras d'immoler mon amant!
Rome qui t'a vu naître et que ton cœur adore!
Rome enfin que je hais parce qu'elle t'honore!
Puissent tous ses voisins ensemble conjurés
Saper ses fondements encor mal assurés;
Et si ce n'est assez de toute l'Italie,
Que l'Orient contre elle à l'Occident s'allie;
Que cent peuples unis des bouts de l'univers
Passent pour la détruire et les monts et les mers;
Qu'elle même sur soi renverse ses murailles,
Et de ses propres mains déchire ses entrailles!
Que le courroux du ciel allumé par mes vœux
Fasse pleuvoir sur elle un déluge de feux!
Puissé-je de mes yeux y voir tomber ce foudre,
Voir ses maisons en cendre et tes lauriers en poudre,
Voir le dernier Romain à son dernier soupir,
Moi seule en être cause, et mourir de plaisir!"

Page 91, line 18.

And go to Athunree! (I cried)

In the reign of Edward the Second, the Irish presented to

Pope John the Twenty-second a memorial of their sufferings under the English, of which the language exhibits all the strength of despair. "Ever since the English (say they) first appeared upon our coasts, they entered our territories under a certain specious pretence of charity, and external hypocritical show of religion, endeavouring at the same time, by every artifice malice could suggest, to extirpate us root and branch, and without any other right than that of the strongest; they have so far succeeded by base fraudulence, and cunning, that they have forced us to quit our fair and ample habitations and inheritances, and to take refuge like wild beasts in the mountains, the woods, and the morasses of the country;—nor even can the caverns and dens protect us against their insatiable avarice. They pursue us even into these frightful abodes; endeavouring to dispossess us of the wild uncultivated rocks, and arrogate to themselves the PROPERTY OF EVERY PLACE on which we can stamp the figure of our feet."

The greatest effort ever made by the ancient Irish to regain their native independence, was made at the time when they called over the brother of Robert Bruce from Scotland. William de Bourgo, brother to the Earl of Ulster, and Richard de Bermingham, were sent against the main body of the native insurgents, who were headed rather than commanded by Felim O'Connor. The important battle which decided the subjection of Ireland, took place on the 10th of August, 1315. It was the bloodiest that ever was fought between the two nations, and continued throughout the whole day, from the rising to the setting sun. The Irish fought with inferior discipline, but with great enthusiasm. They lost ten thousand men, among whom were twenty-nine chiefs of Connaught. Tradition states that, after this terrible day, the O'Connor family, like the Fabian, were so nearly exterminated, that throughout all Connaught not one of the name remained, except Felim's brother, who was capable of bearing arms.

LOCHIEL'S WARNING.

Page 94.

LOCHIEL, the chief of the warlike clan of the Camerons, and descended from ancestors distinguished in their narrow sphere for great personal prowess, was a man worthy of a better cause and fate than that in which he embarked, the enterprise of the Stuarts in 1745. His memory is still fondly cherished among the Highlanders, by the appellation of the "*gentle Lochiel;*" for he was famed for his social virtues as much as his martial and magnanimous (though mistaken) loyalty. His influence was so important among the Highland chiefs, that it depended on his joining with his clan whether the standard of Charles should be raised or not in 1745 Lochiel was himself too wise a man to be blind to the consequences of so hopeless an enterprise, but his sensibility to the point of honour overruled his wisdom. Charles appealed to his loyalty, and he could not brook the reproaches of his Prince. When Charles landed at Borrodale, Lochiel went to meet him, but on his way called at his brother's house (Cameron of Fassafern), and told him on what errand he was going; adding, however, that he meant to dissuade the Prince from his enterprise. Fassafern advised him in that case to communicate his mind by letter to Charles. "No," said Lochiel, "I think it due to my Prince to give him my reasons in person for refusing to join his standard."—"Brother," replied Fassafern, "I know you better than you know yourself: if the Prince once sets eyes on you, he will make you do what he pleases." The interview accordingly took place; and Lochiel, with many arguments, but in vain, pressed the Pretender to return to France, and reserve himself and his friends for a more favourable occasion, as he had come, by his own acknowledgment, without arms, or money, or adherents: or, at all events, to remain concealed till his friends should meet and deliberate what was best to be done. Charles, whose mind was wound up to the utmost impatience, paid no regard to this proposal, but answered, "that he was determined to put all to the hazard." "In a few days," said he, "I will erect the royal standard, and proclaim to the people of Great Britain, that Charles Stuart is come over to claim the crown of his ancestors, and to win it or perish in the attempt. Lochiel, who my father has often told me was our firmest friend, may stay at home and learn from the newspapers the fate of his Prince."—"No," said Lochiel, "I will share the fate of my Prince, and so shall every man over whom nature or fortune hath given me any power."

The other chieftains who followed Charles embraced his cause with no better hopes. It engages our sympathy most strongly in their behalf, that no motive, but their fear to be reproached with cowardice or disloyalty, impelled them to the hopeless adventure. Of this we have an example in the interview of Prince Charles with Clanronald, another leading chieftain in the rebel army.

"Charles," says Home, "almost reduced to despair, in his discourse with Boisdale, addressed the two Highlanders with great emotion, and, summing up his arguments for taking arms, conjured them to assist their Prince, their countryman, in his utmost need, Clanronald and his friend, though well inclined to the cause, positively refused, and told him that to take up arms without concert or support was to pull down certain ruin on their own heads. Charles persisted, argued, and implored. During this conversation (they were on shipboard) the parties walked backwards and forwards on the deck; a Highlander stood near them, armed at all points, as was then the fashion of his country. He was a younger brother of Kinloch Moidart, and had come off to the ship to inquire for news, not knowing who was aboard. When he gathered, from their discourse, that the stranger was the Prince of Wales; when he heard his chief and his brother refuse to take arms with their Prince, his colour went and came, his eyes sparkled, he shifted his place, and grasped his sword. Charles observed his demeanour, and turning briskly to him called out, 'Will you assist me?'—'I will, I will,' said Ronald: though no other man in the Highlands should draw a sword, I am ready to die for you!' Charles, with a profusion of thanks to his champion, said, he wished all the Highlanders were like him. Without further deliberation, the two Macdonalds declared that they would also join, and use their utmost endeavours to engage their countrymen to take arms." —*Home's Hist. Rebellion*, p. 40.

Page 94, line 17.

Weep, Albin!

The Gaelic appellation of Scotland, more particularly the Highlands.

Page 96, line 22.

Lo! anointed by Heaven with the vials of wrath,
Behold, where he flies on his desolate path!

The lines allude to the many hardships of the royal sufferer.

An account of the second sight, in Irish called Taish, is thus given in Martin's Description of the Western Isles of Scotland.

" The second sight is a singular faculty of seeing an otherwise invisible object, without any previous means used by the person who sees it for that end. The vision makes such a lively impression upon the seers, that they neither see nor think of any thing else except the vision as long as it continues; and then they appear pensive or jovial according to the object which was represented to them.

"At the sight of a vision the eyelids of the person are erected and the eyes continue staring until the object vanishes. This is obvious to others who are standing by when the persons happen to see a vision; and occurred more than once to my own observation, and to others that were with me.

" There is one in Skie, of whom his acquaintance observed, that when he sees a vision the inner part of his eyelids turns so far upwards, that, after the object disappears, he must draw them down with his fingers, and sometimes employ others to draw them down, which he finds to be much the easier way.

"This faculty of the second sight does not lineally descend in a family, as some have imagined; for I know several parents who are endowed with it, and their children are not; and *vice versâ.* Neither is it acquired by any previous compact. And after strict inquiry, I could never learn from any among them, that this faculty was communicable to any whatsoever. The seer knows neither the object, time, nor place of a vision before it appears: and the same object is often seen by different persons living at a considerable distance from one another. The true way of judging as to the time and circumstances is by observation; for several persons of judgment who are without this faculty are more capable to judge of the design of a vision than a novice that is a seer. If an object appear in the day or night, it will come to pass sooner or later accordingly.

"If an object is seen early in a morning, which is not frequent, it will be accomplished in a few hours afterwards; if at noon, it will probably be accomplished that very day; if in the evening, perhaps that night; if after candles be lighted, it will be accomplished that night; the latter always an accomplishment by weeks, months, and sometimes years, according to the time of the night the vision is seen.

"When a shroud is seen about one, it is a sure prognostic of death. The time is judged according to the height of it about the person; for if it is not seen above the middle, death is not to be expected for the space of a year, and perhaps some months longer: and as it is frequently seen to ascend higher towards the head, death is concluded to be at hand within a few days, if not hours, as daily experience confirms. Examples of this kind were shown me, when the person of whom the observations were then made was in perfect health.

"It is ordinary with them to see houses, gardens, and trees in places void of all these, and this in process of time is wont to be accomplished: as at Mogslot, in the Isle of Skie, where there were but a few sorry low houses, thatched with straw; yet in a few years the vision, which appeared often, was accomplished by the building of several good houses in the very spot represented to the seers, and by the planting of orchards there.

"To see a spark of fire is a forerunner of a dead child, to be seen in the arms of those persons; of which there are several instances. To see a seat empty at the time of sitting in it, is a presage of that person's death quickly after it.

"When a novice, or one that has lately obtained the second sight, sees a vision in the night-time without doors, and comes near a fire, he presently falls into a swoon.

"Some find themselves as it were in a crowd of people

having a corpse, which they carry along with them; and after such visions the seers come in sweating, and describe the vision that appeared. If there be any of their acquaintance among them, they give an account of their names, as also of the bearers; but they know nothing concerning the corpse."

Horses and cows (according to the same credulous author) have certainly sometimes the same faculty; and he endeavours to prove it by the signs of fear which the animals exhibit, when second-sighted persons see visions in the same place.

"The seers (he continues) are generally illiterate and well-meaning people, and altogether void of design: nor could I ever learn that any of them ever made the least gain by it; neither is it reputable among them to have that faculty. Besides, the people of the Isles are not so credulous as to believe implicitly before the thing predicted is accomplished; but when it is actually accomplished afterwards, it is not in their power to deny it, without offering violence to their own sense and reason. Besides, if the seers were deceivers, can it be reasonable to imagine that all the islanders who have not the second sight should combine together, and offer violence to their understandings and senses, to enforce themselves to believe a lie from age to age? There are several persons among them whose title and education raise them above the suspicion of concurring with an impostor merely to gratify an illiterate contemptible set of persons; nor can reasonable persons believe that children, horses, and cows, should be preëngaged in a combination in favour of the second sight." *Martin's Description of the Western Isles of Scotland*, p. 3. 11.

GERTRUDE OF WYOMING.

Page 142, line 6.

From merry mock bird's song,———

THE mocking-bird is of the form of, but larger than, the thrush; and the colours are a mixture of black, white, and gray. What is said of the nightingale by its greatest admirers is what may with more propriety apply to this bird, who, in a natural state, sings with very superior taste. Towards evening I have heard one begin softly, reserving its breath to swell certain notes, which, by this means, had a most astonishing effect. A gentleman in London had one of these birds for six years. During the space of a minute he was heard to imitate the woodlark, chaffinch, blackbird, thrush, and sparrow. In this country (America) I have frequently known the mocking-birds so engaged in this mimicry, that it was with much difficulty I could ever obtain an opportunity of hearing their own natural note. Some go so far as to say, that they have neither peculiar notes, nor favourite imitations. This may be denied. Their few natural notes resemble those of the (European) nightingale. Their song, however, has a greater compass and volume than the nightingale's, and they have the faculty of varying all intermediate notes in a manner which is truly delightful.—*Ashe's Travels in America*, vol. ii. p. 73.

Page 143. line 5.

And distant isles that hear the loud Corbrechtan roar!

The Corybrechtan, or Corbrechtan, is a whirlpool on the western coast of Scotland, near the island of Jura, which is heard at a prodigious distance. Its name signifies the whirlpool of the Prince of Denmark; and there is a tradition that a Danish prince once undertook, for a wager, to cast anchor in it. He is said to have used woollen instead of hempen ropes, for greater strength, but perished in the attempt. On the shores of Argyleshire, I have often listened with great delight to the sound of this vortex, at the distance of many leagues. When the weather is calm, and the adjacent sea scarcely heard on these picturesque shores, its sound, which is like the sound of innumerable chariots, creates a magnificent and fine effect.

Page 146, line 4.

Of buskin'd limb, and swarthy lineament;

In the Indian tribes there is a great similarity in their colour, stature, &c. They are all, except the Snake Indians, tall in stature, straight, and robust. It is very seldom they are deformed, which has given rise to the supposition that they put to death their deformed children. Their skin is of a copper colour; their eyes large, bright, black, and sparkling, indicative of a subtle and discerning mind: their hair is of the same colour, and prone to be long, seldom or never curled. Their teeth are large and white; I never observed any decayed among them, which makes their breath as sweet as the air they inhale.—*Travels through America by Captains Lewis and Clarke, in* 1804-5-6.

Page 146, line 16.

"Peace be to thee! my words this belt approve;

The Indians of North America accompany every formal ad

dress to strangers, with whom they form or recognize a treaty of amity, with a present of a string, or belt, of wampum. Wampum (says Cadwallader Colden) is made of the large whelk shell, *buccinum*, and shaped like long beads : it is the current money of the Indians.—*History of the Five Indian Nations*, p. 34. *New York edition.*

Page 146, line 17.

The paths of peace my steps have hither led:

In relating an interview of Mohawk Indians with the Governor of New York, Colden quotes the following passage as a specimen of their metaphorical manner : " Where shall I seek the chair of peace ? Where shall I find it but upon our path ? and whither doth our path lead us but unto this house ? "

Page 146, line 22.

Our wampum league thy brethren did embrace:

When they solicit the alliance, offensive or defensive, of a whole nation, they send an embassy with a large belt of wampum and a bloody hatchet, inviting them to come and drink the blood of their enemies. The wampum made use of on these and other occasions, before their acquaintance with the Europeans, was nothing but small shells which they picked up by the sea-coasts, and on the banks of the lakes ; and now it is nothing but a kind of cylindrical beads, made of shells, white and black, which are esteemed among them as silver and gold are among us. The black they call the most valuable, and both together are their greatest riches and ornaments ; these among them answering all the end that money does amongst us. They have the art of stringing, twisting, and interweaving them into their belts, collars, blankets, and mocasins, &c., in ten thousand different sizes, forms, and figures, so as to be ornaments for every part of dress, and expressive to them of all their important transactions. They dye the wampum of various colours and shades, and mix and dispose them with great ingenuity and order, and so as to be significant among themselves of almost every thing they please ; so that by these their words are kept, and their thoughts communicated to one another, as ours are by writing. The belts that pass from one nation to another in all treaties, declarations, and important transactions, are very carefully preserved in the cabins of their chiefs, and serve not only as a kind of record or history, but as a public treasure.—*Major Rogers's Account of North America.*

Page 147, line 20.

As when the evil Manitou——

It is certain the Indians acknowledge one Supreme Being, or Giver of Life, who presides over all things ; that is, the Great Spirit, and they look up to him as the source of good, from whence no evil can proceed. They also believe in a bad Spirit, to whom they ascribe great power ; and suppose that through his power all the evils which befall mankind are inflicted. To him, therefore, they pray in their distresses, begging that he would either avert their troubles, or moderate them when they are no longer avoidable.

They hold also that there are good Spirits of a lower degree, who have their particular departments, in which they are constantly contributing to the happiness of mortals. These they suppose to preside over all the extraordinary productions of Nature, such as those lakes, rivers, and mountains that are of an uncommon magnitude ; and likewise the beasts, birds, fishes, and even vegetables or stones, that exceed the rest of their species in size or singularity.—*Clarke's Travels among the Indians.*

The Supreme Spirit of Good is called by the Indians, Kitchi Manitou ; and the Spirit of Evil, Matchi Manitou.

Page 148, line 12.

Of fever-balm and sweet sagamité :

The fever-balm is a medicine used by these tribes ; it is a decoction of a bush called the Fever Tree. Sagamité is a kind of soup administered to their sick.

Page 148, line 21.

And I, the eagle of my tribe, have rush'd
With this lorn dove.

The testimony of all travellers among the American Indians who mention their hieroglyphics, authorizes me in putting this figurative language in the mouth of Outalissi. The dove is among them, as elsewhere, an emblem of meekness ; and the eagle, that of a bold, noble, and liberal mind. When the Indians speak of a warrior who soars above the multitude in person and endowments, they say, "he is like the eagle, who destroys his enemies, and gives protection and abundance to the weak of his own tribe."

Page 149, last line.

Far differently, the mute Oneyda took, &c.

They are extremely circumspect and deliberate in every

word and action; nothing hurries them into any intemperate wrath, but that inveteracy to their enemies which is rooted in every Indian's breast. In all other instances they are cool and deliberate, taking care to suppress the emotions of the heart. If an Indian has discovered that a friend of his is in danger of being cut off by a lurking enemy, he does not tell him of his danger in direct terms as though he were in fear, but he first coolly asks him which way he is going that day, and having his answer, with the same indifference tells him that he has been informed that a noxious beast lies on the route he is going. This hint proves sufficient, and his friend avoids the danger with as much caution as though every design and motion of his enemy had been pointed out to him.

If an Indian has been engaged for several days in the chase, and by accident continued long without food, when he arrives at the hut of a friend, where he knows that his wants will be immediately supplied, he takes care not to show the least symptoms of impatience, or betray the extreme hunger that he is tortured with; but on being invited in, sits contentedly down, and smokes his pipe with as much composure as if his appetite was cloyed and he was perfectly at ease. He does the same if among strangers. This custom is strictly adhered to by every tribe, as they esteem it a proof of fortitude, and think the reverse would entitle them to the appellation of old women.

If you tell an Indian that his children have greatly signalized themselves against an enemy, have taken many scalps, and brought home many prisoners, he does not appear to feel any strong emotions of pleasure on the occasion; his answer generally is,—"They have done well," and he makes but very little inquiry about the matter; on the contrary, if you inform him that his children are slain or taken prisoners, he makes no complaints; he only replies, "It is unfortunate:" and for some time asks no questions about how it happened. *Lewis and Clarke's Travels.*

Page 150, line 1.

His calumet of peace, &c.

Nor is the calumet of less importance or less revered than the wampum in many transactions relative both to peace and war. The bowl of this pipe is made of a kind of soft red stone, which is easily wrought and hollowed out; the stem is of cane, alder, or some kind of light wood, painted with different colours, and decorated with the heads, tails, and feathers of the most beautiful birds. The use of the calumet is to smoke either tobacco or some bark, leaf, or herb, which they often use instead of it, when they enter into an alliance on any serious occasion, or solemn engagements; this being among them the most sacred oath that can be taken, the violation of which is esteemed most infamous, and deserving of severe punishment from Heaven. When they treat of war, the whole pipe and all its ornaments are red: sometimes it is red only on one side, and by the disposition of the feathers &c. one acquainted with their customs will know at first sight what the nation who presents it intends or desires. Smoking the calumet is also a religious ceremony on some occasions, and in all treaties is considered as a witness between the parties, or rather as an instrument by which they invoke the sun and moon to witness their sincerity, and to be as it were a guaranty of the treaty between them. This custom of the Indians, though to appearance somewhat ridiculous, is not without its reasons; for as they find that smoking tends to disperse the vapours of the brain, to raise the spirits, and to qualify them for thinking and judging properly, they introduce it into their councils, where, after their resolves, the pipe was considered as a seal of their decrees, and as a pledge of their performance thereof, it was sent to those they were consulting, in alliance or treaty with;—so that smoking among them at the same pipe, is equivalent to our drinking together and out of the same cup. *Major Rogers's Account of North America*, 1766.

The lighted calumet is also used among them for a purpose still more interesting than the expression of social friendship. The austere manners of the Indians forbid any appearance of gallantry between the sexes in the daytime; but at night the young lover goes a-calumeting, as his courtship is called. As these people live in a state of equality, and without fear of internal violence or theft in their own tribes, they leave their doors open by night as well as by day. The lover takes advantage of this liberty, lights his calumet, enters the cabin of his mistress, and gently presents it to her. If she extinguish it, she admits his addresses; but if she suffer it to burn unnoticed, he retires with a disappointed and throbbing heart. *Ashe's Travels.*

Page 150, line 4.

Train'd from his tree-rock'd cradle to his bier

An Indian child, as soon as he is born, is swathed with clothes, or skins; and being laid on his back, is bound down on a piece of thick board, spread over with soft moss. The board is somewhat larger and broader than the child, and bent pieces of wood, like pieces of hoops, are placed over its face to protect it, so that if the machine were suffered to fall, the child probably would not be injured. When the women have any business to transact at home, they hang the boards on a tree, if there be one at hand, and set them a-swinging from side to side, like a pendulum, in order to exercise the children. *Weld*, vol. ii., p. 246.

Page 150, line 5.

The fierce extreme of good and ill to brook
Impassive———

Of the active as well as passive fortitude of the Indian character, the following is an instance related by Adair, in his Travels:—

A party of the Senekah Indians came to war against the Katahba, bitter enemies to each other. In the woods the former discovered a sprightly warrior belonging to the latter, hunting in their usual light dress: on his perceiving them, he sprang off for a hollow rock four or five miles distant, as they intercepted him from running homeward. He was so extremely swift and skilful with the gun, as to kill seven of them in the running fight before they were able to surround and take him. They carried him to their country in sad triumph; but though he had filled them with uncommon grief and shame for the loss of so many of their kindred, yet the love of martial virtue induced them to treat him, during their long journey, with a great deal more civility than if he had acted the part of a coward. The women and children, when they met him at their several towns, beat him and whipped him in as severe a manner as the occasion required, according to their law of justice, and at last he was formally condemned to die by the fiery torture. It might reasonably be imagined that what he had for some time gone through, by being fed with a scanty hand, a tedious march, lying at night on the bare ground, exposed to the changes of the weather, with his arms and legs extended in a pair of rough stocks, and suffering such punishment on his entering into their hostile towns, as a prelude to those sharp torments for which he was destined, would have so impaired his health and affected his imagination, as to have sent him to his long sleep, out of the way of any more sufferings. Probably this would have been the case with the major part of the white people under similar circumstances; but I never knew this with any of the Indians; and this cool-headed, brave warrior did not deviate from their rough lessons of martial virtue, but acted his part so well as to surprise and sorely vex his numerous enemies:—for when they were taking him, unpinioned, in their wild parade, to the place of torture, which lay near to a river, he suddenly dashed down those who stood in his way, sprang off, and plunged into the water, swimming underneath like an otter, only rising to take breath, till he reached the opposite shore. He now ascended the steep bank, but though he had good reason to be in a hurry, as many of the enemy were in the water, and others running, very like bloodhounds, in pursuit of him, and the bullets flying around him from the time he took to the river, yet his heart did not allow him to leave them abruptly, without taking leave in a formal manner, in return for the extraordinary favours they had done, and intended to do him. After slapping a part of his body in defiance to them (continues the author), he put up the shrill war-whoop, as his last salute, till some more convenient opportunity offered, and darted off in the manner of a beast broke loose from its torturing enemies. He continued his speed so as to run by about midnight of the same day as far as his eager pursuers were two days in reaching. There he rested till he happily discovered five of those Indians who had pursued him:—he lay hid a little way off their camp, till they were sound asleep. Every circumstance of his situation occurred to him, and inspired him with heroism. He was naked, torn, and hungry, and his enraged enemies were come up with him;—but there was now every thing to relieve his wants, and a fair opportunity to save his life, and get great honour and sweet revenge, by cutting them off. Resolution, a convenient spot, and sudden surprise, would effect the main object of all his wishes and hopes. He accordingly crept, took one of their tomahawks, and killed them all on the spot,—clothed himself, took a choice gun, and as much ammunition and provisions as he could well carry in a running march. He set off afresh with a light heart, and did not sleep for several successive nights, only when he reclined, as usual, a little before day, with his back to a tree. As it were by instinct, when he found he was free from the pursuing enemy, he made directly to the very place where he had killed seven of his enemies, and was taken by them for the fiery torture. He digged them up, burnt their bodies to ashes, and went home in safety with singular triumph. Other pursuing enemies came, on the evening of the second day, to the camp of their dead people, when the sight gave them a greater shock than they had ever known before. In their chilled war-council they concluded, that as he had done such surprising things in his defence before he was captivated, and since that in his naked condition, and now was well-armed, if they continued the pursuit he would spoil them all, for he surely was an enemy wizard,—and therefore they returned home.—*Adair's General Observations on the American Indians*, p. 394.

It is surprising (says the same author) to see the long-continued speed of the Indians. Though some of us have often run the swiftest of them out of sight for about the distance of twelve miles, yet afterwards, without any seeming toil, they would stretch on, leave us out of sight, and outwind any horse.—*Ibid.* p. 318.

If an Indian were driven out into the extensive woods, with only a knife and a tomahawk, or a small hatchet, it is not to be doubted but he would fatten even where a wolf would starve. He would soon collect fire by rubbing two dry pieces of wood together, make a bark hut, earthen vessels, and a bow and arrows; then kill wild game, fish, fresh-water tortoises, gather a plentiful variety of vegetables, and live in affluence.—*Ibid.* p. 410.

Page 150, line 3.

Mocasins are a sort of Indian buskins.

Page 150, line 14.

"*Sleep, wearied one! and in the dreaming land*
Shouldst thou to-morrow with thy mother meet,

There is nothing (says Charlevoix) in which these barbarians carry their superstitions farther than in what regards dreams; but they vary greatly in their manner of explaining themselves on this point. Sometimes it is the reasonable soul which ranges abroad, while the sensitive continues to animate the body. Sometimes it is the familiar genius who gives salutary counsel with respect to what is going to happen. Sometimes it is a visit made by the soul of the object of which he dreams. But in whatever manner the dream is conceived, it is always looked upon as a thing sacred, and as the most ordinary way in which the gods make known their will to men. Filled with this idea, they cannot conceive how we should pay no regard to them. For the most part they look upon them either as a desire of the soul, inspired by some genius, or an order from him, and in consequence of this principle they hold it a religious duty to obey them An Indian having dreamt of having a finger cut off, had it really cut off as soon as he awoke, having first prepared himself for this important action by a feast. Another having dreamt of being a prisoner, and in the hands of his enemies, was much at a loss what to do. He consulted the jugglers, and by their advice caused himself to be tied to a post, and burnt in several parts of the body.—*Charlevoix, Journal of a Voyage to North America.*

Page 150, last line.

From a flower shaped like a horn, which Chateaubriand presumes to be of the lotus kind, the Indians in their travels through the desert often find a draught of dew purer than any other water.

Page 151, line 11.

The crocodile, the condor of the rock,

The alligator, or American crocodile, when full grown (says Bertram,) is a very large and terrible creature, and of prodigious strength, activity, and swiftness in the water. I have seen them twenty feet in length, and some are supposed to be twenty-two or twenty-three feet in length. Their body is as large as that of a horse, their shape usually resembles that of a lizard, which is flat, or cuneiform, being compressed on each side, and gradually diminishing from the abdomen to the extremity, which, with the whole body, is covered with horny plates, or squamæ, impenetrable when on the body of the live animal, even to a rifle ball, except about their head, and just behind their fore-legs or arms, where, it is said, they are only vulnerable. The head of a full-grown one is about three feet, and the mouth opens nearly the same length. Their eyes are small in proportion, and seem sunk in the head, by means of the prominency of the brows; the nostrils are large, inflated, and prominent on the top, so that the head on the water resembles, at a distance, a great chunk of wood floating about: only the upper jaw moves, which they raise almost perpendicular, so as to form a right angle with the lower one. In the forepart of the upper jaw, on each side, just under the nostrils, are two very large, thick, strong teeth, or tusks, not very sharp, but rather the shape of a cone: these are as white as the finest polished ivory, and are not covered by any skin or lips, but always in sight, which gives the creature a frightful appearance: in the lower jaw are holes opposite to these teeth to receive them; when they clap their jaws together, it causes a surprising noise, like that which is made by forcing a heavy plank with violence upon the ground, and may be heard at a great distance. But what is yet more surprising to a stranger, is the incredibly loud and terrifying roar which they are capable of making, especially in breeding-time. It most resembles very heavy distant thunder, not only shaking the air and waters, but causing the earth to tremble; and when hundreds are roaring at the same time, you can scarcely be persuaded but that the whole globe is violently and dangerously agitated. An old champion, who is, perhaps, absolute sovereign of a little lake or lagoon, (when fifty less than himself are obliged to content themselves with swelling and roaring in little coves round about,) darts forth from the reedy coverts, all at once, on the surface of the waters in a right line, at first seemingly as rapid as lightning, but gradually more slowly, until he arrives at the centre of the lake, where he stops. He now swells himself by drawing in wind and water through his mouth, which causes a loud sonorous rattling in the throat for near a minute; but it is immediately forced out again through his mouth and nostrils with a loud noise, brandishing his tail in the air, and the vapour running from his nostrils like smoke. At other times, when swoln to an extent ready to burst, his head and tail lifted up, he spins or twirls round on the surface of the water. He acts his part like an Indian chief, when rehearsing his feats of war.—*Bertram's Travels in North America.*

Page 151, line 13.

Then forth uprose that lone way faring man;

They discover an amazing sagacity, and acquire, with the greatest readiness, any thing that depends upon the attention of the mind. By experience, and an acute observation, they attain many perfections to which the Amerians are strangers. For instance, they will cross a forest or a plain, which is two hundred miles in breadth, so as to reach with great exactness the point at which they intend to arrive, keeping, during the whole of that space, in a direct line, without any material deviations; and this they will do with the same ease, let the weather be fair or cloudy. With equal acuteness they will point to that part of the heavens the sun is in, though it be intercepted by clouds or fogs. Besides this, they are able to pursue, with incredible facility, the traces of man or beast, either on leaves or grass; and on this account it is with great difficulty they escape discovery. They are indebted for these talents not only to nature, but to an extraordinary command of the intellectual qualities, which can only be acquired by an unremitted attention, and by long experience. They are, in general, very happy in a retentive memory. They can recapitulate every particular that has been treated of in councils, and remember the exact time when they were held. Their belts of wampum preserve the substance of the treaties they have concluded with the neighbouring tribes for ages back, to which they will appeal and refer with as much perspicuity and readiness as Europeans can to their written records.

The Indians are totally unskilled in geography, as well as all the other sciences, and yet they draw on their birch-bark very exact charts or maps of the countries they are acquainted with. The latitude and longitude only are wanting to make them tolerably complete.

Their sole knowledge in astronomy consists in being able to point out the polar star, by which they regulate their course when they travel in the night.

They reckon the distance of places not by miles or leagues, but by a day's journey, which, according to the best calculation I could make, appears to be about twenty English miles. These they also divide into halves and quarters, and will demonstrate them in their maps with great exactness by the hieroglyphics just mentioned, when they regulate in council their war-parties, or their most distant hunting excursions.—*Lewis and Clarke's Travels.*

Some of the French missionaries have supposed that the Indians are guided by instinct, and have pretended that Indian children can find their way through a forest as easily as a person of maturer years; but this is a most absurd notion. It is unquestionably by a close attention to the growth of the trees, and position of the sun, that they find their way. On the northern side of a tree there is generally the most moss: and the bark on that side, in general, differs from that on the opposite one. The branches toward the south are, for the most part, more luxuriant than those on the other sides of trees, and several other distinctions also subsist between the northern and southern sides, conspicuous to Indians, being taught from their infancy to attend to them which a common observer would, perhaps, never notice. Being accustomed from their infancy likewise to pay great attention to the position of the sun, they learn to make the most accurate allowance for its apparent motion from one part of the heavens to another: and in every part of the day they will point to the part of the heavens where it is, although the sky be obscured by clouds or mists.

An instance of their dexterity in finding their way through an unknown country came under my observation when I was at Staunton, situated behind the Blue Mountains, Virginia. A number of the Creek nation had arrived at that town on their way to Philadelphia, whither they were going upon some affairs of importance, and had stopped there for the night. In the morning, some circumstance or other, which could not be learned, induced one half of the Indians to set off without their companions, who did not follow until some hours afterwards. When these last were ready to pursue their journey, several of the towns-people mounted their horses to escort them part of the way. They proceeded along the high road for some miles, but, all at once, hastily turning aside into the woods, though there was no path, the Indians advanced confidently forward. The people who accompanied them, surprised at this movement, informed them that they were quitting the road to Philadelphia, and expressed their fear least they should miss their companions who had gone on before. They answered that they knew better, that the way through the woods was the shortest to Philadelphia, and that they knew very well that their companions had entered the wood at the very place where they did. Curiosity led some of the horsemen to go on ; and to their astonishment, for there was apparently no track, they overtook the other Indians in the thickest part of the wood. But what appeared most singular was, that the route which they took was found, on examining a map, to be as direct for Philadelphia as if they had taken the bearings by a mariner's compass. From others of their nation, who had been at Philadelphia at a former period, they had probably learned the exact direction of that city from their villages, and had never lost sight of it, although they had already travelled three hundred miles through the woods, and had upwards of four hundred miles more to go before they could reach the place of their destination. Of the exactness with which they can find out a strange place to which they have been once directed by their own people, a striking example is furnished, I think, by Mr. Jefferson, in his account of the Indian graves in Virginia. These graves are nothing more than large mounds of earth in the woods, which, on being opened, are found to contain skeletons in an erect posture: the Indian mode of sepulture has been too often described to remain unknown to you. But to come to my story. A party of Indians that were passing on to some of the seaports on the Atlantic, just as the Creeks above mentioned were going to Philadelphia, were observed, all on a sudden, to quit the straight road by which they were proceeding, and without asking any questions to strike through the woods, in a direct line, to one of these graves, which lay at the distance of some miles from the road. Now very near a century must have passed over since the part of Virginia in which this grave was situated had been inhabited by Indians, and these Indian travellers, who were to visit it by themselves, had unquestionably never been in that part of the country before: they must have found their way to it simply from the description of its situation, that had been handed down to them by tradition.—*Weld's Travels in North America*, vol. ii.

Page 156, line 12.

Their fathers' dust——

It is a custom of the Indian tribes to visit the tombs of their ancestors in the cultivated parts of America, who have been buried for upwards of a century.

Page 159, line 8.

Or wild-cane arch high flung o'er gulf profound,

The bridges over narrow streams in many parts of Spanish America are said to be built of cane, which, however strong to support the passengers, are yet waved in the agitation of the storm, and frequently add to the effect of a mountainous and picturesque scenery.

Page 169, line 17.

The Mammoth comes,———

That I am justified in making the Indian chief allude to the mammoth as an emblem of terror and destruction, will be seen by the authority quoted below. Speaking of the mammoth or big buffalo, Mr. Jefferson states, that a tradition is preserved among the Indians of that animal still existing in the northern parts of America.

"A delegation of warriors from the Delaware tribe having visited the governor of Virginia during the revolution, on matters of business, the governor asked them some questions relative to their country, and, among others, what they knew or had heard of the animal whose bones were found at the Salt-licks, on the Ohio. Their chief speaker immediately put himself into an attitude of oratory, and with a pomp suited to what he conceived the elevation of his subject, informed him that it was a tradition handed down from their fathers, that in ancient times a herd of these tremendous animals came to the Big-bone-licks, and began an universal destruction of the bear, deer, elk, buffalo, and other animals which had been created for the use of the Indians. That the Great Man above looking down and seeing this, was so enraged, that he seized his lightning, descended on the earth, seated himself on a neighbouring mountain, on a rock on which his seat and the prints of his feet are still to be seen, and hurled his bolts among them, till the whole were slaughtered, except the big bull, who, presenting his forehead to the shafts, shook them off as they fell, but missing one at length it wounded him in the side, whereon, springing round, he bounded over the Ohio, over the Wabash, the Illinois, and finally over the great lakes, where he is living at this day."—*Jefferson's Notes on Virginia.*

Page 169, line 25.

Scorning to wield the hatchet for his bribe,
'Gainst Brandt himself I went to battle forth:

I took the character of Brandt, in the poem of Gertrude, from the common Histories of England, all of which represented him as a bloody and bad man, (even among savages,) and chief agent in the horrible desolation of Wyoming. Some years after this poem appeared, the son of Brandt, a most interesting and intelligent youth, came over to England, and I formed an acquaintance with him, on which I still look back with pleasure. He appealed to my sense of honour and justice, on his own part and on that of his sister, to retract the unfair aspersions which, unconscious of their unfairness, I had cast on his father's memory.

He then referred me to documents, which completely satisfied me that the common accounts of Brandt's cruelties at Wyoming, which I had found in books of Travels and in Adolphus's, and similar Histories of England, were gross errors, and that in point of fact Brandt was not even present at that scene of desolation.

It is, unhappily, to Britons and Anglo-Americans that we must refer the chief blame in this horrible business. I published a letter expressing this belief in the *New Monthly Maga-*

zine, in the year 1822, to which I must refer the reader—if he has any curiosity on the subject—for an antidote to my fanciful description of Brandt. Among other expressions to young Brandt, I made use of the following words:—"Had I learnt all this of your father when I was writing my poem, he should not have figured in it as the hero of mischief." It was but bare justice to say thus much of a Mohawk Indian, who spoke English eloquently, and was thought capable of having written a history of the Six Nations. I ascertained, also, that he often strove to mitigate the cruelty of Indian warfare. The name of Brandt, therefore, remains in my poem a pure and declared character of fiction.

Page 170, line 7.

To whom nor relative nor blood remains,
No!—not a kindred drop that runs in human veins!

Every one who recollects the specimen of Indian eloquence given in the speech of Logan, a Mingo chief, to the governor of Virginia, will perceive that I have attempted to paraphrase its concluding and most striking expression:—"There runs not a drop of my blood in the veins of any living creature." The similar salutation of the fictitious personage in my story, and the real Indian orator, makes it surely allowable to borrow such an expression; and if it appears, as it cannot but appear, to less advantage than in the original, I beg the reader to reflect how difficult it is to transpose such exquisitely simple words, without sacrificing a portion of their effect.

In the spring of 1774, a robbery and murder were committed on an inhabitant of the frontiers of Virginia, by two Indians of the Shawanee tribe. The neighbouring whites, according to their custom, undertook to punish this outrage in a summary manner. Colonel Cresap, a man infamous for the many murders he had committed on those much injured people, collected a party and proceeded down the Kanaway in quest of vengeance; unfortunately, a canoe with women and children, with one man only, was seen coming from the opposite shore unarmed, and unsuspecting an attack from the whites. Cresap and his party concealed themselves on the bank of the river, and the moment the canoe reached the shore, singled out their objects, and at one fire killed every person in it. This happened to be the family of Logan, who had long been distinguished as a friend to the whites. This unworthy return provoked his vengeance; he accordingly signalized himself in the war which ensued. In the autumn of the same year a decisive battle was fought at the mouth of the great Kanaway, in which the collected forces of the Shawanees, Mingoes, and Delawares, were defeated by a detachment of the Virginian militia. The Indians sued for peace. Logan, however, disdained to be seen among the suppliants; but lest the sincerity of a treaty should be disturbed, from which so distinguished a chief abstracted himself, he sent, by a messenger, the following speech to be delivered to Lord Dunmore:—

"I appeal to any white man if ever he entered Logan's cabin hungry, and he gave him not to eat; if ever he came cold and naked, and he clothed him not. During the course of the last long and bloody war Logan remained idle in his cabin, an advocate for peace. Such was my love for the whites, that my countrymen pointed as they passed, and said, Logan is the friend of the white men. I have even thought to have lived with you, but for the injuries of one man. Colonel Cresap, the last spring, in cold blood, murdered all the relations of Logan, even my women and children.

"There runs not a drop of my blood in the veins of any living creature:—this called on me for revenge. I have fought for it. I have killed many. I have fully glutted my vengeance. For my country I rejoice at the beams of peace;—but do not harbour a thought that mine is the joy of fear. Logan never felt fear. He will not turn on his heel to save his life. Who is there to mourn for Logan? not one!"—*Jefferson's Notes on Virginia.*

MISCELLANEOUS POEMS.

Page 194, line 4.

The dark-attired Culdee,

THE Culdees were the primitive clergy of Scotland, and apparently her only clergy from the sixth to the eleventh century. They were of Irish origin, and their monastery on the Island of Iona, or Icolmkill, was the seminary of Christianity in North Britain. Presbyterian writers have wished to prove them to have been a sort of Presbyters, strangers to the Roman Church and Episcopacy. It seems to be established that they were not enemies to Episcopacy;—but that they were not slavishly subjected to Rome, like the clergy of later periods, appears by their resisting the Papal ordinances respecting the celibacy of religious men, on which account they were ultimately displaced by the Scottish sovereigns to make way for more Popish canons.

Page 197, line 15.

And the shield of alarm was dumb,

Striking the shield was an ancient mode of convocation to war among the Gaël.

Page 204.

The tradition which forms the substance of these stanzas is still preserved in Germany. An ancient tower on a height, called the Rolandseck, a few miles above Bonn on the Rhine, is shown as the habitation which Roland built in sight of a nunnery, into which his mistress had retired, on having heard an unfounded account of his death. Whatever may be thought of the credibility of the legend, its scenery must be recollected with pleasure by every one who has visited the romantic landscape of the Drachenfels, the Rolandseck, and the beautiful adjacent islet of the Rhine, where a nunnery still stands.

Page 212, line 14.

That erst the advent'rous Norman wore,

A Norman leader, in the service of the King of Scotland, married the heiress of Lochow, in the twelfth century, and from him the Campbells are sprung.

Page 247, line 11.

Whose lineage, in a raptured hour,

Alluding to the well-known tradition respecting the origin of painting, that it arose from a young Corinthian female tracing the shadow of her lover's profile on the wall as he lay asleep.

Page 260, line 18.

Where the Norman encamp'd him of old,

What is called the East Hill, at Hastings, is crowned with the works of an ancient camp; and it is more than probable it was the spot which William I. occupied between his landing and the battle which gave him England's crown. It is a strong position; the works are easily traced.

Page 264, line 29.

France turns from her abandon'd friends afresh,

The fact ought to be universally known, that France is at this moment indebted to Poland for not being invaded by Russia. When the Grand Duke Constantine fled from Warsaw, he left papers behind him proving that the Russians, after the Parisian events in July, meant to have marched towards Paris, if the Polish insurrection had not prevented them.

Page 276, line 8.

Thee, Niemciewitz,——

This venerable man, the most popular and influential of Polish poets, and president of the academy in Warsaw, was in London when this poem was written: he was then seventy-four years old; but his noble spirit is rather mellowed than decayed by age. He was the friend of Fox, Kosciusko, and Washington. Rich in anecdote like Franklin, he has also a striking resemblance to him in countenance.

Page 277, line 14.

Nor church-bell——

In Catholic countries you often hear the church-bells rung to propitiate Heaven during thunder-storms.

Page 291, line 14.

Regret the lark that gladdens England's morn,

Mr. P. Cunningham, in his interesting work on New South Wales, gives the following account of its song-birds:—"We are not moved here with the deep mellow note of the blackbird, poured out from beneath some low stunted bush, nor thrilled with the wild warblings of the thrush perched on the top of some tall sapling, nor charmed with the blithe carol of the lark as we proceed early a-field; none of our birds rivalling those divine songsters in realizing the poetical idea of '*the music of the grove:*' while '*parrots' chattering*' must supply the place of 'nightingales' singing' in the future amorous lays of our sighing Celadons. We have our lark, certainly; but both his appearance and note are a most wretched parody upon the bird about which our English Poets have made so many fine similes. He will mount from the ground and rise, fluttering upwards in the same manner, and with a few of the starting notes of the English lark; but, on reaching the height of thirty feet or so, down he drops suddenly and mutely, diving into concealment among the long grass, as if ashamed of his pitiful attempt. For the pert frisky robin, pecking and pattering against the windows in the dull days of winter, we have the lively 'superb warbler,' with his blue shining plumage and his long tapering tail, picking up the crumbs at our doors; while the pretty red-bills, of the size and form of the goldfinch, constitute the sparrow of our clime, flying in flocks about our houses, and building their soft downy pigmy nests in the orange, peach, and lemon-trees surrounding them."—*Cunningham's Two Years in New South Wales*, vol. ii. p. 216.

Page 304, line 6.

Oh, feeble statesmen—ignominious times,

There is not upon record a more disgusting scene of Russian hypocrisy, and (woe that it must be written!) of British humiliation, than that which passed on board the Talavera, when British sailors accepted money from the Emperor Nicholas, and gave him cheers. It will require the Talavera to fight well with the first Russian ship that she may have to encounter, to make us forget that day.

Page 316, line 23.

A palsy-stroke of Nature shook Oran,

In the year 1790, Oran, the most western city in the Algerine Regency, which had been possessed by Spain for more than a hundred years, and fortified at an immense expense, was destroyed by an earthquake; six thousand of its inhabitants were buried under the ruins.

THE PILGRIM OF GLENCOE.

Page 326, line 6.

The vale, by eagle-haunted cliffs o'erhung,

The valley of Glencoe, unparalleled in its scenery for gloomy grandeur, is to this day frequented by eagles. When I visited the spot within a year ago, I saw several perch at a distance. Only one of them came so near me that I did not wish him any nearer. He favoured me with a full and continued view of his noble person, and with the exception of the African eagle which I saw wheeling and hovering over a corps of the French army that were marching from Oran, and who seemed to linger over them with delight at the sound of their trumpets, as if they were about to restore his image to the Gallic standard—I never saw a prouder bird than this black eagle of Glencoe.

I was unable, from a hurt in my foot, to leave the carriage; but the guide informed me that, if I could go nearer the sides of the glen, I should see the traces of houses and gardens once belonging to the unfortunate inhabitants. As it was, I never saw a spot where I could less suppose human beings to have ever dwelt. I asked the guide how these eagles sub sisted; he replied, "on the lambs and the fawns of Lord Breadalbane."—"Lambs and fawns!" I said; "and how do *they* subsist, for I cannot see verdure enough to graze a rabbit? I suspect," I added, "that these birds make the cliffs only their country-houses, and that they go down to the Lowlands to find their provender."—"Ay, ay," replied the Highlander, "it is very possible, for the eagle can gang far for his breakfast."

Page 332, line 21.

Witch-legends Ronald scorn'd—ghost, kelpie, wraith,

"The most dangerous and malignant creature of Highland superstition was the kelpie, or water-horse, which was supposed to allure women and children to his subaqueous haunts, and there devour them; sometimes he would swell the lake or torrent beyond its usual limits, and overwhelm the unguarded traveller in the flood. The shepherd, as he sat on the brow of a rock on a summer's evening, often fancied he saw this animal dashing along the surface of the lake, or browsing on the pasture-ground upon its verge."—*Brown's History of the Highland Clans*, vol. i. 106.

In Scotland, according to Dr. John Brown, it is yet a superstitious principle that the *wraith*, the omen or messenger of death, appears in the resemblance of one in danger, immediately preceding dissolution. This ominous form, purely of a spiritual nature, seems to testify that the exaction (extinction) of life approaches. It was wont to be exhibited, also, as "*a little rough dog*," when it could be pacified by the death of any other being "if crossed, and conjured in time."—*Brown's Superstitions of the Highlands*, p. 182.

It happened to me, early in life, to meet with an amusing instance of Highland superstition with regard to myself. I lived in a family of the Island of Mull, and a mile or two from their house there was a burial-ground without any church attached to it, on the lonely moor. The cemetery was enclosed and guarded by an iron railing, so high, that it was thought to be unscaleable. I was, however, commencing the study of botany at the time, and thinking there might be some nice flowers and curious epitaphs among the gravestones, I contrived, by help of my handkerchief, to scale the railing, and was soon scampering over the tombs; some of the natives chanced to perceive me, not in the act of climb ing over to—but skipping over, the burial-ground. In a day or two I observed the family looking on me with unaccountable, though not angry seriousness: at last the good old grandmother told me, with tears in her eyes, "that I could not live long, for that my wraith had been seen."—"And, pray, where?"—"Leaping over the stones of the burial-ground." The old lady was much relieved to hear that it was not my wraith, but myself.

Akin to other Highland superstitions, but differing from them in many essential respects, is the belief—for superstition it cannot well be called (quoth the wise author I am quoting)—in the second-sight, by which, as Dr. Johnson observes, "seems to be meant a mode of seeing superadded to that which Nature generally bestows; and consists of an impression made either by the mind upon the eye—or by the eye upon the mind, by which things distant or future are perceived and seen, as if they were present. This deceptive faculty is called Traioshe in the Gaelic, which signifies a spectre or vision, and is neither voluntary nor constant: but consists in seeing an otherwise invisible object, without any previous means used by the person that sees it for that end. The vision makes such a lively impression upon the seers, that they neither see nor think of any thing else except the vision, as long as it continues; and then they appear pensive or jovial, according to the object which was represented to them."

There are now few persons, if any (continues Dr. Brown,) who pretend to this faculty, and the belief in it is almost generally exploded. Yet it cannot be denied that apparent proofs of its existence have been adduced, which have staggered minds not prone to superstition. When the connection between cause and effect can be recognized, things which would otherwise have appeared wonderful, and almost incredible, are viewed as ordinary occurrences. The impossibility of accounting for such an extraordinary phenomenon as the alleged faculty on philosophical principles, or from the laws of nature, must ever leave the matter suspended between rational doubt and confirmed scepticism. "Strong reasons for incredulity," says Dr. Johnson, "will readily occur." This faculty of seeing things out of sight is local, and commonly useless. It is a breach of the common order of things, without any visible reason or perceptible benefit. It is ascribed only to a people very little enlightened, and among them, for the most part, to the mean and ignorant.

In the whole history of Highland superstitions, there is not a more curious fact than that Dr. James Brown, a gentleman of the Edinburgh bar, in the nineteenth century, should show himself a more abject believer in the truth of second-sight, than Dr. Samuel Johnson, of London, in the eighteenth century.

Page 334, line 12.

The pit or gallows would have cured my grief.

Until the year 1747, the Highland Lairds had the right of punishing serfs even capitally, in so far as they often hanged, or imprisoned them in a pit or dungeon, where they were starved to death. But the law of 1746, for disarming the Highlanders and restraining the use of the Highland garb, was followed up the following year by one of a more radical and permanent description. This was the act for abolishing the heritable jurisdictions, which, though necessary in a rude state of society, were wholly incompatible with an advanced state of civilization. By depriving the Highland chiefs of their judicial powers, it was thought that the sway which, for centuries, they had held over their people, would be gradually impaired: and that by investing certain judges, who were amenable to the legislature for the proper discharge of their duties, with the civil and criminal jurisdiction enjoyed by the proprietors of the soil, the cause of good government would be promoted, and the facilities for repressing any attempts to disturb the public tranquillity increased.

By this act (20 George II., c. 43,) which was made to the whole of Scotland, all heritable jurisdictions of justiciary, all regalities and heritable bailieries, and constabularies (excepting the office of high constable,) and all stewartries and sheriffships of smaller districts, which were only parts of counties, were dissolved, and the powers formerly vested in them were ordained to be exercised by such of the king's courts as these powers would have belonged to, if the jurisdictions had never been granted. All sheriffships and stewartries not dissolved by the statute, namely, those which comprehended whole counties, where they had been granted either heritably or for life, were resumed and annexed to the crown. With the exception of the hereditary justiciaryship of Scotland, which was transferred from the family of Argyle to the High Court of Justiciary, the other jurisdictions were ordained to be vested in sheriffs-depute or stewarts-depute, to be appointed by the king in every shire or stewartry not dissolved by the act. As by the twentieth of Union, all heritable offices and jurisdictions were reserved to the grantees as rights of property; compensation was ordained to be made to the holders, the amount of which was afterwards fixed by parliament, in terms of the act of Sederunt of the Court of Session, at one hundred and fifty thousands pounds.

Page 334, line 14.

I march'd—when, feigning royalty's command,
Against the clan Macdonald, Stair's lord
Sent forth exterminating fire and sword;

I cannot agree with Brown, the author of an able work, "The History of the Highland Clans," that the affair of Glencoe has stamped indelible infamy on the government of King William III., if by this expression it be meant that William's own memory is disgraced by that massacre. I see no proof that William gave more than general orders to subdue the remaining malecontents of the Macdonald clan; and these orders, the nearer we trace them to the government, are thé more express in enjoining, that all those who would promise to swear allegiance should be spared. As these orders came down from the general government to individuals, they became more and more severe, and at last merciless, so that they ultimately ceased to be the real orders of government. Among these false agents of government, who appear with most disgrace, is the "Master of Stair," who appears in the business more like a fiend than a man. When issuing his orders for the attack on the remainder of the Macdonalds in Glencoe, he expressed a hope in his letter "that the soldiers would trouble the government with no prisoners."

It cannot be supposed that I would for a moment palliate this atrocious event by quoting the provocations not very long before offered by the Macdonalds in massacres of the Campbells. But they may be alluded to as causes, though not excuses. It is a part of the melancholy instruction which history affords us, that in the moral as well as in the physical world there is always a reaction equal to the action.—The banishment of the Moors from Spain to Africa was the chief cause of African piracy and Christian slavery among the Moors for centuries; and since the reign of William III. the Irish Orangemen have been the Algerines of Ireland.

The affair of Glencoe was in fact only a lingering trait of horribly barbarous times, though it was the more shocking that it came from that side of the political world which professed to be the more liberal side, and it occurred at a late time of the day, when the minds of both parties had become comparatively civilized, the whigs by the triumph of free principles, and the tories by personal experience of the evils attending persecution. Yet that barbarism still subsisted in too many minds professing to act on liberal principles, is but too apparent from this disgusting tragedy.

I once flattered myself that the Argyle Campbells, from whom I am sprung, had no share in this massacre, and a direct share they certainly had not. But on inquiry I find that they consented to shutting up the passes of Glencoe through which the Macdonalds might escape; and perhaps relations of my great-grandfather—I am afraid to count their distance or proximity—might be indirectly concerned in the cruelty.

But children are not answerable for the crimes of their forefathers; and I hope and trust that the descendants of Breadalbane and Glenlyon are as much and justly at their ease on this subject as I am.

Page 343, line 7.

Chance snatch'd them from proscription and despair.

Many Highland families, at the outbreak of the rebellion in 1745, were saved from utter desolation by the contrivances of some of their more sensible members, principally the women, who foresaw the consequences of the insurrection. When I was a youth in the Highlands, I remember an old gentleman being pointed out to me, who, finding all other arguments fail, had, in conjunction with his mother and sisters, bound the old laird hand and foot, and locked him up in his own cellar, until the news of the battle of Culloden had arrived.

A device pleasanter to the reader of the anecdote, though not to the sufferer, was practised by a shrewd Highland dame, whose husband was Charles Stuart-mad, and was determined to join the insurgents. He told his wife at night that he should start early to-morrow morning on horseback. "Well, but you will allow me to make your breakfast before you go?"—"Oh yes." She accordingly prepared it, and, bring-in a full boiling kettle, poured it, by intentional accident, on his legs!

www.ingramcontent.com/pod-product-compliance
Lightning Source LLC
LaVergne TN
LVHW020914110826
845150LV00004B/669

* 9 7 8 1 4 2 5 5 5 6 4 1 9 *

HOMŒOPATHIC

DOMESTIC PRACTICE,

CONTAINING ALSO

CHAPTERS ON ANATOMY, PHYSIOLOGY, HYGIENE, AND AN ABRIDGED MATERIA MEDICA.

BY

EGBERT GUERNSEY, M.D.

NEW-YORK:
WILLIAM RADDE, No. 322, BROADWAY.
1853.

Henry Ludwig, Printer, 46, Vesey-St., N. Y.

PREFACE.

THE more intimately we are acquainted with our own organization, and the laws of our being, the more readily may we guard against the numerous causes of disease to which we are constantly exposed, and preserve a healthy equilibrium in the system. There are cases, also, where disease presents certain symptoms so distinctly marked, that almost any one possessed of an ordinary knowledge of the human system and of remedial agents, may by the careful administration of medicines, check in the commencement, a difficulty, which if allowed to progress for a few hours, might have gained such headway as to place the patient almost beyond the reach of aid. There are other cases where there is but slight derangement of the system, and the symptoms are so well marked, that the patient will have no difficulty in selecting the remedy, a few doses of which will produce speedy relief.

Thus, with a proper understanding of the laws of nature, and a certain knowledge of remedial agents, all possess the power, to a certain extent, of warding off disease, of relieving a vast amount of suffering, and prolonging their own lives.

In the preparation of this work, I have looked on the human system as a perfect machine of the most beautiful and wonderful character, pervaded by, and the dwelling place of, a spiritual and immortal form. This machine is capable of growth and possesses the power of supplying its own waste, and where there is no violation of nature's laws, moves on in perfect harmony, without discord or pain.

It is very evident that we must understand the structure of the machine, before we know how to apply, judiciously, the remedy when it is deranged, and if we would avoid derangement, we must understand the laws which govern the system, and be acquainted with, and thus know how to avoid the causes which produce disturbance.

I have endeavored in the introductory chapter before proceeding to the treatment of disease to make clear a few points:

1. I have spoken of the anatomical structure of the system, and the beautiful adaptation of the various parts to the duties of life.

2. The physiology of the system, the production from food of bone, and blood, and tissue, and the combustion and chemical changes, which are constantly going on within us.

3. The laws of health and the causes of disease, in which I have glanced at the transmission of disease from parent to child, and the necessity of a correct moral, physical, and intellectual training.

In the introduction I have given some general rules for the proper selection and administration of remedies, for the diagnosis of disease, and the choice of a proper diet.

In the part on the treatment of disease I have aimed

to be as full as is necessary in a work on domestic practice. I have also endeavored to avoid where it could be done, technicalities, and to make the subject as plain and simple as possible. In most cases the quantity of the dose has been given, and the frequency of its repetition, but as this must depend in a measure on circumstances I would urge a careful perusal of the article in the introduction on the administration of remedies.

In part third I have introduced a carefully abridged materia medica, in which the leading indications for a remedy are grouped together under the appropriate head. This will often aid materially in an appropriate selection.

While it has been my aim to prepare as clear and practical a guide as possible for the sick-room and domestic practice, I have had no wish to produce a work to supersede the labor of the physician.

No one who has not devoted years to the investigation of the human system, the causes of sickness, the power of remedial agents, and who is not able to look beneath the surface and trace from apparent unimportant symptoms the true seat and cause of the difficulty, is capable of grappling with all forms of disease and of fulfilling the high and holy duties of the physician. The responsibility which rests on him is a fearful, an awful one. It is no light thing to stand, as it were, between life and death, to rekindle the flickering lamp, almost extinct, to call back the fleeting breath, to arrest the downward course, and drive back that cold shadowy form, whose awful presence is already blanching the cheek and chilling the blood.

In the preparation of this work I have advanced no new, strange and unheard of theory of disease and its treatment, but have aimed to make a plain and practical family guide, in which may be found a description of the human system, hints for the prevention of disease, and its treatment after its seeds have become implanted in the human system. Happy will I be, if any effort of mine shall be the means of diffusing a correct knowledge of the human system "so fearfully and wonderfully made," and of alleviating in the slightest degree the vast amount of human suffering.

TABLE OF CONTENTS.

PAGE

PART II.

DESCRIPTION AND TREATMENT OF DISEASE.

CHAPTER I.

FEVERS.

CHAPTER II.

CUTANEOUS DISEASES.

CHAPTER III.

AFFECTIONS OF THE STOMACH AND BOWELS.

CHAPTER IV.

AFFECTIONS OF THE WINDPIPE AND CHEST.

PAGE

PART III.

CHAPTER I.

CHAPTER II.

CHAPTER III.

REAL AND APPARENT DEATH.

CHAPTER IV.

INTRODUCTION.

Some general directions as it regards the importance of various symptoms, the varieties of constitution and temperament, the detection of the peculiar nature of disease, may appropriately be introduced in this place. In prescribing homœopathically, it is of high importance that the nature and cause of the disease should be understood. In loosing sight of the great landmarks, in seizing hold of an isolated symptom and prescribing carelessly or at random very little good is effected, and sometimes, much positive harm done. Let us make plain then a few prominent points, the correct knowledge of which may enable the patient to understand more readily the character and progress of the disease and the presence of danger.

1. VARIETIES OF CONSTITUTION AND TEMPERAMENT.

A plethoric constitution, is characterized by a florid complexion, frame full and robust, activity and strength of body, and a strong and full pulse. There is an activity in the circulative system, and a predisposition to local or general congestion.

A feeble constitution, is directly the opposite of the foregoing. There is a deficiency in the generation of natural heat, and a tendency to become fatigued from slight exertions. The pulse is feeble and soft. The person is peculiarly subject to diseases characterized by inactivity in certain functions, or great relaxation.

A bilious constitution, is recognized by a dark, or yellow skin, by a predisposition to a derangement and irregularities of the digestive functions, and a tendency to constipation, piles, &c.

An apoplectic constitution may be known by the large head almost buried between the shoulders, short, thick neck, thick set frame, slow full pulse, and tendency of blood to the brain.

A nervous constitution, is characterized by extreme sensitiveness and excitability of body and mind. The pulse is variable, quickly changing from rapid to slow. The patient is liable to nervous disorders, and those spasmodic affections, which are not readily referable to any direct cause.

A lymphatic, or mucous constitution, may be recognized by the light complexion, the frame full and rounded, but the flesh soft and flaccid, and the muscular fibre yielding and relaxed. The circulation is sluggish, the pulse slow, the generation of heat deficient, and there is also a sensitiveness to cold. The patient is subject to slow and sluggish affections, to catarrhal diseases, abscesses, accumulations of water about various organs. Acute diseases are also liable to assume a chronic form and run a slow and tedious course.

The catarrhal or rheumatic constitution, is similar to the last, and is particularly characterized by want of vitality in the skin, which is easily affected by external circumstances.

The consumptive constitution may be known by the clear transparent skin, often with a bright spot on the cheek, flatness of the chest, slender and fragile form, long and spare neck, rapid growth, quick and small pulse, long slender fingers with large joints. The patient is peculiarly liable to affections of the lungs.

There is only one more variety of constitution to which it will be necessary to refer. It is characterized by a tendency to ulcerative sores, particularly of the glands, unhealthy secretions from the skin, and various forms of eruption. Both this and the preceding variety may be considered as modifications of the tuberculous habit.

In the sanguine temperament—generally found in a plethoric constitution—there is great animation and buoyancy of spirits, the bodily health is generally good, but when disease does attack the system it runs a rapid and severe course.

Choleric temperament is generally found in the *bilious constitution*. The increased and altered secretion of bile reacting on the moral and mental faculties has a tendency to engender ill-humour, outbursts of rage, and even a revengeful and malignant temper whenever excited. The complexion is generally of a yellowish tinge, the muscular fibre hard, wiry, and tightly strung. The patient is subject to bilious derangements, which are sometimes even provoked by violent fits of excitement.

The phlegmatic temperament, generally associated with the feeble or lymphatic constitution, is characterized by slow operations of both the mental and bodily functions, and tardiness and weakness of the reactionary power.

A melancholic temperament is readily known by the meditative, gloomy, or retiring disposition. Impressions are deep and lasting, and there is a tendency to look on the dark side and brood often in secret over things, which in the mind of others would be speedily forgotten. The patient is seldom subject to violent impulses or sudden impressions, and is liable to diseases of the stomach and bowels, which often assume a chronic character.

2. THE PULSE.

Not only the frequency, but the peculiar beat of the pulse is of vast importance to the correct diagnosis and proper treatment of disease.

In feeling the pulse, it should be done as gently as possible, as unnecessary parade may needlessly alarms the patient. Three fingers may be placed on the wrist directly back of the root of the thumb and the joint of the wrist, and just within the external bone of the arm. Slightly compressing the wrist with the fingers, and holding there for a moment you will be able to notice not only the frequency but the peculiar character of the pulse. Its rapidity may be easily measured by the second hand of a watch. Notice whether it beats with regularity, full and soft, whether by compression it may be rendered so indistinct as scarcely to be felt, whether it is strong and bounding, almost forcing the fingers from the arm, or hard, or small and wiry like the vibration of a string, or intermittent, striking a few beats and then apparently stopping for one beat, or the pulsations flowing into each other small, and almost imperceptible.

It will of course be necessary to understand the beat of the healthy pulse, and what its different varieties may indicate in disease.

Healthy pulse. The beat of the healthy pulse depends much upon age, sex, constitution and temperament.

In the adult male, of medium size, it generally numbers from 70 to 75 beats in a minute.

In the adult female, it is not generally so strong and full as in the male, and usually numbers from 76 to 84 beats in the minute.

In a person between the ages of seven and fourteen it should number from 80 to 85 beats in the minute.

After teething and until the age of about seven there are generally from 85 to 96 beats in the minute.

In infancy, previous to teething, the pulse varies from 100 to 120 beats in the minute.

After man has reached the prime of life, and enters on the descending scale, which generally takes place in our climate between the ages of forty-five and sixty years, the pulse becomes still slower, numbering in the male about 70 and in the female 75 beats in the minute.

As the person advances to old age, the frequency of the pulse is still further diminished, until in the male there may be only from 55 to 60, and in the female from 65 to 70 beats in the minute.

I have given the usual standard of the pulse in health in the various stages of life, although cases are by no means rare, when in perfect health it may be much lower or higher than I have stated. If, however, the skin is moist and at a natural heat, this would be no indication of disease. The pulse also may vary before or after a meal, and be excited or depressed from exercise or influence of mental emotion. We should of course be cautious in attributing this temporary change to the influence of disease.

VARIETIES OF PULSE IN DISEASE.

The *rapid* or *accelerated pulse* is indicative of inflammation or fever, especially if strong, full and hard, if small and very rapid, it indicates a low state of debility, such as is often present in the latter stage of typhoid fever.

The *slow pulse*, if not habitual, may indicate debility or tendency of blood to the head, or especially, if full and strong, pressure on the brain. It is also generally found in old age.

The *hard* or *wiry pulse* is generally indicative of a high state of inflammation, although in old age it may be occasioned by a hardening or ossification of the arteries.

The *changeable* or *unequal pulse* indicates a derangement of the nervous system, and not unfrequently organic disease of the heart.

The *intermittent pulse* generally shows an organic disease or spasmodic condition of the heart. It is sometimes occasioned by intestinal affections.

The *full strong pulse* indicates a full habit, while the *weak pulse* denotes impoverished blood and a feeble state of the system.

3. THE URINE.

The appearance of the urine in health is slightly varied by age, sex, occupation, food and the season of the year. It should be of a brightish yellow or straw colour, possessed of a slight ammoniacal smell, devoid of unpleasant odour, and precipitating no sediment on standing. In old age, however, the urine may be slightly offensive, and darker in colour than in early life, and in females a slight sediment is not always an unhealthy sign. In persons leading an active life, the urine is of a darker colour than in those of sedentary habits. Different varieties of food may also produce a sensible effect upon the colour and smell of the urine.

The urine should not be examined, until five or six hours after a meal have elapsed, when it should be set aside in a moderate and even temperature for an hour or two.

VARIETIES OF URINE AND THEIR INDICATIONS.

In various forms of disease the appearance, quantity, and smell of the urine, are important diagnostic signs of the state and progress of the disease, and should be carefully observed.

In cases of fever, as the disease approaches a crisis, the previously clear urine becomes thick, and forms a half floating cloud. If this cloud sink, a favourable crisis may be expected, while on the contrary if it remain buoyant near the top, a somewhat unfavourable issue may be anticipated.

As the crisis of the disease declares itself, when the urine has been perfectly clear before, a sediment is now perceptible, and in those cases where the urine has been thick and turbid, the same sediment is perceptible, but the urine above it is clear and transparent. If the sediment is of a smooth, light or greyish colour, and is deposited shortly after emission, it is a favourable indication, but if it should be dark or black, it denotes a putrid state, if bilious or red, it indicates a rheumatic or intermittent type of the disease, and if it is disturbed, heavy, muddy or of a purple colour, forming half of the whole quantity discharged, it is an unfavourable sign.

The red or high coloured urine, if the pulse be accelerated, indicates the presence of fever. Urine of a saffron colour marks the presence of bile in the blood, and shows derangement of the hepatic viscera.

If matter is found in the urine, it shows that suppuration is going on internally.

In children, a milky appearance of the urine is looked upon as an indication of worms in the intestines. A very light or watery appearance of the urine may denote some disturbance of the nervous system.

The appearance of the urine may indicate the presence of Diabetis, or tendency to various forms of calculi in the bladder and kidneys.

The voiding of a large quantity of straw coloured urine of a disagreeable odour and of a sweetish taste, may denote the presence of Diabetis. The *lithic or uric acid calculus* is shown by the red brick dust sediment.

The calculi formed by the combination of phosphoric acid, magnesia and ammonia, is indicated by fetid urine and a whitish *mortar*-like sediment. For a description of the above, together with other forms of calculi, see that subject in the chapter on urinary affections.

GENERAL DIAGNOSIS.

In the investigation of disease, to form a correct idea of its character and the treatment necessary to produce relief, there are several important points to be taken into consideration, aside from the symptoms as they casually present themselves to the eye.

The age and sex of the patient should be borne in mind, and the diseases most likely to occur in the successive stages of life should not be forgotten.

When man lives his appointed time, dying not of disease but of old age, there is a regular ascending scale up to a certain point, which turned, he commences the descending path of life. Each of these several stages or steps is characterized by certain peculiarities.

In the first period of childhood, extending to the time of teething, the little being is extremely susceptible to external influences, and liable to disease from the slightest causes. The whole nervous system is exceedingly sensitive and the little patient peculiarly liable to affections of the brain and spasmodic attacks. This period should be closely watched (see chapter on diseases of children).

In the second and third stages, extending from teething to about the seventh and fourteenth year, there is a want of firmness in the fibre of the system, a susceptibility to fatigue and the consequent necessity of a larger amount of rest than in later years. There is a liability to affections of the brain and respiratory organs.

The next stage, extending to the twenty or twenty-fifth year, during which the system is approaching maturity, is one of the most important periods of our existence. It is during this period that the seeds of constitutional disease are most liable to ripen into a fatal harvest, and now when the passions are strongest, there is danger by their abuse of being thrown from a proper balance, into a too powerful exertion of the mind and body, thus sowing the seeds of diseases, which may be a torment in after life and end in early death.

After a person has reached the age of fifty-five or sixty years, he generally begins to feel that he is growing old; the functions of the body may become less active, and the mind, notwithstanding it may be equally strong, less active in its movements. As year after year rolls away, he is made aware in the stiffness of the joints, in the gradual blunting of the faculties of perception and sensation, that he is rapidly treading the downhill of life. During this stage, he is peculiarly subject to paralysis of various organs, deafness, blindness, apoplexy, asthma, &c. *Constitution and temperament*, are also important points of inquiry, a proper understanding of which will aid materially in the correct selection and administration of remedies. *The cause* of the disease should by no means be overlooked; the previous habits of the patient should be ascertained, and in cases of long standing, or when there is reason to suspect hereditary taint, the health of the parents, and even grandparents, should be known, also whether at any time during the previous life of the patient he has been afflicted with either eruptions, or other diseases, which might not have been entirely eradicated from the system, or whether the medicines given might not have engendered other diseases more painful and lasting than the former. An understanding of the *cause* of the disease will often be a sure guide to the selection of the remedy.

Thus diseases resulting from contusions, sprains, &c., would indicate *Arnica*. In a rheumatic affection produced by dampness, or getting wet, we should think of *Rhus*. Affections produced by grief or chagrin would require *Ignatia*, while those occasioned by fear would indicate *Opium*. Diarrhœa occasioned by cold requires *Dulcamara*. Derangement of the stomach with nausea under certain circumstances would yield to *Ipecac.*, but if the disturbance was occasioned by eating fatty food, the Ipecac would be ineffectual and Pulsatilla be required.

The mind should also be directed to exposures to heat or cold, dampness, unhealthy air, food and clothing, miasmata, contagions, errors of diet, abuse of spirituous liquors, and the various causes which would have a tendency to produce disease.

Finally, the patient should be permitted to explain in his own words, his general sufferings, and the character and location of the pain. It should be ascertained whether the pain comes on at intervals, or is uninterrupted, how long it continues and whether it is worse during the day, or at night, what peculiar symptoms it is associated with; and such other questions, as will guide to an accurate knowledge of the disease. For directions as to the administration of remedies, see the following chapter.

ADMINISTRATION OF REMEDIES.

Too much care cannot be taken in selecting the remedy. The symptoms should be closely compared with those deliniated under the heads of that class of remedies most likely to be indicated. The cause of the disease has also an important bearing in the selection of the medicine. The mind should be directed to the leading symptoms, the pecularities of the disease, and notwithstanding it is not necessary that *all* the symptoms noted should be present, yet the utmost care should be taken, that there are no symptoms present not covered by the medicine, or at least more strongly indicating another. The *totality* of the symptoms, or the symptoms taken as a whole, should be the guide.

THE DOSE AND ITS REPETITION.

No definite rule can be given as to the amount of the dose in all cases. Difference in age, sex, temperament and constitution renders variation both in the quantity of the dose and the frequency with which it is repeated absolutely essential. The idea would be preposterous to give the infant, with its highly excitable nervous organization, the same quantity of medicine and at the same intervals as at a much later period of life, or who would think of giving the highly excitable and nervous temperament or those possessed of acute and exceedingly sensitive feeling the same strength of medicine as would be required by the cold and phlegmatic constitution and temperament?

During the few years of infancy and early childhood the patient is usually quite susceptible to medicinal influence and generally requires the higher potencies. Females are for the most part much more susceptible to medicines than males, therefore the higher potencies may as a general thing be used with them in preference to the lower.

The *sanguine* and *nervous temperaments* are usually quite susceptible to remedies, and may therefore require the higher potencies, while the *bilious*, where there is less susceptibility, requires the lower potencies, given at longer intervals. The *lymphatic* also, being but slightly, in comparison with other temperaments, susceptible to medicines, requires the low potencies given at short intervals.

Some persons are much more susceptible to one class of remedies than another, rendering it absolutely essential that those particular remedies should be given in the high potencies. As a general thing in acute diseases, excepting perhaps in young children, tinctures, and the low potencies should be used, while in chronic cases more benefit may be derived from the higher attenuations.

In my own practice I have generally confined myself to the *tinctures*, and the potencies ranging from the first to the twelfth, more frequently giving the *tinctures* or the *first*, *third*, *sixth*, or *twelfth* attenuation. I am satisfied that in domestic practice the lower attenuations may be used with much greater safety than the higher. In the preparation of the medicines, if tinctures are used, one drop may be placed in a tumbler full of cold water, if intended for a child or a person quite susceptible to medicine, and a teaspoonful given at a dose. If intended for an adult or one not as susceptible to medicine two drops may be prepared in the same way. If the remedy is stronger than is necessary, producing an aggravation of symptoms, a teaspoonful of the mixture, prepared as above, may be mixed with a tumbler full of cold water, a teaspoonful of which may be given at a dose. In the preparation of the remedy, pure water should be used, such as rain, or spring water, and great care taken that the *tumbler and spoon* are perfectly clean. Both should be thoroughly rinsed several times in pure water, and then left to dry.

The medicine should be dropped into the tumbler first, and then the water poured in, turning it from one tumbler into another several times, or stirring it with a spoon until it is thoroughly mixed. The same spoon ought not to be used for more than one remedy until it has been cleanly washed.

If the triturations are used, the size of the dose should be about as much as could be placed on a three cent piece, or taken up by the point of a knife. The remedy should be placed dry on the tongue, and left there until dissolved.

If the globules or pellets are used, unless more specific directions are given in the body of the work in connection with the disease, six of them may be dissolved in a tumbler of water, and a tablespoonful for the adult, and a teaspoonful for the child, given at a dose. The same directions as it regards the tumblers and mixing the medicines may be observed as given in connection with tinctures.

The globules may in some cases act more promptly when given dry on the tongue, hence it is often advisable to give them in that way. By the adult, in these cases, three globules may be taken dry on the tongue. To the child one or two globules may be administered in the same manner.

In acute cases especially, the symptoms should be watched with the utmost care, and the remedy be continued as long as benefit results from its employment. The medicine, if carefully selected, should receive a fair trial, and not be changed frequently, unless there are positive indications that it is doing harm.

Often a medicinal aggravation may be seen, and it is important that the aggravation produced by *medicine* be readily distinguished from that occasioned by *disease*. The medicinal aggravation comes on suddenly and without previous amelioration, while that occasioned by disease is more gradual in its progress, and generally follows an amelioration.

In mild cases one dose will often be sufficient to remove the disease. In the chronic case a long continued administration of a certain remedy may, notwithstanding its clear indication, render the system less susception to its influence. In these cases, a few doses of sulphur, or some other remedy closely resembling the one previously administered may be given, and in a short time, if it be necessary, the patient may again return to the old remedy.

If, either in acute or chronic cases an amelioration follows each administration, the intervals may be gradually increased, and if, as is sometimes the case, susceptibility to its influence should also increase, a higher potency may be given.

The medicines should not be taken within a half hour or an hour of eating, either before or after a meal. The medicines should be kept in a clean dark place, free from odours. Camphor and perfumery of all kinds should be avoided in the sick room, as they have a tendency to antidote the remedy given, or complicate the symptoms of the disease.

RULES FOR DIET.

In the successful treatment of disease, much depends on the proper diet adopted by the patient during the period he is under the influence of the remedy. It is of the utmost importance that the food be of that variety, which will neither stimulate the system too much, nor clog it in its operations, and excite serious disturbances by throwing labour on diseased and weakened organs, which they are unable to perform. Not only should indigestible substances be avoided, but also those articles of food, which are more or less medicinal in their character. By indulging in either, the remedy may be antidoted, or at least new symptoms developed, not at the time distinguishable from those produced by the disease, thus complicating the symptoms, rendering the diagnosis imperfect, and frequently causing the loss of much valuable time. We can only give here some general directions as it regards diet when under treatment, as different articles may be required in different persons, and in the numerous varieties of disease.

ALIMENTS ALLOWED.

Lemonade and other mild acid drinks, water, pure or mixed with currant jelly, raspberry or strawberry, syrup, and sometimes milk, or milk and water, cocoa, unspiced chocolate, arrow-root, farina, barley-water, rice-water. Beef and mutton soup, mutton, beef, venison and most kinds of game, soft boiled eggs and fresh butter.

Occasionally *fish* such as trout, cod, haddock, and fresh scale fish, boiled, or if fried only the white part eaten. Also oysters, unless, as along some parts of the sea-shore they are impregnated with copper.

Among vegetables, potatoes, green peas, cauliflower, spinach, mild turnips, parsnips, carrots, rice, hominy, pearl barley.

Fruits, such as peaches, raspberries, strawberries, oranges, stewed or roasted apples and pears, also prunes, grapes, &c. They should be perfectly ripe and fresh.

Bread, light and not newly baked, and biscuit free from soda or potash.

Puddings such as rice, arrow-root, sago, tapioca, macaroni, vermicelli, &c. Salt and sugar should be used sparingly.

ALIMENTS PROHIBITED.

Rich and highly seasoned soups, such as, turtle or mock turtle; pork, veal, bacon, duck, goose, liver, and all varieties of salt meats and salt fish, also smoked meats, smoked, potted, or pickled fish, eels, lobsters, crabs, and fish not having scales.

Cucumber, celery, onions, garlic, radishes, parsley, horseradish, and asparagus, also all kinds of pickles, salads, and raw vegetables.

Pastry of all kinds, spices, aromatics, and artificial sauces, mustard, vinegar, cheese, confectionary, and almost the whole variety of nuts.

Thus, we perceive, the homœopathic patient is not starved, nor his appetite pampered, or his stomach crowded with articles of food more or less indigestible and capable of creating serious disturbance in the system. But diet plain, healthy, easy of digestion is adapted in all cases, though as I have before stated, different persons require in the varied forms of disease and constitutions, different varieties of food Thus, in cases of diarrhœa, fruits and vegetables should be avoided, while a constipated state of the bowels requires a free use of these articles, also when symptoms of fever are present, meats, butter, eggs, and other stimulating articles of food, should be avoided, confining the diet more particularly to fruits and farinaceous articles.

During treatment, the patient should carefully avoid the use of purgative medicine, salves, perfumery of all kinds, or even aromatic toothpowder.

More specific directions as to diet, will be found in the chapter on Hygeine, and in the body of the work, in connection with the various diseases.

LIST OF MEDICINES.

THEIR ABBREVIATIONS, SYNONYMES AND ANTIDOTES.

1. Acon.—Aconitum Napellus. *Monk's Hood. Antidotes.* Wine, Vinegar, Camphor, Nux-vom.
2. Agar.—Agaricus. Bug agaric. *Antidotes.* Vegetable acids.
3. Alo.—Aloes. *Antidote.* Vinegar.
4. Alum.—Alumina. Oxide of aluminum. *Antidotes.* Bryonia, Cham., Ipecac.
5. Am. c.—Ammonium carbonicum. Carbonate of ammonia. *Antidotes.* Arnica, Camphor.
6. Am. m.—Ammonium muriaticum. Muriate of ammonia. • *Antidotes.* Camphor, Coffea, Hepar sulph.
7. Ant.—Antimonium crudum. Crude antimony. *Antidotes.* Hep. s., Mercury, Pulsatilla.
8. Arn.—Arnica montana. Leopard's bane. *Antidotes.* Camphor, Capsicum, Veratrum, and Vinegar.
9. Ars.—Arsenicum album. Arsenic. *Antidotes.* For its poisonous effects, rust of iron. For medicinal aggravation, Camphor, Ipecac., Nux-vom., Tabac.
10. Aur.—Aurum. Gold. *Antidotes.* Belladonna, China, Mercury.
11. Bell.—Belladonna. Deadly Nightshade. *Antidotes.* Coffee, Hyos., Hepar sulph., Pulsatilla.
12. Brom.—Bromine. *Antidotes.* Coffee, Opium, Camphor.
13. Bry.—Bryonia. White Bryony. *Antidotes.* Acon. Cham., Nux-vom., Ignatia.
14. Calc. c.—Calcarea carbonica. Carbonate of lime. *Antidotes.* Camphor, Nitric acid., Sulphur.
15. Camph.—Camphor. *Antidotes.* Opium, Vinegar.
16. Can.—Cannabis sativa. Hemp. *Antidote.* Camphor.
17. Canth.—Cantharis. Spanish Fly. *Antidote.* Camphor.
18. Caps.—Capsicum. Cayenne Pepper. *Antidote.* Camphor.

19. Carb. v.—Carbo-vegetabilis. Charcoal. *Antidotes.* Camphor, Arsenic, and Coffea.
20. Caust.—Causticum. Caustic. *Antidotes.* Coffea, Nux-v.
21. Cham.—Chamomilla. Chamomile. *Antidotes.* Aconite, Cocculus, Coffea, Ignatia, Nux-vom., Pulsatilla.
22. Chin.—China. Peruvian Bark. *Antidotes.* Arnica, Arsenic, Belladonna, Calcarea, Carb.-veg., Ipecac., Sulphur.
23. Cina. Wormseed. *Antidote.* Ipecac.
24. Coc.—Cocculus. Indian Berries. *Antidotes.* Camphor, Nux-vom.
25. Coff.—Coffea. Coffee. *Antidotes.* Acon., Cham., Nux-v.
26. Colch.—Colchicum. Meadow Saffron. *Antidotes.* Nux-vom., Cocculus, Pulsatilla.
27. Coloc. — Colocynth. Bitter cucumber. *Antidotes.* Camphor, Coffea, Causticum.
28. Con.—Conium. Hemlock. *Antidotes.* Coffea, Spiritus Nitri.
29. Croc.—Crocus sativus. Saffron. *Antidote.* Opium.
30. Cupr. — Cuprum. Copper. *Antidotes.* Belladonna, China, Ipecac., Mercury, Nux-vom.
31. Dig.—Digitalis. Foxglove. *Antidotes.* Nux-v., Opium.
32. Dros.—Drosera. Round-leaved Sun Dew. *Antidote.* Camphor.
33. Dulc.—Dulcamara. Bitter Sweet. Woody Nightshade. *Antidotes.* Camphor, Ipecac. Mercury.
34. Euphr.—Euphrasia. Eye-bright. *Antidote.* Pulsatilla.
35. Fer.—Ferrum. Iron. *Antidotes.* Arnica, Arsenic, Ipecac., Mercury, Belladonna, Pulsatilla.
36. Fer. acet. — Ferrum aceticum. Acetate of Iron. *Antidotes.* Arsenic, Belladonna, Nux-vom.
37. Graph.—Graphites. Black Lead. *Antidotes.* Nux vom., Wine.
38. Hell.—Helleborus niger. Black Hellebore. *Antidotes.* Champhor, China.
39. Hep. s.—Hepar sulphuris. Sulphuret of Lime. *Antidotes.* Vinegar, Belladonna.

40. HYOS.—HYOSCIAMUS. Henbane. *Antidotes.* Belladonna, Camphor, China.
41. IGN.—IGNATIA. St. Ignatius' Bean. *Antidotes.* Pulsatilla, Chamomilla, Camphor, Vinegar, Cocculus.
42. IOD.—IODINE. *Antidotes.* Arsenic, Camphor, Coffea, Sulph., Phos.
43. IPEC.—IPECACUANHA. *Antidotes.* Arnica, Arsenic, China.
44. KALI. B.—KALI BICHROMATUM. Bichromate of Potash.
45. KAL. HYD.—KALI HYDRIODICUM. Hydriodate of Potash.
46. KAL. CARB.—KALI CARBONICUM. Carbonate of Potash.
47. LACH.—LACHESIS. Poison of the Lance-Headed Serpent. *Antidotes.* Arsenic, Belladonna, Nux-vom., Rhus.
48. LYC —LYCOPODIUM. Wolf's Claw. *Antidotes.* Camphor, Pulsatilla.
49. MERC. IOD. Mercury Proto-iodid.
50. *MERC.—MERCURY. *Antidotes.* Arnica, Belladonna, Camphor, Hepar, Iodine, Sulphur, Lachesis.
51. MEZ.—MEZEREUM. *Antidotes.* Camphor, Mercury.
52. MUR. AC.—MURIATIC ACID. *Antidotes.* Large doses of Soap. Small doses of Bryonia, Camphor.
53. NAT. MUR.—NATRUM MURIATICUM. Muriate of Soda. *Antidotes.* Arsenic, Camphor, Nitri-spiritus.
54. NITR. AC.—NITRI ACIDUM. *Antidotes.* Calcarea, Conium, Camphor, Hepar sulph., Sulphur. Soap, in large doses.
55. NUX-VOM.—NUX-VOMICA. *Antidotes.* Aconite, Camphor, Coffea, Pulsatilla.
56. OP.—OPIUM. White Poppy. *Antidotes.* Camphor, Calcarea, Hepar sulph., Sulphur.
57. PETROL.—PETROLEUM. Naphtha. Stone Oil. *Antidotes.* Aconite, Nux-vom.
58. PHOS.—PHOSPHORUS. *Antidotes.* Camphor, Coffea, Nux-vom.
59. PHOS. A.—PHOSPHORIC ACID. *Antidotes.* Camphor, Coffea.
60. PLAT.—PLATINA. *Antidote.* Pulsatilla.

* The varieties of Mercury generally used are the Mercurius solubilis, Mercurius vivus, and Mercurius corrosivus. For the antidotes, see Mercury.

61. Plumb.—Plumbum. Lead. *Antidotes.* Belladonna, Op.
62. Puls.—Pulsatilla. Pasque Flower. *Antidotes.* Chamomilla, Coffea, Ignatia, Nux-vom.
63. Rheum. Rhubarb. *Antidotes.* Camphor, Chamomilla, Nux-vom.
64. Rhus t.—Rhus toxicodendron. Sumach, Poison Oak. *Antidotes.* Belladonna, Bryonia, Camph. Coffea, Sulph.
65. Samb.—Sambucus. Elder. *Antidotes.* Arsenic, Camph.
66. Sab.—Sabina. Savine. *Antidote.* Camphor.
67. Sang.—Sanguinaria Canadensis. Common Blood-root.
68. Sep.—Sepia. Inky juice of the Cuttle Fish. *Antidotes.* Vinegar, Aconite.
69. Sec. corn.—Secale cornutum. Ergot of Rye. *Antidotes.* Camphor, Opium.
70. Sil.—Silicea. Silex. *Antidotes.* Camphor, Hep. s.
71. Spig.—Spigelia. Indian Pink. *Antidotes.* Camphor. Aurum.
72. Spong.—Spongia. Burnt Sponge. *Antidote.* Camphor.
73. Stan.—Stannum. Pure Tin. *Antidotes.* Coffea, Puls.
74. Staph.—Staphysagria. Stavesacre. *Antidote.* Camph.
75. Stib.—Stibium. Tartar Emetic. *Antidotes.* Cocculus, Ipecac., Pulsatilla.
76. Stram.—Strammonium. Thorn apple. *Antidotes.* Belladonna, Nux-vom.
77. Sulph.—Sulphur. *Antidotes.* Aconite, Camphor, Mercury, Pulsatilla, Nux-vom.
78. Sulph. a.—Sulphuric acid. Oil of Vitriol. *Antidote.* Pulsatilla.
79. Tabac.—Tabacum. Tobacco. *Antidotes.* Camph., Ipec., Nux vom.
80. Tereb.—Terebinth. Turpentine. *Antidote.* Camphor.
81. Thuja. Tree of Life. *Antidotes.* Camphor, Pulsatilla.
82. Verat.—Veratrum album. White Hellebore. *Antidotes.* Aconite, Ipecac, Arsenic, Camph., Coffea, China.
83. Kalm. l.—Kalmia latifolia. Laurel.

For a more particular description of the medicines, see Materia Medica at the close of the book.

DESCRIPTION OF THE PLATES.

PLATE 1.

FIG. 1.—A VERTICAL SECTION OF THE EYE. The optic nerve, 1.—The central artery of the retina, 2.—Envelope or sheath of the optic nerve, 3.—The Sclerotic or white coat of the eye, 4.—Transparent cornea, 5.—Union of the Sclerotic with the cornea, 6.—Choroid coat, 7.—Ciliary ligament, 8. —Iris, 10.—Pupil, 11.—Retina, 12.—Vitreous humour, 13.—Crystalline lens, 18.—The anterior chamber of the eye filled with aqueous humour, 19.—The posterior chamber also filled with aqueous humour, 20.

FIG. 2. 1. The Sclerotic coat at the insertion of the optic nerve.—2. The Sclerotic coat has been dissected leaving to view the choroid coat and the nerves which traverse it, and 3. represents their termination in the ciliary ligament. 4. The Iris.

FIG. 3. 1. Ciliary ligament. 2. Iris. 3. Pupil.

FIG. 4.—THE BALL OF THE EYE. 1. Optic nerve. 2. Tendinous attachment of the muscles.

FIG. 5. 1. Ciliary processes. 2. Posterior face of the Iris. 3. Pupil.

FIG. 6.—A GENERAL VIEW OF THE NERVES OF THE FACE, TEETH, AND TONGUE. 6. 8. Represent branches of the dental nerves, and the passage of the filaments into the teeth. 10. Division of the superior maxillary branch into nerves communicating with the orbit of the eye. 11. Branch of the inferior maxillary branch of the fifth pair. 14. The lingual nerve or nerve of the tongue anastimosing also with other nerves. 16. Pneumo gastric nerve. 18. Internal carotid artery. 17. Hypoglossal nerve. Branches of other nerves represented in the cut, it will be unnecessary to point out here.

PLATE 2.

Fig. 1. Is a back view of the human skeleton. *a.* Represents the collar bone or Clavicle. *F.* The shoulder blade or *Scapula.* *b.b.* The shoulder joint. *G.* The large bone of the arm or Humerus. *J.H.* The small bones of the arm or the Ulna and Radius. *g.M.M.* The Pelvis. D. The ribs. N.N. The Femur or large bone of the leg. Q.P. The small bones of the leg or the Tibia and Fibula.

Fig. 2. Represents the bones of the head. 4. Frontal bone or forehead. 3. Parietal, or side bones of the head. 5. Temporal bone. 6. Malar or cheek bone. 7. Bones forming the bridge of the nose. 8. Upper jaw-bone. 9. Lower jaw-bone.

Fig. 3.—The spiral column. 1. 2. 3. 4. Spinous processes. 5. Cervical vertebra. 6. Dorsal vertebra. 7. Lumbar vertebra. 8. The two false vertebra or the Sacrum and coccyx.

Fig. 4.—The chest. The ribs forming the chest are here represented, and at fig. 2 their union by cartileges with the Sternum in front.

Fig. 6.—The bones of the pelvis. 5. The sacrum at its union with the lumbar vertebra. 3. The coccyx. 7. 8. The Innominata or hip bones. 4. The ascetabulum or the cavity into which is inserted the head of the femur forming a ball and socket joint. 9. 10. The seat bones. 6. The Pubis.

Fig. 7.—A view of the bones of the hand. 1. Carpal or wrist bones. 2. Metacarpal bones. 3. 4. 5. Phalanges of the fingers.

Fig. 9.—A view of the bones of the foot. 1. Tarsal or ankle bones. 2. Metatarsal. 3. 4. 5. Phalanges of the foot.

PLATE 3.

Fig. 1. A front view of the muscles of the body.

A. a broad muscle helping to depress the angle of the mouth and also when the mouth is shut draws up the skin with which it is connected below the lower jaw. B. Deltoid muscle, used to raise the arm and assist it in all its motions except depressing it. C. Muscle used to bend the forearm. I. Moves the arm forward and upward toward the sternum. R. Assists in expiration and occasionally in discharging the contents of the stomach and belly. O. Crosses the legs in the manner tailors are used to sit. P. Draws the legs and thigh outward. Q. Helps to bend the leg and assists in bringing it and the thigh inward. T. Pulls the thigh inward. V. W. X. Help to extend the leg. Y. Extends the foot.

FIG. 2. Represents the extensors of the hand and forearm. The tendinous extremities are seen passing under the ligament at the root of the thumb and firmly bound by ligaments to the fingers. They serve to extend the hand and forearm. The flexors placed on the opposite side of the hand not seen in the cut serve to flex the hand and arm, and other muscles in connection with these and the extensors serve to rotate the hand and arm.

FIG. 3. Represents in addition to the muscles on the front of the hand and arm the nerves and arteries. 1. Brachial artery. 2. Radial artery, 3. Cubital artery. 4. 5. 6. 7. 8. 9. 10. 11. 12. 13. 14. 15. The nerves of the arms and hand and their various divisions and branches.

FIG. 4. Represents the muscles of the anterior portion of the leg and foot together with the arteries and nerves. The muscles of the leg may be seen passing under the broad ligament at the ankle, and attached by their tendinous extremity to the foot. These serve to flex the foot, and also to extend and rotate the leg. 1. Tibial artery. 2. The great sciatic nerve which may be seen dividing into various branches along the leg and foot.

PLATE 4.

1. The stomach. 4. Cardiac orifice. 5. Pyloric orifice. 6. Duodenum. 7. Pancreas. 11. Large lobe of the liver. 15. Gall bladder. 16. Duct leading from the gall bladder

to the duodenum. 17. Trunk of the portal vein. 18. Hepatic artery.

1. Circumvolutions of the small intestines. 2. Cœcum receiving the insertion of the small intestines, and presenting at *a* the appendix vermicularis. The colon or large intestine is seen passing around the smaller ones. 3. Ascending colon. 4. Transverse colon. 5. Descending colon. 7. Commencement of the rectum.

PLATE 5.

Fig. 1. Represents the heart, the great aorta passing off from it, and its division into arteries which supply the head and upper extremities with blood, also some of the muscles of the head and face. 1. The heart. 2. 3. Arteries of the heart. 4. Pulmonary artery. 5. The great aorta. 6. The brachial cephalic trunk. 7. The carotid artery branching off from the brachial cephalic on the left side. 9. Division of the brachial cephalic into the subclavian and carotid. 10. Division of the primitive carotid into the internal and external carotid. 11. Thyroid artery. 12. Lingual artery. 13. Facial artery. 16. 17. Arteries of the lips. 26. Vertebral artery. In the face may be seen the muscles by which the various movements of the face may be performed giving to it its varied expressions of life and animation, of joy and sorrow.

Fig. 2. The lungs, heart with its arteries and veins, and the windpipe passing to the lungs. 1. Larynx. 2. Trachea. 3. 4. Lungs. 5. Heart.

Fig. 3. The windpipe is seen with its divisions into larynx, trachea and bronchia. 3. 10. 11. Bifurcation of the bronchia, each branch giving off other branches, which divide into almost innumerable air-cells.

PART FIRST.

ANATOMY, PHYSIOLOGY, HYGIENE, AND THE TRUE THEORY OF CURE.

DOMESTIC PRACTICE.

PART FIRST.

CHAPTER I.

ANATOMY.

The idea is somewhat startling that the dust, which is blown in our faces on a windy day, once formed a part of living beings as active, intelligent, and full of life as ourselves; that the very water we drink has entered into strange and curious combinations.

From the human system, water passes into the air in enormous quantities. The tiny flower that blooms almost unseen and which we may crush by a step, the grass covering the earth with its velvet mantle, the flowering shrub and the foliage of the mighty forest tree, all throw into the atmosphere which envelops the earth a vast amount of moisture. This, collecting in the upper regions of the air, descends again in refreshing showers, or distils upon the earth in gentle dew.

Who can say whether the crystal fluid, which we quaff with such delicious pleasure, may not once have sparkled on the leaf of a rose, or glittered on the swarthy brow of an African sweating at his daily toil beneath a scorching sun. The air, that great reservoir, which surrounds us on all sides, covers alike the negro and the prince, and mingles together the drop which falls from the brow of the dying monarch, and the tear of suffering in the hovel of the poor and lowly. In that vast republic there is no distinction, all are alike.

Man from his infancy to his grave is constantly undergoing change. There are at work within him forces, ever active, never tiring, until the heart ceases to beat and death and decay commence. Yet this change in health is attended with no pain, but is the simple and beautiful process of nature, bringing new materials to take the place of worn out particles, keeping alive within us, that process of combustion, which warms us in winter and cools us in summer, the derangment of which, causes disease and death.

We are to look in this and the following chapter, at the physical organization of man, and unfold step by step, the most wonderful and beautiful mechanism, which ever came from the hand of the Eternal. We are to unveil for a time the human frame, and gaze upon bone, and blood, and muscle, and nerve, and tissue, and examine the various parts which make up this beautiful structure, and inquire into their organization, form and use, the process of health, of regeneration and decay, of life and death. We are to lift the curtain of nature and gaze into her secret chambers. We shall find these chambers irradiated with a pure and holy light, and, stamped upon all, the impress of the most perfect wisdom. We shall learn here a lesson of simplicity, truth and harmony, and admire the wisdom and love of that Being who made so perfect and beautiful an earthly habitation for the deathless soul.

In examining the human system we shall look,

1st, at its bony frame work, or skeleton.
2d, The muscles.
3d, The brain and nervous system.
4th, The organs connected with respiration and circulation.
5th The organs connected with digestion, secretion, excretion and reproduction.

1st, THE BONES OR SKELETON. The bony frame work of the human system consists of two hundred and eight pieces. [*See plate* 2, *fig.* 1]. Of these, eight compose the skull—viz. The *frontal bone or forehead,* the two *parietal bones,* forming the sides of the cranium and meeting at a line directly on the top of the skull, the occipital forming the back part of the skull, *the temporal,* the lower part of the sides of the head around the ears, and the *ethnoid* and *sphenoid.* The former passes from one temporal bone to the other

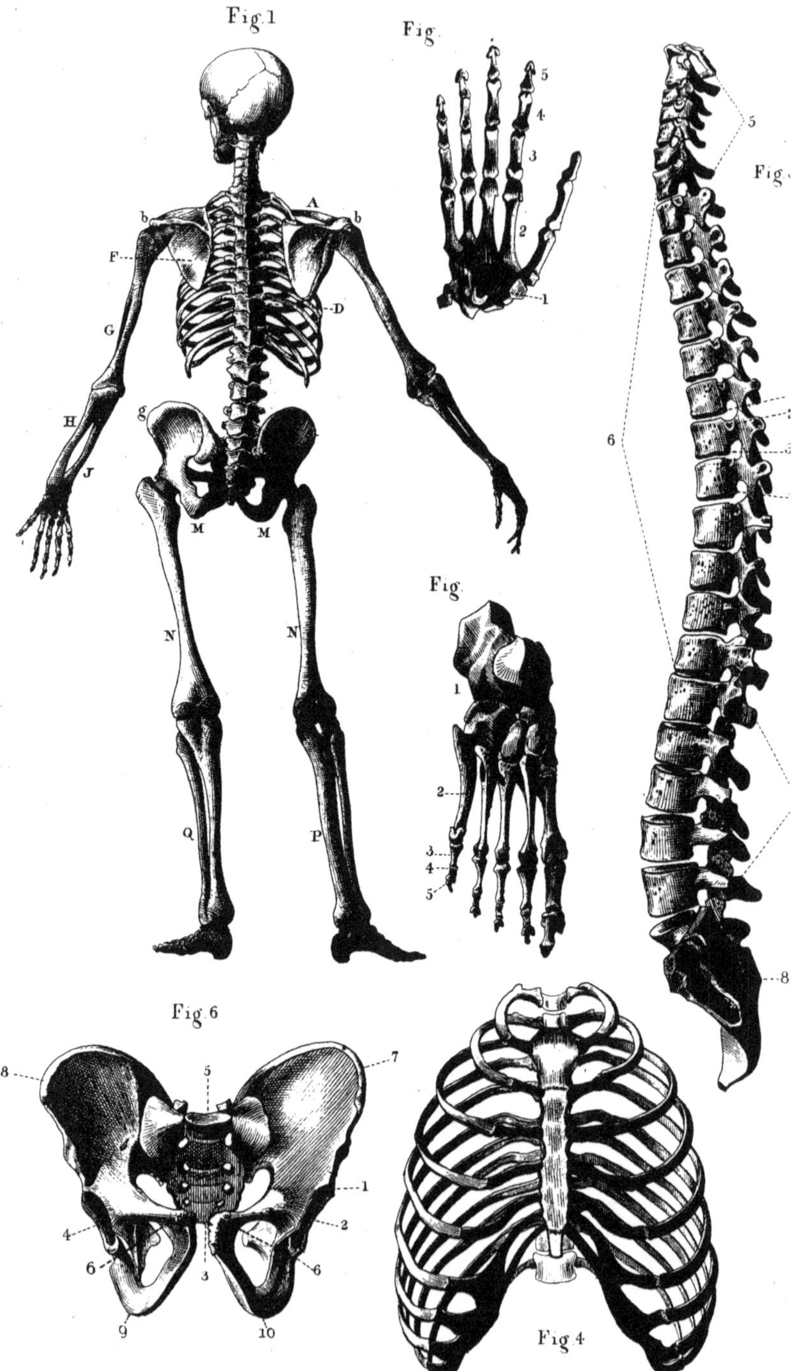
Fig.1
A
b
b
F
D
G
g
H
J
M
M
N
N
Q
P
Fig.
5
4
3
2
1
Fig.
1
2
3
4
5
5
6
8
Fig.6
8
5
7
1
4
2
6
3
6
9
10
Fig.4

across the base of the cranium, and the other is situated in the middle of the anterior portion of the cranium. These bones form a cavity for the brain, which is thus in its bony covering guarded in the most perfect manner from external violence. The edges of the bones are as it were dove-tailed into each other ; they are soft and capable of expansion in infancy, but in after life become solid. The bones of the cranium as well as those of the face are perforated in several places, so that the nerves may pass out from the brain and perform their functions.

THE FACE. The bones of the face [*Plate* 2, *fig*. 2], are fourteen in number. The two *nasal bones*, 7, form the arch or bridge of the nose ; the *vomer* separates the two passages ; the two *malar bones*, 6, form the prominence of the cheek and are generally called *cheek bones*. The *superior maxillary bone*, 8, forms the upper jaw, and the *inferior maxillary bone*, 9, the lower jaw. Of the teeth we shall treat when speaking of their diseases.

THE TRUNK. We are now to notice that curiously contrived and beautifully arranged column, which, while it supports the head and trunk, holding in the centre that great nerve (*Spinal marrow*), which passes off from the brain and gives out other branches to almost every part of the body, still permits us to bend in every direction with the most perfect ease.

This column [*Plate* 2, *fig*. 3], is composed of twenty-four distinct bones with projections, which, forming a canal behind the body of the vertebræ for the spinal marrow, serve also to bind the bones together and as attachments for the muscles. Between the joints of the vertebræ is a highly elastic cartilaginous tissue, which serves as a cushion to break the jar which would otherwise be felt in the brain at every step. With the aid of this elastic cushion and the backward and forward curve of the spine, no direct motion is communicated to the head. The first seven bones are called *cervical* or neck bones, 5, then follow twelve *dorsal* bones, 6, then five *lumbar* vertebra, 7, and last the *sacrum* and *coccyx*. We have thus the spinal column supporting the head as well as giving form and support to the trunk, but another bony cavity is required to contain and guard those vital organs, the lungs, and heart. We therefore find them placed in the *chest or thorax* [*Fig*. 4], which when well developed adds so much to the beauty and noble appearance of the human race. This cavity is formed by twenty-four ribs. Twelve on each side, starting from the twelve dorsal vertebræ and coming forward in a curve, seven of the upper ones on each side unite directly by means of a cartilage with a bone in front, **2**, called the *sternum* or breast bone. Three lower ones united by a cartilage are called *false ribs*, and the two remaining without anterior connection are called floating ribs. The natural form of the chest then resembles a pyramid or cone, the apex of which is at the top. It is not unusual in these days of fashion and artificial beauty, to find the order reversed, and the apex at the bottom. Rest assured, however, that nature's ways are the best, and that she generally contrives to punish severely those, who with fool-hardy temerity seek to fetter or restrain her movements. We have another bony cavity or basin forming the lower extremity of the trunk, essential to the support of the abdomen, as well as to those organs placed in its vicinity. This is called the Pelvis [*Plate* 2, *fig*. 6]. There are posteriorly two bones forming the lower extremity of the spinal column, and sometimes called false vertebræ—viz., the sacrum and coccyx, 3. 5. From these proceed anteriorly in the form of a curve, a larger bone on either side, called the *innominata*, meeting in front at what is called the *pubis*. The upper portion of these bones, 7. 8. are known as the *hip-bones*, the lower portion, 9. 10. as the *seat-bones*.

LOWER EXTREMITIES. At about the middle of the innominata are two cavities, 2. 4. into which are inserted the *thigh bone* or femur, forming what is called a ball and socket joint. The extremity of this bone articulates with the *tibia*, the large bone of the leg, the *fibula*, or smaller bone, being firmly bound to it at the knee, forming a hinge joint.

Over this joint, affording it protection, is placed a smaller bone connected with the femur and leg bones by ligaments and muscles. It is called the *patella* or knee-pan. At the lower extremity of the leg we have the small *tarsal* bones, seven in number, forming the ankle. Articulating with one range of these bones are the *metatarsal*, five in number, to the extremities of these are connected the bones of the toes, called the *phalanges* of the toes.

Fig. 7 represents the bones of the ankle and foot. The tarsal or ankle-bones, 1, the metatarsal, 2, the phalanges of the toes, 3, 4, 5.

THE UPPER EXTREMITIES. The *clavicle* (collar bone) is attached at one extremity to the *sternum* or breast bone, at the other it is united to the *scapula* (or shoulder blade). It keeps the arm from sliding forward. The shoulder blade is situated on the upper and back part of the chest and is held in its position by muscles. The *humerus* is united by a joint with the scapula, and at the elbow it is articulated with the *ulna* of the fore-arm. This bone is on the inside of the arm, while the *radius*, which articulate with the *carpus*, forming the wrist joint, is on the outside. These bones at their extremities articulate with each other, the upper end of the *radius*, rolling on the ulna, and the lower end of the ulna rolling on the radius, thus permitting the varied and beautiful movements of the arm. The *carpus*, or wrist, is composed of eight small bones. Articulating with one range of these, is the *metacarpus*, composed of five bones, forming the body of the hand. United to these are the bones of fingers, called the *phalanges* of the fingers. The articulation of the bones are covered with cartilage, a substance of the nature of bone, yet smooth, solid and much softer. Covering the cartilage, and forming around the joint a shut sack, is the *synovial* membrane. It secretes a serous fluid, which serves to lubricate the joint so that the motion may be free, easy, and without pain. The joints are kept in their position by ligaments or shining, strong, and elastic bands, which generally surround the whole joint.

The bones are composed of animal and earthy matter, the earthy part, giving them strength and solidity, while the animal, imparts vitality. In infancy the animal substance preponderates, causing the bones to be softer and more liable to bend than in old age, when the earthy preponderates, leaving the joints stiff, the bones brittle and liable to break. Over the bones is spread a thin membrane called the *periosteum*. This membrane may become inflamed, when it is peculiarly sensitive and painful.

We have thus the frame work of the human system. The bones are all in their places, but they are only inanimate bones, without life, unable to perform a single movement. Let us then take another step, cover them with muscles, and thus attach to them the bands and pulleys by means of which movement is to be performed.

THE MUSCLES. On this part of the subject we shall of necessity be short, as a minute description would lead us into those dry and technical details, which would be uninteresting to the general reader.

The muscles are composed of bundles of small fibres enclosed in a membranous investment or sheath. Towards the end of the muscles the fibres gradually change into the tendons or cords, by which they are strongly attached to the bones.

The muscles not only enable us to move, perform respiration and the various duties of nature essential to life, but give form and beauty to the frame, form those cavities, within which are enclosed important organs requiring their protecting covering.

The prominent characteristic of the muscles is, *contractility* on the application of the necessary stimuli, and relaxing when that stimuli is withdrawn. The natural stimuli is the *will*, which, flashing like lightning along the nerves, causes the muscles to relax, or contract, and produces those varied and rapid movements of which the body is capable. Each movement or expression is the result of the contraction and re-

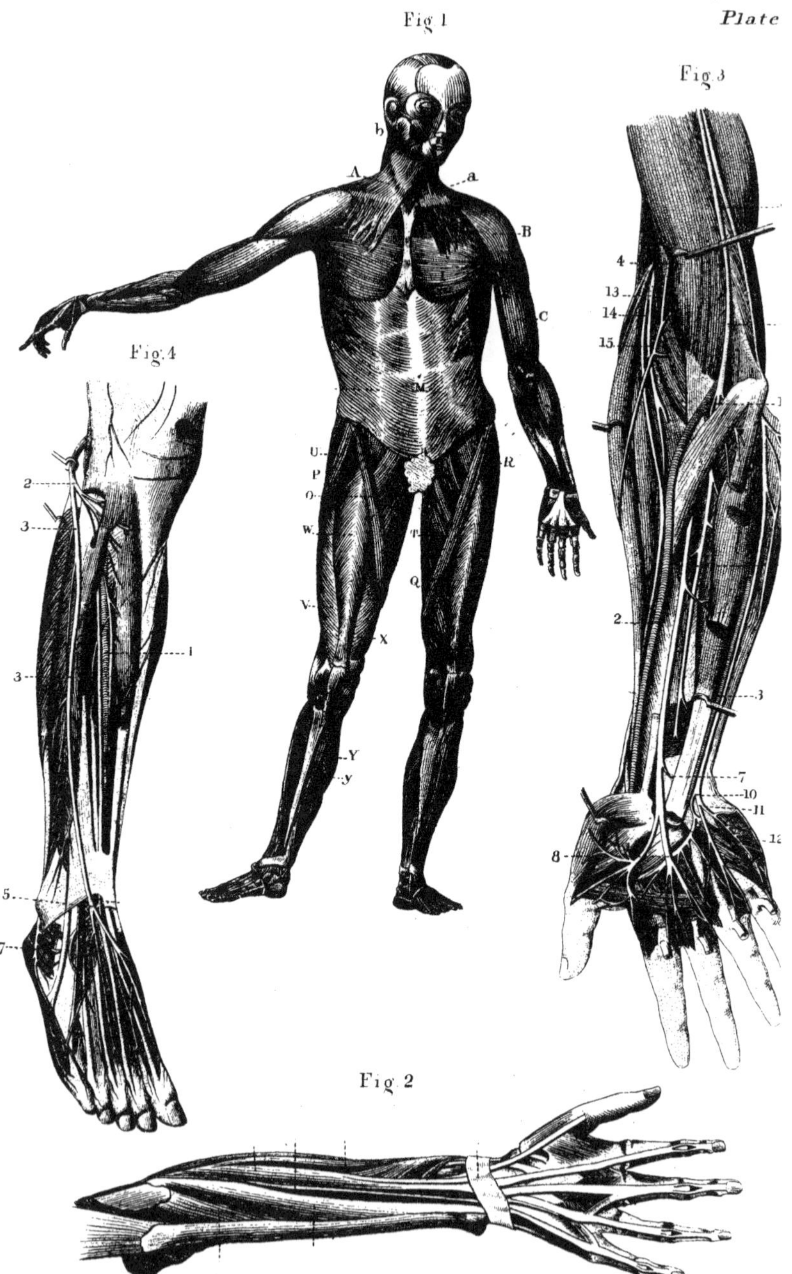

Lith of Schedler & Liebler 161 Brw. New York.

laxing of the appropriate muscles. It is in this way the eyes are opened or closed, the mouth extended, contracted, opened, or closed, the face wears an expression of grief, or is merry with smiles, or convulsed with laughter. The jaw performs its rapid movements in mastication in this manner; breathing is performed by the contraction and expansion of the muscles of the chest and abdomen. The rapid movements of the fingers in the musical performer and the varied and rapid motions of the dancer, show how obedient the muscles are to the mandate of the will. In the upper and lower extremities the muscles which produce flexion and those which produce extension are placed on opposite sides. In the lower limbs the *flexors* are placed on the posterior and the *extensors* on the anterior sides, while in the upper limbs their situation is directly the opposite. The strength and health of the muscles is increased by proper exercise. This fact is familiar to all, although all do not act upon the common-sense lesson it teaches, and take the necessary exercise.

Thus we perceive when the stimuli is applied to one set of muscles, they contracting, flex or draw up the limb. Shut off the nervous stimuli from this class and direct it to another, and their fibres contract, and the limb is extended. Thus, by this beautiful process the chest expands, the bosom rises and falls, we eat, drink, move and live. If the world would more frequently follow the plain and simple teachings of nature, there would be far less sighing and groaning than at present. See Plate 3.

We have now clothed the before naked and unsightly skeleton with flesh, giving it beauty and symmetry of form. Still there is no movement; all is as still and quiet as the form of the dead. The machine is ready for action, but has not yet felt the quickening influence of life. Let us then advance another step and examine the seat of that power, whose quickening influence is infused throughout the system, and whose mandate the muscles hasten to obey.

THE BRAIN AND NERVOUS SYSTEM.

We have seen that a cavity is formed by the bones of the skull and continued through an opening in its base down through the centre of the vertebræ to their extremity. It is to hold within its bony embrace that greyish white, soft and pulpy substance, called the *cerebro-spinal-axis*. Of this, the part passing through the vertebræ, giving off branches to every part of the system, is generally known as the *spinal cord*, while the upper or enlarged portion, also giving off branches, is called the *brain*.

The brain, look at it closely, examine it minutely, bring to your aid, if you please, the powers of the microscope, and what do you see? A soft, pulpy, greyish white substance, and yet this is the seat of the deathless soul, here mind reigns and intellect forges those thoughts, which, like the thunderbolts of Jehovah, scatter ruin and death, rouse a nation to arms, shake a world, or infuse around an atmosphere of purity and love.

Here are conceived the glowing thoughts of the poet, the bright visions and gorgeous pictures of the artist, plans pure and holy, or debasing, polluting, and devilish. This is the fountain of purity and greatness, and of filth, abomination and discord. And yet do we see any of these workings in that mass before us. Do we see how the thought is transmitted along those electric lines, the nerves, to the remotest extremity? Or is the fluid so subtile as to elude our gaze? We feel the blow which fells us to the earth, but can our eyes see that nervous stimuli which induces the action? Is it not natural to suppose, that when an agent so quick and subtile, so powerful in its influence on the system becomes diseased or deranged, it requires not the blow of the hammer to set it right, but rather a power quick and subtile, yet with sufficient strength to restore healthy action?

This cerebro-spinal-centre is enclosed in three membranes. The external one, forming the inside lining of the bone is called the *Dura mater*. On the inner side of the Dura mater is a thin *serous membrane* called the *Arachnoid.* The serous fluid it secretes in a healthy state, seems to lubricate the brain, in a diseased state; this fluid may increase in quantity and oppress that organ. The third membrane investing directly the brain, is highly vascular, composed of a net-work of innumerable vessels held together by cellular tissue. It is the nutrient membrane of the brain, and is called the *Pia mater.*

Not only motion, but life itself depends on the healthy action of the nervous system. The *cerebro-spinal-centre* in its bony cavity guides and controls every action by means of branches of nerves, which ramify throughout every part of the body. Of these branches, the brain proper sends off *twelve pairs.* One pair ramifies upon the membrane lining the nasal passages, creating the delicate sense of smell, and are called the *olfactory nerves.* A second pair, penetrates the coats of the eye, and expands into the retina, forming a surface upon which every object is pictured, and creating the sense of sight. These are the *optic nerves.* The third, fourth, and sixth pairs are distributed among the muscles of the eyes. The fifth pair has three important branches. One branch passes out from the skull at a notch distinctly felt about the middle of the eyebrow, and sends branches to the forehead, eyes and nose. The second branch supplies the the teeth of the upper jaw, and passing out through a notch in the malar (or cheek) bone, sends a branch to the eye and ramifies over the face. The third branch supplies the teeth of the lower jaw by sending a small branch to each tooth. It also sends branches to the muscles of the lower jaw, the ear and the tongue. It is generally in this nerve and its branches that we have that most agonizing of all pain, prosopalgia or neuralgia of the face.

Other nerves supply the ear, the glands of the mouth, the mouth, tongue, throat and muscles of the neck. The tenth or *Pneumogastric* nerve, gives out branches to the respiratory and digestive organs.

As we descend from the brain to the spinal cord, we find

it giving off *thirty-one* pairs of nerves, each arising by two roots, one of which is called the *motor*, the other the *sensitive* root. The motor root arises from a narrow white band on anterior columns of the cord, while the sensitive start from the internal part of the cord.

Five pairs in the vicinity of the shoulder, unite, forming what is called the *brachial plexus*, and again separate into six nerves, which ramify on the muscles and skin of the upper extremities. For the sake of convenience, we may mention, that the first eight pairs of nerves, commencing at the top of the column, are called Cervical, the next twelve Dorsal, the next five Lumbar and the last six Sacral nerves. Besides the *brachial plexus*, above mentioned, there is also a lumbar and sacral plexus, formed in the same manner, supplying the lower extremities, the hips, the abdomen and the organs in the vicinity of the pelvis.

From what has been already said it will be perceived, that the nerves of the spine as well as the brain are of two kinds, the *motor*, or nerves of motion, and the *sensitive*, or nerves of sensation. The nerves of motion communicate principally with the muscular tissues and the various organs of the body, while those of sensation ramify more particularly on the skin. Hence the pain in cutting through the skin is much more severe than in the tissue beneath. If the nerves of motion are injured so that they cannot act on either side, there is an entire paralysis of that side or organ, notwithstanding the sensation may be as acute as ever. So also when the nerves of sensation are paralized, notwithstanding there may be diminution of motion in the part, with which they communicate, yet all sense of feeling is entirely gone. Sever the optic nerve, which is a nerve of sensation, and sight would be entirely destroyed, notwithstanding the motion of the eye would remain uninjured. Yet if the nerve of motion were severed, the sight would remain uninjured, but the eye becomes fixed and motionless ; and so with the other nerves of the head and spine. Hence we are often unable to move some particular part of the body in which feeling may be acute, and on the contrary, sensation may be absent and motion perfect.

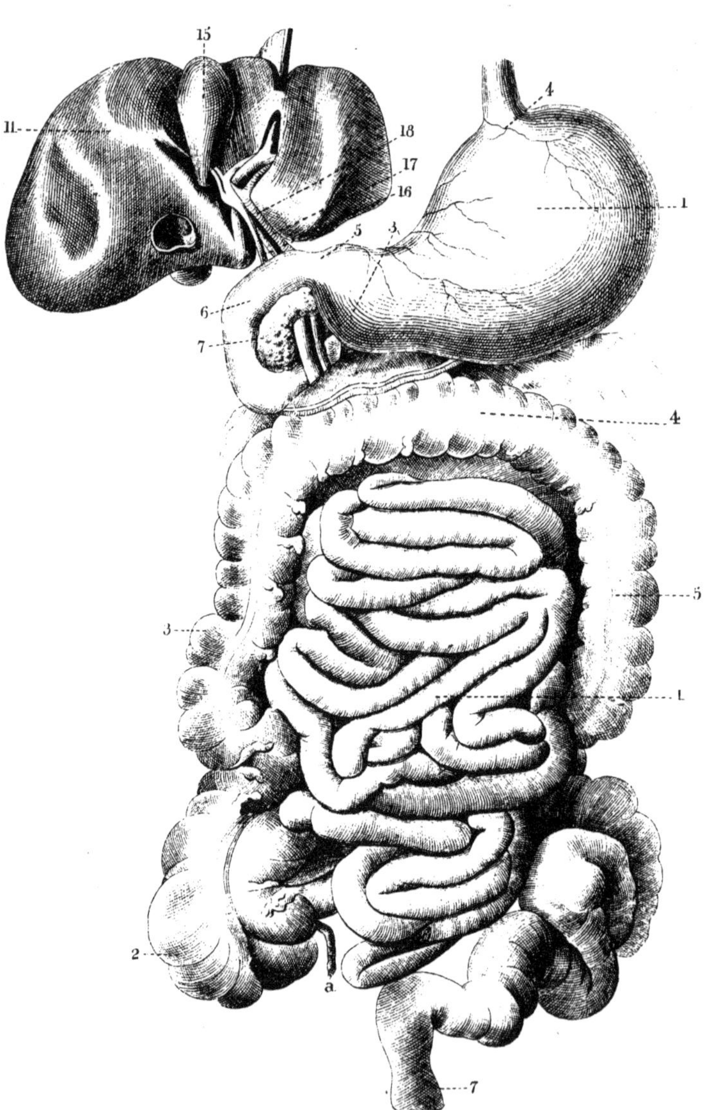

Lith of Schedler & Loebler Bros New York

Besides the nerves already enumerated, there is still another, which performs a most important part in the economy of life, viz.: *The sympathetic nerve.* It consists of a chain of *Ganglia*, or knots, extending the whole length of the spinal column on each side. It communicates by its branches, not only with the spinal but cranial nerves, and all the internal organs of the head and trunk. Every part of the body is more or less under its influence, as filaments from it, accompany all the blood vessels throughout their course. Thus a sympathetic chain is kept up throughout the body both in health and disease.

DIGESTION. A proper understanding of the organs connected with digestion is of course important, as their derangement is the fruitful source of a large share of our physical sufferings.

Situated around the mouth, are six *Salivary Glands*, three on each side of the jaw, the *Parotid*, *Submaxillary*, and *Sublingual*. Their secretion called saliva, is discharged through small ducts into the mouth. Back of the cavity of the mouth, and connecting with it, is a large passage connecting above with the passages of the nose, and below with the *Larynx*, by means of which air is passed to the lungs, and the *Œsephagus*, through which food passes into the stomach, called the *Pharynx*. The *Œsephagus* is a muscular tube extending behind the larynx, heart and lungs, through the diaphragm into the stomach. The Diaphragm is a muscular curtain, separating entirely the organs of the chest from those of the abdomen. It rises and falls with every respiration. The *Stomach* is located on the left side of the abdomen, just below the diaphragm. It has two openings, the upper or *cardiac* orifice connecting with the Œsophagus, and admitting the food, the lower or *Pyloric* orifice, connected with the intestines, through which the food passes after undergoing the action of the stomach.

The Intestines are divided into large and small. The small intestine, which is about twenty-five feet in length, is divided into the duodenum, jejunum, and illium. The large intestine, about five feet in length, is divided into the cœcum, colon and rectum. The duodenum commences at the pyloric orifice of the stomach, and is about twelve fingers in length. Into it open the ducts from the liver and pancreas. The jejunum is a continuation of the duodenum, as is the *illeum* of the jejunum. These forming the small intestines, pass in convolution from one side to the other, until the *illeum* terminates in the colon by a valvular opening near the right hip bone. The cœcum is a blind pouch at the commencement of the large intestines. From this point the large intestine or colon ascends on the right side, crosses the abdomen just below the liver and stomach, descends on the left side to the hip bone, where curving on itself it passes downwards from the rectum and terminates in the anus.

The Peritoneum is a serous membrane adhering to the inner surface of the abdominal cavity, and is reflected over, invests, and supports the viscera of the cavity.

After having completely invested an organ it passes double to the walls of the abdomen, to be there expanded. These duplicatures confine the organs in their place and support them. That which supports the intestines is called the *Mesentery*, and a very large one, hanging loose before them, keeping them warm, is called the *Œmentum.*

The Lactials are small vessels commencing on the mucous membrane of the small intestine, in the upper portion of which they are the most numerous, passing between the membranes of the *mesentery* to several successive ranges of glands, diminishing in number and increasing in size at each successive range until they open into the enlarged portion of the *thoracic duct.* This duct passes through the diaphragm to the lower part of the neck, where it opens into a vein which passes directly to the heart. The food then, after it has been digested by the stomach, passes into the duodenum, and there mingling with the secretions of the liver and pancreas, is tåken up in the form of chyle, as it passes along the intestines, by the innumerable mouths of these little absorbents, the lacteals, by them conveyed to the

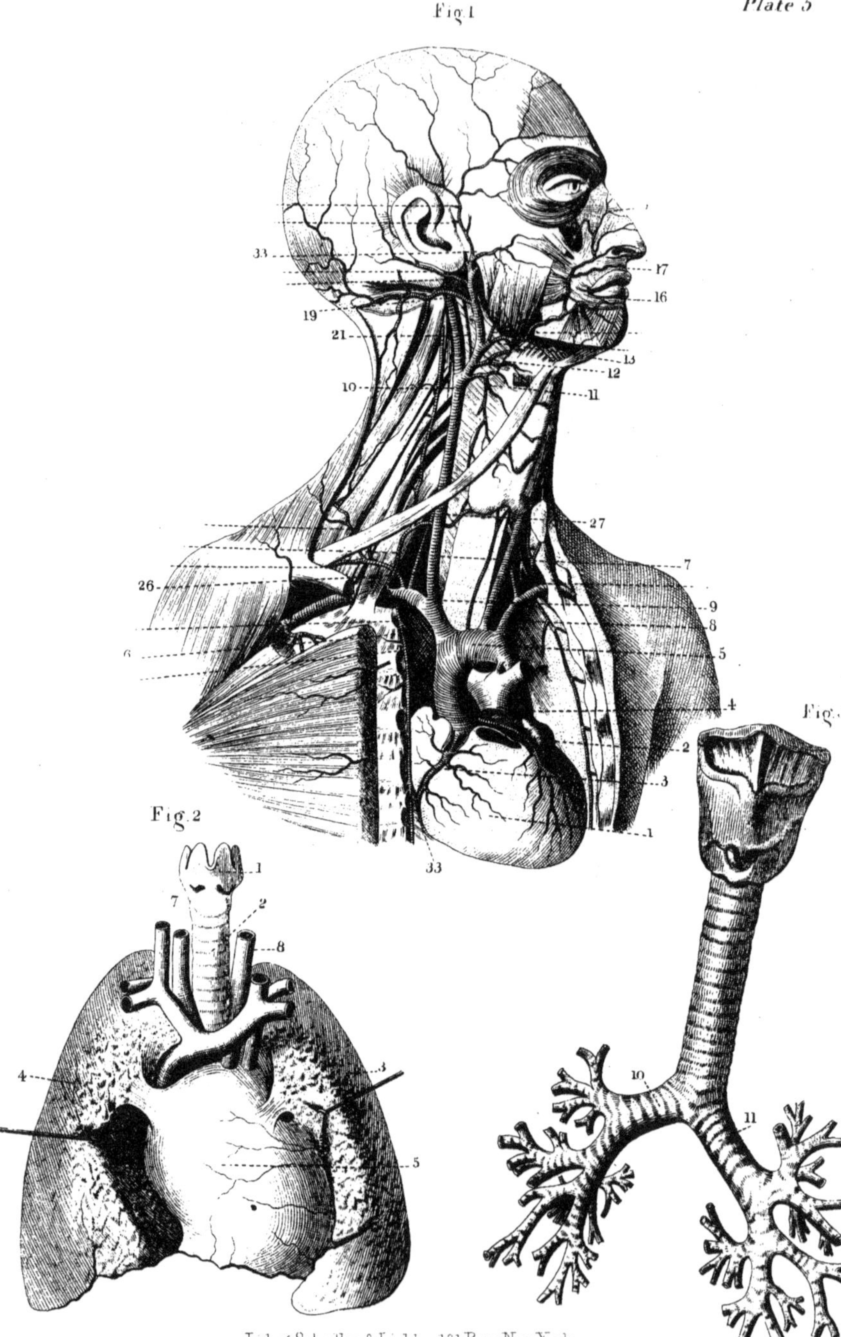

Lith of Schedler & Liebler 181 Brw. New York

thoracic duct, and through it passed into the circulation, and thus conveyed to every part of the system.

The Liver is a large gland, weighing three or four pounds, situated on the right side below the diaphragm. On the under surface is the gall-bladder, which acts as a reservoir for the bile.

The Pancreas is a long gland situated behind the stomach transversely across the posterior part of the abdomen. From it as well as from the liver a duct passes into the duodenum.

The Spleen is a small body situated in the left side. Its use is unknown.

URINARY ORGANS.

The Kidneys, whose office it is to secrete urine, are located on either side of the lumbar vertebræ, below the last false rib. The urine is conveyed from each kidney by a small tube, called ureter, to the bladder. The bladder is the reservoir for the urine, and is located behind the pubis, and above and before the lower part of the rectum. The passage by which the urine passes from the bladder, is called urethra.

We are now very briefly to consider that part of the system by which oxygen is introduced into the body and the elements of life conveyed to every part of it.

RESPIRATION AND CIRCULATION.

The wind-pipe commences at the root of the tongue, and descends in front of the œsophagus to the lungs. Its upper orifice is covered by a valve, called the epiglottis, to prevent the introduction of food, which passes directly over it. Laughter during eating, renders food liable, by the opening of this valve, to pass into the wind-pipe, thus producing violent cough or suffocation. The wind-pipe is composed of cartilaginous rings, united by membranes, and is divided into three parts. The upper portion is called larynx, the middle portion the trachea. The lower part or the *Bronchia* bifurcates from the trachea about the third or fourth dorsal vertebræ, and passes, one to each lung, where it terminates in an innumerable number of air-cells, which exist in every part of the lungs. These air-cells are separated only by a thin membrane from an equal number of cells filled with blood communicating with the heart. The lungs then are of a spongy texture, made up of cellular tissue, and these innumerable air and blood-cells. Respiration consists in filling these cells with air. The lungs are thus distended, and the dark venous blood passing in from the heart on the opposite side, gives off through the thin intervening membrane its carbonic acid and takes in return the oxygen from the air. The air then by the contraction of the proper muscles is forced out and the lungs contract in size. Thus the chest rises and falls with the respiration and expiration of air. There are two lungs, one on each side of the chest, embracing the heart, and separated from each other by a membranous partition. They are suspended in the chest by roots composed of the pulmonary arteries and veins, the bronchial tubes, &c, They are covered by a serous membrane, which is reflected over the wall of the chest, forming a shut sack. This membrane is called the Pleura, and when inflamed occasions that most agonizing disease pleurisy. The lungs rising and falling at each respiration, the inflamed surfaces rub against each other, occasioning the most acute pain.

CIRCULATION. *The Heart* is the great centre of circulation, the mainspring in the beautiful mechanism of the system, its pulsations only ceasing with death. It is situated in the chest between the right and left lung, has two sides, each of which has two chambers or cavities. The upper is called the *auricle*, the lower the *ventricle*. These chambers, the auricle and ventricle, are separated by valves. The right side of the heart is appropriated to the *venous blood*, the left to the *arterial blood*. As the venous blood passes into the right auricle, the auricle contracts and forces it through the valve into the right ventricle. The contraction of the ventricle closes the valve, thus preventing the return of blood, and forcing it into the pulmonary artery, through which it is conveyed to the lungs. Here, in the innumerable cells prepared for its reception, it throws off, through the thin membrane separating it from the air cells, its carbonic acid, and receives in return oxygen from the air; changed now from dark and impure venous blood, to bright and life-giving arterial blood, it passes on through the pulmonary veins to the left auricle of the heart. This chamber, contracting, forces the blood into the lower chamber or left ventricle, from whence it is prevented from returning by a similar valvular arrangement to that found in the right heart. The contraction of the ventricle forces the blood into the great *aorta.* This great artery of the body gives off trunks to the head, the upper and lower extremities and the organs in the abdominal cavity. These branches, dividing and subdividing into innumerable branches, growing smaller and smaller, convey the arterial blood to every part of the system, and at length terminate in a curious network of vessels, called the capillary vessels. The arterial system has fulfilled its duty, conveyed the elements of life and nutrition to every part of the system, and the blood is now ready to be conveyed back to the heart, no longer bright and life-giving, but dark and impure. The veins then, commencing in this capilliary net-work of vessels, at first innumerable in number, collect the blood, and flowing into each other, form at length two large trunks the *ascending* and *descending Vena cava*, by which it is returned to the right auricle of the heart, and from thence in the manner already explained, passes on to the lungs. There throwing off its carbonic acid, and receiving in return oxygen from the air, it flows on to the right heart, when it is again ready to be distributed throughout the system. Thus we have the heart the great central point of the system, the arterial blood flowing outward, freighted with life, to every part of the body and the venous blood, charged with impurities, flowing inward to the heart.

Each cavity of the heart holds two ounces, and as it contracts about seventy times in a minute, more than *two hogsheads* traverse it every hour. And yet performing this mighty labour, it beats on year after year, never tiring, until paralyzed by the hand of death.

For a more minute explanation of the structure of the heart

and the circulation, see "*Diseases of the Heart*," also chapter on Physiology.

THE SKIN. The skin is composed of two layers of membrane, the *Cuticle*, and *True Skin*. The *Cuticle* has neither blood vessels nor nerves, and serves as a protection to the *True Skin*. In the inner layers of the *Cuticle* there is a peculiar colouring matter, *black* in the *Negro*, *copper coloured* in the *Indian*, and in the *White*, so transparent as to be scarcely perceptible. The *True Skin* contains, besides *Arteries*, *Veins*, and *Absorbents*, oil glands, perspiratory glands, and nerves. The nerves ramify on the surface, and render the skin sensitive to the touch. The absorbents are small vessels opening on the inner layers of the *Cuticle*, and through these, poisons being rubbed on the skin are conveyed into the system.

From the *Perspiratory glands*, which separate from the blood the perspiration, spiral ducts pass obliquely to the skin. In health, these glands are constantly in action, pouring out through the ducts an enormous amount of matter in the form of sensible and insensible perspiration. For a more full description of the functions of the skin, *see chapter on Physiology*.

THE TEETH. The Teeth are divided into two parts. The *Crown* rising above the gum is covered with a fine *enamel*, to protect it from decay and wear, and to render it more fit to perform its important functions. The root is of a bony substance, and is firmly inserted in the jaw. Communicating to each tooth through the root, is a small nerve. When this is diseased or exposed by the decay of the tooth, that *exquisite* sensation is produced known as *tooth-ache*.

The first set, twenty in number, appearing in infancy, are only temporary, and are called *milk teeth*. The second, or *permanent* set, appearing between the ages of six and fourteen are thirty-two in number, sixteen in each jaw.

The four front teeth in each jaw are called *incisors*, the next on each side the *cuspid* or eye tooth, the next two, *bi-cuspids*, the next two *molars*, and the last two on each side of the jaw, *wisdom* teeth, from their not appearing until about twenty,

Plate.

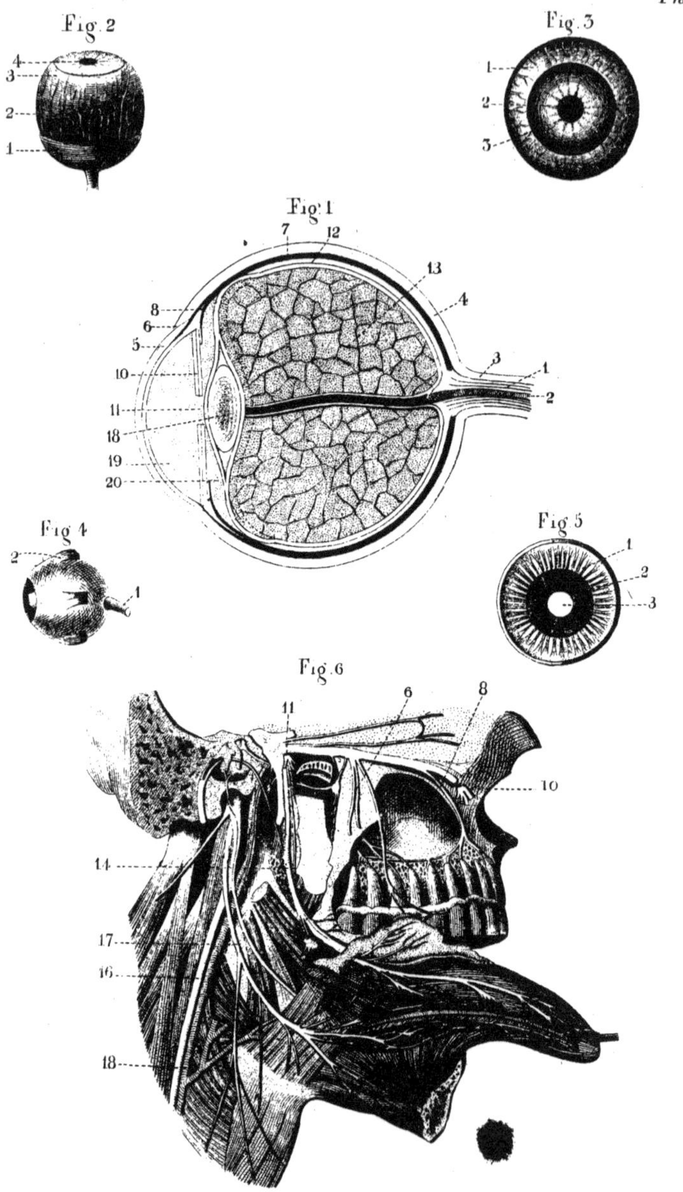

Lith. of Schedler & Liebler 181 Brw. New York.

and then being of short duration. The molars on the upper jaw have three roots, those on the lower two, while the incisors, cuspids and bi-cuspids have each but one root.

See also chapter on *Diseases of Children.*

VISION. The eye is the most perfect and beautiful optical instrument in the world. It consists of a globe, held in its position by means of six muscles attached externally to the *Sclerotic coat* near the *Cornea*, and internally, to the bones of the orbit behind the eye.

The Sclerotic coat, seen in the white of the eye, is dense and fibrous. It is the strong membrane which invests it, except the transparent part in front. This is called the *Cornea.* It is united with the Sclerotica in the same way that the crystal, which it resembles in form, is set in a watch.

Within the Sclerotica there is a vascular membrane called the *choroid* coat. It secretes on its internal surface the *Pigmentum nigrum*, or *black pigment*, giving the dark colour to the pupil of the eye, and is of vast importance in vision. It terminates near the *cornea* in a white circle, called the *ciliary circle.* The internal layer of the edge is thrown into folds, the central border of which, rests on the *crystalline* lens. These folds are called *ciliary processes.*

Starting from the *ciliary circle*, is a beautifully contrived curtain, with an opening in its centre, dividing the anterior portion of the eye into two chambers, the communication between which being at this opening. This curtain is capable of contraction and dilation, thus enlarging the central opening, and is called the *Iris*. The central opening is called the *Pupil.* The two chambers are filled with an *aqueous* humour. Behind the *pupil* is placed a *lens*, clear as crystal, and called the *Crystalline lens.*

Another and last coat within the *Choroid* is called the *Retina.* The optic nerve passes from the brain through the outer coats and expands on this. This is the seat of vision, and here every object we witness is pictured or daguerreotyped, and the impression thus transmitted to the brain. Within the coats already mentioned and back of the crystalline lens, is a chamber forming the larger portion of the ball of the eye, filled with a humour resembling the aqueous, but more dense, called the *Vitreous* humour. Over the eye are the eye-lids, lined on the inside by a delicate membrane, which is also reflected over the ball of the eye, called the *Conjunctiva*. It is liable to become inflamed when it appears blood shot. It secretes a fluid which lubricates the eye.

At the upper and outer angle of the orbit is the *Lachrymal gland*. It secretes the tears which are poured on the ball of the eye, keeping it constantly moist. They pass off through small openings at the internal angle of the eye into the nose.

We have, then, the cornea collecting and bending inward the rays of light; the aqueous humour transmitting the rays and giving free motion to the iris; the iris contracting and dilating, admitting only the necessary rays; the crystalline lens, the focus concentrating the rays which then, crossing each other, are transmitted through the vitreous humour to the retina, which serves as a daguerreotype-plate, upon which the image is pictured, and the impression through the expanded optic nerve transmitted to the brain. What instrument in the world could be more beautiful or perfect in its construction.

CHAPTER II.

PHYSIOLOGY.

The bodies of all the higher animals are composed of a great variety of parts, different in their structure and action, and yet so beautifully adapted to each other as to act in perfect harmony.

In the lowest forms of vegetable life we find a single cell making up the whole fabric. This cell, grows from its germ, absorbs and assimilates nutriment, converts a part of it into its own cell wall, secretes another portion into its cavity, and from a third, produces the reproductive germs that are to continue its race. Having completed the germs, it bursts and sets them free. Each one of these germs is capable of going through the same set of operations.

In the higher forms of vegetable life we find a multiplication of similar cells, among which these operations are distributed, thus producing by the labour of all, a more complete and permanent effect.

At the extremities of the roots of plants we find succulent bodies made up of soft cells, known by the name of *spongioles*. These perform the *absorption* of nutritious fluid, which is conveyed by the vessels of the stem and branches to the leaves, and there in the cells, which make up the parenchyma of those organs, undergoes a change. The watery ascending sap is converted into thick glutinous latex, which like the blood of animals contains the material for the production of new tissue and the elements of the various secretions. This process of conversion comprises not only the *exhalation* of superfluous liquid,the action of light, and the interchange of gaseous ingredients between the sap and air, but a new molecular arrangement of the particles of sap, by which new products are generated. This process, which is such an immense step towards the production of living tissue from the crude material, is called *assimilation*.

As the latex descends in its proper vessels through the

stem, it yields up to the growing parts, the nutrition they severally require. Beside the ordinary tissue, of which most of the fabric is composed, in the growth of which the process of *nutrition* is considered as consisting, there are groups of cells, which separate peculiar products from the sap such as oil, starch, resin, &c., which are stored up against the time they are demanded. These are said to perform the act of *secretion*. All the cells by which the permanent fabric is provided for, have as individuals but a very transitory life. The *absorbents* are continually renewed, some dying, and others forming the solid texture of the root. In the short duration of the *assimilating* cells, we have a convincing proof in the fall of the leaf and the opening buds. The secreting cells undergo a like transitory duration.

The starting point both in the *animal* and the *plant* is the same. The embryo of the animal up to a certain grade of its development, consists, like that of the plant, of nothing else than an aggregation of cells. Among the higher class of animals, however, a large proportion of the fabric consists of tissues in which no distinct trace of cellular origin is apparent, and yet when we subject them to a close analysis, and examine them not only in their complete state but in their development, we find they are reduced to the same category with the tissues of the plants and lower animals. There are tissues peculiar to animals, and these we find referrible to the plastic fluid prepared by the *assimilating cells*, and set free by their rupture. In plants, the tissues principally concerned in the *vital* operations retain their cellular form. We also see distinct groups of cells in the bodies of animals, which have not only the functions of *absorption*, *assimilation*, *respiration*, *secretion*, and *reproduction*, which we also find in plants, but those of *muscular contraction* and *nervous action*, which they alone perform.

The cell originates from a reproductive granule, previously formed by some other cell; this granule attracts to itself, assimilates and organises the particles of the nutrient fluid in its neighbourhood, and converts some of them into the substance of the cell-wall, and draws others into the cavity of the cell. In this way the cell gradually increases in size, and while it approaches its term of life, makes preparation for its renewal, by the development of reproductive granules in its interior, which may become the germs of new cells, when set free from the cavity of the parent by the rupture of the cell-wall. In the *chyle*, *lymph*, and *blood*, we find floating cells, called the *chyle* and *lymph corpuscles* and *colourless corpuscles* of the blood, having no single nucleus, but several scattered particles, each of which is a reproductive granule. These, when set free by the bursting or liquefaction of the walls, float in the current of fluid, and are in their turn developed into cells. In general however, the cells of animal tissue are furnished with a *nucleus*. The nucleus seems to be the chief instrument in the function of the cell. In some cells this function is restricted to the attraction of certain constituents, by which its cavity is filled. These constituents may be of a fluid nature readily passing into decomposition, such as the glandular structure, or they may give solidity to the texture. Thus the cells of the epidermis are strengthened by a deposit of a horny nature, those of shell by the deposit of carbonate of lime, and those of the bones and teeth by mixture of earthy and mineral matter. These cells do not generally reproduce themselves, but successive crops of them are formed as fast as they are required from other sources.

Cells are often elongated, and their cavities occupied by internal deposit, so that they may be mistaken for solid fibres, or the boundary of the cells may be lost by their coalescence with each other. The character of the cell may be completely changed by a solution in its wall in one or more spots so that its cavity is laid open and coalesces with some other. Thus, by the disappearance of the partition between the cells may be formed a tube, and this may coalsce with others to form a capilliary net-work for the circulation of blood.

In the blood we find *two varieties* of cells or corpuscles. The red blood corpuscle owes its colour to a secretion within its walls of a peculiar chemical nature. Notwithstanding, judging from analogy we should suppose that the *red corpuscles* in man and the other mammalia would contain a nucleus, as they do in all other animals, yet they have never been discovered by the most careful microscopic examination. Their principle office seems to be the introduction of oxygen into the blood that circulates through the systemic capiliaries, and the removal of the carbonic acid set free there, serving as a medium for bringing the tissues in relation with air, which is necessary for the maintenance of their vital activity. The colourless corpuscles seem to have a different office to perform. While the red corpuscles are only found in the vertebrated classes and the higher invertebrata, the colourless are found throughout the whole animal scale. Hence we might suppose that the colourless corpuscles are closely connected with nutrition, while the functions of the red corpuscles must be of a more limited character. In animals, in a state of starvation, we find very few colourless corpuscles, while in those that are well fed, they exist in great abundance. In inflammation, colourless corpuscles rapidly increase in the inflamed part. There is then scarcely a reasonable doubt, that elaboration of fibrine is a consequence of this form of cell life, and is one of its express objects.

A class of cells next in independence to the cells in the animal fluid we find on the membranous surface of the body, forming the *epidermis* and *epithelium*. The epidermis is a thin semi-transparent pellicle, covering the entire body in close connection with the true skin. It consists of a series of flattened scale like cells, the outer layers of which are constantly thrown off by desquamation, new ones having formed below. The epidermis is not traversed by nerves and blood, vessels, but is pierced by the excretory ducts of the sebaceous, sweat glands and the hairs. These perspiratory tubes passing from the sweat glands, which are only a short distance beneath the skin, and pouring out an enormous quantity of perspiration are almost innumerable. Each of the perspiratory pores is the aperture of one of these tubes, about a quarter of an inch long. Wilson calculates the average number of these pores to the square inch to be 2800, making in an ordinary sized man 7,000,000. The number of inches of perspiratory tube then would be 1,750,000 or nearly *twenty-eight* miles. What an argument for cleanliness. The office of the epidermis is, to protect the true skin from pain occasioned by slight abrasion, and the irritating effect of air and the changes of temperature.

Other cells mingle with the epidermic and secrete colouring matter instead of horn, these are termed *pigment-cells*. They are not readily distinguished in the epidermis of the fair races of mankind, but in the coloured races they are very marked.

The layer of cells covering the internal free surface of the body is called the ephithelium. The principle forms in which we see them are the *tesselated* and *cylindrical*. The tesselated ephithelium covers the serous and synovial membranes, the lining membrane of the blood vessels, and the tubuli of most glandular structures connected with the skin or mucous membrane. The cylindrical covers the mucous membrane of the alimentary canal, and is also found in the larger ducts of glands which open into it. Both forms of epithelial cells are frequently fringed at their free margin with delicate filaments called *cilia*. These, although of extreme minuteness, are organs of vast importance in the animal economy. Their functions are to propel the secretions, which would otherwise accumulate on the membranes, towards the exterior orifices, whence they may be carried off. The secretions, both in the serous and mucous membrane are carried on through the epithelial cells, and the difference between the two membranes consists principally in the different arrangement of these cells.

Let us now glance at the process of nutrition as it is carried on in the human system, and the various phenomena it produces.

Every hour of our lives a change is going on in our system. Every motion of the hand, every movement of the body, is occasioned by a transformation of the structure or its substance; every mental affection is followed by changes in the secreting fluid; every thought and every sensation is accompanied by a change in the composition of the substance of the brain. We can neither move, nor think without a corresponding change in some portion of the system. The matter which composes the body to-day is constantly passing off in the form of perspiration, urine, or the carbonic acid of the lungs, its place being supplied by new material taken into the system in the air we breathe and the food we eat. In this constant, never-ceasing change not only is nutrition supplied, but force produced. In the closed galvanic circuit, certain changes which a metal undergoes when brought in contact with an acid, produces a current of what we call electricity; so in the human system, in consequence of certain changes undergone by matter which previously constituted a part of the organism, phenomena of motion and activity are produced, which we call *life* or *vitality*. Man from his birth to his death, by night and by day, is constantly taking into his system through the organs of respiration, a vast amount of oxygen. Notwithstanding during the year this amounts to nearly *eight hundred pounds*, yet his weight is not materially increased, but it is oftentimes considerably diminished. The question now arises what becomes of this vast amount of oxygen?

It does not remain in the system, but passes off in the form of a compound of *carbon* or of *hydrogen*. These which once formed a part of the tissue entering into combination with the oxygen, are given off in the form of carbonic acid and water. We find that blood yields 20 per cent. of dry residue; the remaining 80 per cent. is water. In 100 parts of dry residue we find carbon 51.96, hydrogen 7.25, nitrogen 15.07, oxygen 21.30, ashes 4.42. If we take the statement of Lavoisier and Seguin, man receives into his system daily 32½ ounces of oxygen, (46.037 cubic inches = 15.661 grains French weight,) and the weight of the whole mass of blood, of which as we have stated 80 per cent. is water, is 24 pounds. In order to convert the whole of its carbon and hydrogen into carbonic acid and water, 64,103 grains of oxygen are required. This quantity will be taken into the system of the adult in four days and five hours. We cannot then escape the conclusion, that if man takes into his system 32½ ounces of oxygen in a day, he must also receive daily, in the form of nourishment, as much carbon and hydrogen as would make 24 pounds of blood, that is, if the weight of the body remain unchanged, and is in the same condition as it regards health. Experiments have been tried by which the actual amount of carbon consumed in the system during the day has been ascertained with great accuracy. The food of 30 soldiers in barracks was accurately weighed every day for a month, even to the most minute articles, such as pepper and salt, and each article of food was separately subjected to analysis. The feces and urine were also weighed, and the amount of unburnt carbon ascertained and deducted. An adult taking moderate exercise consumes $13\frac{9}{10}$ ounces of carbon daily. This carbon escapes through the skin and lungs in the form of carbonic acid gas, and requires to convert it into that state 37 ounces of oxygen.

As no part of the oxygen taken into the system is given off in other combination than with carbon and hydrogen, and as the carbon and hydrogen must be replaced by the food taken into the system, it is clear that the nourishment required must be in a ratio with the amount of oxygen taken into the body. Two animals which take up an unequal amount of oxygen require in the same ratio an unequal amount of food. The child whose respiration is very active, requires food much oftener than an adult. Deprive a bird of food and it dies in a few days, while a serpent, with its slow respiration, will live without food two or three months. The quantity of oxygen we respire is materially affected by the atmosphere, its density and change of temperature. In summer the air is not only rarified, but contains a vast amount of aqueous vapour, while in winter it is not only dry, but contracted by cold.

Thus the same volume of air contains more oxygen in cold northern climates than in tropical regions, in winter than in summer. The inhabitants of a warm climate therefore would require far less carbon to support life than those, who are compelled to endure the intense cold of the frigid and upper portion of the temperate zones. For the same amount of force far more oxygen is inspired in cold than in warm weather, on the sea-shore than on the summit of high mountains. Nature, with the wisdom which governs all her movements, has so ordained, that the fruits and vegetables which compose a large proportion of the food in tropical climates should contain far less carbon than the food in colder regions, notwithstanding a larger amount in bulk may be used by the former than the latter. The fruit on which the natives of warm climates mostly feed, contains but about 12 per cent. of carbon, while the meat and train-oil in arctic regions contain from 66 to 80 per cent.

From what has been stated, it will readily be perceived, that the true source of *animal heat* is the action between the elements of food and the oxygen conveyed to every part of the body by means of the blood. Carbon cannot combine with oxygen without heat being evolved. The amount of heat of course varies with the amount of oxygen introduced into the system. The temperature of a child whose respiration is very rapid, is higher than that of an adult; the former being 102°, the latter 99.5°. The heat of an adult is the same in every part of the world, where the thermometer continues for weeks at 90° above zero and where it ranges for months from twenty to forty below, amid the ice which encircles the poles, and the rich vegetation which grows with amazing rapidity beneath a tropical sun. This will not appear strange when we look upon the animal body as a heated mass, giving out heat where the surrounding objects are cooler than itself, and taking it in where they are warmer. What an enormous difference there must be in the amount of heat given out in those warm climates where the temperature is nearly the same as the body and in those intensely cold regions where it is 100° lower, and what a vast difference there must also be in the amount of food required to keep up that combustion which produces animal heat. Deprive the native of the south of food, and death would be slow in its progress. Deprive the inhabitant of a frozen region of food, and death would be speedy. The enormous combustion required to be kept up to defend the system against the cold would in a short time exhaust the body of its carbon and death would ensue. There are many tribes of savages who go nearly naked where the climate is intensely cold, but they consume a vast amount of carbon, in the form of meat, train-oil and tallow. Clothes after all are only an equivalent for a certain amount of food. Food is regulated by the number and strength of the respirations, the temperature of the air and the amount of heat given off. The amount of oxygen consumed, depends upon the temperature and density of the air, motion, and the amount and quality off food consumed.

Without detriment to health no more carbon and hydrogen can be taken into the system than is given off in carbonic acid and water, and yet persons accustomed to large quantities of substantial food, on visiting a warm climate, think they must eat the same articles and as much of them as they did when the thermometer was thirty or forty degrees less. On finding their appetite flag and its relish for hearty food subside, they stimulate it, by means of cayenne pepper, mustard, brandy, wine, and a hundred other stimulants. The consequence is, an unnatural state is induced, the carbon is not consumed, disease ensues, and the patient stands a fair chance of paying for his ignorance and folly, with his life. The evils resulting from an abuse of intoxicating drinks have been sketched in such graphic colours as to almost curdle the blood with horror, and yet the question would be by no means a difficult one to decide—which has created more pain, and caused more deaths, intoxicating drinks or errors in diet?

If we hold that the increase of mass in the animal body, the development of organs, and the supply of waste, is dependent on the blood, to ascertain whether a substance contains nourishment, all that is necessary for us to do, is to compare its ingredients with those of the blood.

The chief ingredients of blood will be found to be *fibrine* and *albumen.* Blood, after having been drawn from the body, coagulates and separates into a yellowish liquid, called the *serum,* and a gelatinous mass, adhering to a rod on stirring it, in soft elastic fibres. This is called *fibrine,* and is identical with a muscular fibre purified from foreign matter. The *albumen* is contained in the serum and gives to it the properties of the white of eggs; when heated it coagulates into a white elastic mass.

Fibrine and albumen are shown by chemical analysis to contain the same ingredients in the same proportion. The particles are arranged however in different order, as is shown by the difference of their external properties. They also contain the earth of bones. The serum retains in solution sea salt, and other salts of potash and soda in which the acids are carbonic, phosphoric and sulphuric. The globules of the blood contain not only fibrine and albumen but a red colouring matter, in which iron is an element. Both albumen and fibrine in the process of nutrition are capable of being converted into muscular fibre, and muscular fibre is capable of being converted into blood.

Every part of the body contains nitrogen, also carbon and the elements of water, but the latter in no case in proportion to form water. The blood contains 17 per cent. of nitrogen, and no organ in the body less than that amount. Experiments show conclusively that the body is utterly incapable of producing an elementary body, such as carbon or nitrogen, out of substances which do not contain them. No nitrogen is absorbed from the air, and as it enters into the composition of every part of the body, it is clear that it must exist in all kinds of food fit for the production of any portion of the body.

There is another substance, identical in composition with albumen and fibrine, and that is *caseine.* It is identical also with vegetable caseine, so that certain plants are capable of yielding the same substance that is formed from the blood of the mother. The young animal therefore receives caseine, which is extremely soluble, the chief constituents of its mother blood.

We have said that all the organs in the body contain a certain amount of nitrogen, and that this nitrogen must be taken into the body by means of food. These azotized forms of nutriment, may, in the vegetable world be divided into three parts. When the juices of vegetables are allowed to stand, we find in a few minutes a gelatinous precipitate, which we readily recognize as one of the azotized substances serving as nutriment to animals, viz. *vegetable fibrine.* Heat the remaining fluid to a boiling point, and it coagulates, resembling the white of an egg, or the serum of blood, when diluted with water and heated to the boiling point. This is *vegetable albumen*, or the second nitrogenized substance. From these three azotized substances, *vegetable fibrine*, *albumine*, and *caseine*, are the principal azotized constituents of our food. These three substances, as has already been stated, contain the same organic elements, and are identical in composition with the chief constituents of blood. We have seen that nitrogen exists in every organ of the body, and that those substances necessary for nourishment are generally rich in nitrogen, and yet there are substances, such as sugar, starch, gum, pectine, &c. containing no nitrogen, a certain proportion of which is absolutely essential to our existence, and without which we could not survive.

Milk contains one nitrogenized substance, *caseine;* besides this, its chief ingredients are butter, or fat, and sugar of milk which contain no nitrogen. From the caseine the young animal of course obtains its blood, muscle, cellular tissue, bone and nerve. Why is it then that the other ingredients, the butter and sugar of milk are absolutely essential to life?

By means of these compounds there is added to the nitrogenized constituents of blood an excess of carbon and hydrogen, which are expended in the production of animal heat. The food taken into the body goes in the first place to restore the waste of matter in the various organs, which, in the exercise of their functions are constantly undergoing a change, old particles being consumed and their places supplied by new matter constantly conveyed to all parts of the system by those never-idle channels, the arteries and their ramifications. What then becomes of the new compounds produced by the transformation of the different parts of the body, whose places have been taken by the new material? The never-tiring, never-failing current of the blood constantly performs its office, and when not interfered with performs it well. The arterial blood flowing outward, carrying the principles of life and reproduction, as the transformation in tissues takes place crowds before it the new compounds into the channels prepared for them, the veins, by which in the form of venous blood, it is transmitted in part, to the heart, and from thence passing into the lungs, there subjected to the action of the atmosphere, throwing off its impurities, its character of dark venous blood is changed on the reception of oxygen, to arterial, and is again distributed, divested of its impurities, and freighted with life passes to every part of the system. The venous blood, before reaching the heart, is made to pass through the liver, where there is taken from it those substances that are incapable of nutrition. From the arterial blood, the kidneys take up those new compounds containing the nitrogen of the transformed tissues, which, being no longer of any use, are expelled in the form of urine. Those on the contrary, which contain the carbon of the transformed tissues, are taken up by the liver, and pass into the gall bladder in the form of a compound of soda, *the bile*. This is transmitted through the gall duct into the duodenum, and there mingling with the chyme is taken up in part by the absorbents and returned into the system. By means of the blood a current of oxygen passes into every part of the body. This oxygen in passing through the capilliary vessels, meets with the compound produced by the transformation of tissues, combining with the carbon to form carbonic acid, which passes off through the lungs, and with the hydrogen to form water, which passes off in the form of perspiration. What escapes this process of oxidation is sent back into the circulation in the form of bile, which by degrees completely disappears.

In the vegetable world, the carbon which we find deposited

in seeds and fruits, in the form of oil and fat, was previously a constituent of the atmosphere and was absorbed by the plant as carbonic acid. By the influence of light and the action of the vital force of the vegetable it was converted into fat.

If we turn to the animal world, and examine their food, we are forced to the conclusion, that the fat found in the body, is formed in its organism. In the food of the cow, we find no butter, no suet in the fodder of cattle, and no lard in the food of swine. But we find on separating a certain amount of oxygen, which they contain, from the starch, gum, and sugar, that enter the composition of one class of food, fat is produced. On separating a certain amount of oxygen from fibrine, albumen, and caseine, contained in another class of food, we also obtain fat. In fatty bodies we have on an average for 120 equivalents carbon, 10 of oxygen. In vegetable fibrine, albumen, and caseine for 120 equivalents of carbon there are 36 of oxygen. Therefore we have only to separate 26 equivalents of oxygen from these elements to produce fat. In gum, sugar, and starch, we find the amount of oxygen varies from 100 to 140 equivalents to 120 of carbon, so that to form fat from these substances we have only to separate from 90 to 110 equivalents of oxygen. This oxygen is not given out in a free state, but in combination with other substances, in the form of perspiration, urine and carbonic acid, the result of which combination is of course animal heat. The formation of fat then is occasioned by a deficient supply of oxygen taken into the system to equalize the amount of carbon. For the body to acquire no increase in size it is necessary that the same amount of carbon shall be consumed or given out that is taken into the system. Where a large quantity of carbonized food is taken into the body, and the amount of oxygen is not increased by exercise or labour, of course an accumulation of fat is the result. We have an illustration of this in the Bedouin whose active life would prevent the accumulation of much fat, and in the Turkish and Chinese ladies, where obesity is considered a requisite for beauty, and their indolence and gluttony are favourable to that condition. Whoever heard of a fat Bedouin? The carbon contained in the fat thus deposited is capable of being consumed and entering other combinations for the purpose of supplying *animal heat.*

The substances of which our food is composed then, may be divided into two classes; the nitrogenized, capable of being converted into blood, and thus forming all the organized tissues, which might be called the elements of nutrition, and the *non-nitrogenized*, which are strictly elements of respiration. Let us now look at the process of digestion, and the change necessary for the food to undergo before it can be taken up by the absorbents. All nitrogenized articles of food are undoubtedly converted into albumen before they can contribute to nutrition.

The food, in passing into the stomach, becomes mingled with the saliva, which possesses to a certain extent, the power like the gastric juice, of acting on azotized compounds. With the saliva there is mingled a large quantity of atmospheric air; this entering the stomach, the oxygen aids digestion, the nitrogen passes off in respiration, perspiration, &c. The inner coat of the stomach, in its natural or healthy state is of a light or pale pink colour, varying in its hues according to its full or empty state. It is of a soft or velvet like appearance, and is constantly covered with a thin, transparent, viscid mucus, lining the whole interior of the organ. By applying irritants to the stomach and observing the effect through a magnifying glass, innumerable lucid points and very fine nervous or vascular papille can be seen arising from the villous membrane, and protruding through the mucous coat, from which distils a pure, limpid, colourless, slightly viscid fluid. The fluid, thus excited, is invariably acid, and is called the gastric juice. The gastric juice never appears to accumulate in the stomach when fasting, and is seldom if ever discharged from its vessels, except when excited by the natural stimulus of aliment, mechanical irritation of the tubes, or other excitants.

The quantity of the gastric juice secreted from the walls of the stomach depends on the general requirements of the system rather than the amount of food. The juice refuses to dissolve only a certain amount of food, and when that is accomplished, if an excess has been taken, the residue either remains in the stomach or passes into the bowels in its crude form, becoming a source of irritation, pain, and disease. This abuse of the stomach by introducing into it more food than it can readily digest, is often considered a trouble of but few hours' duration, when in reality the worst effects are not felt at first, but the foundations of a disease are laid, oftentimes exceedingly troublesome and painful, and not frequently terminating in death.

The gastric juice is decidedly acid, containing among other ingredients, a considerable amount of hydro-chloric or muriatic acid. The process of digestion, at one time, looked upon as the result of vital force, is now generally conceded to be carried on by chemical action. The food in passing into the stomach is subjected to a peculiar peristaltic movement, not only producing a thorough intermixture of the gastric fluid with the alimentary mass, but causing the contents to revolve about the interior from point to point.

As the process of digestion goes on, its result in the form of chyme, varying in colour from that of cream to gruel, gradually passes through the pyloric orifice into the duodenum. Here, before it is taken up by the lacteals, it is mingled with the bile and pancreatic juice, the soda in these fluids neutralizing the acidity of the chyme which it has obtained from the gastric juice. The effect of this admixture is to separate the chyme into three distinct parts,—a reddish brown sediment at the bottom,—a whey coloured fluid in the centre,—and a creamy pellicle at the top. The central portion with the creamy pellicle seems to constitute the *chyle* absorbed by the lacteals; the creamy matter being chiefly composed of oily particles, and the wheyey fluid having proteine-compounds, saccharine and saline matters in solution, the sediment, partly consisting of the insoluble portion of the food, and partly of the biliary matter itself, is evidently excrementitious.

Let us now glance briefly at the circulation of the blood. The popular explanation given to the circulation of the blood in man, makes the heart the prime-mover of the mechanism. This organ, they say, is devoted to a double purpose, that of a force-pump, in driving the arterial blood through the arteries to every part of the body, and of a suction-pump, to enable the venous blood to return to the heart. In order to accomplish this twofold purpose, it is furnished with valvular and tubular arrangements, and, at specific periods, contracts and dilates for the purpose of ejecting or sucking up the circulating liquid.

Dr. Draper, professor of chemistry in the New-York University, has advanced another theory, which, to say the least, is plausible and worthy of careful investigation. To keep a continuous flow of a liquid through a capilliary tube it is necessary, either by evaporation, or some chemical action, to remove the superficial portions of the elevated liquid when they stand at the extremity of the tube. Fill a lamp with oil, and unless you light the wick, no oil would be removed. In an alcohol lamp, if the wick should be uncovered evaporation of the alcohol in the upper portion of the capilliary tubes of the wick would take place, and thus a continuous flow of the alcohol would be kept up until the contents of the lamp were exhausted. Take for instance a bladder, which is of course full of capilliary tubes, fill it with alcohol, making the mouth of the bladder tight, so that none of the fluid can escape. On placing the bladder in a vessel of water, you find the alcohol gradually coming out of the bladder into the water, and the water flowing more readily, passing much more rapidly into the bladder, so in a short time you have an accumulation in the bladder which distends it, and finally causes it to burst. Thus a constant current is kept up through the walls of the bladder, that having the most affinity for the tubes flowing more rapidly. Watching these phenomena, Dr. Draper lays down the following principle:

"*If two liquids communicate with one another in a capilliary tube, or in a porous or parenchymatous structure, and have for that tube or structure different chemical affinities, movements will ensue; that liquid having the most energetic affinity will move with the greatest velocity, and may even drive the other liquid entirely before it.*"

Starting from this point, he endeavours to show, that the same forces which cause the circulation of sap in the vegetable world are brought into action in the circulation of blood in the human system; that in both cases the principle is the same.

The arterial blood charged with oxygen, as soon as it reaches its destination in the minute capilliary vessels, begins to carry on its process of oxydation, attacking in a measured way the various tissues through which it is flowing, burning out their effete carbonaceous matter, and in the change of tissue which takes place, causing, as we have already shown, the evolution of heat. While this change is going on in the tissue the arterial blood also undergoes a change, in giving up its oxygen and gaining in exchange the result of the combustion. From crimson, it becomes dark; from arterial it changes to venous blood. On the one side of the capilliary tubes we have of course arterial, on the other venous blood. The arterial blood, bearing its oxygen, ready to burn out any carbon or hydrogen in its way, substances of which the tube or structure is composed, possesses an intense affinity for those structures, which is at last exhibited by their destruction. The arterial blood has therefore an intense affinity for any of the structures with which it is brought in contact, but after its oxygen is exhausted and the arterial is changed into venous blood, this affinity no longer exists.

Referring back to the principle already laid down, what is the phenomena which that principle predicts as arising under these circumstances? Simply, that arterial blood will drive the venous blood before it, and drive it with an inexpressible force. From this train of reasoning Dr. Draper concludes that the true cause of the systemic circulation is the oxygenized action of the arterial blood. In the systemic circulation, upon these principles, the flow must be from the artery to the vein.

In pulmonary circulation we have venous blood presenting

itself in the lungs to atmospheric air. The venous blood has an intense affinity for the oxygen in the air, and the arterial, of course none. Movement therefore must ensue, but as the conditions of the affinity are reversed, so also is the direction of the motion, for now the venous blood drives the arterial before it with great force to the heart. The pulmonary circulation is therefore due to the oxydation of the venous blood.

Those who insist that the circulation is owing to the forcing and suction power of the heart, and to that alone are referred to plants wholly destitute of a heart and yet their juices circulate. There are multitudes of animals in the same predicament. In insects no such central organ appears. In fishes the systemic circulation is carried on without a heart, and in cold-blooded animals movements in the capilliaries take place after the heart is cut out. When we inquire into the condition of the circulation in the earliest periods of existence, we find that the vessels themselves are the first to appear, and the heart is subsequently developed.

What then is the true office of the heart? The systemic circulation originates in the deoxydation of the blood, the pulmonary, in its oxydation. There is no necessary connexion between the chemical changes taking place in the lungs and those in the system. Both are determined by their own proper causes.

If therefore on either of these points of change an excess of action takes place, the result must be a disturbance of the equilibrium of the whole circulation. At some central point therefore, the current, going to the respiratory machine, and that going to the system must be intercepted—and intercepted by an apparatus which could hold both in check and time the movements of one to those of the other. The heart then by periodic muscular contractions serves to adjust the flowing currents to one another, and prevent engorge mentsor deficiencies in any part of the route.

How do these chemical principles apply when the system becomes diseased? Whenever the admission of oxygen into the lungs is stopped, the circulation through them ceases.

What is the cause of that asphyxiated condition? Why does the blood cease to flow. The chemical theory of the circulation of the blood through the lungs points to the oxydation of that blood as the cause of its movement. It is the pressure of the deoxydized upon the oxydized blood that drives the latter along the pulmonary veins to the heart. But should anything intervene to prevent that oxydation taking place, no pressure can arise, and therefore no movement ensue; the conditions for asphyxia are all present; conditions which are removed by the readmission of oxygen into the lungs.

CHAPTER III.

HYGIENE AND THE CAUSES OF DISEASE.

A large class of diseases arise from ignorance; ignorance of the laws of health, of the delicate and beautiful organization of the system, of the great end and aim of existence, of the harmonious play, which should ever exist between all the organs and faculties of our being, between the mind and the body, the spiritual and the physical.

Amid the wild and restless scenes of life, the ceaseless whirl and mad excitement of business, the feverish panting for fame, wealth or power, as well as in the more quiet paths of rural life, or the slothful walks of luxurious ease, but very few maintain that beautiful harmony between all the organs, that equilibrium throughout the system, which is essential not only to health, but true greatness.

As well might we expect ripe fruit amid the cutting winds, the ice and snow of our northern winter, or the rich luxuriance of southern vegetation in our colder northern clime, as to expect health, a happy temperament, and above all a clear and strong mind, unless an equilibrium be kept up in the system and each organ receive its necessary and only its necessary degree of attention and cultivation.

There is no machine in the world so much abused as the human system, or which, if trifled with to the same extent, would last one half as long. It is not generally until often and repeated violations of the laws of health, that nature unable longer to bear the ill treatment, sinks.

We know there is an inexorable sentence passed on all, from which there is no appeal. That sentence is, *death.* This dread conqueror tramples on all. His foot must rest on the necks of all, but must more than half the human race yield to his power in the first flush of life, before they have numbered five summers? Must the strokes of death fall thick and fast on they young, the bright, the gay, the talented, the genius, the statesman, the poet, the scholar, the divine, before even time has marked his wrinkles on their brows or scattered his frosts on their heads? Must earth be piled with the graves of the young? Must the human family, filled with disease and racked with pain, go groaning and sighing through the world, with forms bent, and heavy steps and downcast eyes, and haggard looks? No, we have not thus read the designs of Providence. Great laws have been ordained to govern our physical as well as moral being. The human system is a perfect instrument, which should ever be strung to harmony.

Obey these laws of health, for they were all intended for our physical well-being, maintain a proper equilibrium in the system, and a perfect harmony will pervade the whole, and the notes of this glorious instrument grow clearer and sweeter until it is broken not by disease, but time.

The object of the present chapter, is to unfold some of the great laws of health, to show the causes of disease, and how in many cases it may be prevented, reserving for future chapters the treatment of disease after it has once sown its seeds in the system.

In the investigation of this subject we shall consider

1. *Climate, changes of temperature, &c.*
2. *Impure air, ventilation and cleanliness.*
3. *Diet, exercise, &c.*
4. *Bathing—its different varieties.*
5. *Influence of mind on disease.*
6. *Hereditary taint, predisposition to disease, &c.*
7. *Mental, moral and physical education.*

1. CLIMATE, CHANGES OF TEMPERATURE, &C.

The range of temperature and the amount of cold and heat the human system is capable of enduring is immense. Thus, we find human beings, as well as various forms of animal and vegetable life, flourishing in the intense cold of the frozen regions, when the thermometer sinks to 40 or 50° below zero, and the night is five or six months long, as well as in more temperate regions and in the torrid zone, where the thermometer remains for weeks from 100 to 110° above zero.

The amount of heat and cold, which the human system is capable of enduring under certain ciacumstances has been proved by actual experiment to be so enormous, that had not the statements been well attested, we should have been inclined to doubt their truth. In some experiments tried in the years 1760 and 1761 in France, to devise means to destroy an insect which consumed the grain, a girl entered the oven and after remaining two or three minutes marked the point to which the mercury in the thermometer had risen at 260°. Insisting that she felt no inconvenience, she remained ten minutes longer, during which time the mercury reached the 288 degree, or 76° of heat above water when it boils. On coming out, her complexion was heightened, but her respiration was neither quick nor laboured.

Another girl remained in the oven the same length of time with equal impunity, and even breathed for five minutes air heated to 325° or 113 above boiling water.

At different times physicians and others have entered rooms heated to 240 and 260° and remained some time, sometimes with, and again without their clothes, and without inconvenience. During this time the animal heat, ascertained by placing the thermometer under the tongue, was scarcely increased at all, but the pulse was much quickened. The heat was so great, that pieces of metal about them could hardly be touched; breathing on the thermometer caused the mercury to fall several degrees, and they also cooled their fingers by breathing on them. In the same air, eggs were roasted hard in twenty minutes, and beefsteak well cooked in thirty.

Taking the other extreme, we find the body capable of enduring under certain circumstances an intense degree of cold without injury. Air being a bad conductor, caloric is exhausted much more rapidly when the air is in motion than when still, and therefore a much greater amount of cold can be endured in the latter than in the former case. Capt. Parry mentions that where the thermometer was 55° below zero and no wind stirring, the hands could remain uncovered without inconvenience for a quarter of an hour, while with a fresh breeze and the thermometer at zero, the pain in the same length of time would be intense.

In the recent expedition to the Arctic regions, under command of Capt. de Haven, in search of Sir John Franklin, the degree of cold to which the men were subject in a climate where the thermometer for weeks numbered from thirty to fifty degrees below zero, was beyond what we can well realize. Yet the men were generally healthy. There were but very few colds or inflammatary diseases and I believe no deaths.

Thus we see that the body is capable of enduring under certain circumstances, and for a certain time, great extremes of heat and cold. It was formerly supposed, and is to a certain extent now, that sudden changes of temperature are in all cases hurtful. But this is by no means *always* the case. The inhabitants of Russia are in the habit, while reeking from their vapour baths, of plunging directly into cold water, or rolling in snow, without injurious effects, and Capt. Parry remarked that during his northern expedition they were constantly in the habit in going from the cabin into the external air, of undergoing a change of from 80 to 120° of temperature in one minute without the slightest unpleasant sensations.

The sudden descent from one point to another in atmospheric temperature, must of course vary in its effect, according to the state of the body at that time. We have heretofore explained the generation of animal heat, and shown that in health, nearly the same degree of inward temperature is maintained in every clime. If the external temperature be lower than that of the body, the heat carried off is instantly replaced in health, by the combustion within, together with exercise and clothing. When it approaches the natural heat of the body, sweat breaks out, and the superfluous heat is thus removed by evaporation. The internal evolution of heat is so constant, that an external temperature of 98, which is about the heat of blood in man, when of course the atmosphere cannot abstract heat from the body, is exceeding oppressive. If the heat is carried off just as fast and no faster than it is developed, no particular sensation of either heat or cold is felt. Therefore the sensations must vary in a great measure with the power which different constitutions possess of evolving heat. Thus one person whose power of evolving heat may be less than another, will be cold in a temperature, which the other would consider warm.

If this power of evolving heat, be entire, active, and continuous, no danger need be apprehended even from various alterations of temperature. Great heat of the body, when the cold is applied, is really a condition of safety instead of danger, provided the heat is steady and permanent. Thus, how refreshing to the heated brow is the application of ice, and how grateful during the burning paroxysm of fever affusions of cold water. This principle also holds good of the application of cold, when the body has been heated by exercise, or from any other cause, provided that cause remains steadily in action, there being no local disease, and the body not fatigued, and fast loosing its heat. But, if a person is exhausted and weakened by exercise, if he is perspiring and rapidly parting with heat, if the exercise is over and he remains at rest during, and immediately after the application of cold, then there is danger of mischief. The danger is not from the application of cold, when the body is *hot*, but when the body is cooling after having been heated.

In all those cases where death is occasioned by drinking cold water, it will be found that the body, heated and fatigued by exertion, was rapidly losing heat by profuse perspiration, the person having generally at the time closed his exertions. If the exertion had been continued or at any rate the heat kept at its previous standard, no danger would have resulted. It was in this way, that Alexander lost more of his army, than had ever been slain in his most bloody battle, when they, thirsty, weary, and perspiring with their long march across the desert, rushed wildy into the cold waters of the River Oxus.

Following out the principle we have just laid down we are taught a vast number of useful facts.

The traveler need apprehend but little danger from wet feet, or a wet skin, provided he keep up active exercise, changes his clothes as soon as that exercise ceases, and avoids future applications of cold. It is very common with bathers, after having become heated by a walk or violent exercise, to pause for a while before plunging into the water, and, as they term it, "cool off," after which they rush in and remain some time. This, you will perceive, is not only unwise, but highly dangerous. Far better plunge in at once, paddle about, remain but a few moments, then come out and dress. And so the young lady, fatigued and heated with dancing, had far better get into her carriage, ride home and jump into bed than to stand in this state for a little while and partially "cool off" in the entrance hall before starting. And the gentlemen similarly situated, will feel much better the next day from having put on his over coat and walked briskly home.

Recollect that heat, preternaturally accumulated by exercise, is dissipated by profuse perspiration, and speedily lost, when to this is added rest after fatigue, and that then the application of cold is liable to be followed by unpleasant results.

A very constant effect of continued heat is, to stimulate the organic functions of the body. We have evidence of this in the luxuriant vegetation of warm climates in comparison with the stunted growth of colder regions. As you approach nearer and nearer the poles, not only vegetables, but animals become stunted. The inhabitants of warm climates are much larger than those of frigid regions. Notwithstanding there may not be much difference in point of size between the inhabitants of the torrid and temperate zone, yet the former reach maturity much sooner than the latter, and it is not uncommon to find among them females married, and the mothers of children at the age of twelve or fourteen. Continued heat also produces a depressing influence on the animal functions, causing lassitude and want of energy. Those nations who have most signalized themselves in the world's history, and left the largest record on its pages, have been those, not in equatorial regions, but in the more northern and cold climates. From causes already explained, the prominent affections in warm climates are those of a dysenteric or bilious character.

The effects produced by cold are directly the reverse to those of heat. It acts, when long continued, as a seditive on the animal functions. There is a shrinking of the external parts, and a paleness or deadness of the skin. One of the first effects of cold on the system, is extreme drowsiness, followed by a stupor or sleep, during which the poor victim glides without a pang into the arms of death. This sense of drowsiness is often so great, that notwithstanding the person is conscious, that to sleep is to die, he cannot rouse himself.

There are times, however, when cold not too intense, produces an entirely different effect, acting as a tonic, stimulating, refreshing and invigorating the mind and body. It then becomes a most important curative agent. I have only to instance the well known effect of cold bathing, where it is followed by reaction.

A momentary sensation of cold, however intense, is seldom injurious, but long continued shivering will be very likely to end in disease. The effect of cold is more injurious when applied by currents of air. This is particularly the case when the current strikes only one portion of the body. Better expose the whole body to the same temperature, than have a current playing on one portion. Cold is far more prejudicial to health when accompanied with moisture. Hence a damp cold, foggy atmosphere is much more likely to produce disease, than a clear and dryer one of the same temperature. Wet and damp clothes prolong the sensation of cold, and extract more heat from the body than is generated within, and unless exercise or stimulants are made use of, deranges the circulation and creates internal disturbance.

We have seen that the amount of animal heat remains nearly the same in all temperatures and in all climates. That the air of colder regions is more condensed and with the same number of respirations we inhale a much greater amount of oxygen than in the rarified atmosphere of warmer climates, that it is absolutely essential to life that the rapidity with which animal heat is generated should vary in the different temperatures of the earth.

There is nothing which renders the system more liable to the injurious effects of cold than want of proper nourishment. Dissipation also prostrates the system and in a measure paralizes the power of nature. In cold weather the food of course should be nourishing, the clothing warm, and exercise when in the open air, active. In our northern climates it is generally best to wear flannel next the skin throughout the year, thinner in summer of course than in winter. Being a bad conductor of heat it prevents that of the body from being quickly dissipated, and therefore in a measure guards against the frequent changes ot temperature so common in our climate.

It also absorbs the perspiration, and by its constant friction in movement, gently stimulates the vessels and nerves of the skin. I fully appreciate and insist on the necessity of comfortable warmth to insure health, and yet I have no sympathy with the growing effeminency of the present day. To see the young, who should be full of life and activity, and possess the strongest and most vigorous powers of generating heat, muffled up in cloaks, padded coats and furs, in this climate, forcibly remind one that they may be better acquainted with the reeking fumes of the bar-room, the halls of revelry and the haunts of dissipation, or the heated air of the drawing room, than the healthy, manly, and active duties of life. It certainly bespeaks a ridiculous effeminency, and one from which they themselves will be the greatest sufferers. Pure and healthy recreation, manly and vigorous exercise in the open air, conquering cold by increased physical exertion, nourishing food, and moderately warm clothing, are far better than piles of furs or hosts of mufflers. In addition to this, prepare the system before going out by washing from head to foot in cold water.

But in the training of children particularly, in avoiding effeminency, there is danger of running into the other extreme, and in pursuing what is called "*hardening*," soon harden them into their graves. The constitution of the child should be closely studied, and the utmost prudence observed in the "hardening" process. The child should be sufficiently clothed, and a continued sensation of chilliness never permitted. A cold bath every morning fortifies the body against the cold of the day, but even this should not be indulged in unless followed by a glow of warmth.

In warm climates, if any thing, a greater amount of care is necessary to maintain health under the enervating and debilitating effect of continued heat, the animal functions should be kept naturally active and vigorous, and no organ overtasked beyond its strength. Exposure to the intense heat of the sun may produce fearful congestion, and dissipation of every kind may so impair the functions of nature as to render her an easy prey to the ravages of disease. The same amount of food or the same variety as in a colder climate would not only be unnecessary but highly injurious. The external temperature is nearly if not quite the same as the internal. But little animal heat is therefore required, and but little oxygen in comparison with colder regions is inspired, and consequently if a large amount of nutritious food is introduced into the system it is not consumed, but clogs and fetters the operations of nature. Nature in the abundant fruits and vegetables scattered throughout that climate has designated the proper food for use.

Impure air, ventilation and cleanliness.—A pure atmosphere is essential to life and health, and when it becomes poisoned by decaying vegetable matter or the generation of unwholesome gases, disease is the consequence, either assuming the form of an epidemic, and sweeping over the land like a besom of destruction, or showing its influence in the gradual decay and prostration of the vital powers.

Local causes produce changes in the atmosphere, and give rise to peculiar diseases. Thus at the base of lofty mountains, as the Alps in Switzerland, we more generally find Goître, or swelled neck; the smiling plains of Italy are saddened by the presence of a loathsome cutaneous affection; the Campagna, in the vicinity of Rome, presents a smiling and beautiful appearance, yet its noxious exhalations poison the atmosphere, and often produce in those who have merely passed over its flowery surface, the seeds of an incurable disease. In new countries, where the virgin soil is being turned up to the warmth of the sun, and even in old, where there is much standing water, and in the vicinity of swamps, the air is poisoned by a malaria, which gives rise to the chills and fever. Yet in either of these cases, what chemist is sufficiently skillful to tell the precise amount of this poison sufficient to produce disease. We can neither see, taste, nor smell anything more than usual, and yet we inhale a poison most destructive to health and even life. We sometimes find in nature infinitesimal doses, as well as in our peculiar school of medicine.

The composition of atmospheric air we have already mentioned. When taken into the system its consist of about 78 per cent. of nitrogen, 21 of oxygen, and 1 of carbonic acid, but when expelled from the lungs it is loaded with moisture, and notwithstanding the amount of nitrogen remains nearly the same, from eight to nine per cent. of oxygen have disappeared and been replaced by carbonic acid.

The inspirations of an adult are at least fifteen in a minute, and the average consumption of air not far from 20 cubic inches at each inspiration, so that a single individual requires for respiration at least 300 cubic inches of air in one minute. Therefore in the same time 24 inches of oxygen disappear and are replaced by the same amount of carbonic acid, and in one hour each individual takes in through the lungs at least 1440 cubic inches, the place of which is supplied by the same amount of carbonic acid. Thus each averaged sized adult consumes about 45,000 cubic inches of oxygen, and gives out about 40,000 cubic inches of carbonic acid in 24 hours. The only part of the air capable of supporting life is the oxygen, and when the oxygen of the atmosphere is partly consumed or vitiated by means of the vast addition of carbonic acid, the lungs are deprived of their arterializing power, and respiration consequently is seriously impaired. Take for instance a mouse and confine it in a tight glass jar full of air, and for a short time it seems to suffer no inconvenience, but as the consumption of oxygen, and the exhalation of carbonic acid goes on, the little victim pants as if struggling for air, and in a short time dies convulsed, as if drowned or strangulated. Does it require more than the simple statement of the above facts to convince all of the absolute necessity of pure air, and well-ventilated rooms. The practice of crowding several individuals in tight rooms cannot be too strongly condemned. And yet it is by no means rare to witness several persons occupying one room, and that heated by a tight iron stove, with no way of establishing a current of air or draft in the room. The air is not only vitiated by so many breaths, but the oxygen consumed by the stove.

But a few years since I was called one evening to visit a poor person very sick with the ship fever. I found a kind of hovel, almost surrounded by water, consisting of one room, perhaps fifteen or sixteen feet square, in the centre of which stood a stove almost red hot, in which the cooking of the whole family was done. This room was occupied by nine persons, five of whom were under the full influence of the low, putrid, and sinking *ship fever*. This was by no means an isolated case. Every physician accustomed to practice in our large towns is constantly meeting cases in close and crowded rooms where disease has its full sweep, and where the remedy they require, and without which they will die, is pure air. In cities, particularly among the poorer classes of our population, a fruitful source of crime, sickness, and those frightful epidemics, and pestilential diseases, which are so rife among them, and from them spreads through the community, is impure air, want of cleanliness and nourishing food. The smiling country is open before them with the pure air of heaven eddying around the hill tops and along the valleys. The mighty west, with dark forests, running streams, cool and sparkling fountains, a rich and virgin soil, beckons them to a home of peace and plenty, with less expense than they incur in the crowded rooms and confined air of the city. And yet it is often the case, that the poor prefer the city, with all its deprivations, to the country and plenty. You notice the effect of breathing vitiated air in pale and haggard faces, sunken eyes and cheeks, lassitude, want of energy, and dizziness or pain in the head. Happily the public mind is waking up to the necessity, if they wish to preserve health, of having well ventilated homes, churches, and school rooms.

Cleanliness is absolutely essential to vigorous health, as will be readily seen when we reflect on the intimate sympathy existing between the skin and all the internal organs. When we remember that the skin is perforated with an innumerable number of perspiratory tubes, which carry off from the system in the form of *insensible perspiration* an average amount of *thirty-three ounces* of changed and worn-out material, aside from what is thrown off in the form of visible perspiration, often amounting to two or three pounds in the course of an hour, and that if these pores are contracted or closed by cold or any other cause, this large amount of useless matter must be retained in the system or thrown on other organs, such as the lungs, stomach, liver, and kidneys, we can readily perceive how important it is that the skin should be kept vigorous and healthy.

To avoid this closing of the pores, in the first place be careful to keep the clothing next the skin fresh and clean, as it very soon becomes saturated with perspiration. Clothing worn during the day should in no case be worn at night. The bed also should be thoroughly aired before being prepared for the night.

The head should be kept clean, as a collection of dandruff often produces pain and even eruptions on the scalp. Unguents, and washes of all kinds, with the exception of water should as a general thing be avoided. Many of these preparations contain poisons highly prejudicial to health, and when applied to the hair create pain in the head, and general derangement of the nervous system. Thus, some of these washes and unguents contain arsenic, others Spanish Fly, and others still, lead and a variety of poisons.

Above all to insure a healthy skin, water should be used in abundance. Thorough ablutions of the entire body should be just as much a part of the daily work as eating.

DIET AND EXERCISE.

Pure air, clothing, and cleanliness, are not the only things about which it is necessary to be particular in order to insure health. Without something for the oxygen taken into the lungs to consume, the air would do no good. Hence the amount of food used should be of the proper kind, in the proper quantities, and vary in kind and amount, according to the amount of oxygen inspired, and the quantity of heat necessary to be evolved to insure comfort and support life. We have already explained the evolution of animal heat, and thus, the process of digestion and nutrition. We have seen that the inhabitants of cold climates require food rich in carbon, such as meat and oil, that those of the torrid climate require food containing but little carbon, and should feed more on fruits and vegetables, while in temperate regions a judicious intermixture of both is necessary. We will now mention the time required, as has been ascertained by experiment, for the digestion of some of the prominent articles of food.

				h.	m.
Apples, sweet,	raw	digested in		1.	50.
" sour, hard,	"	"	"	2.	50.
Barley	boiled,	"	"	2.	
Bass, striped, fresh,	broiled,	"	"	3.	
Beans, pod,	boiled,	"	"	2.	30.
" and green corn	"	"	"	3.	45.
Beef, fresh, lean, rare,	roasted,	"	"	3.	
" " steak	broiled,	"	"	3.	
" old, hard, salted,	boiled,	"	"	4.	15.

			h. m.
Beets	boiled,	digested in	3. 45.
Bread, corn,	baked,	" "	3. 15.
" wheat, fresh,	"	" "	3. 30.
Butter	melted,	" "	3. 30.
Cabbage	raw,	" "	2. 30.
" with vinegar,	"	" "	2.
"	boiled,	" "	4. 30.
Cheese, old,	raw,	" "	3. 30.
Chicken,	fricasseed,	" "	2. 45.
Codfish, dry,	boiled,	" "	2.
Duck,	roasted,	" "	4.
Eggs, fresh,	hard boiled,	" "	3. 30.
" "	soft boiled,	" "	3.
" "	raw,	" "	2.
Goose, wild,	roasted,	" "	2. 30.
Lamb,	broiled,	" "	2. 30.
Liver, beefs,	"	" "	2.
Meat and vegetables,	hashed,	" "	2. 30.
Milk,			2.
Mutton,			3.
Oysters,	raw,	" "	2. 55.
"	stewed,	" "	3. 30.
Pork,	roasted,	" "	5. 15.
"	stewed,	" "	3.
Potatoes, Irish,	boiled,	" "	3. 30.
" "	roasted, baked,	" "	2. 30.
Rice,	boiled,	" "	1.
Sago,	"	" "	1. 15.
Salmon, salted,	"	" "	4.
Tapioca,	"	" "	2.
Tripe,	"	" "	1.
Trout, salmon,	"	" "	1. 30.
Turkey,	"	" "	2. 25.
Turnips,	"	" "	3. 30.
Veal,	broiled,	" "	4.
Venison steak,	"	" "	1. 35.

Pork is exceedingly difficult of digestion, while mutton, beef, and venison are not only highly nutritious but easy of digestion.

Veal and lamb are nutritious, but not as easily digested. Poultry is generally easy of digestion, and when young and tender, suitable to invalids.

Eggs and oysters are nutritious, and if not cooked too much, easy of digestion. Rice is nutritious and easy of digestion, as well as sago, arrow-root, tapioca, and farina. The potato is more digestible when roasted or baked than when boiled. Fruits of all kinds are not generally nutritious, although they are refreshing and wholesome. They should be eaten however in the fore part of the day, or at any rate not in the evening. As it regards the use of *coffee*, no particular directions can be given. It is highly injurious to some, while others can use it, not too strong, with plenty of milk, with entire safety. It is strictly prohibited in almost every form of disease, especially when taking medicine. Tea is subject to the same objections as coffee, although black tea can generally be used with safety, while green tea is decidedly objectionable. Cold water is a very excellent substitute for either.

Chocolate is a pleasant drink, preferable to either tea or coffee, when there is no disease of the stomach or abdomen. Milk is highly nutritious, but to persons of plethoric habit it had better be in a great measure avoided.

Exercise is highly important to the health of the organs and the process of digestion. But vigorous violent exercise should not be indulged in immediately before or immediately after a meal, for in either case the harm would be far greater than any benefit which might result. Exercise should be active, to a certain extent in the out-door air, and as regular as possible. Violent fatigue should of course be avoided, the exercise being gradually increased as the strength will bear it. Persons accustomed to a sedentary life should at certain hours exercise the whole system. Among children playing at ball, dancing, or jumping the rope, are pleasant recreations, while among adults, riding, swimming, walking, fencing and dumb bells are equally serviceable. In this way all the organs are kept active and full of vitality, the mind also is clear and capable of greater labour, and the body more robust, better proportioned and capable of greater exertion.

BATHING, ITS DIFFERENT VARIETIES AND USES.

The best time for bathing is undoubtedly in the morning on getting out of bed or two or three hours after breakfast. Simple ablution or any form of cold bathing should be followed by rubbing and exercise. In a swimming or tub bath it is best to remain in for only a short time. Unless reaction comes on, and a warm glow is established, shortly after any of the varieties of bathing, the cold bathing is producing more injury than good, and should therefore be discontinued and tepid water substituted in its place. By gradually decreasing its temperature, the system will soon become accustomed to cold water. In the winter season it is best to have the room slightly warmed, unless the ablution be quickly done, when it may be performed in the cold. Bathing, when followed by fulness of the head, should for the time, be suspended, or warm water substituted. As different forms of bathing are often advisable both in health and disease, and as we shall hereafter have frequent occasion to refer to water applications, we will enumerate some of them here.

Shower Baths.—These are often most refreshing and highly advantageous. If the proper materials be not at hand for constructing one, the contents of a watering-pot poured over the body from a distance of three or four feet will answer every purpose. It acts as a gentle shock upon the skin and nervous system, and stimulates them to the performance of their duty. When the shock is too great they can be taken tepid.

Sitting-Baths (Sitz-baths).—A tub, or better still, a bath prepared for the purpose, made of tin or wood, sufficiently large, that when a person is seated, the water shall come up around the hips to the navel, is all that is required. During the bath the upper as well as the lower part of the body should remain covered, while the abdomen is rubbed with a woollen cloth to increase the action of the skin. The temperature should generally be from fifty to sixty degrees, and the bath continued from five to twenty minutes. The best time for taking it is an hour before dinner or on going to bed. They are particularly serviceable in derangement of organs about the loins, of the hepatic viscera, and to relieve a tendency to congestion, in some of the upper parts of the body.

THE DROP-BATH.—In this bath single drops of water are allowed to fall a distance of five or six feet. It should not be used on any vital part, and seldom continued more than fifteen or twenty minutes. It is frequently of great service in chronic and obstinate paralysis. Active friction should be made over the part between the drops.

THE DOUCHE.—In this bath a small stream of water, of a calibre of from half an inch to four or five inches, is permitted to fall from five to twenty feet, according to circumstances, upon the body. The stream should not be permitted to fall perpendicularly on the head, chest, region of liver, or spine. At first it would be better that it should fall so as to flow over the neck and spine, after which other parts of the body may be exposed to it, particularly the part affected. It should not be taken after a full meal, when fatigued, or in a state of perspiration. The length of time which it may be taken may be from one to ten minutes, and should be followed by active exercise. The douche is a powerful stimulant, but great caution should be exercised in its use. Very weak or nervous persons should avoid it.

WET BANDAGES.—The local application of cold water is of two kinds, viz. when we wish to produce a cooling effect, or warmth and sweating. In the former case, as in inflammation of the brain, several thicknesses of cloth wrong out in ice cold water should be applied to the head, the cloth frequently changed, so that the parts are kept constantly cool. If the cloths are allowed to become warm, the result is worse than if they had not been applied; a still better application, is a beef bladder filled with pounded ice. When warmth or sweating is required as in derangement of the abdomen, stomach, throat, &c. a bandage or napkin, should be wrung out in cold water applied upon the part diseased, and covered with a dry bandage. The warmth of the body soon warms the wet bandage, and the heat, confined by the external dry bandage, the result is a most soothing and excellent form of sweating poultice. In referring to this sweating application of water in the following pages, we shall speak of it as "the wet bandage."

WET SHEET.—This application of water is often highly serviceable in febrile diseases. Two or three blankets are spread on a matress, and over these is spread a linen sheet dipped in cold water and wrung out as dry as possible. The patient, divested of clothing, is now placed on the sheet, which is then carefully folded around as well as the blankets that had been spread on the matress. Cold applications should be made to the head if there be a tendency of fulness there. In acute cases the applications should be changed according to the degree of heat, every quarter or half hour until the dry and hot skin becomes softer and cooler; after each application the body should be washed with cold or tepid water. In chronic cases the patient may remain in the sheet a much longer time. This application may either be made to the whole or part of the body.

Cold, tepid and vapour baths, either applied to the whole or part of the body, as well as the plunge and swimming baths, are all highly serviceable under certain circumstances and conditions of the system. Bathing apparatus should be found in every private dwelling, and particularly in public schools, a good bath to a restless child, who either cannot or will not confine his mind to his studies, will often soothe the system quicker, and invigorate the mind far better, than prosy lectures or any form of punishment.

INFLUENCE OF THE MIND ON DISEASE.

The sympathy between body and mind, and the influence exerted by one over the other, we know exists to a very great extent A man perplexed and annoyed about business-matters, which may be a little out of the regular course of his affairs, is very liable to feel the effect in some physical derangement. Cases are every day occurring where persons unfortunate in business, seeing the fruits of years swept away in some financial crisis, or disappointed in domestic relations, finding friends false, the sanctuary of home outraged, or perhaps the young, lifting the cup of love, bright and sparkling with joy to their lips only to see it dashed to the earth and shattered at their feet, or feeling in the orange blossoms of the wedding wreath the sting of the asp and the poison of death, in every circle of life, in every grade of society, these fearful blows are followed by slow decline, rapid and prostrating disease, the maniac shrieks, or an early death. On many a marble monument, and on many a simple grave-stone, might with truth be traced: "*Died of a broken heart.*"

Could we tear away the veil which hides the working of the mind from outward gaze,—and thank God we cannot,—how many bleeding hearts we should find, hearts crushed and broken, withering away beneath a grief more terrible than death itself. How the painful cause would flash upon us with the brightness of noonday, of many a death, where disease was rapid, defying medical skill, or where, as in slow decline, the poor victim sweetly faded away, or where the last breath was drawn when the light and breath of heaven came in through the grated windows of the home of the insane.

Intense grief, freely indulged, is very liable to undermine the constitution, and also bring on severe and painful forms of disease. Intense grief has in single night blanched the blackest hair to a snowy white. Oftentimes the death of a loved companion, an idolized child, seems to change entirely the current of life, and wither the frame, as if it had been exposed to the poisonous breath of the upas.

There are innumerable cases on record, where persons have died from the effect of fear alone. The history of every pestilence or epidemic shows that in thousands of cases the disease has been induced by fear. In the seventeenth century, when the plague ravaged London, carrying off its victims by thousands, and turning the city into a vast charnel house, simply looking on a person on whom the plague spot had made its appearance was considered almost a sure passport to the grave. Terror and consternation filled the minds of nearly all, and thousands died whose lives might have been spared had they not given way to useless fears.

An Eastern writer illustrates the effect of fear in a very beautiful and striking manner. "A traveler approaching the gates of a city, beheld entering in, a pestilence, and thus accosted it: Whither are you going? Into the city, replied the pestilence, to destroy three thousand lives, and sternly passed in to fulfil his fearful mission. The traveler paused, and soon from the city was heard the death cry, the wailings of friends for friends, and from the gates were carried forth thousands of corpses and hurriedly placed beneath the ground. Finally, the traveler beheld the pestilence stalking forth, and said, why have you exceeded your mission, and destroyed thirty thousand lives instead of three thousand. I have destroyed but three thousand, was the reply—fear has done the rest."

It was common for those who perished by violence to summon their destroyers to appear within a stated time before the tribunal of God, and the guilty ones in many instances have withered away and died as speedily as if smitten by the breath of a pestilence. Pestilence does not kill with the rapidity of terror. The abbess of a convent the Princess Conzaga, and the Archbishop of Rheims, for a jest visited one of the nuns and exhorted her as a person visibly dying. While in the performance of their scheme, they whispered to each other, she is just departing. She departed in earnest, and the guilty pair discovered in the midst of their sport, they were making merry over a corpse. In France, several physicians obtained leave of government to experiment on a criminal who had just been condemned to death. The criminal gladly availed himself of the privilege of being bled to death instead of being executed in public. He was placed in a chair, his eyes blindfolded, his arm slightly pricked with a pin, and a slight jet of water so directed, as to fall on his arm, thence trickling down to fall into a basin prepared for the purpose. The physicians then conversed together on the tragic symptoms, stated the amount of blood in the body, the quantity he had lost, and the length of time he would probably be in dying. In the mean-time the breathing of the victim gradually became fainter, and in a few moments he expired, without having lost one drop of blood. Montaigne tells of a man, who was pardoned on the scaffold, and was found to have expired while awaiting the stroke.

Despair produces a very strong impression on the mind, and thus on the system, and often either drives a person to idiocy, madness, or a speedy death. Almost every physician occasionally meets cases in his practice, when through the injudicious words of friends, or a variety of other causes, all hope vanishes in the patient's mind, and in utter despair he calmy waits what seems to him an inevitable doom. Even now, though it may be at the turning-point of the disease, when a feather's weight may turn the scale for life or death, if he sees around him hopeful countenances, and hears words of encouragement, new life may be infused into his lagging pulse, and he called back from the verge of the grave on which he was trembling.

Keep the lamp of hope burning brightly, unless all ground for hope is over.

The influence of the mind on the system is, as we have already seen, all-powerful, tormenting existence, bringing on and hastening disease and death, or where exerted for good, smoothing the rough pathway of life, and imparting health, vigour and harmony to the whole system.

We cannot look for health and happiness without harmony, and this can only exist where there is a beautiful blending of the moral, the intellectual, and the physical, and where man is in harmony with nature, with his own being, and thus with God.

HEREDITARY TAINT AND PREDISPOSITION TO DISEASE.

Many a child is born tainted with disease. The fountains of life are corrupted in the mother's womb, and the young being is ushered into the world with the seeds of disease and future suffering planted deeply within its system. Disease thus communicated from parent to child, is called *hereditary*. Let us glance at some few of those difficulties, which may as a general thing be classed under this head. We will first notice, that wide-wasting disease found in all classes of society, and which is at the root of a vast amount of chronic difficulties, viz. the class of affections popularly known as Scrofula, but which Hahnemann might call Psora, Hufeland Dyscrasy, but by modern science is more correctly termed *Tuberculosis*. We shall use the latter term in the few remarks we have to make of this class of affections.

Tuberculosis revels in the human family to an extent but little dreamed of by many. Obscuring its origin and masking its real character in a hundred forms, thousands, even when its seeds are rapidly ripening within them, have not the least idea of the real character and cause of their sufferings. It manifests its terrible effects in the early months of fœtal existence, and causes those spontaneous abortions, which destroy one quarter of those affected, before they see the light. After birth it frequently arrests their physical and moral development, and becoming complicated with various diseases, renders the period of infancy and youth full of dangers.

Sometimes it affects particularly the mucous membrane, and frequently extends its effects to the mucous system generally. Hence arise opthalmia, catarrh, affections of the ears, leucorrhœa, intestinal worms, mucous fevers, &c. Sometimes it attacks the skin and produces chilblains in the hands, feet, and face; chronic eruptions of the lips, eyelids, and ears; pustules of various forms scattered over the face, forehead, and chest, and ulcers more or less numerous and extensive.

Sometimes it acts particularly on the cellular tissue, and produces numerous abscesses and profuse suppuration. If it fixes itself on the osseous system, caries, and softening of the bones are among the effects produced. Many of the bones may be affected at the same time, and, as is sometimes the case, the whole skeleton shows the presence of the disease. All these varieties of affections, so apparently dissimilar in their character, are notwithstanding traceable to the same origin and the same cause. It may, as we have before stated, be developed in one patient in the mucous system, in another in the cellular, and in a third, in the bony skeleton, presenting of course a different appearance in each.

Tuberculosis, developing itself in the lungs, the brain, the stomach, the bowels, and in fact in every part of the system, for there is no tissue or organ into which it may not infuse its poison, is the most fearful destroyer of human life, which has ever cursed the world. Lifting its head in almost every clime, infusing its poison in every class of society, not the plague with its unnumbered victims, or the pestilence with its heaps of dead, can compare with it in destruction of human life.

Wherever we find this disease, in its various modifications and developments, whether we see it in loathesome sores, or in the slow or rapid wasting away of consumption, in blindness, deafness, or caries of the bones, we can as a general thing, though not in every case, trace it back to *hereditary taint.*

Notwithstanding the parents themselves may have been apparently healthy, showing no traces of Tuberculosis or a consumptive tendency, yet if we go back two or three generations, we find traces of it, or some affection, which will produce it, in some branch of the family. It is very common for it to have overleaped apparently, one, two, or even three generations, and develop itself in all its virulence in the unhappy victims, whose parents may, as they think, have escaped.

Among the causes of hereditary Tuberculosis we may place Syphilitic taint. Several tuberculous diseases greatly resemble syphilitic maladies. The parent who has contracted Syphilis, and believes himself entirely cured, may through error of treatment still retain in his system, apparently dormant, some portion of the poison, which may be transmitted to his offspring in the form of hereditary Tuberculosis. Thus, the parent, in his thoughtless folly, while running his giddy round of youthful dissipation, digs the grave of his child, poisons its happiness, and in following it to an early grave, or gazing on its weak, puny and diseased form, reaps a bitter harvest for his early sin. Oh, how fearfully do children suffer for a parent's sins.

Abuse of venereal pleasures is another cause of tuberculous children. Instances are by no means rare, particularly among the higher classes of society, where from the manner of living, an artificial excitement usurps the place of the natural, and, as a matter of course, the offspring are weak and puny.

The too early marriages, so common both among the rich and poor, is a fruitful cause of hereditary tuberculosis. For a man to beget healthy children, he must have passed somewhat beyond the age of puberty, and acquired fully his strength and development. These early marriages, where the bride is taken from the parental home at a time when she most needs a mother's care, or the bridegroom perhaps is a mere boy, are perfectly suicidal, and can only result in the broken constitution and feeble health of the mother, or at least, in weak and puny children. The inevitable consequences of these premature marriages are more to be dreaded when men, who have married too young, have previously led dissipated lives, passing, as it were through a period of fifty years in sixteen.

If too early a marriage has a tendency to produce diseased children, so also has a marriage contracted too late in life, when also the reproductive power is deficient in vigour.

Unfortunately, men frequently live, until they are forty-five or fifty, before marriage, and are then connected with those much younger than themselves. The consequence, as a general thing, is feeble children, who often die prematurely.

A considerable disproportion between the ages of parents is another fruitful cause not only of *tuberculous* offspring, but of ill health on the part of one of the parents. In a judicious marriage, there should be but a very few years difference between the ages of the parties. Old age cannot wed with youth with the expectation of vigorous and healthy offspring, any more than winter can mingle with summer. Flowers look sickly and are chilled by winter, and so is youth, when united to age. The young should not sleep with the old, though the difference in age may not be more than fifteen or twenty years, for the vital power in the young is rapidly exhausted by the old. For the same reason the cold and phlegmatic temperament should not sleep with one of warm and nervous temperament, for a similar result is produced. The manifest difference in age, temperament, and constitution, where the parties are placed in so close a relation, are pregnant with disastrous results to the weak and young, as well, if the parties are married, to their offspring.

Marriage should never take place between relations, unless the connection is very remote, for by such a union tuberculous taint existing in one, would be likely to be found in both, and the result would be a frightful harvest of disease in their children. Not for this reason only, but the marriage of relatives, will of itself often be sufficient to develop in their children tuberculous disease, weakness of mind, and even idiocy. Hence the repeated intermarriages of some of the royal families in Europe has produced among them a variety of tuberculous affections, together, sometimes with insanity, weakness of mind, and almost idiocy.

This disease is, as we have already stated, generally hereditary, although it is sometimes the result of moisture, bad air and food, changes of temperature, and also sometimes follows measles, small-pox and hooping cough. Cases are by no means rare in this changeable climate, when it is developed in those whose ancestral blood has been untainted with the disease, as far back as they can trace. Persons of robust and strong constitutions, showing no predisposition to consumption, have fallen victims to it from undue exposure to changes of temperature or too violent exertion of the chest.

Notwithstanding *tuberculosis*, as a general thing, is hereditary, we should be very sorry to believe, that the descendants of a family, in whose systems are lurking the seeds of this poison, must necessarily be tainted, generation after generation, that there is no escape, no dispersing the dark cloud, which hangs like a pall over their future. If this were the case, it would indeed be a curse so dark and fearful, that the poor victims might well pray for death.

But this is not the case. By a proper marriage, a marriage in which enlightened reason shall be called into action and not blind passion, a passing fancy, or pecuniary interest, and where in the physical and mental education and training of the children from the time of their birth, there is brought to bear a clear enlightened mind, and a proper understanding of the laws of health, I see no reason why such children may not be healthy and in the course of one or two generations all predisposition to the disease be removed.

A person of consumptive habit, marrying one of tuberculous diathesis, will be pretty sure to give birth to tuberculous children.

In selecting a partner for life, fitness of mind and disposition are not the only things to be taken into consideration. There is another question quite as important, and that is health, predisposition to disease, and the prospect of having healthy children, for all on entering the marriage state expect, sooner or later, to become parents.

These are questions of vast importance, and should not be lightly answered. Many a young mother after having given birth in rapid succession to several children, is called on to follow her husband to the grave, and weep in widowhood over blighted hopes, and feel that for years her existence must be a prolonged struggle to obtain the necessaries of life for her helpless children. Many a father looks upon children weak and puny, and follows his wife to the grave at a time, when they most need a mother's care, and he the comfort and solace of a wife.

And yet in the selection of a wife or husband, how little attention is paid to health, physical development and the probability, that in two or three years they will not be separated by death.

We have seen in the investigation of this subject, that *tuberculosis* is developed not alone, as is sometimes supposed, in the chest in the form of pulmonary consumption, but in every part of the system, and in an hundred forms.

Among the other forms of disease, to which there may be an hereditary predisposition, we have only space to mention gouty and rheumatic difficulties.

MORAL, INTELLECTUAL, AND PHYSICAL EDUCATION.

The harmonious blending, and proper education and training of this "Trinity" of our being is essential not only to health and happiness, but to true greatness. The name of Washington, of Howard, and Hahnemann stand out in bold relief as glorious examples of the truth of this principle.

There have been more powerful intellects than Washington's, more wily and skilful diplomatists, minds more skilled in conceiving and arranging the minutia of war, more quick and rapid amid the thunder and carnage of the battle-field, but never did there exist a purer patriot, or one in whom self was more quickly and sternly sacrificed to his country's weal. Never since our Saviour, did there exist one in whom the patriot, the philanthropist, the christian and the statesman were so beautifully blended. Had Napoleon added to his daring genius, his almost superhuman intellect, the moral force of Washington, the down-trodden nations of Europe might not now gaze in silent horror, as the blood of their purest patriots streams from the scaffold, and the last scene of his eventful life might have closed more brightly, than in his ocean-girt prison.

True greatness consists, not in the powerful development of

any one faculty of the mind without regard to the others, but in the harmonious blending of all, to ensure which, the moral, the intellectual, and physical must be properly trained and educated. The great lessons of life are to be taught in childhood, and those principles inculcated, which will grow and expand into a ripe harvest of honour and usefulness.

But this preparation for the training of the child should date previous to its birth, as a lasting impression is produced upon it, by the health of the father as well as the mother at the time of conception. The child is often punished and made to suffer keenly in the early days of its childhood for faults inherited directly from the parents. The health of the mother, the tone of her mind, her feelings, tastes, and pursuits, during the time she is carrying her child, are all important to the future condition of the unborn babe.

Dr. Gregory, in speaking of the influence of the parental stock, says: " Parents frequently live over again in their offspring, for children certainly resemble their parents not merely in countenance and bodily conformation, but in the general features of their minds and in both virtues and vices. Thus, the imperious Claudian family long flourished in Rome, unrelenting, cruel and despotic, it produced the merciless and detestible tyrant Tiberius, and at length ended, after a course of six hundred years, in the bloody Caligula, Claudius, and Agrippina, and then in the monster Nero." And thus we frequently see the vices and follies of the parents flourishing in luxuriant growth in the child.

When speaking of hereditary taint, I referred particularly to the diseases developed, and sufferings produced by improper marriages. Even in our northern clime, nothing is more common, than for young ladies to enter the marriage-state at the age of fifteen, sixteen or seventeen years. Not only unhealthy children are the result of this early marriage, but as a general thing, the young wife is totally unfit for the duties and responsibilities of her station. What does she know of i fe and its stern duties, which all, the rich and kindly nurtured as well as the poor and lowly, should know how to fulfil.

She, whose form has scarcely changed to womanhood, and on whose cheek still lingers the down of childhood, where has she learned the great lesson of life, that she should boldly venture out on the untried ocean before her. And when the young infant lies in her arms, a pure and holy thing, whose little heart beats quietly in happy innocence, can she take it by the hand and lead it safely past those quicksands, which are so thickly scattered around its path. And then the mind, can she in her young girlhood direct it aright, at a period when its whole future may depend, in part on her guidance?

Need we wonder, as we look around upon society, and see so many rash and foolish marriages, that there are so many still-born children, that so many of the rising generation are pale, sickly, and feeble, that so much vice abounds, that the peace of so many families is wrecked, that so many children are left motherless, and that so many young mothers are placed beneath the green sod? What else could we expect from this violation of the laws of their being, from this offering themselves on the altar of fashion and blind passion.

The gloomy records of the grave show, that nearly one-half of those born into the world perish before reaching the age of five, and one-third before the age of three years. How very few live to a good old age, and how mighty that throng, from ths ranks of infancy, childhood, and middle age, who follow each other in rapid succession into the realms of death. From these periods of life death reaps his richest harvest. Among those, who bright and joyous with the elasticity of youth and vigour of manhood, whose brilliant aspirations seem about being realized, death scatters his shafts and the cold waters of that river, which lies between us and the grave, freezes with its icy current the warm pulsations of the young heart, and bears onward on its dark bosom all there is of life to the vast ocean of eternity.

Look at the infant in its mother's arms, what does it know of sin, what of life, and how has it transgressed against, and excited the anger of its Maker? And the child, surrounded by the golden haze of its young life, just as it begins to delight the parent's eye and gladden their hearts by its opening beauties, and stir within them the pure and holy depths of an affection, which none but parents can feel; just as the light of thought begins to gleam from the bright eye and set its impress on the expanding brow, the bright eye becomes dim, the flushed cheek pale as marble, the whole being withers beneath a blight, which stagnates the youthful blood, lays a hand of ice on the heaving breast, and quenches in the darkness of death, bright hopes and glorious aspirations.

Why is it, that earth is thus piled with the graves of the young? Why is it, that death riots and revels in the haunts of childhood, and changes the joyous prattle and merry laugh of innocence to the wild wail of deep and bitter agony?

See the mother, with bleeding heart, clasping in deep and untold anguish the cold and pulseless form of her child to her heaving bosom, and hear her murmur with pallid lips, "my child, my bright, my beautiful, my loved one, how can I give you up, how take you from my warm bosom and lay you in the cold, dark, damp grave." And the father, the strong man, the iron will, he, who has struggled manfully and bared himself to the stern conflicts of life. Oh! how he bends now, like a broken reed, how the cold drops start from the forehead, as he gazes with glazed eye, and in speechless misery, for he cannot weep, on the little being, cold and pulseless before him.

Hear that prayer, which daily goes up from thousands of bleeding hearts, "*oh God! let this bitter cup pass from me.*"

Glance for one moment at this misery, at this deep anguish, at those mourning weeds, at these sweet buds nipped by the frosts of death, and then lift your eyes in reverence to heaven, and say if you can, *if you dare*, "Thou, oh Father, in mercy, kindness and love, hast done it all. Thou, in mercy or in wrath, hast sent thy fearful messenger death, through the earth to wither with his icy breath, the brightest fairest flowers in their first bloom."

The doctrine of "Divine Providence" as sometimes understood at the present day, is very convenient for physicians to hide behind, as a shield for their ignorance, or for patients or friends to preach, as an excuse for dereliction from duty.

But reflect whether you are not blaspheming, a pure and holy God by charging all this wo and misery on him, the result by far too often, of your own ignorance, folly or wickedness.

In a reverence for the Supreme Being, and in a firm belief in his Providence, I yield to no one, but my soul shudders and sickens at the proneness of the human race, while madly or blindly rushing on in their own way, heedlessly trampling on laws, which form the basis of their existence, to make a "Divine Providence" accountable for the result of their own disobedience. If the parents had been properly trained, had given way to no dissipation during youth, and had entered the marriage-state as rational, intelligent beings, might not a large portion of this disease have been prevented? Cases of sickness however are frequently seen, where there has been no known disobedience of nature's law, but are the result of circumstances, apparently beyond our control.

We can lay down then with perfect safety this broad principle. —

If the human race were properly educated, mentally, morally, and physically, and would follow closely the teachings of nature, appealing so strongly to the God implanted reason and common-sense within them, cultivating harmony in themselves and with the world, not only a large portion of disease which now devastates the earth would vanish, but we should have a race in beauty and intellect such as the world has never seen since the fall of man.

The influence exerted by the mother on the child during the period of gestation, the general rules which should regulate her habits, as well as the treatment of the babe during the first few months of infancy will more appropriately come under the head of "*Affections of women and children*," which will be found in the latter part of the work.

Commencing with the child as it emerges from the nursery, leaving its peculiar diseases and training during infancy, for a future chapter, let us glance at some of the prominent points deserving attention not only during childhood, but amid the bustle, the stern duties and active scenes of life.

The food of the child is of vast importance. It should be plain, simple, nourishing and in sufficient variety and quantity. The more simple its preparation the better. Spices, tea, and coffee, rich gravies and fatty food should be avoided. Pastry, rich cake, and confectionary of all kinds should form no part of its diet. Fruits and vegetables, perfectly ripe and fresh, can generally be eaten with safety.

Pure air and cleanliness are at no time more important than in childhood. The rooms and bed should be well aired daily. Feather beds are as injurious to children as to adults and should therefore be avoided. The clothing should be loose, to give ample play to the limbs and muscles, and of sufficient warmth to ensure comfort.

Bathing the entire body every day should also be practiced, the temperature being guided by the strength and temperament of the child. (*See bathing.*) Out-door exercise in the open air is absolutely essential. There are a hundred harmless and innocent sports in childhood, which can be safely indulged, such as playing at ball, jumping the rope, skating, swimming, &c. Contrast the buoyant and elastic step, the ruddy cheek, the sparkling eye, the well developed form of the boys and girls who are accustomed to vigorous exercise in the open air, with those weak and puny children on whom the breath of heaven is scarcely permitted to blow.

At the age of six or seven, and not before, by which time the physical system should have received a fair start, the child may be sent to school. Previous to this period, the physical should be developed, and its teachers be, the mother and nature. Learn it to think, inculcate habits of observation, and when studying in nature's temple, check not with a careless word its eager questionings. Let the great book of nature be the volume studied, and through it the holy principle of love and beauty so strongly stamped on every page, be infused into the mind with every breath, and every gaze on the bright world around.

Sometimes immense harm is done in chaining the young mind, at too early an age, to books and abstract rules. The physical should first be permitted to become strong and healthy, or at least, developed to such an extent, that the mind may be brought into activity with safety. You will find in almost every family, at least one child, that gives bright promise of a brilliant future. The parents, in the pride of their heart, determine it shall win a glorious name, and therefore, instead of at first holding back the mental, and fostering the physical, preserving a healthy equilibrium between them, the mind is pushed and goaded on, its pride constantly flattered by praise, until the brain by too violent exercise looses its elasticity, and sinks into a state of dulness, or like the mettled courser, goaded on by the spur, it rouses itself for a new effort, and then falls dead on the field. Thus, not unfrequently, is the pride of the parent doomed to a bitter disappointment. To no one is out-door exercise more absolutely essential to health, than the student, and hence swimming, riding, fencing, dancing, and those gymnastic exercises, which contribute so much to health and a proper development of the form, should hold a conspicuous rank in the education of all. Look into our colleges, and among those who study hard, and take but little care of their bodily health, and you will see pale and sickly countenances, bent forms, sallow or hectic cheeks, with disease and death stamped upon them in perfectly legible characters. What can we call these men, who thus trample on the laws of their being, dig their own graves, and write their own death warrants, but madmen and suicides. What can they expect but disease and death. Unless the machinery of the body be kept unclogged, in vigorous health, and each part perform its proper functions, its infirmities will tinge with a sickly and unhealthy hue the strongest mind and the brightest genius. To have a healthy mind, there must be a healthy body, and with both, almost any purpose, however difficult, may be accomplished.

In female education, the heart should be educated as well as the head. The cold and selfish reasoning of fashion, that female education should be confined to those superficial accomplishments and graces, which will enable them to shine in the drawing-room, should be denounced in the strongest terms. These accomplishments are very well in their place, but without a solid basis, they form a poor support in the stern duties of life. The time may come when they will require something to make their home happy and their life pleasant, besides a superficial knowledge of drawing accomplishments. They should be taught the great laws of their being, and the duties they will be called on to fulfil as wives and mothers. No false modesty should prevent their understanding thoroughly those great truths, which must have such an immense influence on their future happiness, and the welfare of their children.

Equal care should be taken of the physical training as in the other six, and out-door exercise is of quite as much importance. Swimming, skating, riding, dancing, walking, and those other exercises which give ease and freedom to the movements, and strength, elasticity and health to the whole form, should occupy a certain portion of their time.

The influence exerted on the child beneath the parental roof is as enduring as life. The seed planted then, will in after years yield a ripe harvest of good or evil. The child should be made to feel, that its home is the purest, sweetest place on earth, and that its parents are its best friends. Above all, it should never be permitted to witness there, wrangling, disputing and contention, bitterness and heart-burning, or to hear from its parents one angry word or unjust charge. Make the home happy, and let its atmosphere be one of love and harmony. I have often felt indignant at the treatment children meet with at the hands of those from whom they should only receive kindness and affection.

As I have heard the harsh and angry word, the heavy blow, the bitter tone of rebuke and denunciation, the unjust and often foul-mouthed charge, and seen the flashing eye, and the cheek flushed with passion, I have felt like telling the unnatural paents or guardians they were training the child for a future of crime and bitterness. Need we wonder at the awful and terrible fruits of human passion, when its fearful lessons are instilled into the young mind in the sanctuary of home. If we cannot have unbounded confidence between parent and child in the family circle, where on this sin-stained earth can it be found?

If this confidence existed, and the child were made to feel that its parent's ears were ever open to its troubles, in them it had warm and ready sympathisers, kind advisers, and hearts whose strongest anxieties were for its future welfare, what untold misery and suffering might be avoided. Thousands would be prevented from entering on a career of vice and crime, and hundreds, instead of finding the dream of their youth blighted, their purest affections trampled on, would be saved from a career so dark and fearful. On the harmonious training of the child in its parental home, depends, in a measure, the career of the man, and the greatness and prosperity of the nation.

From what has been already said, it will be readily seen, that a false system of education, incorrect training of the child, and ignorance of the laws of health, beget a large amount of the vice and crime, which devastate society.

Look at the various avenues to vice in every part of the land, the gambling, and scenes of debauchery and crime, at which even devils might blush! Here in the city of *New-York* alone, with its churches and benevolent institutions, its untold wealth, and untold misery, the central point of the arts and sciences, literature and refinement, we find gambling and drinking saloons in almost every street, and a population of at least TWENTY THOUSAND, who have sold themselves, body and soul, into a slavery bitter as death, who eat their bread from the wages of *prostitution*.

It is a hard thing, oh parent, to believe, that you are training that son for disease and death, for the penitentiary or the gibbet.

It is a hard thing to believe and bitter to realize, that you are training that daughter, so bright and gay, so beautiful and joyous, for disease, pain and an early grave, for a childless wife, for the mother of children weak and puny, for contention, for a cold and heartless life with no aim but self, no God but fashion, for the halls of prostitution, and the lowest brothels of the depraved. But go into our prisons and among the haunts of vice, and read a secret page in the history of crime. Go beyond the deed, to the imperceptible steps, which led to the crime ; get at the moral, physical, and intellectual training in youth, and you will find there notes of discord and jarring strings.

We build prisons, huge stone walls, with gloomy cells, in which to confine those, who have been convicted of outraging law ; we build the scaffold, and twist the rope, which is to send the victim into eternity ; we found hospitals, the clergy hurl the anathemas of God against vice, while it lifts its unabashed head and laughs at these puny efforts, these baby blows on its citadel. The victims of crime have but practiced the lessons taught them by society, and in their homes, and less cunning or more venturesome than others have been detected in the act, and punished. They are punished for yielding to temptations, which society itself spreads out before them. After scattering traps all over the community, those who dare fall into them and are detected are punished for their folly.

Year after year the abandoned women who throng our streets descend to the grave by hundreds, and their ranks are filled with new victims not from the city alone, but from country towns and rural villages. Year after year the young and beautiful go down to early graves, genius flashes out for a brief moment, when death seizes its victim, children fall by thousands, in the homes where should be peace, happiness and contentment, is discord and contention, the prisons groan with victims, the scaffold trembles beneath its weight, and society sleeps on, wondering at the amount of crime, and trying to lop off some of the branches of that mighty tree, whose dark shadow is cast over the earth.

Let us strike at the root of this difficulty, let us make the intellectual, the moral and physical to move on in perfect harmony, each performing its proper duty, each leaning on the other, and all forming one glorious whole. Until we accomplish this, in attempting to arrest vice, we but beat the air. Until we accomplish this, disease will continue to devastate the earth, continue to pile it with graves, and fill it with weeping and sorrow. Abuse of either the moral, physical or intellectual, undermines health and happiness. It is only in the proper blending and use of all we are to look for weapons, which will batter down prison walls, make the gibbet a thing that was, and in the place of sorrow, darkness and gloom, light up the lamp of joy and happiness.

CHAPTER IV.

TRUE THEORY OF CURE.

Nature, in all its operations, in all its movements, is characterized by the utmost simplicity, order and harmony. There is no confusion, no discord. Creation itself is like a mighty instrument, its parts composed of worlds and systems of worlds. Touched by the hand of God, it gives forth only notes of music and of harmony.

If, with the aid of the telescope's mighty power we look upon the heavens, world on world, and system beyond system start into view, stretching far away into the depths of space, even beyond the assisted gaze of man. And yet these unnumbered worlds, to which in point of size, our earth is but a pigmy, roll on in silent majesty from year to year, and from age to age, sweeping through the heavens on their viewless track, almost with the lightning's swiftness, crossing and recrossing on their silvery paths, without interfering one with the other, but in the utmost harmony and order. The comets wander off into unknown regions, returning at their appointed time after centuries of absence. Sweeping backward and forward through the heavens, they may rightly be called the pendulums of the universe, marking the hours of eternity. If we look at the vegetable world, at the tree, which striking its roots deep into the ground, has wrestled with a century's storms and tempests, at the ivy, which twines around its trunk, at the flowers which bloom in wild and sweet profusion over the face of nature, at the green grass which forms a yielding carpet beneath our feet, we find them all obeying fixed and positive laws. In all the combinations of matter, which are every hour going on about us, how harmonious the progress, and marriage, if I may so speak, of matter, how beautiful and grand the result!

In the vast laboratory of nature, how simple the elements we see at work, yet how stupendous and mighty the result. Each particle of matter obeys a principle it cannot transgress, and combines in beautiful proportion with the element necessary to complete the plan. Each combination in nature, each step in the mighty plan of creation, is in obedience to fixed, unalterable laws. Science is unfolding one glorious truth after another, revealing in dazzling light, the beauty, harmony and simplicity of nature, and the causes of her various phenomena. We see what causes have been at work to upheave the mountain, form the channels of rivers, dot the ocean with islands, and cover the earth with vegetation and beauty; why spring is followed by summer, and summer by winter; why to-day we feel the soft and gentle breezes of the south, and to-morrow swelter beneath the rays of a burning sun, tremble before the storm, or shiver in the cold winds from the north.

Nature works by fixed laws. There is no chance, no guesswork in her combinations and movements. Science is gradually unfolding these principles and laws, and now, guided by those laws which have been already unfolded, we daily penetrate deeper and deeper into the temple of nature, and bring to light new wonders and glories. The chemist in pursuing his labours, has fixed data to work upon, data the result of experience and close and accurate observation. At each step of his progress he feels that he is treading on firm ground, that his pathway is surrounded with light, that the science he is cultivating is a positive science, and whenever he directs his footsteps into unexplored regions of investigation he goes forth with confidence, confidence in immutable and unchangeable laws, and finds in all his researches, in all the glorious truths he brings to light from nature, no clashing with laws already known, no contradiction of the true science of the past, but a beautiful harmony reigning through all.

In what an endless labyrinth did the theories of the ancients involve them as it regards the movements of the heavenly bodies and the various phenomena of nature. Contradiction met them at every step, and they found themselves at every effort becoming more and more entangled in a net-work of mysteries. At length the philosopher detects in "Attraction of Cohesion and Gravitation" the great levers which move worlds, and going on step by step, he discovers other truths, and finds in all, principles which are to guide him and cast light on his path in all future investigations. And now the astronomer, with his telescope, can calculate the movements of the heavenly bodies, predict with unerring certainty the return of the comet from its far off wanderings, and unroll before our eager gaze the glorious map of the starry heavens.

If we look back upon the history of medicine, what proofs do we find, until within the last half century, of its having any claim to a rank among the positive sciences. We find the whole medical profession groping in fog, striving to catch shadows, and vainly searching in the midst of bogs and quagmires for firm ground on which to stand. Now and then, as a ray of sunlight penetrates the mist by which they are surrounded, they perceive their error, and start off into another, and equally fuitless path. Thus confusion treads upon the heels of conjecture. Theory after theory is born, flourishes its brief span, and is then crowded from the stage to give place to another equally wild and fruitless. The theory of to-day is renounced to-morrow, consigned to the tomb to be exumed by some modern Æsculapius, clad in new garments, and proclaimed to the world with a flourish of trumpets as his own offspring. Time and space would fail us, and indeed it would be a useless task to attempt a description of the theories of disease, and its treatment, which have been advanced by the medical philosophers of the world from the days of

Hippocrates to the present. Let us briefly glance at the treatment the patient receives at the hands of the so-called, old or allopathic school of medicine, with its boasted antiquity, and its experience of thousands of years.

Floating about on the wild sea of conjecture, without any leading principle to guide to the appropriate remedy, the treatment of disease is as various as the almost innumerable theories, which have been advanced.

Minute and highly important symptoms are disregarded, and facts are compelled to give way, that clashing theories may triumph. "Break down the disease, if in so doing, you break down the patient," is too often the result, although not generally the open preaching of the allopathic school.

We will suppose a patient sick with fever, and glance at the treatment he would be likely to receive at the hands of different physicians. The cause of the disease to the unbiassed mind should be apparent, and the case perfectly plain and simple. Prostrate on his bed, the head dizzy and throbbing with pain, the heart beating with violence, the pulse quick and wiry, and the whole frame burning with fever, the patient tosses from side to side, eagerly watching for the approach of his physician, filled, as his fancy pictures him, with the accumulated wisdom and experience of centuries, whose magic skill is to soothe the tortured frame, cool the fevered blood, and call back the pulse of health.

At length the physician enters, looks at the flushed face, places his finger on the pulse, and says, unless we reduce the vital power, and deplete the patient, he will die. The arm is bared, and the blood spouts from the vein until weakened by its loss, a faintness almost amounting to insensibility is felt. Bind up the arm, give a smart purgative, follow it by nauseating doses of antimony, and to-morrow, if no better, put in again the lancet and cathartics. As he leaves the room, he gives the comfortable assurance, that in addition to these pleasing remedies, the patient is to have for the coming few days, nothing to eat.

But, perchance, a physician is called in having a different theory. The fever, he says, undoubtedly arises, in this case, from an irritation of the intestinal canal. Clear out the canal then, with a gentle purgative, keep the patient perfectly quiet, and give him cooling drinks.

But, still another physician may have been called in, and he says, that the fever is caused by an irritation of the brain, and we must deplete valiantly, bleed from the arm, apply leeches to the temples, put ice to the head, and be sure not to forget the cathartics.

And these physicians, and a host besides, agreeing in a plain simple case, as to the cause of the disease and the treatment necessary, about as well as oil agrees with water, are all ranged under the worn and time-honoured flag of allopathy. Godly allopaths all, steeped in the wisdom of the past, how their souls revolt at quackery, and their lips curl in scorn at those, who tired with the restless waves on which they had been tossing, of the shifting sands in which they had been enveloped, dare to set their feet on firm ground and drink of pure waters.

But we will suppose, the fever was in reality produced by an inflammation of the brain. The capillaries of the brain are congested, and to relieve their congested state a large amount of blood is drawn from the system. The strength is reduced, but the congestion still continues. An artificial inflammation must now be produced in some healthy part of the system, which shall supersede that already existing in the brain. Put on the blisters then, and ply drastic purgatives.

But what effect do you produce by this treatment, and how do you touch beneficially the true seat of the disease? The serous vessels of the brain, from their loss of irritability and tone, are prevented from performing their functions aright, and no cure can take place, until this tone and irritability is restored. Can you, by the most active depletion, prevent the red globules, freighted with oxygen, from entering the relaxed and enfeebled capillaries, and the whole remaining mass of blood from circulating through the brain every few moments?

Certainly not, and by thus reducing the strength you take away one of the most important stimulants to these enfeebled vessels. And also by creating new inflammations, you reduce the chance of recovery by weakening the system and taking away a portion of its power to struggle against disease. And more than this, you by your drugs may create new diseases frequently more serious than the old, diseases, which in their long duration and the torture they produce in the system, often make the patient long to lay his weary head in the quiet of the grave.

One would suppose that the Allopath might devoutly pray, "Oh for some rest to this tossing bark, Oh! for some rock on which to stand, some ray of light to penetrate this gloom, or one thread to guide me through this tangled maze."

But lest the reader should suppose the picture is overdrawn, let me quote from one whose virgin heart has never wandered from the shrine of Allopathy or become tainted with heresy. Dr. Bushnan in a little work, published in London, in 1850, on "cholera and its cures," paints us the following exquisite picture of Allopathy. In speaking of the different remedies used in cholera by the "*regular profession*," he says: "Let us pass in review these remedies, so as to obtain a bird's eye view of them. They defy classification. Omitting for a moment the complex method by which cholera was to be vanquished, what were the simple specifics that were to cure, infallibly cure, the fearful enemy?

"Water of every temperature. Wrap the cholera patient in a cold sheet, says one. Dash cold water repeatedly over the sheet in which he is enveloped, says another. Ply him well with cold water internally, says a third. Freeze him; cool his blood to thirty below zero, adds a fourth. Fools that ye are, exclaims a fifth, 'thus to treat a patient half dead with cholera—I say, wrap him in sheets soaked in boiling water; and having thus half-cooked the shivering wretch, conclude the process by placing him over the boiler of a steam engine.'

"Sage advice, learned Thebans! the blood is dark, and the surface cold. 'My theory,' shouts one man, is that oxygen reddens the blood, and by its action on that blood, generates heat; therefore make the patient inhale oxygen.' 'Nay,' rejoins another, 'the blood in the lungs is too bright; oxygen has nothing to do with the generation of heat; stifle him with carbonic acid.' 'There are cramps present, which cause much suffering, and therefore are they the symptoms especially to be treated, Chloroform annihilates pain—let him breathe chloroform.'

"'It is evident,' avows one sapient doctor, 'that there is no bile in the stools; therefore calomel should be administered.' 'It is plain,' says another, 'that diarrhœa is the great evil; therefore let him have opium, that is the drug which effectually prevents a free flow of bile.' 'He is cold and depressed—what so natural as to stimulate.' The wisdom of the proposal is proved by the numbers who recommended its adoption—the folly of the many is manifested by the proportion who died under the use of stimulants. 'Give him alkalies,' vociferates one man. 'Nay,' says another, 'lemon-juice, and acids are the true remedies.'

"'It is simply a stage of intermittent fever,' maintain some; 'therefore,' they add, 'the drug for its prevention, and its cure is quinine.' 'Not half potent enough,' whispers a supporter of the same theory, 'give him arsenic.'

"Certain fanatics refused the use of medicine, but in the course of their religious mummeries, administered to the credulous a cup of olive oil. A patient recovered, and 'Eureka!' shout the populace. *Vox et præterea nihil,* say those who wait awhile before they decide.

"Opium, in one man's mind, is a specific in small doses, the twentieth of a grain frequently repeated. 'Nonsense,' says another, 'opium *is* a specific, but let it be given in doses of from six to twelve grains.' The latter has one advantage; if the power of absorption yet remains to the stomach, the patient will assuredly be saved all further pain, and, if he be a good man, mercifully provided for in a better world.

"'Calomel is the specific that will stay every symptom of the cholera, bring back the pulse, and restore life almost to the dead, if given,' says one, 'in twenty or thirty grains at a dose.' 'No,' says another, 'give it in that way, and you will kill the patient. It must be given in small doses at short intervals.'

"Then come other infallible specifics—pitch, sulphur, phosphorus, and carbon; gold, silver, zinc, and lead; strychnine, salicine, morphine, and cannabine; hachshish, and zorabia; abstraction of blood and injection of blood; perfect repose and incessant motion; to the skin irritation the most severe, applications the most soothing; stimulants the most violent, sedatives the most powerful."

And this is *medical science.* Medical science to which man is to turn for relief when the body is racked with pain, and in which he is to find hope when disease with stealthy footsteps enters his home. Oh! what a parody on true science, what a mockery of suffering humanity. But does the medical history of the past two thousand years present no bright spots, has it placed no trophies in the temple of truth? Have the thousands of noble and self-denying men who have filled its ranks accomplished no good. On the contrary, the history of medicine is full of brilliant discoveries, but they have mostly been in the field of physiology. Here great truths have been developed, and the way prepared for the introduction of a law of cure of so beautiful and perfect a character that it is destined to banish all adverse theories from the field. Notwithstanding theories of disease almost innumerable have been advanced, but one law of cure has ever been established. Let us briefly examine this law, which we may do by answering the question of

WHAT IS HOMŒOPATHY?

The disturbance created in the system by morbific causes produces in the organism a mass of symptoms, which represent the actual malady or disease. The object of the medicine then is to annihilate these symptoms, in doing which the internal change on which the disease is founded is also removed. The object is not by means of opiates to palliate for the time, or by active depletion to decrease the severity of the symptoms,—for in either case the cause is not removed,—but to remove thoroughly, and effectually, in fact, annihilate the symptoms, and thereby eradicate the disease.

How is this to be done? There surely must be some principle to guide us in the selection of a remedy and its appropriate administration. It cannot be possible that we are left to grope in the dark, striking about us at random in the hope that some of our blows will hit the mark. If this were the case, we should be far more likely to hit the wrong than the right place, and be pretty sure of doing more injury than good. But this is not the way in which nature performs any of her operations. There is no chance, no guess-work, no confusion, in any of her movements. And certainly we should not expect to be thrown on the broad ocean of conjecture, where man, the noblest and most beautiful of all its works is concerned. No, there is a law by which we are to be guided in the removal of disease, as immutable and unchangeable as the laws which govern the heavenly bodies. No cure can be performed, unless in obedience with this law, from which, if we depart, we embarrass, instead of aid nature in its operations.

This law is perfectly plain and simple. A medicine taken into the healthy system produces a certain disturbance, which acting on the organism, gives rise to a peculiar class of symptoms. In other words, a disease is produced by artificial means, creating a peculiar disturbance in the system, and producing a particular class of symptoms. Now, where a disease is produced by other causes, with symptoms similar in every respect to those produced by the drug, we of course conclude, that there is a similar disturbance in the system, a similar internal change, in fact, a like disease to that developed by artificial means.

If then, we now give this drug, it is evident we produce an artificial disease, occasioning the same disturbance, producing the same internal change, giving rise to the same symptoms, in fact, precisely similar to the one already existing in the system. But these affections cannot exist together, for the more intense or powerful will destroy the weaker. If then with our drug we produce an artificial affection, a little more intense or powerful than the old, we of course demolish the old intruder, and expel it from the system. In a word, a weaker dynamic affection in man is permanently extinguished by one that is similar, of greater intensity, yet of a different origin. A reaction of nature is excited by the drug, and thus the disease expelled. Of course, the remedy must be allowed to produce its specific effect, and be given unmixed with any other. If two or three remedies are mixed together, and given at the same time, it is clear, that you get the pure effects of neither. The drug given must cover, or be capable of producing in health, not one symptom alone, but the entire group.

An affection produced artificially, *dissimilar* to the one existing in the system, does not destroy that affection, but if more powerful, simply causes its suspension until the new disease performs its course, or is cured, when the old disease re-appears. Thus the stronger may suspend the weaker, but they never cure each other reciprocally. Therefore the method frequently adopted in Allopathy of producing contrary symptoms is wrong, and cannot cure.

If then, as has been already said, disease is removed by giving drugs, which when taken into the healthy system produce a train of symptoms similar to those existing in the diseased, the absolute necessity of a pure Materia Medica will be readily perceived. Each drug must be tried on the healthy system, and the symptoms developed under its use carefully noted down. And this has been done not by one alone, but by hundreds, who have gladly endured the suffering to which they have thus submitted themselves, that in so doing they might be the better enabled to alleviate human suffering, and check the fearful desolations of disease. These investigations have been carried on by different persons, in countries widely separated from each other, at the same time. Thus the proving of the same drug may have been going on at the same time in Germany, France, England, and America, and the progress of each unknown to the other until the whole was finished. When compared they have been found to agree in every important particular. Thus, by thoroughly proving each drug on the healthy system, the only pure Materia Medica ever made has been prepared. Each drug has been submitted to a laborious and painful investigation, and in no other way can a Materia Medica be produced on which any reliance can be placed.

How different a Materia Medica thus prepared, from the loose, uncertain, and guess-work affair of Allopathy. We know from actual experiment, that a drug will produce such and such symptoms. In Allopathy there is no such certainty. Not a drug has been thoroughly investigated in the only correct way, that of a trial on the healthy system. The Allopath then has no sure ground on which to stand. Somewhere he has read or heard that a certain drug will benefit in a certain disease, but how does he know the symptoms indicating it are present, or that his informant might not have received it from as uncertain a source as himself.

We have presented a principle which experience has clearly established as the only law of cure ever discovered. On this broad principle has been produced the only pure Materia Medica the world has seen. Such then is Homœopathy. The corner-stone of the edifice, the broad platform upon which is reared the whole glorious structure is "*Similia Similibus curantur*," or "like is cured by like." This is the great law of cure, the law through which all cures must be performed, the principle for which we contend, which is inscribed on all our banners, and which will as surely triumph throughout the world as truth will triumph over error.

This is Homœopathy. Is there any thing so terrible about it? Anything so contrary to reason, so awful and pernicious as to bring down upon it the vials of Allopathic wrath? But is it said, I did not suppose this was Homœopathy? I thought that it consisted in infinitesimal doses. Then there never has been a greater mistake. Upon this man of straw have been poured vials of wrath and torrents of indignation. Homœopathy consists not in the amount of the dose, but in that dose being given in obedience to the great principle already stated.

The question then is, how large a dose, given strictly homœopathically, is necessary to produce a cure with the greatest safety, and in the least amount of time. Hahnemann, when he commenced the practice of his new system gave his medicines in the ordinary-sized doses to which he had been accustomed in the Allopathic school. But he very soon ascertained, that where medicines were given after a close and accurate study of the symptoms, and were intended to act specifically, this course would not answer. He must from an inevitable necessity, if he wished to cure his patient, obtain the drug in its purest form, and give it in minute doses. Hence arose the system of infinitesimal doses. It was the work of necessity, the direct result of the homœopathic law. And yet this system of infinitesimal doses, without regard to the great homœopathic law of which it is the natural result, has been held up as *homœopathy*, and been made a target against which have been hurled the sneering and contemptible shafts of ridicule, falsehood, and misrepresentation. The sapient Allopath, to show the inertness of homœopathic medicines, has heroically swallowed a dozen of the medicated globules, never dreaming that in so doing, he was only showing his own ignorance and folly, for it is the great law of our system, that for these globules to produce their legitimate effect, a peculiar class of symptoms must be present, to which the remedy is homœopathic. The diseased state of the system also far increases its susceptibility to medicines.

Let us briefly examine this system of infinitesimal doses, and see if reason and experience do not teach us, that even small things, so far as appreciable quantity is concerned, are capable of producing a tremendous effect. It must be borne in mind, that in homœopathy, the drug, in addition to its being administered in obedience to a fixed law, is obtained in its purest form, and, unmixed with any other medicinal substance, is allowed to produce its specific effect. This is not the case in Allopathy. There, as they themselves have often lamented, but very little dependence can be placed on their drugs, as it is almost impossible to obtain them pure, and as if this were not enough to destroy the little specific action they might exert, three or four medicines are often combined together, thus, the one destroying in a great measure the effect of the other. Where can be the necessity of pouring into the stomach an enormous quantity of drugs, when, if given in a pure state, a much smaller amount would produce a more decided effect. Who would think of crowding the stomach with crude Peruvian bark, when the curative principle of the bark is at hand, in the form of quinine?

But let us look at nature, from whose vast store-house we can draw such glorious lessons of wisdom and truth. Let us glance at those silent operations, which are capable of producing such mighty changes in the world of matter. It is true, our Creator might, if he chose, have made this world, which now moves on in such order and harmony, to have creaked and groaned in every joint, he might have made the smallest fly to have buzzed thunder, but He had no such absurd idea of order and power. Let those who ridicule the fact, that an infinitesimal amount of matter so small as to possess no appreciable weight, or taste, can exert any influence, creep out of their narrow shell, and open their eyes to the wonders going on around them every day and every hour.

The earthquake is on its fearful march, and the earth trembles before its mighty power. Cities are overwhelmed and mountains rent and torn like paper. Volcanic fires burst from the quaking earth, and with tongues of flame and lava flood deluge in fiery ruin the surrounding country. Touch, taste and weigh in human scales these subtile forces, which produce such tremendous power. The electric current strikes the traveler dead to the earth. Gather up the particles and tell us their weight and measure. Standing in New-York a message is transmitted with lightning speed along the telegraphic wires to New-Orleans. Tell us the amount and size of the electric particles, which bear the message on to its destination.

When vegetable substances are subjected to heat and moisture, certain atoms or molecules are set free, which diffused in the atmosphere, may infect hundreds with intermittent fever. And yet do those moving through a miasmatic district, smell, taste or see the subtile poison, which is so powerfully to affect them? Can the chemist detect it by any process of analysis with which he is acquainted?

Minute particles are constantly escaping from persons affected with small-pox, scarlet fever, and other diseases, which passing into the air are capable of affecting hundreds and thousands of persons with the same disease. Cases are on record where a letter merely written in a house, where a person was sick with the small-pox, and transmitted through the mail hundreds of miles, has communicated the disease at the end of the route and infected a whole neighbourhood.

In whatever part of the world we go, we find the needle of the compass pointing toward the magnetic pole, showing that the molecules or atoms, which escape from this magnetic deposit pervade the whole universe. Can we see or taste them, or if they were all collected together, could we weigh them?

The dog, as well as other animals, traces its prey by the sense of smell for miles, and a single grain of musk scents the room for days without any appreciable diminution in quantity. Gold may be divided into particles of $\frac{1}{1.500.000.000}$ of a square inch and still possesses the colour and other characters of gold. A single drop of a solution of indigo, colours 1000 cubic inches of water, so that the particles of indigo must be smaller, than the twenty-five hundred millionth of a cubic inch. Linen yarn has been spun, a pound of which was 1.432 English miles in length. A visible portion of such thread could not have weighed more than $\frac{1}{127.080.000}$ of a grain.

If we look through the microscope, we discover animals, living and perfect in all their parts, so minute that it would require the heaping together of millions on millions to be visible to the naked eye.

In all vegetable substances the real strength remains latent in the crude state, and requires certain preparation to develop it. The more completely the essential principle is separated from the crudity, by which it is surrounded, the more powerful it becomes. It has been clearly shown by science, that by friction, mixture, &c., principles of immense power may be liberated from substances, which in their crude state are entirely inert.

Inasmuch as the active properties of a medicinal substance is developed from its surface, to develop its full powers, we must make it cover over as large a surface as possible. A grain of matter thoroughly triturated with one hundred grains of sugar of milk, may be made to pervade every part of it, and the matter may be still farther diffused by taking one grain of this substance and combining it in the same manner with another quantity of the medium. The drug thus separated, retains in each atom of its minute subdivision the power of exerting a specific influence on the system.

We have thus endeavoured to make clear two points, viz. the great homœopathic law, and the system of infinetisimal doses, and trust we have succeeded in showing that the former is the only true law of cure, and the latter not quite so ridiculous, as some, who are not accustomed to think, seem inclined to suppose.

We have said, that the law of "Similia similibus curantur," is the only law of cure, and when cures are performed, they are in obedience with this law, no matter, who the physician or what the drug given. Let us bring the Allopathic school themselves to the bar, and apply the test to some of their cures.

Nitric acid is a favourite remedy for salivation and ulceration of the mouth produced by mercury, and yet this drug is capable of exciting salivation and ulceration of the mouth. Preparations of *copper* are also given in cases of *chorea* and *epilepsy*, and yet the administration of copper produce symptoms precisely similar.

Rhubarb and calomel are favourite Allopathic remedies for diarrhœa and dysentery, and yet given in large quantities during health, produce inflammation of the tissues of the bowels, griping pain and frequent discharges. Cubebs and cantharides given in health, produce inflammation of the mucous membrane of the urinary organs, and yet they are unhesitatingly prescribed when this state exists in disease. Ipecac. given in twenty or thirty grains produces vomiting, but the Allopath has found by experience, that given in the tenth or twentieth part of a grain it will relieve vomiting.

Mercury in all those cases where it is found indispensible by the Allopath, is capable, if taken in large doses in health, of producing precisely a similar state. To an ordinary inflammation of the eye, they frequently apply a mild solution of nitrate of silver, and yet this drug applied to the healthy eye, produces that inflamed state. Castor oil, is given to cure diarrhœa, and yet its primary effect is a diarrhœa. The mother has learned by experience, that when her child is injured by a burn, to produce relief, she must hold it to the fire, or apply alcohol, or oil of turpentine. And so we might go on enumerating, and we should find in every case, where a cure is performed by means of drugs, it is in obedience to the homœopathic law.

From what has been already said, we find, that in disease, where the disturbing causes are slight, nature is sufficient of itself to produce a healthy reaction, but when the aid of medicines are required, those medicines must be given in obedience to the law of " Similia similibus curantur."

The vital force reacts with far more power against impressions caused by specific medicinal influences, than against those produced by morbific agents, hence those produced by the latter, often assume a serious character and run on for a long time, while those produced by the former, result in rapid spontaneous recovery.

The medicine acts directly on the part affected, so that as a general thing an exceedingly minute dose is all-sufficient to produce a cure.

In conclusion we have only to say, that homœopathy, founded as it is on truth, on an immutible, unchangeable law, is destined to triumph throughout the world. In Europe, Asia, Africa, America, and the islands of the ocean, its influence is felt and acknowledged. In every land and in every clime it is working its rapid way, the current daily increasing in strength and size, bearing down before it all opposition, and those who are now rash or foolish enough, to oppose its progress must soon either fall in with its current, or be swept away before its rushing tide.

PART SECOND.

TREATMENT OF DISEASE.

CHAPTER I.

FEVER.

In another chapter we have shown, that the human system is like a perfect, beautiful, and harmonious instrument, each particle of matter having its own proper duty to perform, and when that duty is performed correctly, when each organ does its proper work, then the perfect machinery of the body quietly, silently fulfills its duty. There is no aching head, no throbbing pain, no burning fever, but the eye sparkles with health, the cheek is flushed with its rosy hue, the pulse bounds with vigorous life and with strong and elastic step man treads life's pathway, until this glorious temple crumbles away by the slow and undermining influence of age, and, liberating its etherial spiritual form, returns to the dust from whence it sprang.

When, from various causes, any part of the system is clogged in its operation, and is thus prevented from performing its functions aright, the struggle which takes place between the vital, living principle within us, between nature in its effort to throw off this clog, to remove this friction, to restore the organ to its proper tone and strength, produces fever and its accompanying train of symptoms. Therefore fever, instead of being the *disease itself*, is merely occasioned by *vital reaction against* the disease, by the struggle of nature to throw off those clogs which prevent its free action. This struggle, as a matter of course, causes an increased combustion, an increase of heat is therefore the natural consequence, as well as an increased rapidity in the circulation of the blood.

You have seen the important part that the skin performs in the economy of nature, how every part of it is perforated with minute tubes which throw off into the external world in the form of perspiration, not however always perceptible, worn out particles of matter which have performed their part in the economy of life. Close up these minute tubes, either by the sudden action of cold, by being exposed to a draft of air, or by any of the various causes of disease, and you at once disturb the whole economy of nature. Combustion is still going on, chemical changes are constantly taking place, but those particles which should be thrown off are kept within. Now commences, or should commence a contest between the *vital principle*, *nature*, or whatever you please to call it, against those causes which prevent its free action, and the result of this struggle is fever, the torturing pain, the rapid pulse and those various phenomena of disease to which different names have been assigned.

You know the absolute necessity of keeping the organs of respiration in a free and healthy state. Through them we receive oxygen, the life-giving principle of air in exchange for the carbonic acid of the blood, the result of the chemical changes going on in the system. Restrict the action of these organs either by cold, heat, sudden change of temperature, compression of the chest, or any of the varied causes which produce disturbance there, and you cause inflammation, sometimes of a violent form, producing the most agonizing pain, or it may be of a more passive character, ending in suppuration and consumption.

Take if you please the digestive organs. Fill the stomach with food it cannot assimilate, pay no attention to its powers of digestion, when it flags goad it on by stimulants, and you break down its strength, you render the liver torpid, you paralize the intestinal canal, or deprive it of proper action, you force into the system more fuel than is required for the production of animal heat and the sustenance of life. And now the whole machinery of the body is out of order. Nature has been hampered in her movements, abused, trampled on, and yet she rises in all her strength and struggles manfully to vindicate her rights. But the disturbing cause may be too great for her unassisted strength, and she sink paralized, or, roused into too violent action, a highly inflammatory state is the result. In the former case, the disease is of a low, sinking character, in the latter, highly inflammatory. In both cases, the progress is full of danger and the end may be, *death*.

Now is the time for human skill to step in and aid nature in her efforts for relief. How is this to be done? By binding her hand and foot, by opening a vein and drawing away her life, by producing violent action on the bowels, by depleting and paralyzing her every effort at relief, by dragging her down, shorn of her strength until she is perfectly helpless? No! common sense, outraged nature cries no, a thousand times, no. If you cannot aid nature, do not, in the name of heaven, throw obstacles in the way, and thus deprive the poor victim of the last chance of life. If you must meddle with something, meddle with inanimate matter, but oh! trifle not, tamper not with human life.

In disease, nature has an important part to perform. Unassisted, its efforts are to bring about a crisis sufficient for the extermination of the disease. Failing in this, death is the inevitable consequence. Do we aid nature, if we take away her vital power to wrestle with disease? How is it that in violent acute diseases, *Pleurisy* or *Pneumonia*, for instance, in which the patient has been bled, perhaps to fainting, where the depleting system has been carried on heroically? The patient gains, it may be, present relief, but in a short time the fever returns with almost, if not quite its former violence. Nature has been prostrated for the moment, the disease remains untouched, and the blow, which should have been aimed at the cause of the disturbance, is directed against nature. Instead of putting out the robber, who seeks to steal your life, the watchful sentinel, who warns of danger and struggles to repel the intruder, is stricken down at his post. For a moment it is paralized, but then rouses and renews, but with diminished strength, the contest. How much more philosophical and in accordance with nature, to assist her efforts in removing gently, yet surely, the causes of disease. Homœopathic remedies act upon the disease oftentimes in such a specific way, as to remove the trouble without giving rise to any perceptible crisis. A crisis may however take place, in perspiration, diarrhœa, increased flow of urine, or eruption, the particulars of which will be given in their appropriate place.

In the *simple or irritative* form of fever the efforts of nature are generally adequate to the removal of disease.

In the *inflammatory form* the efforts of nature are more powerful, than is necessary, and the termination of the disease, unless human aid steps in, may be fatal.

In the *torpid* form, nature requires aid, but from a different cause. In this case nature is prostrated and has not sufficient power to wrestle with disease.

Before treating directly of the various forms of fever, some remarks are necessary as to general treatment, which is alike advisable in all varieties.

Absolute rest both of the mind and body are very essential. The food should be light in its character, easy of digestion, the patient abstaining carefully from the more solid and stimulating articles of diet. It is fortunate, that in most cases the stomach craves but little food, while there is a constant desire for drink, generally craving cold water, than which there can be nothing better. Ice-water, or even ice held in the mouth, when desired, can be given in small quantities with perfect safety. Toast water, or even lemonade, can also be given, save in looseness of the bowels, or while under the influence of aconite, when acids should be avoided. Should the fever be high, frequent ablutions in cold water are highly refreshing to the patient. The room should be well ventilated, the temperature kept as nearly as possible at an even rate, say from sixty to seventy degrees, according to comfort. The patient should be placed on a matress, lightly covered with blankets, and kept at as comfortable a temperature as possible. The covering should of course be regulated by the feelings of the patient. Cleanliness should be carefully observed, and to this purpose the linen should be frequently changed. In nearly all cases, save where the bowels are disordered, fruits, but little if any tart, such as roast apples, oranges, strawberries, raspberries, and peaches, are, in moderate quantities, allowable. We now proceed to treat more directly of the different varieties of fever.

SIMPLE FEVER.

(FEBRIS SIMPLEX.)

CAUSES.—This fever, unless the forerunner of some other disease, is exceeding simple in its character, generally terminating in the course of two or three days and often running its entire course in twenty-four hours. It is generally occasioned by sudden change of temperature, or undue exposure to heat or cold.

DIAGNOSIS.—A sensation of shivering, followed by heat; thirst, quick pulse, and often an aching sensation in the head and limbs.

TREATMENT.—Aconite, two drops in a tumbler of water, a tablespoonful administered every two hours, the patient remaining quiet, and covered up in bed; perspiration will as a general thing be produced in a few hours, and the patient be entirely relieved in twenty-four hours, unless some other disease should be developed, such as Scarlatina, Measles, &c.

Should there be soreness of the throat, aching of the head and limbs, Belladonna may be given in alternation with the Aconite, a dose of each every four hours.

INFLAMMATORY FEVER.

(FEBRIS INFLAMMATORIA, SYNOCHA.)

CAUSES.—This fever may arise from suppressed perspiration, sudden changes of temperature, external or internal injuries, exposure to heat, damp, or cold. We may generally expect a favourable termination, unless, as is often the case, when treated allopathically, it runs into some other disease, or the patient sinks from exhaustion.

DIAGNOSIS.—Violent chill, preceded by lassitude and followed by great heat, hard, full, quick pulse, dry skin, dry and slightly coated tongue; heaviness of the head, soon passing into an aching pulsative pain particularly in the forehead; red face, sparkling eyes, great thirst, dry hot breath, sometimes hurried and anxious breathing; red and scanty urine, restlessness and anxiety. The symptoms are worse in the evening, generally abating after midnight.

TREATMENT.—The great remedy in controlling the fever is undoubtedly *Aconite.* It acts more directly and powerfully and certainly with far less future harm to the patient, than leeches, blood-letting and cathartics. A dose, prepared as in *simple fever*, may be given every two hours.

Should there be fulness and heat in the head, vertigo, pain in the forehead, flushed face, and sensitiveness to noise or light, red shining eyes, *Belladonna* should be given in alternation, a dose of the first one hour, and of the other the next.

Bryonia, is particularly indicated, where there is tearing, shooting, or aching in the limbs, violent pain in the head with vertigo on rising or moving; delirium, pressure at the pit of the stomach, constipation; violent thirst and burning dry heat mingled with chills. We should look to it as the prominent remedy, where there is oppression, shooting pain in the chest, short cough and difficult breathing. It should be given prepared as the *Aconite*, every two hours, or if there should be much fever, as would most likely be the case, be alternated with *Aconite* a dose of each every two hours.

NERVOUS OR TYPHOID FEVER.

(TYPHUS.)

This disease is of a low sinking character, the nervous system being particularly involved. Under this head we may include the dreaded, and so often fatal, *ship* and *hospital fevers.* They are in reality a violent form of Typhus.

This fever may assume from the commencement the form of Typhus, or, as is very often the case, especially under the prostrating treatment of the Allopathic school, other varieties of fever may run into this low sinking and more dangerous malady. Besides the two forms already mentioned, there are three forms of Typhus, more or less distinct, notwithstanding the general symptoms may be the same. These are;

1. *Cerebral Typhus*, or *Typhus cerebralis*, affecting principally the brain and the nervous system.

2. *Typhus Abdominalis*, or *abdominal Typhus*, where some part of the abdomen is the principal seat of the disease.

3. *Pneumo Typhus*, or *Typhus of the lungs. Typhoid lung fever*, or *Typhoid Pneumonia*, affecting the organs of the chest.

Typhus in its progress may indicate a high state of nervous action (*Typhus versatalis*), or the patient may be constantly inclined to stupor (*Typhus stupidus*), or it may be of a putrid character (*Typhus Putridus*), where there is a strong tendency to disorganization and decay. This is the most alarming form of the disease.

Causes.—The causes are numerous, and some of them remote. It may arise from hunger, bad food, ill-ventilated apartments, where numbers are crowded into a small space and the air rendered highly impure, exposure, want of cleanliness and those hundred causes, to which the poor are exposed. It may arise also from chagrin, sadness, grief, care, disappointed love, disappointment in business, violent exertions of the mind and body, venereal excess, depressing emotions, excessive heat, prostration from disease, or from medical treatment, which may be worse than the disease ; dampness, cold, and a peculiar state of the atmosphere, which may fail to give sufficient sustenance to the vital forces, and thus develop epidemic Typhus.

The progress of the disease is often slow, sometimes lasting 21 or 28 days, and even longer. The convalescence is also slow, and the patient, unless great care is used, very liable to a relapse. The precursory symptoms, headache, lassitude and a general derangement of the system, unless controlled by appropriate remedies, not unfrequently last for days and even weeks. Perfect quiet, great cleanliness, a room well ventilated and not too dark, are absolutely essential. There are several indications which every good nurse can watch, and which will indicate to a certain extent the danger, or immediate prospect of convalescence.

1. *The Pulse.* Should this gradually become quiet and

even, hope would naturally and justly brighten, but the more accelerated it becomes, the more the danger to the patient increases. A constant variation in the pulse is a worse indication even than its frequency.

2. *The Urine.* Should it be clear, thick, brown, bloody, or with a cloud floating or rising towards the surface, or with a sediment, with the urine turbid above it, the danger is great, but should there be a gradual clearing up of urine previously thick, or previously clear urine become turbid, improvement is indicated.

3. *Hemorrhages*, especially by urine and stool, diarrhœa, putrid, fetid smell, are indicative of putrid dissolution. Deafness, though naturally exciting alarm in the friends, is by no means an unfavourable symptom.

Diagnosis.—This disease, notwithstanding it steals on, as a general thing, slowly, yet it firmly and surely gains a footing, unless arrested by appropriate remedies, and may in a short time so prostrate the system as to render the prospect of recovery extremely hazardous. During the premonitory stage, the patient is languid, easily tired; he loses his appetite, the tongue becomes white, and inclined to tremble. There are wandering pains in the head, chest, back, abdomen or extremities, fulness and giddiness of the head, drowsiness, and unsound and unrefreshing sleep at night. These precursory symptoms may last for days or weeks. The commencement of the fever is marked, not by a violent chill, but by slow chills alternating with heat, and sometimes violent headache. The expression of the face is dull and heavy, and there is no desire for exertion either of the mind or body. On pressing heavily on the abdomen near the right hip, a sensation of pain is distinctly felt. As the disease progresses, the skin becomes dry and hot, the appearance of the tongue is exceedingly variable. At times it may be clean, smooth and red, then again slightly furred, the tip and edges red, with a dark brown almost black streak in the centre, or the whole tongue become dark and excessively dry. Sordes form about the teeth. Delirium, generally of a low muttering kind, although sometimes more violent in its character, a vacant or indifferent look, perfect indifference to every thing, stupor, gradually sinking down in the bed diarrhœa, &c. are among the symptoms which may be developed during the progress of the disease.

TREATMENT.—Perfect quiet, cleanliness, a room well ventilated and not too dark, cold water, or toast water, whenever desired, are of course essential. If during the precursory symptoms there should be chilliness, lassitude, with alternate heat, headache, giddiness, rheumatic pains, pain in the back, furred tongue and restlessness at night, *Bryonia* and *Rhus*, two drops in a tumbler of water may be used in alternation two hours apart. These will often be sufficient to arrest the disease, but should inflammatory symptoms set in, such as a dry and burning skin, hard full pulse, restlessness, thirst, congestion of blood to the head, *Aconite* should be administered every two hours.

Belladonna is indicated in the commencement of the disease, where it is occasioned by fright or chagrin, where convulsive twitching of the limbs, and a general feeling of restlessness is present, especially in the limbs; or where it commences with fainting turns which are followed by extreme sensitiveness of all the organs; or where there is a continual drowsiness increasing to lethargy, with snoring, during which the countenance changes from cold and pale to red and hot, disturbed sleep, anxious and restless when awake, with internal heat and headache. Where also the inflammatory symptoms indicating Aconite are present, the two remedies should be given in alternation, a dose of each every two hours.

Belladonna, is also particularly indicated where in the progress of the disease the delirium becomes more furious; there are visions while awake, starts as from affright, internal burning heat, without thirst, distension of the veins and throbbing of the arteries of the head, pressing pain in the temples, intolerance to noise; the eyes may be congested; the tongue is red, burning hot, and parched, the mouth and throat dry, deglutition difficult, abdomen distended and sensitive to the touch, and frequent diarrhœic stools. Where these symptoms appear Belladonna should be given every two hours.

Bryonia is a most valuable remedy in Typhus, and is frequently indicated. It is often appropriate in alternation with *Rhus.* Its indications are a bruised, aching sensation throughout the whole body. The most downy bed would feel hard. Beating, pressing pain in the forehead from within outward, particularly painful when looking up or moving the eyes, burning sensation of the head, notwithstanding the forehead may be covered with a cold sweat, moaning during sleep, heat and frightful dreams. In the commencement of the disease where heat alternates with chilliness, the former in the morning, the latter in the afternoon, and where there is moderate thirst, vertigo, increase of headache and excessive erethism of the nervous system, and where gastric symptoms are present, such as bitter taste, yellow coating of the tongue, nausea, vomiting, and difficult stool, *Bryonia* is strongly indicated. This remedy is also indicated where in the progress of the disease the heat becomes permanent, and is accompanied with delirium, but little complaint of pain, yet grasping at the head, delirious talk of business, face red and bloated, lips dry and cracked, white miliary eruption and constipation.

Dose.—Prepared as before directed, and given once in two or three hours.

Rhus tox. is a very important remedy, particularly in the "*versatile*" and stupid forms of Typhus, especially the latter, and also where the convalescence is slow, the pulse continuing feverish, and the diarrhœa and oppression of the chest not entirely removed.

In the precursory stage there is chilliness even near the fire, colic and diarrhœa, bruised sensation in various parts, white-coated tongue, nausea, vomiting of mucus, and vertigo; a stiff and lame sensation when at rest, numbness of the parts on which the patient lies, and a stinging, drawing and rigidity in the nape of the neck and back. As the disease advances there is great weakness and prostration, sleeplessness, great restlessness at night with anguish or heavy sleep, with murmurs, snoring, dry heat, sleep disturbed by troublesome dreams, frequent starting and throwing off the clothes. Talkative delirium, frequent desire to run away, stupifying headache, vertigo on rising up. As abdominal typhus gradually develops itself, the heat and violent delirium become continuous, the cutting in the abdomen and diarrhœa are followed by pain in the limbs, great weakness, tongue and lips blackish, cheeks burning red, sopor, with muttering, snoring and small accelerated pulse. The eyes are red and uninfluenced by outward impression, the odour from the mouth is fetid, the stools involuntary, and the urine whitish and turbid. Oppression of the chest strongly indicates *Rhus.* It should be given prepared as *Bryonia*, a dose every two hours, unless in alternation with *Bryonia* or some other remedy, when it should be taken every four hours.

Opium.—Is indicated where there is a constant desire to sleep, or a lethargic sleep with laboured respiration and snoring, hard full pulse. It should be given, prepared as *Bryonia*, a dose every two or three hours.

Hyosciamus.—Excessive wildness, great nervous excitability, furious delirium with visions, or apathy and stupidity, fixed and dull eyes, surrounded by a livid circle, or red and sparkling eyes with pupils either dilated or contracted.

DOSE.—Same as Opium.

Strammonium.—Violent pain in the head, with fainting, delirium, violent tossing, illusions of sight, loss of consciousness, dilated and insensible pupils, lethargic sleep and snoring. Dose, same as Hyosciamus.

Phosphorus, is principally indicated when the disease arises from cold or onanism. In the precursory stage there are rheumatic pain in the limbs, worse morning and evening, and aggravated by cold air or the touch, and sometimes accompanied with a general sensation of sickness, a weary bruised feeling, tightness of the head, palpitation of the heart, and pain in the stomach and bowels. As the disease progresses, there is a small, hard, quick pulse, profuse sweat; sleep interrupted by shrieks, moaning, stitches, and rattling in the chest, oppressive cough and bloody expectoration, painfulness of every part of the body. The above group of symptoms occurring in Typhoid Pneumonia are very accurately covered by this remedy. There may also be painful sensitiveness in the abdomen near the right hip, sometimes accompanied by half liquid bloody stools, beating pain in the head, and discharge of blood from the nose.

DOSE.—A powder or three globules every two or three hours.

Phosphoric acid.—Great prostration, flighty, even when awake, aversion to conversation, always on the back, in a drowsy state, replying to questions incoherently or not answering at all, low muttering delirium, dryness of the tongue, dry and burning skin, loose evacuations generally passed involuntarily and sometimes bloody, frequent, weak, and sometimes intermitting pulse. The remedy should be alternated with *Rhus*, a dose every three hours.

Arsenic.—If in connection with the above symptoms there is a rapid sinking of the vital powers, great prostration of strength, countenance deathly, eyes dull and glassy, pulse scarcely perceptible, burning thirst and diarrhœa, give *Arsenic* every hour. Should the evacuations be fetid, cold perspiration on the face and extremities, rattling respiration, *Carbo veg.* should be given in alternation, a dose of each every hour.

DOSE.—Same as *Phosphorus*.

Muriatic acid is an important remedy in Typhus stupidus where there is sliding down in the bed, with moaning and groaning during sleep, and constant muttering when awake, with inability to collect the senses, paralytic condition of the tongue, with dryness of the mouth and fauces. Where these symptoms occur it is generally best to give the acid in alternation with *Opium*, a dose of each every four hours. Where the acid is given alone, it should be given once in three hours. Sufficient may be dissolved in a tumbler of water to make it slightly tart, and a tablespoonful given at a dose.

Besides the remedies already enumerated, we will mention a list which may at times be found highly serviceable. For particular indications, see Materia Medica at the close of the book. *Arnica*, *Camphor*, *China*, *Coffea*, *Cantharides*, *Cocculus*, *Ipecac*, *Ignatia*, *Lachesis*, *Lycopodium*, *Nux-vom.*, *Pulsatilla*, *Mercurius*, *Veratrum*, *Sulphur*.

For *Cerebral Typhus* or *brain fever* the principal remedies are *Acon.*, *Bell.*, *Bry.*, *Hyos.*, *Op.*, *Rhus.*

For *Typhoid lung fever. Ip.*, *Bry.* and *Rhus*, or *Ars.*, *Chin.*, *Hyos.*, *Phosphor* , *Phos.-ac.*, *Sulph.*, *Laurocerasus.*

For *Abdominal Typhus*, *Rhus* or *Bry.* or *Ars.*, *Chin.* and *Merc.*, or *Arn. Carb. v.*, *Nux-vom.*, *Puls.* and *Sulph. Canth.* and *Phos.*

YELLOW FEVER.

This disease prevails principally in warm climates and is peculiarly fatal where it attacks persons who are not acclimated, and who, coming from a colder region, seem to forget, that a change of climate would naturally indicate a change in habit, dress and diet. In a previous chapter we have spoken of the different amount of oxygen contained in a warm and moist climate, where the heat continues for months, and in the colder regions of the temperate and frigid zones, where the intense heat is of but few days or weeks' duration. The amount of food, both in kind and quantity, should be materially different in warm climates from that in regions at greater distance from the equator. In the rarified air of the former, a less amount of oxygen is taken into the system, and therefore less solid nourishing food is required than in colder regions, where the air is more condensed, thus necessarily containing more oxygen. Food introduced into the system and not consumed, remains as a clog and irritant, encumbering the organs, cramping their operation, and sowing in the body the seeds of decay. Hence, in these warm climates great caution is necessary not only as it regards diet, but also clothing and exposure to the heat of the midday sun and the dampness of the night.

Causes.—Animal and vegetable substances exposed to continued heat in a moist atmosphere soon decay, and fill the air with a poisonous miasmata. This miasm, may give rise to yellow fever, especially where it is produced by the decaying animal and vegetable substances found in close streets, the crowded and ill-ventilated rooms and cellars, and the necessarily confined air of the populous city or village. The chemist, perhaps, would hardly undertake to detect the subtile poison in the atmosphere, by which the life-springs of thousands are tainted, and yet he can laugh right merrily at the folly and absurdity of infinitesimal doses. Other prominent causes, are exposure to the heat of the sun, mental anxiety, want of cleanliness, dissipation, a fondness for stimulants both in food and drink, in reality a greater love for the palate and stomach, than for life and health. This is one great cause, why the disease is more frequent and much more fatal among that class of residents who foolishly persist in indulging in the same variety of food, the same style of living, the same habits they were accustomed to in their colder home.

Diagnosis.—This fearful pestilence is looked upon as almost as fatal as that terrific scourge, the Cholera. Sometimes the patient is taken down when at his daily avocations, without warning, and in a few hours is a corpse. In other cases the disease approaches more slowly, the premonitory symptoms being well marked. The severity of the disease, as we have before stated, depends much upon the constitution, habits and temperament of the patient.

The first symptoms are generally want of appetite, constipation, oppression of the stomach, giddiness and debility. Where the attack comes on with violence, there is cold, shuddering, headache, nausea and vomiting. This is followed by severe pain in the back, and tearing pain in the limbs, sometimes amounting to cramps. These sensations last for a few hours, and are followed by violent reaction. The breathing becomes difficult, the breath burning, the pulse hard, full, and quick, the checks red and turgid, the conjunctiva injected, violent pain in the head and throughout the body, skin dry and hot, burning thirst, nausea and vomiting. The abdomen becomes hard and painful, and a sensation of great suffering is felt in the stomach. This period, lasting in severe cases from twelve to twenty-four hours, although sometimes it continues three or four days, is followed by what seems to the patient almost an entire remission. For a few hours the patient is comparatively comfortable, notwithstanding there may be some nausea and distress about the stomach, but this rest is speedily followed by a return of many of the old symptoms with increased violence. The skin and eyes acquire a yellow tinge. The tongue is parched and covered with a dark fur, the skin clammy, the head confused, the pulse sinks, delirium may set in, the retching increase in violence, the matter vomited presents a darker and thicker appearance, and the stomach is painful and sensitive.

This stage may last from twelve to forty-eight hours, sometimes with slight remissions towards the termination, when it is followed by the third stage, when the symptoms increase at a fearful rate. The strength fails rapidly, there is extreme prostration, the tongue and lips are parched and cracked, the gums soft and livid, exuding black blood; there is intense suffering in the stomach, great anxiety, hiccough, the dreaded *black vomit*, getting darker and darker, and more and more frequent, until death closes the painful scene. On the setting in of the third stage, the patient is generally beyond the power of earthly aid.

Treatment.—The most important remedies are,—in the *first stage*, and sometimes in the second, *Aconite*, *Ipecac.*, *Belladonna*, *Bryonia*, *Pulsatilla* and *Nux-vom.* In the *second* and *third* stage, *Nux-vom.*, *Mercurius-sol*, *Arsenicum*, *Argent-nit*, *Digitalis*, *Phos.-ac.*, *Rhus-tox.*, *Verat.*, *Canth*, *Carb.-veg.* and when there are black dejections, *Hellebore.*

Ipecac.—Is generally indicated in the first stage, where slight chills, general pains, uneasiness in the stomach, nausea and vomiting, together with a sensation of faintness are present.

Dose.—A powder, or three globules dry on the tongue every two hours.

Aconite.—Should the symptoms after a short time remain unabated, or change for the worse, other remedies are indicated, and the treatment should be of the most prompt and decided character. *Aconite* is indicated where there is violent febrile reaction; dry and hot skin, great thirst, full and rapid pulse, short and anxious respiration, restlessness and anguish; eyes red and sensitive, mouth dry, great internal heat; pain in the forehead and head, also in the back and limbs, heat and sensitiveness of the stomach; nausea, vomiting, and a general sense of prostration.

DOSE.—This remedy is particularly indicated in the first and sometimes in the second stage of the disease. It is often indicated in alternation with Belladonna, when it should be given two drops of the tincture, or six globules, dissolved in a tumbler of water, a tablespoonful every two hours. When given alone, it should be taken every two or three hours, according to the violence of symptoms.

Belladonna.—Indicated mostly in the first stage of the disease, where there are sharp shooting pains or violent throbbing in the head; face bloated and red, eyes sparkling and red, or fixed, glistening and prominent, pulse variable, burning thirst and heat, tongue loaded with whitish yellow or brown coating; nausea or vomiting; aching and cramplike pains in the loins, back and legs; during the fever, great restlessness and anguish.

DOSE.—The same as Aconite.

Bryonia.—Headache increased by movement, pains in the back, loins, and limbs; pulse rapid, full or weak; great thirst, tongue dry with white or yellow coating; yellow skin; eyes painful on motion, red, or dull and glassy, or sparkling and filled with tears. Pain and burning in the stomach, or fullness and oppression; vomiting or nausea, particularly after drinking; restlessness, anxiety and delirium.

DOSE.—The same as Aconite. Give every two or three hours. Sometimes the remedy can be alternated with *Rhus.*

Rhus.—Dull, glazed, and sunken eyes; dry and black tongue, pulse quick and small; talkative delirium, or partial stupor; moaning and great restlessness, particularly at night. Violent pain and burning in the stomach; spasms in the abdomen; numbness or partial paralysis of the lower extremities; nausea and vomiting, colic, diarrhœa, and difficult deglutition.

DOSE.—Same as Bryonia.

Nux-vom.—Eyes yellow or inflamed; yellow skin; pulse

variable ; tongue dry, cracked and brown, or coated with a white or yellow fur ; vertigo ; pains in the head ; pressure, cramp-like or burning pain in the stomach ; hiccough ; bilious or acid vomiting ; tremors of the limbs ; great desire for stimulants ; frequent movements of slimy, bloody, or bilious matter ; coldness, cramps, and numbness in the lower extremities.

DOSE.—A powder or three globules every two hours.

Mercurius.—Tongue moist and white, or dry and brown, pulse very changeable, now quick, strong and intermittent, and again weak and trembling ; loss of strength and feeling of fatigue ; vertigo or pain in the head ; convulsive vomiting of bilious matter ; extreme tenderness of the stomach ; coldness and cramps in the arms and legs ; constipation or loose mucous, bloody or bilious discharges.

DOSE.—Same as *Nux.*

Arsenic.—Changeable expression of countenance, generally a yellowish, bluish, or deathly cast ; sunken eyes, surrounded by a dark circle ; lips and tongue brown or black ; nose pointed ; cold clammy sweat, pulse irregular, generally quick, weak, and small, or trembling, indicating great prostration ; burning pains, especially in the region of the stomach and liver, sometimes with oppression of the stomach, and vomiting, particularly after drinking ; diarrhœa sometimes with pain and tenesmus, though often involuntary ; pain in the abdomen as from a weight ; oppression of the chest, with rapid and anxious respiration. Delirium, low muttering, or talkative ; loss of consciousness. This remedy is peculiarly applicable in the second and third stage, where there is a rapid sinking of the vital power.

DOSE.—Give a powder, or dissolve six globules in a tumbler of water, and give a tablespoonful every half hour or hour, as the symptoms may indicate.

Veratrum.—This remedy is principally indicated in the second and third stage, where there is a general coldness, particularly of the hands and feet, which may be covered with a cold perspiration ; cramps in the upper and lower extremities, and in the stomach and abdomen ; frequent loose evacuations ; pain in the abdomen and stomach ; vertigo ; great thirst ; severe vomiting, sometimes of bile and mucus, and again of black bile and blood. Loss of sense, stupor or violent delirium.

Dose.—One drop or six globules in a tumbler of water, a tablespoonful every half hour, hour, or two hours, according to symptoms.

Phos. ac.—Stupidity ; aversion to conversation ; great prostration, stupid expression, with glassy hollow eyes ; sleeplessness, restless, or sleepiness, or delirium, with picking the clothes. Cold perspiration, with anxiety and oppression of the chest.

Dose.—Six globules in a glass of water, a tablespoonful every hour.

Besides the remedies we have already enumerated, *Canth.*, *Carb. veg.*, *Lach.* and *Sulph.* may also be serviceable. For particular indications, see Materia Medica, at the close of the book.

BILIOUS REMITTENT, REMITTENT OR BILIOUS FEVER.
(FEBRIS REMITTENS.)

Causes.—In this country, this form of fever is most violent, and prevails to a greater extent in the southern and western states. It is the endemial fever of warm climates, particularly where the soil is marshy, the country new, and the vegetation rich. It is by no means rare however in more temperate climates, particularly in the autumn or during a summer of great heat ; it sometimes develops itself in the winter and spring. In addition to causes already named, we may mention dissipation, either in eating or drinking, exposure to changes of temperature, anger, fear, or grief, and in fact, any of the numerous causes by which the digestive organs are disturbed.

Diagnosis.—This fever holds perhaps an intermediate place between the intermittent, and the Typhoid, into which, either from bad treatment or the weakness and temperament of the patient, it often runs. There are generally premonitory symptoms, such as headache, unpleasant sensation of the stomach, and general uneasiness. A chill, more or less severe, is followed by flushes of heat; mouth clammy and dry; thirst, nausea, and occasionally vomiting; pain in the head, back, and limbs, with hurried respiration and frequent, small, and sometimes irregular pulse. These symptoms are speedily followed by great febrile heat. There is a dry skin, violent and throbbing pain in the head, flushed face, full and rapid pulse, and sometimes delirium. The tongue is white, there is a tenderness of the epigastrium, with occasional vomiting; the urine is high coloured, and the bowels generally constipated. In twelve or fourteen hours a remission of the symptoms generally takes place, although the fever does not entirely subside. After a calm of two or three hours the exacerbation again takes place, becoming shorter in duration, and less violent as the disease abates. In the more severe forms of fever the remission may be scarcely perceptible, yet there are certain indications always present,—viz., gastric irritability, a sense of oppression, and distress of the epigastrium, pain in the head, back, and limbs, and prostration of the strength early in the disease. Convalescence is indicated by the remissions becoming more distinct, the pulse full, soft, and less frequent, and the bowels and stomach more regular and healthy in their action. The disease may continue fourteen days or even longer, although under the judicious use of homœopathic remedies, it not unfrequently disappears in a very few days.

Treatment.—As we have before stated, there are generally premonitory symptoms, before the fever sets in, indicating a derangement of the stomach and bowels, sometimes lasting several days. Taken in hand now, a few doses of medicine will often remove every symptom of disease, and thus prevent a sometimes long and tedious fever.

In cases of indigestion, where there is fulness and weight of the stomach, nausea and vomiting, *Ipecac.* and *Pulsatilla* are the prominent remedies. *Pulsatilla* is particularly indicated where these symptoms arise from the use of fatty food. The latter remedy, if nausea still continues after a short time, can be followed by *Ant. crud.*

Where the disease is occasioned by changes of temperature, *Bryonia*, *Rhus* and *Stibium* are indicated. *Chamomilla* when occasioned by anger, and *Ignatia* if by vexation, grief, or shame.

Aconite.—Is strongly indicated on the setting in of febrile symptoms, where there is high fever, rapid pulse, great thirst, yellow coating on the tongue; bitter taste; bitter, greenish or slimy vomiting, painfulness in the region of the stomach and the liver, and severe headache. Either *Bryonia*, *Belladonna* or *Pulsatilla* may be indicated in alternation with *Aconite.* Mix two drops in a tumbler of water, and give a tablespoonful every two hours.

Bryonia.—Where there is aching or tired sensation in the head, back, and limbs; constipation; bilious vomiting especially after drinking; great heat, or shivering with heat in the face; great desire for acids, and aversion to food, bitter or insipid taste; dry, brownish-yellow tongue.

Belladonna.—Violent pain in the head, particularly the forehead; dry mouth; yellowish or white tongue; heat about the head with thirst, alternating with chills; vomiting of sour or bitter substances; sopor in the day time, and sleepless nights.

Pulsatilla.—Whitish tongue; flat, pappy, or bitter taste; bitter and offensive belching; aversion to food, and desire for acids; nausea; vomiting of food, mucous or sour and bitter substances; pressure in the stomach, and difficult breathing; inclination to diarrhœa and frequent shivering.

Chamomilla.—Bitter taste, fetid smell from the mouth; loss of appetite; nausea, and sour or bitter vomiting; anguish, tightness, and pressure in the stomach; flatulent colic; constipation; diarrhœa with greenish or sour stools; restlessness, and ill-humour; heat of the face and eyes, with red cheeks, or heat with shivering.

Veratrum.—Great debility after a stool; bilious vomiting and diarrhœa; pain in the abdomen, and coldness of the extremities.

DOSE.—The above class of remedies should be given, one drop of the tincture, or six globules in a glass of water, a tablespoonful every one, two or three hours, as severity of the symptoms indicate.

Ipecac.—More particularly in the first part of the disease, where there is loathing of food, nausea, ineffectual efforts to vomit, or vomiting; pressure and painful fulness in the pit of the stomach; diarrhœa; aching in the forehead; heat with thirst or shiverings.

Nux-vom.—Dry and white or yellowish tongue; bitter taste; nausea, and vomiting, particularly when in the air; cardialgia; tightness, and pressure in the region of the stomach; spasmodic colic; constipation with frequent and ineffectual urging to stool, or with slimy or watery stools; aching in the forehead with vertigo; ill-humour; heat with shivering; bruised sensation in the limbs.

Mercurius.—Moist, white, or yellowish tongue; painfulness of the stomach and abdomen, particularly at night, with anguish and restlessness; sleepy in the day, and wakeful at night; ill-humour.

Arsenicum.—Great debility; burning sensation and sensitiveness of the stomach, often with nausea and vomiting.

Colocynth.—Violent colic, particularly after eating, sometimes with diarrhœa; cramp in the calves.

Stibium.—A prominent remedy in bilious fever, generally in alternation with Bryonia. Nausea, gagging and vomiting, aching pain in the forehead, bruised sensation in the limbs; oppression of breathing, dry heat and rapid pulse.

Carb. veg.—Acidity of the stomach; fulness of the head; putrid diarrhœa and great prostration.

Antimonium.—Following Ipecac. or Pulsatilla, where those remedies are not sufficient.

Rhus is often indicated in alternation with Bryonia; for its particular indications as well as for those of Sulphur, see Materia Medica.

Dose.—Six globules, or a powder dry on the tongue; or one drop of the tincture in a glass of water, a tablespoonful every one, two, or three hours, according to symptoms.

INTERMITTENT FEVERS.

Chills and Fever. Fever and Ague.

FEBRES INTERMITTENS.

The symptoms of this fever are so marked, that there is no difficulty in distinguishing it from all other forms. In Remittent Fever, the fever is never entirely absent during the remission, while in Intermittent the paroxysm comes on, and in a few hours, passes entirely off, leaving the patient without any perceptible trace of the fever.

It prevails more extensively in marshy countries, particularly at the south and west, where the land is being drained, forests leveled, and the rich soil turned up by the plow. The air is poisoned with a miasm so subtile in its character as to defy detection, and yet so powerful as to prostrate the strongest man. It may also be developed after other diseases.

Diagnosis.—The paroxysm is generally marked by three distinct stages, viz. 1st, *cold;* 2d, *fever;* and 3d, *sweating stage;* although these stages sometimes seem commingled together. The symptoms in this disease are exceedingly variable. In some cases, the paroxysms appear every day, in others, every other day, and again, once in three or four days or even one or two weeks apart.

The cold stage is preceded by headache, languor, and a stretching sensation; blueness of the nails, and numbness of the toes and fingers. The coldness and shivering of the limbs and back gradually increase and pervade the whole body, the teeth chatter, the shivering is so violent as to shake the bed; the application of external warmth produces no immediate effect. There is oppression of the chest, pain in the head or stupor and delirium. The pulse is weak and oppressed.

This stage varies in violence and duration, lasting from half an hour to three hours, when it is followed by the *hot stage.*

This stage is characterized by violent fever, quick, wiry, and rapid pulse, great thirst, dry skin, flushed face, pain in the head, and sometimes delirium, hurried breathing, and oppression of the chest.

It lasts from three to twelve hours, when it terminates in

the sweating stage, or, as is sometimes the case in warm climates, runs into Remittent, or continued fever.

Sweating stage. The violence of the fever begins to abate and is succeeded by profuse perspiration : the pulse becomes less frequent, soft and full, and the aches and pains rapidly disappear, until all traces of the former violent paroxysm have entirely subsided.

TREATMENT.—The remedies indicated are numerous, and should be selected with great care. No disease requires more care in the selection of remedies than this. A prominent remedy in distinctly marked Intermittent, where all three of the stages are clearly and distinctly defined, is undoubtedly,

Quinine.—Those of our Allopathic friends, who cure Intermittent, without leaving after unpleasant consequences, would be somewhat surprised, if told the action of that drug is purely homœopathic, and their patient is cured strictly on the homœopathic principle.

DOSE.—Ten grains may be thoroughly triturated with twice the amount of white sugar, or sugar of milk, and made into ten powders, one of which can be taken every three hours, during the intermission of the paroxysm, or five grains may be dissolved in ten tablespoonfuls of water, and a tablespoonful taken in the same way. During the paroxysm, the remedy must be discontinued. Even if it should not return, a powder should still be given every day for five or six days.

In addition to the above remedy, one or more of the following well selected, are frequently sufficient to produce a speedy cure. *Acon., Ars., Ant.-crud., Ipecac., Nux-vom., Puls., Bry., Verat., Sab., Ignatia., Cham., Lach., Rhus., Caps., Sulph , Op., Carbo-veg., Cocc., Bell.*

Ipecac. is often highly beneficial in connection with *Nux*, particularly in the commencement of the disease.

DOSE.—A powder, or three globules, should be given every three hours between the paroxysms, and a powder or three globules of *Nux.* immediately after the attack. If the next attack should be equally violent, of course another remedy should be selected. If the tincture is given, one drop may be dissolved in a tumbler half full of water, and a tablepoonful taken at a dose. The particular indications for Ipecac. are — much shivering with but little heat, or the contrary; shivering increased by external warmth; oppression of the precordial region; nausea, vomiting. It is also particularly indicated in that variety, where the third or sweating stage is scarcely perceptible.

Nux-vom.—This remedy as well as *Verat.*, *Bry.*, *Bell.*, *Coc.*, *Puls.* and *Ipecac.* will be found useful, where the bowels are constipated, and when errors in diet give rise to bilious symptoms. It is more particularly indicated in those fevers, where the paroxysm comes on every day or every other day, generally in the afternoon, evening, or night, and where there is aching pain in the forehead, vertigo, nausea, and bitter taste; spasms of the stomach, and great weakness. We shall also find it useful, where there are, particularly at the commencement of the disease, paralytic weakness of the limbs, giddiness and prostration; difficult breathing, palpitation of the heart, shivering, followed by anxiety and warmth; violent headache, increased by walking and the open air; burning, itching, and sometimes delirium.

Dose.—Same as *Ipecac.*, with which it may be compared.

Belladonna.—Violent headache with dizziness; shivering, with moderate heat, or the contrary. Heat with redness of the face and pulsation of the arteries.

Dose.—Two drops or six globules, dissolved in a tumbler of water, a tablespoonful every two hours, during the paroxysm; where the fever has been of long standing, every six hours during the intermission.

Arsenic.—Is a prominent remedy in this disease, particularly where the stages are not distinctly marked, but are in a measure commingled; or where there is burning heat, with anguish, restlessness, and great thirst; great prostration of strength; nausea, retching and vomiting; severe pains in the stomach and throughout the body. Preceding the chilly stage, there is often stretching, yawning, headache, vertigo, with stupefaction; between the chilly and hot stage, debility and sleep, vertigo, thirst, nausea and vomiting.

Dose.—Same as *Ipecac.*, given during the intermission of

the fever every three hours. (Compare Chin. *Ipecac.* and *Verat.*

Veratrum.—Is indicated in those fevers which consist simply of external coldness, or internal heat, with dark urine, or when a warm sweat is present, soon becoming cold, accompanied with vertigo, nausea, and great pain in the back.

Dose.—Same as Belladonna. Give every two hours during the continuation of the symptoms.

Pulsatilla.—Will be found beneficial, where there is vomiting of mucus ; moderate thirst, pain in the head, and oppression of the chest, during the cold stage, and shivering when uncovered, during the hot and sweating stage ; aggravation in the afternoon or evening ; gastric or bilious affections with their accompanying symptoms between the paroxysms.

Dose.—Same as Belladonna. Give during the intermission of fever every two or three hours.

Ant.-cr.—Has a close resemblance to Pulsatilla. The perspiration is simultaneous with the heat, and suddenly disappears leaving dry heat, thirst, want of appetite, nausea, vomiting, pressure in the stomach, and pain in the chest.

Dose.—Same as *Ipecac.* Give same as *Belladonna.*

Bryonia.—Where the paroxysms occur daily or every other day, particularly in the morning, preceded by vertigo, pain in the forehead ; coldness and shivering more prominent than heat. During the chilly and hot stage, dry cough, stinging in the chest, asthma, nausea.

Dose.—Same as *Belladonna.*

Opium.—Particularly in young and old persons, where there is great drowsiness, snoring sleep, flushed face. Give a tablespoonful every two hours, during fever.

Dose.—One drop or six globules in a tumbler of water.

Rhus.—Is nearly related to Bryonia, with which it can often be given in alternation. The chilliness is sometimes attended with pain in the limbs, headache, vertigo and nausea. There is generally great restlessness and thirst ; gastric symptoms, nettle rash ; convulsions and hardness of hearing.

Dose.—Same as *Belladonna.*

Ignatia.—Coldness, alleviated by external warmth ; thirst, only in the chilly stage ; confusion, or bruised pain in the head, pressure in the pit of the stomach, debility, pale countenance snoring sleep, thirst after the fever.

Dose.—Same as *Belladonna.*

Sabadilla.—Paroxysms recur at the same hour; short, chilly stage followed by thirst, then heat; fever, consisting entirely of chills; chilliness during the intermission of fever, want of appetite, nightly dry cough, pains in the chest, oppression of breathing.

Dose.—Same as *Opium.*

Carb.-veg.—Chills principally in the evening or night; thirst only during shivering; during the hot stage, vertigo, nausea, headache, oppression in the chest and pain in the stomach, abdomen and bowels; rheumatic pains in the teeth and limbs before and during the fever.

Dose.—Same as *Ipecac.*

Capsicum.—Prevalence of the chilly stage, during which alone there is thirst; heat and sweat simultaneous; restlessness, headache or confusion of the head, sensitive to noise, vomiting of mucus, pain in the chest and back, tearing in the limbs, diarrhœa with slime and burning fæces. (Compare with Carb.-v.)

Dose.—Same as *Belladonna.*

Nat.-mur.—Pains in the bones and back, headache, debility and yellow livid complexion; loss of appetite and painful sensitiveness of the stomach. During the chilly stage shortness of breath, yawning, drowsiness, and thirst. (Compare with Caps, and Carb.)

Dose.—Same as *Ipecac.*

China.—Before the fever, nausea, headache, anxiety, palpitation of the heart. Shivering alternating with heat, or heat long after the chill. Uneasy sleep, yellow complexion, and general gastric symptoms.

Dose.—Same as *Belladonna.*

Aconite.—When the paroxysms of fever are violent, *Aconite* should be given, two drops in a tumbler of water, a tablespoonful every hour.

For general directions as to the administration of remedies, see page 12.

CHAPTER II.

CUTANEOUS DISEASES.

The skin is liable to an almost innumerable class of diseases, some affecting also other organs, and even the whole system, accompanied with severe pain, violent fever and often delirium, ending, unless speedily relieved, in death. Others are of a more chronic character, attended with but little, if any fever, oftentimes tedious in their cure, and generally far more annoying than dangerous. Among the former class we may mention, *Scarlet Fever*, *Erysipelas*, *Measles*, and *Small-Pox*.

Scarlet Fever, Measles, Chicken-Pox, and Small-Pox, are infectious, and generally prevail as epidemics. Very seldom is a person attacked with either of the above diseases more than once. The danger of infection is greatest after death. Infection seldom if ever takes place before the eruption appears, but from that time until the pustules have fairly dried up, or the eruption has in a great measure subsided, the infectious matter is being constantly thrown from the system.

For the sake of convenience, we shall divide eruptive diseases into two classes. 1. *Eruptive Fever*. 2. *General Cutaneous Diseases.*

1. ERUPTIVE FEVERS.

NETTLE RASH. URTICARIA.

This rash is seldom dangerous, although excessively tormenting. The eruption resembles very much that produced by the sting of the nettle, hence its name, *Nettle Rash* or *Urticaria; Urtica,* being the Latin for nettle. It consists of an irregular. pale red, or whitish eminence, surrounded by a rosy hue. Its appearance is preceded by restlessness, and accompanied with heat, burning and tingling in the spots, itching and irritation, The blotches are constantly changing their position, disappearing in a few hours in one part of the body, and reappearing in another. They are generally brought out by cold, and disappear in warmth.

It is occasioned by cold, changes of the temperature, excessive eating and drinking, and in many persons produced by the use of shell-fish, oatmeal, almonds, strawberries, and other kinds of food.

TREATMENT.—External applications should be avoided. If the rash is produced by a cold, is preceded by a stinging sensation, *Dulcamara* is the proper remedy, a dose every six or twelve hours. If the rash is accompanied by a little fever, is of burning stinging character, *Rhus* should be given. *Rhus* may be alternated with *Bryonia* once, when the rash is occasioned by damp weather, and is accompanied with shivering. A dose may be given in alternation every three, six, or twelve hours.

Pulsatilla and *Nux-vom.* are the prominent remedies, when the disease is occasioned by indigestion, *Pulsatilla* being particularly indicated, when it arises from the use of fatty food.

DOSE.—Of the first, a drop or three globules may be dissolved in a tumbler half full of water, and a teaspoonful taken every three or six hours. Of the last, if in tincture or globules, give as above; if in powder, give dry on the tongue, at the same intervals.

Ipecac. is also useful, when the rash is accompanied with nausea. Should it assume a chronic character, *Calcarea, Sulphur, Mercurius,* or *Nitr.-acid* may be given.

DOSE.—A powder or three globules of the Ipecac. may be given every two or three hours. Of the latter remedies a powder or three globules may be taken morning and night.

Should unpleasant symptoms arise from the rash striking in, a dose of *Ipecac.* may be given, followed in two hours by *Bryonia*, a dose every two hours until it has been taken three or four times.

DIET AND REGIMEN.—The diet should be plain and simple, abstaining from every thing of a heating or stimulating character. The above remedies will also generally be successful in the treatment of other simple forms of rash unconnected with any other disease, with the addition, perhaps of Aconite, where there is much increase of the circulation, and *Chamomilla*, when occurring in children.

For more particular directions as it regards the administration of remedies, see page 10.

SCARLET RASH. PURPLE RASH. MILIARIA PURPUREA.

Scarlet Rash is frequently developed in connection with Variola, Measles, and Scarlet Fever. It is not unfrequently mistaken for the latter disease, to which it has a considerable resemblance, and from which it is important, that it should be distinguished as the treatment is entirely different. Happily this can very readily be done; the small granular elevations easily felt on passing the hand over the skin, the dark redness of the efflorescence, and no white imprint being left after pressure with the finger are sufficient marks of distinction.

Precursory symptoms are chilliness alternating with heat, heaviness and fulness in the head, vertigo and aching pain in the forehead. These symptoms generally last but a short time. The eruption shows itself in no particular place, but is more frequently seen on the covered parts, and about the bend of the joints. Sore throat may be felt previous to the eruption, but entirely subsides while the eruption is out. Should, however, the eruption recede, the throat becomes highly inflamed, and the disease may immediately assume a dangerous type. There is great danger of this disease striking in, thus producing derangement of the brain, or some other vital organ, causing death. The disease is contagious, and those who have had it once, are still liable to have it many times again.

Treatment.—When this disease exists alone, *Aconite* is almost a specific remedy.

Dose.—One drop or six globules dissolved in a tumbler of water. A tablespoonful given once in two or three hours according to the severity of the symptoms, until five or six doses have been taken, will often be sufficient. Should, however, there be a whining mood, great restlessness, pain in the head, back, and extremities, *Coffea* will be indicated and may be given, generally in alternation with *Aconite*, two hours apart.

Dose —Same as *Aconite*.

Should the eruption be slow in making its appearance or suddenly disappear, *Ipecac.* and *Byronia* may be given in alternation, in the former case, every two hours, and in the latter, every half hour, until relief is obtained.

Dose.—Same as *Aconite*.

Belladonna will be required, should symptoms of cerebral disturbance occur, with starting on closing the eyes, fulness of the head, and blood-shot eyes.

Dose.—One drop, or eight globules in a tumbler of water, a tablespoonful every hour.

Should there be stupor, *Opium* would be required, administered in the same way as *Belladonna*. When the disease is of a malignant character, or complicated with *Scarlet Fever*, the treatment should be similar to that indicated in Scarlet Fever.

Diet and Regimen.—The diet should be of a light farinaceous character, and great care observed to prevent taking cold.

SCARLATINA.

Scarlet Fever.

Scarlatina, is generally a contagious epidemic, seldom attacking persons but once, and more frequently seizing its victims from the ranks of childhood. The cheek of many a mother has paled with terror as she heard the news of its approach, and gathering her babes around her, she has fled from the neighborhood tainted by its presence, as from the breath of a pestilence. In severe cases the rapidity of its progress, often running its course in two or three days, and where the termination is not fatal, the danger of its leaving behind some chronic difficulty, are enough to cause it to be dreaded in every community. The treatment of this disease with a success hitherto unknown, and in many cases its prevention did much towards turning the attention of the public to Hahnemann, and that great law of cure, which is now pervading every land.

Diagnosis.—The genuine Scarlatina seldom attacks persons beyond the age of twelve, and is now generally met with in complication with sçarlet rash or some other disease. The eruption is like the redness of erysipelas, of a fiery bright, scarlet red, or resembling the color of a boiled lobster, turning white under pressure of the finger, but speedily, on the finger being removed, resuming its original color. The boundaries of this redness are not distinctly defined, but are imperceptibly lost in the surrounding white parts. The red skin is perfectly smooth and glossy, the redness from time to time increasing or diminishing in extent and intensity. The eruption commences on the uncovered parts, or those slightly covered, as the face, neck, hands, arms, chest and feet, is accompanied with swelling, and gradually spreads over the body. Simultaneous with the redness, the heat and fever appear, continuing, in simple cases, three or four days, and in malignant ones, about seven, when the eruption gradually becomes paler and paler until it entirely disappears. The more extensive and intense the redness, the more violent the fever. With the disappearance of the redness and the abatement of the fever commences the stage of the desquamation, when the epidermis peals off in large patches. In connection with the fever, dryness of the mouth, severe soreness and often ulceration of the throat exist.

If the disease is combined with *scarlet rash*, instead of the skin presenting a smooth shining appearance, the roughness of the eruption is distinctly felt on passing the hand over the surface. This disease was formerly, frequently mistaken for *measles*, but to the careful observer the distinctive marks are sufficiently plain. Independent of the eruption, the *soreness of the throat* present in scarlatina, is absent in measles, and the *catarrhal* symptoms, which are present at the outset of measles are not observed in the commencement of scarlet fever.

Treatment.—*Belladonna* is the specific in the true form of this disease, a few doses of which will often afford decided and permanent relief. There is fever, quickness of the pulse, dryness of the mouth and thirst, throat highly inflamed and swollen; spasmodic contraction of the throat, danger of suffocation, and inability to swallow the least liquid; thirst, red and dry tongue, inflamed and painful eyes; pressure over the eyes or shooting in the head; starts and jerks on closing the eyes, sleeplessness with great nervous excitement. The external redness does not always appear, but in these cases the throat is swollen and painful, and the tongue presents a bright red appearance.

Dose.—Two drops, or six globules, of the remedy should be dissolved in a tumbler of water and a tablespoonful given every two or three hours, according to the severity of the symptoms. Should the symptoms be accompanied with fever, dry heat, bilious vomiting, &c., especially in the commencement of the disease, *Aconite* may be alternated with the *Belladonna*, one or two hours apart. *Stibium* may also be indicated in the same manner, a powder given in alternation with Belladonna, when the Aconite proves unavailing, and when there is a soporose condition; great heat, nausea, vomiting, convulsions or spasmodic jerks and imperfect development of the eruption. If the symptoms should become worse shortly after the administration of the *Belladonna*, it may be suspended, and the article in the Introduction, on the administration of remedies, be consulted. If the increase of symptoms are an aggravation of the remedy, the system will soon react, if however they are aggravations of the disease, other remedies will be necessary.

Mercurius.—Is a prominent remedy in the malignant form of the disease, where there is great inflammation about the throat, swelling and ulceration of the glands, accompanied by an offensive smell, salivation and ulceration of the mouth. It may be given after or in alternation with Belladonna, two hours apart.

Dose.—A powder, or three globules, dry on the tongue.

If after the expiration of twelve or fourteen hours no improvement is manifest, but the restlessness increases and the saliva becomes more offensive, *Lachesis* and *Arsenic* may be given in alternation, in the same manner as the Mercurius, one or two hours apart, until five or six doses of each have been taken.

Arsenic.—Will be indicated, where there is great prostration of strength, distorted features, nightly burning fever, gangrene of the throat, as well as in the various forms of dropsy caused by this disease.

Dose.—A powder, or three globules, may be given every three hours.

Capsicum is also a useful remedy, when there is redness of the face, alternating with paleness; violent sore throat, painful swallowing, and contraction and spasm in the throat, pains in the neck, sneezing, hoarseness, hacking cough and accumulation of tough mucus in the throat.

Dose.—One drop, or six globules, may be dissolved in a tumbler of water, and a spoonful given every two or three hours.

Coffea.—Is often indicated in alternation with Belladonna, when there is great restlessness, irritability, and whining mood, particularly at night. They may be alternated one or two hours apart.

Rhus.—Will be found useful, when the disease assumes a vesicular form, and is accompanied with restlessness, starts, thirst, and dry tongue.

Dose.—Same as *Belladonna.* Give every one or two hours.

Muriatic-acid is another prominent remedy in the malignant form of this disease, as well as in certain varieties of Typhoid Fever. It is indicated, where there is severe ulceration of the throat, fetid breath, acrid discharge from the nose, soreness and blisters about the nose and lips, efflorescence of an irregular and faint color, changing to a dark red, frequently intermixed with petechiæ; flushing of the check, and dull redness of the eyes. It is more frequently indicated after Mercurius and Lachesis, particularly if those remedies have in a measure failed of producing good results.

DOSE.—Sufficient of the *Muriatic-acid* may be put in a tumbler of water, to make it very slightly tart, and a teaspoonful given every two or three hours.

Nitric-acid.—May also be thought of, when the swelling and ulceration are severe.

Opium.—This remedy will be found useful where there is snoring sleep, great restlessness, sometimes with vomiting or constipation, burning heat, soporous stupefaction.

DOSE.—Same as *Belladonna.* Give once in two or three hours.

Sulphur.—Will prove beneficial where there is lethargic sleep, starts or constant delirium, puffed red face ; red, dry and cracked tongue, great thirst ; cerebral affections, which do not yield readily, to *Belladonna.*

DOSE.—A powder, or three globules, may be given every two or three hours.

SECONDARY DISEASES SUCCEEDING SCARLATINA.—Severe pain in the ear will generally be relieved by *Pulsatilla,* one drop, or four globules, dissolvedin a glass of water, and a tablespoonful taken every two or three hours, until four or five doses have been taken. If this not does produce relief, alternate *Belladonna,* prepared in the same manner, and *Hepar Sulph.,* a powder, or three globules, one hour apart.

The running at the ear will generally be controlled by *Calcarea,* a powder, or three globules, every six hours.

Fetid discharge at the nose, and pain in the nasal bones will be relieved by a few doses of *Aurum,* a powder, or three globules, at intervals of four or six hours.

Mercurius will be found beneficial, where there is ulceration of the face or throat; a powder, or three globules, three times a day to be followed, if necessary, after three or four days, by *Sil. Calc. Hep.-s., Sulph.* or *Iod.*

Should there be symptoms of *dropsy of the brain,* such as, great heat about the head, cold extremities, vomiting on moving, *Belladonna* and *Hellebore* may be given, one drop, or six globules, dissolved in a glass half full of water, and a teaspoonful administered in alternation every two hours.

In cases of dropsical swelling of the body, or the extremities, I have found great benefit from an alkaline bath. The water, comfortably tepid, is made sufficiently alkaline, to be perceptible to the taste, by dissolving in it *Pearlash* or *Saleratus*. In this bath the patient may be placed once or twice a day, being permitted to remain four or five minutes.

Hellebore and *Belladonna*, as directed above, may be given in alternation four hours apart, until four or five doses have been taken. Should the difficulty still continue, *Arsenic* or *Phos.-ac.* given at intervals of six hours, will generally complete the cure.

Croupy cough will be relieved by a few doses of *Hepar-s.* given every four hours. During the administration of these remedies, the patient should be very careful, to avoid taking cold.

PREVENTION.—During the prevalence of the scarlet fever, the attack may frequently be warded off entirely, or the disease rendered comparatively harmless, by administering every evening three globules of *Belladonna*, for one or two weeks. I have always found as a preventative the higher attenuations of this remedy far more beneficial, than the lower.

DIET and REGIMEN.—Diet should be simple such as gruels, toast, &c., returning gradually and carefully to more nourishing food. The room, of course, should be well ventilated, and yet the patient strictly guarded against taking cold. A particular caution is also necessary about going out too early as often serious secondary disturbances are occasioned by a want of proper prudence.

MEASLES.

Morbilli.

This is generally an infectious epidemic, occurring, more particularly among children, where it is seldom fatal, unless badly treated, or it becomes complicated with other difficulties. In persons, more advanced in years, it may assume a severe and even dangerous character, from its power of arousing and developing into full and fatal action germs of disease which may have been slumbering in the system for years.

Diagnosis.—The progress of the disease may be divided into three stages. At first the symptoms of an ordinary catarrh are perceived, such as slight inflammation of the eyes, sneezing, discharge of water from the nose, dry, short cough, difficult breathing, pain in the forehead, back, and perhaps diarrhœa, accompanied with fever of a remittent character, gradually increasing until the eruption appears on the skin. This is the first or *febrile stage.*

The second or *eruptive stage*, commences on the third or fourth day. The eruption first appears on the face and arms in the form of small, red spots, and for three or four days gradually increases and extends over the body. On the fourth day the eruption grows paler, and the symptoms abate. On the sixth or seventh day the third stage or, *stage of desquamation*, commences. If the eruption is slight, the scaling may be scarcely perceptible, and all morbid phenomena terminate in the critical sweat, diarrhœa, or urine. During this stage, the cartarrh may increase to pneumonia, and perhaps, in scrofulous subjects, be followed by consumption.

A long train of unpleasant difficulties may follow measles, such as, severe inflammation of the eyes, swelling of the glands, consumption of the bowels, pain in the ear, deafness, and tormenting chronic eruption.

Treatment.—The two great remedies in the treatment of this disease are *Aconite* and *Pulsatilla.* Very often a few doses of either one or both of these remedies will be all the patient requires. One drop, or six globules, may be dissolved in a tumbler of water, and a tablespoonful taken in alternation every two, three, or four hours. The febrile symptoms, inflammation of the eyes, giddiness and confusion of the head, strongly indicate *Aconite*, while *Pulsatilla* is particularly useful, where gastric symptoms are present, when the cough is worse toward evening or in the night, is accompanied by yellowish or whitish expectoration, sometimes followed by vomiting, or there is a yellowish or greenish nasal discharge, and is almost a specific, where the eruption delays in making its appearance. When given alone, it may be taken every three hours.

Dose.—One drop, or six globules, in a tumbler of water, and a tablespoonful every two, three, or four hours.

Should there be great restlessness, an occasional dose of *Coffea* may be given. Should the eruption strike in, or sickness at the stomach and oppression of the chest be present, a few doses of *Ipecac.* alone, or in alternation with *Bryonia,* prepared in the same manner as the *Aconite,* given one or two hours apart will produce relief.

Bryonia.—Will also be found of great value, when the cough is dry and attended with shooting pain in the chest, difficult breathing, &c., when it may be alternated with *Aconite* as directed for *Aconite* and *Pulsatilla.* Rheumatic pains in the limbs, and constipation also indicate this remedy.

Belladonna.—Will prove beneficial, where there is severe pain in the head, sore throat, dry cough, twitching of the limbs, and great restlessness.

Dose.—Two drops, or six globules, in a tumbler of water, a tablespoonful every two hours. If much fever is present, it may be given in alternation with *Aconite,* two or three hours apart.

Should the eruption be slight, and severe inflammation of the eyes be developed, or violent pain in the ear, with purulent discharge be present, *Sulphur,* in alternation with *Pulsatilla,* given at intervals of two, three, or four hours, will generally produce speedy relief.

Diseases occasioned by Measles.—Typhoid symptoms not unfrequently set in after measles, in which case, if there are dry, dark tongue and lips, burning heat, vomiting, or diarrhœa, *Arsenic,* a powder, or six globules, in a tumbler of water, may be given, a teaspoonful at a dose, once in two or three hours. If there should be loss of consciousness, watery diarrhœa, great weakness, cough, inclination to vomit, *Phosphorus* may be given in the same manner.

Severe *pain in the ear* will generally be relieved by a few doses of *Pulsatilla*, given as heretofore directed, at intervals of one or two hours, and if much purulent discharge be present, it may be followed by four or five doses of Sulphur, one every four hours, and this, if necessary by three or four doses of Carb.-v. at the same intervals. *Croupy symptoms* will be relieved by *Hepar-s.* or *Spongia*, and the remaining cough by *Puls.*, *Sulph.*, *Dros.*, *Hyos.*, *Bry.*, *Phos.* Should the measles be followed by disturbance about the head, irritation of the eyes with intolerance of light, *Belladonna* or *Strammonium* as directed heretofore, may be given at intervals of three or four hours.

Swelling of the glands below the ear (Mumps), will be relieved by *Rhus.* and *Arnica*, prepared in the same manner as *Aconite*, and alternated every three or four hours.

Constipation should create no alarm, as it generally passes off in a short time without medicine. Should a mucous diarrhœa set in, *Puls.*, *Merc.*, *Chin.*, or *Sulph.* will speedily remove it. (See Materia Medica.)

Diet and Regimen.—Same as in Scarlet Fever. The same care also should be taken to prevent unpleasant consequences from cold. During convalescence the patient should use the eyes but little, for fear of inflammation.

During the prevalence of measles, *Aconite* and *Pulsatilla* may be taken in alternation, three globules at a dose, two days apart.

ERYSIPELAS.

St. Anthony's Fire. Rose.

Diagnosis.—Previous to the attack, gastric symptoms may be present, as well as a general sensation of languor and dullness. The actual attack very frequently commences with distinct shivering. The erysipelatous redness suddenly makes its appearance on different parts of the body, accompanied with swelling, heat and tingling. In severe cases, the parts become very much swollen, the skin presenting a deep red, shining appearance, the patient suffering intensely from a burning heat, tingling, and a painful sensation of tension.

The redness and swelling gradually, and sometimes very rapidly extends, and when it appears on the face, as is most frequently the case, unless checked in its progress, covers the entire head. In these cases delirium is frequently present. Sometimes the inflamed surface becomes covered with vesicles or blisters, resembling those occasioned by a scald. In these severe cases, which are often attended with much danger, particularly when it attacks the head, there is a high fever, thirst, pain throughout the body, gastric derangement, sometimes vomiting, severe headache, sleeplessness, great nervous excitability, and a sensitiveness to the slightest noise. The erysipelatous inflammation often wanders, changing from one ear to the other, or from one side of the face to the other, or perhaps confining itself to the nose and eyes. Perhaps there is no disease which produces such a complete change, for the time being, in the appearance of the face as erysipelas. Those who pride themselves on their beauty, would shudder could they see in the closed lids, the swollen cheeks, the inflamed nose, the fearful change which a few hours has wrought in their appearance.

Causes.—It may be occasioned by gastric derangement, or, as is most frequently the case, by sudden suppression of perspiration. It is also very frequently found in females during menstruation. It may also be produced by certain kinds of food at particular seasons of the year, as the different varieties of shell-fish, and also from the abuse of spirituous liquors. We also see it developed in mechanical injuries, and not unfrequently setting in after the operation of the surgeon, with such violence as speedily to destroy life. It sometimes seems to prevail as an epidemic to such an extent, that the surgeon hesitates to perform even the most necessary operations. The physician, at these times, is often exceedingly annoyed at finding it set in with great severity in the arm of the child after vaccination.

Treatment.—The prominent remedies are, *Aconite*, *Belladonna*, and *Rhus*, also *Pulsatilla*, *Bryonia*, *Arsenic*, *Lachesis*, *Sulphur*. The presence of considerable fever, with dry, hot skin, would indicate *Aconite*.

Dose.—Two drops, or six globules, in a tumbler of water, a tablespoonful every two hours.

Belladonna will be indicated if the redness expands in rays, and severe shooting pains with great heat are felt, aggravated by movement, particularly if the inflamation is in the face, and is accompanied with severe swelling, burning heat, violent headache, delirium, restlessness, thirst, dry and hot skin. It is frequently alternated, with great benefit, with *Aconite* or *Rhus.*

Dose.—Two drops, or six globules, in a tumbler of water, a tablespoonful once in two hours.

Rhus is particularly indicated, when vesicles or blisters are perceived, or where there is great swelling, a tendency to spread, or extend to the brain, and where there is great restlessness and delirium. This remedy is frequently given in alternation with *Belladonna* or *Aconite.* The combination of symptoms mentioned under those remedies will be a sufficient guide.

Dose.—Two drops, or six globules, in a tumbler of water and a tablespoonful given every one, two, or three hours, according to the severity of the symptoms.

In severe cases, particularly if there is a dryness or pain in the throat, or the swelling or vesicles show a suppurating tendency, a powder, or three globules, of *Lachesis* may be given at intervals of three hours, until four or five doses have been taken, after which the *Belladonna* and *Rhus* may be again administered. If at night there should be great restlessness, and no disposition to sleep, two or three doses of *Coffea* may be alternated with *Belladonna,* one hour apart.

A constant desire to sleep will be controlled by one or two doses of *Opium,* prepared the same as *Rhus.*

Pulsatilla may be given, where the disease affects the ear, where the skin is of a bluish red, or the spots wander from one place to another, and also in those cases, which arise from injurious articles of food.

Dose.—Same as *Belladonna.* Give every two or three hours.

Bryonia, will be found useful where the inflammation occurs about the joints.

Dose.—Same as *Pulsatilla*.

Rhus, *Sulphur*, *Arsenic* and *Lachesis* are important remedies, where the disease has terminated in ulceration ; the two former or the two latter in alternation twelve hours apart.

Arsenic is also indicated, where the disease affects the scrotum, or where the vesicles are of a blackish character, and show a tendency to pass into gangrene, where there is great prostration of strength or black diarrhœa sets in. It may be alternated with *Carb.-v.* or *Lachesis*, a powder, or three globules every three or four hours.

Where the disease assumes a chronic form, *Graphites Sulphur* or *Nit.-ac.* may be consulted.

Diet and Regimen.—The diet should be of a simple character, similar to that in fevers. Great pains also should be taken to prevent cold during convalescence, as it often occasions troublesome dropsies.

CHICKEN-POX.
Varicella.

This is a disease, confined almost entirely to childhood, running its course rapidly, and is attended with but little, if any danger. It is somewhat similar to Small-Pox, but is distinguished from it by its mild character, and rapid course. In Small-Pox the face never escapes, while in Chicken-Pox it is but slightly affected, the eruption appearing more on the scalp, shoulders, neck, and breast. The fever, before the eruption, is also of short duration, seldom lasting more than twenty-four hours, and notwithstanding there may be headache, the swimming in the head and backache, which are characteristic symptoms in Small-Pox, do not appear.

The eruption is composed from the first, of transparent vesicles or blisters, having but one cavity, the liquid seldom becoming turbid, but shrivels upon a spongy crust, while in Small-Pox the pustule has a dent on the top of it, contains cells like an orange, and in the commencement, presents the appearance of a little point like the head of a pin.

TREATMENT.—Often no medical treatment is required, but if considerable fever is present, *Aconite* may be given every two hours. Should there be great heat and pain in the head, *Belladonna* may be given in alternation with the *Aconite*, two hours apart, until better.

Great nervous excitement, restlessness, anxious and disturbed sleep with dreams and moaning, will be relieved by three or four doses of *Coffea*, given at intervals of two or three hours. Should there be spasms, as is often the case during dentition, *Belladonna* and *Ignatia* may be given in alternation, one hour apart, until two doses of each have been taken. (See also convulsions.) The tenesmus, which is sometimes present, will be relieved by a few doses of *Mercurius*, given at intervals of two or three hours. The stranguary will be relieved by *Cantharides*. The disease in its mild form may be very much shortened by *Pulsatilla*, administered three or four times a day.

DOSE.—A powder may be taken dry on the tongue, or if tinctures or globules are used, two drops of the former, or six of the latter, may be dissolved in a tumbler of water, and a tablespoonful given at a dose.

SMALL-POX.

Variola.

This loathesome and highly dangerous disease has ever been looked upon with the utmost horror. The earliest accounts we have of it, we find it making its appearance in Egypt and Arabia, about the middle of the sixth century. From these nations it gradually spread throughout the old world, in the thronged cities and villages, numbering its victims by thousands, and every where reaping a rich harvest. Wherever it appeared, the air seemed to bear on its wings its poisonous breath, and whole neighborhoods were desolated.

In 1517, twenty-five years after the discovery of this western world by Columbus, it was introduced on this continent. So fatal did it prove, that in a very short time after it reached Mexico, three millions and a half of people were destroyed in that nation alone. One of the most sad and melancholy scenes in its fearful, desolating march was the death of the emperor, the brother and successor of the brave but unfortunate Montezuma.

After a time it was found, that where the disease was communicated by inoculation, it was far less violent in its character, being attended with but little danger. Many persons in every community were therefore inoculated, so that instead of the disease decreasing, hundreds, even in country places, exposed to the contagion and not having guarded against it by inoculation, took it in its most violent form. In England the deaths by Small-Pox amounted to about 45,000 annually.

At length in 1798, *Dr. Jenner*, an English physician, announced to the world a discovery, which has been the means of saving thousands of lives, and has checked in a great measure the ravages, of what was then considered, one of the most loathesome scourges which had ever desolated the earth. That discovery was, that *Cow-Pox* is almost a sure preventive to the Small-Pox. This doctrine at first was received with ridicule, contempt and the most violent opposition ; but what are ridicule and opposition to the stubborn array of facts, and the ultimate triumph of truth ? But few years elapsed before the doctrines of Jenner, became universally popular, and vaccination for Cow-Pox was introduced into almost every nation. Careful observation has shown however, that it is well to renew the vaccination every ten or fifteen years. With this precaution, there is but little danger of exposure to the Small-Pox.

Diagnosis.—This disease has four distinct stages, each of which generally requires different remedies.

1. *The febrile stage.*—This stage usually commences from eight to fourteen days after exposure to the contagion, and continues from two to four days. It sets in with shivering followed by fever, heat, and dryness of the skin, hard and frequent pulse, pain in the stomach and back, nausea and

vomiting, aching in the bones, and bruised sensation of the flesh, swimming and severe pain in the head, and sometimes wild delirium and convulsions. Cough and sensitiveness of the eyes to light are also usually present. Vomiting and pain in the back are characteristic symptoms of Small-Pox, and when these are very severe, the pain in the small of the back exceeding acute, and the vomiting extends into the eruptive stage, a severe attack may be apprehended.

2. *The eruptive stage.*—From the second to the fourth day the eruption makes its appearance in the face, in the form of small red points, increasing in extent an elevation from hour to hour, and distinguished from other eruptions by a small pimple about the size of a millet seed in each point. On the second day it appears on the hands, and on the third on the feet and the rest of the body.

3. *The suppurative stage.*—In this stage the pustule completes its development, becomes as large as a split pea, and is filled with a yellowish fluid, which gradually changes its color, until it assumes a turbid appearance. It is surrounded by a red circle, and has on the top a blackish depression or dent. As the pustules first appear on the face, and lastly on the extremities, they may have reached maturity in one part of the body, while they are still filling in another. During this stage, which lasts three or four days, fever, more or less swelling, and salivation are present.

4. *The stage af Desiccation.*—The pustules present on the top a brown appearance, and some of them burst, forming scabs. The fever and swelling gradually subside, the scales peel off, leaving at first a deep red stain. All danger is over, when the process of desiccation has ceased in the face.

The more violent, or *confluent* form of the disease, where the pustules are so numerous as to run into each other, forming an immense scab, is longer in duration, and attended with more violent symptoms and danger.

TREATMENT.—During the sixteenth century and even later, in the treatment of this disease the great object was to expel the humour by means of perspiration. To accomplish this, the patient was confined in a hot room, dosed with hot drinks, and warmly covered in bed; notwithstanding under this treatment a majority of the patients died, when Sydenham introduced, what is now called the cooling regimen, throwing away the hot drinks, using light covering, keeping the patient cool, and having the room freely ventilated, he was attacked on all sides by the learning and bigotry of the age, but without avail, for reason and common-sense in the end are sure to triumph.

Febrile Stage.—*Aconite* may be given every two or three hours; in alternation with *Belladonna*, if there is severe pain in the head, intolerance of light or delirium. Should there be considerable stupor, two or three doses of *Opium* given at intervals of hours will produce relief.

Dose.—Two drops, or eight globules in a tumbler full of water, a tablespoonful at a dose.

Bryonia and *Rhus* may be alternated two or three hours apart, if after four or five doses of the *Aconite* have been taken, there should be aching and bruised sensation in the bones and flesh, and severe pain in the back. Sometimes, where the fever is high, and the above symptoms exist, either Bry. or Rhus may be alternated with Aconite.

Dose.—Same as *Aconite.*

Stibium should be given if nausea or vomiting is present.

Dose.—A powder every hour until the nausea is relieved, or until three or four doses have been taken. If there is great restlessness and inability to sleep, a few doses of Coffea may be required, given at intervals of an hour, and prepared in the same manner as *Aconite.*

2. *The Eruptive Stage.*—During this stage I have found the most benefit from *Strammonium*, two or three drops in a tumbler of water, a tablespoonful every two, three, or four hours, according to the severity of the symptoms. It is particularly useful where the eruption is slow in its appearance and progress.

Should there be cough and indication of considerable trouble about the lungs, *Stibium* may be alternated with the *Strammonium* two hours apart.

Sometimes, where the pustules are filling well, and the disease is progressing rapidly, the *Strammonium* may be omitted, and *Stibium* and *Thuja.* (the latter prepared as directed for *Aconite*), given in alternation, three hours apart.

3. *Suppurative Stage.*—If there should be but little fever, a simple regimen alone will be required. If, however, an ulcerative fever is present, attended with abundant salivation, affection of the eyes, nose, and throat, *Mercurius* will be required.

Dose.—A powder, or three globules, every three hours.

If the Pox become black, and typhoid symptoms set in, *Muriatic acid* may be given every two hours, or if considerable stupour is present, it may be alternated with *Opium*, two hours apart.

Dose.—Same as *Aconite.*

Rhus or *Arsenic* will be indicated, when the skin around the pustules is of a livid color, and burning thirst and great exhaustion are present. If diarrhœa should set in, *China* will be required.

Dose.—*Rhus* and *China*, same as *Aconite. Arsenic*, same as *Mercurius.*

4. *Stage of Desiccation.*—Simple ablution with tepid water will generally be all that is required. A powder, or three globules of *Sulphur*, given morning and evening for three or four days, will frequently be serviceable. If as is sometimes the case, other diseases set in, *see symptomatic index*, and diseases under their separate heads.

Diet and Regimen.—The room should be thoroughly ventilated, and kept at a moderate temperature. The patient should be placed on a matress or straw-bed, be lightly covered and the room considerably darkened. The diet should be cooling, such as, water, lemonade, oranges, roasted apples, stewed prunes, strawberries, gruels, toast, &c., avoiding the lemonade and fruit, if diarrhœa should be present. Animal food should not be used in any form until the disease is pretty thoroughly over.

VARIOLOID.

By this term is generally understood a modified form of Variola or Small-Pox, occurring sometimes even after Cow-Pox. The pustules are few in number and the treatment, if any is required, is similar to Small-Pox.

2. GENERAL CUTANEOUS DISEASES.

Under this head might be arranged a large variety of cutaneous difficulties, more or less troublesome. The limits of a work like this, however, preclude the possibility of detailing the treatment of all these various classes, and indeed it would be in a measure unprofitable to the general reader. We shall therefore only speak of those less complicated difficulties, most frequently met with in family practice.

ITCH.

Scabies.

King George 4th once remarked, in the peculiarly chaste and elegant language which characterized that monarch, "that none but kings ought to have the itch, it was such a luxury to scratch." A wish with which the community in general would very gladly concur.

Diagnosis.—It appears, in the form of small vesicles, filled with a clear fluid, and surrounded by a red border, between the fingers, on the wrists, and in the bend of the joints. Sometimes, if the disease continues some length of time, it extends over the body, with the exception of the face, which is entirely free. The itching is aggravated in the evening by the warmth of the bed, or on coming from cold into warm air. As the vesicles become broken up by scratching, they may form thick scurfs.

Cause.—The disease, the cause of which is a small animalcule burrowing in the skin, is generally communicated by contact, either from individuals, or handling filthy articles, such as, dirty wool, cloth, &c.

Treatment.—First, ascertain that the disease is really the itch. Second, remember that if suppressed or not thoroughly cured, it may lead to chronic difficulties of an exceedingly troublesome or painful character, and that salves and greasy ointments are not the best to thoroughly eradicate the affection, but may often drive it in, and should therefore as a general thing be avoided.

Sulphur.—This is the most important remedy, and will often be alone sufficient to produce a cure. A powder of the first, or one drop of the tincture, may be taken morning and night for a week, when it will be well to discontinue the remedy, and give a sulphur-bath at intervals of two or three days, until three or four have been taken, when, if necessary, the *Sulph.* may be recommenced, given in alternation with *Mercurius.* In connection with the internal use of *Sulphur*, five or ten drops of the tincture, may be dissolved in a tumbler half full of water, and the worst parts bathed with it, morning and night.

Carb. v. or *Hepar-s.* may be required, if, after one week the *Sulphur* and *Mercury* should not be followed by decided relief.

DOSE.—A powder, or three globules, night and morning.

In the *humid* variety, characterized by yellow pustules, which are met with not only on the hands and feet, but about the body, *Sulphur* and *Lycopodium* may be alternated, one in the morning, and the other at night for one week, when, if not materially better, *Mercurius* may be substituted for Lycopodium, and the remedies given as before.

DOSE.—Same as *Carb. v.*

Besides the remedies already mentioned, *Causticum* or *Graphites* will sometimes be required.

ITCHING OR IRRITATION OF THE SKIN.

Prurigo.

This consists of a fine colorless, almost imperceptible eruption under the cuticle, itching excessively, particularly when warm in bed. It may be occasioned by the abuse of fatty food, extremes of heat and cold, and also be developed in connection with other diseases, when it must be treated accordingly.

Treatment.—Bathing the parts with Alcohol, diluted one half, will often produce decided relief.

Sulphur may be given, if the itching is severe or worse in the evening, or in bed.

Dose.—A powder, or three globules, morning and night.

Ignatia, where the eruption resembles flea-bites, and is relieved by scratching.

Dose.—Two drops, or six globules, in a tumbler of water, a tablespoonful morning, noon, and night.

Pulsatilla, when it comes on in bed, and is aggravated by scratching.

Dose.—Same as *Ignatia*.

Mercurius, where *Pulsatilla* seems to be indicated, and yet does not produce relief, and also where the parts bleed easily after scratching.

Dose.—Same as *Sulphur*.

Rhus, where the itching is attended by a burning sensation. If after three or four doses no relief is obtained, it may be followed by *Hepar-s*. If the itching appear on undressing, *Nux* may be alternated with *Arsenic*, one in the morning, the other at night

Dose.—*Rhus*, same as *Ignatia*. *Hepar-s.*, *Nux*, *Arsenic*, same as *Sulphur*.

In obstinate cases *Sulphur* in alternation with *Carb. v.*, or *Lycopodium*, *Graphites*, *Silicea* may be indicated. In old persons *Opium* will be serviceable, a dose every night.

If the eruption shows itself around the anus or private parts, *Sulph.*, *Nit. ac.*, *Sep.*, *Calc.*, *Dulc.*, or *Thuj.* may be required.

SCALD-HEAD.

Tinea Capitis. Favus.

This disease, frequently called "*Ringworm of the Scalp*," occurring principally among children, is highly contagious and excessively obstinate. It is often communicated, by means of the comb and brush, or the towel. Pustular ringworm is not alone confined to the scalp, but frequently appears on other parts of the body.

There are several varieties, but a general description will

only be necessary here. The affected parts become red, hot, painful, and elevated, accompanied with swelling of the glands of the neck and head. After a few days, small round pustules start up, gradually filling with a yellowish white, thick fluid, smelling badly on being discharged. As the pustules break, the hairs become glued together, and in a short time, scaly, thick and hard crusts are formed. Frequently the roots of the hair are entirely destroyed. Violent external treatment may, by driving the disease in, occasion serious disorders, which not unfrequently terminate in death.

CAUSES.—Want of cleanliness, keeping the head too warm, scrofulous disposition, coarse and indigestible food, close and filthy dwellings, and contagion, are among the numerous causes.

TREATMENT.—Avoid of course, as much as possible the causes which produce the disease.

Rhus is the prominent remedy during the inflammatory stage, especially where there is secretion of greenish pus and nightly itching.

DOSE.—One drop, or eight globules, in a tumbler of water, a tablespoonful morning and night.

Sulphur may be given, should dry scabs be formed.

DOSE.—A powder, or three globules, morning and night.

Should the pus assume a corrosive character, thus causing new ulcers, and therefore an extension of the disorder, *Arsenic* may be given in the same manner as the *Sulphur*, again returning to *Rhus.* after five or six doses have been taken.

The lighter form of the eruption may be controlled by *Hepar-s.* especially when it is not confined to the head, but is found on the neck and face, also when it is accompanied by affection of the eyes.

DOSE.—Same as *Sulphur.*

Staphisagria, will be very beneficial, where the disease is of a humid, fetid character, with itching, and swelling of the glands of the neck.

DOSE.—Same as *Rhus.*

Dulcamara, will prove of benefit where the glands of the

neck as well as other parts of the body are swollen, or *Bryonia*, if they are highly sensitive.

DOSE.—Same as *Rhus*.

Besides the remedies enumerated above, *Calc.*, *Graph.*, *Lyc.*, *Acid mur.*, or *Phos.* may be indicated.

DIET AND REGIMEN.—Strict attention should be paid to diet and cleanliness. It would be advisable to remove the hair in the commencement of the disease.

MILK CRUST.

Crusta Lactea.

This disease principally attacks infants between the seventh and eighth month after birth, and during the first period of dentition. Where the child is naturally healthy, often no treatment is required, except perhaps a change of air.

DIAGNOSIS.—The eruption consists of yellowish white pustules on a red surface, breaking in three or four days, and forming whitish yellow crusts. As the secretion continues these crusts become darker and thicker. The eruption first appears on the forehead and cheek, and gradually extends over the face, covering it like a mask, sometimes also covering the entire scalp and ears.

The prominent remedies are *Rhus*, *Sulph.*, *Hep.-s.* *Staph.*, *Sep.* and *Ars.* For their separate indications, see *Tinea Capitis.* The inflammation of the eyes, which not unfrequently accompanies this disease, yield to *Euphrasia*, *Hepar-s.* or *Belladonna.* See *Materia Medica.*

CRUSTA SERPIGNOSA.

This may be considered as a variety of the *Itch*, although it was formerly looked upon as identical with *Crusta Lactea.* Like that, it is confined to children, but differs from it, in appearing first on the ear, breaking out in small pustules, filled with some kind of fluid, and attended with violent itching, particularly at night, while the Crusta Lactea appears first on the forehead in irregular large pustules, and is attended with but slight itching.

TREATMENT.—This form of eruption is much more obstinate than the other variety, and should generally be treated by a skilful physician. *Sepia*, *Calc.*, *Sulph.*, *Merc.*, *Staph.*, *Graph.* are among the prominent remedies.

DOSE.—One drop, or eight globules, in a tumbler of water, a tablespoonful morning and night; or a powder, or three globules, dry on the tongue.

RINGWORM.

Herpes Circennatus.

In this disease there is an eruption on a slighly inflamed basis, in the form of small rings or circular bands, the vesicles occupying the circumference. Within, the skin at first looks healthy, but gradually becomes rough and scales off, as the eruption dies away. It generally occurs in summer and in warm climates. It frequently disappears in the course of a week, or it may last all summer.

TREATMENT.—A few doses of *Sulphur*, given morning and night, may be sufficient. If after a week no improvement is perceptible, *Sepia* may be given, followed if necessary, by *Causticum* in the same manner.

DOSE.—Same as in *Crusta Serpignosa.*

In this form of *Herpes*, Dr. Metcalf has given *Tellurium* with the most happy results. A powder may be taken morning and night.

HERPES.

Tetter.

This is a non-contagious affection of the skin, characterized by the eruption of clusters of globular vesicles on inflamed patches, of irregular or rounded form and of small extent. After a few days, the vesicles may subside or burst, forming a thin brownish scab.

Of the numerous varieties of this disease it will only be necessary to mention three.

1. HERPES PHYLETENODES.
2. HERPES CIRCENNATUS, or *Ringworm.*
3. HERPES ZOSTER, or *Shingles.*

1. *Herpes Phylctenodes.*, This variety is characterized by clusters of globular and transparent vesicles, appearing in variable numbers upon red patches over different parts of the body. The appearance of the eruption is generally attended with considerable itching and smarting. We not unfrequently see varieties of this group appearing on the face, hands, body, extremities, and private parts.

HERPES ZOSTER, ZONA, or *Shingles.* This variety usually attacks one side of the body in the shape of a semicircular belt or band, formed by several clusters of agglomerated vesicles. It is more commonly seen on the abdomen, where it begins in some part of a line, extending down the centre of the abdomen, and proceeds outwardly around the body, until it about reaches the vertebræ, thus forming a sort of half girdle. It is generally attended with considerable itching, and sometimes with more or less fever.

TREATMENT.*—*Rhus*, should there be much restlessness and fever, may be given morning, noon, and night. The ordinary forms of the disease will generally be controlled by *Sulphur*, *Sepia* or *Causticum*, given in the same manner as directed in *Herpes circennatus.*

Should the eruption assume *a dry* character, *Sepia*, *Sulphur*, or *Silicea* may be given.

Where there is a tendency to *ulceration*, it may be controlled by *Merc.*, *Rhus.*, *Sulph.* or *Sep.*

If violent itching is present, *Nit.-ac.* or *Graphites* or *Staphysagria* will produce relief, or if warmth increases the difficulty, *Clematis* may be given.

Besides the remedies already enumerated, *Dulc.*, *Ars.*, *Carb.-v.*, *Phos.*, *Mez.*, *Canth.*, *Hep.* may be indicated. (See Materia Medica.)

DOSE.—One drop, or eight globules, in a tumbler of water, a tablespoonful morning and night, or a powder, or three globules, dry on the tongue at the same intervals.

* For general directions as to the administration of remedies, *see page* 10.

ACNE.

A peculiar eruption consisting of hard, inflamed tubercles, is frequently seen, in persons of a sanguine temperament, on the forehead, temples, face, and chin, and sometimes on the neck, shoulders, and upper parts of the chest. They frequently suppurate, but sometimes scale off without perceptible suppuration, leaving a purple spot.

To effect a cure, particular attention should be paid to diet. Among the remedies, *Staphysagria* will be found useful for stinging itching pimples, with pain when touched, and *Sulphur* when the round blotches are covered with white yellowish scurfs.

Dose.—A powder, or three globules, every other night. Another variety of this disease consists of a number of black points, which when pressed, discharge worm-shaped, indurated mucus.

This variety also requires particular care, as it regards diet. A powder, or three globules, of *Sulphur*, *Sepia* or *Nit.-acid.* may be taken every other day.

CHILBLAINS.

Perniones.

This inflammation generally appears on feet and hands, which have been frost bitten. It is attended with more or less burning and itching, and sometimes ulceration takes place, when the parts are exceedingly troublesome and painful.

Treatment.—*Arnica Court Plaster*, covering the inflamed surface, often produces prompt relief, and is particularly useful, where the difficulty is caused by pressure or friction ; or five or six drops of the tincture may be put in a tablespoonful of water, and the parts bathed with the mixture. If the inflammation be superficial with slight red swelling, burning and itching in the warmth, a few doses of *Nux*, taken morning and night, will produce relief.

If however the chilblains should be very painful, *Nit.-ac.* or *Phosphorus* may be given in the same manner. Should the parts present a blue-red and swollen appearance, accompanied with severe throbbing pains, *Pulsatilla* will be indicated, morning, noon, and night, followed, if relief is not obtained after five or six doses, by *Belladonna*, taken in the same manner.

When the chilblains are blue-red and accompanied with violent itching, *Kali-carb.*, may be given morning and night, and if the itching should be more violent in warmth, *Sulphur* given in the same manner.

Should blisters form on the inflamed part or ulceration set in, *Arsenic* or *China* may be taken morning and night. The ulceration may be dressed with some mild and soothing application as, simple cerate or a poultice. In severe cases *Petrol.*, *Agar* and *Carb.-v.* may be consulted.

Dose.—One drop, or eight globules, in a tumbler, a tablespoonful at a dose, or a powder or three globules may be given dry on the tongue.

EXCORIATION.

Intertrigo.

This is often the result of a want of cleanliness, although it not unfrequently originates from some internal cause.

To produce a cure, often nothing more is required than a tepid bath every day. If however the difficulty still continues, *Arnica*, *Nux*, *Lycopodium* or *Sulphur* may be given a dose every night, especially where it occurs during summer.

The *chafing of bed ridden patients* may be bathed with *Arnica*, ten drops of which may be dissolved in four tablespoonfuls of water, and applied two or three times a day with a soft cloth.

Where there is a disposition to *fester*, as is often the case after the slightest injury. A dose of *Hepar-s.*, *Silicea*, *Lachesis*, or *Sulphur* may be given every night.

Chapped hands, (Rhagades) which so often occur on the hands of those who work in water, may be relieved in such cases by *Calcarea*, *Hepar-s.*, *Sulphur* or *Sepia*, taken in the manner indicated above.

When the difficulty manifests itself in the winter, a few

doses of *Sulphur* or *Petroleum*, given in the same manner, will produce relief.

WHITLOW.

Felon. Panaris.

We understand, by this term, an abscess, more or less deeply seated, forming about the end of the finger. The pain, when the disease is fairly developed, is agonizing, often depriving the patient of rest.

The difficulty may frequently be removed, when it is first noticed by dipping the finger in water as warm as can be borne. If this should fail to produce relief, give *Mercury* every four hours, applying at the same time a bread and milk poultice. If no relief is obtained after four or five doses, *Hepar-s.* and *Silicea* may be alternated four hours apart. Should the pain become severe and there be pretty plain indications of the presence of matter, the abscess may be freely opened with a sharp knife. The parts should be frequently washed with warm water.

DOSE.—A powder, or three globules, dry on the tongue.

ULCERS.

The presence of ulcers indicate a diseased state of the system, being in reality the outlets formed by nature to carry off matter, which, unless removed, might produce serious disturbance of some internal organ. The treatment should be directed to remove the disturbing cause, and where this is done, the ulcer will generally heal of itself.

1. *Simple Ulcer.*—The simple, purulent, or healthy ulcer, is characterized by pus of thick consistency and white color, readily separating from the surface of the sore. Healthy granulations, small, florid and pointed at the top, speedily follow, and the sore is soon covered by a new skin. But little treatment is necessary, excepting to bathe the parts frequently with tepid water and cover with soft linen lint to absorb the matter.

2. *Irritable Ulcer.*—The surrounding skin is jagged, ter-

minating in a sharp edge. The ulcer generally presents quite a cavity, undermining the skin and discharging a fluid more or less thin and ichorous. The slightest touch may produce pain or cause the ulcer to bleed. The pain may be either constant, slight, or severe, or coming on in paroxysms.

3. *The gangrenous or sloughing Ulcer* is generally only a stage of the irritable one. In this the edges of the sore have a livid appearance, with small vesicles on them. The surface is dry, and more or less fever is present.

TREATMENT.—The irritable ulcer should be bathed freely with tepid water. Dry soft linen lint may be placed in the cavity, or the ulcer may be covered with a compress dipped in either cold or warm water, as is most agreeable to the patient.

If the ulcer presents a livid aspect, or bleeds readily, secreting an ichorous fluid, mixed with blood, and especially if there is burning pain, *Arsenic* may be given in alternation with *Carbo-v.*, a dose of one in the morning, and the other at night. *Lachesis* may be substituted for the *Carbo* in case the surrounding parts present a mottled appearance.

In ordinary cases, the external soothing treatment and internal use of *Sulphur* and *Silicea*, or *Sepia* in alternation, a dose of one every night, will be sufficient to effect a cure.

3. *Indolent ulcer.*—The irritable ulcer frequently runs into this variety, or may, in some degree be complicated with it. Fomentations, such as bread and milk poultice, applied for two or three days, will often so stimulate the ulcer as to cause it to put on a healthy appearance. *Sulphur* and *Silicea* may be alternated in the same manner as indicated above, for one week, when, if improvement is not perceptible, *Calcarea* and *Sepia* may be substituted. Should an ulcer proceed from a diseased state of the bone, *Mercury* and *Sulphur* may be given in the same manner, followed if necessary by *Calcarea* and *Lycopodium.*

A very obstinate ulcer not unfrequently forms on the lower limbs, occasioned by swelling of the veins. This is called a *Varicose ulcer*. *Sulphur* is here a prominent remedy, given as above, or *Lycopodium* and *Lachesis* may be alternated.

Syphilitic ulcers, cancerous difficulties, &c. will be treated in their appropriate place. (See also symptomatic index).

DOSE.—A powder, or three globules, taken as directed above.

BOILS. CARBUNCLES.

Boils are characterized by a hard elevation of a round or cone-like form, having an inflamed appearance, attended with pain more or less severe. They are slow in suppurating and discharge, on breaking, pus mixed with blood, and after a little while a core.

There is sometimes a constitutional tendency to this difficulty, but very frequently they appear as critical discharges. particularly after fevers and eruptive diseases, and not unfrequently form the termination of chronic eruption, such as, itch, &c. Derangement of the system from abuse of food and torpidity of the circulation often causes them.

TREATMENT.—The external application of a bread and milk, flaxseed, or slippery-elm poultice, is not only very soothing but hastens the cure.

Arsenic may be given, a dose morning and evening, but should there be much swelling, and the boil present an inflamed and fiery red appearance, attended with considerable pain, *Belladonna* may be alternated with *Mercury*, four or five hours apart.

After matter has formed, which may be indicated by the softness of some portion of the tumor, *Hepar-s.* may be given every four or five hours until the tumor breaks.

Should the boil assume a malignant character, becoming blue, painful and increasing in size, *Lachesis* and *Arsenic* may be alternated four or five hours apart.

The Carbuncle is often exceedingly dangerous, especially when it appears on the head, as it is very liable to run into mortification. It is large in size, presents a hard and livid appearance, is exceedingly painful, and on breaking, instead of presenting a central core like the ordinary boil, discharges an offensive matter mixed with blood, from several openings.

Silicea in the less severe forms of carbuncle, a dose every four or five hours, will generally be alone sufficient; but should it assume a very painful and severe character, *Lachesis* should be alternated with *Arsenic* three or four hours apart. The parts may be frequently bathed with tepid water.

To prevent the return of boils or to eradicate the affection, *Sulphur* may be given every second night.

DOSE.—Two drops, or eight globules in a tumbler of water, a tablespoonful at a dose ; or a powder, or three globules, dry on the tongue.

ABSCESS. SWELLING OF THE GLANDS.

The glands in different parts of the body are liable, from various causes, to become swollen and suppurate, causing frequently not only considerable pain, but more or less general disturbance throughout the system. Hence we frequently have swelling of the glands of the neck, arm-pit, groins, &c.

One of the various poultices already enumerated may be applied, and, if the swelling is attended with considerable pain, *Belladonna* and *Mercury* alternated four or five hours apart. If the swelling is slow in its progress, *Hepar-s.* or *Silicea* may be given, one in the morning, and the other in the evening. Should the patient be scrofulous, a dose of *Iodine* may be given every night.

After the abscess has opened, a few doses of *Hepar-s.* in alternation with *Silicea*, given morning and night, may be required. Enlargement of the glands about the neck require *Dulcamara* and *Mercury* in alternation, a dose every evening, and after suppuration has commenced, *Hepar-s.* and *Silicea* in the same manner.

Sulphur every second night will often remove a tendency to this difficulty, or eradicate the relics of the disease.

DOSE.—A powder, or three globules, dry on the tongue, as directed above.

WARTS.

These little fungous growths, appearing frequently on the hands, do not add materially to their beauty, and are somewhat annoying.

Touching them three or four times a day with the tincture of *Thuja*, will generally cause them to rapidly disappear. If after a week's trial no effect is perceived, *Rhus* may be used in the same way.

Should it be necessary to resort to internal remedies, *Causticum* or *Calcarea* may be given, a dose every other night for two weeks, if necessary.

CORNS.

Clavi Pedis.

To prevent their formation, do not cramp the feet, but wear boots and shoes made easy and comfortable. This, however, will not always prevent their formation, for we sometimes find them when this fault cannot be charged to the patient.

The corns should not be permitted to become large and hard, and should therefore occasionally be pared down as much as possible, and covered with *Arnica plaster*, or ordinary adhesive plaster. They may also be bathed, where there is considerable pain, with *Arnica*. Should there be a sensation as if needles were running through the corn, *Ant. crud.* may be taken, a dose every evening for a week. *Calc.*, *Sep.*, *Sil.* may be required, if there is considerable pain ; a dose every evening, commencing with *Calc.* and following in a week's time, if necessary by another remedy.

CHAPTER III.

AFFECTIONS OF STOMACH AND BOWELS.

DISPEPSY.

This is one of the most common difficulties in the whole list of disease. It includes most of those undefinable, and sometimes inexpressible sensations popularly classed under the head of "bilious derangement." It is in this way that the stomach generally speaks, when it has been crowded with more food than it can manage, or when the food is not of the proper quantity, or taken at the proper time, or when its strength has been tasked by stimulants and dissipation. The result of this violent action, is of course, weakness of the digestive organs.

Derangement of the stomach is followed by a long train of unpleasant and distressing symptoms. A sympathetic action is felt in the head and in fact in every part of the body. Thus we have violent headaches, intolerable dulness, great vertigo, general lassitude, pain in the abdomen, constipation, diarrhœa, and a host of diseases.

Causes.—The human system is fond of order and regularity, and when this order is interfered with, derangement is the result. This may arise, as it regards the stomach, from either taking too much and too rich food, or not enough; by eating whenever convenient, instead of at regular hours, by eating food not easily digested, or too great a variety at one time; by indulging in the free use of stimulants, such as, spices, liquors, &c., and by the immoderate use of tobacco, coffee, and tea, as well as by various other causes. The stomach is not unfrequently weakened by large doses of medicine, and continues in this debilitated state for years.

Diagnosis.—Sensation of weight in the stomach, especially after eating, loss of appetite, bitter taste in the mouth, sour rising, flatulence, nausea, and sometimes vomiting of acid or mucus, drowsiness, particularly after a meal.

TREATMENT.—Abstain from unnatural stimulants, which generally only produce temporary relief, and make use of food, easy of digestion, at regular intervals. The free use of cold water in chronic derangement, in the form of the wet bandage, (see page 80) is also recommended. Recent cases of dyspepsy are generally controlled by means of *Pulsatilla*, *Ipecac.*, or *Nux-Vomica*, while those of longer duration are not unfrequently entirely removed by means of *Hepar-s.* and *Sulphur.*

When occasioned by the use fat things, *Pulsatilla* is generally indicated, or sometimes *Ipecac.* or *Carb.-veg.*

Occasioned by cold water, ices, or fruits: *Puls.*, *Caps.*, *Ars.*, *China*, *Ipecac.*, or *Verat.*

In *children*, *Ipecac.*, *China*, *Puls.*, *Nux-vom.*, *Sulph.*, *Cham.*

In *old people*, *Ant.*, *Carb.-veg.*, *Chin.*, *Nux-vom.*

Occasioned by a *sedentary life*: *Bry.*, *Nux-vom.*, *Sep.*, *Sulph.*

By *prolonged watching*: *Arn.*, *Carb.-veg.*, *Nux-vom.*, *Puls.*, *Verat.*

By *debilitating losses* from purging, bleeding, &c.: *Chin.*, *Calc.*, *Carb.-v.*, *Ruta.*, *Phos.-ac.*

By *sexual excess*: *Calc.*, *Merc.*, *Nux-vom.*, *Staph.*

Gluttony: *Ant.*, *Ars.*, *Ipecac.*, *Nux-vom. Puls.*

Spirituous liquors: *Carb.-v.*, *Nux-vom.*, *Sulph.*, *Chin. Puls.*

Abuse of *Coffee*: *Nux-vom.*, *Ignatia.*

Abuse of *Tea*; *Fer.* or *Thuja.*

Abuse of *Tobacco*: *Ipecac.*, *Nux-vom.*, *Puls.*

From *Grief*: *Nux-vom.*, *Bry.*, *Chin.*, *Ignatia.*

From *Meat*: *Fer.*, *Ruta*, *Sil.*, *Sulph.*

From *Milk*: *Bry.*, *Calc.*, *Nux-vom.*, *Sulph.*

As it regards the particular indications of remedies, *Nux-vomica* is perhaps one of the most prominent, particularly at the commencement of the treatment, and where there is a predisposition to constipation or piles, or a temperament which is restless, irritable, lively and choleric.

There is generally a sour, bitter taste in the mouth, hunger, or repugnance to food, with craving for spirituous liquors ; nausea, sour eructation ; or else vomiting of food, flatulence, dulness, vertigo, lassitude and disposition to sleep, tenderness of the stomach when touched, with a sense of weight or fulness; sufferings from drinking, coffee, tobacco, abuse of food, and the various forms of dissipation; water-brash, heaviness and dulness of the head; constipation, heat and redness of the face; yellow or earthy complexion. It is frequently desirable to alternate it with *Sulphur*, the *Sulphur* in the morning, and the *Nux* at night.

DOSE.—A powder, or three globules, night and morning. If in alternation with *Sulphur*, as directed above.

Sulphur.—More particularly indicated in the beginning of the treatment, in chronic dyspepsy, or in persons of nervous and irritable temperament after *Nux-v.* or *Pulsatilla*. There is repugnance to food, craving for acids ; sufferings from meat, acids, fat, milk, and sweetened food ; shortness of breath, nausea, vomiting of food, eructations, pain in the stomach after eating; acidity, water-brash, flatulence, &c.

DOSE.—Same as *Nux*.

Pulsatilla.—Indicated in the commencement of the disease, particularly when occasioned by fatty food. There is dislike to cooked or hot food, and a craving for acids, spices, wines and rich food; nausea, eructations or vomiting, dyspnœa and sadness after a meal; water-brash; bitter or sour eructations; frequent loose evacuations, sometimes with colic. This remedy is particularly suited to women, and can often be followed by *Sulphur*.

DOSE.—Two drops, or eight globules, in a tumbler of water a tablespoonful at a dose. For directions as to giving the medicine, see *administration* at the close of this disease.

Bryonia.—Particularly indicated in damp and warm weather, and where there is constipation; painful sensibility of the stomach to the touch, sometimes with colic, a sense of fulness, or vomiting of food after a meal; aversion to food and craving for stimulants; empty, sour, or bitter eructations. It may frequently be alternated with *China* or *Rhus*.

Dose.—Same as *Pulsatilla.*

China.—In marshy districts in the spring or autumn, or where the system has been debilitated by blood-letting purging, &c.; and where there is indifference to food, craving for stimulants; acid, or bitter taste; uneasiness, drowsiness, fulness, distensions, eructations; great weakness; sensibility to currents of air; disturbed sleep. It is sometimes alternated with *Bryonia* or *Rhus.*

Dose.—Same as *Pulsatilla.*

Rhus.—Its indications are similar to *Bryonia*, with which, or with *China*, it is generally advisable to alternate it. There is an unnatural taste; repugnance to food and craving for dainties; disposition to sleep, lassitude and nausea after a meal; painful but abortive eructations; distension of the stomach, gastric sufferings and uneasiness, particularly at night.

Dose.—Same as *Pulsatilla.*

Hepar-s.—Is a valuable remedy in chronic cases, particularly if *Mercury* has been freely given, or if almost all kinds of food disagree, with craving for stimulants; nausea, particularly in the morning, sometimes with vomiting of sour, bilious or mucous substance; pain in the abdomen; sensation of fulness and distension, with a desire to have the clothes loose about the stomach.

Mercury or *Lachesis* are often indicated after Hepar-s., or they may be given in alternation.

Dose.—Same as *Nux.*

Lachesis.—Variable appetite; nausea, vomiting of food, particularly after eating, together with pain, drowsiness and a feeling of fulness and distension; flatulence; dyspnœa; constipation; fulness and tenderness of the region of the stomach to the touch. *Mercury* is sometimes required after *Lachesis.*

Dose.—Same as *Nux.*

Mercurius.—Unpleasant taste in the morning; aversion to hot, and craving for cool food and drink; painful sensibility of the stomach with nausea, eructations, fulness and tension; constipation with tenesmus.

Dose.—Same as *Nux.*

Calcarea.—Acid or bitter taste; thirst with little appetite; dislike for meat and hot food, with craving for dainties; nausea, water-brash, acidity, fulness and tenderness of the stomach to the touch; debility, pain in the head with sensation of coldness. Frequently given after *Sulphur.*

Dose.—Same as *Nux.*

Arsenicum.—Burning pains or colic in the stomach and abdomen, sometimes with chilliness and anguish; stomach sensitive to the touch; fulness or aching sensation, great debility; nausea, vomiting and diarrhœa, particularly after drinking, and every motion of the body.

Dose.—Same as *Nux.*

Ipecac.—Loathing of food with desire to vomit; violent straining or easy vomiting, nausea, pains and pressure or sense of fulness in the stomach; aching sensation in the forehead or head; chilliness; colic and diarrhœic stools.

Dose.—Same as *Nux.*

Carb.-v.—Loss of appetite; nausea and vomiting after a meal; acidity and pains in the stomach; heaviness and dullness of the head; peculiarly sensitive to changes of the temperature, cold, hot, dry or damp weather.

For particular indications for other remedies, see Materia Medica, at the close of the book.

Dose.—Same as *Nux.*

Administration.—I have already mentioned (page 12) in the introductory chapter, which I trust the reader will carefully peruse, the manner of preparing and giving medicines, so that it will be unnecessary to enter into the minutiæ here. Two drops may be mixed in a tumbler of water, a tablespoonful given at a dose, or a powder or three globules taken on the tongue. In recent cases of derangement of the stomach, the remedy carefully selected, may be given, a dose once in from one to four hours, according to circumstances. In chronic cases the intervals should be longer, say every six, or twelve hours, generally morning and night. I would again urge upon the attention of the reader, the necessity of closely studying the case, of being particular in the selection of a remedy, and after its selection, giving of it a fair trial.

Diet and Regimen.—The diet should be plain and simple, the habits regular, the mind cheerful and easy, and those causes, which tended to produce the disease, carefully avoided. Bathing and friction, moderate exercise in the open air, cheerful conversation, avoiding unpleasant and gloomy thoughts, and indulgence in those things which will give a healthy tone to the mind, and life and animation to the body, will often effect a cure without resorting to internal remedies. Late suppers, rich and stimulating food and drinks, and the artificial manner of living, which seems to be so pleasing to some, are not pleasing to the stomach, and are followed, oftentimes, by indigestion running into violent fevers and chronic dlfficulties, which undermine the constitution and sap the foundations of life.

LOSS OF APPETITE.

Anorexia.

This is occasioned by a derangement or weakness of the nerves of the stomach, and is generally symptomatic of other difficulties, vanishing when those difficulties are removed. When it seems to be the only symptom present, the remedies under the head of dyspepsy may be consulted, or with but few exceptions, it may be entirely removed by the use of water, in the form of bathing, exercise and a proper attention to diet. (See pape 78.)

MORBID APPETITE.

Bulimy.

This affection is also occasioned by a derangement of the nerves of the stomach, and instead ofbeing a disease itself, forms a part of some other disease, with which it may be treated. The remarks respecting *loss of appetite*, are applicable here.

NAUSEA. VOMITING.

These difficulties may be occasioned by errors in diet, in which case vomiting should be encouraged by the use of warm water, until the disturbing cause is ejected. They more generally, however, form part of a group of symptoms, indicating a derangement of various organs, and will be treated in connection with the diseases of which they form symptoms. When it so far predominates over other symptoms as to require particular attention, the prominent remedies are, *Stibium, Ipecac, Pulsatilla, Nux, Arsenic, Cuprum, Veratrum.*

Vomiting of blood may require: *Acon., Fer., Arn., Hyos., Ipecac., Nux-v., Amm.-c., Carbo-v., Caust., Chin., Mill., Puls.*

Of food: Ars., Fer., Hyos., Nux-v., Puls., Sulph, Bry.

Black vomiting: Ars., Calc., Chin., Verat., Ipecac., Nux-v.

From *indigestible food* or overloading the stomach: *Ipecac., Puls., Stib., Bry., Nux-v., Sulph., Ars., Bell., Fer., Rhus.* *See also Dyspepsy.*

For *Vomiting of Pregnant females*, see diseases of *Pregnancy*. Of *Drunkards*—see Delirium Tremens. Consult also the index, and the disease indicated by the group of symptoms.

ADMINISTRATION.—Two drops, or six globules, in a tumbler of water, a tablespoonful at a dose; or a powder, or three globules, may be taken dry on the tongue. Give a dose in from one to three hours.

DIET.—Light farinaceous food, such as, toast water, toast, gruel, farina, &c.

SEA SICKNESS.

This is a most distressing difficulty, and one unfortunately, in which the patient receives but very little sympathy. Its severity and duration, depend very much upon temperament and the condition of the person at the time. Some are sick from the motion of a carriage, or on the water, when it is simply rippled by the wind, while others experience no unpleasant sensations even in the wildest storms of the ocean.

CAUSE.—It may arise from a peculiar impression, produced on the brain and nervous system by the motion of the body, or by the objects we are passing; or again by the abdominal viscera, with the motion of the vessel rising and falling against the stomach, and from a variety of causes. The intense nausea, violent vomiting and disregard for life render it unlike any other disease.

TREATMENT.—Some advise the use of a bandage drawn around the body very tightly, just below the stomach, but all agree in the propriety of not crowding the stomach with a large amount of food just before going aboard. Brandy, lemons, ale, herring, &c., generally agree. The patient should remain in the open air, avoiding the bed, or the confined air of the cabin as much as possible. The remedies which will sometimes afford relief, are:

Cocculus.—When with the nausea there is an extreme sensitiveness of smell; loathing of smoking; hunger, but no appetite. It is indicated by the nausea, and vomiting occasioned by the motion of a carriage, especially in delicate females.

DOSE.—One drop, or six globules, in a tumbler of water, a tablespoonful every one, two or three hours, or if it be preferred, three globules may be taken dry on the tongue at the same intervals.

Nux-vom. and *Arsenicum* may be taken in alternation every two or three hours, particularly, when the symptoms are slight, or commence just after embarking.

DOSE.—A powder, or three globules, dry on the tongue.

Tabacum.—When the nausea is excessive, aggravated by the slightest motion of the head and body, and when the symptoms are relieved in the air.

DOSE.—Same as *Cocculus.*

Arsenicum.—When the excessive nausea is accompanied by great prostration, violent retching, burning sensation in the throat and stomach. It should be given between the paroxysms. After the severity of the paroxysms have subsided, the nausea and giddiness is frequently removed by *Tabacum* or *Cocculus.*

DOSE.—Same as *Nux.*

Ipecac.—Vomiting unattended by weakness.

DOSE.—Same as *Nux.*

Pulsatilla.—The patient is relieved in the open air.

Petroleum.—A prominent remedy particularly when there is debility.

Dose.—Same as *Nux.*

Constipation during a voyage is controlled by *Nux-vom. Op., Cocc., Sulph.* And if accompanied with bloody gums and putrid taste, *Staphysagria.* A dose once in twelve hours will generally be sufficient.

SPASMS, AND PAIN IN THE STOMACH.

Gastralgia, Cardialgia. Neuralgia of the Stomach.

This disease is excessively tormenting, and often slow and tedious in its progress.

Diagnosis.—Pain in the region of the stomach, varying in character and severity; at times violently constrictive, cutting, tearing, gnawing and beating; sometimes so violent as to cause the patient to bend double, at others, dull and heavy. It frequently extends to the breast and back, and is felt between the shoulders. Hard pressure from without generally relieves the pain. The paroxysms vary in duration from a quarter of an hour to a day. As the disease progresses, they increase in frequency and intensity until the pain is felt nearly all the time. There is often distressing vomiting, hiccough, flatulence, obstinate constipation, and palpitation of the heart. Toward the end of the paroxysm the patient is frequently relieved by bilious, acrid, or mucous vomiting.

Causes.—Any cause which has a tendency to derange the nerves of the stomach, as irritation of the liver, spleen, &c. Errors of diet, abuse of coffee and tea, fatigue, emotion, cathartics, abuse of ardent spirits, as well as other stimulating articles. Suppression of cutaneous eruption and cold in the stomach, when the body is heated. Exposure to cold, damp or changeable weather, especially in gouty and rheumatic persons. It is often particularly violent in females at the menstrual or critical period, when it may cause vomiting of blood.

Treatment.—Flannel should be worn next the skin, the feet should be kept warm, and particular attention paid to the diet. All stimulants, such as wines and spices, as well as coffee and tea, excepting perhaps weak black tea, should be avoided. Rich food and gravies, uncooked vegetables, new bread or warm cakes, sweetmeats, cheese and all of that class of food should be strictly prohibited. *Gastralgia*, occasioned by *abuse of coffee* may indicate: *Cham.*, *Cocc.*, *Ign.*, *Nux-v.*

Caused by moral emotions, such as, *anger*, *grief*, *&c.*. *Cham.*, *Coloc.*, *Nux-vom.*, *Ign.*, *Staph.*

By debility from nursing, purgatives, loss of blood, &c.: *Carb.-v.*, *Chin.*, *Cocc.*, *Nux-vom.*

By indigestion: *Bry.*, *Nux-vom.*, *Puls.*, *Carb.-v.*, *Chin.*

By intemperance: *Carb.-v.*, *Nux-vom.*, *Calc.*, *Sulph.*

By suppressed eruption: *Sulph.*

During *Catamenia*: *Cham.*, *Cocc.*, *Nux-vom.*, and particularly *Puls.*, *Sep.*

Catamenia too weak: *Cocc.*, *Puls.*

Catamenia too profuse: *Calc.*, *Lyc.*

Torpor of liver and bowels from want of exercise: *Carb.-v.*, *Nux*, *Sulph.*

Nux-vom. is one of the most important remedies, particularly indicated towards the commencement of the disease. A few doses, followed perhaps by three or four doses of Carb.-v. will often effect a complete cure. If, however, notwithstanding the similarity of the symptoms to *Nux*, decided relief is not obtained in a short time, *Pulsatilla*, *Chamomilla*, *Ignatia*, or *Cocculus* may be consulted with advantage.

The particular symptoms indicating *Nux*, are contractive, pressive, and spasmodic pains in the stomach; aggravation of pains after a meal or from coffee; oppression of the chest, with pain extending into the back; nausea, water-brash or vomiting of food during the pain; flatulence, constipation, hæmorrhoidal sufferings; irritable, morose and changeable temper; palpitation of the heart; pain in the head, or pressive pain in the forehead.

Dose.—A powder, or three globules, dry on the tongue; or one drop of the tincture in a tumbler of water, a tablespoonful at a dose. In acute and severe cases it may be given once in two hours until relief is obtained. In chronic cases it may be taken morning and night.

Carb.-v. particularly after *Nux*, and where there is violent contractive spasmodic pain, worse on lying down; water-brash, nausea, repugnance to food, flatulence, oppression of the chest and constipation; painful burning pressure with anxiety, aggravated at night or after a meal.

DOSE.—A powder, or three globules, morning and night.

Chamomilla.—Distension of the abdomen, with heavy pressing sensation, oppression of the chest and shortness of breath; worse after a meal or at night; great anguish, sometimes relieved by coffee; pulsative pain in the top of the head, particularly at night. It may be alternated with *Coffea*, and followed, when notwithstanding the similarity of the symptoms relief is not obtained, by *Belladonna.*

DOSE.—Two drops, or six globules, in a tumbler of water, a tablespoonful once in two or three hours.

Cocculus.—Often of benefit after *Nux-vom.*, or *Chamomilla*, where but slight relief has been obtained by them, and when the pain is relieved by emission of flatulence; also where the symptoms seem to indicate *Nux*, and yet are not relieved by that remedy.

DOSE.—Same as *Chamomilla.*

Pulsatilla.—Shooting pains, aggravated by walking, and in the evening, when they are also increased by shivering; spasmodic pain either from fasting or overloading the stomach, with nausea or vomiting; pulsation or tension in the stomach; sour or bitter taste, diarrhœic stools; mild disposition, sad and tearful. It is of decided service in menstrual difficulties.

DOSE.—Same as *Chamomilla.*

Belladonna.—Especially in women and delicate persons, and where the necessary relief has not been obtained from *Chamomilla*; violent aching or spasmodic tension or pain, so violent as to deprive of consciousness, great thirst, yet worse during and after drinking; sleeplessness at night, and sometimes the opposite during the day.

DOSE.—Same as *Chamomilla.*

Bryonia.—In the less violent forms of the disease. There is pressure in the pit of stomach, during and after a meal, together with a sensation of swelling; the pressure, sometimes increasing to pinching or cutting, is relieved by external pressure which creates belching of wind; headache and constipation.

Dose.—Two drops, or six globules, in a tumbler of water, a tablespoonful at a dose; or three globules, dry on the tongue. Give once in three or four hours.

Platina.—Particularly serviceable during profuse menstruation, generally in alternation with *Belladonna.*

Dose.—A powder, or three globules, every three hours.

China.—When occasioned by debility, such as that resulting from hemorrhage, sexual excess, cathartics, emetics, &c. Flatulence, water-brash; fulness and pressure after a meal; violent attacks, with sense of repletion, oppressive aching pain, eructations and empty retching.

Dose.—Three drops in a tumbler of water, a tablespoonful morning and night.

Ipecac.—Nausea, retching, vomiting, dull stitches in the stomach.

Dose.—One drop, or six globules, in a tumbler of water, or three globules dry on the tongue. Give a dose every two hours until relieved.

Sulphur.—Pressive pain as from a stone, especially after a meal, with nausea, vomiting and water-brash; acidity, eructations; tendency to hæmorrhoid or mucous derangement of the digestive organs; disposition to anger, grief, or melancholy.

Dose.—A powder, or three globules, morning and night.

Causticum.—Pressure, spasmodic constriction and clawing, shuddering when the pain increases, acidity and water-brash.

Dose.—One drop, or six globules, in a tumbler of water, or three globules dry on the tongue. Give every two or three hours.

Ignatia.—Particularly after *Pulsatilla*, or when it has been occasioned by grief or fasting; also pressive pain like a stone, after a meal or at night; weakness, emptiness, or burning in the stomach, which is sensitive to the touch; hiccough, repugnance to food, drink, or tobacco.

Dose.—Same as *Causticum.*

Calcarea.—Principally in plethoric persons and women subject to profuse menstruation, or where *Belladonna* has given but slight relief, and where there is compressive spasmodic pain, worse after a meal or at night, with vomiting of food, acidity, nausea and painful sensibility to the touch; constipation and hæmorrhoidal difficulties.

Dose.—Same as *Sulphur.*

Argent-nit.—Useful with females weak and irritable, when the menses are early and profuse; the spasmodic pain is very violent and is accompanied with retching and vomiting of acrid, yellow, greenish bitter mucus.

Dose.—A powder, or three globules, every two or three hours.

Arsenic.—Burning pain in the stomach; vomiting on drinking the smallest quantity; violent pain, or dull and heavy; great prostration.

Dose.—A powder, or three globules, dry on the tongue, every two or three hours. Where, in acute cases, the pain is excessively violent, the remedy carefully selected may sometimes be given once in half an hour or an hour. The external application of warm cloths may also be advisable.

COLIC.

Diagnosis.—Pain more or less severe; griping, tearing, cutting, grumbling or rumbling in different parts of the abdomen, but particularly about the navel; the pain generally comes on in paroxysms. The abdomen is sometimes drawn in, at others distended and tense; the pain is generally relieved by pressure, the bowels seldom being painful to the touch, unless the disease is gradually assuming the character of inflammation of the bowels. These symptoms are frequently attended by vomiting, more or less violent; the bowels, as a general thing, in simple colic, are constipated.

1. Inflammation of the stomach, and Hernia may be mistaken for simple colic, and yet, with a little care, they may very readily be distinguished. The absence of fever, except in exceedingly violent paroxysms, the pain being relieved by

pressure, the aspect of the countenance, and the quiet, soft pulse, will distinguish it from *inflammation of the bowels.* It may very readily be distinguished from hernia by the absence of the small *hernial tumour*, which is present in the latter affection.

CAUSES.—Among the prominent causes we may enumerate, errors in diet, dissipation, mental trouble, constipation, flatulent food, cold, and all those causes which have a tendency to produce inaction of the bowels and derangement of the digestive organs.

It may arise also from "*Intersusception*," in which a small portion of the intestine passes within itself, forming a stricture, which presents an impassible barrier to the passage of food, when unless relief is speedily obtained inflammation may set in ending in mortification and death. In this, there is at first no fever, but an obstinate, unyielding constipation; vomiting, gradually becoming worse, and pain, which at first is circumscribed to a small space. This form of the disease is by no means of frequent occurrence.

2. *Flatulent Colic.*—This is very frequent in children, improperly fed, and in dyspeptic persons, particularly those who are poorly nourished, or are addicted to the use of spirits. There is seldom but little sickness, not often constipation, but a painful retention of flatus, an occasional rumbling sensation in the bowels, with emissions of flatulence.

3. *Bilious Colic.*—In this form of colic, prior to the appearance of the characteristic symptoms, the patient usually suffers under symptoms of disordered stomach and intestines such as, bitter taste, yellow fur on the tongue, nausea and vomiting. There is thirst, anxiety, restlessness, severe cutting and screwing pain. Bilious vomiting supervenes, and the bowels are freely moved, the evacuations being mixed with bile. The symptoms gradually abate, only the severer forms being attended with much fever, and in those it sometimes terminates in inflammation of the bowels, and death.

4. *Painter's Colic.*—This variety is known by a variety of names, viz. *Colica Pictonum*, *Devonshire Colic*, &c.

It is occasioned by being exposed to the action of lead, and is very common among painters, who use the white lead in their paint, as well as among plumbers, and those engaged in smelting ores, or in lead manufactories. At first, there is a loss of appetite, restless nights, and disturbance of the nervous system. This is followed by vomiting, pain in the abdomen, at first in paroxysms, but gradually increasing until it becomes almost constant. There is little or no fever, but headache, pain in the limbs, obstinate constipation, and, after the severe symptoms have passed away, frequently paralysis of the extremities. An almost invariable symptom of Lead Colic, is a bluish line, extending along the edge of the gums. Sometimes this bluish-grey tinge extends over the mouth.

TREATMENT.—A warm bath will often produce speedy relief. If convenient, the patient may be seated in the bath, the water coming up to the stomach, the upper part of the body being covered so as to confine the steam, and permitted to remain in this situation ten or twelve minutes. He can then be taken out and covered warm in the bed, bottles of hot water being placed to the feet. When this form of bath is not convenient, warm cloths can be placed over the abdomen.

The prominent remedies are: *Belladonna*, *Colocynth*, *Nux*, *Pulsatilla.*

For *Flatulent Colic:* *Nux*, *Bell.*, *Carb.-v.*, *Calc.*, *Cham.*, *Chin.*, *Puls.*, *Sulph.* *Cocc.* may be consulted.

For *Bilious Colic:* *Nux*, *Coloc.*, *Bry.*, *Merc.*, *Puls.*, *Cham.*

For *Painter's Colic:* *Opium*, *Bell.*, *Alumina*, *Platina.*

With *constipation:* *Op.*, *Nux*, *Bryonia.*

From *Indigestion:* *Cham.*, *Coloc.*, *Sulphur.*

From cold damp weather: *Pulsatilla.*

From *Bathing:* *Nux.*

From a *strain* or a blow: *Arnica*, *Bryonia*, *Rhus.*

See also SYMPTOMATIC INDEX.

The particular indications are:

Nux-vomica.—Obstinate constipation; pressure in the abdomen as from a stone with flatulence; pinching, contractive, or compressive pains; pressure, fulness and tension in the stomach and abdomen; coldness of the extremities, or numbness during the pain; griping and flatulence; pressure on the bladder and rectum; pain in the loins or pressive headache. Particularly indicated in persons of plethoric habit and accustomed to rich living.

Dose.—One drop, or eight globules, in a tumbler of water, a tablespoonful at a dose; or three globules, or a powder, dry on the tongue.

Colocynth.—A prominent remedy, expecially where there is violent cutting and griping pains; tenderness and bruised sensation of the abdomen; cramps in the calves of the legs; restlessness and tossing from the pain; constipation or diarrhœa, and bilious vomiting, particularly after eating.

Dose.—Same as *Nux*.

Pulsatilla.—Shooting pain; uneasiness, heaviness, fulness, tension, and bruised sensation in the stomach and abdomen, incarcerated flatus, with rumbling, pinching, griping, aggravated by touch; worse in the evening or on lying down; general heat; pain in the loins when rising; nausea; diarrhœa; paleness of the face; pressive headache.

Dose.—Two drops, or eight globules, in a tumbler of water a tablespoonful at a dose; or three globules dry on the tongue.

Belladonna.—Pinching and drawing with a pressure downward, increased by motion; swelling between the stomach and navel, relieved by pressing; or pain in the stomach as if the intestines were grasped by finger nails; or spasmodic constriction in the abdomen with burning and pressure in the small of the back; or congestion of blood to the head, redness of face, and pain of the most violent character. *Mercury* or *Hyosciamus* are often suitable after *Belladonna*.

Dose.—Same as *Pulsatilla*.

Chamomilla.—Particularly in children, or when the attack is brought on by violent anger or chagrin. There are tearing, drawing pains, with restlessness; nausea, bitter vomiting, or bilious diarrhœa; bruised pain through the loins; incarcerated flatus with anguish, tension, and fulness in the stomach: pressing down; cheeks alternately pale and red.

Pains worse at night, in the morning, or after a meal. *Pulsatilla* suits well after *Chamomilla*.

DOSE.—Same as *Pulsatilla.*

Arsenicum.—Violent pain with great anguish; griping, spasmodic, corroding pain, with great burning, or sensation of cold in the abdomen; nausea or vomiting; thirst, shivering and debility; worse at night or after eating or drinking.

DOSE.—A powder, or three globules, dry on the tongue, every two or three hours.

Carb.-veg.—Distension of the abdomen with incarcerated flatus, rumbling, belching of wind; pressive pain in the head; general heat, obstinate constipation, hemorrhoids.

DOSE.—Same as *Arsenic.*

China.—Distension of the abdomen with fullness and pressure; or spasmodic constrictive pains, incarcerated flatulence; especially when the pains appear at night, or in those who have been weakened by debilitating losses, as diarrhœa, loss of blood, &c.

DOSE.—Same as *Pulsatilla.* Give morning, noon and night.

Cocculus.—Constrictive spasmodic pains, with flatulence, nausea, shortness of breath and distension of the stomach; or sensation of emptiness in the abdomen; tearing and burning in the intestines with clawing in the stomach; nausea, constipation, anguish, and nervous excitability.

Hyosciamus.—Similar to *Belladonna.* Pain in the head, restlessness, tenderness, hardness and distension of the abdomen, griping or spasmodic pain with vomiting.

Coffea.—Violent almost delirious pain; agitation, grinding of the teeth, oppression of the stomach, convulsions, coldness of the limbs and suffocation.

Phosphorus.—Flatulent colic, deep in the abdomen.

Ignatia.—Nightly colic, shooting in the vicinity of the spleen; incarcerated flatulence with difficult emission.

Mercurius.—Tenderness of the abdomen, when touched; pains worse at night, particularly after midnight; hiccough, morbid appetite; nausea, salivation, eructations or slimy diarrhœa; tensive burning or shooting pains, or violent and contractive, with distension and hardness of the abdomen, especially around the navel.

Sulphur.—In hæmorrhoidal colic, if the desired effect has not been obtained from *Carb.-v.*, or *Nux-vom.*; or in bilious colic, when neither *Chamomilla* or *Colocynth* has produced relief; or in flatulent colic after *Cham.*, *Cocc.*, *Nux* or *Carb.-v.*

Lycopodium.—Enormous quantity of flatulence, especially after eating; with pressure, distension, and fullness in the stomach and abdomen; constipation.

Calcarea.—In flatulent colic, or where it arises from acidity of the stomach.

Bryonia.—In bilious rheumatic attacks; after taking cold, with diarrhœa. Alternate with *Rhus.*

Opium.—Especially in *Painters' colic*, heaviness in the abdomen, which is hard and distended; obstinate constipation with vomiting or involuntary stools.

Veratrum.—Burning in the abdomen, tenderness, and cutting pains; rumbling and flatulence with difficult stools. Alternated with *Arsenicum*, or *Coffea.*

Platina, especially in lead colic, or in consequence of fear, or anger; contractive pain in the abdomen and stomach, with sensation of bearing down; sad, melancholy mood. Particularly indicated for females.

Administration.—In violent cases of colic, particularly where there is *Intersusception*, in bilious colic with obstinate constipation, injections may be necessary. If so, a pint of cold, or tepid water, may be thrown into the bowels. If this does not answer, it can be again repeated with the addition of a teaspoonful of salt, the water made sweet with molasses.

In violent cases, the remedies, prepared as directed for *Pulsatilla* or *Arsenic*, may be given every twenty or thirty minutes, gradually increasing the time, as the symptoms are relieved, to two or four hours. If after four or five doses have been given, no relief is obtained, the medicine should be changed.

Diet and Regimen.—Food, easy of digestion, carefully avoiding all flatulent diet, and food which the patient has found at times to disagree with him.

INFLAMMATION OF THE LIVER.

*Hepatitis.**

This disease has an acute and chronic form. Both of which, under homœopathic treatment, are generally quickly relieved without the development of various difficulties so common under Allopathic treatment, particularly in hot climates, such as abscess of the liver, which often terminates in death or in adhesion to some other organs.

Diagnosis.—There is generally an enlargement distinctly felt below and under the short ribs on the right side, where a sensation of tightness is also felt. The patient cannot lie on the left side, is troubled with fever, shortness of breath, cough and often vomiting and hiccough. The pain is seated, at times violent, burning, sharp, cutting, tensive, extending into the region of the stomach or thorax, at other times dull and aching, felt only during a deep inspiration, cough, or on external pressure. The region of the liver is extremely sensitive, hot, throbbing, and swollen, pain is also felt in the top of the right shoulder and arm, sometimes with a sensation of paralysis in the whole of the right side.

The fever, which is generally violent, is sometimes intermittent or remittent. Gastric or bilious symptoms are also present, such as hiccough, aversion to food, eructations, nausea and vomiting, fullness, burning and anguish in the pit of the stomach, bitter taste, jaundiced appearance, constipation or clayey stool.

Causes.—It may be occasioned by violent emotions, by emetics, or drastic cathartics; by cold in the abdomen, particularly when great heat alternates with dampness, or cold weather, or immediately by a cold drink, by indigestion, ardent spirits and the passage of gall stone. It may also be occasioned by mechanical injuries, such as a blow or heavy fall, also by sup-

* For a description of the liver, *see page* 39 *and* 56, also Plate 4.

pression of piles, of chronic eruption, erysipelas, diarrhœa, dysentery, &c. It is very common in the hot weather of warm climates.

TREATMENT.—The external application of the *wet bandage*, (*see page* 80) will often be of service in relieving the heat and pain. The remedies particularly indicated in the acute form of this disease are *Aconite*, *Belladonna*, *Mercury*, *Nux*, *Bryonia*, *Chamomilla*, *China*, *Lachesis*, *Pulsatilla*, and *Staphysagria*.

The chronic form of this disease is characterized by a class of symptoms similar to the acute, although in a modified degree. There is a continued pain in the right side, occasional cough with expectoration, and sometimes enlargement of the liver; yellow complexion, occasional feverish and dyspeptic symptoms, wasting of flesh and loss of strength. The prominent remedies are: *Nux-vom.* and *Sulphur*, which are often given in alternation, *Mercury*, *Iodine*, *Silicea*, *Lycopodium*.

*Aconite** is almost always indicated in the commencement of the disease. There is violent inflammatory fever, shooting pains in the parts affected, great restlessness, moaning and anguish.

DOSE.—Two drops, or eight globules, in a tumbler of water, a tablespoonful at a dose; or three globules, dry on the tongue. Give a dose every hour, or two hours, in all cases gradually increasing the intervals as the symptoms abate.

Belladonna.—Congestion of the head, with vertigo, fainting, clouded sight, burning thirst, great restlessness, sleepiness, dry cough, shortness of breath; stinging pain aggravated by pressure, inspiration, cough, or by lying on the side affected, sometimes extending to the shoulders or neck. Sometimes distension of the pit of the stomach, and tightness across the abdomen above the navel. A prominent remedy in the acute form either after *Aconite*, or in alternation with that remedy or *Mercury*, and in the chronic form, when the above

* For general directions as to the administration of remedies, *see page* 10.

symptoms exist in a modified state, in alternation with *Bryonia*, *Chamomilla*, *Pulsatilla*, *Aconite*, or *Mercury*.

DOSE.—In the acute form same as Aconite; in chronic cases once in four or six hours.

Chamomilla is a prominent remedy where the disease is occasioned by violent chagrin with gastric or jaundiced symptoms. It is also indicated, when there is more anguish than pain, which is not increased by pressure, motion or breathing; pressure in the stomach, tightness of the upper part of the abdomen, oppression of the chest, yellow color of the skin, and bitter taste in the mouth.

DOSE.—Same as *Aconite*.

Pulsatilla may be of benefit, if there should be green, slimy, diarrhœic stools, or disposition to vomit, oppression of the chest, and the paroxysms of anguish more frequent at night.

DOSE.—Same as *Aconite*, a dose every two or three hours.

Bryonia is an important remedy where the inflammation is attended with constipation and spasmodic symptoms of the chest. It is of great value in all congestive inflammations with violent fever, great vascular and nervous excitement; or for inflammations occasioned by cold or chagrin, worse at night, on waking, or during motion. It is particularly useful, when there is swelling in the region of the liver with burning, stinging pain during contact, cough or breathing. It may be given alone or in alternation with *Aconite*, *Belladonna*, or *Mercury*.

DOSE.—Same as *Aconite*.

China.—Aggravation every other day, with shooting pressing pains, hardness and swelling in the region of the liver and stomach; headache, bitter taste, and yellow tongue.

DOSE.—Two drops, or twelve globules, in a tumbler of water; or six globules dry on the tongue. Give morning, noon, and night.

Nux.—Shooting, pressive pain, with great sensitiveness in the region of the liver to the touch; constipation; bitter, sour taste, nausea, vomiting; short breath, headache, vertigo, thirst, red urine, and paroxysms of anguish. Sometimes in alternation with, or followed by *Sulphur*.

Dose.—Same as *Aconite*. Given once in three or four hours.

Mercurius.—Bitter taste, chilliness, aching pain in the region of the stomach and liver, sensitive to contact, unable to lie on the right side, jaundiced appearance and frequent paroxysms of anguish. *Lachesis* is frequently suitable after or in alternation with *Mercury*, particularly when the difficulty has been occasioned by ardent spirits.

Dose.—A powder, or six globules, once in three or four hours.

Sulphur.—Towards the close of the disease or where other remedies have failed in producing the desired effect. In chronic Hepatitis it is often desirable to alternate it with *Nux*.

Dose.—A powder, or six globules, once in six or twelve hours.

It should be remembered, that in administering the remedies, the intervals should be gradually increased as the violence of the symptoms abate, while in the chronic forms of the disease, a dose once in six or twelve hours, will generally be sufficient.

Diet.—Similar to that in fevers. No meats or soups, but gruels, toast, panada and light farinaceous articles; toast water, cold water, lemonade, baked apples, prunes, sweet oranges, peaches, raspberries, strawberries, &c., may be allowed.

JAUNDICE.

Icterus.*

There are several varieties of this disease; the chronic, acute, and that which occurs in infancy. It may continue from a few days to several weeks, but generally terminates favorably, except it may have arisen from abuse of *Mercury*, or in infancy, where it may have continued for some time, and there is present a dark brass color of the skin, distended ab-

* See page 39 and 56.

domen, spasms, sopor, putrid vomiting, stomach hot and painful, when it usually terminates fatally.

DIAGNOSIS.—There is a suppressed or limited secretion of bile in the liver, and consequently as we have explained in the chapter on physiology, there is a yellow color of the skin, the eyes even having a yellow tinge, and the liver stained yellow from the perspiration; there is sometimes an appearance of bile in the urine. The taste is frequently bitter, with inclination to vomit, or vomiting of mucous or bilious substance, the abdomen distended; sometimes pain in the region of the liver, a scanty white, gray or clayey stool. If there is fever, the chilliness is of short duration, and the fever has distinct remissions in the morning.

The disease may be occasioned by errors in diet, by taking cold when the skin is covered with perspiration, by drinking freely of cold water, or using ice, when the body is heated, by abuse of China, cathartics, mercurial and sulphur ointment, and from intermittent fevers. It sometimes becomes an epidemic disease when a hot atmosphere is suddenly cooled by a thunder-storm.

TREATMENT.—The *wet bandage*, (see page 80) around the body, over the stomach and liver, as well as general bathing, will be found of advantage. The patient should be kept in a warm and even temperature, and perspiration encouraged as much as possible.

*China** will be useful where there has been abuse of *Mercury*, and where there is pressure at the the stomach, distension of the abdomen, vomiting, diarrhœa, and great debility.

Mercurius is indicated after abuse of *China*, and in tuberculous individuals, when asthmatic symptoms, painfulness of the liver, rheumatic pains in the muscles of the chest are present. It is generally best to give it in the commencement of the disease, a dose morning, noon, and night.

Sulphur.—When occasioned by suppression of eruption, and in tuberculous and psoric individuals, after abuse of *Mercury*.

* For general directions as to the administration of remedies, see page 10.

Iodine.—There is a dingy yellow skin, irritable temper, thick coating of the tongue, thirst, turns of nausea, white diarrhœic stools alternating with constipation, dark, yellow-green, corrosive urine. It is also indicated after abuse of *Mercury*.

Chamomilla.—When occasioned by cold, chagrin, anger or when the body is sensitive to the open air, with sleeplessness, restlessness during sleep, distension of the abdomen, discharge of undigested food.

Digitalis.—Particularly indicated when the whole skin is yellow; there is loathing, empty retching, sensitiveness and pressure in the stomach and region of the liver, distension of the abdomen, sluggish, gray, clayey or chalky stools, turbid, yellow-brown urine.

Pulsatilla.—After abuse of *China*, *Chamomilla* or *Sulphur*, and from overloaded stomach. Frightful dreams, nocturnal anguish, sad, whining mood, bitter eructations, bitter, or sour, or bilious vomiting, throbbing in the pit of the stomach, difficult stool with straining.

Nux.-vom.—When occasioned by chagrin and anger, by abuse of spirits, coffea, tobacco, opium, &c.; or by sudden change of temperature, in individuals with irritable, melancholy, hysteric disposition, or who are very sensitive to the open air.

Administration.—Two drops of the tincture, or twelve globules in a tumbler of water, a tablespoonful at a dose; or three globules or a powder on the tongue; in severe cases give every three or four hours, according to symptoms. In slow chronic cases, a dose morning and night will generally be sufficient.

Diet.—Food easy of digestion, fruits, farinaceous articles, &c. Meats, plainly cooked, may be used judiciously, in the more chronic forms of the disease.

INFLAMMATION OF THE SPLEEN.

Splenitis.

Diagnosis.—Tensive, throbbing pains in the region of the spleen, extending to the shoulder, oppression of breath, constriction of the stomach, worse on turning to the left side or during motion; sometimes perceptible enlargement in the region of the spleen, painful when touched. Oppression, anguish, cough, dyspeptic symptoms, vomiting, eructations, &c. There may be vomiting of blood even at the commencement. The fever is attended with great thirst, and is generally of a remittent character.

Causes.—The causes producing inflammation of the spleen, are similar to those already enumerated under the head of inflammation of the liver. We may also mention the abuse of quinine, and living in a marshy region. It is more frequent among persons of middle age and old people, and also in men, than in women.

Treatment.*—In acute *splenitis,* accompanied with much fever, *Aconite* is an invaluable remedy and should be given alone every one or two hours, or if in alternation with some other remedy indicated, such as, *Bryonia*, *Belladonna* or *China*, every two or three hours. If the pain still continues after the fever has in a measure subsided, the appropriate remedies should be given.

Dose.—Two drops, or twelve globules, in a tumbler of water, or three globules, dry on the tongue, given as above directed.

Nux-vom. is indicated, where there is a sensation of swelling, and increase of the stinging pain to contact or motion; nausea, aversion to food, fainting spells, vomiting of blood, pains in the stomach, retention of stool, dyspeptic symptoms, &c. It is particularly useful after *China* or *Arnica*, where these remedies have only produced a temporary amelioration, the constipation and pressing gastralgia continuing nearly the same.

* For general directions as to the administration of remedies, see page 10.

China is a very important remedy and may often be given at the very commencement of the disease alone, or in alternation with *Aconite*. It is generally however given after the fever has been in a measure subdued by *Aconite*, and where the frequent vomiting of blood has produced great weakness, and also when there are lancinating, tearing pains with hardness and painful swelling of the spleen, the patient being unable to lie on the affected side. The fever is frequently of an intermittent character, and characterized, by dry, burning heat, aversion to food, nausea, and bitter taste, thirst, and restlessness.

Arnica.—Generally after *China*, when that is not quite sufficient; and when there are pressive shooting pains, typhoid symptoms, apathy and stupor.

Arsenicum.—May be useful after *China;* or where there are diarrhœic stools with discharge of dark coagulated blood, burning pain in the spleen with anguish and pulsation in the pit of the stomach.

Bryonia.—Particularly, if the constipation and sticking pains continue after the use of *China*, *Arnica* and *Nux*. *Pulsatilla* may with advantage be alternated with *Bryonia*, where there are sticking pains, increased by motion, and the part is visibly swollen.

In the chronic form of the disease. *Nux*, *Mercury*, *Bryonia*, *Sulphur*, *Calcarea*, *Carb.-v.* or *Iodine* may be given.

Dose.—Two drops of the tincture, or twelve globules, in a tumbler of water, a tablespoonful at a dose, or three globules, or a powder, dry on the tongue. In acute cases give every two or three hours, gradually increasing the intervals as the symptoms abate. In the chronic form of the disease a dose may be taken morning and night.

Diet.—Same as in *Inflammation of the liver.*

INFLAMMATION OF THE STOMACH.

*Gastritis.**

This disease is exceedingly painful and violent, running its course with great rapidity. It is astonishing, when we con-

* For a description of the stomach, see plate 4, and page 37 and 58.

sider the ill-treatment the stomach receives at our hands, that it is not much oftener affected with violent inflammation.

Diagnosis.—In the more violent forms of *Gastritis* there is a constant burning, gnawing, sticking, constrictive pain in the stomach, occasioning shortness of breath, and aggravated by breathing, contact, or pressure ; the desire for cold drink is excessive, notwithstanding if taken, even in the smallest quantity it is immediately vomited. The pulse is small, wiry, suppressed, frequently intermitting; the stool and urine scanty or suppressed. In the milder forms, the above symptoms are present in a less violent degree. The vomiting is less frequent, and the pain less severe. The position which the stomach occupies in relation to other parts of the system renders inflammation of that organ exceedingly dangerous. It requires prompt and vigorous treatment to arrest the rapidity of its progress. There is also in connection with other symptoms great anxiety, prostration, small, thread-like pulse, cool extremities and often fainting fits and convulsions. Death may take place either by *gangrene* or *nervous paralysis*. In the former case, the sudden cessation of pain, one of the heralds of death, is often looked on by surrounding friends with joy, as an indication of returning health, but the accompanying symptoms, the small, scarcely perceptible, remittent pulse, and coldness of the extremities, dashes the cup of joy to the earth, and chills them with the shadow of approaching dissolution. The latter termination, or "*nervous paralysis*," is generally accompanied with spasms, fits of fainting, and the utmost debility. The acute form not unfrequently passes into chronic inflammation, spasm and ulceration of the stomach.

Causes.—This disease may be occasioned by mechanical injuries, the introduction into the stomach of acid or corrosive poisons, the use of cold drinks, when the stomach is heated, stoppage of bilious diarrhœa, and suppression of eruptions ; inflammation of adjoining organs and metastasis of inflammation of other organs to the stomach.

TREATMENT.*—In Gastritis, occasioned by poisons—see *Poisons*.

Aconite is indicated at the commencement of the disease, where there is violent inflammatory fever and great pain, and particularly when occasioned by chills or cold drinks.

Ipecac.—When vomiting predominates and when occasioned by indigestion or chill, and when *Aconite* is insufficient. The tongue is clear.

Stibium.—Indications similar to *Ipecac.* with the exception of a white or yellow coated tongue.

Bryonia.—More particularly after *Aconite* or *Ipecac.*

Pulsatilla.—When caused by indigestion, or chill in the stomach from ice, particularly after *Ipecac.* or *Bryonia.*

Arsenic is perhaps the most important remedy in the treatment of the disease. It may often be given in alternation with *Veratrum.* There is a burning pain, vomiting, rapid prostration of strength, paleness of the face and coldness of the extremities.

Veratrum.—There is also vomiting, severe pain in the stomach, sometimes cramps, or spasms, prostration of strength, and coldness of extremities.

Hyosciamus.—When there are dropsical sufferings, or cerebral symptoms, with talkative delirium, loss of consciousness or stupor.

Belladonna.—When *Hyosciamus* does not produce the desired relief.

Opium and *Camphor* in alternation where there is prostration of strength, drowsiness and stupor.

Nux is of benefit in those cases, where *Aconite, Ipecac., Bryonia,* or *Arsenic* may be indicated and prove insufficient, particularly in persons accustomed to ardent spirits.

DOSE.—A powder, or three globules, dry on the tongue; or two drops of the tincture, or twelve globules, in a tumbler of water, a tablespoonful at a dose.

In the more violent cases give every fifteen or thirty minutes

* For general directions as to the administration of remedies, *see page* 10.

until relief is obtained, when the time can gradually be increased to one, two, or three hours, or, if after eight or ten doses, there is no change of symptoms, another remedy should be selected. Fomentations of hops over the stomach, or the application of cloths wrung out in hop water, will often produce a soothing effect.

DIET.—As almost every thing taken into the stomach is vomited, but very little, at first should be taken, and that should be of the lightest and simplest character ; cold water or toast water, in small quantities, not more than a tablespoonful at a time may be given, and gruels, as the symptoms gradually abate.

INFLAMMATION OF THE BOWELS.

*Enteritis.**

This disease like *gastritis* is exceedingly painful and rapid in its progress. In its idiopathic form or setting in from the commencement as an inflammation of the bowels, it is by no means of frequent occurrence, yet as a *symptomatic* affection, setting in during the progress, or the sequele of some other disease, such as the various forms of fever, it is of very frequent occurrence. We are apt to find the *symptomatic* form existing to a greater or less degree in almost every variety of acute inflammation.

DIAGNOSIS.—Where the peritoneal coat is the principal seat of the disease, it is called "*Peritonitis,*" and is accompanied in a greater degree, in addition to the usual symptoms of *enteritis*, with high fever, violent pain and an extreme sensitiveness of the abdomen to the touch. One variety of this disease we shall refer to under puerperal fever. In the acute form of *enteritis*, involving the sub-mucous tissue and peritoneal coat, as well as the mucous membrane, we have violent burning, cutting pain, generally in one spot, especially in the region of the navel, and gradually extending over the abdomen, increased by the slightest pressure with tightness, heat and

* For a description of the intestines, *see plate* 4, *and page* 38.

distension of the abdomen. The patient lies on the back, with the knees drawn up, and using only the muscles of the chest in breathing, avoiding, on account of the intense pain, every motion of the body. There is obstinate constipation; nausea and vomiting, so violent that not only every thing taken into the stomach is thrown up, but even fæces; constant desire for cold water, which, however, produces aggravation of pain. The pulse, as in all acute abdominal inflammations is small and wiry, or weak and like a thread. As the disease advances, there is hiccough, the pulse beats irregularly, the extremities grow cold, the features are sharpened and ghastly, and cold sweat breaks out. Delirium may occur toward the last, but generally the intellect remains clear. When the disease ends in death, similar symptoms occur to those mentioned in *gastritis*, terminating in gangrene. The pain ceases, the pulse becomes weak and scarcely perceptible, the extremities cold, and the impress of death is seen stamped in visible characters on the face, in the sharpening features, the glazing eye and the cold breath. The less acute form of this disease, or that developed by other diseases, is not characterized by the same violent symptoms, but may end in obstinate constipation, perforation of the intestines and gangrene. In this variety, the pain is more diffuse, and diarrhœa of a slimy or bloody character may also be present.

Causes.—It may arise from mechanical injuries, errors in diet, abuse of ardent spirits, the pernicious practice of eating chalk, magnesia, &c.; from cold, suppressed eruption, drastic cathartics, worms, parturition, and in connection with other diseases such as the malignant fevers.

Treatment.—The utmost quiet is of course essential, and in those cases where the patient can not bear the lightest pressure on the abdomen, it may be protected from the weight of the bed-clothes by a light frame-work not allowing the clothes to touch the skin. A warm bath, if the patient is able to bear it, or sponging the abdomen with hop water, will be found advantageous. The obstinate constipation being occasioned by inflammation, will not be relieved by the most violent cathartics, and when that inflammation subsides, the constipation ceases or is readily controlled.

Aconite should commence the treatment as directed in gastritis, and be continued so long as the fever is intense, the skin hot and parched.

Arsenicum is a prominent remedy in the severe forms of this disease; there is prostration of strength, intense burning pain. It may be given either alone or in alternation with *Veratrum*. For particular indications, see *Gastritis*. It is also a prominent remedy in the less acute forms of the disease, where there is burning heat, thirst, increase of pain after cold drink, nausea, fetid diarrhœa, and extreme debility.

Belladonna.—Red and smooth tongue, or coated in the centre with red tip and margin; dry and hot skin, thirst, delirium, particularly at night; sensation of soreness in the abdomen, with tenderness on pressure. *Belladonna* is a prominent remedy in the severe forms of this disease, and is very often indicated in alternation with *Mercurius*.

Dose.—Two drops, or twelve globules, in a tumbler of water, a tablespoonful at a dose; or six globules dry on the tongue. Give every one or two hours.

Mercurius.—The tongue is foul, coated white or brown; dry or covered with thick mucus; great thirst, abdomen tender to the touch, hard and distended; watery, bilious, and offensive stools; urging to stool, followed by severe straining and the passage of blood. There may be prostration of strength, chilliness, and disposition to perspire during the night.

Dose.—A powder, or six globules, every two or three hours.

Nitric acid is serviceable where *Mercury* has proved insufficient, particularly in chronic cases, where there is tenderness and tenesmus, especially where the disease occurs in those persons who have taken large quantities of calomel.

Dose.—Two drops of the first dilution, in a tumbler of water, a tablespoonful once in six or twelve hours.

Opium and *Plumbum* are the prominent remedies where

there is vomiting of fæces, spasmodic pain about the stomach or abdomen.

DOSE.—Of the former one drop, or twelve globules, in a tumbler of water; of the latter a powder, or three globules dry on the tongue. Give every three or four hours.

Nux-v.—There is soreness with burning heat in the abdomen, loss of appetite, vomiting of food, pain on drinking, constipation, flatulence, or watery or bloody stools with straining. *Sulphur* is frequently indicated in alternation.

DOSE.—A powder, or six globules, every four, six or twelve hours.

Besides the remedies already enumerated, *Bryonia, Colocynth, Chamomilla, Pulsatilla, China, Cantharides, Rhus, Phosphorus* may also be consulted. As the more common forms of inflammation of the bowels occur in connection with other diseases, the particular indications of many of the remedies will be given when speaking of those diseases. Consult *Worms, Gastritis, Hepatitis, Diarrhœa, Dysentery.*

DIET.—Same as in *Gastritis.*

DIARRHŒA.

Diarrhœa is generally a symptom of, or is developed in connection with, some other disease. It may at times be looked upon as a dangerous and even alarming symptom, and again as the precursor of returning health, the welcome indication that the *crisis* is favorable, and that the disease is leaving the system. The favorable *crisis* of a disease not unfrequently shows itself in a diarrhœa. This diarrhœa is an indication that nature is reacting, bursting the fetters of disease, which have hitherto bound it, preventing its free action, and is returning to a healthy equilibrium. In these cases no particular treatment is necessary.

Another form of diarrhœa mentioned above, and by far the most common, is that which is developed in connection with some other disease. In these cases it is generally an unpleasant, and not unfrequently an alarming symptom, as in consumption, typhoid fever, &c., where the powers of nature are rapidly prostrated. There is no difficulty in distinguishing between the favorable diarrhœa of the *crisis*, and the unfavorable one of disease. In the former case, there is a perceptible amelioration of severe symptoms, the fever is sensibly diminished, and the pulse becomes more slow, soft and full, while in the latter case the pulse becomes weaker, the system more prostrated, or at any rate there are no ameliorating symptoms.

It will be unnecessary to refer to the treatment of this variety here, as it forms only one of a group of symptoms in other diseases, and will be treated in connection with those diseases, under their appropriate heads. *See also* SYMPTOMATIC INDEX.

It remains then in this place only for us to speak of *diarrhœa*, when it occurs as a primary affection. In its duration, it may vary from a day to several days or even weeks, often running into a chronic form lasting for months or years. The peculiar symptoms are familiar to all. The attack is sometimes preceded by precursory symptoms of a gastric affection, and is ushered in by an increased and more frequent discharge from the bowels, the color varying more or less from the natural.

There are often nausea, flatulence, griping pain in the bowels, succeeded by stools of a fluid, watery, bilious, mucous, or bloody consistency. The tongue may also be furred and the breath foul, but in simple diarrhœa, there is generally but little, if any fever.

Diarrhœa sometimes, as in bilious difficulties, and where it arises from indigestion or dissipation, may be highly beneficial, being the effort of nature to throw off those indigestible and irritating substances, which, unless expelled in this manner, might create violent fever and serious disturbances. It may again be the result of cold, occasioned by dampness or changes of temperature, impurities of the air and impure food, or the effect of the mind on the body, the prostration of fear, or the violent excitement of anger. The bowels, as well as the stomach, sympathise with almost every organ in the body, and give indications of uneasiness, when those organs are deranged.

Diarrhœa is of itself indicative of some disturbed action about the bowels, and when this disturbance is of such a character, as to need medicine to relieve it, the remedy should be directed so as to remove irritation, restore the proper tone to the bowels and cause them to act in obedience with nature. Much harm is often done by suddenly suppressing a diarrhœa, by means of brandy, opium, and the general class of astringents. The disease is not removed any more, than a putrid sore, covered with a plaster; it may be concealed from sight, but the irritating cause is still untouched.

Treatment.—*Dulcamara.*—Is the prominent remedy in diarrhœas occasioned by cold, particularly in the summer and fall, and where the evacuations are of a green, yellow slimy or sour character, occurring particularly at night, preceded by colic and followed by debility; there may also be nausea, retching, restlessness, thirst and griping or lancinating pain in the bowels.

Dose.—Two drops, or twelve globules, in a tumbler of water, a tablespoonful at a dose; or six globules dry on the tongue. Give every three, four, or six hours.

China.—If the diarrhœa is of a debilitating kind, occurring particularly after eating or in the night, and containing undigested food.

Dose.—Same as *Dulcamara.* Give morning, noon and night.

Bryonia.—When occasioned by the heat of summer, or when caused by cold, as drinking cold water, or when occasioned by vexation or passion, particularly if rheumatic symptoms are present. The evacuations may be almost involuntary, have a fetid smell, and be accompanied with flatulence or fermentation.

Dose.—Same as *Dulcamara.* Give every four or six hours.

Chamomilla.—Slimy, bilious, or watery diarrhœa of a yellowish or greenish color, resembling chopped eggs; there is thirst, tearing colic, griping and fullness in the pit of the stomach; the abdomen is hard and distended, the evacuations frequent and sometimes attended with nausea or bilious vomiting. It is a prominent remedy in diarrhœa during dentition, and is often accompanied with cries, restlessness, and anguish. (See diseases of children.)

DOSE.—Same as *Dulcamara*. Give every three or four hours.

Ipecac.—Watery diarrhœa, of a slimy, yellowish or greenish character, with nausea, or vomiting of watery or green mucus; or putrid, bloody, or slimy, with white flakes and tenesmus (see dysentery); tearing colic, with restlessness, cries and tossing. Particularly useful in children. (See Cholera Infantum.)

DOSE.—A powder, or three globules, every two, three, or four hours, according to the severity of the symptoms.

Pulsatilla.—Particularly in diarrhœas from disordered stomach, or indigestion, and when there is watery, bilious, or slimy evacuations; tongue coated white, nausea, or slimy, bitter vomiting, colic and cuttings, especially at night; sometimes the evacuations are mixed with blood or change their color to yellow white or green.

DOSE.—Two drops in a tumbler of water, a tablespoonful at a dose; or three globules on the tongue. Give every three or four hours.

Rheum.—A prominent remedy when the evacuations have a sour smell, are of a liquid, slimy, fermented or greenish character, accompanied with colic, frequent ineffectual efforts to evacuate, and tenesmus, or profuse evacuation with vomiting; restlessness, anguish, and cries. A prominent remedy in children (see diseases of children). *Chamomilla* is often suitable after it.

DOSE.—Same as *Pulsatilla.*

Mercury.—Particularly when there is danger of its assuming a dysenteric form, and where the stools are watery, slimy, or bilious, or of a bloody or greenish character, preceded by colic and griping, and followed by tenesmus and straining; there may also be nausea, shivering and shuddering.

DOSE.—A powder, or six globules, every three hours.

Colocynth.—Watery or bilious diarrhœa with violent

griping colic, particularly when caused by vexation or passion; where *Chamomilla* has not produced relief.

Arsenic.—Burning evacuations of a watery, slimy, putrid or brownish character, with burning, griping or tearing pains in the abdomen, especially after midnight; thirst, nausea, or vomiting; emaciation and weakness; hollow eyes, pale cheeks. Coldness of the extremities, colic pains, distension of the abdomen, in alternation with *Veratrum.*

DOSE.—Same as *Mercury.*

Ferrum.—Painless evacuations, especially at night, or after eating or drinking; thirst, emaciation, pain in the stomach, back and anus.

DOSE.—Same as *Mercury.* Give morning, noon and night.

Sulphur.—In those obstinate cases, where other remedies seem to have failed, and particularly where the evacuations occur at night,—with colic, tenesmus, shortness of breath,—of a slimy, watery, frothy, putrid, bloody or sour character; easily renewed on taking cold.

DOSE.—Same as *Mercury.* Give every four or six hours.

Secale.—Where the evacuations are painless and are expelled with great violence, often involuntarily and without premonitory symptoms, and followed by weakness.

DOSE.—Three globules, once in four or six hours.

Carbo-veg.—Diarrhœa of a putrid, fetid smell, or in wet weather, after taking cold. (See also Cholera.)

DOSE.—A powder, or six globules, every four hours.

Ignatia.—Diarrhœa with rumbling in the bowels, occasioned by grief.

DOSE.—One drop in a tumbler of water, a tablespoonful once in two hours; or three globules dry on the tongue at the same intervals.

Nux-vom.—Scanty evacuations with griping pain, colic and tenesmus.

Phosphorus.—I have found this a highly valuable remedy in chronic diarrhœa with painless evacuations, debility and emaciation.

DOSE.—A powder, or six globules, once in six hours.

Belladonna.—Small stools with bearing down pain, flushed face, and congested feeling in the head.

Veratrum.—Diarrhœa with symptoms resembling cholera (which see), or where there are cutting, griping pains, and debility. These symptoms we frequently see during the diarrhœas, developed in fevers.

In classifying some of the various remedies, we find where Diarrhœa occurs without pain, *Fer.*, *Chin.*, *Phos.*, *Secale* are particularly indicated.

Diarrhœa with *Colic: Coloc.*, *Merc.*, *Nux-v.*, *Cham.*, *Bry.*, *Ars.*, *Sulph.*, *Puls.*, *Rheum.*

With *Tenesmus: Ars.*, *Ipecac.*, *Merc.*, *Nux-v.*, *Bell.*, *Sulph.*

With *vomiting: Ars.*, *Ipecac.*, *Verat.*, *Puls.*

With prostration of strength: *Ars.*, *Chin.*, *Verat.*, *Phos.*, *Sec.*

Chronic diarrhœa: Calc., *Fer.*, *Phos.*, *Chin.*, *Nit.-ac.*, *Sulph.*

In consequence of an *eruption: Ars.*, *Chin.*, *Sulph.*, *Merc.*, *Pulsatilla.*

In *aged* persons: *Secale*, *Phos.*, *Bryonia.*

In tuberculous persons: *Iodine*, *Calc.*, *Sep.*, *Sil.*, *Sulph.*, *Phosphorns.*

From taking cold: *Dulc.*, *Chamomilla.*

From cold drinks: *Ars.*, *Carb.-v.*, *Puls.*

From sudden emotion—joy; *Coff.*, *Acon.*, *Pulsatilla.*—Fright: *Cham.*, *Veratrum.*—Grief: *Phos.-ac.*, *Ignatia.*—Disappointment or anger: *Cham.*, *Coloc.*, *Nux-vom.*

The result of indigestion: *Ant.*, *Coff.*, *Ipecac*, *Nux*, or *Pulsatilla.*

The result of a debauch: *Carb.-v.*, *Nux-v.* Of milk: *Bryonia*, *Sulphur.* Of fruit: *Ars.*, *Chin.*, *Pulsatilla.*

Abuse of medicinal substances: *Mercury*, *Hep.-s.*, *Carb.-v.*, *Chin.*, *Nit.-ac.* Of magnesia: *Puls.*, *Rheum.* Of tobacco: *Cham.*, *Pulsatilla.*

For more minute classification and special indications, see *Materia Medica* and *symptomatic index.* In chronic cases a dose of the remedy morning and evening will be sufficient.

Diet.—Rest is advisable, particularly in severe cases.

Fruits and acidulated drinks should be avoided, and the diet consist of light unirritating food, such as salep, farina, gruel, arrow-root, &c. In chronic cases the food may be nourishing, yet easy of digestion.

DYSENTERY.

Bloody Flux.

This disease is intensely painful and requires prompt and vigorous treatment to prevent its assuming a highly dangerous form. The suffering has often been represented as similar to that endured by the mother in child-birth. It is generally attended with fever, sometimes accompanied with thirst, headache, nausea and vomiting. The dysenteric attack may be preceded by diarrhœa or rheumatic symptoms, or from the commencement assume the form of a decided dysentery. It cannot be looked upon as a diarrhœa, from which it may readily be distinguished, but it is essentialy an inflammation of the mucous membrane of a certain portion of the intestine. No fæces are discharged but mucous or bloody stools, accompanied with straining and tenesmus and generally preceded by severe griping pain in the bowels. The appearance of fæces, though they may be mixed with blood, indicates that the inflammation is subsiding, reaction taking place, and that the patient is decidedly advancing towards convalescence. The discharges at first, may be of a whitish or jelly-like mucus, resembling the scraping of the intestines, (called *Dysenteria alba*) or white dysentery) speedily followed by the *bloody flux* or red dysentery, of a mucus and bloody character, from the inflamed surface of the intestines, mixed with membranous shreds, and morsels that resemble flesh. The evacuations may vary in color, green, black, and reddish, like the washings of meat, and very fetid. During this state there is of course a continuance of febrile symptoms, great restlessness and intense anguish.

The disease may terminate in mortification and exhaustion, in a chronic dysentery, or in health.

Dysenteries are particularly violent in warm climates,

sometimes developed in severe epidemics, not only there, but, generally in a less violent degree, in our more temporate regions. It is the pest and scourge of the army, exposed as the soldiers are to every variety of hardship, to-day engaged in the fierce strife of battle, and to-night sleeping perhaps on the cold damp ground, with the rain pouring in torrents upon them. In two years and a half the British army lost in Spain nearly 5000 men by this disease. Hundreds of our own army, during the campaign in Mexico, died with it, or returned home only to lay their bones among their kindred. It may be caused by indigestible food,errors in diet, and tainted or impure food, abuse of spirituous liquors, and by taking cold, particularly when the perspiration is suddenly suppressed. Unripe or decayed fruit is also injurious, but fruit perfectly ripe and fresh may be eaten with safety. The disease is more liable to occur in the latter part of the summer, autumn, and fall, and is particularly severe in damp miasmatic and marshy districts.

Treatment.—To those of us, who have formerly been Allopathic physicians, it is refreshing to contrast our present treatment of this disease with our old practice, and if it is pleasant to us, it is much more so to the patient. Under the homœopathic treatment a death by dysentery when taken in time is exceedingly rare, while in other treatments it is an every day occurrence. We have seen in this disease, that the mucous membrane of the intestines is highly inflamed, often coming away in shreds, while from the highly inflamed and irritated surface blood is freely discharged. The great object is of course to relieve this irritation and re-establish a natural and healthy action. How is this to be done? An Allopath would pour into those irritated, inflamed and bleeding bowels, cathartics, mercury, castor-oil, opium, astringents, such as sugar of lead, &c. And as they pride themselves on appreciable doses, the dose would consist of a considerable amount of the drug. A homœopath, by remedies acting gently, in obedience to a fixed law, would remove the febrile irritation, control the spasms and severe distress, as we shall hereafter show, gently, yet quickly and effectually.

The prominent remedies are: *Aconite*, *Bryonia*, *Belladonna*, *Rhus*, *Mercurius*, *Colocynth*, *Ipecac*, *Nux*, *Sulphur*, *Carb.-v.*, *Nit.-ac.*, *Plumbum*, *Pulsatilla*.

*Aconite** is indicated particularly in the commencement, where there is fever, shivering, heat and thirst, and in dysentery, during warm weather with cold nights; attended with rheumatic pains in the head, neck and shoulder.

In the early stage of the disease, *Aconite* will often be sufficient to break up the attack.

DOSE.—Two drops, or six globules, in a tumbler of water, a tablespoonful every two or three hours.

Aloes.—Violent evacuations with bloody stool, colic, heat in the rectum, tenesmus, and faintness, when at stool.

DOSE.—A powder, or three globules, once in three hours.

Belladonna.—After, or in alternation with *Aconite*, where, in addition to the febrile symptoms, the exacerbation comes on in the afternoon, the patient is restless, the face red, the head hot; colicky, or cutting burning pain, constant urging to stool, and discharge of bloody mucus.

DOSE.—Same as *Aconite*.

Mercury is one of the most important remedies in the treatment of this disease. Violent tenesmus, straining before and after the evacuation, as if the intestines would be jerked out, which only produces a passage of blood, or of blood-mixed with a substance resembling chopped eggs. During the evacuation, colic, nausea, and shivering.

Colocynth is second only to Mercurius in the treatment of most forms of dysentery. The prominent symptoms are bloody stools, fullness and pressure in the abdomen, and particularly, severe *griping colic*, so violent as to cause the patient to bend double. In most forms of dysentery, where Mercury is required, I have found the griping colic also present indicating *Colocynth*. In these cases I have generally given

* For general directions as to the administration of remedies, see page 10.

them in alternation, two or three hours apart, or even at shorter intervals, if the symptoms are very violent.

DOSE.—A powder, or six globules of the *Mercury* may be given, and one drop, or twelve globules of *Colocynth*, mixed in a tumbler of water, a tablespoonful at a dose, given as directed above. These remedies, if their good effect seem to cease, may be followed by two or three doses of *Colchicum* with advantage.

Ipecac.—A very important remedy, particularly in the dysenteries of autumn and after *Aconite;* or when there is nausea, violent tenesmus and colic, stools, first of a slimy, then a bloody mucus. It may sometimes be indicated in alternation with or followed by *Colocynth*, or *Mercury.*

DOSE.—One drop in a tumbler of water, a tablespoonful at a dose; or a powder, or six globules, dry on the tongue. Give every two or three hours.

Arsenic.—The indications for this remedy are similar to those of *Carb.-veg.*, with which it is generally best to alternate. There is burning pain in evacuating the bowels, rapid prostration, coldness of the extremities, cold breath, putrid and offensive discharge of urine and fæces, often involuntary.

DOSE.—A powder, or six globules, every two or three hours.

China is useful where the disease occurs in marshy countries, and where the sinking putrid symptoms still continue after the use of *Arsenic* and *Carb.-v.*

DOSE.—Three drops in a tumbler of water, a tablespoonful every four hours.

Nux-v.—Small, frequent evacuations, of bloody slime, with tenesmus, violent cutting about the umbilical region, heat and thirst. Particularly useful when brought on by the heat of summer, or when *Arsenic* only aggravates the putrid smell of the evacuations.

DOSE.—Same as *Arsenic.*

Pulsatilla.—Mucus streaked with blood, nausea, vomiting of mucus, shivering and cutting in the bowels.

Dose.—Two drops, or eight globules, in a tumbler of water, a tablespoonful once in three or four hours.

Nitric-acid.—Constant pressing in the rectum without evacuation, or evacuation of mucus after which tenesmus continues, followed by tensive pressure in the head, heat, thirst, and intermittent pulse.

Dose.—Same as *Pulsatilla.*

Plumbum.—I have found this a valuable remedy in those very violent cases not relieved by *Mercury* and *Colocynth.* Nothing but blood is passed, the pain is intense, and the tenesmus continues even after the stool.

Dose.—A powder, or three globules, every three hours.

Bryonia and *Rhus* deserve attention when the disease occurs during the heat of summer, and is occasioned by a chill, or accompanied with rheumatic pains. (See Diarrhœa.)

Sulphur.—After other remedies have failed, Sulphur often removes the disease, or arouses the system, so that it is more susceptible to the action of other remedies.

Dose.—A powder, or six globules, may be given every three hours until three doses have been taken.

Diet.—The patient should keep in a reclining posture in the bed, and when the disease is violent use the bed-pan instead of getting up. The drink should consist of cold water, toast water, rice coffee, black tea; and the food, of toast softened in tea, or water, salep, arrow-root, farina, &c. All kinds of animal food and wines should of course be avoided even during convalescence.

CHOLERA MORBUS.

The sporadic or bilious cholera, known as *Cholera Morbus,* differs materially from that fearful pestilence *Epidemic* or *Asiatic Cholera,* notwithstanding there is something of a resemblance in appearance. It occurs principally in the summer and autumn, and is common in all parts of the country.

Diagnosis.—The attack may be preceded by the ordinary symptoms of bilious derangement, such as, languor, nausea, oppression about the stomach, colicky pains, &c. More frequently, and as a general rule, it comes on suddenly, without any precursory symptoms. There is nausea, sudden and repeated vomiting, with a violent diarrhœa, first of fæces, then of a watery, bilious fermenting liquid, accompanied with tenesmus, violent burning, cutting, griping colic, particularly about the navel. The vomiting consists at first of the contents of the stomach, but at length a watery, slimy, or bilious fluid is discharged in larger or smaller quantities. Even after the vomiting has ceased, painful retching and gagging may continue. In violent cases, if the disease is not promptly checked, there may be a rapid prostration of strength, cold sweat, pale and haggard face, spasmodic and scarcely perceptible pulse and convulsions.

CAUSES.—Taking cold suddenly in hot weather, intense heat long continued, violent emotions, unripe fruit, acrid, non-fermenting drinks, fat, rancid food, powerful cathartics, suppressed menstruation, gout or cutaneous eruptions.

TREATMENT.*—The principal remedies in the treatment of this disease are: *Ipecac.*, *Chamomilla*, *Arsenic*, *Colocynth*, *Veratrum*, *China*, *Dulcamara*, *Pulsatilla*. The precursory symptoms, if there are any, will generally yield to one or two doses of *Chamomilla*. Should however nausea and vomiting with diarrhœa exist, a dose of *Ipecac.* repeated every hour or two, will be indicated. If these do not relieve in four or five hours, or the attack becomes fully developed, other remedies should be consulted, as *Veratrum*, *Colocynth*, &c.

PARTICULAR INDICATION.

Chamomilla.—When the attack is occasioned by a chill or fit of passion, and where there is yellow-coated tongue, bilious diarrhœa, cramps in the calves of the legs, colic pains, or pressure about the navel.

Ipecac. is an important remedy, particularly in the commencement of the disease, when the vomiting seems to predominate.

Veratrum.—If, notwithstanding the use of the preceding

* For general directions as to the administration of remedies, see page 10.

remedies the disease becomes fully developed, this is a most important remedy. The vomiting and diarrhœa are very violent, the countenance is pale and expressive of deep suffering, the abdomen is tender to the touch; excruciating pains in the region of the navel, cramps in the calves of the legs and fingers, coldness of the breath and extremities, and rapid prostration of strength. It alternates well with *Ipecac.*

Colocynth is also an important remedy and is indicated by violent griping colic, bilious vomiting, green, bilious or watery diarrhœa.

Arsenic.—Rapid prostration of strength, violent and painful vomiting, diarrhœa almost constant, small, weak, intermittent pulse, spasms in the fingers and toes, clammy perspiration, burning sensation in the region of the stomach, &c.

Dulcamara.—Caused by changes of the temperature, iced drinks, &c.; griping or cutting pain in the bowels, greenish diarrhœa and bilious vomiting.

Pulsatilla.—In mild cases, where there is mucous diarrhœa, and where the attack was caused by indigestible food.

China.—When the disease was occasioned by indigestible substances, unripe fruit, and where it occurs in marshy districts. There is prostration, vomiting, pressure about the abdomen, and brownish evacuations, containing indigestible food.

Dose.—Three drops may be mixed in a tumbler of water, and a tablespoonful taken at a dose; or a powder or six globules may be taken on the tongue. In violent cases, a dose may be given every twenty or thirty minutes, until three or four doses have been taken, when, if indicated, other remedies may be selected, or those given in longer intervals, varying from one to three hours.

Diet and Regimen.—The patient should be kept warm by means of blankets, bottles filled with warm water should also be applied to the feet, and in violent cases dry hot cloths, or a mustard poultice, may be applied over the stomach. The drink should consist of cold water, and the food of gruels.

ASIATIC CHOLERA.

Epidemic Cholera.

We proceed now to the investigation of one of the most fearful diseases which has ever ravaged the earth. Confined to no nation and no clime, the breath of this pestilence has sped on its mission of death from land to land and from nation to nation, numbering its victims by thousands. In the East Indies, and the southern portions of Asia, along the banks of their mighty rivers, in their crowded cities, and valleys teeming with the rich luxuriance of tropical vegetation, it has reaped a rich harvest for many years.

In Madras from 1818 to 1822 23⅓ per cent. of the army were attacked, and of these 22¾ per cent. died. In 1821, one-sixth part of the inhabitants of a province on the Persian Gulf perished, and in the same year in another province, in a few weeks time 18,000 fell victims. In September, 1830, in Moscow, 54 per cent. of all attacked died. In Paris, in 1832, 18,000 perished, and in Palermo in a population of 120,000, 25,000 perished.

In the United States, in 1832, it filled the land with terror and carried consternation and mourning to thousands of family circles. In New-York city alone there were 5,547 cases, and of these 2,782 died, being one-half of all that were attacked. In 1821–2, twenty-five of the Allopathic hospitals in Italy and France give a ratio of 63 deaths out of every one hundred patients, and in this country, in 1832–4, their success was but little better.

A fearful pestilence speeds as with the wing of a destroying angel, from land to land, marking its pathway with graves, mocking the skill and science of those who claim to be "the medical world," pursuing its dark and conquering path almost unchecked.

A dark picture indeed, and well might we tremble at the approach of so dread a disease.—But it is not all dark, not all conquering, for a system based upon nature and experience steps in, rolls back the swelling tide, and abates its fearful ravages.—It is in diseases like this, diseases which have planted the Earth with graves, and which laugh to scorn the efforts of old systems to check their progress, that *Homœopathy* wins its most glorious victories, and secures its most brilliant and lasting triumphs. The success of Homœopathy in the treatment of Cholera and other violent diseases, has contributed more than aught else to its rapid advancement all over the world. In 1832, there were treated allopathically in Vienna, 4,500 Cholera patients, and of these 1,360 or 31 per cent. died. There were treated homœopathically 581 patients, of whom 49 died ; being only 8 per cent.

Dr. Quin, of London, gives the result of the treatment of ten Homœopathic physicians. The patients treated were 1,093, and of these only 95 died, thus twenty-one out of every twenty-three were saved.

Dr. Rath, sent by the King of Bavaria to ascertain the results of the Homœopathic treatment of Cholera, reports the treatment of 14 physicians in Prague, in Hungary and Vienna. The number of cases treated was 1,269, the number of deaths only 85.

In Austria, Berlin, Russia and Paris there were treated homœopathically 3,017, of which ten out of every eleven were cured. Hon. Alex. Eustaphieve, the Russian Consul-General, makes a similar statement, as it regards the success of the Homœopathic treatment in various parts of the Russian Empire, and the venerable Admiral Mordvenow, President of the Imperial Council, says, "not a single death has occurred, when Homœopathic treatment was resorted to in the incipient stages of Cholera."

But we need not go beyond our own country, for here we have ample proofs of the splendid triumphs won by Homœopathy, particularly in the Cholera of 1849. Under Homœopathic treatment the loss did not exceed from two and a half to three and a half per cent. And the cases reported by Homœopathic physicians as Cholera, were in reality such, decided and well marked cases. The mortality under the

Allopathic system was similar to that already mentioned in Europe.

DIAGNOSIS.—There may be precursory symptoms, such as inclination to diarrhœa, rumbling in the bowels, debility, general feeling of uneasiness, but as a general thing, the attack comes on suddenly, and runs its course with great rapidity, not unfrequently terminating in death in ten or twelve hours.

There is sudden prostration of strength, diarrhœa and vomiting, gushing forth in large quantities. The discharges follow each other in rapid succession becoming more and more watery and fluid, until after three or four discharges, they present the appearance of rice-water, and are without smell. These are the rice-water discharges of Cholera. There is also a painful burning in the stomach, sometimes extending behind the sternum, frequently connected with a sighing, and with it an insatiable thirst, anxious breathing, accompanied with a constant desire for cold water, which however produces but slight relief, and is almost immediately, particularly when taken in large quantities, thrown up in vomiting. The prostration rapidly increases, the patient becomes restless and anxious, and in a short time the fearful and agonizing cramps are developed in the limbs and frequently the bowels and breasts. They generally commence in the calves, toes, and fingers.

There is also an increasing oppression of the chest, and an excessive smallness of the pulse. The movements become painless and may be either very frequent or few in number. If the stools diminish in number while there is also a decrease in the strength and pulse, a speedy dissolution is indicated. No trace of bile can be found in the evacuations, but they are accompanied by a great sense of exhaustion, which soon amounts to utter prostration. As the disease progresses, the last stage or that of collapse sets in. Besides the above symptoms which may be present, particularly the cramps, a coldness commencing at the lower limbs gradually spreads over the body, resisting all external means of warmth; the face and lips become pale, blue, and cold, the body and tongue present a shriveled appearance, the breath becomes cold, a cold, clammy perspiration bedews the skin, the circulation apparently ceases, as often no pulse can be felt for hours before death. The voice is peculiar, being feeble, fine, somewhat hoarse, hollow or without resonance. The patient at length sinks into a stupor, the face presents a frightful ghostlike appearance, the eyes may be blood-shot, and turned up in the head, and death speedily closes the scene.

Causes.—The medical world is still to a certain extent in obscurity, as it regards the cause of this fearful pestilence. It attacks people of all ages and of every condition in life, but is more frequent and fatal among those who are pent up in ill-ventilated rooms, exposed to the effluvia of decaying vegetable matter, uncleanly in their persons, and imprudent in their diet, or among that class, whose chief delight is in the luxuries of the table and the exhilaration of the wine cup.

We cannot look upon this disease as a diarrhœa, for no fœcal matter is seen in the discharges. It is rather a decomposition of the blood, occasioned by some unknown cause, aided by a variety of circumstances, such as fear, debility, as well as the causes mentioned above, in which the watery part or serum of the blood, separating from the coagulum, escapes from the blood vessels into the stomach and bowels from whence it gushes in torrents.

This decomposition may be the work of days or hours, or as in the cases of dry cholera, which are the most violent, and are unattended with discharges, be the work of a few moments, accompanied from the commencement with violent and continued cramps. These cramps are occasioned by a cessation of arterial action on the muscles and of course cease when that action is reestablished. Need we wonder then at the rapid prostration of the cholera patient, when we remember, that these rice-water discharges, which gush forth in such torrents, consist in reality of the white part of the blood?

Prevention.—Cholera prevails as an epidemic, often desolating a town or city while villages within the distance of a few miles entirely escape. By some it is considered contagious, but this view I think is entirely erroneous. In a somewhat extended observation of Cholera I have never seen or read any adequate proof of its contagion.

Cleanliness, pure air, a healthy diet, and above all, a calm and even mind, are of course essential in warding off the attack. Giving way to fear, in this, as in every other disease, debilitates the system, and thus renders a person far more liable to its fatal effects. The gates are opened by the trembling victim, and all the disease has to do, is to enter and take possession. Any thing which would have a tendency to weaken the system, should be avoided, and yet a healthy vigorous action of the mind and body are of the utmost importance.

A sudden breaking up of habits, injurious in themselves, yet long persisted in, may cause too violent a shock of the system at a period, when violent shocks are dangerous. Thus, persons accustomed for a long time to the use of liquors or tobacco, may continue to use them, but in diminished quantity. The diet should be plain and simple, yet nourishing. Beef, potatoes, and bread, also *ripe* and *fresh* vegetables and fruit should constitute the principal part of the diet—the latter in moderate quantities.—Melons and green fruit and vegetables are not to be used.

The best beverage as a general thing is cold water. It may be advisable to wear a flannel bandage over the bowels. The utmost regularity should be observed in all things, eating, sleeping, or exercise, and mental or physical excesses should be carefully guarded against.

Treatment.—There is often previous, or after the attack, a diarrhœa with rumbling in the bowels, and a general feeling of prostration or uneasiness. This is called *Cholerine*, and is generally easily relieved. Where it has been occasioned by cold, and is accompanied with pain in the limbs, headache, shivering, &c., a few doses of *Bryonia* and *Rhus*, given in alternation every two or three hours, will produce relief. If occasioned by debilitating causes either mental or physical a few doses of *Phos.-ac.* or *China*, given at intervals of three or four hours, may be taken. If occasioned by fear, *Chamomilla* would be indicated, and if there should be present much nausea, *Ipecac.* may be given. A dose every two or three hours.

When the attack fairly commences, the *rice-water discharges* being present, *Camphor* is the all-important remedy, and should be immediately given. The patient should be covered up in bed, and a drop of the tincture of *Camphor* given on a lump of sugar every three, four, or five minutes. As soon as reaction takes place, and the patient becomes warm, the doses may be given less frequently, and when full perspiration commences, cease entirely. A little brandy and water may now be given.

If after the use of *Camphor* headache should come on, a few doses of *Belladonna* will relieve it. Should however *cramps* commence, which are not removed, or are only modified by the *Camphor*, we must turn our attention to other remedies ; these are *Cuprum* and *Veratrum*, which are the most important, and can frequently be given in alternation. The cramps, coldness of the body or extremities, prostration, and discharges, clearly indicate these remedies. *Veratrum*, particularly when the cramps are exceedingly violent in the calves and bowels, and *Cuprum* when the vomiting is preceded by spasmodic constriction of the chest. *Veratrum*, two drops of the tincture may be dissolved in a tumbler of water, and a teaspoonful given in alternation with a powder of *Cuprum*, ten, fifteen, or twenty minutes apart, gradually increasing the intervals as the symptoms are relieved. If after five or six hours the vomiting has nearly or quite ceased, there are cramps in the extremities, particularly the calves, and the evacuations still show no trace of bile, the prostration and coldness still continuing, *Secale*, a drop dissolved in a glass half full of water, and a teaspoonful may be given at intervals of half an hour, until three or four doses have been taken.

In this stage *Phos.-ac.* is often a valuable remedy, particularly where chest symptoms are prominent, oppression of breathing, pain in the chest and side, anguish and restlessness. Two drops of the first dilution may be mixed in a glass half full of water, and a teaspoonful given every fifteen or twenty minutes.

During this stage, the covering may be governed by the feelings of the patient, who generally prefers to be well covered. Small lumps of ice may be taken, the drinks may be either cold or warm, according to the feelings of the patient, and injections of cold water may be thrown into the bowels, when they are severely cramped. Friction also should be made with the warm, dry hand, particularly over those parts violently cramped. Should the disease pass into the last stage, or that of *collapse*, *Arsenic*, or *Carb.-veg.* are the prominent remedies. *Veratrum* and *Secale* may also be indicated, and *Camphor*, if that remedy has not before been given. This stage may last from a few hours to two or three days with but slight alteration, and terminate in convalescence, death, or some other disease, particularly Typhoid Fever.

Carb.-veg. should be given every three hours, particularly if stupor is present, or there is oppression of the chest or head, and should there be a sensation of intense burning in the stomach, with frequent desire for water, it may be alternated with *Arsenic* every two hours, gradually increasing the intervals to six hours, as the returning pulse shows signs of reaction. Should the burning sensation be the prominent symptom, *Arsenic* may be given alone at intervals of an hour. *Arsenic* is also indicated when the disease sets in with great violence, and when there is violent burning in the stomach, bowels, and throat, with great thirst and debility. The covering should be governed by the feelings of the patient, who generally prefers but little if any. The application of external warmth in this stage is entirely useless.

I have thus endeavored to delineate the development and progress of Asiatic Cholera, as well as the treatment I found most successful in my own practice during the prevalence of this disease in 1849.

As has already been seen *Camphor*, *Cuprum* and *Veratrum*

are the prominent remedies, one or the other of which may be indicated in every stage of the disease, as well also as preventatives. *Phos.-ac.*, *Ipecac.*, *Arsenic*, *Carbo-v.*, *Secale*, *Hellebore*, are also important remedies and deserving of particular attention.

During the prevalence of this epidemic, every family should be provided with a small case, containing a vial of the tincture of *Camphor*, one of *Veratrum*, one of the powder of *Cuprum*, and another of *Ipecac.* The premonitory symptoms should be promptly checked. At the commencement of the attack, until the physician arrives, the friends should not hesitate in their course, but administer the remedies with promptness and decision.

The day is not far distant, when as the great Homœopathic law shall be acknowledged throughout the world, as the only law of cure, and it requires no prophet's eye to foretel the speedy arrival of that day, this now withering pestilence will no longer be looked upon as a scourge and a desolater of mankind.

CONSTIPATION. COSTIVENESS.

This most troublesome and obstinate difficulty more frequently exists as a symptom of some other derangement. When however it seems to be the principal symptom, it requires patience and care in the use of remedies to effect its removal. It may arise from inaction of the liver, a general derangement of the digestive organs, causing weakness of the bowels, from mental difficulty, and an almost infinite variety of causes. Thus we frequently see it in persons of sedentary habits, as a result of dissipation, or mental anxiety, in pregnant females, and in various forms of disease.

It can frequently be removed by means of a change of diet, fresh air, judicious exercise, perfect regularity in eating and the time of stool. Looking at this trouble in its true light, we very readily perceive the injurious effects produced by cathartics. The bowels, inactive and debilitated, are roused to violent action only to settle back into a state of greater weakness and inactivity than before. The experience of all accustomed to cathartics shows, that their secondary effect is almost always *constipation*. Hence they should be avoided entirely or only resorted to in extreme cases. Where mechanical means are necessary, injections of cold or tepid water may be used, or if the case is urgent, or these should fail, a tablespoonful of sweet oil and a teaspoonful of salt may be added.

Water is also an exceedingly valuable remedy both as a drink and as an external application. The *sitz-bath*, or a *shower-bath*, the water falling obliquely over the abdomen, and perhaps stomach and liver, are not unfrequently highly advantageous. (See page 80.) The diet also should be simple, easy of digestion and of an opening kind. Hence, bread made of unbolted flour, fruits and vegetables perfectly fresh and ripe, may be eaten freely, together with a moderate amount of meat simply cooked. Late suppers, highly seasoned food, &c. should of course be strictly prohibited. The general directions given in treating of dyspepsy may also be observed here.

How much more consistent with common sense is the doctrine, which teaches us that when the bowels or digestive organs are weakened, or in a measure paralyzed so as to be unable to perform their functions aright, that we should by gently stimulating nature, rouse it from its torpor to its natural and healthy action, rather than by strong mechanical means weaken it for a moment, only to render it by the violence of its action more helpless than before?

If we only reflect, that constipation is generally the result of a torpor, or want of action in the intestinal canal and digestive organs, we should hardly think of removing the difficulty by those means, the unavoidable tendency of which would be to weaken those organs.

The prominent remedies in the treatment of this disease are: *Nux-v.*, *Sulphur*, *Bryonia* and *Opium*. Besides these *Sep.*, *Lach.*, *Lyc.*, *Plat.*, *Calc.*, *Phos.*, *Ant.*, *Sil.*, *Coc.*, *Alumina*, *Veratrum*, *Puls.*, *Carb.-v.*, &c., are also frequently indicated.

For persons of sedentary habits: *Bry.*, *Nux-v.*, *Sulph.*, *Lyc.*, *Op.*, *Plat.* are generally indicated.

That of *drunkards*, *Nux-v.*, *Opium*, *Sulphur.*

Following *diarrhœa* or *purging*: *Nux-v.*, *Opium*, *Ant.*, *Lachesis.*

In old persons, often alternating with diarrhœa: *Ant.*, *Op.*, *Phos.*, *Bry.*, *Lachesis.*

In pregnant women: *Nux-v.*, *Op.*, *Sep.*, *Alum.*, *Bry.*, *Lyc.*

In Lying-in-women: *Ant.*, *Bry.*, *Nux-v.*, *Plat.*

In Infants: see diseases of children.

When traveling in a carriage: *Plat.*, *Alum.*, *Opium.*

During a sea-voyage: *Cocc.*, *Silic.*, *Tab.*

For other varieties, see *Symptomatic Index.*

PARTICULAR INDICATIONS.*

Alumina.—I have found great benefit from this remedy in cases of obstinate constipation, when the fæces were dry and hard, great inactivity of the large intestines, and the movements were accompanied with considerable straining, and also when attended with hæmorrhoidal tumors. It may frequently be given in alternation with *Bryonia.*

DOSE.—A powder, or three globules, every night.

Bryonia.—Particularly indicated in those of an irritable, passionate character, and also in rheumatic persons; in warm weather, or when occasioned by a disordered stomach with chilliness and headache. It alternates well with *Nux-v.* or *Alumina.*

DOSE.—One drop, or six globules, in a tumbler of water, a tablespoonful every night.

Nux-vom. is an important remedy in constipation, especially in chronic cases, occasioned by coffee, dissipation, or from sedentary habits, also in persons subject to *hæmorrhoids*, or in consequence of indigestible food, or a too hearty meal; and especially when there is nausea, distension, pressure and heaviness about the abdomen, headache, ill-humor, and full-

* For general directions as to the administration of remedies, see page 10.

ness about the head, disturbed sleep, and general sensation of dullness, frequent and ineffectual effort to evacuate, with a sensation as if the anus were contracted. It is frequently advisable to alternate it with *Sulphur; Sulphur* in the morning, and the *Nux* at night.

A powder, or one globule of the 12th, may be given at a dose.

Sulphur.—In cases of habitual constipation, particularly if there is a tendency to hæmorrhoids, or uneasiness about the abdomen, with ineffectual efforts to evacuate.

Dose.—Same as *Nux*, with which it may often be alternated.

Opium.—More particular in recent cases, or in old persons, and frequently in chronic cases occasioned by sedentary habits. There is headache, determination of blood to the head, redness of the face, want of appetite, weight in the abdomen, sensation as if the anus were closed, and the intestinal canal paralyzed.

Dose.—One drop, or six globules, in a tumbler of water, a tablespoonful morning and night.

Pulsatilla.—Similar indications to those of *Nux;* especially useful in persons of a mild, cold, phlegmatic temperament, or when occasioned by derangement of the stomach from fatty food.

Dose.—Same as *Opium.*

Sepia.—Particularly suitable to females, where there is irregularity of the menses, and also where there is a derangement of the circulation of the liver, accompanied with languor, heaviness, and pain in the head; hard, bullet-shaped fæces; also indicated in rheumatic persons. It is frequently suitable in chronic cases after Nux and Sulphur.

Dose.—A powder, or three globules, morning and night.

Platina.—Obstinate constipation and ineffectual desire to evacuate, accompanied with pain in the abdomen and stomach; excessively difficult evacuations, with tenesmus and tingling in the anus.

Dose.—A powder, or three globules, morning and night.

Plumbum.—Very obstinate constipation, either painless, as if the bowels were paralyzed, or accompanied with severe colic, particularly about the navel, or when there is ineffectual effort to evacuate with painful sensation of constriction about the anus. Particularly useful in persons affected with palsy, epilepsy, dropsy or emaciation.

Dose.—A powder, or three globules, morning and night.

Silicea.—Especially in scrofulous constitutions, in verminous difficulties, and where dyspeptic symptoms are present. There may be ineffectual effort to evacuate, and colic.

Dose.—Same as *Platina.*

Veratrum.—Severe constipation, headache, flushed face; nausea, tenderness of the abdomen to the touch, and especially in bilious, gastric and hypocondriacal individuals.

Dose.—Two drops, or six globules, in a tumbler of water, a tablespoonful morning and night.

Lycopodium.—Particularly where there is a scrofulous constitution, and also from long continued dyspepsy, or abuse of medicines.

Dose.—A powder, or six globules at night.

Conium.—In old people or females, and where there is ineffectual effort to evacuate.

Dose.—Same as *Opium.*

In recent cases of constipation, the remedy should be given more frequently than in the chronic form. In the former, where the accompanying symptoms are violent, it may be necessary to give it every three or six hours.

HÆMORRHOIDS. PILES.

An obstruction in the circulation of the hæmorrhoidal artery, thus producing a congested state of the rectum, particularly about the anus, gives rise to small tumors or lumps, called piles. These lumps may be external, or so far within the rectum as to be imperceptible to sight, and they may or may not bleed, and are therefore spoken of as either external, internal, bleeding, or blind piles.

They may be occasioned by a constitutional taint, in which

case, if partially removed, they are liable to return at any time. They may give rise to, or be combined with, various forms of chronic disease, when close and careful observation is necessary to produce permanent relief.

The exciting causes are, use of stimulants, such as, spirits, coffee, spices, &c., or frequent use of cathartics; constipation or the contrary; depressing emotion, great mental exertion, sedentary life, riding on horseback. They frequently occur during pregnancy, from wearing tight clothes, or from worms. They are generally attended with considerable heat, burning, tearing, or cutting pain, and weakness and pain about the small of the back.

The food should be such as to keep the bowels moderately open; heating or stimulating drinks should be avoided, cathartics consigned to oblivion, and the surgeon's knife allowed to rest quietly in its case. The habit of cutting off these tumors, is not only revolting treatment, but generally productive of far more evil than good.

TREATMENT.*—I have found in these cases great advantage in the use of the sitz-bath. (*See page* 80.) It has a tendency to reduce the inflammation, and remove in a great degree the sufferings of the patient.

Nux-v. is a prominent remedy in almost every form of this disease, and particularly useful when occasioned by constipation, abuse of stimulating drinks, sedentary life with mental exertion, worms, compression of the abdomen, swelling of the abdominal organs, and in pregnancy.

DOSE.—A powder, or six globules, may be taken every six or twelve hours according to the symptoms.

Sulphur is also a prominent remedy, particularly in blind or flowing piles of a chronic nature. It is also strongly indicated for hæmorrhoidal colic with contractive pains about the umbilicus.

DOSE.—Same as *Nux*, with which it may often be alternated, the *Sulphur* in the morning, and the *Nux* at night.

* For general directions as to the administration of remedies, *see page* 10.

Belladonna is an excellent remedy in bleeding piles, especially where there is severe pain in the small of the back. It may be followed with advantage by *Hepar-s.*

Dose.—Two drops, or twelve globules, in a tumbler of water, a tablespoonful every six hours.

Sabina is also a valuable remedy, especially in bleeding piles, with discharge of bright, red blood, or blood mixed with mucus.

Dose.—Same as *Belladonna.*

Capsicum, *Carb.-v.*, *Arsenic*, and *Pulsatilla* are also useful in flowing piles. In old and distressing tumors, *Nit.-ac.*, *Mur.-ac.*, *Calcarea*, *Lycopodium* are frequently indicated.

The various forms of this disease, and its combination with other difficulties, render it advisable, particularly in chronic cases, to employ the skill and experience of the physician, rather than trust to home treatment.

CHAPTER IV.

AFFECTIONS OF THE WINDPIPE AND CHEST.*

We now proceed to the investigation of a class of diseases exceedingly common in our variable and ever-changing climate, and which, neglected, often lead to serious consequences. In the chapters on Anatomy and Physiology I have shown the important part which the organs connected with respiration perform in the economy of life, the beauty and regularity with which they perform their functions in health, and the necessity of their being well developed, vigorous and active, unclogged in their movements, to secure beauty of form and maintain a healthy and harmonious equilibrium in the system.

A slight irritation of a certain portion of the windpipe may destroy the music of the sweetest voice, and the seeds of that wasting *consumption*, which has saddened so many a hearth and blighted so many sweet buds of promise, may be sown by a slight cold, at the time easily removed, but neglected, planting its roots so deep and strong as to sap the fountains of life, and lay its victim in the grave.

Serious disturbances of the chest of course require the aid of the careful and skilful physician, but many of the incipient symptoms are so plain, that not unfrequently a few doses of medicine, properly selected by the patient, may remove the whole difficulty, and prevent the development of what might have been a serious disease.

For the sake of convenience, we shall divide the diseases treated in this chapter into two classes.

1. *Affections of the Windpipe and Lungs.*
2. *Affections of the Heart.*

---

* For a description of the organs included under this head, see plate 2, fig. 4, and plate 5. Also page 30, and 39.

1. AFFECTION OF THE WINDPIPE AND LUNGS.

HOARSENESS.

Aphonia. Raucitas.

When this difficulty, which is an affection of the mucous membrane of the larynx exists, as it often does in connection with other diseases, such as, measles, influenza, and severe disturbances about the chest and windpipe, its treatment will be given in connection with those diseases under their appropriate heads.

When however it exists alone or combined with cough, or, it runs into a chronic form, thus paving the way for more serious disturbance, of course, specific treatment is required.

TREATMENT.*

Pulsatilla.—Where there is almost complete extinction of the voice (*Aphonia*), loose cough, and discharge from the nose of thick yellow mucus. It is frequently necessary to follow it by *Sulphur.*

Nux-vom. is a prominent remedy, and particularly indicated where the hoarseness is worse in the morning and is accompanied with dry, rough, fatiguing cough. (*See Influenza.*)

Mercurius is particularly useful after *Nux*, or *Pulsatilla*, and where there is profuse perspiration, especially at night, a hoarse, rough voice, and a burning, tickling sensation in the larynx. (*See also Influenza.*)

Capsicum.—Obstruction with sensation of tickling in the nose; violent cough, worse towards evening, and pain in the head or abdomen.

Rhus.—Where there is a sensation of rawness in the throat and chest, chilliness, pain in the limbs, hoarseness, worse after talking, difficult breathing, with sneezing, and watery discharge from the nose. It alternates well with *Bryonia*, a dose three or four hours apart.

Drosera.—Hoarseness with low, hollow voice.

* For general directions as to the administration of remedies, see page 10.

Chamomilla.—Particularly in children, with accumulation of mucus in the throat, cough, worse at night, and often toward evening; slight fever and restlessness.

Sambucus.—Deep, hollow cough; oppression of the chest, &c.

Sulphur.—Particularly in cold, damp weather; roughness, and scraping in the throat; watery discharge from the nose in obstinate or chronic cases, where the voice is almost extinct. It will be frequently indicated after *Pulsatilla* or *Mercury.*

Hepar-sulph. is particularly indicated where mercurial preparations have been used; where the cough is worse at night and accompanied by a sensation of soreness in the throat and chest. *Causticum,* which is also indicated by the above symptoms, may be given, if, after four or five doses of *Hepar-s.* no relief is obtained.

Carb. v.—In chronic hoarseness, aggravated by talking, and worse in the morning and evening, also in wet weather.

Phosphorus is a valuable remedy, particularly in chronic hoarseness, where there is a dryness in the throat and chest, sometimes with sensation of soreness, and voice almost extinct. It is not unfrequently indicated in alternation with *Carbo-v.* or *Hepar-s.*

Administration.—In acute cases the remedy should be taken every four or five hours, until five or six doses have been taken, when if no relief is obtained, another remedy should be selected.

In chronic cases, a dose every six or twelve hours, may be given, changing the remedy in three or four days, if no improvement is perceptible.

Two drops, or eight globules, in a tumbler of water, a tablespoonful at a dose; or a powder, or six globules, dry on the tongue.

Diet and Regimen.—The wet bandage, (see page 80) around the throat at night will materially aid the cure. The food should be plain and simple, abstaining from spices and wines.

INFLUENZA.

There are but few persons in our ever-changing climate, who have not had practical experience of the sensations, produced by this disease. It very commonly, though not always, exists as an epidemic, frequently prevading a whole community.

For the sake of clearness and convenience, we divide it into three varieties.

1. *Coryza,* or cold in the head.*
2. *General Influenza.*
3. *Typhoid Influenza.*

1. CORYZA.

Diagnosis.—The difficulty may commence with shivering, and feverish sensation, and is accompanied with pain in the head, particularly over the eyes and about the root of the nose, obstruction of, or running at the nose, watering of the eyes, sometimes with pain and redness. If these symptoms are not checked, the irritation may travel downward to the larynx and lungs, giving rise to other varieties of influenzas and colds, most of which commence in this way.

Treatment.—If taken promptly, a few doses of *Camphor* will generally alone be sufficient to produce a cure. Two drops may be mixed with four tablespoonfuls of water, and one spoonful taken every three hours. Next to *Camphor*, *Arsenic* is the prominent remedy. It is indicated by obstruction of the nose, accompanied by, or in alternation with, profuse watery discharge, sometimes with burning in the nose and excoriation of the adjacent parts.

Dose.—A powder, or six globules, every two or four hours, according to the severity of the symptoms.

Mercury is of great value, where there is frequent sneezing, profuse watery discharge, swelling, redness, and excoriation of the nose, itching or aching pain, on pressing the nose;

* For general directions as to the administration of remedies, see page 10.

pain in the limbs, restlessness, shivering, or feverish heat and thirst. Frequently indicated in alternation with *Nux*.

Dose.—Same as *Arsenic.*

Nux-v. is indicated, where there is dryness with obstruction of the nose, headache with heaviness in the forehead, or shooting, tearing pains; running of the nose in the morning, with dryness in the evening or night; constipation and sensation of weariness.

Dose.—Same as *Arsenic.*

Hepar-s.—Particularly if *Mercury* has not produced relief, or the patient has before been drugged with calomel; also where cold air renews the difficulty, causing headache; or the cold only attacks one nostril, and the headache is made worse by movement.

Dose.—Same as *Arsenic.*

Pulsatilla.—Loss of appetite, taste and smell; secretion of thick and offensive mucus; sneezing; heaviness and confusion of the head, particularly in the evening, in the warmth of the room, with obstruction of the nose; better in the open air.

Dose.—Two drops, or twelve globules, in a tumbler of water, a tablespoonful once in four or six hours.

Chamomilla.—Particularly useful in children,either alone or in alternation with *Belladonna* or *Pulsatilla.* After suppressed perspiration; heaviness of the head with stupor; shivering with heat; acrid and smarting mucus in the nose.

Dose.—Same as *Pulsatilla.*

Sulphur.—Obstruction and dryness of the nose, or profuse secretion of thick, yellowish and puriform mucus; sneezing, loss of smell, &c.

Dose.—A powder, or six globules, every six hours.

Euphrasia is useful where the eyes are red and watery.

Dose.—Same as *Pulsatilla.*

Administration.—Where persons are constantly liable to this affection on the slightest exposure, it can often be prevented by bathing the head and neck every day in cold water.

If the discharge from the nose should suddenly stop and be

attended with headache, *Aconite*, three or four doses, given at intervals of three hours, followed, if necessary, by *Pulsatilla*, will produce relief.

Should difficulty of breathing be developed, *Bryonia* and *Ipecac.* in alternation, three hours apart, may be given, followed by *Arsenic*, if no relief is obtained after two doses of each have been taken.

2. GENERAL INFLUENZA.

In addition to the symptoms mentioned under *Coryza*, there is more or less shivering, alternating with flashes of heat, violent headache, drowsiness, rheumatic pains, difficult breathing, generally cough, more or less severe, painful and red eyes, and general debility.

TREATMENT.—In the commencement of the disease *Camphor* is the prominent remedy, a drop of which may be given every hour, until three or four doses have been taken.

Arsenic is also strongly indicated in the first stage of the disease, three or four doses of which may be given at intervals of two or three hours.

Mercury is particularly useful, where head symptoms preponderate. There is sneezing, running at the nose, rheumatic pains, or red, watery eyes, sore throat, loose cough, slimy diarrhœa, with straining.

DOSE.—A powder, or six globules, once in two or four hours.

Stibium.—Dry and hard cough, sometimes with rattling in the chest, alternation of shivering and flashes of heat, frequently with pain in the forehead, tightness about the nose, and pressing pain over the eyes. Should there be considerable pain about the chest, hoarseness and difficulty in drawing a long breath, *Phosphorus* may be alternated with the *Stibium*, two hours apart.

DOSE.—Same as *Mercury*.

Belladonna may be alternated with *Mercury*, where there is soreness of the throat, pain in the head, rheumatic pains, &c., given two or three hours apart.

Dose.—Two drops, or twelve globules, in a tumbler of water, a tablespoonful at a dose.

Nux-v.—Hoarse, hollow cough, excited by tickling in the throat, accompanied with headache, pain in the lower part of the back, constipation, obstruction of the nose, and sensation in the chest of excoriation.

Dose.—A powder, or six globules, morning, noon and night.

Causticum.—Particularly where *Nux* seems indicated, yet does not produce relief, and where the cough is worse at night with severe excoriating pain in the chest, and the aching pains in the limbs are aggravated by movement.

Dose.—One drop in a tumbler of water a tablespoonful, or six globules on the tongue, at a dose.

Pulsatilla.—Cough worse on lying down; discharge from the nose of thick offensive mucus, loss of appetite and insipid taste. Frequently required in alternation with *Mercury.*

Dose.—Same as *Causticum.*

Stannum.—In protracted cases with easy expectoration.

Dose.—A powder, or six globules, morning and night.

Ipecac., when the cough is accompanied with vomiting, or where the attack is followed by difficulty of breathing. A powder, or six globules, every two hours, until better. (See also "*Coughs.*")

3. TYPHOID INFLUENZA.

The third, and last form of influenza we shall notice, is by far the most severe and dangerous.

Diagnosis.—There is at first shivering, sometimes mixed or in alternation with flushes of heat. The pulse becomes rapid, the skin dry and hot, there is great fullness and severe pain in the head, particularly over the eyes and in the forehead. Sometimes the head seems as if it would burst, and the blood not unfrequently starts from the nose, or there may be a dull heavy stupor, or the patient be wild with delirium. The voice is unnatural, and there is generally considerable obstruction about the nose; cough may or may not be present.

Treatment.—Cloths dipped in cold water and placed on

the forehead, are not only exceedingly grateful, but contribute much to allay the congested state of the head.

In the commencement of the disease the treatment should commence with *Stibium.* A powder of the 1st may be given every two hours. Should there be great fullness about the head, *Opium* may be given in alternation, an hour and a half or two hours apart. *Hyosciamus*, *Bryonia*, *Veratrum*, *Rhus*, *Arsenic*, are also prominent remedies, for particular indications of which, see "*Typhoid fever, and coughs.*"

Diet and Regimen.—In the milder forms of influenza no particular directions are necessary as regards diet, with the exception that stimulating and highly spiced food and drink should be avoided, adhering to water as a drink, or a little weak black tea, and taking care that the food be light and easy of digestion.

In the severe form of Typhoid Influenza, the diet should be the same as in fever.

COUGH.

Cough may be occasioned by a slight irritation of the air-passages and be simply *catarrhal*, or it may exist only as one of a group of symptoms, indicating a deep-seated disease of the lungs and throat, or it may be *sympathetic*, produced by a derangement of some other important viscera.

Thus, we not only have coughs produced by the various diseases of the chest, but occasioned by teething, dyspepsy, worms, growing too fast in children, and various other causes.

The character of the cough, and the group of symptoms connected with it, are to be our guide in detecting the seat and severity of the disease, and consequently the appropriate remedy.

The treatment of cough, when it is developed in connection with derangement of important viscera, will be given in connection with those diseases in their appropriate place. We shall here give the indications for several of the prominent remedies, where *cough* is the principal symptom.

*Aconite.**—Violent short cough, with feverish heat and sometimes pain in the chest and difficult breathing.

* For general directions as to the administration of remedies, see page 10.

Stibium.—Deep, hollow cough, or loose cough with rattling in the chest, rapid and difficult breathing, feverish sensation; cough with nausea or vomiting. In alternation with *Phosphorus* where there is much pain about the chest. (See Pneumonia. See also *Influenza* and *Croup.*)

Ipecac.—Spasmodic coughs, frequently accompanied with nausea and vomiting, worse at night, or in cold air; oppression of breathing, as if the lungs were filled with mucus; and in children violent coughing until the face becomes livid and the body stiff. (See Hooping Cough.)

Hepar-s.—Dry, hoarse, or deep cough, frequently excited by talking, stooping, or much exertion; worse at night and aggravated by exposure of any part of the body to the cold. Generally in alternation with *Phosphorus.*

Phosphorus.—Cough excited by lying on the left side; dry cough from tickling in the throat; hoarseness and pain in the chest as from excoriation. (See Pneumonia.)

Carb.-v.—Dry, spasmodic cough, sometimes producing vomiting, aggravated by damp, cold weather, and worse in the morning or towards evening, accompanied with a burning excoriating pain in the chest. (Alternate with Phosphorus.)

Nux-vom.—Dry, hoarse, fatiguing or spasmodic cough, worse in the morning and during the day. Oppression of the chest in the night, and on lying down, with a feeling of heat and dryness in the mouth. Cough excited by tickling, scraping sensation with feeling of roughness or rawness in the throat, accompanied with hoarseness, severe pain in the head, and bruised sensation about the stomach. Sometimes aggravated by eating, or meditation, and not unfrequently producing vomiting. Particularly beneficial in persons of an energetic, sanguine temperament.

Sulphur.—Particularly in obstinate cases, where the cough is dry, frequently excited by food or a deep inspiration, worse during the night. Cough with expectoration of thick, or fetid mucus, or pus, of a salt or sweetish taste; headache, pain in the chest, abdomen, and loins.

Chamomilla.—Dry cough, particularly in children, excited

by constant tickling in the throat and chest, worse at night, or in the morning and evening, and aggravated by talking; cough during sleep, sometimes with fever, and so violent as to threaten suffocation. Fretfulness, cough after crying, or a fit of passion; fever towards evening.

Bryonia.—Dry catarrhal cough, particularly in winter, and on coming into a warm room, excited by irritation in the throat, and frequently accompanied with shivering, followed by fever, and rheumatic or aching pains in the head and limbs. Dry, nervous cough, or loose cough with yellowish expectoration.

Rhus.—Short, dry cough, excited by tickling in the chest, worse in the evening before midnight, and attended with restlessness and shortness of breath; cough with shooting pains in the side and chest, sometimes with expectoration of blood.

Belladonna.—Violent spasmodic cough; dry, short, and hacking cough at night, renewed by the slightest movement; dry cough, almost without intermission, day and night with redness of the face, and sensation as if something were in the windpipe; pains in the abdomen, neck, and head; frequently an attack of coughing, followed by sneezing.

Hyosciamus.—The symptoms indicating this remedy are similar to *Belladonna,* which it can follow, if that fails to produce relief. I have found more benefit, however, from *Hyosciamus*, where the cough is incessant, worse on lying down, and seems to be excited by a tickling in the throat, sometimes with rattling.

Capsicum.—Cough, worse towards evening and in the night, severe pain in the head, as if it would burst, aching throughout the body, and an aching, smarting sensation in the throat, as from eating pepper.

Ignatia.—Particularly in persons of a mild or variable temperament. Short hacking or shaking cough as from the tickling of a feather. Cough, worse after eating, on lying down at night, or rising in the morning. Dry cough, with running at the nose.

Mercury.—Hoarse, catarrhal cough, with watery discharge

from the nose, or diarrhœa, and frequently bleeding at the nose. Dry cough, worse towards evening or in the night, increased by talking, and sometimes attended with retching and expectoration of blood.

Drosera.—Deep, hollow, hoarse cough. Dry, spasmodic cough, worse on lying down and at night, aggravated by laughing, and sometimes followed by retching and vomiting. (See Hooping Cough.)

Stannum.—Cough with expectoration of a sweetish or saltish taste, attended with debility and perspiration. Dry, shaking cough, worse at night, and increased by speaking or laughing. (See Consumption.)

Dulcamara.—Loose cough after taking cold; cough excited by drawing a deep breath, worse when at rest. Sometimes expectoration of blood.

Amm.-carb.—Rough voice; dry, tickling, suffocating cough, worse in the morning and in damp, cold weather, accompanied with sensation of burning behind the breast-bone.

Pulsatilla.—Severe shaking cough, worse at night, and frequently attended with retching and vomiting. Loose cough with aching in the chest, hoarseness, cold in the head, and expectoration of bitter mucus. (See Influenza.)

China.—Asthmatic cough at night, with pain in the chest, or cough from ulceration of the lungs, or loss of blood. (See Consumption.)

Arsenic.—Asthmatic cough and breathing; dry cough worse at night, and sometimes with bloody expectoration, and a burning sensation over the body. (See Asthma.)

Sepia.—Dry, spasmodic cough, worse at night, or on lying down, and sometimes attended with nausea and vomiting. It is particularly useful in persons of a scrofulous constitution, and in chronic cough with thick or puriform expectoration.

Cina.—Principally in children. Dry, spasmodic cough, pale face, moaning, restlessness, and crying. (See Worms).

DOSE.—Two drops, or twelve globules, in a tumbler of water, a tablespoonful at a dose; or a powder, or six globules, on the tongue.

In recent cases the remedy may be given once in from two to four hours, until five or six doses have been taken, then wait five or six hours, and if no relief has been produced, select another remedy. In cases which have assumed a chronic character, a dose once in six or twelve hours, will be sufficient.

Diet and Regimen.—The same as in chronic diseases, unless considerable fever is present, when abstain from meats and fatty food. The predisposition to cold can often be overcome by bathing freely every day with cold water. Cough should be taken in hand at once, as cases are by no means rare, where neglected, it has laid the foundation of disease, which has mocked the efforts of human skill to eradicate.

For Croup and Hooping Cough, see Diseases of Children.

PLEURITIS.

Pleurisy.

By consulting the chapter on Anatomy, (page 30, and also plate 5) an idea will be obtained of the position of the lungs and their investing membrane, which will aid materially in a correct understanding of the character of this disease.

Diagnosis.—Pleurisy consists of an inflammation of the serous membrane covering the lungs, which is also reflected over the inner wall of the chest, forming as we have already explained a shut sack. Thus it will be perceived, one part of the membrane covers the soft and compressible lung, which is suspended in the chest, the firm walls of which are lined with the other part of the membrane. These opposed surfaces freely moving upon each other, of course when inflamed produce a train of symptoms not only exceedingly painful, but unless promptly and carefully treated often highly dangerous.

This inflamed membrane may pour out from its diseased surface a large amount of serum, or a watery fluid, or coagulable lymph, pus or blood. Thus the *pulmonary pleura*, or the membrane which invests the lungs, may by this coagulable lymph be firmly glued to the *costal pleura*, or the membrane which covers the walls of the chest, thus attaching the lung to the chest, preventing all lateral movement between them and obliterating the pleural cavity. Or the lung may be compressed to a very small compass, and the chest distended by the large amount of serous fluid, sometimes amounting to several pints, which has been poured out by the inflamed membrane into the pleural cavity, or one portion of the pleura may be united by coagulable lymph in some places, and separated by the effused fluid in others.

DIAGNOSIS.—The pain, which is frequently preceded by chill and fever, generally commences in a spot just below one or other of the breasts, from whence it radiates to other parts, but is sometimes felt in other places, as along the sternum, beneath the collar bone, and not unfrequently extends over the whole side of the thorax. The pain is sharp and stabbing, as if at each inspiration a sharp instrument were thrust into the chest at a particular point, the patient is unable to take a long breath, being able to fill the lungs only to a small extent, the breath is quick and hurried, the face flushed, the skin hot, the pulse quick and feverish. Pressure on the side increases the pain ; the patient is at first unable to lie on the side affected, and as the disease advances if much serous effusion has taken place, he is also unable to lie on the other side from the fluid passing round to that side, compressing the healthy lung, so as to produce suffocation. The urine, at this stage, is generally offensive, and has a sediment. Cough is also present, small, dry, half-suppressed and ineffectual; the expectoration if any is very slight. Should much frothy mucus be expectorated, the disease is complicated with bronchitis, and if rust colored sputa be brought up, it is complicated with pneumonia.

CAUSES.—The most common cause of *pleurisy* is exposure to cold and dampness. It is, however often occasioned by mechanical violence or by the accidental extension of disease from other parts. Thus it may be excited by the splintered ends of a broken rib, by a wound penetrating into the chest, or by a perforating ulcer of the pulmonary pleura, the extension of a tubercular excavation. Of course the cause should be taken into consideration in the treatment of the disease.

TREATMENT.*—*Aconite* and *Bryonia* are the two great remedies in this disease. If the attack is violent, they may be given two or three doses of each in alternation, twenty or thirty minutes apart, afterwards one hour apart, gradually increasing the intervals to two or three hours as the symptoms become better. Two drops of the tincture, or twelve globules, may be mixed in a tumbler of water, and a tablespoonful given at a dose. After the pain has been removed by *Bryonia*, or the fever still continues notwithstanding the use of *Aconite*, a few doses of *Sulphur* will generally complete the cure. *Sulphur* may also follow the above remedies, if after twenty-four hours, no relief has been obtained by them, or if the disease is complicated with Pneumonia, and there is danger of solidification of the lung taking place. A powder or three globules may be given once in two or three hours.

Mercurius is of great benefit, where the fever has been subdued, but the pain and shortness of breath still continue, and the patient is becoming exhausted by copious night sweats. Give a powder or six globules once in two or three hours. If during the night the patient should be very restless and sleepless, a few doses of *Coffea* or *Belladonna* given at intervals of one hour will generally produce relief.

DOSE.—Same as *Aconite.*

Arsenicum is of use if considerable effusion has taken place, and there is prostration of strength, impeded and asthmatic respiration.

DOSE.—A powder, or three globules, once in two or three hours.

Pleurisy, as we have already said, may be complicated with pneumonia (pleuro-pneumonia), or with bronchitis, in which cases *Hepar-s.*, *Phosphorus*, *Carb.-v.*, *Belladonna*, *Rhus*, *Lachesis*, *Sulphur*, *Lycopodium*, *China*, or *Sepia* may be indicated. Consult also those diseases.

DIET AND REGIMEN.—As in fevers.

* For general directions as to the administration of remedies, see page 10.

PLEURODYNIA.

False Pleurisy.

Diagnosis.—Notwithstanding this disease is often mistaken for pleurisy, with a little care it can be very readily distinguished. It is a rheumatic affection of the intercostal muscles, generally preceded by pains in the neck and shoulders, and accompanied with but little if any fever or thirst. The pain is often severe in the side, but the cough is slight, only hard pressure between the ribs increases it, while in pleurisy the side is exceedingly sensitive to a slight touch, and the cough is dry and painful.

Treatment.—*Arnica,* two or three doses, given at intervals of three hours, will often be sufficient to produce a cure. If then, relief is not obtained, the *Arnica* may be alternated with *Pulsatilla,* two hours apart, until three or four doses of each have been taken.

Dose.—Two drops, or twelve globules, in a tumbler of water, a tablespoonful at a dose.

Bryonia.—Where the pains are sharp and cutting, exceedingly violent during inspiration.

Dose.—Same as *Arnica,* give every two or three hours.

Nux-v.—Shooting pain, with great sensibility of the external parts of the chest to the touch, aggravated by movement and by deep inspiration.

Dose.—One drop in a tumbler of water, a tablespoonful given; or a powder, or three globules taken on the tongue.

Ranunculus-b.—I have frequently found this remedy very efficacious, where the pains were sharp and cutting, increased by movement, and where other remedies had failed to produce a beneficial result.

Dose.—Same as *Bryonia.*

External application of warmth in the form of hot cloths, or even a cloth wrung out in Alcohol, and slightly sprinkled with Cayenne pepper will frequently produce relief.

Diet and Regimen.—Should there be much fever, as in fevers generally.

PNEUMONIA.

Inflammation of the Lungs.

This disease generally commences with chilliness, followed by heat. The breath is frequent, difficult, painful and anxious, and where both lungs are inflamed, performed through the action of the abdominal muscles and the diaphragm. Pain in the chest and taking a long breath. Cough dry and deep, or quick on spontaneous, or excited by deep breathing, talking or swallowing. Expectoration tough, sticky, at first partially transparent and slimy, afterwards bloody, saffron or rust colored. The patient dislikes to talk, does not wish to be disturbed, and generally prefers lying on the back. Sometimes the face of the patient becomes very red, the head painful, the tongue parched, the skin dry and hot, accompanied with excessive thirst. The fever after a time may assume an intermittent type, disappearing in the morning and coming on in the afternoon with renewed violence. Or it may assume a Typhoid form, accompanied with prostration, low muttering delirium, &c. (See Typhoid fever.) When the breathing becomes easy, the skin moist, the expectoration natural, the patient may be looked upon as in a fair way to recovery.

Causes.—Sudden changes of temperature, exposure to cold, north or northeast wind, sudden cooling after violent exertion, mechanical injury, or inhalation of acrid or noxious gases.

Treatment.*—The prominent remedies are *Aconite*, *Stibium*, *Bryonia* and *Phosphorus*.

Aconite is the prominent remedy, during the chilliness and fever, especially if the pulse is quick, the pain in the chest violent and the respiration oppressed.

Dose.—Two drops, or twelve globules, in a tumbler of water, a tablespoonful once in one or two hours.

Bryonia.—Particularly where the difficulty has been occasioned by exposure to cold or violent muscular exertion.

* For general directions as to administration of remedies, see page 10.

There is oppression and pain in the chest, aggravated by movement, with constant desire to cough. The cough is generally loose, and the expectoration white, slimy and streaked with blood, or of a brick dust color. There is often rheumatic pain about the extremities, thirst and constipation. It is frequently indicated in alternation with *Aconite.*

Dose.—Same as *Aconite.*

Belladonna will be a valuable remedy, where there is congestion of blood to the brain, delirium and danger of typhoid symptoms. Generally in alternation with *Aconite*, one hour apart.

If no relief follows the administration of *Aconite* and *Bryonia*, and the disease passes into the second stage, *Stibium* and *Phosphorus* should be administered, generally in alternation, one or two hours apart. The *Stibium* is indicated by great oppression of breathing, cough, with much mucous rattling, profuse expectoration, dry, hard cough, and sometimes nausea. *Phosphorous* symptoms are severe sticking pains in the chest, excited or aggravated by breathing or coughing, shortness of breath, dry cough and rust colored expectoration. Where the attack is severe *Phosphorus*, is frequently required at the commencement of the disease, either alone or in alternation with *Aconite* or *Belladonna.*

Dose.—A powder, or six globules, may be given every two or three hours.

Should typhoid symptoms set in, which are characterized by extreme restlessness, delirium and stupor, quick and irregular breathing, thread like pulse, rattling of mucus and prostration of strength, the disease is assuming an alarming character.

Phosphorus is here also an invaluable remedy ; should there be indications of solidification of the lungs, detected by the greater difficuly of breathing, depression of the mental faculties, bland delirium, grasping at flocks, rapid prostration, feeble pulse, difficult cough, short and difficult breathing, with oppression and anguish.

Dose.—A powder, or three globules, once in two or three hours.

China.—Where the patient has been weakened by a loss of blood, or when there is palpitation of the heart on breathing, or coughing, stitches in the sides and chest, and great weakness.

Dose.—Three drops in a tumbler of water, a tablespoonful every three or four hours.

Sulphur is beneficial in rendering the system more susceptible to the action of remedies. Where the appropriate remedies fail to produce an effect, a few doses of *Sulphur* may be given, returning afterward to the previous remedies.

Dose.—A powder, or six globules, once in three or four hours.

Veratrum.—Small, weak pulse, cold extremities ; vomiting, diarrhœa, rapid prostration of strength and delirium.

Bry., *Rhus*, *Hyos.*, *Op.*, *Bell.*, *Phos.-ac.*, *Lach.*, and *Lyc.* are also sometimes indicated in this stage of the disease. For particular indications, see Typhus Fever.

Pneumonia unless properly relieved, may become chronic or terminate in consumption. *Mercury*, *Sulphur* or *Stannum* will generally be sufficient, to break up this chronic tendency. See also consumption.

Diet and Regimen as in fevers.

PNEUMONIA NOTHA.

This variety of Pneumonia, sometimes called false pneumonia, more generally affects old people, and not unfrequently terminates in complete paralysis of the lungs. The symptoms at first are those of an ordinary cold. The cough is generally moist, the expectoration white, yellow and slimy, sometimes streaked with blood ; pressure, stinging and burning sensation in the chest, increased on going up-stairs, or turning to either side. The fever, if present at all, is generally slight.

Treatment.—*Arnica* is a valuable remedy, where there is a bruised sensation in the chest, slight cough, with blood streaked, slimy expectoration.

Dose.—Three drops in a tumbler of water, a tablspoonful every three or four hours.

Bryonia.—Increase of symptoms at night great heat in the chest, violent racking cough and expectoration of dingy-reddish mucus.

Veratrum and *Ars.*—If there are cold extremities and rapid prostration.

Belladonna.—Flushed face, short, dry cough and difficult breathing.

Dose.—Same as *Arnica.*

Phosphorus and *Stibium* may also be indicated. See Pneumonia. For other symptoms see also Pneumonia.

Diet and Regimen.—If much fever is present, the same as in Pneumonia, otherwise articles of a more nourishing character, such as, broth, &c.

LARYNGITIS.

Cynanche Laryngia.

This disease in its acute form requires prompt and energetic treatment, as it is frequently exceedingly dangerous, running its course with alarming rapidity. It has numbered among its victims many distinguished men, among the rest Washington. Taken at its commencement, it is generally easily relieved by skilful homœopathic treatment. It is occasioned by inflammation of the parts composing the larynx, and particularly of the mucous membrane covering the laryngeal cartilage, including the epiglottis.

Diagnosis.—There is a sore throat, and on looking into it a redness of the fauces and uvula is perceptible, not enough however to account for the excessive restlessness and anxiety, and the great difficulty of deglutition. To the difficulty of deglutition is shortly added great difficulty of breathing. The respiration is attended with a throttling noise, and the act of inspiration is protracted and wheezing, as if the air were drawn through a narrow tube. The distress seems to be situated in the vicinity of the *Pomum Adami* or Adam's apple. **If there is cough, it is with a harsh, husky and abortive** sound. The voice is hoarse or sinks to a scarcely perceptible whisper. The face is flushed, the skin hot and dry, the pulse hard. As the disease advances, the distress increases, the countenance becomes pale, or livid, anxious and ghastly; the eyes protrude, the restlessness is extreme, the difficulty of breathing becomes greater, there is a constant desire for air, and unless relieved, death by strangulation speedily ensues. This disease occurs in both sexes, and at all ages.

Causes.—It is generally occasioned by exposure to cold, or to cold and dampness. It is sometimes produced by mechanical violence or chemical injury done to the larynx, and not unfrequently by children attempting to swallow boiling water from the spout of a tea-kettle.

Treatment.—The external application of the wet bandage is often advisable. (See page 80.) The severity of this disease, and the rapidity with which it runs its progress, renders it highly important, that, if possible, it should be treated by a skilful physician.

Aconite is indicated, when the symptoms of inflammatory fever first declare themselves. It may be given, until the febrile symptoms abate, or until other symptoms set in.

Dose.—Two drops, or twelve globules, in a tumbler of water, a tablespoonful every hour or two hours.

Spongia follows well after *Aconite*, and is indicated as soon as the breathing becomes shrill, and the pain and sensibility in the upper part of the windpipe becomes more decided. There is also an increase of hoarseness and difficulty of articulation.

Dose.—Same as *Aconite*.

Hepar-s. may follow *Spongia*, when that remedy ceases to produce a good effect; or it may follow *Aconite*, when, notwithstanding the administration of that remedy, the febrile symptoms remain unabated. I have often found it advisable to alternate *Spongia*, and *Hepar-s.*, one or two hours apart.

Dose.—A powder, or six globules, every one or two hours.

Bromine will prove beneficial, where there is hoarseness,

extreme sensitiveness of the throat, dry and harsh cough, sometimes almost suffocative. It may be given once in two or three hours.

Stibium is also a prominent remedy, where the symptoms commence with severity; hoarseness, dry, harsh, and ringing cough, sometimes almost suffocative. A powder may be given every hour.

Belladonna will likewise prove beneficial, where there are spasms in the throat, causing an inability to swallow liquids; the throat on looking into it presents a swollen and highly inflamed appearance.

Dose.—Same as *Aconite*.

Diet and Regimen.—Same as in fevers.

BRONCHITIS.

This is an inflammation of the mucous lining of the *Bronchia*, or air-tubes of the lungs.

It presents itself under two forms: *the acute and chronic;* both of which will be treated separately.

1. *Acute Bronchitis.**—This form of disease very often succeeds Coryza, or cold in the head, although in those whose lungs are highly susceptible, it may commence at once in the bronchia. At first a feeling of roughness is felt in the trachea, which soon amounts to such a degree of titillation, as to excite frequent cough, which is at first dry and hard. Hoarseness is also present as well as uneasiness of breathing, tight feeling across the chest frequently amounting to pain, particularly on coughing. There is generally fever, pain in the limbs, shivering and rapidity of the pulse. The cough increases in severity and is accompanied with expectoration of froth or viscid mucus, which after a time may become streaked with blood.

When the disease terminates favorably, the first symptoms of improvement are, greater freedom of breathing, remission of fever, and expectoration diminished in quantity, and be-

* For a description of the windpipe, see plate 5. For general directions as to the administration of remedies, *see page* 10.

coming thicker. Where it terminates unfavorably, the breathing becomes more and more difficult, rapid prostration and collapse takes place.

TREATMENT.*—As a preventative the free, daily external use of cold water is highly beneficial.

Aconite.—During the inflammatory stage of the disease, and where there is obstructed respiration, dry and frequent cough, excited by a tickling sensation in the throat and chest, hoarseness, hot and dry skin, with rapid pulse.

DOSE.—Two drops, or twelve globules, in a tumbler of water, a tablespoonful may be taken every three or four hours. Sometimes *Stibium* is preferable, a powder given at the same intervals.

Spongia and *Hepar-s.*, generally in alternation after the use of *Aconite*, when there is hoarseness, burning, tickling in the larynx, anxious, laborious respiration, hollow dry cough.

DOSE.—Of the former one drop, or twelve globules, in a tumbler of water, a tablespoonful at a dose; of the latter a powder, or three globules, on the tongue. Give three or four hours apart.

Phosphorus.—This is a very prominent remedy, particularly after the inflammatory symptoms have subsided, and also where the disease assumes a chronic character, or where there is danger of the lungs being involved. There may be oppression of breathing, hoarseness, dry cough, pain in the throat and chest.

DOSE.—A powder, or three globules, every three or four hours.

Belladonna is frequently useful, where there is violent pain in the head, soreness of the throat, short and rapid respiration, dry and fatiguing cough, and oppression of the chest.

DOSE.—Two drops, or twelve globules, in a tumbler of water, a tablespoonful once in two or three hours. Among the other remedies useful in this disease, we may enumerate

* For a description of the windpipe, see plate 5. For general directions as to the administration of remedies, see page 10.

Lach., *Bry.*, *Puls.*, *Ipecac.*, *Ars.*, *Sulph.* and *Mercury.* See Materia Medica.

2. *Chronic Bronchitis.*—This variety of the disease may follow the acute form, or it may steal on gradually, until, before the patient is really aware of his situation, he is fully under its influence. In its advanced stage it is nearly as serious a disease as phthisis, to which it not unfrequently leads, and with which its symptoms correspond so closely, that there is sometimes difficulty in distinguishing between them. As this disease is somewhat long in duration, and generally requires the treatment of a judicious physician, it will be only necessary to mention here some of the prominent remedies; among them we may enumerate: *Phos.*, *Caust.*, *Hepar-s.*, *Stan.*, *Sep.*, *Lyc.*, *Bar.-c.*, *Lach.*, *Ars.*, *Sil.*, *Con.*, *Prot.-iod-hyd.*, *Nit.-ac.*, *Sulph.* and *Calcarea.*

HÆMOPTYSIS.

Hæmorrhage from the lungs.

The hawking or coughing considerable quantities of blood, or the welling up of the crimson current, as from a fountain, often produces such consternation in the minds of the patient and surrounding friends, as to render them entirely unfit for those prompt and decided steps so essential to safety, and upon which, in fact, the life of the patient may hang. The hæmorrhage arising from the nose, mouth, or throat may create unnecessary alarm, and lead to the supposition, that it is really from the lungs. A very slight inquiry into the attending circumstances will be sufficient to detect the difference.

Diagnosis.—It will only be necessary for us here to speak of two kinds of hæmorrhage.

First, That which depends on congestion to the lungs, and

Second, that occasioned by consumption, where ulceration gradually consumes the lung, and in its progress causes the rupture of some of the larger blood vessels. This latter variety not unfrequently dashes to earth delusive hopes, and startles the patient with the alarming fact, that a disease, the very name of which excites a thrill of terror, is weaving its meshes around the fountain of life, and drawing its victim swiftly on into the arms of death. It arouses him to the necessity of either doing something, if it be nothing more than a change of air, or be content to die.

The *first* variety mentioned, or that which depends on congestion of blood to the lungs, may be occasioned by lifting, violent exertion, mechanical injury, or the inhaling of poisonous gases or breathing an air filled with injurious dust, as metal filings, or the dust from lime, tobacco, &c., or it may be constitutional, or produced by rapid changes of temperature, or the abuse of spirituous drinks. It is frequently occasioned by suppression of blood from other organs. Thus we find it caused by the sudden disappearance of the piles, in ladies by the stoppage of the menses, and during pregnancy, by the pressure upward produced by the enlarging womb. Hæmorrhage more frequently occurs between the ages of 16 and 40.

The most dangerous of this variety of hæmorrhage is the apoplectic, when the symptoms of an apoplectic fit are present, the patient loosing consciousness and bloody froth issuing from the mouth.

Treatment.*—In severe cases, perfect repose in a half sitting, half lying position is essential, the patient should not be permitted to speak, and no unnecessary noise or confusion allowed in the room. In the absence of other remedies a teaspoonful of ordinary table-salt may be carefully given, so as not to produce choaking, in water, every ten minutes, or five or ten drops of Sulphuric acid, mixed with a tumbler of water, and a tablespoonful given in the same manner, until relieved.

Aconite is an important remedy in the commencement of the difficulty. There is generally a fullness and burning pain in the chest, palpitation of the heart, feeble wiry pulse, pale

* For general directions as to the administration of remedies, *see page* 10.

face, restlessness and anxiety. The blood is discharged in large quantities, at short intervals.

Dose.—Two drops, or twelve globules, in a tumbler of water, a tablespoonful may be given every twenty or thirty minutes, but if after two or three hours no relief is produced, another remedy should be chosen.

Ipecac.—If after the administration of the Aconite a taste of blood should remain in the mouth, or there should be present a slight hacking cough, with expectoration, streaked with blood.

Arsenicum.—Anxiety, palpitation of the heart, seething of blood in the chest, worse about midnight, and spreading a burning heat over the body; after *Hyosciamus*, in drunkards.

Arnica.—Particularly in those cases occasioned by mechanical injuries or violent exertion, and where with but slight exertion, blackish, coagulated blood is discharged, accompanied with stitches, burning, contracting pain in the chest, seething of blood, palpitation of the heart and debility, or where with a cough excited by irritation under the sternum, there is a discharge of bright red, frothy blood, sometimes mixed with lumps of mucus.

Millefolium is a prominent remedy, particularly where there is a discharge of blood, with but slight, if any cough, fermenting sensation in the chest, with sensation as of warm blood rising in the throat. Often after *Aconite*, a dose every half hour.

Belladonna.—Slight cough produced by tickling in the throat, with aggravation of the hæmorrhage, sensation as if the chest were full of blood with shooting pains ; worse by movement.

China.—Where the patient is debilitated from the loss of blood, or where there is violent dry and painful cough, with taste of blood in the mouth, shivering with flushes of heat, cloudiness of sight and bewilderment of the head.

Hyosciamus.—Where it is preceded by a dry cough, particularly at night, or in drunkards after *Opium* or *Nux-vom.*

Opium.—Particularly in intemperate persons, or where there are expectoration of thick and frothy blood, stifling or shortness of the breath and anguish, trembling of the arms, sleepiness and anxious starts.

Dulcamara.—Especially when occasioned by cold.

Rhus.—Restlessness, tingling in the chest, discharge of bright, red blood, increased by the least moral emotion.

Pulsatilla.—In obstinate cases, with expectoration of black coagulated blood, anxiety and shivering, particularly at night; also when the difficulty is produced by suppression of the catamenia.

Nux-v.—Frequently after *Ipecac.* or *Arsenicum* and in drunkards after *Opium*, or where there is tickling in the chest with cough, worse towards morning; also when occasioned by cold, anger, or a sudden suppression of hæmorrhoidal discharge.

Carb.-v.—Particularly in persons who have taken Mercury, and where there is burning pain in the chest, and where the patient is very susceptible to changes of weather.

Sulphur, *Ignatia*, *Sabina*, *Stannum*, also deserve attention.

Dose.—In violent cases same as *Aconite*, where the discharge is slight every six or twelve hours. In apoplectic cases *Aconite* should be given immediately, either in alternation with, or followed by *Opium*, in half an hour's time, if no relief is obtained.

Diet and Regimen.—The patient should be kept cool. Stimulating food and drink should be avoided, and both food and drink given invariably cold. If the feet should become cold, they may be put in warm water.

CONGESTION OF THE CHEST.

Determination of blood to the chest is not an unfrequent difficulty with young people when the form is being rapidly developed, and also in persons of a phthisical habit.

Diagnosis.—Palpitation of the heart with short and oppressive breathing, fullness and weight in the chest, coldness of the extremities. Slight cough is sometimes present.

TREATMENT.*—*Nux-v.* is a prominent remedy when produced by a sedentary mode of life, abuse of spirits, or continued mental exertion, and where there is palpitation of the heart, short panting breath, oppression, anxiety, asthmatic distress, heat and burning in the chest, particularly at night, with great restlessness and agitation; also sensation around the chest, as if the clothes were too tight.

Belladonna.—Palpitation of the heart and strong pulsations in the chest affecting the head; shortness of breath, short cough, internal heat and thirst, and sometimes slight spasms in the chest.

China.—Especially where there have been debilitating losses, with palpitation of the heart, dyspnœa and oppression, with great anguish.

Aconite.—Great heat and thirst, shortness of breath, with violent oppression, and palpitation of the heart.

Phosphorus.—Oppression with heaviness, fullness, and tightness in the chest; palpitation of the heart, and sensation of heat ascending to the throat.

Mercury.—Anxious oppression, with desire to take a long breath, burning in the chest, palpitation of the heart, cough with expectoration of blood.

Spongia.—Where the difficulty is produced by fatiguing exercise, is accompanied with prostration and nausea, or where it is brought on by the slightest movement or exertion.

Pulsatilla.—When it occurs before menstruation, or when that has suddenly stopped.

Bryonia.—When there is constipation or piles, which have been suddenly suppressed. It may frequently be alternated with *Pulsatilla.*

DOSE.—Two drops, or twelve globules, in a tumbler of water, a tablespoonful at a dose, or a powder, or three globules, may be given on the tongue. Give once in four or six hours.

* For general directions as to the administration of remedies, see page 10.

PULMONARY CONSUMPTION.

Phthisis Pulmonalis.

We come now to speak of a disease which in our ever-changing climate is constantly scattering its seeds over the land, gathering its victims alike among the poor and lowly, the sons and daughters of toil, and the gay votaries of fashion, the lovers of luxurious ease, and the mighty throng which ever crowd the various paths of dissipation. Consumption, ghastly messenger of death, how many cheeks have paled as thou with stealthy footsteps and almost noiseless tread hast glided into the sanctuary of their home; how many young mothers hast thou laid in an early tomb; how many bright golden links, uniting hearts in fond affection, severed with thy corroding touch; how many barks freighted with the wealth of genius, of beauty, of deep and holy love, have gone down into the dark ocean of death at thy bidding!

To move on, day after day, week after week, and perhaps month after month, your friends feeling that with each revolving sun the hectic flush is growing brighter, the step more feeble, the form more attenuated, and the stern and perhaps unwelcome truth at length forcing itself upon your own mind, for the victim is too often buoyed up with a delusive hope, and the last to awake to his real situation, that the sands in your hour-glass are fast running out, that death is drawing you on, slowly it may be, yet with a strength, you cannot resist, to his cold embrace, into that dim and shadowy spirit-world, where *his* power ends, and the roar of time's waves is never heard—*this is consumption.*

In another chapter it has been necessary for me to refer to the causes of this disease, and to urge the importance of watching for its first stealthy footsteps, and thus guarding against its entrance, or eradicating it before it has become so deeply planted as to defy control.

I have spoken of it in the chapter on the causes and prevention of disease, as the result of hereditary taint, slow perhaps in its progress, as the sequele of other diseases, as produced by dissipation, exposure to sudden changes of temperature, imprudence in living and dress, and various other causes.

Diagnosis.—The incipient stage of consumption *can be cured*, and even where it is hereditary, I am strongly inclined to believe, that by means of proper physical, moral, and mental training, a proper education of the whole system in childhood, in very many cases at least, the children may escape the doom of the parents. I say that consumption in its incipient stage may be cured, but beware how you allow it to fasten its fangs deep in the system, how you disregard the slight hacking cough, the growing sensation of languor, the weakness of the chest, the increasing flush on the cheek, and those other symptoms which perhaps at first may be easily removed, but which, disregarded, are like the easy gentle motion of the boat gliding along the outer circles of the *maelstrom*, the victim unconscious of danger, until, rushing on with increased rapidity he is startled, when alas too late, by the roaring vortex below.

The general symptoms of phthisis are, cough, dyspnœa, expectoration, hæmoptysis, night-sweats and wasting, hectic fever, hoarseness, or loss of voice, diarrhœa, and various other symptoms, marking the different stages of the disease.

Cough is one of the earliest symptoms. It is at first generally slight and dry, occurring particularly on getting into the bed at night, on getting up in the morning, or after any unusual exertion. It soon becomes more troublesome, and is attended with more or less expectoration. Hæmoptysis, another symptom is a kind of expectoration; the expectoration of blood. This is a common symptom, but I have already spoken of it under a separate head. As the disease progresses, the patient is troubled with shortness of breath after but very little exertion, and particularly on going up-stairs or ascending even a slight eminence.

Hectic fever gradually steals on. The patient may in the evening feel chilly, and at night flushed and hot, the skin, particularly the hands and feet, dry and burning, followed during sleep and towards morning by profuse and exhausting perspiration. This perspiration is generally more copious on the upper part of the body, the chest and head, and almost invariably comes on during sleep, the patient on awakening often finding himself drenched.

Diarrhœa is another very common symptom, more frequently, however occurring during the latter part of the disease, and rapidly prostrating the strength of the patient. The voice sometimes for months is almost entirely extinct, the patient grows weaker and weaker, until at length he glides almost without a struggle into the arms of death. Or perhaps for a time the unpleasant symptoms may abate, the strength begin to return, and brightening hope whisper to the soul promises of returning health, when the blow falls and all is over. In tubercular consumption, the tubercles may exist for years without disturbing the health, when by proper treatment they can be removed, but at length they soften and produce ulceration. The rapid form of consumption, which is frequently seen among the young, and after debilitating diseases, is rightly called *galloping consumption*, for its course is short.

In tuberculous persons, syphilitic, and eruptive diseases, there is often a transfer of the disease from external organs to the lungs, developing a consumption, which speedily carries off the patient.

TREATMENT.—The treatment of this disease in all its stages covers so broad a field as to render it not only impossible but unnecessary to go into the particulars here, as the skill and care of a judicious physician are necessary in its treatment. For the appropriate remedies in the incipient stage, consult "*cough*," "*inflammation of the lungs*," *&c.* In the more advanced stages, among the prominent remedies are, *Arsenic*, *Stan.*, *Merc.*, *Phos.*, *Calc.*, *Carb.-v.*, *Hepar-s.*, *Kal.-carb.*, *Nit.-ac.*, and *Iodine.*

DIET AND REGIMEN.—Cleanliness, fresh air, and as even a temperature as possible, are of course essential. Often simply a change of air, going from a cold to a warmer or more temperate climate will be sufficient to arrest a disease which seemed almost hopeless. In selecting the food, the wishes and feelings of the patient should be consulted, taking care, however, that while the food is as nourishing as may be, it is as little stimulating as possible.

ASTHMA.

This is a spasmodic disease, producing a constriction of the bronchial tubes, often hereditary, incident to both sexes, but more common in men than in women. The air tubes of the lungs are encircled by minute bands of muscular structure, which like other muscular fibres may be affected by spasms. These spasms of course contract the air tubes, and the difficulty of breathing and the wheezing respiration is occasioned by the air being forced through the narrowed channels for respiration.

Diagnosis.—There is great difficulty of breathing; coming on in paroxysms and accompanied with loud wheezing respiration, passing off in a few hours with more or less expectoration.

If the patient has ever suffered from an attack, there are generally premonitory symptoms sufficiently prominent to indicate its approach, such as loss of appetite, languor, drowsiness, oppression, and chilliness. The dyspnœa more generally comes on after midnight, but not unfrequently occurs during the afternoon and evening. There is a sense of con striction about the chest, and urgent desire for fresh air, often causing the patient to rush to the open window, however cold may be the night, and a loud wheezing respiration. These symptoms often last for several hours, when remission gradually takes place. The attacks may return at longer or shorter intervals, and when they cease with little or no expectoration, the case is said to be one of *dry asthma*, but when expectoration is copious, it is called *humid* or *humoral asthma.* Asthma is often connected with organic disease of the heart and large blood vessels.

Causes.—This disease, as we have already said, may be hereditary, or it may be occasioned by certain states of the atmosphere irritating the surface of the air-passages, or by certain influences, which affect in a peculiar way the nervous system; thus nearly all the exciting causes of catarrh may produce asthma. Some breathe with the most freedom in the keen air of the mountain top, others in moist, low places; not unfrequently the breathing will be exceedingly difficult in one street and perfectly easy in another not half a mile distant. A person at a hotel in Paris could sleep perfectly well in a room in the front of the house, but found it impossible to sleep in the back part, from the asthma.

TREATMENT.—Before giving the symptomatic indication for the different remedies it may present the treatment in a clearer light, to classify the remedies according to the exciting causes of the disease.

When occasioned by a congestion of blood in the chest, *Acon.*, *Bell.*, *Nux-v.*, *Phos.*, *Cupr.* or *Puls.* may be consulted.

By a derangement of the menses: *Bell.*, *Cocc.*, *Nux-v.*, *Puls.*, *Sep.*, *Cuprum.*

By flatulence: *Cham.*, *Chin.*, *Nux-v.*, *Sulph.*, *Veratrum.*

When it simply presents the form of cramps in the chest: *Bell.*, *Coc.*, *Cupr.*, *Moschus*, *Nux-v.*, *Stram.*, *Stibium* and *Bryonia.*

When occasioned by inspiration of dust: *Calc.*, *Sil.*, *Sulph.*, *Ipecac.*

When the result of a chill: *Dulc.*, *Acon.*, *Bell.*, *Bry.*, *Ipecac.*, *Arsenic.*

In consequence of moral emotions: *Ignatia*, *Coff.*, *Cham.*, *Nux-vom.*

From suppressed catarrh: *Ars.*, *Ipecac.*, *Nux-v.*, *Samb.*, *Stibium.*

In hysterical women: *Coff.*, *Ignatia*, *Moschus*, *Stram.*, *Asa.*, *Ipecac.*, *Ars.*, *Pulsatilla.*

In aged persons: *Con.*, *Op.*, *Camph.*, *Carbo-v.*, *Arsenic.*

When moist with accumulation of mucus in the bronchia: *Ipecac.*, *Ars.*, *Bry.*, *Puls.*, *Sulph.*, *Stan.*, *Phos.*, *Stibium.*

SYMPTOMATIC INDICATIONS.—*Ipecac.*, *Arsenic* and *Bryonia* are the most prominent remedies, and perhaps more frequently indicated, than any other. If the attack should come on suddenly, it would be safe to give a dose of *Ipecac.*, until the remedy most indicated could be ascertained.

Ipecac.—Nocturnal paroxysms of suffocation, spasmodic constriction of the larynx, rattling in the chest from mucus; great anguish; short dry cough, redness and heat, or paleness and coldness of the face alternately; nausea with cold perspiration on the forehead, anxious, rapid and moaning respiration, or respiration short and obstructed, as from dust. It may be followed or alternated with *Arsenic*, *Bryonia* or *Nux.*

Bryonia.—Obstructed respiration, increased by talking or movement, particularly at night or toward morning, frequent cough with pressure or shooting pain in the chest, aggravated by movement; palpitation of the heart; difficult, moaning anxious respiration, intermixed with deep inspirations.

Arsenicum.—Obstructed respiration, cough, and accumulation of thick mucus in the chest; oppression at the chest and want of breath at every movement; constriction in the chest and larynx with painful pressure on the lungs, worse in a warm room. Suffocative fits, particularly at night or in the evening in bed, with panting or wheezing respiration, great anguish and cold perspiration. Remission of the attack on the appearance of cough, and renewal during rough weather, and changes of temperature. The attacks are often accompanied with great weakness and burning pain in the chest. *Arsenic* is frequently required after *Ipecac.*, and is indicated in most cases of chronic as well as acute asthma.

Nux-vom.—Where *Arsenic* fails to produce relief, and where the constriction is in the lower part of the chest, even the clothes producing a sensation of tightness and oppression; short cough with difficult expectoration; sputa tinged with blood; congestion toward the chest, with heat, burning, palpitation of the heart, and general uneasiness; asthma relieved by lying on the back, turning, or sitting up.

Belladonna.—Particularly in children, and women subject to spasms, with congestion and pulsation in the head and chest; oppressed breathing and want of breath; dry cough at night; anxious and moaning respiration, at times deep, at others short and rapid; constriction of the larynx with danger of suffocation, and sometimes loss of consciousness.

Pulsatilla.—Especially in children after the suppression of a miliary eruption; and in hysterical persons after the cessation of the catamenia or from taking cold: rapid, short and rattling respiration; choking as from the vapor of sulphur; paroxysms of suffocation, with anguish, palpitation of the heart, spasmodic constriction of the larynx and chest, particularly at night or on lying in a horizontal position; short panting cough, expectoration of sanguineous mucus, tension, fullness, pressure and shooting in the chest. Asthma aggravated by movement.

Phosphorus.—Dyspnœa, obstructed respiration and oppression of the chest, especially in the evening and during movement; great anguish or spasmodic constriction in the chest; nocturnal attacks of suffocation as from paralysis of the lungs; palpitation of the heart, short cough, shooting pain, heaviness, fullness, and congestion of blood to the chest. Alternate with *Belladonna,* and where there is danger of paralysis of the lungs, with *Stibium.*

Stibium.—Especially in children and aged persons, and where there is anxious oppression, dyspnœa; choking, and paroxysms of suffocation in the evening or morning, with rattling of mucus in the chest, violent cough, palpitation of the heart, and congestion of blood to the chest.

Sulphur.—Particularly in chronic cases, where there are nocturnal paroxysms of suffocation, and obstructed respiration, fullness, painful weariness, burning, and congestion in the chest; expectoration of mucus, detached with difficulty and sometimes of a bloody appearance; spasms in the chest, constriction and pain in the sternum, short respiration and inability to speak.

Sambucus.—Principally in children, and where there are choking when lying down; wheezing and rapid respiration, nocturnal paroxysm of suffocation with spasmodic constriction, great anguish rattling of mucus in the chest, and paroxysms of suffocating cough.

Aconite.—Principally in sensitive persons and young girls of plethoric habit, especially if occasioned by moral emotion, and where there is dyspnœa, suffocative cough at night, anxious, short, and difficult respiration, congestion in the head with vertigo.

Cuprum.—In children and hysterical persons, after a fright, anger, a chill, and before the catamenia; spasmodic constriction of the chest; obstructed respiration on walking; short, spasmodic cough with paroxysms of suffocation, and whistling on trying to take a deep inspiration.

China.—Dyspnœa and oppression with inability to breathe on lying with the head low; wheezing in the chest when drawing breath; spasmodic cough and noctural paroxysms of suffocation; sanguineous sputa; palpitation of the heart, and prostration of strength.

Cocculus.—Especially in hysterical persons, where there is dyspnœa, constriction in the throat and chest, with oppression, particularly at night.

Chamomilla.—In children after a cold or a fit of passion, and when there are paroxysms of suffocation, swelling about the pit of the stomach, agitation and cries.

Moschus.—For hysterical persons and children, and where there is oppression and spasmodic constriction of the chest and larynx, particularly after a cold.

Opium.—Deep stertorous and rattling respiration; obstructed breathing, choking, suffocating cough, and paroxysms of suffocation during sleep, like nightmare.

Calcarea.—In chronic cases, and where there is obstructed respiration, and frequent dry cough, as from dust, particularly at night.

Ignatia.—Especially when occasioned by fright, grief or indignation.

DOSE.—Two drops, or twelve globules, of the selected remedy, in a tumbler of water, a tablespoonful at a dose; or a powder, or six globules on the tongue.

In severe cases, give from every half hour to three hours, and in chronic cases, two or three times a day.

DIET AND REGIMEN.—Persons subject to the asthma should bathe the chest morning and night, at first with tepid water, gradually lowering the temperature until it reaches the natural coldness. Coffee and greasy substances should be avoided. Often when the paroxysm is excessively severe, it may be relieved by strong coffee, tobacco, or strammonium smoke.

2. AFFECTIONS OF THE HEART.

These affections we shall divide into two classes:

a. Acute. b. Chronic.

a. ACUTE DISEASE OF THE HEART.

Acute inflammation of the heart seldom exists alone, but is nearly always connected with rheumatism. So generally is this the case that it is sometimes called "*rheumatic inflammation of the heart.*"

DIAGNOSIS.—The patient, suffering perhaps from rheumatism, becomes anxious peevish and flightly. There is an oppression and hurried beating of the heart, palpitation, and perhaps a dry cough. Pain is felt on pressing over the region of the heart, and is increased by a deep inspiration. The pulse is very irregular, generally weak, small and contracted.

The head is of course considerably affected, and not unfrequently is mistaken for the seat of the disease. The patient may become very obstinate, cunning, or taciturn, or excessively stupid, and at length perhaps maniacal, exceedingly restless, or shaken with convulsions.

CAUSES.—Besides being frequently the result of the transition of rheumatism to the heart, this disease may arise from cold, violent blows, injuries, &c.

TREATMENT.—The prominent remedy is *Aconite*, a dose every half hour, in alternation with, or followed by *Bryonia*, *Nux-v.*, *Cocc.*, *Ars. Cannabis*, *Dig.*, *Bell.*, *Phos.*, *Spigelia*, may follow, a dose once in from one to three hours.

b. Chronic Affections.

Diagnosis.—Difficulty of breathing, and palpitation of the heart, particularly on ascending an eminence. Shortness of breath, violent beating of the heart like the blows of a hammer; the beating extends over a larger space than usual; occasional pain, although neither this nor palpitation are always present. Pulse sometimes intermittent, at others excessively irregular; slow, weak, and faltering, or quick and fluttering. There are generally headache, irritability of temper, sometimes cough, spitting of blood, and dropsical swelling of the legs.

Causes.—We have already described, in the chapter on anatomy, the formation and functions of the heart, but to impress the matter still more strongly on the mind of the reader, we will recapitulate some facts here. The heart, the great central point, the balance-wheel of the circulation, contains four chambers; into these the blood passes from every part of the body, and by their contraction is forced out, and conveyed through the appropriate channels, arterialized and charged with life, to the most remote parts of the system.

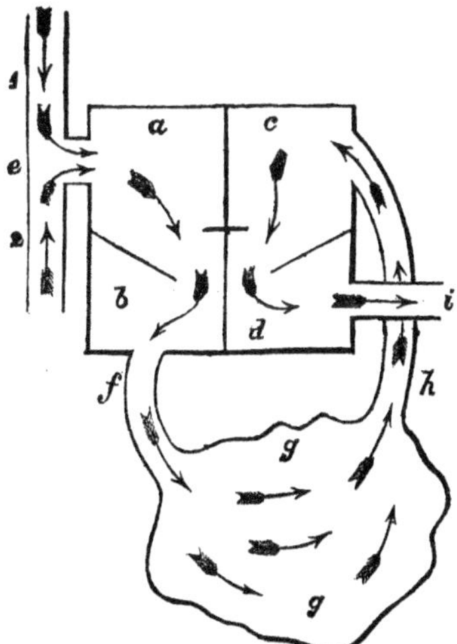

To make the matter still more plain let the foregoing diagram represent the passage of blood through the heart.

For the sake of convenience I have represented the heart in the form of a square. This, however as the reader is well aware is not the case. The arrows represent the current of blood. *A* and *b* represent the right heart, divided into two chambers by the valve or folding-door which is seen partly open, the blood passing through, as represented by the arrows.

1 indicates the vein through which venous or defiled blood enters the heart from the head, and 2 represents the vein through which the venous blood from all the rest of the system, ascending, mingles with the descending blood from the head at *e* and enter together.

Into the first chamber, or *auricle,* of the right heart, *a,* we have then entering the blackened and impure blood from every part of the system. Passing through the valve or folding-door, it enters the lower chamber or *ventricle* *b,* and from thence at *f* passes into the lungs *g,* and there undergoing a chemical change, in which its impurities are exchanged for oxygen, the life-giving property of air, it quits the lungs at *h,* ascends behind the great artery *i* and enters the first chamber of the left heart *c,* descends through the folding-door or valve into the lower chamber *d,* and now, having passed through the entire suit of rooms, thrown off its impurities and become again charged with life, it passes from the heart into the great *aorta* *i,* and is conveyed on its mission of life to every part of the system.

We have seen that the blood is forced from one chamber to the other by the contraction of these chambers or pouches, how is it then, for instance, that on the contraction of the lower chamber of the right heart, the blood is not forced upward into the upper chamber as well as downward into the lungs? This is obviated by the valve which is seen opening downward. The contraction of the chamber closes this valve, and prevents the blood ascending.

The same arrangement also exists at *f* and *i,* thus preventing the blood returning to the heart. It will very readily be perceived that the heart has a most important function to perform, and that any derangement of its machinery is speedily felt throughout the system. These valves must play with the utmost nicety, these chambers must contain the requisite amount of strength, and where this mechanism is prevented from the full performance of its duty, serious results are the consequence.

We are now prepared to look at the cause of some of the diseases of the heart.

The valves it has been seen, to perform their functions aright, transmitting the blood from one chamber to the other, and preventing its return, must open and close with the utmost freedom, and fit with the greatest nicety. They, however, sometimes lose their soft and flexible character and become stiff, bony and immoveable. The valve or door between the upper and lower (*a* and *b*) chamber of the right heart, remaining perhaps half open, and fixed in its position, prevents the blood from passing with the freedom, it would have done if the valve had remained wide open, into the lower chamber, and on the contraction of that chamber, is no obstacle to its being forced into the upper chamber as well as into the lungs.

The consequence therefore is, that a deficient amount of blood is forced into the lungs, a portion being driven back into the upper chamber. Thus it will readily be seen, that the upper chamber is constantly gorged and distended with blood, and this partial stoppage or stagnation of course produces a like stagnation of the blood flowing into this chamber. It will very easily be perceived then that there can be no free transmission of venous blood from the brain through the stagnant vein opening into the upper chamber, and the choked up and congested state of that chamber must, as a matter of course, produce congestion and engorgement of the brain. The vessels of the brain are engorged, because they cannot empty themselves into the already engorged vein (1), which is gorged because it cannot empty itself into the distended chamber *a*, distended, because the blood not only cannot pass freely into the lower chamber, but a portion of what does pass, is driven back.

A large portion of the blood from the lower parts of the

body in returning to the heart passes through the liver. The vein (2) not being able, for the reasons expressed above, to empty its contents into the upper chamber of the heart as rapidly as necessary, a similar state of engorgement of the liver and the lower organs may take place, from the same cause as in the brain.

When the valve of the left heart is affected in the way just described with the right heart, the same consequences result to *the lungs*, as we have just seen are produced on the brain, liver, and other organs. The chamber *c* becomes gorged in the same way as the chamber *a*, just described, so that it will admit but sparingly the blood flowing through the lungs (*h*). The vessels of the lungs therefore, being unable to empty themselves, congestion is the result.

These valves are subject to various other difficulties besides ossification, alike serious in their results, and productive of many of the same symptoms. Thus, the valves may be prevented closing, from warts or fleshy excrescences growing on their edges, or they may be too small, or perhaps holes may be ulcerated through them.

Similar valves or doors to those already mentioned are situated at *f* and *i*, where the blood passes out of the heart into the lungs and out of the other chamber into the great *aorta*. Supposing the valve where the blood flows out of the chamber *d* into the great artery *i* be diseased either by ossification or otherwise, so that the current of blood out of the heart into this vessel be obstructed, the chamber *d* of course becomes gorged and distended with blood, the heart contracts more strongly, and from the increased muscular exertion, the sides become hardened and swollen; thus constituting *hypertrophy* or enlargement of the heart. Congestion of the lungs is also the almost inevitable result. In the same manner by derangement of the valve *f*, *hypertrophy* of the chamber *d* is produced, together with congestion of the brain, liver, &c.

Surrounding the heart, which as we have before said, is lined both inside and outside by a smooth polished membrane, is a bag, applied loosely and allowing the heart to dilate and contract without the slightest impediment. This membrane may become inflamed, and in this state become firmly glued to the sides of the heart. The free movement of the heart is thus prevented, its action is hampered, and it vainly struggles, and throbs to escape its imprisonment. The heart, thus cramped in its movements, the effect on the circulation will readily be perceived.

TREATMENT.—See *symptomatic indication.*

PALPITATION OF THE HEART.

Perhaps this is as proper a place as any to introduce this unpleasant and very common variety of heart difficulty. It is frequently, as we have seen, a symptom of some severe form of heart disease, and yet it is not uncommonly a very slight trouble easily relieved. The young, during the growing period, are often troubled with it, and the old from ossification of the valves.

It may also arise from derangement of the nervous system, produced by violent mental emotion, the abuse of ardent spirits, coffee, &c. It is of very common occurrence in persons of plethoric habit; during pregnancy, also by overloading the stomach, or eating at improper times.

TREATMENT.—If occasioned by *congestion of the blood, or plethora: Acon., Bell., Coff., Op., Nux-v., Lach., Phos.*

In *nervous persons: Asa., Cham., Coff., Nux-v., Puls.*

After moral emotions: Cham., Coff., Ign., Op., Nux-v.

After a fright; Op., or *Coff.*

From disappointment: Cham., Ign., Nux-v.

From joy: Coff.

Fear, or anguish: Verat.

After *loss of blood: Phos.-ac., Chin.*

After the *suppression of an eruption: Ars., Caust., Lach., Sulph.*

SYMPTOMATIC INDICATION.—I have chosen, for the sake of easy reference by the patient, to note under the above head the symptomatic indication of some of the different remedies for the various diseases of the heart which I have described, both acute and chronic.

Spigelia.—An all important remedy in most forms of heart disease. Inflammation of the heart, with and without articular rheumatism. Tumultuous pulsation with suffocative sensation and spasms in the chest, particularly when lying or sitting, aggravated by motion. Chronic affection of the heart, after inflammation, or with articular arthritis. Audible palpitation, increased on sitting down, bending the chest forward, and frequently accompanied with pain and oppression of the chest. Valvular disease, hypertrophy, dilation of the heart with their accompanying symptoms. Tremulous motion of the heart.

Aconite.—Palpitation of the heart with great anguish, general heat, great soreness and debility of the limbs. Palpitation in young plethoric persons. Quick and rapid pulsations of the heart, notwithstanding the pulse is slow and intermittent. Oppressive aching in the region of the heart, sometimes as if a heavy load were pressing upon it. Difficult respiration in the erect position from shooting pain. Inflammation and chronic affections of the heart with fullness in the chest and sensation of congestion in the head.

Aurum.—Violent palpitation of the heart, coming on in paroxysms, and attended with oppression. Shaking sensation of the heart on motion. Arthritic metastasis and organic affections of the heart.

Arsenic.—Palpitation of the heart, irregular, with anguish, excessively violent, particularly at night, and when lying on the back. Inflammation and organic disease.

Belladonna.—Great anguish about the heart, oppressed sensation, tremor with anguish and pain and a kind of bubbling sensation in going up-stairs. Palpitation with intermittent pulse, also when at rest, increased by motion.

Lachesis.—Palpitation with anxiety or weakness ; felt in the back, debilitating with nausea ; chronic, particularly in girls, also accompanying other affections, and frequently followed by oppressive pain in the chest. Irregularity of the pulsations. Great anguish about the heart with heaviness in the chest in rheumatism ; constrictive sensation.

Arnica.—Quivering pulsations, oppression or stitches in the heart with fainting fit. Pain as if the heart were squeezed together.

Natrum-mur.—Pains in the heart, particularly at night. Palpitation from the slightest motion, sometimes accompanied with anguish. Fluttering motions in the heart, irregularity or intermittent pulsations.

ADMINISTRATION.—Two drops, or twelve globules, of the selected remedy, in a tumbler of water, a tablespoonful at a dose ; or three globules, or a powder, on the tongue. In acute cases, a dose once in from a half hour to three hours. In chronic cases, once in from four to twelve hours.

DIET.—Violent mental excitement and strong physical exertion, should of course be avoided. The nervous system should be kept as quiet as possible, and all strongly stimulating articles either of food or drink should be strictly prohibited. Pure air and a moderate amount of exercise are essential.

CHAPTER V.

AFFECTIONS OF THE MIND.

INSANITY.

A feeling of awe steals over us as we wander along the silent and deserted streets of some ancient city and gaze upon the crumbling temples, the broken columns, the rubbish choking up the palaces of kings, relics of power, grandeur and beauty, the only monuments of a past age, voices faint and murmuring, whispering to us through the long dim lapse of buried centuries, of nations mighty in their strength, but long since numbered with the dead. Sadness is upon us as we thus tread amid the dust of buried empire.

But what are the ruins of matter, the upheaving of thrones, the wreck of nations, *to the ruins of mind.* What the desolation of a temple reared by man to one fashioned by the *Eternal God.* Mind, immortal mind, reeling upon its throne, without helm, without chart or compass, drifting hither and thither upon a stormy ocean, or tossed upon its waves a helpless, hopeless wreck, how sad, how awful! See the maniac flying in terror from his best friends; clinging to his bitterest enemies, with strange cunning gliding from his room at the dark hour of night, to murder his helpless babes, or steep his hands in the blood of his wife. Listen to his maniac laugh, his wild shrieks and fearful curses!

Allowing the term insanity its strict signification, we should find hundreds with whom we mingle every day, yea, thousands in all grades of society, in every department of life, statesmen, clergymen, business-men, laboring under some form of mental derangement, and the world itself somewhat of a crazy world. A lunatic, who had been for some time confined in one of our asylums, was one day asked by a visitor, what he was sent there for. He very shrewdly replied, it was all owing to a difference of opinion. The world insisted, that *he* was crazy, while he as strenuously maintained, the shoe was on the other foot, and the *world* was crazy ; the world being in the majority and having the power in their own hands, carried the day and shut him up. Perhaps both were partially correct.

We can hardly believe, that a perfectly sane man will violate with impunity every law of nature, that he will sacrifice reputation, the esteem of the good, health, an easy conscience, and a home pervaded with an atmosphere of love for the gratification of selfish or sensual passions. We can hardly look upon either the spendthrift, foolishly squandering his wealth, or the miser, hoarding up his gains and denying himself even the necessaries of life, as perfectly sane ; and we certainly must look upon the mother, who trains her daughter in that cold and selfish school, where the warm feelings of the heart are frozen, and nature compelled to give place to art, in which, alas, too many of our daughters are educated, as possessing, to say the least, an extremely ill-balanced mind.

But our object here is to look upon insanity in a medical light, only so far as it assumes the perceptible character of a disease. However interesting the subject may be, we shall only have room to glance at it here. We may look at it under three divisions :

1. *Moral insanity*, consisting in a morbid perversion of the natural feelings, affections, temper, habits, &c., but without any maniacal hallucination, or any particular lesion of the intellect or reasoning faculties.

2. *Intellectual insanity*, attended with hallucination, when the patient believes in some unreal event, repugnant to his former experience and common-sense, and acts under the influence of this erroneous conviction.

3. There is another form, which might with propriety be called *incoherent madness*, in which the ideas follow each other with astonishing rapidity, but in a state of the most complete incoherence and confusion.

1. *Moral Insanity.*—There are thousands of persons at large throughout community, who are affected more or less

with this modification of insanity. They are generally persons of singular, wayward, and eccentric character. On inquiry it will frequently be found, that habit, temper, and disposition seem gradually to have undergone a change. This may first be noticed after some severe shock, or a violent attack of sickness, or it may have been coming on for years, and is merely an increase of peculiarities always more or less natural or habitual. Certain forms of this variety of insanity are exceedingly difficult to detect, and sometimes, notwithstanding friends might be perfectly satisfied themselves, that the patient was really of unsound mind, they would still find it almost impossible to bring forward sufficient proof to satisfy a jury. The patient might be capable of reasoning with the greatest clearness on almost any topic, and accounting with great ingenuity and even plausibility for his eccentricities of conduct. He often thinks and acts under the influence of strongly excited feelings, during which time we may obtain a clue to his mental derangement.

I well recollect a case which occurred during my childhood in my native town and created considerable excitement. A Portuguese, by the name of *Rabello*, murdered a boy about ten years of age, the son of his employer, in a most horrid and savage manner. With an axe the head was severed from the trunk, the chest laid open and the boy literally chopped to pieces. *Rabello* had been looked upon as possessed of a morose and irritable disposition, but had by no means been considered insane. The indignation of the community was so strongly excited by this brutal and cold blooded murder, that law-abiding and law-loving as they were, they could hardly be prevented from hanging the victim without judge or jury. The proof of the murder was positive, and there seemed to be not the slightest chance for the prisoner of escape from the gallows.

Hon. Truman Smith, since a member of the U. S. Senate, from Connecticut, believing the man deranged, undertook his defence, and on the trial so indefatigable was he in his exertions, that he succeeded in obtaining a verdict of insanity.

Perhaps the indignation of the community was now about equally divided between Mr. Smith and the prisoner; both were denounced in the strongest terms, and the wiseacres shook their heads, mourned that justice had departed from the land, and the basest crime could now go unpunished. The prisoner was properly confined, and scarcely six weeks had passed away, before he might have been seen chained to his cell, a raving madman. Had it not been for the enlightened efforts of his council on his trial, notwithstanding his insanity, he would have been condemned to death.

In this variety of insanity there are often violent outbursts of passion breaking out without cause, and leading oftentimes to the commission of crime. Cases are also exceedingly frequent where persons allow their feelings to become strongly and bitterly excited against others without proper cause or provocation; constantly brooding over fancied wrongs, misconstruing even acts of kindness, looking upon those who are really friends, as foes, ever finding fault with others, but seeing none in themselves, these feelings of malevolence and hatred may grow deeper and stronger, until the most ridiculous and absurd ideas obtain full possession of the mind, or perhaps the darker thoughts of murder creep in, at first scarcely whispered, but growing stronger and stronger, ever haunting them, and hurrying them on by an invisible force until the bloody deed is consummated. This is one form of *moral insanity*.

There is another class of cases in which there is a disposition to melancholy and dejection of the mind without any illusion of the understanding connected with it. Surrounded by every comfort, a feeling of gloom and sadness shrouds all their prospects. Their darkened sky is illumined by no golden ray of hope, nature has no cheering word for them, but crushing, dark despair and melancholy weighs them down.

Sometimes the chilling thought of suicide, steals in upon them, or there arises in their mind a fear that they shall be led to the commission of some great crime. This thought continually gains strength, haunting them whenever alone, hurrying them on with an almost irresistible power, until at length, too often, alas, the fearful deed is consummated.

A propensity to theft is often a distinctive feature of moral insanity, and not unfrequently the sole characteristic of the disease. Cases are on record where persons possessed of wealth, surrounded by every comfort, would steal every thing they could lay their hands on, even articles they could never use, and the use of which they were entirely ignorant. A case is on record where a lady, beautiful, amiable, highly educated and accomplished, surrounded by every luxury wealth and taste could furnish, the mother of two beautiful children, a devoted husband ready to supply every want, yet would pilfer whenever she had an opportunity, articles too, she could never put to any use. Her husband, devotedly attached to her, reasoned with her upon the guilt of her conduct. With bitter tears she would confess the fault and solemnly promise never to be guilty of the like offence again, and yet the very next hour, if opportunity offered, commit the same offence. She became known throughout the community, and in the stores she was watched on making her appearance, and if after leaving, any little article was missed, a bill was made out, sent to her husband, and immediately paid.

Another form of moral insanity displays itself in an entire want of self-government, in constant excitement, and thoughtless and extravagant conduct. These persons frequently become drunkards, their drunken attacks being followed by periods of raving madness. After the attack has passed off, they will again in a short time indulge in intoxicating drinks, notwithstanding they know the inevitable consequence.

2. *Intellectual insanity*, or madness attended with hallucinations. When a morbid delusion is impressed on the mind, but little doubt can be entertained of the existence of insanity. There are two entirely different states of disease attended with this symptom. In the one case the understanding, when exercised on most subjects, is comparatively clear, and the morbid impressions only partial; in the other, the disturbance of the intellectual faculties involves all the other operations

of the mind. The former is called monomania, the latter, mania.

Monomania.—It is very common to see persons perfectly sane on every subject but one, but touch that and you open wide the floodgates of insanity. Some persons are deranged on the subject of religion, and display the utmost bitterness, and indulge in the harshest invective against all who dare to differ from them. Others are deranged on some particular science, or upon some of the great moral and philanthropic questions of the day. It is denounced by some as wild fanaticism, and is in reality a species of insanity, properly classed under the head of monomania.

The patient laboring under this affection, is often gloomy, morose, and excessively melancholy.

Mania.—The characteristics of this variety of insanity are too well known to require much description. They may either be highly excitable, raving in violent delirium, or perhaps the insanity may be of a milder kind; they are generally firmly convinced that they have either performed some mighty deeds, that they are some illustrious characters or troubled with other illusions equally devoid of truth. Thus, one believes he is Jesus Christ, another that he is Jehovah, and another perhaps, that he is Mahomet, or a king.

3. *Incoherent madness.*—In this form of madness the disease commences with great excitement; the patient is restless, active, and generally sleeps but little. Ideas follow each other in the most astonishing rapidity, but without the slightest connection. Words and sentences are half uttered, and this unmeaning jargon is kept up almost constantly, the patient scarcely allowing himself to eat or sleep. This state of excitement, after having continued for some time, frequently gradually decreases; the patient becomes more quiet, obtains sleep, and may in time become perfectly rational.

Causes.—The causes of the various forms of insanity are exceedingly numerous. One fruitful cause is an erroneous and unsuitable method of education. The bad qualities are nurtured and allowed to grow without restraint, until they choke the good, or the good feelings of the heart are warped and bittered, by an iron will and the cold harsh control of narrow and prejudiced minds. But I have already referred to this matter in the chapter on the "*Causes of Disease*."

Among the other causes of insanity we may enumerate abuse of ardent spirits, blows on the head, and exposure to the heat of the sun, intestinal irritation; irregularity of the uterine functions, not unfrequently produce temporary derangement, especially where the catamenia is suppressed, irregular, or attended with agonizing pain. Insanity of a violent form is sometimes developed in connection with child-bearing.

Of the moral causes of insanity it will be unnecessary for me to speak here. Cases are familiar to all, where disappointments in business, or love, the workings of a troubled conscience, ill-judged religious advice, tending alone to excite fear, have sent the poor victim to the madhouse for life.

All experience shows that civilized man is far more subject to insanity than the savage, and the inhabitants of large cities, as a general thing, than those of the country.

Treatment.—The condition of the violently insane now and half a century ago is entirely different, then they were treated more like brutes, loaded with chains, scourged, abused in every way, and seldom met with kindness. Now they are treated like human beings, unfortunate it is true, but yet deserving care and kindness.

It will be impossible to detail fully in a work like this, the treatment required in the various forms of insanity, and indeed, it would not be necessary as this disease is one that requires the skill of the physician, of one too who is versed in human nature, and knows how to administer to a mind diseased.

The patient should be surrounded by a proper moral influence, blending firmness with the utmost kindness, and watching the leading traits of character developed, acting accordingly. Mental alienation occasioned by *oppressing emotions*, such as anger, fear, mortification, or vexation, usually requires: *Bell.*, *Hyos.*, *Ign.*, *Phos.-ac.*, *Nux-v.*, *Plat.*

When the result of *excessive study*: *Lach.*, *Plat.*, *Stram.*, or *Nux-v.*, *Op.*, *Sulph.*, *Bell.*, *Hyos.*

From *religious notions* attended with melancholy; *Lach.*, *Sulph.*, *Verat.*, or *Ars.*, *Aur.*, *Bell.*

For the delirium of drunkards: *Nux-vom.*, or *Op.*, or *Hell.*, *Hyos.*, *Stram.*, and *Puls.* (See also Delirium Tremens).

In Females, from a derangement of the sexual functions: *Acon.*, *Bell.*, *Plat.*, *Puls.*, *Stram.*, and *Verat.*, or *Cup.*, *Sec.* (See also Diseases of Females.)

Melancholy, of an excessively gloomy character, may require: *Ars.*, *Aur.*, *Lach.*, or *Nux-v.*

Melancholy, of a more gentle and placid character, may require: *Cocc.*, *Bell.*, *Ign.*, *Hell.*, *Con.*, *Phos.-ac.*, *Puls.*, *Sil.*

SYMPTOMATIC INDICATIONS.—*Belladonna.*—Great distress with agitation and inquietude. Frightful visions, fear of death, repugnance to conversation and society; haggard eyes, fixed and furious look, burning thirst, trembling of the limbs, sleeplessness with agitation; or gloomy, tearful humor, with apathy and indifference.

Hyosciamus.—Paroxysms of violent delirium, alternating with epileptic fits; sleeplessness with constant talking, great anguish and fear, visions of the dead; jealousy; fury with impulse to kill.

Lachesis.—Talkative delirium with rapid change of ideas; suspicion, jealousy or pride, and fear of death; or despondency and great disposition to give way to grief.

Nux-vom.—Anguish and inquietude, with disposition to wander abroad; congestion, bewilderment and heaviness of the head; pressure or fullness in the abdomen and stomach; constipation or watery diarrhœa; sleeplessness with starts.

Opium.—Great drowsiness; visions of mice and scorpions, convulsive movements; inability to sleep, notwithstanding there is sleepiness, constipation, congestion of the head, epileptic fits.

Platina.—Ravings of past events, with singing, dancing, or weeping; quarrelsomeness; contempt for others, with great self-esteem; increased sexual desire; dread of death and frightful visions.

Stramonium.—Dizziness or loss of consciousness, belief that the body is divided into two parts; delirium with frightful visions; religious movements; lascivious ideas, or affected manners; conversation with spirits, ridiculous antics, or wild and ungovernable fury; bloatedness of the face with silly expression.

Veratrum.—Great anguish and despondency; taciturn with violent oaths on the slightest provocation; loss of consciousness with singing, whistling, and religious mania, lascivious ideas, proud and haughty.

Arsenic.—Great anguish; fear of spectres, robbers, solitude, &c. Aversion to conversation; inclination to commit suicide, or dread of death, tearfulness and fear of offending.

Cantharis.—Violent rage; renewal of paroxysms at the sight of water; excitement of the sexual organs.

Pulsatilla.—Stupor, nocturnal delirium, sleeplessness with anguish, or agitated sleep with anxious dreams; great melancholy with weeping; despair of eternal happiness with constant prayers. Tendency to fear and disposition to hide.

Sulphur.—Confusion of the intellect, indifference, apathy, or uneasy about domestic or religious affairs.

Cuprum.—Want of moral energy; imaginary occupations; wildness and redness of the eyes, during the paroxysm, tears, anxiety and disposition to hide.

Administration.—Two drops, or twelve globules, in a tumbler of water, a tablespoonful at a dose; or a powder, or three globules on the tongue. In violent cases give once in from one or three hours. In cases less violent, or where the symptoms are comparatively mild, or the affection only partial, every twelve or twenty-four hours.

VARIOUS AFFECTIONS OF THE MIND.

Consequences of *fright and fear: Op., Bell., Ign., Puls* may be consulted.

Excessive joy: Coff., Op., Pulsatilla.

Grief: Ign.
Home sickness: Phos-ac., Staphysagria.
Jealousy: Hyos., Nux-v.
Violent anger: Nux-v., Chamomilla.
Chagrin: Cham., Nux-v., Ign., Platina.
Insult and mortification: Bell., Ign., Plat., Pulsatilla.
Unhappy love: Phos-ac., Ignatia.

For symptomatic indications and administration, consult Insanity.

HYSTERIA.

Hypochondria.

The two names above, indicate the same disease, the former being applied to the affection when found in the female, the latter in the male.

Hysteria has characters peculiar to itself, but is also apt to assume the form and mimic the symptoms of diseases of a much graver nature.

The hysterical paroxysm resembles somewhat an epileptic fit, yet is very easily distinguished from it. There are strong convulsive movements of the limbs and trunk; the head thrown backward, the face flushed, the eyelids closed and tremulous, and the jaws firmly shut. If the hands are left at liberty, she will often strike her breasts, tear her hair, and rend her clothes. After a short time a calm may take place, which, however, is generally followed by another spasm, and the whole attack not unfrequently terminates in an explosion of tears, sobs, and convulsive laughter.

Another variety of this form of paroxysm, is when the patient suddenly sinks insensible, and without convulsions; there is a slow, interrupted breathing and flushed cheeks; she recovers, fatigued and in tears.

In another form of *hysteria*, there is a sensation of a ball rolling about the abdomen and stomach, and sometimes ascending the throat, so as to impede deglutition.

The hysterical seizures are confined almost entirely to women, generally between the ages of fifteen and forty, and are as a general thing, connected with some derangement of the sexual functions.

The variety of serious diseases which may be so accurately mimicked by *hysteria* as to defy detection except by the practiced eye of the physician, is truly astonishing. Among the rest we find, palsy—perfect hemiplegia or pariplegia—entire loss of voice, *laryngitis*, and pain in the breasts, resembling that of cancer. We also find a peculiar kind of cough, loud, harsh and dry, resembling croup, hiccough, violent vomiting, sometimes of blood. Hysterical affections of the bones, joints, and back, are exceedingly common, in which the pain is extremely severe, and the symptom such as to lead friends and sometimes physicians to believe that a serious difficulty is present. The limbs are often drawn up and immoveable, and the system so filled with pain on the slightest movement, as to lead the patient to suppose that death would be the result of any attempt to walk, and yet, let the house take fire, or some violent shock take place, they would run for their life and be surprised to find themselves when the excitement wore off, perfectly recovered. I was once called to see a patient who had never moved from her bed for nine months. She ate well most of the time, yet insisted every morning she should not live till night, and every night persisted in taking a weeping farewell of her friends. I ordered a small pistol to be placed at night at the foot of the bed, so arranged that it could be discharged from another room by a slow match, and when discharged would set on fire a quantity of cotton, upon which had been poured some turpentine. When all was quiet, the pistol was discharged, the cotton blazed up, and the poor girl, screaming with terror, jumped from her bed and rushed from her room. I need not say, the next day on calling I found my patient entirely well. She has since married, and is the mother of two children, but ascertaining by some means or other the hand I had in the trick, she has never forgiven me.

Treatment.—The application of cold water in the form of a shower-bath, or during the paroxysm, cold water dashed into the face or poured on to the head from a pitcher, will be found serviceable. The patient also may be allowed to smell from time to time of *Camphor*.

Nux-v.—Aversion to life, ill-humor, aching and dullness in the head, exhaustion from walking, unrefreshing sleep, pain in the stomach and bowels, constipation and piles.

Sulphur.—Great bodily and mental indolence, depression of spirits, constipation and restlessness.

Nat-mur.—Depression of spirits, weeping and disposition to be alone; ill-humor, aversion to life, headache with want of appetite.

Acon., *Bell.*, *Bry.*, *Op.*, *Moschus.*, *Hyos.*, *Valerian*, may be consulted, as well as the other remedies mentioned under the head of insanity.

CHAPTER VI.

AFFECTIONS OF THE HEAD.

HEADACHE.

Cephalgia.

The head sympathises with the derangements of nearly all the other parts of the system. The causes of headache are exceedingly varied, rendering it necessary, to ensure success in its treatment, that the symptoms shall be carefully noted, and the cause of the difficulty ascertained as nearly as possible. With a little care in selecting the appropriate remedy, persons can frequently relieve themselves of this troublesome affection, so common to all, without the aid of a physician. We shall speak of some of the prominent causes, and mention the appropriate treatment under their several heads.

1. *Headache from congestion to the head.*
2. *From catarrh or cold in the head.*
3. *From constipation and gastric derangement.*
4. *From rheumatism.*
5. *From external causes.*
6. *Sick headache.*
7. *Nervous headache.*

1. *Headache from congestion to the head.*

Some of the prominent symptoms are, violent throbbing of the arteries of the head; fullness and heaviness of the head, accompanied by giddiness, particularly on stooping or walking in the sun; also fullness and pain above the eyes, increased by stooping; heat about the head.

Treatment.—Abstain from highly stimulating food and drinks, such as ardent spirits, tea, coffee, &c. Bathe the head freely in cold water, placing if necessary, a cloth wet with cold water on the temples.

Congestion caused by *chagrin* requires: *Chamomilla.*

By *suppressed grief* or *mortified feelings ; Ignatia.*

By *anger: Nux-v., Chamomilla*, or *Bryonia.*

By *fright: Opium.*

By *constipation: Aloes, Nux-v., Opium.*

From *gastric derangements: Sepia, Nux-v., Ipecac, Bryonia, Sulphur.*

From the use of *intoxicating liquors: Nux-v., Opium.*

From *a blow: Arnica.*

From *joy: Coff.*

From *a cold:* (*See Influenza.*)

From *suppressed menstruation: Bell., Puls., Acon., Verat., Bry., Sepia.*

From *sedentary habits: Aloes, Nux-v., Sulphur.*

SYMPTOMATIC INDICATION.—*Nux-v.*, is an invaluable remedy when the difficulty is caused by abuse of ardent spirits, sedentary mode of life, and severe mental labor, also when the following symptoms are present. Heat and redness of the face, throbbing of the arteries of the head, paroxysms of vertigo, violent headache, particularly in the forehead over the eyes, increased by stooping or coughing.

Belladonna.—In the more severe forms, when the veins about the head are distended, accompanied with paroxysms of stitching pain on one side, aggravated by motion, noise or light; not unfrequently scintillations before the eyes, and obscuration of sight; buzzing in the ears, and sopor. Violent aching pain, bloodshot eyes, delirium, worse on moving the eyes and head, and great sensitiveness to light or noise. The symptoms are generally developed by disturbance or derangement of some other organ, as during dentition, from cold or derangement of the menses.

Aconite.—When the symptoms are violent, accompanied by heat and considerable pain, violent throbbing, heaviness and fullness in the head, delirium, sensitiveness to light or noise, and aggravated by motion. Alternate with *Belladonna.* These remedies, if the symptoms commence with considerable violence, should be given at the beginning of the attack.

DOSE.—Two drops, or twelve globules, in a tumbler of water, a tablespoonful at a dose; or six globules dry on the tongue. Give once in two or three hours.

Bryonia.—Compressive pains in the head, or sensitive on stooping, as if every thing would protrude through the forehead. Bleeding at the nose, burning and watery eyes, constipation.

DOSE.—Same as *Aconite.* Give once in three or four hours.

Rhus.—Burning pulsative pains, with fullness in the head, fluctuation of the brain as from a fluid rolling inside, weight in the back part of the head; particularly if pains occur after a meal. Frequently in alternation with *Belladonna,* or *Bryonia.*

DOSE.—Same as *Bryonia.*

Opium.—Severe tearing pains, heaviness and beating in the head. Muddy sensation of the brain with stupor. Wandering look, constipation.

DOSE.—Same as *Aconite.* Give once in four or six hours.

Pulsatilla.—Pressive and distressing pain in the side of the head, commencing in the back of the head and extending into the root of the nose, or *vice-versa.* Relieved by binding something tight around the head, or walking, and aggravated by sitting or looking upward; heaviness of the head; paleness of the face and vertigo; tearful humor, particularly in females, shivering, anxiety. It suits those of a cold or lymphatic temperament.

DOSE.—Same as *Aconite.*

Gloenine has been found highly beneficial when there is fullness and severe pain, almost causing delirium. Three globules may be given once in three or four hours.

Mercury.—Fullness in the head as if it would split, or as if it were compressed with a band. Worse at night, with burning, tearing, boring pains, easy and profuse perspiration.

DOSE.—A powder, or six globules, once in four or six hours.

Veratrum.—Pressive throbbing pain; sensation as if the

brain were bruised, or constrictive pain; rigidity of the nape of the neck, nausea and vomiting.

DOSE.—Same as *Bryonia*.

2. HEADACHE FROM CATARRH, OR COLD IN THE HEAD.

Aconite.—Where the fever is intermixed with chills, running at the nose and eyes, and pressing, dull feeling over the eyes. Frequently followed by *Stibium*.

DOSE.—Two drops, or twelve globules, in a tumbler of water, a tablespoonful once in three hours.

Nux-v.—Constipation with chilliness, or feverish heat in the head, heaviness in the forehead.

DOSE.—A powder, or three globules, once in four or six hours.

Mercury.—Pressing pain over the root of the nose; frequent sneezing and running at the nose, chilliness and pains in the limbs. (See also Coryza, or cold in the head.)

DOSE.—Same as *Mercury*.

3. HEADACHE FROM CONSTIPATION AND GASTRIC DERANGEMENT.

Headache occasioned by constipation will generally be relieved by *Nux-v*., *Bry*., *Op*., *Sulph*., or *Aloes*., (see *Nux-vom*., *Bry*., and *Opium*, under headache from congestion to the head.)

Besides these I have found great benefit from *Sepia*, where there is constipation occasioned by derangement of the portal circulation, and where there are shooting and boring pains in the head with nausea and vomiting; headache, worse in the morning; intolerance of light with inability to open the eyes; congestion of blood with heaviness and confusion of the head. Particularly in females and where there is a derangement of the menstrual functions.

DOSE.—A powder, or six globules, once in six hours.

Silicea.—Throbbing pain with heat and congestion in the head, worse in the morning or afternoon, aggravated by intellectual labor, speaking or stooping; sensation as if the head would split; pain on one side, shooting, tearing, and extending over the face ; tubercles on the head, tenderness of the scalp, and falling off of the hair.

Dose.—Same as *Sepia.*

Sulphur.—Pressure and heaviness in the head, shooting pains, particularly in one side ; severe pain over the eyes ; throbbing, bubbling pain with heat in the head, worse in the morning, at night, or in bed, also increased by thinking or in the open air.

Dose.—Same as *Sepia.*

Where occasioned by gastric derangement, *Bry.*, *Puls.*, *Nux-v.*, and *Ipecac.* are the prominent remedies. *Pulsatilla* will be found beneficial where the headache has been occasioned by eating too freely, particularly of greasy food, and where there is considerable nausea. *Ipecac.* is also frequently beneficial where there is considerable nausea, and violent headache. (See gastric derangement.)

4. HEADACHE FROM RHEUMATISM.

The prominent remedies in this variety of headache are *Bell.*, *Puls.*, *Bry.*, *Rhus.*, *Nit.-ac.*, *Spig.*, *Nux-v.*

For the symptomatic indications of *Bell.*, *Puls.*, *Bry.*, *Rhus.*, and *Nux-v.* (See Headache from congestion.)

Nit.-ac. is indicated where there is sharp shooting, or sore and aching pain about the head, particularly where it occurs after, or in connection with, a rheumatic attack in some other part of the body.

5. HEADACHE FROM EXTERNAL CAUSES.

The external causes, which may produce headache, are exceedingly numerous. It will only be necessary to enumerate a few, with the prominent remedies, under their respective heads.

When produced by a *fall*, or *blow : Arnica.*

From abuse of *spirituous liquors* : *Carb.-v.*, *Nux-v.*, *Coff.*, *Pulsatilla.*

From a *chill : Bell.*, *Bry.*, *Dulc.*, *Nux-vom.*

When produced by *bathing : Ant.*, or *Pulsatilla.*

From *cold drinks : Bell.*, *Ars.*, or *Pulsatilla.*

From *changeable weather:* *Bry.*, *Rhus.*, *Carb.-v.*, *Nux-v.*, *Rhododendron.*

From *Tobacco:* *Ant.*, *Ign.*, *Aconite.*

From *prolonged watching:* *Cocc.*, *Nux-v.*, *Pulsatilla.*

From *heat:* *Acon.*, *Bell.*, *Bry.*, *Carb.-v.*

DOSE.—In sudden and violent attacks of headache it may be necessary to give the remedy once in from half an hour to two hours. Where it is long continued or habitual, a dose may be given every night, changing the remedy, if after five or six doses but little benefit has been derived.

6. *Nervous Headache.*

This variety of headache is generally confined to one side of the head, or the pain is developed above the root of the nose. The pains are of a neuralgic character, violent, throbbing, darting and stinging, worse at night, and attended with thirst, flushed cheeks, and great sensitiveness to light, noise, or touch.

Belladonna is a prominent remedy, where the pains are of a violent burning, shooting, or rending character, commencing sometimes gently, but increasing to a fearful intensity. There is often a roaring and buzzing in the ear, and sensation as if water were fluctuating in the head.

Bryonia, *Ign.*, *Nux-v.*, *Puls.*, *Coff.*, *Cham.* are also prominent remedies in this affection. (See Headache from congestion.)

7. *Sick Headache.*

This troublesome difficulty is generally dependant on gastric derangement, and in some persons it seems to be periodical, returning at stated times, at intervals either more or less frequent.

There is generally sickness at the stomach, swimming in the head, or violent aching pain, not unfrequently coming on in the morning, and continuing until relieved at night by sleep.

The prominent remedies are, *Ipecac.*, *Bell.*, *Bry.*, *Nux-v.*, *Spig.*, *Acon.*, *Sep.*

Where the symptoms commence with nausea and vomiting and are accompanied with bruised sensation about the head, *Ipecac.* is the appropriate remedy and should be given immediately at intervals of half an hour.

Nux-v. is also a prominent remedy for the indications of which as well as the other remedies. (See Headache from Congestion.)

The tendency to sick headache is often removed by taking a dose of *Nux*, when the first symptoms are noticed. A dose of *Nux*, *Sepia*, or *Silicea* taken every other night for a week or two, will often entirely eradicate the tendency to this extremely painful complaint.

DOSE.—A powder, or six globules, may be given on the tongue as directed above.

VERTIGO.

This is generally symptomatic, disappearing when the cause is removed, yet it is sometimes the prominent symptom.

When occasioned by a derangement of the stomach, *Ant.*, *Bell.*, *Nux-v.*, *Cham.*, *Merc.*, *Puls.*, and *Rhus* may be consulted.

By *nervous affections*: *Arn.*, *Bell.*, *Chin.*, *Hep.-s.*, *Nux-v.*, *Puls.*, *Mosch.*, *Rhus.*

When occasioned by *congestion of blood*: *Acon.*, *Bell.*, *Chin.*, *Con.*, *Op.*, *Puls.*, *Nux-v.*, *Sulphur.*

Suppressed *ulcers and eruptions*: *Calc.*, or *Sulphur.*

The *motion of a carriage*: *Hep.-s.* and *Sil.*, or *Cocc.* and *Petrol.*

Aconite.—Vertigo on rising from a recumbent posture or stooping, nausea or cloudiness of the eyes, loss of consciousness and whirling in the head.

Antimonium.—Disordered stomach with nausea and vomiting.

Arnica.—When occasioned by too full a meal, and attended by nausea, cloudiness of the eyes, and whirling in the head.

Belladonna.—Vertigo, with anguish, dizziness, cloudiness,

or sparks before the eyes, or with staggering, nausea, trembling and recurrence of the attacks on stooping or rising up.

Conium.—Whirling vertigo, causing the patient to fall sideways, heaviness and fullness of the head, weakness of memory.

Hepar-s.—Produced by the motion of a carriage or moving the head, with nausea, fainting, and dizziness. If not sufficient, follow by *Cocc.*, *Petrol.*, or *Silicea.*

Lachesis.—With paleness of the face, fainting and bleeding at the nose, particularly in the morning.

Nux-v.—During and after a meal, when walking in the open air, in the morning, or in the evening in bed, or when lying on the back, with whirling or wavering in the head, buzzing in the ears, cloudiness of the eyes or fainting,

Opium.—Coming on when rising up in bed, or caused by fright, and attended with trembling, dizziness, and humming in the ears.

Pulsatilla.—Vertigo on raising the eyes, or when seated, or stooping, or in the evening in bed, or after a meal, with nausea, heaviness in the head, humming in the ears, paleness of the face.

Silicea.—Vertigo in the morning, on elevating the eyes, from the motion of a carriage, or mental emotion, with nausea and retching.

Sulphur.—Vertigo when sitting, in the act of ascending, after a meal, in the morning, at night with nausea, fainting and bleeding at the nose.

ADMINISTRATION.—Two drops, or twelve globules, in a tumbler of water; or a powder, or three globules, on the tongue. Give once in from one to four hours, according to circumstances.

APOPLEXY.

DIAGNOSIS.—The attack is generally preceded by precursory symptoms, which if promptly met by the appropriate remedies, often readily yield, and thus the attack itself, for the time is warded off. There is dullness and heaviness of the head, obscuration of sight, buzzing in the ears, hardness of hearing, great disposition to sleep, which however is unrefreshing and disturbed by dreams; derangement of the memory, heat and throbbing of the arteries of the head, and sometimes severe shooting pain; cold hands and feet, pulse slow, full, and intermittent, and not unfrequently torpor of the abdominal organs.

When total apoplexy of the brain takes place, the patient falls down without consciousness, totally, or partially paralyzed; the breathing is stertorous and slow, the pulse hard, full and slow, the eyes are staring and protruded, speech difficult, or entirely lost, the face is livid, and vomiting frequently takes place.

In some cases the patient complains of a sudden and violent headache, vomiting sets in, the pulse is at first soft, the face pale, and the patient in a kind of stupor; gradually the stupor increases, the face becomes red, the patient answers with difficulty, coma sets in, from which every effort to rouse the patient is unsuccessful.

Causes.—Apoplexy is more frequent among males than females, and generally occurs after persons have passed the prime of life. A predisposition to apoplexy is indicated by a stout short body, large and short neck, corpulence, dark, red countenance. The predisposition is increased by rich living, piles, and sedentary habits.

It is also frequently induced by sudden changes of temperature, strong mental emotion, abuse of spirituous drinks, or narcotic substances, tight cravats, and organic affections of the heart.

Treatment.*—In the treatment of this disease the homœopathic plan is much more successful than any other. If taken during the premonitory symptoms, as I have already stated, the attack can generally be warded off.

The first step should of course be to remove the exciting causes. Tight dresses should be loosened, the patient placed

* For general directions as to the administration of remedies, see page 10.

in a cool place, where there is plenty of fresh air, and the head and trunk raised. Should the attack have been produced by poison, this should at once be antidoted. (See chapter on Poisons and their Antidotes.)

The premonitory symptoms require principally, *Acon.*, *Bell.*, *Opium*, *Nux-v.*, *Ipecac.*, *Coff.*, and *Mercury.*

Belladonna is an important remedy, where there is severe pain in the forehead, and heat in the head, drawing, tearing, or heaviness and dullness of the head, vertigo, illusions of the senses, great restlessness, sopor, stertorous breathing, dilated pupils.

Coffee.—When produced by mental emotion; sad and whining mood, great nervousness and sleeplessness, heaviness and tightness of the head, with pain as if bruised.

Opium.—Particularly in old persons, and when occasioned by ardent spirits. Stupor, coma, stertorous breathing, red, bloated face, moaning, motion of the lips as if to talk, full and slow pulse, with throbbing of the arteries of the head.

Hyosciamus.—Sudden attack, accompanied by convulsive motions and followed by stertorous breathing. The precursory symptoms are characterized by languor, occasional loss of consciousness, disposition to sleep, from which he starts in affright, small and feeble pulse, violent vertigo, illusions of the sight, sad and peevish mood.

Nux-vom.—In the precursory stage, in persons of sedentary habits, or addicted to the use of ardent spirits, particularly when there is vertigo and dull heavy pain on the right side.

Arnica.—Particularly when occasioned by mechanical injuries and where it appears after a meal.

Mercury.—Distensive pain in the head as if it would burst, throbbing of the arteries, uneasiness and heaviness of the limbs, languor and lassitude from the least exertion, blackness of sight, with vertigo. Frequently in alternation with *Belladonna.*

Administration.—In violent cases where the attack has actually commenced, do not trust too much to your own reresources, but send immediately for a physician, giving in the mean time a dose of the appropriate remedy every fifteen, twenty, or thirty minutes. For the precursory symptoms a dose may be given three or four times a day. Mix two drops, or twelve globules of the remedy in a tumbler of water, giving a tablespoonful at a dose; or place three globules, or a powder, on the tongue.

DIET AND REGIMEN.—The diet where premonitory symptoms are present, is all important. It should be light and spare, and consist entirely of bread, fruit, and vegetables, and in very moderate quantities.

INFLAMMATION OF THE BRAIN.

Encephalitis. Meningitis. Arachnoiditis.

The position of the brain and the membranes which invest it, has already been explained in the chapter on Anatomy. Inflammation of the brain itself, is called *Encephalitis* of the Dura Mater or membrane next the skull, *Meningitis*, of the covering next the brain, *Arachnoiditis*. As it would be difficult to discriminate between these varieties of inflammation, and not essential to the treatment, it will be only necessary to give some of the prominent symptoms which characterize inflammation of the brain and its investing membranes.

DIAGNOSIS.—The attack may come on suddenly, with but little pain, but characterized by a drowsy sensation and great stupor, sensitiveness to light, dizziness, and contracted pupil. This is more frequently the form of attack in old persons. More commonly however there is severe pain, heat and fullness in the head; throbbing of the arteries, irritability, vertigo, sleeplessness, or restless sleep, with disturbed dreams, or starting as in affright, stupor, unsteady gait. The pulse is full, sometimes suppressed, but generally rapid. As the disease increases and assumes a distinct character, the pain in the head may become dull and heavy, and be aggravated by the slightest movement, the head hot and burning, the countenance flushed and wild, the eyes shining and red, the pupils contracted; great sensitiveness to light, grating of the teeth, great stupor and stertorous breathing, delirium, mild, or wild and raving. The deeper the interior of the brain is affected, the more the senses become stupefied, until the patient may become entirely unconscious. The thirst is intense, the skin dry and hot, and the pulse generally small, frequent, and tremulous.

TREATMENT.*—External application should be made to the head of cold water, taking care to remove the cloths frequently before they become warm, or what is still better, the application of a bladder, filled with pounded ice. The latter is much the best as the cold is continuous.

Aconite.—Particularly at the commencement of the disease, and when there is violent inflammatory fever, burning pains in the head, redness of the face and delirium. It is often indicated before or in alternation with *Belladonna.*

Belladonna is a very important and in fact the principal remedy in this disease. Where there are violent burning and shooting pains in the head, together with great heat and violent pulsations in the head, and redness of the face. Red, sparkling eyes, with furious look, loss of consciousness, sometimes low mutterings, at others furious delirium, convulsions, spasmodic constriction of the throat, vomiting, &c. The patient buries the head in the pillow and is exceedingly sensitive to light or noise. In alternation with *Aconite*, or perhaps *Hyosciamus*, or *Stramonium.*

Hyosciamus.—Drowsiness, loss of consciousness, wild and talkative, or muttering delirium, talking about his own affairs, dilation of the pupils, picking the bed clothes, redness of face; inarticulate speech.

Stramonium.—Constant jerks of the limbs, moans, and tossing during sleep, and frequently absence of mind on waking; timidity and fear.

Bryonia.—Prolonged shiverings, with heat in the head, thirst; constant inclination to sleep, with delirium, starts, cries, pressive burning or shooting pain in the head.

Opium.—Lethargic sleep, with snoring, half open eyes,

* For general directions as to the administration of remedies, *see page* 10.

dizziness on waking, frequent vomiting, entire apathy and indifference to every thing.

Administration.—Two drops, or six globules, in a tumbler of water, a tablespoonful every one or two hours, and sometimes in exceedingly severe cases every half hour, until the severity of the symptoms abates.

Diet and Regimen.—The same as in fevers.

SUN-STROKE.

Coup-de-Soleil.

This is a kind of inflammation of the brain produced by exposure to the strong heat of the sun. It is quite common in India, and other warm climates. The head may be bathed with brandy, and a small quantity given internally occasionally, until the prominent symptoms are relieved.

Camphor may be given, one drop at a dose, at intervals of five or ten minutes, to be followed after four or five doses have been taken, by *Belladonna*, alone or in alternation with *Carb.-v.*, or *Lachesis*, half an hour apart.

FALLING OFF OF THE HAIR.

Alopecia.

Consult a physician if possible, if not, avoid the cause, if you can discover it, and examine some of the following remedies.

Where it is occasioned by severe acute disease: *Hepar-s.*, *Calcarea*, and *Silicea* may be consulted.

In *Lying-in-Women: Calcarea*, *Sulphur.*

From *Debilitating losses: China*, *Ferrum*, or *Mercury.*

From *Grief: Phos.-ac.*, or *Ignatia.*

From frequent attacks of *headache: Hepar-s.*, *Nit.-ac.*, *Phosphorus*, *Sepia.*

From abuse of Mercury: *Hepar-s.*, or *Carb. v.*

When there is a strong tendency of the hair to turn grey: *Phos.-ac.*, *Sulph.-ac.*, or *Graphitis.*

When there is much scurf on the head: *Calcarea*, *Graphitis.*

The head should be bathed frequently with cold water but oily applications should as a general thing be avoided. The great object is, to keep the scalp clean and gently stimulate the hair bulbs, which may be done in the manner described above, but which oily applications seldom accomplish. It is some times advisable to put five or six drops of *Cantharidis* into a tumbler half full of water, and wash the head once or twice a day. A dose of the medicine may be taken every night, or night and morning.

CHAPTER VII.

AFFECTIONS OF THE EYES, EARS, AND NOSE.

1. AFFECTIONS OF THE EYES.*

The eyes are subject to various disorders, but the extreme delicacy of the organ renders it highly important that as a general thing they should be treated by a careful and scientific physician or occulist. The step from sight to blindness is so short, that often the utmost care and caution are necessary to ward off serious consequences. Examine particularly the article on the eye in the chapter on Anatomy.

Lotions should as a general thing be avoided, confining external application to pure soft water, milk and water, or a mixture made from pouring water upon quince seeds. These applications may be made either cold or tepid, according to the feeling of the patient. If the redness is occasioned by external injury, or is slight and the result of a simple cold, six drops of *Arnica* may be placed in a cup half full of water, and the eye washed with it three or four times a day.

WEAKNESS OF SIGHT.

Amblyopia.

Under this head we shall include *Amaurosis*, and the various forms of weakness of sight, most frequently met in practice.

The causes are exceedingly numerous, and sometimes difficult to detect. It may arise, as in amaurosis, from a weakened, paralyzed, or diseased state of the retina or optic nerve. It may be occasioned by inaction or derangement of some of the various branches of nerves, which pass to different parts of the eye, and not unfrequently by gastric, nervous, or catarrhal derangement, or general weakness of the entire system, occasioned by disease, too frequent sexual indulgence, and

* For a description of the eye, see plate 1, also page 43.

self-pollution, long-continued watching, great mental anxiety or trouble. It may also be occasioned by too great labor of the eyes, exposure to strong light, constant reading, especially in the twilight, and that variety of employment which requires close application.

Amaurosis, sometimes coming on gradually, at others running its course with great rapidity, may end in partial or entire blindness. If neglected too long there is but little hope of relief, yet if taken in time, it can speedily be removed by a judicious homœopathic treatment. There may be more or less pain about the eyes and the head, a dimness of sight, every thing looking thick and muggy, or appearing as if seen through a net work, black specks before the eyes like moats or cinders, multiplying in number until the whole becomes dark, or the first symptoms may be a remarkable diminution of the apparent size of objects ; thus a horse may not appear larger than a dog.

TREATMENT.*—In all forms of weakness of sight particular attention should be directed to the general health, the causes of the trouble should be carefully avoided, and the utmost care taken to live in accordance with the laws of nature. Pure and bracing air, out-door exercise, healthy nourishing food, frequent bathing, and a cheerful disposition, are of vast importance. As it regards some of the various causes, where the disease has been produced by employement in *fine work*, *Bell.*, *Ruta*, *Calc.*, or *Spig.* may be consulted.

Where the result of *Debilitating causes : Natr.-m.*, *Chin.*, *Phos.-ac.*, *Nux-v.*, *Sulphur.*

From abuse of *Spirituous liquors : Chin.*, *Lach.*, *Nux-v.*, *Opium.*

The result of a cold : *Bell.*, *Dulc.*, *Euph.*, *Pulsatilla.*

From *debilitating causes : Chin.*, *Phos.-ac.*, *Nat.-m.*

In *aged persons : Aur.*, *Con.*, *Op.*, *Secale.*

In *scrofulous persons : Bell.*, *Calc.*, *Merc.*, *Sulph.*, *Aur.*, *Hep.-s.*, *Iodine.*

* For general directions as to the administration of remedies, see page 10.

The result of *rheumatism: Cham., Euph., Merc., Puls., Rus, Hell., Spig., Causticum.*

Of *suppressed eruption: Calc., Caust., Sil. Merc., Sulphur.*

Abuse of Mercury: Aur., Nit.-ac., Bell., Sulphur.

Connected with congestion to the head: *Op., Bell., Hyos., Nux-v.*

With disease of the *ear: Nit.-ac., Petrol., Pulsatilla.*

With Gastric or abdominal affections: *Caps., Cocc., Nux-vom., Puls., Staphysagria.*

With *uterine* derangement: *Plat., Sep., Con. Cic., Sulph.*

With *pulmonary* affections: *Calc., Hep.-s., Iod., Sil., Phosphorus.*

Symtomatic Indications.—*Aurum.*—Flames and sparks or black points before the eyes; appearance of objects as if they were divided horizontally.

Belladonna.—Dilated or insensible pupils; great intolerance of light; flames, black points or colored or silvery spots before the eyes; nocturnal blindness commencing at sunset; pressive and shooting pain, extending to the orbit and forehead.

Calcarea.—Confusion of sight as if looking through a mist, especially when reading; intolerance of light; dilated pupils.

Cicuta.—Frequent suspension of vision, vertigo, wavering of objects before the sight, and apparent movement of letters when reading.

Hyosciamus.—Nocturnal blindness, dilated pupils, strabismus, and illusions of sight.

Mercury.—Cloudiness of sight; black points, sparks and dancing moats before the eyes; sudden attacks of blindness; great sensibility of the eyes; shooting or pulsative pain.

Nux-v.—Sparks or spots before the eyes; sensibility to the brightness of day; heaviness and contraction of the eyelids.

Phosphorus.—Sudden attacks of blindness; objects appear as if covered with a grey veil; sensibility to the brightness of day, and black spots before the eyes.

Pulsatilla.—Confused sight as if looking through a fog, or something which might be removed by rubbing; intolerance of light with shooting in, or flaming circles before the eyes; contraction of the pupils, and profuse discharge of tears.

Ruta.—Confusion of sight as if looking through a mist; dancing black points before the sight, and pressing, burning pains in the eyes, especially when fatigued.

Silicea.—Momentary attacks of blindness, confusion and pale appearance of letters when reading; black spots before the eyes, intolerance of light, and discharge of tears.

Sulphur.—Confusion of sight as if looking through a mist, or a black veil were before the eyes; intolerance of light; sudden attacks of blindness by day; sparks, dancing moats and black spots before the eyes; profuse discharge of tears or excessive dryness of the eyes.

Agaricus.—Incipient amaurosis; indistinct sight; every thing appears obscured as from muddy water, or surrounded with mist, or as if covered with cobweb; double sight, black moats hovering before the sight. Consult also *Opthalmia.*

Administration.—Two drops, or twelve globules, in a tumbler, a tablespoonful at a dose; or a powder, or six globules, dry on the tongue. A dose may be administered from once to three times a day.

OPHTHALMIA.

Inflammation of the eyes.

In inflammation of the eye, the irritation generally extends also to the lids, as the conjunctiva or external membrane of the eyeball is, as we have already shown, reflected over the inner surface of the eyelids.

External applications may consist of either cold or tepid water, or milk and water, or a mucilage made by pouring water on quince seeds. The room should be darkened, and the patient kept as quiet as possible. Care also should be taken that matter from the diseased eye should not be transmitted to those of the attendant, as a similar inflammation would be the result.

The prominent remedies in *Ophthalmia* are, *Bell.*, *Arn.*, *Euphrasia*, *Acon.*, *and Merc.* These remedies may be indicated in almost every variety of the disease. In treating this disease, we shall for the sake of clearness, speak of it under the following heads.

a. *Catarrhal Ophthalmia.*

b. *Rheumatic and Arthritic Ophthalmia.*

c. *Scrofulous Ophthalmia.*

d. *Syphilitic Ophthalmia.*

a. Catarrhal Ophthalmia.

This is generally the result of a cold, frequently affects both eyes, and may be attended with cough and fever. The redness gradually extends over the whole conjunctiva, at first there is profuse discharge of tears, then more or less secretion of mucus. The eye is sensitive to the light; pressure in the eyes with burning, shooting pains, and sensation as if sand were lodged between the lids, are also present.

Aconite is an important remedy in the commencement of the treatment, either alone or in alternation with *Belladonna* or *Chamomilla.*

Chamomilla is serviceable when there is slight catarrhal fever, sensation of pain on opening and closing the lids, which are often closed with mucus.

Belladonna is an invaluable remedy, where there is congestion to the head, great redness and dryness of the eyes, and sensitiveness to light. It is particularly indicated where there is a profuse watery discharge from the nose, accompanied with the usual catarrhal symptoms.

The indications of *Euphrasia* are similar to those of *Belladonna*, with the exception that with the former there may be a profuse discharge of tears and mucus, which is not characteristic of *Belladonna.* The *Euphrasia* is also more particularly indicated where the inflammation is violent and extensive, or where little ulcers may have formed around the cornea.

Ignatia will be of service where there is but little apparent inflammation, but severe aching pain in the balls, accompanied with great sensitiveness to light, and profuse lachrymation and coryza.

A disposition to catarrhal Ophthalmia on every change of the weather, can frequently be relieved by a few doses of *Sulph.*, *Calc.*, or *Nux-v.*

In the first stage of the disease, four drops of *Arnica* may be placed in a cup of water, with which the eye may be bathed.

b. Rheumatic and Arthritic Ophthalmia.

This variety of Ophthalmia is generally connected with rheumatic and gouty difficulties, and is attended with severe pain. There are sticking, tearing or boring pains in the eyeballs, orbits, and not unfrequently in the temples, aggravated by change of weather. Great redness ofthe eye, sensitiveness to light, and sometimes profuse lachrymation are also present. This is a highly dangerous variety of Ophthalmia, as the inflammation is liable to extend to the internal membranes, and create ulceration of the cornea, and frequently loss of sight.

The prominent remedies, are *Acon.*, *Bell.*, *Spig.*, *Col.*, *Euph.*, also *Puls.*, *Bry.*, *Rhus*. *Sulphur*, *Calc.*, *Hep.*, *Caust.*, *Merc.*, may also be consulted.

Treatment.—In the commencement of the difficulty, if the inflammation should be slight, and the disease evidently of a rheumatic character, *Bryonia* and *Pulsatilla* may be given in alternation, and if there should be considerable fever present, and the pain be more severe, *Rhus* and *Aconite* may be alternated in the same way.

As a general thing, where the usual inflammatory phenomena are present, *Aconite* should commence the treatment, either in alternation, or followed by *Belladonna*, if there should be indications of congestion to the brain, violent pain about the eyes and profuse lachrymation.

Belladonna is particularly useful, when beside the symptoms already mentioned, there are severe aching pain over the eyes, with pain in the balls as if they would be torn out or pressed into the head ; sparks and flashes before the eyes ; intolerance of light, confusion of sight, &c.

Euphrasia is a valuable remedy where the pain is severe, the inflammation extending to the cornea, or if ulcers have formed there, and the pupil become contracted.

Spigelia is suitable when the eyeballs feel swollen and exhibit a number of enlarged vessels; the pain is violent, sticking, boring, and digging, and proceeds from the interior of the eye; on opening the eyes objects seem to float in fire.

Colocynth is an invaluable remedy where the pains are seated in the eyeballs, and are of a burning, cutting character, and where there is congestion of the head, intolerance of light, lachrymation, pressing and tearing pain in the whole brain, most violent in the forehead on moving the eyes.

Sulphur is also of importance near the close of the disease, or to quicken the action of the other remedies. See also, *Inflammation of the eyelids* and *weakness of sight*.

c. Scrofulous Ophthalmia.

This is a common form of *Ophthalmia*, but generally is confined to children. The eyeball is very red and bundles of enlarged vessels run towards the cornea; there is intolerance of light, profuse discharge of corrosive tears, increased secretion of mucus, and an aggravation of symptoms towards morning; the eyelids are generally reddened, and if the cornea is affected, it becomes dim and sometimes ulcerates.

Pulsatilla will be found useful in the commencement of the disease, followed perhaps by *Euphrasia* or *Nux*. *Hepar-s.* is also a prominent remedy, particularly when the cornea has become dim.

Belladonna is suitable in the more advanced stage of the disease, when the bundles of enlarged vessels have formed and extend into the cornea, and where there is a painful pressure in the eyes, and also the presence of the symptoms enumerated under *Catarrhal Ophthalmia*. It may sometimes be followed by *Sulphur* and *Calcarea*, *Sepia* or *Causticum*. See also *Tuberculosis*.

d. Syphilitic Ophthalmia.

This variety of *Ophthalmia* may arise from suppressed gonorrhœa or syphilis, and from a transmission of the matter to the eye. The treatment should commence with *Aconite*, followed after the fever is somewhat subdued, by *Mercury*, and this after eight or ten doses have been taken, if decided relief is not obtained, by *Nit-ac.*, *Sulph.*, or *Thuja*.

A physician should be consulted immediately, as prompt and skilful treatment is necessary to avoid serious consequences.

Administration.—Two drops, or twelve globules, in a tumbler of water, a tablespoonful at a dose; or a powder, or three globules, dry on the tongue. In severe cases a dose in one or two hours, but as the symptoms gradually abate, the intervals may be extended to four or six hours. In the milder forms of the disease, a dose once in four or six hours will be sufficient. See also page 10.

Diet and Regimen.—The patiênt should be kept perfectly quiet, and the room more or less darkened, to suit the feelings of the patient. The diet should be simple, as in fevers.

Inflammation of the Eyelids.

Aconite.—Where the eyelids are swollen, hard and red, with heat, burning, and dryness; or where there are burning and tensive pain, pale and shining swelling, intolerance of light, fever, &c. *Bell.*, *Hep.*, or *Sulph.*, are often suitable after this remedy.

Belladonna.—Eyelids swollen and red, burning and itching, bleeding on opening them, or with the margins everted, or paralytic heaviness of the lids.

Calcarea.—Incisive, burning or smarting pain, especially when reading, with red, hard and large swelling, copious secretion of humor, and nocturnal agglutination.

Euphrasia.—Ulceration and itching of the margin of the eyelids, redness and swelling and agglutination by night; coryza and pain in the head.

Hepar-s.—Redness of the eyelids, with pain as from ulceration, or as from a bruise when touched; nocturnal agglutination. Often after *Aconite* or *Mercury*.

Mercury.—Eyelids hard, with swelling, difficulty in opening them, ulcers on the margin, pustules on the conjunctiva, scabs round the eyes, pain and itching, or absence of pain.

Pulsatilla.—Inflammatory redness of the conjunctiva, secretion of mucus, appearance of styes, nocturnal agglutination.

Sulphur.—Redness of the eyelid, with burning pains, discharge of humor; ulceration of the margin, pustules and ulcers around the orbits. It may be followed or alternated with benefit by *Calcarea.*

ADMINISTRATION.—In acute cases the remedy may be taken once in from three to six hours; in chronic cases once or twice a day. One drop, or six globules may be mixed with a tumbler of water, and a tablespoonful taken at a dose; or a powder, or six globules, may be taken dry on the tongue. See also page 10.

STYE ON THE EYELID.

A swelling or ulceration of the meibomian glands, situated in the margin of the eyelid, is called a stye. This difficulty is exceedingly annoying, but of short duration.

On the first appearance of the swelling, *Pulsatilla* is the prominent remedy, a dose three times a day. Should however ulceration take place, a powder, or three globules, of *Mercury* may be alternated with the same amount of *Hepar-s.*, one dose of each during the day.

For a predisposition to these swellings, or where they present a hardened appearance, *Staph.*, *Calc.*, or *Sulph.* may be given one dose, or six globules, each day.

WATERY EYES, OR WEEPING.

As we have already explained, in speaking of the anatomy of the eye, ducts or little tubes, called the lachrymal ducts, pass from the inner canthus of the eye into the nose, carrying off the water secreted by the tear-glands. When these little ducts are either partially or entirely closed by some obstruction, the tears, unable to pass off by the usual channel, must of necessity flow over the lids upon the cheek. This difficulty, to say the least, is exceedingly annoying, rendering an almost constant wiping of the eye necessary.

The prominent remedies are, *Calc.*, *Iod.*, *Puls.*, *Bell.*, *Sil.*, *Petrol.*, and *Sulphur.* The two first may be given in alternation, a dose of *Calcarea* one day, and of the *Iodine* the next. If the attack is recent and accompanied with swelling, &c. *Belladonna* and *Pulsatilla* may be alternated in the same way.

DOSE.—A powder, or six globules, dry on the tongue; if the tincture is used, one drop may be prepared and administered as heretofore directed.

NEAR-SIGHTEDNESS.

Myopia.

This, when of long continuance is often occasioned by a too great prominence of the eye-ball, and may frequently be entirely removed by gently pressing it with the finger daily, so that it gradually assumes the more flat or natural form. In aged persons and even in others, debilitated by disease, where the sight is weakened, the eye may be too flat, and with the finger gently compressing the ball not unfrequently the original prominence is given to the eye, and the natural sight restored.

The prominent remedies in short sightedness are, *Puls.*, *Sulph.*, *Phos.-ac.*, *Nit.-ac.*, and *Carb.-v.*

When occasioned by ophthalmia, *Pulsatilla* or *Sulphur* may be given every other night; when caused by *abuse* of *Mercury: Carb.-ac*, or *Nit.-ac.*, and from debilitating losses, *Phos.-ac.*, in the manner indicated above.

DOSE.—Same as in "Watery eyes, or weeping."

FOREIGN SUBSTANCES IN THE EYE.

If particles of dust enter the eye, they can generally be removed by bathing it in cold water, or turning the head on one side, gently opening the lids and dropping three or four drops of water into the outer canthus. The water flows inward over the eyes and washes out the particles. If the matter is not removed in this way, raise the lid, gently bringing it forward over the other, at the same time looking towards the nose. If a hard particle should become imbedded in the membranes of the eye, a silk handkerchief or the point of a needle will generally remove it. The inflammation caused by the irritation may be removed by washing the eye in cold water or with a mixture, composed of six drops of *Arnica* to a cup of water.

FALLING OF THE LID.

Frequently bathing the eye with cold water and using as much as possible the muscles on that side of the face where the affection exists will be found advantageous.

The prominent remedies are, *Veratrum*, *Zinc*, *Nit.-ac.*, *Belladonna*, *Pulsatilla*, and *Sepia*. A powder, or three globules, of the selected remedy may be given every third day.

2. AFFECTIONS OF THE EARS.

MUMPS.

Parotitis.

Perhaps this is as appropriate a place as any to introduce this oftentimes troublesome and painful, though seldom dangerous disease. It consists in an inflammation of the large gland lying under and in front of the ears. It more frequently occurs in children and seldom attacks a person but once.

TREATMENT.*—In its simple form it requires but little treatment, except placing a handkerchief around the neck, and keeping the patient in the house.

Mercury in most cases will be found a specific. A powder, or three globules, may be taken two or three times a day. If the tumor should suddenly disappear, and sharp pain be felt in the brain, with lethargy and delirium, *Belladonna* should be given every hour, followed after three or four doses, if necessary, by *Hyosciamus*.

* For general directions as to the administration of remedies, see page 10.

DOSE.—Two drops, or twelve globules, in a tumbler of water, a tablespoonful at a dose; given as directed above.

Should the swelling assume an erysipelatous character, attended with considerable restlessness and fever, *Belladonna* and *Rhus* may be alternated two or three hours apart. If there should be a metastasis to the stomach, or if the voice should become hoarse, *Carb.-veg.* may be given, in the same manner as *Belladonna*, also if there is *slow fever* and the tumor begins to harden, *Mercury* having proved insufficient. If there is a metastasis to the testicles, as is often the case, the testicles swelling and becoming excessively painful, *Pulsatilla*, *Nux-v.*, or *Mercury* are the appropriate remedies, given at intervals of from two to four hours, according to the severity of the symptoms.

DIET AND REGIMEN.—The patient should be confined to fruit and light farinaceous articles of diet, avoiding all animal food and stimulating drinks.

INFLAMMATION OF THE EAR.

Otitis.

This is an exceedingly painful disease, attended with heat, redness and swelling, burning, stinging, lacerating and throbbing pain, aggravated by motion, frequently extending over the whole head, and often affecting the brain, accompanied with the usual symptoms of cerebral inflammation. There is generally considerable fever, often delirium, and not unfrequently in children, vomiting, coldness of the extremities, and convulsions.

This affection is generally the result of cold, but sometimes occasioned by the inflammation of an adjoining organ, or the suppression of some cutaneous eruption.

Pulsatilla is the most important, and in fact almost specific remedy in inflammation of the ear, a dose of which at first may be given every hour, gradually increasing the intervals as the pain subsides.

Belladonna, however will be required should symptoms of inflammation of the brain set in, either with or without convulsions; if violent fever is present, it may be alternated with *Aconite*, one or two hours apart.

Should there be confused noise or sensation as of water rolling in the head with throbbing pain, or if there is yellowish discharge from the ear, *Mercury* may be required, at intervals of three or four hours, until better.

DIET AND REGIMEN.—Same as in fever.

DOSE.—Two drops, or twelve globules, in a tumbler of water, a tablespoonful at a dose; or a powder on the tongue. See also page 10.

EAR-ACHE.

Otalgia.

There is often pain more or less severe in the ear, even when but little if any perceptible inflammation is present.

When of a *rheumatic character*, *Belladonna*, *Mercury*, or *Pulsatilla* are the prominent remedies.

When the result of a chill or suppressed perspiration, *Chamomilla*, *Dulcamara*, *Pulsatilla*, *China* or *Sulphur* may be consulted.

Belladonna.—Digging and boring pains, tearing and shooting, sometimes extending into the throat, with roaring and humming in the ears; great sensibility to noise; severe pain in the head and eyes, together with fullness and heat in the head and face.

Pulsatilla.—Jerking and lacerating pains as if something were endeavoring to pass out through the ears; redness, swelling, and heat of the external ear, or shooting and lacerating pains, excessively violent, extending over the whole side of the head; particularly in females of a chilly disposition or easily moved to tears.

Chamomilla.—Cutting, as from knives; sensation of stoppage about the ear; great sensibility to noise, and extreme sensitiveness to pain.

Mercury.—Shooting pains, extending into the cheeks and teeth; sensation of coldness in the ear, and aggravation of pain in bed; spasmodic pain with inflammatory redness of the ear.

Nux-v.—Lacerating or shooting pain extending into the forehead and temples, with lacerating in the bones of the face, worse in the morning or evening.

Platina.—Spasmodic pains; rolling and thundering in the ears; coldness of the ears and tingling, extending over the face.

Spigelia.—Pressive pain as if caused by a plug, with aching and tearing in the bones of the face.

ADMINISTRATION.—Two drops, or twelve globules, in a tumbler of water, a tablespoonful every one or two hours until relieved. If, notwithstanding the administration of the appropriate remedy, the pain is not entirely removed, a few doses of *Sulphur*, given at intervals of four or six hours, will generally complete the cure. See also page 10.

DEAFNESS.

Difficulty in hearing.

Hardness of hearing may be produced by cold, mechanical injury, various diseases, and in many cases, as where it occurs in the aged, be developed without pain, and give to the patient no clue to its cause.

Sometimes from birth, the ears are impervious to all sound, and consequently the child, having no guide in the sound of others' voices for the modulation of his own, is not only *deaf* but *dumb*. This condition at first thought so dreadful, is now through the interposition of science and our various excellent asylums, deprived of half its terrors.

We shall only have space to give some of the leading indications for the treatment of the various forms of deafness, yet sufficiently full however for domestic practice, as it is often complicated with other difficulties rendering the skill of the physician essential. Derangement of hearing, the result of *catarrhal* or *rheumatic* affections, produced by a *chill*, generally requires, *Arsenic, Belladonna, Mercury, Pulsatilla, Calcarea, Causticum, Hepar-s., Nit.-ac.*, or *Sulphur*.

Occasioned by *suppressed eruption: Sulphur* or *Antimony.*

The result of *measles: Pulsatilla* or *Carb.-v.*

Of *Scarlatina: Belladonna* or *Hepar.*

Of *Small Pox: Mercury* or *Sulphur.*

Of abuse of *Cinchona* in *Intermittent Fever: Carb-v., Calcarea, Pulsatilla.*

Of abuse of *Mercury: Nit-ac., Aurum, Carb-v., Sulphur.*

Of *Fevers, Nervous Affections, &c.: Arnica, Phosphorus, Veratrum.*

When produced by a suppressed discharge from the ears or nose: *Hepar-s., Lachesis, Belladonna.*

Symptomatic Indications.—*Calcarea.*—Deafness as if the ears were obstructed; humming, rolling or tinkling, singing, and noise, or throbbing and heat in the ears. Dryness of the ears or purulent discharge; pressive headache in the forehead.

Causticum.—Vibration of sound, even the patient's voice in the ear; sensation of obstruction, with rumbling, humming, and roaring in the ears; discharge from the ears; rheumatic pain and great sensitiveness to cold.

Graphites.—Dryness in the ears or purulent discharge; singing, whistling, tinkling or humming, and thundering in the ears, particularly at night, eruption around the ears.

Lachesis.—Often after *Causticum,* and where there is dryness in the ears, painful pulsations or cracking, rolling, drumming and reverberation of sound in the ears; excoriation around the ears.

Mercurius.—Sensation of obstruction, ceasing when swallowing or blowing the nose; reverberation of sound in the ears; tinkling, roaring and humming, particularly in the evening; discharge from the ear, sometimes with ulceration; rheumatic pain in the ears and head, and great tendency to perspiration.

Nitric-acid.—Dryness or discharge from the ears; sensation of obstruction, with grumbling, throbbing, or cracking; frequent toothache, with affections of the gums.

Phosvhorus.—Great difficulty in hearing sounds, and yet

excessive reverberation of sounds in the ears, with resonance in the head; throbbing and pulsations in the ears.

Pulsatilla.—Tinkling or chirping in the ears, or sensation as if they were stopped, with roaring and humming; shooting pains in the ears; hard, black or liquid wax, and sometimes discharge of pus or blood.

Sulphur.—Difficulty of hearing, especially the human voice; closing up of the ears, particularly when eating, and blowing the nose; gurgling, as if caused by water, or humming and roaring; discharge from the ears, and disposition to colds in the head.

Consult also *Inflammation* and *Running* of the ear.

ADMINISTRATION.—Deafness is sometimes caused by a collection of hardened ear-wax, in which case, have it carefully removed. A powder, or six globules, may be given morning and night, every night, or every other night, according to circumstances. See also page 10.

NOISES IN THE EARS.

This difficulty seldom exists alone, but is generally connected with some other affection, as deafness, inflammation of the ears, or running at the ears. See those diseases.

RUNNING OF THE EARS.

Otorrhœa.

Running of the ears, is frequently found in scrofulous persons, and is often the result of a cold, and of other diseases, particularly affections of the ear.

If the result of acute inflammation of the ear, *Pulsatilla, Mercury, Sulphur*, are the prominent remedies.

If occasioned by cold, *Belladonna, Mercury* or *Pulsatilla* will be required.

Occurring after *Measles* or *Scarlatina: Belladonna, Hepar-s., Mercury, Pulsatilla.*

After *Small Pox; Mercury, Sulphur, Carb.-v.*

From abuse of *Mercury: Aurum., Nit-ac., Silicea.*

In *Scrofulous* persons: *Hepar-s., Mercury, Sulphur, Iodine.*

When the discharge is of a *purulent character: Hepar-s.,*

Mercury, Pulsatilla, Silicea, Calcarea, Nit-ac., or *Aurum* may be required.

Bloody: Mercury, Pulsatilla, Lachesis, Silicea, or *Sulphur.*

Offensive: Carb-v., Hepar-s., Mercury, Pulsatilla.

A sudden suppression of the running may be followed by exceeding unpleasant symptoms, such as swelling of the glands in the throat, neck, or testicles, and violent headache and fever.

If swelling of the glands of the neck commences, *Belladonna, Mercury*, or *Pulsatilla* should be given. If there is violent headache, *Belladonna*, or *Bryonia*; if the suppression is occasioned by cold, *Dulcamara*, or *Mercury;* and if the testicles should commence swelling, *Mercury, Pulsatilla*, or *Aurum* will be required. The remedy selected, should be given every three or four hours, until better.

Administration.—Give the remedy once, or twice a day, if the symptoms are urgent, for six or eight days, when, if no improvement is perceptible, another remedy should be selected. Two drops, or eight globules, should be mixed with a tumbler of water, a tablespoonful given at a dose; or a powder, or six globules, on the tongue.

FOREIGN SUBSTANCES IN THE EAR.

In every part of our body, we perceive the most wonderful evidence of design and wisdom. Were it not for the excessive bitterness of the wax in our ears, they would be constantly liable to be invaded by insects; as it is, so far as the ears are concerned, they seldom give us any trouble. When however, insects do get into the ear, with a little care they can be removed. If the substance should be of a hard nature, as a bean, pea, or seed, care should be taken not to crowd it farther in, but, bending the point of a pin or needle in the form of a hook, it can generally be inserted, and the offending substance drawn out, after which, if the ear should be inflamed, it may be washed by a mixture, composed of two drops of *Arnica*, to one tablespoonful of water.

3. AFFECTIONS OF THE NOSE.

The nose is liable to numerous affections, but as they are mostly connected with other troubles, the treatment as a general thing, is given in connection with those diseases. The symptoms and treatment of *Coryza*, or cold in the head, which frequently involves the nose, has already been given in connection with *Influenza* and *catarrhal difficulties*.

INFLAMMATION OF THE NOSE.

This may arise from a bruise, when it can be relieved by *Arnica*, or *cold water*. It is often produced by cold, abuse of ardent spirits, scrofulous and syphilitic affections, and a variety of other causes.

If there is swelling, soreness, heat or erysipelatous redness about the nose, a few doses of *Belladonna* will generally produce relief. For the indication of other remedies, see *Coryza*, or cold in the head.

Where there are *ulcerations* or *scabs* in the nostrils: *Alum.*, *Aurum*, *Borax*, *Mercury*, *Nit-ac.*, or *Sulphur*, may be given.

A discharge of pus generally indicates, *Aurum*, *Mercury*, *Sulphur*.

Syphilitic inflammation requires *Mercury*, or if that remedy has already been used to excess, *Nit-ac.*, *Aurum*, or *Thuja*.

If arising from abuse of spirituous liquors; let liquor alone, and take, *Arsenic*, *Calcarea*, *Belladonna*, *Phosphorus*.

In *Scrofulous* persons: *Aurum*, *Calcarea*, *Mercury*, *Phosphorus*, *Sulphur*.

Warts on the nose: *Causticum*.

ADMINISTRATION.—The remedy may be taken one, two, or three times a day, according to the severity of the symptoms. Two drops, or eight globules, should be mixed with a tumbler of water, a tablespoonful given at a dose; or three globules, or a powder, taken dry on the tongue.

BLEEDING OF THE NOSE.

Epistaxis.

Bleeding at the nose is not unfrequently an accompanying

symptom of various diseases, particularly in fevers, where there is a strong tendency of blood to the head. When it occurs on what is called the critical days, it is looked upon as favorable. It is sometimes constitutional, and is very often produced by the disturbance of some other organ.

When it arises from *congestion to the head: Aconite, Belladonna, or Rhus,* will be required. *See congestion to the head.*

Occurring during *Coryza: Arsenic,* or *Pulsatilla. See that affection.*

In children subject to *verminous difficulties: Cina, Spigelia, Mercury.*

Preceding *Catemenia: Lachesis, Pulsatilla.*

In women when the *Catemenia* are too feeble: *Pulsatilla, Sepia, Secale.*

In women where they are too *profuse: Aconite, Crocus, Sabina.*

In women, *absence of Catemenia: Bryonia, Pulsatilla, Sepia.*

From *great weakness: China, Secale, Ferrum.*

From being *over-heated: Aconite, Belladonna,* or *Carb-veg.*

From abuse of *spirituous liquors: Nux-v., Bell., Carb-v.*

From *great exertion: Arn. or Rhus.*

Tendency to *bleed* from the slightest cause: *Calc., Carb-v., Silicea, Sepia.*

Cold water, or ice water, should be applied to the root of the nose, and the head be kept elevated as much as possible.

Administration.—One drop, or eight globules, in a tumbler of water, a tablespoonful at a dose; or a powder, or six globules, on the tongue. In severe cases, the remedy should be administered every fifteen or twenty minutes.

Heating or stimulating food, until the tendency to the attack has subsided, should of course be avoided. See also page 10.

ULCERATION OF THE NOSE.

Catarrh.

In this disease, an ulcer is formed in the upper part of the nose, and sometimes in the cavity of the cheek bone, discharging a pus-like substance, or pus mixed with blood. As the ulceration spreads, a sensation of tightness and obstruction is felt about the nose, severe aching pain is also felt about the root of the nose, and over the eyes ; as the disease increases, unless arrested, the cartilage and even the bones of the nose may become involved, and frightful deformity ensue. The discharge is sometimes exceedingly fetid, and seems to drop into the throat, causing nausea, and sometimes vomiting. This disease requires the attention of a careful physician. The treatment may, however, commence with *Belladonna*, at intervals of six hours, followed after three or four doses by *Mercury*, morning and night, and that in like manner by *Sulphur* or *Aurum*. If the pain is exceedingly severe in the evening, and there is reason to expect syphilitic combination, the treatment may commence with *Mercury*, a dose two or three times a day, or if that remedy has been taken in excess, *Aurum*, *Nit-ac.*, or *Sulphur*, may be given in the same manner.

Scabs in the lower part of the nostrils generally require, *Lachesis*, *Calcarea*, *Carb-v.*, *Graphites*, *Silicea*. A dose every night.

CHAPTER VIII.

AFFECTIONS OF THE TEETH, MOUTH AND THROAT.

Sound and healthy teeth depend in a great measure upon bodily health. Persons who have always been healthy, who are never troubled with derangements of the stomach or bowels seldom have aching or decayed teeth. Derangement of the stomach and bowels, from whatever cause it may be produced, is exceedingly liable to affect the teeth, producing slow or rapid decay, and those torturing pains, the most agonizing to be borne, and yet for which the patient receives the least sympathy.

Some teeth even in apparently healthy persons seem to be extremely brittle, and far more liable to decay or crumble away than others. We have already explained the formation of teeth, their connection with the nerve, and the cause of some of the torturing pains, to which they give rise when diseased. As the teeth, strictly speaking, come under the province of the Dentist rather than the physician, it will be only necessary to give some general directions how to preserve them, and how to alleviate the sufferings they produce when in a diseased state.

Pay strict attention to the general health, keep the stomach and bowels in a natural state, and above all, even if you are still wandering in the boggy and cloudy regions of Allopathy, avoid taking large quantities of various nostrums, cathartics, mineral acids, &c. Keep the mouth sweet and clean by rinsing it with pure cold water, and brushing the teeth in the morning, and after each meal, avoid also exposing them to sudden changes of heat and cold, as drinking cold water, when the mouth is filled with hot food. If *tartar* forms on the teeth, have it carefully removed. If the teeth become diseased, consult a judicious and skilful dentist, and do not because they ache a little have them extracted forthwith. Your own teeth, however poor they may be, if they do not affect your general health, and can be prevented from paining you, are generally far better, than any artificial teeth, however beautiful or skilfully prepared. Teeth are often extracted because the patient is vexed with long continued pain, and the dentist is willing to indulge the whim, partly because it saves him future trouble, because it gives him a fine opportunity to display his skill, and pocket a good fee, in preparing an artificial set, when even a greater amount of skill might be displayed in patching up the tooth and saving it, if only for two or three years.

Dentistry in this country has reached a state of perfection far superior to that of any other in the world, and in point of beauty almost rivals in its work nature itself. The thought is very consoling, when we see our teeth making their exit one after the other, that art has given us the means of replacing them by others equal in beauty, though not quite as serviceable.

Treatment.—*Bell.*, *Cham.* or *Merc.* may be given in most cases of toothache, until the more specific remedy is ascertained.

Pains affecting several teeth at once usually require, *Cham.*, *Merc.*, *Rhus* or *Staphysagria.*

Affecting also the bones of the face : *Hyos.*, *Merc.*, *Sulphur.*

Extending to the eyes : *Pulsatilla.*

To the ears: *Cham.*, *Merc.*, *Pulsatilla.*

To the head: *Cham.*, *Nux-v.*, *Merc.*, *Rhus*, *Pulsatilla*, *Belladonna.*

With *swelled face* or *gums:* *Arn.*, *Cham.*, *Merc.*, *Puls.*, *Sep.*, *Sulph.*, *Aur.*, *Bell.*, *Bryonia.*

For *rheumatic toothache :* *Acon.*, *Bell.*, *Bry.*, *Puls.*, *Rhus*, *Cham.*, *Staph.*, *Sabina.*

Of a *nervous character:* *Bell.*, *Cham.*, *Coff.*, *Hyos.*, *Ign.*, *Plat.*, *Spig.*

Occasioned by abuse of *Mercury:* *Carbo-v.* or *Nit.-ac.*

From a *cold;* *Bell.*, *Bry.*, *Rhus*, *Puls.*, *Merc.*, *Dulcamara.*

Occurring at the period of *Catamenia: Calc., Carbo-v., Chamomilla.*

During *Pregnancy: Bell., Calc., Nux-v., Puls., Sep., Staph.*

In Hysterical persons: *Ign.* or *Sepia.*

In children: *Calc., Bell., Cham., Coff., Ignatia.*

SYMPTOMATIC INDICATION.—*Aconite.*—If there is considerable fever, congestion, heat and swelling of the gums and face, with great restlessness. Frequently in alternation with *Belladonna.*

Belladonna.—Drawing, lacerating or shooting pain in the teeth, face, and ears, worse at night, in the evening, and on lying down. Swelling of the gums and cheek; heat and redness of the face; salivation or dryness of the mouth and throat with great thirst. Pains worse in the open air, from contact with food, or mental exertion. After this remedy *Hepar-s., Mercury, Chamomilla* or *Pulsatilla* may be indicated.

DOSE.—Two drops, or twelve globules, in a tumbler of water, a tablespoonful once in from half an hour to two hours.

Chamomilla.—Violent, drawing, jerking, pulsative or shooting pains, almost insupportable, particularly at night, when warm in bed, with heat and swelling of the face; violent semi-lateral pains, sometimes affecting the whole side of the face, aggravated by eating or drinking; great restlessness and weakness.

DOSE.—Same as *Belladonna.*

Mercury.—Lacerating, pulsative or throbbing pain, shooting in decayed teeth or in the roots, sometimes affecting the entire side of the face and extending into the glands and ears, aggravated at night, by cool damp air, or eating and drinking, especially anything cold, and almost insupportable in the warmth of the bed. Salivation and swelling of the cheek, gums or glands. Sensation as if the teeth were too long; ulceration, bleeding and discoloration of the gums. Frequently indicated after, or in alternation with *Belladonna* or *Dulcamara.*

DOSE.—A powder, or three globules, once in two or three hours.

Pulsatilla.—Particularly in persons of a mild and timid character, with disposition to shed tears. Toothache with earache and semi-lateral headache, drawing, shooting or jerking pain, or pulsative and gnawing pains with pricking in the gums, pains extending to the face and head, to the eye and ear of the side affected, with shivering and shortness of breath, aggravation in the evening, after midnight, when warm in bed, and from hot food, mitigated sometimes by cold water or cool air.

DOSE.—Two drops, or twelve globules, in a tumbler of water, a tablespoonful once in one or two hours.

Nux-vom.—Particularly in persons of a lively choleric temperament, with florid complexion, and in those who freely indulge in coffee and spirituous liquors, or who lead a sedentary life. Pains extending over the head, jerking, drawing as from excoriation, in the teeth and jaws ; gums swollen and painful, with pulsation ; painful enlargement of the glands, pain worse at night, in the morning on waking, or when engaged in intellectual labor ; irritable and peevish temper.

DOSE.—Same as *Mercury.*

Calcarea.—Toothache especially during pregnancy or at the period of catamenia ; congestion in the head, particularly at night ; pulsative pains and feeling of excoriation ; swelling and bleeding of the gums ; pains increased by a current of cold air, or by drinking anything cold or hot.

Bryonia.—Jerking, drawing pain, with looseness of the teeth, and sensation as if they were too long, particularly on eating ; pain rendering it necessary to lie down, worse at night or on taking anything hot into the mouth, or when lying on the side affected.

DOSE.—Two drops, or twelve globules, in a tumbler of water, a tablespoonful every one or two hours.

China.—Debility, occasioned by nursing or loss of fluids and when the pain is increased by the slightest contact, or after eating, or at night; sometimes relieved by clenching the teeth.

DOSE.—Same as *Bryonia.* Give every two or three hours.

Ignatia.—Especially where there is a tendency to indulge in grief, and when the pains are aggravated by coffee or tobacco smoke, in the evening after lying down, or in the morning on waking. Often indicated after *Cham.*, *Nux.v.* or *Pulsatilla.*

DOSE.—Same as *Bryonia.*

Mezerium.—Particularly where there are drawing, shooting pains, extending to the bones of the face and temple; pains in carious teeth, aggravated by touch or movement; shivering and congestion to the head.

Rhus.—Especially in persons disposed to melancholy, and where there are tearing, jerking, shooting or tingling pains, worse in the open air or at night, and relieved by the external application of heat.

DOSE.—Same as *Bryonia.*

Spigelia.—Jerking, pulsative or tearing pain, especially in carious teeth, coming on after a meal or at night, aggravated by cold water or exposure to cold air; frequently existing in connection with heart symptoms.

DOSE.—Same as *Bryonia.*

Staphysagria.—Where there is a disposition of the teeth to decay and break, with paleness, whiteness, ulceration and swelling, and tenderness of the gums, swelling of the cheek and glands; tearing, drawing pain even in the healthy teeth, and in the gums; aggravated during or immediately after eating, or drinking anything cold, and from contact or exposure to the cold.

DOSE.—Same as *Bryonia.*

Sulphur.—Tearing, jerking and pulsative pain, especially in carious teeth; congestion to the head and pulsative headache; constipation; pain worse at night, or on exposure to cold air; swelling and bleeding of the teeth and gums. Frequently serviceable after *Coffea* or *Aconite.*

DOSE.—A powder, or three globules, once in three or four hours.

Coffea.—Violent pain with tears, trembling and excessive anguish ; worse at night, or after a meal.

DOSE.—Two drops, or twelve globules, in a tumbler of water, a tablespoonful every hour or two hours.

Arsenicum.—Painful looseness and elongation of the teeth. Insupportable pain, aggravated by lying on the side affected, and relieved by the warmth of the fire.

DOSE.—A powder, or six globules, in two hours.

Carbo-v.—Frequently after *Ars.* or *Merc.*, and where there is bleeding and ulceration of the gums, exceedingly sensitive to the touch and looseness of the teeth.

DOSE.—Same as *Sulphur.*

Silicea.—Violent pain in the jaw, pain worse at night; ulcerative tendency of the skin.

DOSE.—Same as *Sulphur.*

Nit.-ac.—Pulsative and drawing or shooting pain, mostly in the evening, or when in bed.

DOSE.—Three drops of the 1st dilution, in a tumbler of water, a tablespoonful once in two or three hours.

Platina.—Pulsative and digging pains in the teeth ; sensation of cramp and torpor on the side affected.

DOSE---A powder, or six globules, once in three hours.

Sabina.—Particularly when connected with menstrual functions ; sensation as if the tooth were splitting ; aggravated by the warmth of bed. Besides the above *Hepar-s.*, *Hyosciamus*, *Sepia*, *Veratrum*, *Aconite*, it may also be consulted.

If no relief, is obtained after five or six doses, another remedy should be carefully selected.

OFFENSIVE BREATH.

Offensive breath and bad taste in the mouth are almost invariably only symptomatic of some other difficulty. When they arise from decayed teeth, the teeth should be cleansed, and the cavities properly filled by a dentist. If no dentist can be consulted conveniently, clean out the cavity yourself, and fill it with wax. If it should arise from derangement of the stomach, consult the disease under which it occurs. See also *Symptomatic Index.*

GUM-BOIL.

Abscess in the gums.

Should there be considerable heat, pain, and swelling, *Aconite* and *Belladonna* may be alternated three or four hours apart. If there is considerable throbbing, pulsative pain, *Mercury* and *Hepar-s.* may be alternated in the same way. After matter has formed, *Mercury* or *Silicea* may be given once in four or five hours.

DOSE.—The *Aconite* and *Belladonna* may be given two drops, or twelve globules, in a tumbler of water, a tablespoonful at a dose. The *Mercury*, *Hepar-s.*, and *Silicea*, a powder, or three globules on the tongue.

SCURVY.

Scorbutus.

This is a very common disease among sailors, and those who have been a long time at sea, deprived of fresh provisions, particularly vegetables, and also among those, where the air is damp and impure, the food scanty, and the small amount of vegetables used, stale and unhealthy. There is evidently a great impoverishment of the blood and an absence of some of its most important constituents.

Notwithstanding we have introduced it in this place, it is not solely a disease of the mouth, but pervades the whole frame. It is characterized by great fetor of the breath, sponginess, turgidity, hæmorrhage and ulceration of the gums and mouth; the gums recede, and the teeth become so loose as to fall out. There are livid subcutaneous spots and hæmorrhages in different parts of the body, particularly at the roots of the hairs, and frequently contraction of the limbs. As the disease progresses, the limbs swell, and ulcers appear on various parts of the body.

Scorbutic ulcers differ materially from others. Instead of pus they excrete a thin, fetid, sanious fluid, mixed with blood;

their edges are generally of a livid color, spongy and puffed up.

TREATMENT.—A change of diet is of vast importance, and with this alone a cure may generally be affected. Fruits, vegetables, lemon juice and other acid drinks should be used. Potatoes are particularly beneficial as an article of diet, and where a person can be well supplied with them, of a good quality, there is generally but little fear of the scurvy.

Mercury is a highly useful remedy, if it has not been previously used to excess. It is particularly indicated where the gums are red, fungous, detached, ulcerated and readily bleeding, with burning pains at night; inflammation and ulceration of the tongue and mouth; fetid smell and discharge of offensive or sanguineous saliva; swelling of the tongue and loose scalding evacuations.

Nit.-ac.—Particularly where much *Mercury* has been taken, and where there is bleeding, whiteness and swelling of the gums; salivation, looseness of the teeth, and putrid odor in the mouth.

Nux-v.—Especially in lean persons, who lead a sedentary life, and are of a lively temperament, and where there are putrid and painful swelling of the gums with burning and pulsative pains; fetid ulcers in the mouth, nocturnal salivation, bloody saliva, putrid smell of the mouth, discolored face, emaciation and constipation. Generally in alternation with *Arsenic*.

Arsenic.—Swelling and bleeding of the gums, looseness of the teeth; ulceration on the margin of the tongue, apthæ, with violent burning pains; great debility.

Carb.-v.—Especially where considerable *Mercury* has been taken, and where there are retraction, pain and ulceration of the gums, with profuse bleeding, looseness of the teeth, and fetid ulcers in the mouth.

Sulphur.—Swelling and bleeding of the gums with pulsative pain; vesicles and apthæ in the mouth and on the tongue; offensive and sour smell of the mouth.

Sulphur-ac.—Apthæ in the mouth, swelling, ulceration, bleeding of the gums, and profuse salivation.

ADMINISTRATION.—Two drops in a tumbler, a tablespoonful at a dose; or a powder, or six globules on the tongue. Give every four or six hours, increasing the intervals as the symptoms change for the better.

CANKER OF THE MOUTH.

This is a very common disease, particularly among children. White ulcerated spots are seen on the inside of the mouth and throat, and also on the tongue, gums, lips, &c. The gums swell, are spongy and recede from the teeth. These symptoms are generally preceded by feverishness, and more or less derangement of the stomach and bowels. There is often swelling of the glands of the throat and mouth, and a profuse secretion of acrid, putrid saliva.

TREATMENT.—*Mercury* is the most prominent remedy, unless the disease has been caused by an abuse of that drug, when *Nit.-ac.*, or *Carb.-v.* should be taken. For the symptomatic indications of these remedies, also *Ars.*, *Nux-vom.*, *Sulph.*, *Carbo-v.*, *Nit.-ac.* *See Scurvy.*

Borax.—Ulceration of the gums, mouth, and tongue; acrid, fetid, urine. Particularly useful in children.

Capsicum.—Principally in plethoric persons who lead a sedentary life, and where there are burning vesicles in the mouth and on the tongue, and swelling of the gums.

ADMINISTRATION.—Same as in *Scurvy.*

SALIVATION.

Ptyalism.

This disease is almost always connected in our mind either with an abuse, or a free administration of *Mercury*, yet it frequently owes its origin to other causes, as colds and the various forms of fever, particularly the cutaneous variety. The mucous membrane of the mouth, and the salivary glands connected with it, which in health secrete only the necessary amount of saliva, when irritated, swollen and inflamed by disease, may discharge it in large quantities. To effect a permanent cure then, the glands and mucous membrane of the mouth must be brought back to a healthy state.

Mercury produces the most frightful ulceration of the mouth and surrounding parts, as well as profuse salivation. The appropriate remedies in these cases are, *Nit.-ac.*, *Sulphur*, *Hepar-s.*, *Iodine*, and *Belladonna.*

When occasioned by cold, fevers, &c., *Mercury* is the prominent remedy, a powder, or three globules, once in four or six hours.

Dose.—Two drops, or twelve globules, in a tumbler of water, a tablespoonful at a dose; or a powder, or three globules on the tongue. Give once in four or six hours.

See also *Canker in the mouth*, and *Materia Medica.*

INFLAMMATION OF THE TONGUE.

Glossitis.

This disease is exceedingly painful, and, as might naturally be supposed, attended with great anguish. Fortunately however it is of rare occurrence. It may be occasioned by cold, derangement of adjoining organs, abuse of Mercury, ulcers, poisons, mechanical injuries, the sting of a bee, &c. The tongue swells to an enormous size, so as to fill the whole cavity of the mouth, and even protrude beyond the teeth, and unless speedily relieved, suppuration, gangrene, or hardening of the tongue may take place.

Treatment.—When occasioned by mechanical injuries or by the sting of a bee, eight or ten drops of *Arnica* may be put in four tablespoonfuls of water, and the mouth rinsed with it three or four times a day.

Should there be considerable inflammation and fever, *Aconite* should be given, a dose every hour, followed if there is much pain, swelling, and tendency to suppuration, by *Mercury* and *Belladonna* in alternation one or two hours apart.

Arsenic and *Lachesis* may be alternated in the same manner, should there be danger of gangrene.

When the difficulty arises from the abuse of Mercury, *Nit.*-

ac., or *Hepar-s.* may be administered two or three hours apart.

If produced by a burn, *Urtica Urens* is the appropriate remedy, administered in the manner indicated for *Arnica.*

DOSE.—Two drops, or twelve globules, in a tumbler of water, a tablespoonful at a dose ; or a powder, or six globules on the tongue. Give as above directed.

RANULA.

Swelling under the tongue.

This is occasioned by an obstruction of the ducts, through which a portion of the saliva passes from the salivary glands into the mouth. It presents the appearance of a bluish eminence, and is generally without pain.

The prominent remedies are *Calcarea, Mercury, Thuja,* commencing with the first, and giving a powder, or three globules every night for one week, when, if not better, administer the next remedy, and so on in the same manner. Externally it may be washed by a solution of ten drops of *Arnica* in a tea-cup of water, once a day.

DEFECTS OF SPEECH.

Stammering, &c.

This may be the result of disease, such as paralysis, congestion to the head, or fever; in which case, see the respective diseases. It however very often exists without any apparent cause, and in these cases a certain mental training, particularly in childhood will prove far more beneficial than any medical treatment, and will as a general thing be entirely successful.

The patient should be advised to read aloud, slowly and distinctly, enunciating clearly each word and syllable, at the same time, beating time with the finger or foot. When talking, he should avoid excitement, keep the mind perfectly clear, and pronounce every word clearly, slowly, and distinctly. A course of mental training like this, will if taken in time, be sufficient to break up the habit.

Should however there be great sensitiveness of the nervous system. A dose of *Belladonna*, *Hyosciamus*, *Strammonium*, or *Lachesis* may be taken twice a week, until five or six doses have been taken. See page 10.

SORE THROAT.

Angina, Cynanche.

There are numerous varieties of this disease, such as quinsy, simple, ulcerated, and chronic sore throat. It may consist of a slight inflammation of the fauces and palate attended with but little pain, or the swelling may be so great as almost to choke up the passage, accompanied with fever and severe pain, and if not relieved terminate in extensive ulceration.

TREATMENT.—In the commencement of the disease the wet bandage, (see page 80) or a cloth wrung out in cold water, bound around the throat, covered with a dry flannel, is an invaluable remedy, and in simple cases with the addition of a few doses of *Belladonna*, will be the only treatment required. It should be applied at night or during the day, if the patient remain in the house.

In persons subject to throat difficulties, the chest and throat should be freely sponged with cold water morning and evening, taking care, however to rub the parts perfectly dry.

The treatment can generally be commenced with *Belladonna*, or if considerable inflammation and pain are present, *Mercury* may be alternated with the *Belladonna*, from two to four hours apart, gradually increasing the intervals as the symptoms are relieved.

SYMPTOMATIC INDICATIONS.—*Aconite.*—Violent fever, dry heat, great thirst, restlessness, deep redness of the parts affected, pain and difficulty in swallowing or speaking, burning and pricking sensation. Frequently in alternation with *Belladonna* or *Mercury.*

DOSE.—Two drops, or twelve globules, in a tumbler of water, a tablespoonful every two hours.

Belladonna.—In almost every variety of sore throat, especially where there are excoriating pains, scraping, dryness, burning or shooting in the throat, particularly when swallowing; pains shooting to the ears; spasmodic constriction of the throat, with great difficulty in swallowing; inability to drink, the fluid escaping through the nostrils, or violent thirst with dread of drinking; bright or yellowish redness of the parts affected, without swelling, or severe swelling and redness of all the parts with suppuration, and rapidly spreading ulcers; accumulation of mucus in the throat; swelling of the muscles and glands of the neck; fever, hot, red and swollen face, and aching in the forehead. *Mercury* is generally suitable either after or in alternation with this remedy.

DOSE.—Same as *Aconite*. When alternated with *Aconite* or *Mercury*, they may be given either one or two hours apart, according to the severity of the symptoms.

Mercury.—Violent shooting pain in the throat, especially when swallowing, extending to the ears and glands of the neck; excoriating pain, swelling and great inflammatory redness of the parts affected; difficult swallowing, especially drinks, which escape through the nostrils, yet a constant desire to swallow. Ulcers and tendency to suppuration in the throat; elongation of the palate; rheumatic symptoms in the head and nape of the neck; sometimes with shivering. In the commencement of the disease it may be indicated in alternation with *Belladonna*, if however there are strong symptoms of suppuration or ulcerations, it should be alternated with *Hepar-s.* or *Lachesis*, and after the abscess is broken, with *Hepar-s.* or *Silicea*.

DOSE.—A powder, or six globules, every two hours.

Lachesis.—Particularly where *Belladonna* or *Mercury* seem indicated and yet prove insufficient, and especially if there are excoriating pains, burning and dryness in the throat in circumscribed places, extending to the ears, larynx and tongue, with shortness of breath and danger of suffocation; swelling and redness of the throat; sensation of a tumor or lump in the throat, inducing a constant disposition to swallow, which however is painful and difficult; symptoms aggravated in the afternoon and morning, and by the slightest touch of the neck. Compare with *Belladonna* and *Mercury*.

Dose.—A powder, or six globules, once in two or three hours.

Chamomilla.—Particularly in children, where the disease is caused by checked perspiration, and where there are swelling of the glands of the throat, burning pain and sensation of enlargement in the throat; difficulty of swallowing solid food; tickling in the larynx, producing coughing and hoarseness, fever in the evening, with flushes of heat, alternating with shivering.

Dose.—Two drops, or twelve globules, in a tumbler of water, a tablespoonful once in two or three hours.

Nux-v.—Particularly after *Chamomilla*, or in persons lean and bilious, or of a sanguine temperament; pain in the throat as from excoriation, especially when swallowing; sometimes with a sensation as of a plug, or a sense of constriction in the throat; swelling of the throat, dry cough, headache; small ulcers with a putrid smell.

Dose.—Same as *Lachesis*.

Pulsatilla.—In females or persons of a mild character, and where there is a redness of the throat, with a sensation as if the parts were swollen; scraping pain and dryness in the throat, without thirst; shooting in the throat, particularly when swallowing, accumulation of tenacious mucus; shivering toward evening.

Dose.—Same as *Chamomilla*.

Bryonia.—Hoarseness, cold in the head, dry cough and oppressed respiration; constipation; pricking and painful sensibility of the throat, when touched, on turning the head or swallowing; shootings and sensation of dryness in the throat; fever or shivering and coldness. After or in alternation with *Aconite*.

Dose.—Same as *Chamomilla*.

Hepar-s.—Frequently after or in alternation with *Belladonna* or *Mercury*, and where there are lancinating pains in the throat, especially when swallowing or coughing; difficult swallowing; swelling and violent pressure in the throat with danger of suffocation, in alternaion with *Mercury*.

Capsicum.—Tingling sensation in the throat, as if produced by pepper. Inflammatory pain with painful pressure or contraction, particularly during swallowing; violent pain in the glands of the neck in paroxysms; ulceration in the mouth and throat, dry hacking cough, hoarseness, &c. Often of decided benefit in epidemic maladies, and where the difficulty is complicated with gastric or rheumatic ailments, also in those cases where *Cham.*, *Bry.*, *Ign.*, *Nux-v.* and *Puls.* seem indicated, yet prove insufficient.

DOSE.—Same as *Chamomilla.*

Ignatia.—Red and inflammatory swelling of the throat with severe pain and great difficulty in swallowing; sensation of a plug in the throat, or shooting to the ears; ulceration of the throat. Compare with *Cham.*, *Nux-v.*, *Puls.*, *Bell.*, *Merc.*

DOSE.—Same as *Chamomilla.*

Sulphur.—Swelling, dryness, excoriating or lancinating pain in the throat; swelling of the glands of the neck; painful sensation of constriction with difficulty in swallowing.

DOSE.—A powder, or six globules, once in four or six hours.

Cocculus.—Sensation of roughness and burning in the throat, extending into the chest, sensitiveness of the neck, inability to swallow, excessively violent cough at night, gastric derangement.

DOSE.—Same as *Chamomilla.*

Nit.-acid is a valuable remedy, where the throat is filled with superficial ulcers, or where the throat-difficulty is occasioned by abuse of *Mercury*, or is the result of *Syphilis.*

DOSE.—Three drops of the first dilution in a tumbler of water, a tablespoonful once in four or six hours.

Merc.-Iodatus is an exceedingly valuable remedy in certain varieties of throat disease. There may be swelling of the glands of the throat, ulcers scattered over the gums and along the margin of the tongue, with red edges, and an ashy grey centre; severe inflammation of the throat, assuming as it advances, a deep scarlet or even purple color, or as it passes into the chronic form, showing itself in patches, covered with a secretion of yellowish mucus, inducing constant coughing. Sometimes where the inflammation is intense, as in malignant scarlatina, the parts present a smooth shining glazed appearance, the voice sinks into a whisper, or is entirely extinct, an aching sensation is felt in the throat, particularly on pressing the larynx, also under the sternum and clavicles, with weariness and oppression.

Dose.—A powder, once in three hours.

In malignant or putrid sore throat, where the disease sets in with great violence and often runs its course with frightful rapidity, in addition to the remedies already enumerated, the following deserve attention; consult also *Scarlatina*.

Sulphuric-Acid.—Sudden and rapid prostration of strength, frequent chills, pain in the throat, with sensation of swelling, deep bluish red spots or patches re-covered by a membrane, beneath which is seen more or less suppuration.

Dose.—Two drops in a tumbler of water, a tablespoonful once in three or four hours.

Arsenic.—Particularly where the inflammation is of an erysipelatous character, or where it assumes a typhoid form; great prostration of strength, burning heat, cold hands, great restlessness and anguish, ulceration, discharging fetid matter and strong tendency to gangrene.

Dose.—A powder, once in three hours.

Conium is also a valuable remedy, where the parts have assumed an ash grey color and a blackish aspect, whitish eruption on the skin, swollen tongue, bloody and involuntary stools, together with the presence of symptoms indicating *Arsenic*.

Dose.—Two drops in a tumbler of water, a tablespoonful once in two or three hours.

In the treatment of this variety should the ulcers assume a more healthy character, it may be well for a time to cease the remedies previously given, and substitute *Sulph.* a powder, or three globules, once in four or six hours.

Where the disease is of a chronic or constitutional character, sometimes combined with bronchial and chest difficulties, the remedies deserving particular attention are, *Alum.*, *Arg.-nit.*, *Bar.-c.*, *Calc.*, *Hep.*, *Lach.*, *Sulph.*, *Nitr.-ac.*, *Natr.-m.*, *Nux-v.*, *Sabad.*, *Sen.*, *Staph.*

Where the disease is caused by an abuse of *Merc.*, *Bell.*, *Carb.-v.*, *Hep.*, *Lach.*, *Sulph.*, *Nit.-ac.*

From a syphilitic cause: *Merc.*, *Nit.-ac.*, *Thuj.*, *Sulph.* As it regards external application, where the glands are much swollen, and suppuration is apparent, poultices of flaxseed or slippery elm may be applied. The mouth and gums may be washed or swabbed with cold water or tepid milk and water. In certain varieties of throat disease great benefit has been derived from swabbing the throat with a solution of nitrate of silver, but this should not be applied, unless by the hands of a careful physician. In chronic cases the remedy may be given once in six or twelve hours.

Diet and Regimen.—Same as in fever.

SWELLING OF THE TONSILS—OF THE PALATE.

We have included the treatment of these diseases in the preceding article. In some there is a tendency to enlargement of the tonsils on taking even a slight cold, also to swelling and elongation of the palate. The treatment indicated above, together with gargling the throat with cold water, and the wet bandage, will generally be sufficient to remove the difficulty. The prominent remedies are, *Nux-v.*, *Bell.*, *Merc.*, *Calc.*, *Arg.-nit.*

CHAPTER IX.

AFFECTION OF THE URINARY AND GENITAL ORGANS.

The difficulties we shall enumerate under this head will be more readily understood by carefully reading that part of the chapter on anatomy, which refers to these organs, and thus gaining a correct idea of the anatomical relation of the parts. See page 39.

INFLAMMATION OF THE KIDNEYS.

Nephritis.

DIAGNOSIS.—A dull or acute pain is felt in the loins, on one or both sides of the spine, between the hips and short ribs, and frequently extending over the whole of the lumbar region. The pain extends along the ureters to the bladder, and is sometimes attended with nausea, vomiting, and colic. The region of the kidney is hot and painful, the pain is aggravated by motion and even deep breathing, and the patient is unable to lie on the affected side. The urine is generally of a fiery-red appearance, and may be either diminished or suppressed, or be mixed with pus or blood, and its emission attended with burning pain. In the male, the testicle is drawn up, and in most cases the thigh of the affected side is numb. The fever is more or less severe, and sometimes assumes the typhoid form. The urine may be entirely suppressed and violent vomiting, delirium, or stupor set in. If the inflammation is not arrested, ulceration may set in, the pus being discharged with the urine.

TREATMENT.*—The prominent remedies are, *Aconite*, *Canth.*, *Cann.*, *Nux-v.*, *Bell.*, *Hepar-s.*, *Pulsatilla*, *Mercury*, and *Cocculus.*

* For general directions as to the administration of remedies, see page 10.

Aconite is indicated, where there is considerable fever present, generally in alternation with *Cantharides* or *Cannabis.*

The most important remedies are, *Cantharides* and *Cannabis*, which are often given with advantage in alternation.

Cantharides is indicated by the presence of sticking, tearing and cutting pains in the region of the kidneys, aggravated by motion, and coming on in paroxysms. Painful emission of urine, sometimes almost impassible, passed drop by drop, attended with violent burning pains, and mixed with blood. There is considerable fever, violent thirst, and constant urging to urinate.

Cannabis.—The indications for this remedy are similar to those of *Cantharides*, with the addition of a drawing, ulcerative pain from the kidneys to the groins.

If the disease should be caused by suppressed hæmorrhage or abuse of spirituous liquours, *Nux-v.* is a prominent remedy.

Belladonna will be found of benefit, where there is burning, stinging pain in the region of the kidneys, extending along the ureters to the bladder, and recurring in paroxysms, extending to the abdomen, aggravated by contact; colic, heat in the region of the kidneys, restlessness, constipation, &c.

Hepar-s. is often of advantage after *Belladonna.*

Mercury will be of service, where there are throbbing, pulsative pains, or the emission of pus. See *Gravel.*

Administration.—Three drops, or twelve globules, in a tumbler of water, a tablespoonful at a dose; or a powder, or six globules on the tongue. Give every hour or two hours, according to the severity of the symptoms. Where the paroxysms of agony are excessively severe, the remedy may be given until three or four doses have been taken, every half hour.

Diet and Regimen.—Same as in fevers.

INFLAMMATION OF THE BLADDER.

Cystitis.

Like *Nephritis*, inflammation of the bladder commences with chills, hot and dry skin, nausea, and vomiting, scanty and highly colored urine and constipation. As the inflammation progresses, the pain becomes deep-seated, burning and cutting, sometimes extending over the whole abdomen, and into the penis or rectum. The urine is discharged drop by drop, or entirely suppressed, is thick, dark-red, and turbid, mixed with blood or mucus. The pain in the region of the bladder is intense, aggravated by the slightest motion, in attempt to pass water, or alvine evacuations.

There is violent thirst, hot and dry skin, great restlessness, and anguish, and frequently, cerebral and typhoid symptoms. Convulsions and fainting may also be present.

CAUSES.—This inflammation may exist in connection with derangement of the kidneys, or be produced by stone in the bladder. It may also be produced by cold, stimulating drinks, gonorrhœa, mechanical injuries, or derangement of the womb.

TREATMENT.*—The selection of the remedy must be guided by the cause of the disease. When occasioned by abuse of spirituous liquors, *Nux-v.* is the appropriate remedy. When produced by the use of *Cantharides,* one drop doses of *Camphor,* given at intervals of two hours, will speedily produce relief.

Aconite is indicated during the presence of fever, either alone, or in alternation with some other remedy, especially *Cannabis*, or *Cantharides*.

Cannabis.—Complete retention of urine, or a desire to urinate, principally at night, with burning pain; or emission drop by drop of bloody urine.

Cantharides.—Emission of urine, drop by drop, with shooting, burning pains, or violent and ineffectual desire to urinate; extreme sensitiveness of the region of the bladder to the touch. In alternation with *Aconite* or *Cannabis.*

Digitalis.—When the neck of the bladder is principally affected, and where there is constrictive pain and retention, or painful desire to urinate, with emission of only a few drops.

Dulcamara.—Particularly in chronic cases, aggravated or

* For general directions as to the administration of remedies, see page 10.

brought on by slight cold, or where the urine deposits a slimy sediment.

Hyosciamus may be given, where there are spasms of the bladder, three drops in a tumbler half full of water, a table-spoonful every half hour until relieved. *Pulsatilla*, *Sulphur*, *Thuja*, *Terebinth*, and *Copaiba* may also be consulted. See *Nephritis*, also *Symptomatic Index*.

Administration.—Where the inflammation is intense, and the sufferings severe, the remedy prepared as directed in *Nephritis* may be given every hour, gradually increasing the intervals as the symptoms abate, to two or three hours.

Diet and Regiment.—As in fevers. Avoiding particularly wines, liquors, and all kind of stimulating and heating drinks.

SUPPRESSION, AND RETENTION OF URINE.

Suppression and retention of urine although frequently producing similar symptoms are entirely unlike.

In *suppression of urine* there is no secretion of urine, the secreting function of the kidneys being for the time either partially, or entirely destroyed. This variety is attended with considerable danger, the brain being exceedingly liable to become diseased, and if the suppression be total, serious cerebral difficulty generally sets in, in the form of delirium, succeeded by coma and effusion. In these cases the saliva, sweat, and water effused on the brain, have a urinous smell and taste.

The suppression may arise from inflammation of the kidneys, when it is attended with febrile symptoms, nausea, vomiting, pain in the region of the kidneys, tenderness of the abdomen to the touch, frequent desire to urinate, but if any is secreted, it passes in small quantities, and is accompanied with severe pain; or it may be occasioned by the presence of gravel or calculi in the kidneys, giving rise by their irritation to inflammation, when the symptoms are similar to those described above. Sometimes it may depend on paralysis of the kidneys, when there may be no desire to urinate, an absence of pain and febrile symptoms, but the unpleasant cerebral symptoms set in none the less rapidly.

In *retention of urine*, the urine is secreted as usual, but from some cause, such as the presence of stone in the bladder, inflammation or stricture of the urethra, paralysis of the bladder, enlargement of the prostrate gland or the presence of tumors, it is prevented from passing out. The symptoms of course are exceedingly varied according to the cause of the disease. There is distension of the bladder, which can be distinctly felt, elevated above the pubis,—and by this symptom alone the difficulty may be distinguished from suppression of urine,—pain in the region of the bladder, and constant but ineffectual desire to urinate, attended with severe pain, except in cases of paralysis, where there is an absence of febrile symptoms and pain. This difficulty seldom exists alone, but generally in connection with some other disease. If not relieved, the bladder may become so distended as to be ruptured, discharging the urine into the bowels, causing gangrene, and resulting in death.

TREATMENT.—The use of the catheter may be frequently required, but as this should be used by the practiced hand of the physician, it will be unnecessary to speak of it here. The cause of the disease should be ascertained as nearly as possible; whether the result of stricture, of inflammation, of mechanical injury, of paralysis or gravel.

External application, such as, warm baths, poultices, warm cloths, or if much heat is present, cold water will be found not only in this complaint, but in *Cystitis* and *Nephritis*, valuable auxiliaries. See also *wet bandage*, page 80. The prominent remedies are: *Canth.*, *Cann.*, *Acon.*, *Bell.*, *Rhus*, *Nux-v.*, *Terebinth*, *Ars.*, *Asparagus*, *Arnica.*

Where in inflammation of the kidneys or bladder there is considerable fever: *Aconite* is indicated and may be followed after the fever, abates by *Cantharides* and *Cannabis*, one or two hours apart.

Where it is occasioned by *mechanical injury*, or the *irritation of calculi*, *Arnica* is the proper remedy.

When produced by *metastases of gout or rheumatism*, *Rhus* or *Belladonna* may be given, if accompanied with much fever, in alternation with *Aconite*.

When the result of paralysis, *Nux-v.*, *Arsenic*, or *Terebinth*.

Spasmodic retention may be relieved by *Camphor*, *Belladonna*, or *Aconite*.

ADMINISTRATION.—Three drops, or twelve globules, in a tumbler of water, a tablespoonful at a dose; or a powder, or six globules on the tongue. In severe cases a dose may be given every hour, increasing the intervals as relief is obtained, to two or three hours.

URINARY CALCULI.

In the investigation of this disease particular attention should be directed to the urine, as its color, smell and sediment will afford a pretty correct guide to the character of the calculi.

The *lithic urine* lays the foundation for a large proportion of the calculi which are formed in the bladder or other parts of the urinary organs. It is characterized by the spontaneous deposition of *lithic acid*, constituting the principal part of what is generally termed the *sand*, or *brick dust sediment* of urine.

Next in frequency to the variety just mentioned, are those composed of a combination of *Phosphoric-acid*, *Magnesia* and *Ammonia*. The urine is fetid and the sediment deposited of a white color resembling mortar.

Another variety, less frequent, however, than either of the above, is the *mulberry* calculus. It is of a dark brown color and is very heavy and hard. There are several other varieties of *calculi*, varying in appearance and in chemical combination, but it will be unnecessary to particularize here.

It is worthy of remark that this disease is more generally found in the male than in the female sex, and is principally confined to youth and old age, and is seldom if ever seen either in the *frigid* or the *torrid* zones. It is especially liable to attack those in whom there is any hereditary tendency to gout.

Diagnosis.—The urine, as a general thing, shows some kind of sediment, and there may also be frequent desire to urinate. Often no pain is felt for some time unless after severe physical exertion. An attack may come on suddenly, in which the stone, if situated in the kidneys, may pass into the bladder. The pain is of the most intense and violent character, the urine high colored, or mixed with blood. Where the stone is already in the bladder, the symptoms are varied. There may be stoppage of water, great heaviness about the region of the bladder and general uneasiness.

Treatment.—One great object must be to prevent if possible, the formation of *Calculi*, by correcting those secretions on which the morbid sediments depend. After the stone is already formed, the physician must either dissolve it by means of medicines administered internally, or remove it by an operation. Among some of the prominent causes of this disease, we may mention derangement of the digestive organs, from errors in diet, abuse in spirituous liquors, &c., lime water, mental and bodily fatigue, and tendency to gout and rheumatism. A sea voyage to either a hot or cold climate, will often produce entire relief. In all cases, a plain and simple diet, and a cheerful temperament, are of the utmost importance.

In the *lithic acid* diathesis, baths and friction should be freely used, every thing of an acid nature avoided, and animal food form a principle article of diet.

The *phosphatic diathesis* requires, on the contrary, a vegetable diet, and the free use of acids and fruits.

The prominent remedies are, *Cannabis*, *Cantharis*, *Nux Vomica*, *Lycopodium*, *Sarsaparilla*, *Calcarea*, *Phosphorus*, and *Asparagus*.

Cannabis and *Cantharis*, during a paroxysm of pain from the gravel, are prominent remedies. There is a burning, scalding, and painful sensation when making water, as well as after; the urine is sometimes slimy or bloody, and violen pain may also be felt in the region of the kidneys and bladder.

Dose.—Three drops of the remedy, may be dissolved in a tumbler half full of water, and a tablespoonful given in alternation, during the paroxysm, half an hour apart. The external application of warmth during the severe paroxysm, will frequently aid in producing relief.

Nux-vomica will be found highly advantageous, when the disease originates in errors of diet, abuse of stimulants, and chronic derangement of the digestive organs, also where there are acute and spasmodic pains.

Dose.—If the paroxysm is severe, a powder, or six globules, may be taken once an hour, but as a general thing, once every twelve or twenty-four hours, will be all that is necessary.

Lycopodium is especially useful in persons of a lymphatic temperament, and those who have been troubled with affections of the mucous membrane. The pain is principally in the urethra, and is of a burning, smarting character, during the passage of water. The urine is fetid, is of a dark red color, and deposites a red or yellowish sediment.

Dose.—Same as *Nux.*

Calcarea is useful where the affection is developed in scrofulous children. The pain in the urinary organs, and the desire to pass water, are worse during the night; the urine is fetid, and deposites a white sediment.

Dose.—Until four powders have been taken, a powder, or six globules, every twelve hours, after this, once in twenty-four hours.

Phosphorus.—This remedy will be found highly advantageous in old and debilitated subjects, and where there is great prostration of strength, also where the patient has no control over the urinary organs, and where the urine has a strong smell of ammonia, and deposits a whitish, or brick dust sediment.

Dose.—A powder, or six globules, may be taken every twenty-four hours.

Asparagus is a valuable remedy where there is a fetid smell to the urine, depositing a whitish sediment; frequent desire to urinate, pain on passing water, and cutting pain in the urethra and kidneys.

Dose.—Three drops, or twelve globules, may be mixed in a tumbler of water, and a tablespoonful given once in twelve hours.

DIABETES.

In this disease, there is an increased flow of straw-colored urine, of a sweetish taste; or not an unusual secretion of urine, but what there is, strongly charged with saccharine (*sugar*) matter. The disease may continue for months, or years, and in many cases, terminate at length in death.

As the disease progresses, derangement of the digestive organs is perceptible, and the memory becomes impaired; there is great emaciation, coldness of the extremities, and dropsical effusion.

Treatment.—Vegetables should be carefully avoided, and a nutritious diet enjoined of animal food. The external application of water, in the form of the sponge bath, or wet sheet, is highly advantageous. See page 80.

The patient should place himself under the care of a judicious physician without delay. The prominent internal remedies are *Phos-acid*, *Carb-veg.*, *Muriatic-acid*, *Conium*, and *Nux-vom.*

ENURESIS.

Incontinence of Urine.

This may be occasioned by a weakness of the muscles concerned, or a partial or entire paralysis. In the latter case, the bladder is unable to retain for a moment the urine secreted, which constantly dribbles away, drop by drop, very much to the annoyance of the patient. Where there is merely a weakness, or partial paralysis, it gives rise to that difficulty so common among children, *wetting the bed.*

Treatment.—Where enuresis is occasioned by either partial or entire paralysis of the muscles, the application of electricity along the lower portion of the spine, and over the neck of the bladder, will be found beneficial. The prominent internal remedies are, *Hyosciamus*, *Causticum*, and *Conium*. The sitz-bath will also be of service. See page 80.

Dose.—Two drops, or twelve globules, in a tumbler of water, a tablespoonful morning and night.

Enuresis in children, in the form of *wetting the bed*, may arise from some other difficulty, such as worms. The cause should be ascertained as nearly as possible, before any treatment is adopted.

When there is a peculiarly strong and horse like smell about the urine, a powder of *Benzoic-acid* may be taken every night.

Cantharides may be found of benefit, one drop, or six globules, given every evening for three nights, stopping it immediately should there be pain in passing water. If after a week no change is apparent, a powder, or six globules of *Silicea*, may be given every second night, until six doses have been taken, when if no improvement is perceptible, *Sepia* and *Carb-veg.*, may be given in the same manner.

SEMINAL EMISSIONS.

These frequently occur in the young; just after reaching the age of puberty, and are generally occasioned by a morbid imagination, combined perhaps, with irregularity of habits, and errors of diet. The patient should strive to live more in obedience to nature, and cultivate a healthy frame of mind. The external application of the sponge-bath will be found beneficial. Three globules of *Phos.-acid* may be given every other night.

GONORRHŒA.

Not every discharge from the urethra is gonorrhœa. In gonorrhœa when infection takes place, in from two to four days after an impure connection, a tingling or itching sensation is felt at the orifice of the urethra, especially when urinating. Soon the lips of the urethra become red and swollen, the inflammation extending an inch or two up the urethra; the emission of urine is attended with a scalding, burning pain, more or less severe. A discharge takes place at first of a mucous character, but if the inflammation increases, changes to a yellow or greenish color, and if exceedingly violent, may assume a bloody character. Erections, or cordee, of an exceedingly painful character, frequently come on at night.

TREATMENT.—Quiet, a plain and non-stimulating diet, and an absence of ardent spirits of every kind, are of great importance. During the inflammatory period, characterized by burning, scalding pain, on the emission of urine, copious discharge, &c. *Cannabis* and *Cantharides* are the proper remedies. One drop of each may be given in alternation, four hours apart, until the inflammatory symptoms have in a measure subsided, when *Mercury* and *Sulphur* may be substituted and administered, a powder on the tongue, at the same intervals. *Mercury* is more particularly indicated, when the discharge is of a greenish character, and *Sulphur*, where it presents a whitish or serous appearance.

When the disease is allowed to run on for several weeks, it becomes chronic, and is called "*Gleet.*" There is no pain, but a slight discharge. The prominent remedies are, *Sulphur*, *Mercury*, *Capsicum*, *Nit-ac.*, or *Thuja.*

DOSE.—A powder, or six globules, may be taken on the tongue; or two drops mixed with a tumbler half full of water, a tablespoonful at a dose. Give every night for a week, when if not better, another remedy may be selected.

SYPHILIS.

This disease may remain lurking in the system for years, be transmitted from parent to child, and lay the foundation for diseases ending in deformity, misery and death. It will only be necessary here to give some of the prominent indications, as after it has passed the primary stage, it frequently becomes complicated with a variety of diseases, and requires all the skill of the practiced physician to detect the cause and apply the appropriate remedy.

DIAGNOSIS.—All sores on the penis are not by any means syphilitic, but the primary chancre or syphilitic sore usually presents itself on some part of the end of the penis, in from three to eight days after infection, in the form of a red and slightly itching pimple. In a short time matter forms in the centre of the pimple, and a deep ulcer with ragged edges, and yellowish surface is gradually formed. This ulcer may be slight and superficial, or perhaps deep and rapidly spreading, attended with severe pain, and rapidly destroying the adjacent parts. The most simple form, by bad treatment, such as the administration of Mercury in large and repeated doses, may be changed into sores of the most violent character, and the poison scattered over the system, producing the most fearful consequences. In connection with the chancre, swelling in the groin or *bubo* may set in, sometimes ending in ulceration.

Where the disease is not checked in the primary stage, the poison may become diffused through the system, giving rise to *secondary* and *tertiary* symptoms. The throat may become deeply ulcerated, the voice and nose destroyed, and deep and loathsome sores form in different parts of the body. A copper-colored eruption also may be developed on the skin, generally commencing on the face and hands. Another terrible result of neglected syphilis is an affection of the bones and their periosteal covering. The covering of the bones become swollen, and if the disease is allowed to run on, osseous deposits form beneath it, producing the *venereal node*. These generally exist on the head and the bones of the leg. The pain where the bones and their covering are affected, is often agonizing, generally coming on in the latter part of the afternoon, and continuing until midnight.

Treatment.—It is highly important in this disease that a careful physician be consulted as soon as possible, as neglect or injudicious treatment may be attended with the most unpleasant symptoms. Syphilitic taint may, as we have before remarked, lurk in the system for years, laying the foundation of various diseases, which require the closest scrutiny on the part of the physician to detect the real cause. It may also be transmitted from parent to child, developing in the young frame diseases which fill the body with pain and end in deformity and death. Hence the vast importance of eradicating the disease thoroughly from the system.

The almost specific remedy for primary chancre is *Mercury-sol.* This should be given a powder of the first or third trituration, morning and night for eight or ten days, when, if improvement is perceptible, the intervals may be gradually increased.

Should however but little improvement take place, and other remedies be required, it may be followed by *Thuja* in the same way for three or four days, and this in its turn by *Nit.-ac.*, two drops in a tumbler of water, a tablespoonful at a dose. Where ulcers are developed in the throat, *Mercury* is still the appropriate remedy, given as before mentioned, but if after five or six doses no improvement is perceptible, it should be followed by *Nit.-ac.*, one drop in a tumbler of water, and a tablespoonful given three times a day.

The eruption, pain in the bones, ulceration of the throat and nose, and other secondary symptoms can generally be controlled by *Mercury*, *Nit.-ac.*, *Thuja*, *Aurum*, given as above directed.

CHAPTER X.

GENERAL AFFECTIONS.

RHEUMATISM.

This exceedingly painful disease is quite common in our ever-changing climate, and is alike the dread of the physician and patient, especially when developed in those in whom there is an hereditary predisposition to this kind of affection. Its constant liability to change from one part of the system to another, and even to attack some vital organ, renders it not only excessively painful, but highly annoying under any form of treatment. Notwithstanding Homœopathy has shorn it of half its terrors, and abolished from the sick-room the painful and disgusting treatment so much in vogue in the allopathic school, yet under any treatment it is a disease to be dreaded, and one in which in violent cases we cannot always with certainty predict a speedy recovery.

Rheumatism is essentially, inflammation of the fibrous tissue,—sometimes however involving, as the disease extends, other tissues,—and most commonly seizes the fibrous parts, which lie around the joints, particularly the larger joints, although the inflammation frequently commences in the head, neck, chest, or arms, and extends to other parts of the body. So long as it is confined to the extremities, the pain may be excessive, deformity may ensue, but notwithstanding the severity of the symptoms but little danger to life is apprehended. Should however the disease strike some vital organ the danger is imminent.

Diagnosis.—In *acute rheumatism*, languor, slight chills and general uneasiness are followed by swelling of some part of the system, accompanied with pain, heat, and generally more or less redness. The pains are exceedingly variable in character, sharp, lancinating, dull and throbbing, or numb aching, gnawing, or boring, aggravated by the slightest movement.

The weight of the bed clothes is sometimes oppressive, and it is impossible to move the joints. The fever is high, pulse bounding and full, face flushed, the head aches, the urine is high colored, turbid, acid, and sedimentious, and the patient is frequently drenched in sour smelling perspiration. The tongue is red at the tip and edges, but the centre of it is covered with a whitish fur.

Acute rheumatism generally occurs between the age of fifteen and forty, although it is sometimes seen in children as early as three or four.

Chronic rheumatism differs materially from the *acute* form in the absence of fever, in the little or no constitutional disturbance, and in the pain being far less severe. In one form there is some heat and pain, and sometimes swelling of the joints. The pain is increased by pressure, motion, or warmth, but the appetite is good. In the other form there is a sense of coldness and stiffness in the painful joints.

CAUSES.—Exposure to wet, cold, damp or changeable temperature, and sudden suppression of perspiration are the prominent causes.

TREATMENT.—In the acute form where there is considerable swelling, heat and pain, frequently bathe the part affected with tepid water or with a mixture composed of ten drops of Arnica to six tablespoonfuls of water. If cold water is applied, see "*wet bandage*," page 80.

Aconite will be of advantage, where there is a dry skin, violent fever, thirst, redness of the cheeks, shooting, tearing pains, worse at night.

ADMINISTRATION.—It may be given every hour or two hours, according to the severity of the symptoms. It is frequently indicated in alternation with *Bell.*, *Rhus*, or *Bry.* when the remedies may be given either one or two hours apart.

Belladonna.—Violent fever, congestion in the head, redness of the face and eyes; swelling with shining redness, shooting, burning pains, aggravated at night or by movement. Particularly indicated when the difficulty is felt in the upper extremities. It is often especially useful either after or in alternation with *Acon.* or *Puls.*

Bryonia.—Tearing, shooting pains on moving the parts, or pain flying about from one part to another; red and shining swelling; pains worse at night, or increased by the least movement; coldness and shivering or febrile heat, headache, bilious or gastric sufferings, stitching pain in the region of the liver, and pulsative headache. Frequently indicated after *Acon.* or *Rhus.*

Rhus.—Drawing tensive and dragging, or wrenching, gnawing and boring pain; paralytic weakness and tingling in the affected parts; red and shining swelling; pains worse at night, during rest or in changeable weather. Frequently indicated after or in alternation with *Arn.* or *Bry.*

Pulsatilla.—Pains passing rapidly from one part to another; drawing, tearing, or jerking pains, worse at night, in a warm room or on altering a position, sensation of paralysis in the parts affected, feeling of coldness on a change of weather; pain relieved by uncovering the limb to the open air.

Colchicum.—An important remedy both in acute and chronic rheumatism. There are lancinating, jerking or tearing pains, worse at night, and aggravated by motion or anxiety; or there may be only stiffness in the joints when attempting to walk, with swelling of the parts in the vicinity of the inflammation.

DOSE.—Two drops, or twelve globules, in a tumbler half full of water; in acute cases a teaspoonful every two or three hours, but in chronic cases, once in six or twelve hours.

Chamomilla.—Dragging, tearing pains with a sensation of numbness or paralysis in the parts affected; pains worse at night; fever with burning or partial heat, preceded by shuddering; great agitation and tossing, with shivering and a desire to remain lying down. Dragging and rheumatic pains in the extremities, worse at night; aching pains on waking.

DOSE.—Two drops, or twelve globules, in a tumbler of water, a tablespoonful once in three or four hours.

Mercurius.—Pains of a shooting, tearing or burning character, aggravated by the warmth of the bed and by cold or damp air, and worse towards morning; swelling and sometimes a sensation of coldness in the parts affected; profuse perspiration but without producing relief. The pains principally affect the joints and bones.

Dose.—A powder, or six globules on the tongue, once in three or four hours.

Nux-v.—Sensation of torpor and numbness in the parts affected with cramps and palpitation in the muscles, sensitiveness to cold, constipation and gastric sufferings. The pains also may be of a tensive or drawing character, and be particularly confined to the chest, loins, and back.

Dose.—A powder, or six globules, once in three or four hours.

It is frequently advisable to alternate it with *Chamomilla.*

Rhododendron.—Pains worse during repose, and aggravated by rough or damp weather.

Dulcamara.—Rheumatism following a severe attack of cold and manifesting itself at night or during repose, and unattended with fever.

Causticum.—Insupportable pains in the open air, relieved in bed or in the warmth of a room; or paralytic weakness or rigidity of the part affected.

Arsenicum.—Burning, tearing pains, worse at night, aggravated by cold air, and relieved by heat.

China.—Pains increased by the slightest touch, with perspiration and paralytic weakness of the part affected.

Ignatia.—Contused or wrenching pains as if the flesh were torn from the bones, worse at night and relieved by a change of posture.

Phosphorus.—Pains excited by the slightest chill, and accompanied with headache and oppression of the chest.

Sulphur.—An exceedingly valuable remedy in nearly all forms of chronic rheumatism, and particularly useful to rouse the system when it has in a measure lost its susceptibility to the appropriate remedy.

Dose.—Of the above remedies two drops, or twelve globules may be mixed with a tumbler of water, and a tablespoonful given at a dose; or a powder, or six globules, may be taken on the tongue. Give once in three, four, or six hours.

Nitric-acid has been a very successful remedy in my own practice both in the acute and chronic forms of rheumatism. The prominent indications are, severe drawing and lacerating pains all over the body; or pains particularly affecting the joints, bones, and the upper and lower limbs. The joints feel weak and bruised, and are exceedingly sensitive, especially after exertion. Pains aggravated by cold or damp air; trembling or numb sensation in the limbs.

DOSE.—Three drops of the first dilution in four tablespoonfuls of water, a tablespoonful once in four or six hours.

In the chronic forms of rheumatism *lemon juice*, or *lemonade* may be given, often with the most happy results. Great benefit may also be derived, especially in chronic cases, where there is a tendency to paralysis, or rigidity of the joints, by the proper application of the "*magnetic battery.*" The poles of the battery should be so applied that a continuous current will pass through the limb or joint, and also through the muscles affected from one end to the other. *Thuja*, *Veratrum*, *Carb.-v.*, *Ferrum*, *Lachesis*, or *Colocynth*, may also be indicated in certain varieties of rheumatism.

DIET AND REGIMEN.—When fever is present, the diet should be similar to that in fevers. Those who are liable to attacks of rheumatism will often find it advantageous to wear next the skin, silk undershirts and drawers.

GOUT.

Arthritis.

A gentleman who had suffered intensely, both from *rheumatism* and *gout*, made quite an appropriate comparison between the two. "Apply," he says, a "thumb-screw to the thumb, and turn it until the pain is as severe as can possibly be endured, and that is *rheumatism*. Now give it one more turn, and you have *gout*.

The nature of the inflammatory action, both in gout and

rheumatism, is undoubtedly the same. An attack of gout is almost always preceded, or accompanied by gastric derangement, and sometimes diarrhœa. The inflammation may attack any of the small joints, although it is generally situated in the ball of the great toe. The integuments are swollen, the pains severe, of a darting, throbbing, burning, or aching character, increased by contact, or movement. The pains are aggravated at night; the urine is passed in small quantities, is high colored, and becomes turbid on standing, the patient is exceedingly restless and irritable. When the paroxysms of gout are of frequent occurrence, a thickening of the articular membrane is produced, calcareous deposits are formed about the joints, and the disease is liable to assume a chronic form.

The disease, as a general thing, though not in all cases, may be looked upon as hereditary. The exciting causes are, high living, abuse of stimulants, particularly wines, want of sufficient exercise, loss of rest, and irregularities in eating. It is generally confined to middle age, or more advanced life.

TREATMENT.—Those in whom there is a strong predisposition to the disease, should be careful to avoid the causes which are liable to produce it. The treatment in all its stages, is similar to that indicated in rheumatism. Consult that disease.

PAIN IN THE SMALL OF THE BACK AND LOINS.

Lumbago.

DIAGNOSIS.—Violent pain of a rheumatic character in the small of the back and loins, either periodical or permanent, and sometimes accompanied with fever. It is frequently produced by cold or strain, and may come on suddenly, without a moment's warning, on suddenly rising from a stooping posture, and cause the most excruciating pain on every attempt to turn, or on the slightest motion. This kind of rheumatic pain often affects the neck, producing what is called *kink* or *crick* in the neck.

TREATMENT.—*Aconite* is the prominent remedy in the commencement of the disease where considerable fever is present.

Dose.—Two drops, or twelve globules, in a tumbler of water, a tablespoonful once in two or three hours; or three globules on the tongue at the same intervals.

Bryonia.—Severe aching or darting pain in the back, causing the patient to walk in a stooping posture, aggravated by the slightest motion, or a draught of cold air, and sometimes attended with a sensation of chilliness.

Dose.—Same as *Aconite.*

Rhus.—Pains of a shooting or dragging character ; severe aching, as from a sprain or bruise ; sensation of stiffness or tension in the affected part on movement ; pain aggravated by rest. A prominent remedy in cases of long standing, and frequently indicated after, or in alternation with *Bryonia.*

Dose.—Same as *Aconite.*

Belladonna.—Deep-seated pains, producing a sensation of heaviness, gnawing or stiffness.

Dose.—Same as *Aconite,* and frequently in alternation with that remedy.

Nux-v.—A valuable remedy in obstinate cases. Pains increased by motion and turning in bed at night, and attended with weakness; pains resembling those produced by a bruise or fatigue ; irritable temper and constipation.

Dose.—A powder, or three globules, once in four or six hours.

Pulsatilla.—Particularly useful in females, or individuals of mild, sensitive, or phlegmatic temperament. Pains resembling those mentioned under the head of *Nux,* but producing a sensation of constriction in the affected parts.

Dose.—Same as *Aconite.* Give once in four or six hours.

Mercurius.—Pains resembling those indicating *Nux,* but aggravated at night.

Dose.—Same as *Nux.* Where the affection is of long duration, the above remedies may be given at longer intervals.

NEURALGIA. PROSOPALGIA. TIC-DOLOUREUX.

This disease may attack every system of nerves, and be developed in every part of the body. Being purely an affection of the nerves, the pain may become most intense and agonizing, sometimes producing delirium. It assumes different names, when developed in different parts of the body. Thus, we have *Prosopalgia*, *Tic-doloureux*, *Nervous headache*, *Angina pectoris*, *&c.* all of which are only varieties of neuralgia.

For Neuralgia of the Stomach, see page 185. Neuralgia of the Abdominal nerves, see *Colic*, page 189. For Nervous headache, see *headache*, page 200.

Of the other forms of neuralgia we shall treat of

1. Facial Neuralgia, sometimes called Prosopalgia or Tic-Doloureux.
2. Angina Pectoris, or neuralgia of the heart.
3. Neuralgia of the spinal marrow.
4. Sciatica.

1. *Neuralgia of the face.*

DIAGNOSIS.—The pain is not continuous, but comes on in paroxysms at irregular intervals. At first it may be slight, like the commencement of a common toothache, but it gradually increases in severity, until the patient may become almost wild with the pain. The pain is of a lancinating, tearing, beating or boring character, and follows the course of the nerve. After the pain has continued a certain length of time, it gradually subsides. The more severe the paroxysm, the shorter its duration. Where the pain commences at a point in the eyebrow directly over the middle of the eye, it generally extends to the eyebrow, forehead, eyelids, and frequently deep in the orbit of the eye. If it commences at a point about the middle of the cheek bone, it may extend over the cheek, lower eyelid, upper lip, and radiate to the teeth, palate, and tongue. Where the pain commences about the middle of the chin, it may extend to the lips, teeth, sides of the tongue, and the soft parts under the chin. Thus, whatever nerve is affected, the pain may be traced along its branches. There may also be a reflex action of the nerves of motion, producing an involuntary twitching of the muscles of the affected part.

The intervals between the paroxysms may be of hours, days, or even weeks' duration, but the longer they continue the more frequent they become, until at length the nerves may become so sensitive that the paroxysm is excited by the slightest emotion, or by the least touch, or exposure to cold air.

CAUSES.—It may be complicated with rheumatism, or be the result of cold, wounds, contusions, affections of the teeth and abdominal organs, suppressed chronic eruptions, carcinomatous, psoric, or syphilitic dyscrasia.

TREATMENT.—*Aconite.*—In inflammatory or rheumatic prosopalgia, where there is considerable heat and swelling. The pain is throbbing, burning, shooting or stitching, worse at night, appearing in paroxysms and accompanied with great sensibility of the whole nervous system.

Belladonna.—Paroxysm commencing with an itching in the affected part, and changing to a violent lancinating, aching, crampy or drawing pain in the check and nasal bones; the pain is on one side, and is frequently accompanied with an increased secretion of saliva or tears. Aggravation of pain from the slightest movement, noise, warmth of a bed, or a current of air. Twitching of the muscles of the face.

DOSE.—Two drops, or twelve globules, in a tumbler half full of water, a tablespoonful during the violence of the paroxysm every half hour or hour, gradually increasing the intervals as the pain abates.

Bryonia.—Particularly in rheumatic persons, and where the pains are of a pressing, drawing, lacerating or piercing character; mitigated by moving the part affected; pains in the limbs, and sometimes chilliness followed by fever.

DOSE.—Two drops, or twelve globules, in a tumbler of water, a tablespoonful every hour or two hours.

Chamomilla.—Great sensibility and extreme restlessness; swelling of the face; redness of one cheek and paleness of the other; drawing, tearing or pulsative pain, with sensation of torpor in the part affected.

DOSE.—Same as *Bryonia*.

China.—Stitching, pressive, or beating pains, particularly in the cheek bones, aggravated by the slightest contact; sensation of torpor, and paralytic weakness in the parts affected.

DOSE.—Same as *Bryonia.*

Colocynth.—Violent rending, or darting pains, principally on the left side of the face, and extending to the ears, temples, nose, and teeth, and all parts of the head, aggravated by the slightest touch.

DOSE.—One drop, or twelve globules, in a tumbler half full of water, a tablespoonful once in one or two hours.

Coffea.—Insupportable pain, and great excitability of the nervous system.

Arsenicum.—Violent burning, or tearing pain, worse at night, or during repose, and relieved by the application of external heat. Great prostration, and sometimes a sensation of coldness in the affected parts. Tendency to periodicity in the attacks.

DOSE.—A powder, or six globules, once in two or three hours.

Hepar-s.—Pains in the bones of the face, aggravated by the slightest touch; aggravation in the evening.

Platina.—Sensation of coldness, or torpor in the affected part, with severe spasmodic pain; or tensive pressure in the bones adjoining the ear, with a sensation of creeping or crawling; worse in the evening, or at rest.

DOSE.—A powder, or six globules, once in two or three hours.

Spigelia.—Violent tearing or jerking pain, aggravated by the slightest touch, or by movement of the parts, or pains appearing to shoot from the centre of the brain to the sides of the head; pains of an aching, pressive character, sometimes with glossy swelling of the affected part.

DOSE.—Same as *Belladonna.*

Rhus.—Stinging, burning, or drawing pain, or pain as from subcutaneous ulceration; worse during repose and in the open air, and relieved by movement or warmth.

DOSE.—Same as *Bryonia*, with which it may sometimes be alternated.

Mercurius.—In rheumatic persons, with aggravation of pain at night, and nightly perspiration; sensation of coldness in the parts affected, and great debility.

DOSE.—A powder, or three globules, once in two or three hours.

Nux-v.—Especially in persons addicted to spirituous liquors, and those of a lively and choleric temperament, or those who lead a sedentary life. Drawing and jerking pain, aggravated in bed, in the cold air, and during meditation.

DOSE.—A powder, or three globules, once in three or four hours.

Pulsatilla.—Lacerating and pulsative pain on one side, worse on lying down and during repose; relieved in the open air. Particularly useful in women and persons of a mild or timid character.

DOSE.—Same as *Bryonia.*

Sabina.—Pains of a violent lacerating and throbbing character, occurring during menstruation.

DOSE.—One drop, in a tumbler of water, or three globules on the tongue. Give every hour or two hours.

Kalmia.—This remedy has been given with marked success in the more violent forms of Prosopalgia, where the pains are of a violent lacerating or throbbing character.

DOSE.—Three drops, in six tablespoonfuls of water, a tablespoonful every hour.

Where the pain is excessively violent, it may be advisable to bathe the parts with a mixture, composed of six parts of *Aconite*, to four tablespoonfuls of water. *Staphysagria* may also be applied in the same manner. The external application may be warm or cold, according to the feelings of the patient.

2. ANGINA PECTORIS.

Neuralgia of the heart.

Diagnosis.—Intense and terrible pain in the region of the heart, coming on in paroxysms, and extending over the chest, neck, and arms, and accompanied with sensation of fainting. The pain varies in intensity, the breathing may be apparently arrested, or be exceedingly difficult and attended with moaning; the pulse is generally small and feeble, and during the paroxysm, the face and extremities may be covered with a cold sweat.

Causes.—It may arise from abuse of spirituous drinks, errors in diet, dyspepsy, rheumatism or gout, and is not unfrequently connected with organic disease of the heart.

Treatment.—During the paroxysm the patient should remain perfectly quiet, in an erect position, and be relieved from all external pressure.

Arsenicum.—This is a valuable remedy, where the patient is unable to breathe, except with his chest bent forward; oppressive stitching in the region of the heart, with fainting and anguish; the attack is renewed or aggravated by the least motion.

Digitalis is indicated where the action of the heart is violent, or where the disease sets in suddenly, and there are present, drawing or spasmodic pains in the left chest and sternum, the neck and arms, and sometimes a deathly anguish.

Belladonna.—Difficult and hurried respirations with moaning; tensive shooting or pressive pain in the vicinity of the heart; tremor of the heart, with anguish and an aching pain.

Rhus.—Violent pulsative stitches, in the region of the heart, sometimes with painful lameness and numbness of the left arm; palpitation of the heart; difficulty of breathing.

Spigelia.—Great difficulty of breathing. Dull or oppressive stitches in the region of the heart; cutting, lacerating, or tensive and drawing pain; violent palpitation of the heart.

If other remedies are required, *Iodine*, *Mercury*, *Phospho-*

rus, and *Veratrum*. See also "Facial Neuralgia," and "Materia Medica."

Dose.—Two drops, or twelve globules, in a tumbler of water, a tablespoonful at a dose; or six globules, or a powder, on the tongue. In violent paroxysms, give every half hour or hour, gradually increasing the intervals as the pain abates.

3. *Neuralgia of the Spinal Marrow.*

Diagnosis.—Pain in the back, with convulsive paroxysms in the internal body, or in the organ in relation with the affected portion of the spinal marrow. When the disease is in the upper portion of the marrow, it may affect the head, causing severe pain there, dizziness, amaurosis, buzzing in the ears, deafness, delirium, and stiffness of the neck. If the affection is in the lower cervical portion, its effects are felt in the chest, arms, and throat, producing serious pain and paralysis, spasms of the throat, hiccough and oppression, or palpitation of the heart. If the upper dorsal portion be affected, we have spasmodic cough, palpitation of the heart, fainting fits, moaning and pains below the false ribs. If the lower dorsal portion is diseased, there may be pain in the stomach, derangement of the digestive functions, and difficulty in urinating. If the lumbar portion is affected, we may have colic, almost paralysis of the limbs, and drawing in the testicles.

As this disease may be somewhat complicated in its character, it will always be best to consult a physician. Among the prominent remedies, we may enumerate, *Belladonna*, *Rhus*, *Staphysagria*, *Conium*, *Veratrum*, *Sabina*, *Colocynth*, *Aurum*, and *Nux-v*. See Neuralgia of the face, also Materia Medica.

4. SCIATICA.

Pain in the Hip.

Diagnosis.—Pain in the region of the hip, frequently extending to the knee and foot, and following the course of the sciatic nerve. By its severity it may not only produce violent pain, but stiffness and contraction of the limb. The pain manifests itself not only during motion, but also during repose.

This, as well as other diseases of the hip, and also of the knee-joint, should not be neglected, but the advice of a physician immediately obtained.

TREATMENT.—When the attack is accompanied with considerable fever, *Aconite* may be given, if the pain is violent, in alternation with *Belladonna*, or *Bryonia*.

Belladonna.—Where the slightest motion increases the pain; the skin of the part affected is red and shining, and burning fever may be present.

Bryonia.—The symptoms are similar to those indicating *Belladonna*, with the exception that the parts affected are not as red, but quite as painful; constipation may also be present.

Rhus.—The pains are darting, tearing or dragging, attended with tension and stiffness in the muscles, and aggravated during rest; painful sensibility of the joint when rising from a sitting posture.

Ignatia.—Pains of an incisive nature, particularly on moving the limb. It is highly useful where the disease occurs in persons of a mild or melancholic temperament.

Colocynth.—Sensation as if a tight band were around the hips and back, the pains running down from the regions of the kidneys into the legs; pain excited or aggravated by anger or indignation.

Pulsatilla.—Pains worse toward evening, during the night and when seated, but relieved in the open air.

Nux-v.—Pains aggravated toward morning, and attended with a sensation of stiffness and contraction, also of paralysis, torpor and chilliness, in the parts affected.

Arsenicum.—Burning pains or sensation of coldness in the affected parts; acute dragging pain, with great restlessness, occasional intermission of pain, with periodical returns; pain relieved by external warmth; weakness and disposition to lie down.

Among the other remedies sometimes indicated, we may mention: *Veratrum*, *Chamomilla*, *Conium*, *Staphysagria*, *Hepar-s.*, *Phosphorus*, and *Sepia*, *Sulphur*, *Mercury*, and *Lachesis*.

DOSE.—Two drops, or twelve globules, in a tumbler, of water, a tablespoonful at a dose; or a powder, or three globules on the tongue. In severe cases give a dose every two or three hours. If the disease assumes a chronic character, a dose once in six or twelve hours will be sufficient.

PARALYSIS.

Palsy.

DIAGNOSIS.—There is a partial or total loss of voluntary motion and sometimes of sensation. Certain portions of the body may be in a state of paralysis and other parts as active and vigorous as ever. Thus the arm may be paralyzed, and also certain muscles of the face. Where it follows apoplexy there is generally paralysis of the whole of one side of the body from the head to the feet. This is called *Hemiplegia.*

When there is a loss of voluntary motion only, the affected parts become soft from want of action and wither away.

TREATMENT.—Consult a physician without delay, for if taken in time a cure may often be affected, while, if the disease is allowed to run on, it may soon be out of the reach of aid.

Rhus.—An important remedy where there is great sensitiveness to cold air, general debility and languor; tingling or itching in the paralyzed parts. Lameness in the extremities and joints, with stiffness, worse on rising, after having been seated for some time. Paralysis of one side or of the lower extremities, with dragging, slow, difficult walking. Particularly useful when caused by nervous fevers.

Nux-v.—Paralysis, particularly of the lower extremities; trembling of the limbs; cramps and spasmodic twitching of the parts; heaviness and stiffness of the limbs, sensitiveness to cold air. Especially when brought on by the use of stimulants, narcotics, or from a too sedentary life.

Among the other important remedies, we may enumerate: *Belladonna, Bryonia, Cuprum, Secale, Plumbum, Cocculus, Stannum, Kali-carb., Natrum-mur.,* and *Sulphur.*

Cuprum is a prominent remedy where the attack sets in after Asiatic cholera, nervous or typhoid fever, or apoplexy.

Secale where the paroxysms are of frequent recurrence. *Natrum-mur.* is a valuable remedy where the paralysis is caused by sexual debauchery, onanism, violent passion, anger or chagrin. The electro-magnetic battery will often establish a cure when all other means fail.

Dose.—The remedy may be given once or twice a day.

EPILEPSY.

There are convulsive motions, with entire loss of consciousness; falling down with cries and foam at the mouth; the thumbs are flexed into the palm of the hand. The attacks occur in paroxysms, each paroxysm having two stages. The first or convulsive stage may last from a few minutes up to two or three hours, when it passes into the second or the soporous or apoplectic stage. Sometimes the attack comes on without any premonition, when the patient, no matter where he may be, falls senseless to the earth, as if struck by lightning. Sometimes, however, there are premonitory symptoms, such as, headache and nausea. The attacks may come on at certain periods but more frequently at indefinite times. The disease is difficult to cure and the attacks may continue through life, ending in weakness of the mental faculties, and sometimes almost idiocy. It must be borne in mind that in epilepsy, the convulsions, however weak they may be, are attended with entire loss of consciousness, while convulsions, even of the most violent character, if the patient still retain a certain amount of consciousness, are not epileptic.

Treatment.—In the treatment of this disease almost every thing depends in getting at the correct cause, hence the case should be submitted to a careful physician. During the paroxysm particular pains should be taken to prevent the patient hurting himself from his violent motions. A small piece of pine wood or a piece of cork may also be placed between his teeth. Two drops of *Belladonna* may be mixed in a tumbler half full of water, and a teaspoonful given as soon as he can swallow, every fifteen or twenty minutes. During the second or soporous stage, *Opium* may be given in the same way, a dose once in a half hour or hour.

CHOREA.

St. Vitus's Dance.

This disease may occur as an epidemic, particularly when large crowds meet, some of whom are laboring under some violent excitement. It most frequently, however occurs in the female at the time of development of puberty, from the seventh to the sixteenth year.

There are involuntary motions of single members, or the whole body, wandering from one part to the other. These motions are exceedingly variable in their character. Sometimes there are violent jerks of different parts of the body; if of the arm, whatever is in the hand at the time is thrown down with violence; sometimes there are violent contortions of the muscles of the face, again the patient may, against his will dance for hours, or run for miles until completely exhausted. It differs from epilepsy in one important particular, the convulsions are *never* attended with loss of consciousness.

It would be impossible in a work like this to detail the treatment of this disease, as the practiced judgment of the physician is necessary to conduct the cure. The galvanic battery will be found an important remedy. The system should be strengthened, and to this end, the body should be bathed with cold water, out-door exercise taken, and violent excitement avoided.

TETANUS.

Trismus, or Lockjaw.

By tetanus we understand sudden contractions or cramps, long-continued and violent twitching of the voluntary muscles of various parts of the body. Generally the muscles most easily affected are those of the neck, jaws, and throat. The patient feels an uneasiness in bending or turning the head, at length there is difficulty in opening the mouth, and this is shortly followed by closing of the jaws, either gradually, but with great firmness, or suddenly, and with a snap. Soon the muscles connected with swallowing become affected, and this is shortly followed by a severe acute pain in the lower part of the sternum, piercing through to the back. The pain is subject to aggravation in paroxysms, the spasms extending to the muscles of the *trunk*; to the large muscles of the *extremities;* the muscles of the *face*, and so on until all the voluntary muscles of the body may become fixed. As the disease advances, the spasms increase in frequency and violence, and are attended with intense pain. Where the contractions or spasms are confined to the lower jaw, the disease is generally called "*trismus* or *lockjaw*."

CAUSES.—The most common causes are punctured and lacerated wounds, which injure one or more of the nerves. It is more liable to follow punctured wounds in the extremities than in the trunk. Taking cold in wounds, the irritating effects of splintered bones and foreign substance, such as, dirt, rust, &c., also blows upon the back may lead to *tetanus*. It sometimes, although much more rarely, follows suppressed menstruation, low fevers and violent exertion of the mind and body.

TREATMENT.—The exciting cause should be ascertained and removed if possible.

Nux-v.—This is a highly important remedy in almost every variety of tetanus. It is especially indicated where the spasms are frequent and short, and there are cramp-like pains in the region of the stomach, constipation and loss of appetite. If the patient has been addicted to the use of spirituous liquors, the indications for the remedy will be still more apparent.

DOSE.—A powder, or six globules on the tongue every hour.

Arnica.—This remedy may be used with advantage as an external application in those injuries which threaten to lead to tetanus. Six drops may be mixed with three tablespoonfuls of water, and the wound washed with the mixture three or four times a day. Two drops also may be mixed in a tumbler half full of water, and a tablespoonful given at the same intervals.

Belladonna may be given where the disease affects principally the extremities, and where it is occasioned by deranged menstruation and difficulties connected with the utero-genital system; also where delirium is present.

DOSE.—Two drops, or twelve globules, in a tumbler of water, a tablespoonful every two, three, or four hours. *Pulsatilla* may be given with advantage after *Belladonna*, at the same intervals.

Should there be great rigidity of the extremities, wild and fixed look, and difficult respiration and deglutition, *Stramonium* will be indicated in alternation with *Hyosciamus*. Give every hour or two hours, prepared same as *Belladonna*.

Warm bathing and the external application of hot fomentations are often productive of decided relief. Among the other remedies which may be indicated we may enumerate, *Veratrum*, *Hydrocianic-acid*, *Phosphorus*, and *Camphor*.

HYDROPHOBIA.

This is one of the most fearful and agonizing diseases on record, and what adds still more to the terror inspired by its name, but very little success has as yet been met with, in its treatment.

DIAGNOSIS.—The disease follows the bite of a rabid animal, not however immediately. The wound may seem perfectly healthy, and heal as kindly as if no poison had been infused into it by the bite of the animal. In the course however of a period, varying from three weeks to eighteen months,—and some say years may elapse,—the premonitory symptoms set in. The bitten parts present a livid and slightly swollen appearance, which is accompanied by burning heat and sharp pain, extending toward the central part of the body. Very soon after this local irritation commences, sometimes even in a few hours, the specific constitutional symptoms begin. The patient is hurried and irritable; there is pain and stiffness about the neck and throat, and every attempt to swallow fluids brings on a paroxysm of choking and sobbing. As the disease advances, the eyes become red and brilliant, and highly sensitive to light, the cramps about the throat, neck, and chest, more and more violent, until the sight of liquid or any shining substance, or even the passing of a gust of wind over the face, produce the most painful paroxysm. A viscid saliva is constantly secreted, and notwithstanding the most intense thirst is present, the patient cannot drink for fear of bringing on the fearful spasm. As the disease advances, the old wound opens and discharges an offensive substance, respiration becomes more difficult, the countenance is haggard, the eyes sunken, but still brilliant; there is delirium of a wandering or violent character, constant inclination to bite, loss of voice, sinking of the pulse, until at length, death comes, as a welcome messenger to relieve the poor victim of his tortures.

TREATMENT.—Where a person has been bitten by an animal supposed to be rabid, the bitten part should be immediately cut out or cauterized with caustic potash or some other burning substance. *Belladonna* may be used as a preventative and also during the disease. As a preventative, six globules may be taken every other night for two weeks. During the disease two drops, or twelve globules, may be mixed with a tumbler of water, and a tablespoonful given every hour or two hours.

Nux-v., *Stramonium*, *Hyosciamus*, *Lachesis*, and *Veratrum* may be of service given as in *tetanus*.

DELIRIUM TREMENS.

Mania à potu.

This disease is so well known as to require but slight description here. It is met with in every grade of society, from the high to the low, among the rich and the poor. Among the so-called higher classes of society, it very often receives the name of nervous fever, or inflammation of the brain, while among the poor it is called by its blunt and appropriate name, "*delirium tremens.*"

This disease, as a general thing, is produced by a long-continued use of spirituous liquors. We sometimes find it, however, in those who are not in the least addicted to this detestable vice, but whose nervous system has been overstrained by other modes of strong excitement. Thus, the long-continued mental anxiety in which gamblers and great speculators are accustomed to live, may cause it.

Diagnosis.—This disease is sometimes mistaken for inflammation of the brain, yet when observed even with but little care, the difference is very apparent.

The face may be red and the eyes blood shot. There is a rapid pulse, wildness of look and constant fidgeting with the hands, and sometimes tremor of the limbs. The delirium is generally a *busy* delirium; whatever he does is done in a hurried manner, and with a sort of anxiety to perform it properly. There is great sleeplessness, frequently an entire absence of sleep for several days and nights; constant chattering. The tongue is moist and creamy, the pulse though frequent, soft, and the skin moist. Ask the patient a question, and he may answer it properly, but immediately his thoughts are wandering to things which exist only in his imagination. His thoughts are generally distressing and anxious; he is giving orders about his business or persons who are absent, or devising plans of escape from some imaginary enemy, or starting in terror at the hideous reptiles which he thinks he distinctly sees all around him. He seldom meditates harm, the delirium more frequently being combined with a mixture of cowardice and fear.

Treatment.—*Opium.*—This is one of the most prominent remedies in the treatment of this disease. There are rapid and constant motions; wild and staring expression; tremor of the hands and limbs; frightful or fantastic visions, confusion of ideas, and sometimes stupefaction and inclination to commit suicide.

Nux-v.—Trembling of the limbs; spasmodic twitching in different parts of the body; vomiting or pressure and burning in the stomach; constipation, headache, coldness of the extremities; depression of spirits; constant uneasiness, anguish, and desire to run away; troublesome visions.

Belladonna.—Congestion of blood to the head, flushed face, injected eyes, boisterous delirium; great nervous excitement; trembling of the limbs, and visions.

Stramonium and *Hyosciamus* are also valuable remedies, especially where there are convulsive movements, great excitability, rapid motions, picking at imaginary objects, and muttering delirium.

DOSE.—Two drops of the remedy, in a tumbler of water, a tablespoonful every hour, until relief is obtained.

TUBERCULOSIS. SCROPHULOSIS.
Scrofula.

We have already referred to some of the varieties of this disease, and the causes which contribute the most to its development. (*See page* 84.) It might with propriety be called "*Parent of diseases,*" as it is the fruitful source of almost an innumerable variety. It is, as a general thing hereditary, taints the whole system, and may be developed in any organ of the body; even the bones furnish frightful evidences of its ravages. It may remain latent in the system for years, but be developed in all its virulence in some weakened organ, or in a system prostrated by disease, anxiety, or dissipation.

A tuberculous constitution may be indicated by the following appearances; large head, short, thick neck, light hair, fair skin and rosy cheeks, generally blue eyes and large pupils; the form may be full and rounded, but the flesh is soft and flabby; frequent bleeding at the nose, and accumulation of mucus in the lungs, trachea, nose, and intestinal canal.

The prominent symptoms are, glandular swellings and indurations on the neck, below the jaw, the nape of the neck, axilla, groins, and finally in almost every part of the body. The swellings are at first soft, painless and moveable, but afterward become larger, harder, painful, inflamed, and finally suppurate and form scrofulous ulcers. As we have said before, almost every tissue and organ of the body may be attacked by this disease.

It may attack the mucuous membrane of the nose, commencing with a swelling and redness about the wings of the nose, and attended with a thin offensive discharge which frequently blocks up the nose.

The stomach and liver may also be the seat of tuberculosis, as well as the spleen, intestines, throat, lungs, brain, spinal marrow, eyes, ears, bones, joints, &c. A frequent form in which scrofula is developed is *Scrofulous Ophthalmia*; in this variety there is an extreme sensitiveness to light, even the slightest ray producing intense pain. An eruption generally appears during the inflammation on the cheeks near the eyes, into which they frequently extend, producing ulcers which may destroy sight.

White swelling and Hip disease, are other forms of scrofula in which the joints and the membrane which surrounds them are diseased. These diseases are generally slow in their progress, at first pain only being felt after exercise. As the disease advances, the cartilages and other substances which compose the joint, become so thickened that the joint becomes immoveable. If the disease is still allowed to progress, suppuration takes place, accompanied with emaciation, hectic fever, great prostration, and night-sweats soon terminating in death.

Rachitis or *Rickets*, is another variety of scrofula affecting principally the bones, and usually making its appearance between the ninth month and the second year. This is a morbid alteration of the bones, characterized by swelling, softening and deformity. The head is large and heavy, and sinks on the shoulders. The softened bones are unable to retain their shape; hence the shoulders stand out, the spinal column is curved, and lasting deformity of different parts of the system may be the result, as well as serious diseases occasioned by the contraction of internal organs.

I have already spoken of the tubercles of the lungs, in the article on Pulmonary Consumption. It would be impossible in our limited space, to go into the minutiæ of the almost innumerable variety of diseases produced either in part, or entirely by a tuberculous taint. It will be only necessary to refer the reader to the diseases under their respective heads, and to the "*Symptomatic Index.*"

CAUSES.—The prominent causes of hereditary tuberculosis have been given in the chapter on the causes of disease. See page 84. But the disease as we there remarked is not always hereditary. It may be produced in childhood by nursing from a scrofulous or syphilitic nurse, or even be introduced into the child by vaccination, the pus being taken from one in whom there was a constitutional taint. Living in impure, damp, or moist cold air; in a general neglect of cleanliness, and eating heavy indigestible food in the first years of infancy. Violent astringent medicines which impede and stop the salutary motions of nature, and measles, small pox, scarlet fever, and those other diseases which tend to weaken the lymphatic system, may also produce it.

TREATMENT.—The treatment should be in a great measure constitutional. The food should be healthy, and easy of digestion, but highly nutritious. Vegetables combined with animal food may be used, but rich gravies and highly oily substances should be avoided. A moderate use also of porter, ale, and light wines may be advisable. Cleanliness, bathing the entire body daily, and a daily change of linen are essential, as well as pure air, and active muscular exercise.

The most prominent remedies in the treatment of the various forms of Scrofula are, *Sulphur*, *Calcarea*, *Iodine*, *Ferrum*, *Mercury*, *Aurum*, *China*, *Belladonna*, *Conium*, *Hepar-s.*, *Sepia*, *Barita*, *Dulcamara*, and *Rhus.*

Sulphur.—Its prominent indications are, ulcers on various parts of the body; humid eruptions on the head, behind the ears, and discharge from the ears; eruption about the eyes, and inflammation of the eyes, sometimes with ulcers on the cornea, great intolerance of light and swelling and inflammation of the lids; swelling and sometimes suppuration of the glands; white swelling of the knee and pain in the knee and hip joints; pulmonary cough, with sticking pains in the chest and purulent expectoration; swelling of the nose with offensive discharge.

Dose.—In acute cases, a powder, once in six hours, in chronic cases, every night.

Rhus.—Eruptions and soft tubercles on the scalp; inflammation of the eyes, with eruption around them, and great sensitiveness to light; eyelids itch, are swollen and inflamed; scurfy eruptions on different parts of the body; swelling of the glands about the neck and throat; enlargement of the bones and inflammation in the hip and knee-joints; stiffness and lameness of the limbs, and sensitiveness to the air; stitches in the chest, and short painful cough; crusty eruption in the nose and about the mouth.

Dose.—Six globules, once in twelve or twenty-four hours.

Iodine.—Enlargement and induration of the glands; rough and dry skin and emaciation; inflammation of the knee, with swelling, catarrhal affections of the mucous membrane; inflammation and swelling in the liver; abdomen tumid, with pain on pressure; cough and pain in the chest; swelling and pain in the bronchial glands, and hectic fever.

Dose.—Same as *Rhus.*

Calcarea.—This is an exceedingly valuable remedy in almost every stage of tuberculosis, particularly in glandular swellings and softening of the bones. It is also highly indicated in the scrofulous ophthalmia of children, especially where there are ulcers on the cornea; also scrofulous eruptions and ulcers in children. It follows well after *Sulphur*, *Mercurius*, or *Hepar-s.*, and may be followed with advantage by *Silicea*, or *Iodine.*

Dose.—A powder, or six globules, morning and night.

Hepar-s.—Particularly where the tumors and enlarged glands are in a state of suppuration, and where the ulcers discharge a thin and offensive matter; also in Ophthalmia where there is a profuse secretion of tears, and a considerable mucous discharge.

Dose.—Same as *Calcarea.*

Mercury will be found of great advantage where there is inflammation of the eyes, with danger of ulceration; inflammation, pain, and swelling of the glands; eruptions and ulcers on the body, and affections of the bones and joints.

DOSE.—Same as *Calcarea*.

Belladonna.—Glandular swelling, with inflammation and suppuration. Inflammation of the eyes, with heat, redness, and great sensitiveness to light, severe pain in the ball of the eye; swelling of the bones, of the lips, nose and tonsils, bleeding of the gums; roaring in the ears, soreness of the throat, &c.

DOSE.—Two drops, or twelve globules, in a tumbler of water, a tablespoonful in acute cases, every three or four hours; in chronic cases every night.

Baryta.—Scrofulous affections of the ears, with discharge of purulent matter; pain in the joints and bones; sore throat, especially after a cold; chronic inflammation of the eyelids; scrofulous eruptions and ulcerations.

DOSE.—A powder, or six globules, at night.

Sepia is particularly useful in females affected with derangement of the menstrual functions, and *Aurum*, *Ferrum*, and *Phosphorus* will be found of great advantage in obstinate cases, especially where the strength is running down.

DOSE.—Same as *Baryta*.

Bryonia will be found a most valuable remedy in tuberculous affections of the chest, characterized by rheumatic or aching pain in the chest and cough.

DOSE.—Same as *Belladonna*.

CANCER.

Carcinoma.

This malignant disease may be correctly classed under the head of Dyscrasia. Like tuberculosis, taken in its incipient stage it can be in a measure held back if not entirely eradicated, but permit it once to fasten its talons firmly in the system, and its progress is as a general thing steadily onward, notwithstanding the utmost effort of human skill to arrest its march, until its victims, are relieved from pain by the welcome summons of death.

Cancer may properly divided into three species, viz., scirrhus; encephaloid or brain-like cancer; and colloid or gum-like cancer.

Scirrhus is characterized by great hardness. It is as firm as a cartilage, and creaks when divided by a knife. The surfaces, exposed by its division, present a glistening, satiny appearance and a white, or grey, or bluish-white color.

The *encephaloid cancer* is composed in a great measure of a soft white, opaque pulpy substance, very closely resembling, both in color and consistency, that of the healthy brain. This pulp is traversed and circumscribed by fibrous septa. In the *colloid* or gum-like cancer, there is exhibited an appearance of small portions of a greenish-yellow transparent gum, or jelly, arranged in regular cells. Hence it is sometimes called *alveolar* cancer.

These three varieties may, notwithstanding the dissimilarity of their appearance, coexist in different organs of the same individual. If a tumor of one growth be amputated, and, as is often the case, a fresh growth springs from the same place, this secondary growth may be of another species. Occurring in any one part of the body, they are exceedingly prone to multiply in other parts, so that if one is removed by the surgeon's knife, the probability is that the disease will soon be developed in some other part of the body, if not in the same spot.

Cancerous growths are attended during some portion of their progress with severe pain; they enlarge in bulk sometimes slowly, at others with great rapidity, changing tissues and eating away contiguous parts, breaking out when near the surface into repulsive ulceration and ultimately destroying life. Vital parts are slowly disorganized by the corroding extension of these tumors and sometimes large blood-vessels are laid open, producing death by hæmorrhage.

This disease is liable to attack every organ and tissue of the body: the brain, the eye, the lip and face, the lungs, the stomach, the intestines, the liver, the kidneys, the breast, the womb, the testicles, the bones, all may suffer from its frightful ravages. Among the parts, however, which are more frequently attacked than others, we may mention, the female mammæ, the uterus, the stomach, liver and testicle.

The edges of a cancerous ulcer are generally hard, ragged, unequal and very painful. The whole surface of the sore is also unequal. The discharge is a thin, dark-colored, and fetid ichor, and in the advanced stages considerable blood is lost. A burning heat is felt over the ulcerated surface, and shooting or lancinating pains. When it occurs in the female breast, it is more liable to commence at that period, when the uterine functions are about to cease.

In *cancer of the stomach*, there is but little perceptible difference between its earliest features and those of common nervous dispepsy. In both, flatus, acid eructations, and weight in the stomach are present. At length, in cancer, decided pain is felt, in a little time becoming oppressive and shooting from the stomach into the back and loins, down the thighs. Nausea sets in, and the food is rejected, mixed with quantities of ropy mucus, by which the pain and oppression are relieved. The appetite cannot be indulged in to satisfaction from the aggravation of symptoms, which full meals and certain kinds of food induce. The bowels are generally costive. In this first stage of the disease under the influence of some cause evident or undiscovered, all, or nearly all the symptoms may rapidly vanish and continue suspended for weeks or months, but at length a time arrives, when the disease takes firm possession.

A visible wasting now sets in, increasing as the malady advances to a frightful emaciation. The pain in the stomach may become constant, but aggravated after a meal. If the appetite still remain, the wretched patient fears to satisfy the craving, from the violent pain produced by the entrance of food, and the vomiting he knows will ensue. The vomiting no longer produces relief, but increases the distress, and may be brought on by the smallest quantity of food. Suffering now becomes habitual, and unmistakeable signs of anguish are planly stamped on every feature. Beside the food vomited, various other matters are thrown from the stomach. Of these, the most common are fluids, containing a dark substance like coffee-grounds, uncoagulated blood, a thick poraceous matter, or finally a dark green serum. Debility gradually seizes on all the functions, until at length the patient, wasted almost to skin and bones, the pain and vomiting cease, and death comes without a struggle, a welcome messenger to free the poor victim from the agony he has so long endured.

TREATMENT.—Very much depends on the proper treatment, during the percursory stage. Then, the disease may be held in check or perhaps entirely eradicated, while, if allowed to go on, it becomes so firmly seated, as in the majority of cases to terminate fatally.

Arsenic is undoubtedly the prominent remedy in all forms of cancer. Where the cancer attacks the face, lips, checks, nose, or tongue, its indications may be seen in the burning swelling in the nose, painful to the touch; ulceration of the nostrils with discharge of fetid ichor; ulcers in the whole face; wart-shaped ulcer on the check; ulcerated eruption around the lips, with burning pain, particularly when the parts become cold; spreading ulcer on the lip, tearing and smarting during motion.

When the disease is in the stomach, its indications are equally apparent. There is a burning, corrosive and gnawing pain in the pit and region of the stomach, oppressive anguish, cutting and tearing pain, alternating with the corrosive and burning pain. Great prostration, vomiting of food and mucus, and aggravation of symptoms after a meal.

Nux-vom. is indicated in cancer of the stomach, where there are pressive griping or crampy sensation; oppression and sensation of constriction of the chest; nausea, belching up of sour or bitter fluid, constipation, palpitation of the heart and flatulence.

Mezerium will also be of benefit in this variety of cancer, where there are burning, corrosive pains in the stomach; sensation as if the food remained a long time undigested, and sometimes vomiting of blood.

Plumbum may produce relief, where there is obstinate constipation; vomiting without relief, consisting of greenish, blackish, or bitter substances, and paroxysms of burning, constrictive pains in the stomach.

Dose.—A powder, or three globules, of the above remedies dry on the tongue, morning and night.

Aurum may be indicated in most forms of cancer, especially when not only the soft parts, but the bones are affected.

Calcerea.—Polypi in the nose, which may degenerate into cancer; also pimples, scurfs, and ulcers high up in the nostrils and around the lips, accompanied with swelling, which by their long duration may end in cancer.

Silicea has been found of great benefit, when there are suppurating glandular swellings, scirrhous indurations, putrid spreading ulcers, scurfs and ulcers in the nose, on the lips, and face.

Dose.—A powder, or three globules, dry on the tongue, every night.

Besides the remedies, already enumerated, we may mention as deserving attention: *Conium, Sepia, Sulphur, Hepar-s., Thuja, Nitric.-ac., Mercury, Staphysagria* and *Lachesis*.

Diet and Regimen.—The diet should be nourishing and easy of digestion. Meats and the more solid articles of food should be preferred to watery vegetables. The character of the food also must be guided in a great measure by the feelings of the patient, carefully avoiding those varieties, experience has proved injurious.

DROPSY.

Dropsy is a common term, signifying effusion into the cellular tissue, or into any of the natural cavities of the body. To enter into an explanation of the causes of this effusion would lead us into a broader field, than the design of this work would admit, a field, which would be in a measure uninteresting to the general reader. It will only be necessary for us then to briefly describe some of the varieties of this disease and the treatment. We shall here speak of three varieties:

1. *Anasarca, or cellular Dropsy.*
2. *Ascites, or Abdominal Dropsy.*
3. *Hydrothorax, or Dropsy of the chest.*

1. ANASARCA, OR CELLULAR DROPSY.

This variety generally first manifests itself in the lower extremities, especially after standing or walking, gradually extending upwards, until the cellular tissue of the whole system becomes involved. The swelling is generally soft and doughy, leaving a dent on pressure, and the skin white and shining. When confined to the lower extremities, it may exist for years with but little danger, but it seldom pervades the whole system, unless the system has become seriously impaired.

CAUSES.—It is frequently produced by abuse of *Arsenic* and *Mercury*. Loss of blood, abuse of stimulants, derangement of the womb, scarlatina, measles, pulmonary consumption, &c.

2. ASCITES, OR ABDOMINAL DROPSY.

Dropsy of the belly is often the result of inflammation of the bowels, or peritoneal inflammation, or it may come on almost imperceptibly from some constitutional disturbance. There is a gradual enlargement of the abdomen, generally commencing in the vicinity of the stomach, and afterwards extending over the entire abdomen. There is difficulty of breathing on taking exercise, sallow complexion, dry skin, and scanty secretion of high-colored urine. Also a general feeling of languor and debility, and stiffness, particularly when attempting to bend the body.

3. HYDROTHORAX, OR DROPSY IN THE CHEST.

The most common causes of this affection are, organic disease of the heart, and protracted pleuritic inflammation.

The symptoms are the most urgent when the patient has remained for some time in a recumbent posture. The breathing is rapid and labored, and the countenance distressed, pallid and wax-like. Shortness of breath occurs from the slightest exercise, and the pulsations of the heart are irregular. Dropsy of the heart is a frequent attendant on hydrothorax.

TREATMENT.—The prominent remedies in the cure of dropsy are *Apis mel*, *Apocynum cannabium*, *Arsenicum*, *Digitalis*, *China*, *Hellebore*, *Colchicum*, *Asparagus*, *Cantharides*, *Hyd. potassa*, *Mercurius*, *Crotalus* and *Dulcamara*.

Apis mel.—This is a most important remedy in general dropsy, but particularly in *ascites* and *hydrothorax*. The prominent symptoms are anxious respiration and sensation of fullness and constriction in the chest; fullness and tenderness of the abdomen, harsh, dry skin, diminished secretion and sometimes painful emission of urine, impaired appetite and debility.

DOSE.—A powder every six or twelve hours, according to the severity of the symptoms.

Apocynum can. is a very valuable remedy, particularly in abdominal dropsy, after the use of *Quinine*, in intermittent fevers, in general dropsy, succeeding scarlet fever, and also in other varieties of the disease.

DOSE.—Three drops in a tumbler of water, a tablespoonful once in six or twelve hours. In acute cases once in three or four hours.

Arsenicum.—In the different varieties of dropsy, especially when they are accompanied by an earthy or pale and greenish color of the skin; great weakness and general prostration; dryness and redness of the tongue; asthmatic sufferings, with suffocating sensation when lying on the back, coldness of extremities; great thirst; loss of appetite, tenderness of the abdomen, small secretion of urine, with frequent desire to urinate; difficult respiration; blisters or dark colored spots on different parts of the body.

DOSE.—A powder, or six globules; in acute cases, once

in three or four hours; in the chronic form every twelve hours.

Digitalis.—Scanty secretion of high colored urine, strong pulsations of the heart, irregularity of the pulse, pale face and blue lips; vertigo, distension of the abdomen, frequent desire to urinate, stitches in the region of the heart. This remedy is strongly indicated in hydrothorax, occasioned by disease of the heart.

Hellebore.—Swelling of the face and lips; fluctuating swelling in the abdomen; great debility, nausea, piercing pains in the extremities; throbbing or compressive pain in the head; frequent desire to urinate with an almost entire suppression of the secretions.

Dose.—Two drops, or eight globules, in a tumbler of water, a tablespoonful once in from four to twelve hours.

Dulcamara.—Particularly for dropsy, occasioned by suppressed perspiration, and where the skin is dry and hot, the whole body bloated, the urine small in quantity, turbid and fetid; great thirst, constipation and aggravation of symptoms at night.

Dose.—Same as *Hellebore.*

Crotalus.—General dropsy, swelling of the whole body; oppression of the chest, not permitting a recumbent position, and hydrothorax in old people.

China.—Pale, sallow or sickly countenance; debility, derangement of the liver and stomach, with pain and tenderness in those organs; coldness of the surface of the body; great sensitiveness to cold, weariness of the limbs, restless nights, difficult and suffocative respiration, scanty urine. This remedy is particularly useful where the disease has been occasioned by loss of animal fluids and prostrating diseases.

Dose.—Three drops in a tumbler of water, a tablespoonful once in six or twelve hours.

Diet and Regimen.—These are of the utmost importance. A warm, dry and pure air is necessary. In acute dropsy the diet should be the same as in other acute diseases; in the chronic form the food should be light and nourishing, not much at a time, but taken frequently. In *ascites* particular attention should be paid to the digestive organs. The excessive thirst of which the patient complains may be gratified, provided the beverage does not interfere with the medicine. Cold water, milk, and buttermilk may be used, also diuretic drinks sometimes, such as, decoctions of parsley, asparagus, &c.

CHAPTER XI.

DISEASES OF WOMEN.

The female sex, from their physical organization, are subject to a large class of affections peculiar to themselves. When the female is in a state of health and all the organs fulfil their duty correctly, the successive steps of nature are attended with but little if any pain, and but slight functional disturbance. But let the system become deranged, from almost any cause, and a disturbance is very liable to be created in the generative organs. Diseases of these organs, more or less severe, are exceedingly common, and are attended with prostration and sometimes severe pain.

At the age of fourteen or fifteen *menstruation* should commence, and continue at intervals of about twenty-eight days until the age of forty-five or forty-six, lasting from three to five days at each time, and throwing off from four to six ounces of fluid. During gestation and *lactation*, these monthly periods, as a general thing, cease. Menstruation commences earlier in warm climates than in cold, and the time may vary even in health, in all climates, and also the intervals between the periods may be a week shorter in some than in others.

In a perfectly healthy female these periods should return with the utmost regularity, and be attended with but little if any pain, but owing to a variety of causes, the menstrual functions are liable to serious derangements. These derangements are often brought on either through the carelessness or ignorance of the patient. In certain circles of society, obeying the arbitrary dictates of foolish and absurd fashion, does much to undermine health, and scatter, broad cast, in the young frame, those seeds which soon ripen in a harvest of disease and suffering, terminating often, after years of suffering in death. We pity the poor, who poorly fed and badly clothed, living in damp and unhealthy air, sink into an early grave. But what shall we say of those who with the luxuries of life at their command, clothe themselves in garments which cannot afford sufficient warmth, walk the streets with shoes impossible to protect their feet from the dampness of the ground, and with the absurd idea of adding beauty to their form and complexion, compress the chest with corsets, and smear their face with cosmetics. The more comfortably a person is clad, and the more closely she obeys the laws of health in every respect, the less liable will she be to this variety of disease. See also the chapter on Hygiene and the causes of disease.

AMENORRHŒA.

Retention, or Suppression of the Menses.

There are two distinct classes of Amenorrhœa; one where the catamenia have never appeared, and the other where they have continued regular for some time, and then ceased.

In retention of the menses, where their appearance is delayed beyond the proper age, the countenance generally presents a sickly appearance; the appetite is variable, and there is often nausea, great debility and lassitude, and sensation of fatigue even after the slightest exertion. Palpitation of the heart, headache, constipation, derangement of the stomach, pains in the small of the back, head, limbs and side, and hysteric symptoms may also be present; hæmorrhages may also take place in different organs. Not unfrequently the mind sympathises with the disturbance; the temper may be irritable, or there may be a sad, weeping, or desponding mood.

Suppression of the menses, may be of two kinds, *acute* and *chronic*. The acute form may arise from cold caught by wet feet during the time of menstruating; from a bodily or mental shock received, either just previous to, or during the menstrual flow; from mental distress or the depressing passions; from fever, or any serious disease setting in at that time.

In some cases no ill effects follow for some time this sudden suppression, but more generally a degree of fever arises, with headache, hot skin, quick pulse, thirst, nausea, &c.; or the patient may be attacked by local inflammations either of the brain, lungs, intestinal canal, or of the womb itself.

Chronic suppression may be the issue of an acute attack, or it may arise from the gradual supervention of delicate health, from disease of the ovaries, uterus, or other parts. The time may become irregular, and the quantity gradually diminish until it ceases entirely. More frequently however the menses are gradually supplanted by a white discharge, until in time, the leucorrhœa becomes permanently established.

Some of the prominent causes of amenorrhœa we have already enumerated. It may arise, however, from congenital deformity, but here the skill of the surgeon will be required.

TREATMENT.—*Pulsatilla* is especially adapted to females of a mild and easy disposition, and particularly when it arises from taking cold, from violent passions and emotions, and in partial obstruction, accompanied with hysteric and dyspeptic symptoms. The prominent symptoms are languor; pain across the small of the back and in the lower part of the abdomen; palpitation of the heart, loss of appetite, nausea and vomiting; sensation of fullness in the head and eyes, and disposition to general coldness; alternate crying and laughter, or sadness and melancholy. The symptoms are generally worse in the afternoon, and may change from one place to another.

Cocculus—Great derangement of the nervous system, pinching and contracting pain in the lower part of the abdomen; also against a scanty discharge of black blood, or when the patient is very weak, with agitation, sighing, groaning, &c.

Cuprum.—A valuable remedy, in cases of spasms, with nausea and vomiting, or where cramps in the extremities are present.

Phosphorus.—In persons of delicate constitutions and weak chest, and where, in place of menstruation, expectoration of blood occurs in small quantities, with hacking cough, and pain in the chest.

DOSE.—A powder, or six globules every second day.

Arsenicum.—Great prostration; swelling of the feet, ankles or face, especially around the eyes, with paleness of the face.

Dose.—A powder, or six globules, once in twelve or twenty-four hours.

Sulphur.—After Pulsatilla, and also after other of the above remedies, when they seem indicated yet prove insufficient.

Dose.—A powder, or six globules, every night.

Bryonia will prove of benefit, where the suppression is attended with swimming or heaviness, or pressure in the head; pains in the chest, or in the small of the back, dry cough, bleeding at the nose, and constipation.

Dose.—Two drops, or eight globules, in a tumbler of water, a tablespoonful once in six or twelve hours; or three globules on the tongue at the same intervals.

Sepia—Sallow complexion; nervous headache and debility; giddiness, toothache, melancholy and sadness; pain in the limbs, as if they were bruised; frequent colic and pain in the loins.

Dose.—A powder, or six globules, once in six or twelve hours.

Ferrum and *China* are the prominent remedies where there is constitutional debility, seen in the sickly complexion, emaciation, pain in the chest, back, limbs, and loins, palpitation of the heart, debility, languor, derangement of digestion, and often leucorrhœa.

The remedy may be given every night or every other night.

Aconite may be alternated with *Bryonia* where there has been a sudden suppression of the menses, producing congestion to the head or chest, with throbbing and acute pains.

Dose.—Two drops, or eight globules, may be mixed with a tumbler of water, and a tablespoonful given once in one or two hours.

Besides the above remedies, we may enumerate *Belladonna*, *Veratrum*, *Calcarea*, *Graphitis*, *Conium*.

Diet and Regimen.—Exercise in the open air is of importance. The diet should be simple yet nourishing. Warm foot-baths may be used, or a tepid sitz-bath. Great care should be taken to avoid the causes which might produce the disease.

DYSMENORRHŒA.

Painful menstruation. Menstrual colic.

This painful affection may occur at any menstrual period, and in some cases it may be traced back to the commencement of menstruation. The amount of pain varies; in some cases it may be moderate, lasting only a few hours, in others so excessively severe, as to cause fainting or delirium.

Causes.—This painful affection may be of a neuralgic character, or be produced by the smallness of the mouth of the womb, or as is mostly the case with plethoric persons, be occasioned by a congested state of the secretory vessels of the womb. A fruitful cause of the deranged state of the womb may be traced to those almost innumerable instances, where the patient has violated some of nature's laws. The digestive organs are impaired by an unnatural state of living, and this, together with the buckram and whalebone used to compress certain portions of the body, impedes the natural circulation.

Treatment.—The most prominent remedies in this affection are, *Aconite, Pulsatilla, Secale, Belladonna, Nux-v., Platina, Cocculus, Sabina, Ferrum, Conium,* and *Veratrum.*

Aconite will be required if there are febrile symptoms present, quick pulse, thirst, rapid respiration, headache, and restlessness. It may frequently be alternated with *Pulsatilla* or *Belladonna.*

Dose.—One drop, or twelve globules, in a tumbler of water, a tablespoonful once in two or three hours.

Pulsatilla.—Menses retarded, with discharge of black and coagulated, or pale and serous blood. Also when there are colic, abdominal spasms, severe pains in the small of the back, sometimes passing down the thighs, nausea, vomiting and shivering sensation. It is particularly indicated, when attended with sadness or melancholy, or when caused by exposure to wet or cold, grief, mortification, or fright.

Dose.—Same as *Aconite.*

Belladonna.—Violent pain in the back, and sensation in

the lower part of the abdomen, as if the organs would be forced out, accompanied with congestion of blood to the head or chest, pulsative pain in the head, and heat and redness of the face. Particularly suitable in persons of plethoric habit.

DOSE.—Same as *Aconite.*

Cocculus.—Early appearance of the menses, with abdominal spasms, or discharge of small quantities of dark coagulated blood, with pressive colic and nausea; paralytic weakness and spasms in the chest, or convulsive movements of the limbs.

DOSE.—Same as *Aconite.*

Secale.—Menses profuse and of long duration, with tearing and incisive pain, coldness of the extremities, and great weakness.

DOSE.—One drop, or six globules, in a tumbler of water, a tablespoonful once in three or four hours.

Ferrum and *Platina* are indicated where there is profuse menstruation, but severe pain in the back and loins, cramps in the abdomen, discharge of dark blood, mixed with membraneous shreds.

DOSE.—A powder, or three globules, once in two or three hours.

Nux-v.—Where there is gastric derangement; writhing pains in the back, with nausea; pains of a spasmodic character, felt in the abdomen and neck of the bladder.

DOSE.—Same as *Ferrum.*

Graphitis.—Menses feeble and of short duration. Griping and abdominal spasms; violent headache, nausea, pain in the chest and rheumatic pain in the limbs.

DOSE.—A powder, or six globules, once in three or four hours. It would be well to give a dose of the appropriate remedy, every third night during the interval between the monthly period.

MENORRHAGIA.

Profuse Menstruation.

If the menstrual discharge is excessive, and continues longer than usual, it will be necessary to check it by means of the appropriate remedies.

Ipecac. is the appropriate remedy, where there is a profuse discharge of bright red blood, sometimes attended with dullness or nausea.

DOSE.—One drop in a tumbler of water, a tablespoonful at a dose; or a powder, or three globules on the tongue. Give at first every hour gradually increasing the intervals as the symptoms abate to two or three hours.

Crocus is a highly important remedy, particularly where the menses have returned too soon, and the discharge is dark colored, clotted and too copious.

DOSE.—One drop, or twelve globules, in a tumbler of water, a tablespoonful at first every hour, increasing the intervals as the symptoms abate.

Sabina.—Menorrhagia during and often miscarriage, or at the menstrual period; profuse discharge of bright red, or dark and coagulated blood, accompanied with rheumatic pains in the head and limbs; also pains like labor-pains.

DOSE.—Same as *Crocus.*

China.—Great debility from copious or long continued discharges; also when the discharge has been checked, but weakness still remains.

DOSE.—Three drops in four tablespoonfuls of water, a tablespoonful once in three or four hours.

Secale.—Where the hæmorrhage arises from want of tone in the uterus, and from passive congestion and debility of that organ; there may be pale face and coldness of the extremities; tenesmus in the rectum and bladder; discharge of dark and offensive blood, increased by motion, sneezing, or coughing.

DOSE.—Two drops, or twelve globules, in a tumbler of water, a tablespoonful once in two or three hours.

Pulsatilla.—Discharge of blood at intervals; black and mixed with clots, with pains like labor-pains; particularly during pregnancy, at the critical age and also confinement.

DOSE.—Same as *Crocus*.

Belladonna.—In persons of a plethoric habit; determination of blood to the head; dizziness and pain in the head; pressing pain in the small of the back and abdomen; flushed cheeks, brilliant and congested eyes.

Platina.—Profuse and too frequent menstrual discharge, consisting chiefly of thick, dark colored blood, and attended with bearing down pain like labor-pain.

Besides the remedies already enumerated, *Arnica*, *Chamomilla*, *Ignatia*, *Nux-v.*, *Ferrum*, *Sepia*, and *Sulphur*.

In connection with the internal administration of remedies it will be necessary that the hips be elevated, and the head lowered, and the patient kept cool and quiet. Where the hæmorrhage is profuse, the external application of cloths wet in cold water, or even a bladder filled with pounded ice, over the region of the womb, will be advisable.

IRREGULAR MENSTRUATION.

The treatment necessary in the various forms of menstrual irregularities has already been given.

For menses too frequent or too early, *see menorrhagia*. For menses too late or insufficient, *Amenorrhœa*. For menses mixed with leucorrhœa, *see Leucorrhœa*.

CESSATION OF MENSES. CHANGE OF LIFE.

This change generally takes place about the forty-fifth or forty-sixth year, although it may occur several years earlier, or even later. In a very few cases it has been delayed until the age of sixty, and in a few instances even till seventy. Persons of delicate constitution, or those accustomed to sedentary habits or a high style of living, generally experience the change earlier than those of robust constitution, or accustomed to much exercise.

The change of life is one of the most important eras in a

woman's existence, second only to the first appearance of the menses. This period, safely passed, and continued health and a long life are generally before her, but now her path is surrounded with danger, and she must tread it with careful footsteps. It is at this period that the seeds of much future suffering may be sown in the system, and those old predispositions to disease, perhaps long forgotten, spring up in luxuriant growth. The menses become irregular both as to time and quantity, returning once in two or three weeks, or delaying three or four months, at times the discharge scarcely perceptible, at others so profuse as to amount to a hæmorrhage. Sometimes the menstrual fluid is mixed with mucus.

In most females during the progress of this change, there s more or less general disturbance of the system.

There may be great nervousness, severe attacks of headache, dizziness, flushes of heat, or paleness and debility; there may also be derangement of the urinary organs, the urine at times scanty and high colored, at others frequent and in large quantities; the patient may also experience pain in the back, loins, and abdomen, swelling of the abdomen or extremities, piles, and violent itching of the privates, palpitation of the heart, and hysteric spasms. Sometimes the menses gradually cease without any unpleasant symptoms, and in almost all cases, where the female safely passes through this period and no after difficulties are developed, her health is more firmly established than before.

The prominent remedies are *Pulsatilla* and *Lachesis*, given in alternation three days apart. Should the discharge be frequent and very profuse, consult *menorrhagia*. If attended with much pain, see *dysmenorrhœa*, and for the other affections which may arise, consult the respective chapters in which these diseases may be found.

Particular attention should be given to diet, exercise, clothing, &c. The room should be well ventilated, and if possible, daily exercise in the open air taken; daily bathing should also be practiced. The food should be nourishing, but easy of digestion, and articles of a highly stimulating character carefully avoided. The clothing should be warm and comfortable. . Strong mental or physical excitement should be avoided and a cheerful state of mind cultivated.

CHLOROSIS.

Green Sickness.

This disease is confined principally to female youth, but not unfrequently occurs in married women, and occasionally in the young and delicate of the male sex.

DIAGNOSIS.—Chlorosis has generally three distinct stages; the incipient, the confirmed and the inveterate. The first stage steals on the patient insidiously, and is usually but little observed by parents or friends. There is slight paleness and languor, fatigue more easily produced by the ordinary occupations, restless nights, and heavy mornings. With these changes there is a confined state of the bowels, morbid appetite, deranged condition of the bowels, fetid breath and a white and pasty tongue; there is recurrent headache, pain in the left side, and palpitation. The menses are also, when present, of a lighter character.

In the second or confirmed stage all the symptoms are aggravated. The whole system, especially the face and fingers, seem absolutely without blood, sometimes presenting a pearly, at others a yellow hue. The eyelids are sometimes slightly swollen, the tongue apparently without blood, the teeth liable to decay, the nails brittle, the hair dry and harsh, and the ankles swollen. As the disease progresses, the menses grow scanty and pale, until they entirely cease, the stomach is oppressed after eating, and a pecular morbid appetite is present. The friends may be deceived, as it regards the character of the disease, from the occasional appearance of severe headache, pain in the side or breast, and the various symptoms found in hysteria. The second stage gradually passes into the third, when dropsical symptoms set in, and the disease assumes a more dangerous form. There may also be in each stage of this affection a peculiar tendency to hæmorrhage from different organs in the body.

Causes.—The most usual exciting causes are, delicate and sedentary habits, especially in persons of a lympathic constitution, impure air and unhealthy food. Servants and especially cooks are particularly liable to this disease, but the delicate and inert habits of the rich not less frequently lead to this affection. In all, there is the same torpor of the bowels, the same defective digestion, assimilation and formation of blood.

Treatment.—Pure air, frequent bathing, moderate outdoor exercise, and digestible and nutritious diet, are of the utmost importance in this disease. Daily bathing should be practiced, commencing with tepid baths, gradually increasing the temperature of the water, as the strength of the patient will permit. (See *bathing*.) Bathing in sea-water and a sea-voyage to some warm climate will also prove of benefit. The blood is impoverished and needs enriching, and this must be done by nutritious articles of diet, easy of digestion. The use of wine, porter, and Scotch ale, at the meals, may also be advisable.

The most prominent remedies in the treatment of this affection are, *China*, *Sulphur*, *Sepia*, *Ferrum*, *Arsenicum*, *Calcarea*, *Pulsatilla*, *Platina*, and *Nux-v*.

Pulsatilla.—Especially adapted to persons of a mild, timid or sad disposition, who have been irregular in menstruation, or where there is total suppression of menses, with pain in the small of the back, chilliness, &c.; also if the disease was produced by cold or dampness. There may be beating and cutting pain in the stomach and abdomen; severe pain in one side of the head or in the forehead, pale face; green, slimy or bloody stools; suppression of the menses or scanty menstrual discharge; acrid, thin leucorrhœa; nausea, loss of appetite; pain and weakness in the small of the back; weight in the abdomen; general sensation of fatigue, palpitation of the heart, and periodic expectoration of dark coagulated blood.

Sepia.—When *Pulsatilla* has proved insufficient, and where there are painful beating in the head, swollen and puffy face, pain in the region of the liver, and difficulty of breathing; colic, pain in the limbs as if bruised, and weakness and pain in the small of the back; sensitiveness to cold air, and restlessness during the night. This remedy is particularly indicated in females of a nervous temperament, and thin and delicate skin, and in those in whom there is a great tendency to irregularity of the menses.

Sulphur.—Pressive fullness and heaviness in the stomach and bowels; emaciation, violent appetite, and burning or sour eructations; irregularity of the bowels, pain in the loins, and difficulty of breathing, congestion to the head, with throbbing pain; pain in the back of the head, or humming in the head; eruption around the mouth and on the forehead; general nervous irritation; acrid or burning leucorrhœa; swelling of the feet and ankles; glandular swellings about the neck. Symptoms aggravated by motion.

China.—Pale or livid countenance; swelling of the limbs; leucorrhœal discharge; yellowish skin; scanty menses, or suppression of them; sensitiveness of the whole nervous system, and dread of cold air; unnatural appetite; lassitude and debility. It is particularly indicated where the disease is accompanied or produced by hæmorrhage, leucorrhœa, or masturbation, and where there is great weakness of the whole system, fetid breath, pale or yellowish skin, and derangement of the stomach and bowels. There may be headache, vertigo, ringing in the ears, nausea, bitter or sour taste, flatulence, hæmorrhoids, asthmatic respiration, trembling of the limbs, and sensitiveness of the skin. It is particularly indicated in persons of sedentary habits, or in those who have indulged freely in wines or coffee.

Bryonia.—Congestion to the head, chilliness, sometimes alternating with heat; dry cough, colic, constipation, and sometimes bleeding at the nose.

Ferrum and *Calcarea* may be important remedies, where there are emaciation, swelling of the extremities, and great debility.

Dose.—Six globules, or a powder, may be given morning

and night; or if the liquid is given, two drops may be mixed in a tumbler of water, and a tablespoonful taken at the same intervals.

LEUCORRHŒA.

Fluor Albus. Whites.

Leucorrhœa is one of the most troublesome and obstinate, as well as the most common of the whole class of female diseases. The causes are various. It may be produced by cold, by a sudden suppression of the menses; by severe labor, where the vagina has been kept for a long time on the stretch, by constipation, free use of tea and coffee, ascarides in the rectum, excessive sexual indulgence, exertion soon after delivery, violent exercise, or not sufficient exercise, frequent childbearing, and also as a symptom of various affections of the womb. The most frequent causes of leucorrhœa, however, may be traced to errors in living, imprudence in dress, and that artificial life so common in certain classes of society. How often do we see the simple teachings of nature rejected, and mind and body warped and compelled to bend to the dictates of fashion, or follow the lead of an absurd and diseased imagination? Need we wonder that where the passions are stimulated, and the mind excited by the luxuries and stimulants of the table, the excitements of the ballroom or theatre, and the glowing and sometimes impure pages of a certain class of fiction, a reaction should be produced both on the mind and the body.

Diagnosis.—Leucorrhœa may be of two kinds. It may either be an affection of the mucous membrane of the vagina, in which case it is called *vaginal leucorrhœa*, or it may be a morbid action of the lining membrane of the uterus, when it receives the name of *uterine leucorrhœa*. Both of these varieties may have an acute or chronic stage. It will not be necessary in this place to draw the precise line of demarcation between the varieties of the disease, and we shall therefore include all under the one head of, leucorrhœa.

The milder forms are frequently allowed to run on for a

long time before any medical advice is taken. The character of the discharge depends upon the seat and severity of the disease. When the discharge is considerable, and of some standing, decided effect is produced on the system. The countenance becomes pale and sallow, the frame weak, the appetite impaired or capricious, the spirits languid, and exertion is attended with fatigue; the bowels are irregular, and digestion disordered; pain in the back is also felt when fatigued, and a peculiar dragging, bearing down and weary sensation. The discharge in these cases is of a mucous character, and may not be very abundant.

The most acute form of leucorrhœa, generally the effects of a cold, or some irritating cause, consists of a profuse watery or purulent discharge, attended with local soreness and pain. The vagina is hot and tender to the touch; fever is also present. When the discharge is more scanty and glairy, or creamy and opaque, it is an indication that the neck of the womb is affected. All the varieties of leucorrhœa may end in the chronic form, when the discharge is more or less profuse and constant, mucous or purulent, or a mixture of both; it may also become green and purulent. The quantity may also be abundant, amounting in some cases to a pint in twenty-four hours, and expelled in gushes on every change of posture. In these cases there is great emaciation and debility. There may be dragging pain in the back, palpitation of the heart, night-sweats, difficult respiration, and swelling of the feet.

Treatment.—In the successful treatment of this disease, very much depends on the physical and mental condition of the patient. The food may be nourishing, but taken at the proper time, and be as little stimulating as possible. Late suppers, wines and all kinds of dissipation should be avoided. Moderate exercise in the open air will be productive of good, but care should be taken to avoid much fatigue. Particular attention also should be given to the dress. The feet should be well protected from the damp ground, the clothing warm and comfortable, fitting loosely to the body, and the skirts instead of being permitted to hang upon the hips, held up by the shoulders by means of shoulder-straps or braces. Above all, cultivate a healthy tone of mind. Cast aside the exciting romance, and mingle only in those amusements which will have a tendency to produce a healthy action on the mind and body.

Water is a most important remedial agent in this affection. A daily hip-bath should be taken, (see page 80,) and the entire body thoroughly bathed. Cold water thrown up the vagina by a syringe prepared for that purpose, may also be highly advantageous.

China, is a valuable remedy in the commencement of the treatment, and in those cases where the disease has been produced by debilitating causes, and is of long standing.

Pulsatilla.—Especially when the affection occurs during pregnancy, and when the discharge is thick like cream, or milky, or thin, acrid and burning, and when it is associated with indigestion. Particularly useful in persons of a lymphatic temperament, in whom the monthly flow is irregular.

Calcarea.—When *Pulsatilla* seems indicated, but yet has not produced the desired effect; and also in females in whom the monthly turn is excessive, and when the affection occurs at the turn of life, and is attended with severe itching; particularly suitable in chronic leucorrhœa, affecting weak and scrofulous females.

Sepia.—Particularly indicated in sensitive and delicate persons; the discharge is yellow or greenish, more or less acrid or corrosive, generally watery, and most abundant just before or just after the menses, and attended with itching in the parts.

Alumina.—Where the menstrual flux is scanty, and the discharge profuse, corrosive, and attended with itching and burning.

Nux-v.—Where the affection is induced by abuse of stimulants, or indigestible food, and the discharge is profuse, and of a bloody, yellowish or fetid mucous character, and is attended with constipation and cramp-like pains in the abdomen.

Sulphur.—In obstinate cases, and where it results from repelled eruptions; also where the discharge is of a yellowish, burning and corrosive character, and preceded by colic.

Agaricus.—Particularly when occasioned by a torpid state of the liver, and where there is pain in the small of the back, weariness of the limbs and sensation as of a pressing weight in the lower part of the body, intense itching and burning in the genital organs.

Kreosote.—In most forms of chronic leucorrhea.

DOSE.—A dose of the selected remedy may be taken once in twenty-four hours, until five doses have been taken, when if necessary it may be changed.

Besides the remedies above enumerated, *Cocculus*, *Causticum*, *Graphitis*, *Iodine*, *Ipecac.*, *Nitric-ac.*, *Natr.-mur.* may also be of benefit.

PROLAPSUS UTERI.

Falling of the womb.

Falling of the womb is a very common affection, especially among females, who have borne children, although it is occasionally met with in unmarried females and those who have never given birth to children. It is occasioned by a weakness of the ligaments, which give support to the womb, and also by a weakness of the walls of the vagina. We frequently find it the result of sitting up too soon after delivery, and also occasioned by violent vomiting, coughing, or sneezing, by lifting heavy weights, and a general weakness of the system.

The patient complains of a sensation of fullness in the pelvis, of weight and bearing down and dragging from the loins and umbilicus. There is more or less pain in the back, extending round the groins. The patient is worse in the evening than in the morning, and the symptoms are aggravated by much exertion. Leucorrhea is generally an attending symptom, although the discharge may vary, occasionally very profuse, sometimes slight, but in all cases diminishing the strength of the constitution.

TREATMENT.—The sitz-bath (*see page* 80) will be highly beneficial, also general bathing. Rest in the recumbent position will be advisable, or at least, the patient should avoid being on the feet, as much as possible.

In the commencement of the difficulty, a powder, or six globules of *Nux-v.* may be alone sufficient to produce a cure. If this remedy fails of producing the desired effect, it may be followed by *Belladonna*, *Sepia*, *Calcarea*, or *Aurum* in the same manner, changing the remedy for another, if in a weeks' time no effect is produced. In severe cases the patient will of course perceive the propriety of consulting her physician.

It will be unnecessary to speak here of various other affections of the womb, such as, cancer and a variety of ulcerations and tumors, as the experience and skill of the physician or surgeon will be necessary to produce relief.

PREGNANCY.

The birth of a child, is at once the most wonderful, and sublime act of existence. Existence itself assumes a mightier import to the mother as she gazes on the little being, whose pure eyes are turned to her's, whose form, clasped to her bosom, thrills through all her being, and unseals the fountains of a deathless love. Springing from herself, a part of herself, for two hundred and seventy days nourished in her womb, commencing from an almost imperceptible germ, and growing on day by day, drawing life itself from her, until at length a miniature human being, it is folded in her arms, with a body, a part of herself, and a soul a part of God, *deathless*, *eternal.* Another ripple is started in the great ocean of life, whose widening circles are lost from mortal gaze in the ocean of eternity.

Parturition is a crisis in a woman's existence. It is no disease, no chance of life, but the healthy action of nature, and one great end of her being. Safely carried through this crisis, and the equilibrium of the system becomes more perfect, and the health more firmly established. It is one of the strange things of nature that this crisis so complete, producing such a tremendous revolution in the whole system, should, in such a vast majority of cases, terminate favorably. The danger in the majority of cases, is in proportion to the previous health of the mother, and her obedience of the laws of nature. Those who daily violate nature's laws, who forget the mighty responsibility which rests upon them, and the fearful crisis through which they are about to pass, need not wonder at being the victims of a train of evils, which may end in death.

To one class the period of gestation seems like a dark and thorny path; others, less sensitive, or more philosophical, or enthusiastic in their nature, forget the present, in the bright anticipations for the future, or look upon it as something over which they can have no control, and therefore give way to indolence, or freely indulge in all the luxuries and extravagances a morbid appetite can induce.

The mother should never forget that her own health, and thoughts, and feelings, during the period of gestation must produce a marked influence on the child.* Her condition, mental as well as physical, when carrying the child is all important to its future welfare. Cases are by no means rare, where the excessive anxiety or sadness of the mother during the period of gestation is shown in the after life of her child. It has been observed that in a large proportion of cases, where children are born out of wedlock, the delivery is premature, or if the mother reaches her full time, she gives birth to a still-born child. The agony of the mother, the thought of the brand of shame which will ever after cling to her, the withering of life's brightest flowers, the hissing tongue of the world's scorn, marking her out as an object fit only to be trampled in the dust, all this is enough not only to destroy the child but the mother also.

There is no period of life when a woman stands in such need of sympathy as at this time. It is now, when sensitive in the extreme, she needs the watchful and soothing care of affection. Let her at other times contend, and wrestle, if it must be so, with the stern, harsh and cruel exactions of a cold and selfish world, and there are times when a woman's spirit

* I have alluded to this subject in the chapter on the causes of disease, page 90.

and nerve are stronger than man's, but now surround her with an atmosphere where the tumultuous heavings of the world, with its passions and troubles, are as little felt as possible. Make the path as smooth and easy as unwearied kindness, patience and affection can accomplish.

The extreme sensitiveness at these times, often renders the utmost tact and forbearance on the part of friends, absolutely essential. She should be surrounded with every comfort, and every means taken to secure cheerfulness and an easy, happy mind. To secure this, it is not necessary she should be surrounded by useless luxuries, and every ridiculous whim, the result of a morbid imagination gratified. This would produce the thing you wish to avoid.

Gloomy and harrassing thoughts and impressions should be guarded against, and every means taken to preserve a healthy and vigorous tone to the mind and body. The mother should by no means yield to indolence or indulge in dissipation. Cheerful conversation, pleasant friends, agreeable books, and the soothing charm of music, as well as daily out-door exercise and household duties, all should contribute their share to promote comfort and enjoyment. The cases are very rare, where it is essential for the mother to give up her household duties entirely. She will be much happier by continuing to be mistress of her own household. Large ventilated rooms, and pure air are of the utmost importance.

Great cleanliness should also be strictly practiced. It is essential that the pores in the skin should be kept constantly open, a healthy and even circulation induced, and an equilibrium kept up as much as possible throughout the system. The body should be washed from head to foot once every day in moderately cold water, taking particular pains afterward to rub it quite dry, or a tepid bath can be taken every two or three days.

Another important point which should by no means be overlooked is dress. We occasionally see mothers who attempt to conceal the rotundity of their form, either from shame or some other reason, with tight dresses and corsets tightly laced. For a married woman in this situation, to be ashamed of her form, bespeaks a weakness of which I trust but very few of my countrywomen are guilty. What situation in life is there more holy, and in the name of heaven, what is there for which a pure and virtuous woman should be ashamed. The dress should be made perfectly easy, either warm or cool as the weather may indicate, fitting lightly to the body. The slightest compression of the abdomen and chest should be avoided, so that the utmost freedom may be given to the organs and muscles of respiration. Dr. Eberle in speaking of this subject, makes use of the following excellent remarks. "The custom of wearing tightly laced corsets during gestation cannot be too severely censured. It must be evident to the plainest understanding, that serious injury to the health of both mother and child must often result from a continual and forcible compression of the abdomen, whilst nature is at work in gradually enlarging it for the accommodation and development of the fœtus. By this unnatural practice, the circulation of the blood throughout the abdomen is impeded, a circumstance which, together with the mechanical impression of the abdominal organs, is peculiarly calculated to give rise to functional disorders of the stomach and liver, as well as to hæmorrhoids, uterine hæmorrhage, and abortion. The regular nourishment of the fœtus also is generally impeded in this way; a fact which is frequently verified in the remarkably delicate and emaciated conditions of infants born of mothers who have practiced this fashionable folly during gestation. It may be observed, that since the custom of wearing tightly laced corsets has become general among females, certain forms of uterine disease are much more frequent than they were sixteen or eighteen years ago."

Lycurgus, whose laws were sometimes a little arbitrary, although generally characterized by sterling sense, ordained a law, that pregnant women should wear wide loose clothing, and a similar law prevailed among the Romans. By attending particularly to dress, mothers would not only escape much of the pain of child-birth, but find themselves after the crisis had passed more quickly convalescent, and without those lingering and prostrating complaints, which do so much to undermine the constitution.

DIET.—A proper diet is all-important. Plain, simple and nourishing, easy of digestion, and free from exciting and highly stimulating compounds. The idea generally prevails that as the growth of another being depends on the food taken by the mother, the amount of food should be greatly increased, and to satisfy this double demand of nature, a very generous diet should be substituted for the ordinary manner of living. Hence mothers are often urged to drink porter, and partake freely of stimulating food, spurring on the appetite when it lags, by some new delicacy. They forget that notwithstanding there is an increased expenditure of substance necessary for the development of the child in the mother's womb, yet nature which understands its duty perfectly well, has in a measure provided for it, by suppressing the usual periodical discharge, which ceases at the close of the period of child-bearing. Nature we have said understands her duty, but we must be careful not to confound her voice with the whisperings of a morbid appetite and imagination, indicative of disease. When during gestation the general health, the appetite and digestion improves, an increase of food would not only be advantageous but highly necessary. As a general thing, where the diet has been plain, simple and sufficiently nourishing, no increase or change is necessary. There may be a morbid appetite, but unless the health and digestive powers improve, if the appetite is indulged in to its full extent, and even stimulated, as is often the case, exactly contrary to the object aimed at will be gained, the stomach will be overloaded with food it cannot digest, and the appetite will either give way, or a long train of painful symptoms follow, such as, nausea, heartburn, colic, constipation, and piles, disagreeable breath and perspiration, difficulties which the mother is accustomed to bear in righteous resignation as a part of her lot. Even if the digestion should remain unimpaired, and larger amount of nourishment is taken into the system than is necessary, a sense of fullness will follow, producing difficulties about the head or some other organ, and not unfrequently miscarriage.

There is less danger of running to the opposite extreme and taking too little food, in this country than among some of the thickly populated districts of the old world. There, where life is a continual struggle for bread, and where hundreds die from a want of the proper nourishment, the babe is often born weak and puny, and the mother from lack of nourishment herself is unable to furnish it to her child, and the poor child dies of what the world is pleased to call some infantile disease, but which in reality is neither more nor less than *starvation*. In our own happy country there are but very few who cannot obtain the necessaries of life. It makes but little difference whether the system lacks nourishment either from a want of food, or from too great abundance of it, so as to impair the organs of digestion and render them unable to perform their functions aright.

Longings, which are so often observed in pregnant females for strange and even ridiculous things, by many are watched with a great deal of interest, and the absolute necessity of indulging them for fear of producing an effect on the child is considered an important duty. Sometimes an urgent desire is felt to eat earth, or feast on a tallow candle, and a hundred such unnatural whims. I need not say that these longings are peculiar to delicate, irritable, and nervous women, whose minds are *unemployed*; we should hardly expect to find them in the healthy woman, whose mind is employed and made cheerful by reading, conversation, or any healthy exercise. The proper remedy is, not to gratify the whim—unless it be for some harmless thing, for longings of this kind are common to all—that would only tend to increase the disease; but to make use of plain and simple food, such as the stomach can easily digest, and above all, give pleasant employment to the mind, take moderate exercise, and be as cheerful as possible.

DERANGEMENTS DURING PREGNANCY.

In about nine months, or two hundred and seventy days from the time of conception, *labor* commences, terminating in the birth of the child. The child may be born, however, as early as the seventh month, and yet live, and in some cases nine months and a half may elapse, before the birth of the child. In the latter case, labor is more difficult on account of the increased size of the child. But delivery earlier or later than two hundred and seventy days, is an exception to the general rule, and is attended with more or less danger to the mother or child.

During pregnancy, the female is liable to numerous troublesome affections, some of which we shall now enumerate.

MORNING SICKNESS.

In most females, nausea, vomiting, and heartburn are present, some portion of the time during their pregnancy. They generally come on about the fourth or fifth week after conception, and continue for ten or twelve weeks, when they make their exit to return again during the last month. In some few cases they do not appear at all, and in others continue through the whole period. They generally come on in the morning shortly after getting out of bed, last two or three hours, and perhaps re-appear in the evening for the same length of time.

TREATMENT.—*Ipecac.* will produce relief, where there is bilious vomiting, or vomiting of drink and undigested food, or nausea and vomiting, with uneasiness in the stomach.

Nux-v.—Nausea or vomiting in the morning; acid and bitter eructations, hiccough, heartburn; sensation of weight in the pit of the stomach; depraved appetite or craving for chalk, earth, &c. Constipation and irritable temper.

Pulsatilla.—Nausea after a meal; vomiting of food, heartburn, eructations bitter or acid; depraved appetite, a longing for acids, beer, wine, &c.

Arsenicum.—Excessive vomiting after eating or drinking, with attacks of fainting; prostration and emaciation.

Natrum-mur.—In obstinate cases where there is loss of appetite, waterbrash, acid stomach, &c. Particularly after *Nux.*

DOSE.—A powder, or six globules of the selected remedy may be given morning and night. If the liquid is administered, two drops may be mixed with a tumbler of water, and a tablespoonful given at the same intervals. When the symptoms are exceedingly violent and long continued, the remedy may be given once in three hours until relieved.

CONSTIPATION.

During pregnancy, the bowels are very liable to become constipated. As a general thing, the difficulty may be controlled by taking moderate exercise in the open air, and eating freely of brown bread and ripe fruits. Should the constipation still continue, a few doses of the appropriate remedy will produce relief, unless it is occasioned by mechanical obstruction.

Nux-v.—Particularly where there are symptoms of derangement of the stomach, headache, and sometimes frequent inclination for stool, without result.

Bryonia or *Ignatia* may follow *Nux*, or be taken in alternation with it, one in the morning, and the other at night.

Opium, Sulphur, and *Lycopodium* are also valuable remedies.

For particular indications, see Constipation, page 230.

DIARRHŒA.

Diarrhœa occasionally occurs during pregnancy, when it should be speedily checked, or the strength may become prostrated. *Lycopodium, Sulphur, Nux-v., Dulcamara*, and *Ipecac.* are prominent remedies.

For particular indications, see Diarrhœa, page 210.

VERTIGO AND HEADACHE.

There are frequently giddiness, fullness or pain in the head during pregnancy. There is sometimes sensation of weight on the top of the head, or in the back of the neck; palpitation of the heart, and great nervous excitability. The symptoms are generally worse in the morning. The prominent remedies are, *Aconite*, *Nux-v.*, *Belladonna*, *Opium*, *Platina*, *Pulsatilla*, and *Sulphur*.

Aconite is indicated in persons of plethoric habit, and nervous temperament, especially if there is giddiness on rising from a seat as if intoxicated, determination of blood to the head, stupefying pain, redness of the eyes, and intolerance of light.

Belladonna.—Congestion to the head; pain in the forehead over the eyes, and in the top of the head; throbbing in the temples, redness of the eyes, and intolerance of light and noise.

Nux-v.—Particularly in persons of a sedentary habit, worse in the morning, and relieved in the open air; giddiness and feeling of confusion in the head, or jerking, tearing, or periodical pains; constipation; acid or bitter taste.

For particular indications of other remedies, consult Headache, page 290.

Dose.—A powder, or three globules, may be taken once in three or four hours; or two drops, or twelve globules, may be mixed with a tumbler of water, and a tablespoonful taken at the same intervals.

FAINTING AND HYSTERIC FITS.

These are very common in persons of nervous temperament and delicate constitution. They are generally unattended with danger, and pass over in a short time. The causes which produce them should be carefully avoided. During the attack, the face should be sprinkled with cold water, and fresh air freely admitted.

Belladonna and *Aconite*, may be given in alternation, six or twelve hours apart, in plethoric individuals, or where there is congestion of blood to the head.

Chamomilla, when the attack is produced by a fit of anger.

Dose.—Two drops, or twelve globules, in a tumbler of water, a tablespoonful once in six or twelve hours; or three globules, at the same intervals.

Nux-v.—When produced by derangement of the digestive organs.

Dose.—Same as *Chamomilla.*

Coffea.—Great nervous excitability; spasmodic pain in the bowels, oppressed respiration, cold perspiration.

Dose.—Same as *Chamomilla.* Give once in three or four hours.

Pulsatilla.—Disposition to hysteria; depression of spirits, &c.

Dose.—Same as *Chamomilla.*

Ignatia.—Severe headache as if a nail were driven into the head; sadness, concealed melancholy and sighing.

Dose.—Same as *Chamomilla.* Give at first, once in three hours.

Consult also Hysteria, page 287.

TOOTHACHE.

This is of very common occurrence during pregnancy, frequently commencing in a sound tooth, extending to the whole set, and the pain sometimes shooting to the face and head. The pain is exceedingly severe, sometimes making the patient almost delirious.

The prominent remedies are, *Calcarea, Sepia, Belladonna, Mercurius, Staphysagria, Nux-v., Chamomilla,* and *Pulsatilla.*

For particular indications, see Toothache, page 226.

PRURITIS.

During pregnancy, the female is occasionally annoyed with excessive itching in the privates, sometimes so violent as to bring on miscarriage. It is generally occasioned by an acrid or vitiated secretion of the walls of the vagina. Sometimes the parts are covered with a white substance, resembling the thrush of infants, and is easily rubbed off; or the parts may assume a dark red hue, accompanied by a thin watery secretion, and the most intolerable itching.

The parts should be frequently bathed with cold water. A weak solution of borax in water, applied three or four times a day, will generally remove the itching, without the aid of other remedies. *Sepia*, *Silicea*, *Sulphur*, and *Rhus*, may also be consulted. See Materia Medica.

VARICOSE VEINS.

This disease is not confined to the period of pregnancy, although it most commonly occurs at that time. It seldom occurs in first pregnancy, but in subsequent pregnancies it is liable to come on the first months.

It consists of a distension and dilation of the superficial veins, which at first assume a reddish hue, but afterwards a bluish or leaden color. They become larger from standing on the feet or allowing the limb to hang. They generally commence in the ankle, and are usually confined to one or both of the lower limbs. After delivery, the pressure of the pregnant uterus on the large veins of the abdomen being removed, the swelling disappears, and the veins regain their natural size. When the distension is slight, it is not painful, but if it should continue to increase, it may not only become painful, but the veins may burst.

If the limb should be painful, the patient must remain in a recumbent position a few days. It may be necessary also to apply the laced stocking, or bandage the limb. If this is done, it should be applied in the morning when the veins are the least distended, commencing at the toes and progressing upwards.

If medicines are required, *Arnica*, *Nux-v.*, or *Pulsatilla* may be given, commencing with the first, and giving six globules every other night for a week, and then, unless relieved following with the next in the same manner.

HÆMORRHOIDS. PILES.

This troublesome affection is not confined to pregnancy, although it frequently occurs then and after delivery, in those who are never troubled with it any other time. It is occasioned by the pressure of the impregnated uterus on the hæmorrhoidal artery and the veins of the abdomen.

For treatment, see Hæmorrhoids, page 232.

PAINS IN THE BACK AND SIDE.

An aching pain or a dull heavy pressure in the small of the back or in the side, just under the short ribs, is often experienced during pregnancy, particularly between the fifth and the eight month.

The pain in the back will generally be relieved by a few powders of *Kali-carb.*, taken at intervals of twelve hours. Should other remedies be required, *Bryonia*, *Rhus*, *Belladonna*, *Pulsatilla*, or *Nux* may be selected, giving a dose every night, and changing it, if after the expiration of four or five doses no relief has been obtained.

For pain in the side, *Aconite*, *Chamomilla*, *Pulsatilla*, *Bryonia*, or *Phosphorus* will produce relief, given as directed above.

CRAMPS.

We frequently find this painful affection coming on about the fourth or fifth month, and again towards the end of pregnancy; they may attack the muscles of the abdomen, hips, back, and the lower extremities.

When they attack the muscles of the abdomen, *Belladonna*, *Pulsatilla*, or *Nux-v.* will produce relief.

The back: *Ignatia*, *Opium*, or *Rhus*.

The hips: *Colocynth*, or *Stramonium*.

The thighs: *Hyosciamus*.

The legs: *Calcarea*, *Chamomilla*, *Nux-v.*, or *Sulphur*.

The remedy may be taken, when there is predisposition to cramps, every night, and also on the first indications of their approach. For particular indications, see Materia Medica.

DERANGEMENTS OF THE URINARY ORGANS.

There is often, during pregnancy incontinence of urine, frequent desire to pass water, sometimes attended with pain.

For the treatment of the various affections of the urinary organs, see affections of those organs, page 342.

For other affections of pregnancy, see their respective headings in their appropriate place.

MISCARRIAGE.

Miscarriage may occur at any period during gestation but is more frequent about the third or fourth month. If it occurs after the sixth month, it is called premature labor. Miscarriage coming on at a late period, is often attended with considerable danger, and where a female has miscarried once, there is a great liability of its recurrence.

The causes are numerous, but the most common are, dissipation, such as a free use of stimulating food and drinks, and late hours; a too sedentary mode of life, neglecting to take exercise or fresh air; great physical exertion; purgative drugs; violent and sudden mental excitement; and mechanical injuries, such as a fall or a blow.

The attack is generally preceded by certain symptoms, which if taken in time, may sometimes be controlled, and the miscarriage prevented. The precursory symptoms are usually chilliness followed by fever, and bearing-down pains; pains in the abdomen or loins, and pains resembling labor-pains; discharge of mucus and blood, sometimes followed by emission of a watery fluid.

At the first symptom of an approach of the attack the patient should be placed in a recumbent position, and remain there as quiet as possible until all danger is over. A physician of course should be obtained as speedily as possible.

TREATMENT.—*Arnica* should be given when the symptoms arise from a fall or blow or from great physical exertion.

Secale.—Constant expulsive efforts with profuse discharge of dark liquid blood, followed by debility; and also where miscarriage has occurred before, and in debilitated persons.

Sabina.—Dragging and forcing pains extending to the back and loins, with profuse discharge of bright red blood.

Chamomilla, particularly when occasioned by a fit of passion; also where the pains are periodical, and are followed by a discharge of dark colored or coagulated blood, or blood mixed with mucus; violent pain in the bowels; coldness and shivering.

Crocus, particularly in protracted cases and where there is a discharge of dark clotted blood brought on by the slightest motion.

Hyosciamus should be given where there are spasms and convulsions of the whole body, with loss of consciousness.

China.—In weak and exhausted persons, and where there are spasmodic pains in the uterus, or bearing-down pain with discharge of blood at intervals ; giddiness, fainting, coldness of the extremities and prostration.

Ipecac.—Spasms but without loss of consciousness ; continuous discharge of bright red blood with pressing downward ; nausea or vomiting, pain in the abdomen and sometimes faintness.

Belladonna.—Particularly in the commencement and where there are violent bearing-down pains, severe pain in the abdomen, loins, and small of the back ; flushed face and profuse discharge of blood.

Platina.—If *Ipecac*. fails to relieve and where there are pressing bearing-down pains ; pain in the back passing into the groins, and discharge of dark, thick or clotted blood.

Dose.—Two drops of the selected remedy, or twelve globules, in a tumbler of water, a tablespoonful, where the attack is urgent every half hour or hour ; or six globules may be taken on the tongue at the same intervals.

For further directions as it regards *flooding*, see *Menorrhagia*.

PARTURITION.

In about 270 days after impregnation, labor generally commences. There are certain signs by which the female is able to calculate with tolerable certainty about the time she may expect to be confined. Perhaps the most correct mode of calculating is, 280 days from the last menstrual period till confinement; another calculation is, from the period of *quickening*, or the first sensation of fetal life, which is usually perceived about four months and a half after conception. During the last month also the child sinks lower down in the abdomen, and the waist becomes smaller. As the time approaches when a woman expects to be confined she of course sees that every thing necessary for the occasion is prepared, and placed convenient and in order, so that at the time everything may be in readiness, and all confusion avoided. Previous to the setting in of labor she frequently suffers from what are called

FALSE PAINS.

These do not always exist, and when they do, they usually precede labor but a few hours; sometimes however they come on days and even weeks before delivery. They differ from labor-pains in being unconnected with uterine contractions, not increasing in intensity as they return, and are principally confined to the abdomen. If medicines are required, a few doses of *Bryonia*, *Nux-v.*, *Pulsatilla*, or *Dulcamara*, will generally be sufficient.

Bryonia may be given if the pains in the abdomen are followed by dragging pain in the back and loins, with constipation and irritable temper. *Nux-v.* where there are similar symptoms to those indicated by Bryonia, also a bruised sensation in the region of the pubis. *Pulsatilla* where there are pains in the abdomen or loins, with stiffness and painful dragging and aching in the thighs. *Dulcamara* where the pains are seated in the small of the back, and are thc result of a cold or dampness; and *Belladonna* where the pains are of a spasmodic character.

Dose.—Two drops, or six globules, of the selected remedy may be mixed in a tumbler of water, and a tablespoonful taken once in three or four hours.

LABOR.

Preceding labor there are often premonitory symptoms, such as, nervous trembling, sadness, looseness of the bowels, flying pains through the abdomen, frequent inclination to pass water, followed by a slight discharge of reddish mucus. But at length pains, bearing down, come on at regular intervals, gradually increasing in intensity and frequency until the little being is ushered into the world. During the progress of the labor, cold water may be taken if desired. As the labor progresses there may be

CRAMPS, CONVULSIONS, AND SPASMODIC PAINS.

Chamomilla may be given, where the pains are acute, and are attended with spasms.

Belladonna, if there are violent bearing-down pains, with convulsive movements of the limbs, congestion to the head, red and bloated face.

Hyosciamus, where there are severe convulsions, with loss of consciousness, anguish, cries, and oppression of the chest.

Stramonium.—Trembling of the limbs and convulsions without loss of consciousness.

Cocculus.—Cramps and convulsions in the limbs and the whole body; cramps in the lower part of the abdomen.

TREATMENT AFTER DELIVERY.

After delivery the patient should remain perfectly quiet, and be made as comfortable as possible, without disturbing her. At the expiration of an hour or two, if every thing goes on well, she may be changed, and put to bed. If flooding sets in after delivery, see *Menorrhagia*.

AFTER PAINS.

These pains come on after delivery and are more and more severe after each successive labor, seldom occurring with first children. They are occasioned by the efforts of nature to expel the clots of blood which may remain in the womb, and where they are not very violent nor of long duration, no treatment is necessary. Should, however, they be very severe and long continued, one of the following remedies will produce relief.

Arnica should be first given, followed after three or four doses, if necessary, by *Pulsatilla*. If relief is not soon obtained, and the pains are severe, accompanied with great restlessness, *Nux-v.* and *Chamomilla* may be taken in alternation,

Secale and *Cuprum* may be alternated, where the pains are very violent, especially in those who have borne many children.

Dose.—Two drops in a tumbler of water, a tablespoonful once in one or two hours; or six globules on the tongue at the same intervals.

DURATION OF CONFINEMENT.

The first five or six days should be spent in bed, during which time the mother should remain perfectly quiet, her food of a light farinaceous character, consisting of toast, black tea, panada, farina, roasted apples, &c. At the expiration of this time she may be permitted to set up a little while, if every thing goes on well, increasing the period each day. If the secretion of milk has become fairly established, and all febrile symptoms subsided, her diet may gradually assume a more nourishing and substantial character.

There is generally a torpidity of the bowels for several days, but this should create no alarm, as for a few days, on account of the great change going on in the system, no evacuation is necessary. The constipation can as a general thing be controlled by the food, which should consist in part of fruit, such as roasted apples. If there should be no movement after six or seven days, three or four doses of *Bryonia*, at intervals of four hours, followed if necessary by *Nux*, or *Sulphur*, will usually produce relief. If however after two or three days no relief is obtained, a tepid water injection may be given. The diarrhœa which sets in sometimes after delivery, will be relieved by a few doses of *Rheum.*, *Phos-ac.*, or *Pulsatilla*, and if occasioned by a cold, *Dulcamara*, given at intervals of four hours.

THE BREASTS.

If, for several weeks previous to the birth of the child, particular attention is given to the breasts, much future suffering and trouble may be avoided. The breasts should be bathed with cold water daily, and afterwards rubbed dry. Should there be tenderness or slight excoriation, they may be bathed with weak brandy and water twice a day. Should there be aching pain in the nipples, a few doses of *Aconite* may be given. If there are cracks or excoriations, a powder of *Silicea* may be taken in the morning, and *Hepar*, at night.

MILK FEVER.

About the third day after delivery, the breasts become filled with milk. The fever which usually attends this profuse secretion, generally lasts but two or three days, and is called the "*milk fever.*" As a general thing, it passes off without serious injury, requiring no other treatment than good and careful nursing. Should, however, there be much soreness and hardness of the breasts, they may be bathed two or three times a day, with a lotion composed of six drops of *Arnica*, to a tablespoonful of water.

If considerable fever is present, attended with restlessness, and also if the breasts are knotted and hard, a few doses of *Aconite* may be given, at intervals of two or three hours. *Bryonia* may follow *Aconite*, if that is insufficient, and should there be oppression of the chest, and pain in the head. *Pulsatilla*, or *Rhus*, may be given, should there be heat and hardness of the breasts, with rheumatic pains in the chest and limbs. If the breasts are very much distended and painful, they may be relieved by the breast pump.

DOSE.—Six globules on the tongue, or two drops, in a tumbler of water, a tablespoonful at a dose.

SUPPRESSED SECRETION OF MILK.

In some cases there is a deficiency of milk. This difficulty may generally be obviated by taking nourishing food, and those drinks which have a tendency to increase the secretion of milk, such as, milk, milk punch, or beer.

Again, owing to some mental or physical disturbance, there may be a suppressed secretion of milk, followed by local congestion, determination of blood to the head, &c. In these cases, *Pulsatilla* should be immediately given, two drops, or twelve globules, in a tumbler half full of water, a teaspoonful once in two or three hours. This may be followed after three or four doses, if necessary, by *Bryonia* and *Belladonna*, in alternation two hours apart. Should there be in connection with the above symptoms, considerable fever, together with great nervous excitement, *Aconite* and *Coffea* may be alternated as above.

SORE NIPPLES.

The mother is frequently tormented with sore nipples, which are so painful as to render it almost impossible to nurse her child. They may be bathed two or three times a day with weak brandy and water, or alum-water; or with a lotion composed of six drops of *Arnica*, to a tablespoonful of water, taking care however, after either of these applications, to bathe them with tepid milk and water before nursing. If there is a constant pain, *Chamomilla* may be given once in three or four hours, until relieved. Should suppuration or ulceration commence, a powder of *Silicea* may be taken morning and night, followed in four or five days if necessary, by *Mercury*, *Calcarea*, or *Hepar*.

GATHERED BREAST. AGUE IN THE BREAST.

The mother sometimes suffers severely from these troubles, which if not controlled, may produce serious derangement and severe suffering.

Taken in the commencement, a few doses of *Bryonia*, two drops, or twelve globules, in a tumbler half full of water, a spoonful every two hours, will generally be sufficient. Should, however, considerable fever set in, and the breasts be swollen, painful, and very tender, *Aconite* and *Belladonna* may be alternated, two hours apart; warm cloths also may be applied, or Stramonium leaves be placed over the breasts. Should gathering or suppuration commence, indicated by hard swelling and throbbing pain, *Hepar* and *Silicea*, may be given in alternation, a powder, six hours apart, followed if necessary after two days, by *Mercury*, and *Lachesis*, at the same intervals, until the abscess breaks. When the suppuration has pretty well advanced, poultices of bread and milk, slippery elm, or flax-seed may be applied. After the abscess has opened, give a powder of *Sulphur* every night.

THE LOCHIA.

This discharge, which follows confinement, resembles at first menstruation, but gradually grows lighter colored, becoming before it ceases, yellowish or whitish. It is sometimes thin and scanty, ceasing in a few days, at others profuse, lasting for weeks, but its general duration is about ten days. If long continued and very profuse, it weakens the system, and should be checked. If it ceases too soon, and at the same time there is a suppression of milk, serious disturbances may be apprehended.

If it is long continued and very profuse, see *Menorrhagia.*

When it is suppressed: *Bryonia*, *Pulsatilla*, *Dulcamara*, *Opium*, *Platina*, or *Belladonna*, will be required.

Bryonia is indicated, where the suppression is accompanied by severe headache, fullness and throbbing in the head, and aching in the back.

Pulsatilla, where there is sudden suppression from mental emotion, or dampness, followed by fever, headache, &c.

Dulcamara, when occasioned by cold or dampness, in alternation with *Pulsatilla*.

Platina.—From violent mental emotion, with great sensitiveness of the sexual organs.

Dose.—Two drops, or six globules, in a tumbler half full of water, a teaspoonful once in four hours.

PUERPERAL FEVER.

This fever, sometimes called "*Child-Bed Fever*," is the dread of mothers, and is often attended with serious danger. A physician should be consulted without delay, for if allowed to go on, it may gain a fearful ascendency.

Diagnosis.—The attack may commence even before delivery, though these cases are rare, but they generally are developed in from twenty-four hours to three days after. The attack generally comes on with rigors or shivering, followed by thirst, quickened pulse, and flushed face. The pulse during the disease is rapid, small and wiry, varying from 110 to 140 in a minute. To these symptoms succeed, pain in the head, coming on gradually, nausea, vomiting, and increased sensibility about the uterus. Pain in the abdomen soon attracts notice, generally commencing in the lower part, on either side, and radiating over the abdomen. The pain at first is attended with considerable tenderness of a portion of the abdomen, which becomes very great as the inflammation extends, until at length the patient may not be able to bear the slightest pressure.

There is generally a suppression of the *lochia*, and the urine is usually diminished in quantity, turbid or high colored. During the disease, there may be present at times, great excitement of the nervous system, attended with spasms. This fever frequently prevails as an epidemic.

TREATMENT.—It will be impossible, and in fact it would be unnecessary, to go into the details of treatment here, as the watchful care of the physician will be required to arrest its progress.

Aconite should commence the treatment, in alternation with *Bryonia* or *Belladonna*. The specific indications for *Aconite* are, fever with dry burning heat, thirst for cold drinks, redness of the face, short and oppressed breathing; tenderness of the abdomen to the touch, and scanty, bloody, and fetid lochia.

Belladonna.—Distention or excessive tenderness of the abdomen, sometimes with shooting and digging pains; spasmodic colic; painful pressure on the genital organs; shivering in some part with heat in others, or burning heat with redness of face; pressive headache; great sleeplessness with agitation, or constant inclination to sleep, or delirium and other cerebral symptoms; scanty lochia, or profuse discharge of coagulated and fetid blood.

Bryonia.—Sensitiveness of the abdomen to the touch on the slightest movement; constipation, with shooting pain in the abdomen; high fever with great thirst for cold drinks, and burning heat over the body.

Chamomilla.—Particularly where the fever is brought on by a fit of passion, or a chill, and where the lochia is profuse, abdomen sensitive to the touch, colic-like labor-pains, great agitation and nervous excitability.

Nux-v.—Sudden disappearance of lochia, with heaviness and burning in the genital organs; or profuse discharge with severe pain in the small of the back, and difficulty in urinating. Constipation; nausea; pain in the thighs and legs with numbness; confusion of the head, or pressive headache with vertigo.

Rhus, is a valuable remedy where there is great restlessness, particularly at night, and where the white lochia becomes bloody, with discharge of clotted blood.

Dose.—One drop, or six globules, in a tumbler half full of water, a teaspoonful at a dose; or a powder, or three globules on the tongue. Give once in one, two, or three hours.

Diet and Regimen.—The patient should be kept as quiet as possible, and everything which might produce excitement, be strictly prohibited. The diet should be similar to other varieties of fever.

CHAPTER XII.

TREATMENT OF CHILDREN.

THE INFANT.

The child, while in the womb, is in reality a part of the mother, receiving its nourishment from her and existing in a kind of passive state. The various organs of the body are in a state of complete repose, becoming prepared however for the duties they will have to perform when this passive state is over.

The muscles, the bones, the kidneys, liver, lungs, bowels, and the whole nervous system having no duties to perform remain in a state of almost complete repose. But when the child is ushered into the world, it immediately commences a new existence. Now every organ is aroused and called into action. The lungs move, the bowels act, the kidneys perform their duty, the nervous system begins to show signs of action, and the whole machinery of life moves on in harmony.

Before, surrounded by a fluid of unvarying warmth, and nourished by the mother's blood; now, introduced into a colder and ever-changing atmosphere and wrapped in clothing, however soft it may be, still subjecting it to much harder pressure than it ever before sustained, and compelled to digest its own food and throw out its own waste, the change is speedy, and the effect on the system necessarily great. The very suddenness of the change is necessary to call into action the organs of the body, and thus secure the life of the child. If respiration is not established before the maternal circulation ceases, the child dies as if from suffocation.

The child is of course exceedingly sensitive, and the shock produced by the sudden transition of temperature from 98° to 100° in the mother's womb, to 65° or 75° in the atmosphere, calls into activity respiration. The effect produced is similar to the panting and sighing, which almost every one has noticed on plunging into a cold bath. The sensation to the child of this sudden change of temperature is so disagreeable, that generally the first intimation the mother has that her child is living, is a *lusty cry*, and none but the mother can tell the gushing love which that cry awakens in her heart, or its quick pulsations of joy.

The extreme sensitiveness of the child to external influences is its greatest safeguard. Changes of temperature, hard or harsh clothing, want of cleanliness, and errors in food, may be the means, however trifling they might appear to the more hardy frame, of producing local disease. Hence the child gives utterance to its complaint in a warning cry of distress, the only way in which it can make its complaints known.

We have seen in a preceding chapter, that aside from a venous and arterial circulation, by which the blood is conveyed, charged with nutrition to every part of the system and returned back to the heart charged with impurities, there is a pulmonary circulation, by which the dark impure venous blood is thrown into the lungs from the heart, and there, changed by the action of the air in the air-cells, having received the elements of nutrition in the chyle, conveyed through the thoracic duct, becomes arterialized, and is thrown into the right side of the heart, and from thence conveyed to every part of the system.

In the unborn child the pulmonary circulation does not exist. The arterial blood is received direct from the mother, and as respiration does not exist, there is no necessity of the blood passing through the lungs. It therefore passes directly through, from the right to the left auricle of the heart, by what is called the *foramen ovale*, or oval hole. With the first gasp of the child on emerging into the air, the muscles of respiration begin to act, the blood passes into the lungs, and a new circulation commences. The foramen ovale, no longer of any use, gradually closes up, and the whole volume of blood passes through the lungs. Heretofore the child has lived through the mother, its arterial and venous circulation carried on through the umbilical cord, but now it must breathe, and eat for itself. The lungs and heart are at first small, but they continue to expand and increase in size from year to year.

Partly on account of the small size of the chest, and partly from the extreme nervous sensibility, the circulation of the blood in infancy is much more rapid than later in life. While in an adult the heart contracts and the pulse beats from 60 to 80 in a minute, during the first months of life it is nearly double that number, and varies from 120 to 130. Hence we should be on our guard about mistaking a perfectly natural for a feverish pulse.

It is very obvious that the rapid circulation of the infant and its quick respiration, render it more liable, by increasing the nervous excitability, to various forms of acute diseases, than at a more advanced age, where the circulation and respiration are less rapid. Therefore an even temperature and a pure atmosphere are absolutely essential to the health of the child.

Another condition indispensable to the life of the child is the supply of animal heat. This, before birth has been obtained through the mother, but now the child occupies a comparatively independent position, and the preparation of animal heat must be carried on in its own body and by its own organs. The evolution of animal heat we have fully explained in a preceding chapter. It is the same in the child as in the adult. It depends upon *respiration*, *digestion*, and *nervous excitement.* The power of generating animal heat, contrary to what is supposed by many, is far less in the young than in the adult. The reasons are very obvious. The lungs are small, therefore respiration is less full and active; the diet consists of watery and unstimulating milk, and the infant is of course prevented by weakness from making use of much exertion; and lastly the nervous system is not fully aroused, the child, during the first months of its life, sleeping a large portion of the time. A temperature of about 98 is essential to man, and this we find he has, if in a state of health, whether he inhabits a land where the thermometer is 100° above zero or 20° below. This uniform temperature of the body is much warmer as a general thing than the surrounding atmosphere, and unless the internal fires were kept burning, the body would soon cool down to the same temperature as the medium by which it is surrounded. The power of generating animal heat is smaller in early life, than at any other period of existence, and therefore the power of resisting external cold is far less at that period. The pernicious effects of highly heated and impure air, and allowing the limbs of the child, both in the house and out of doors, to be destitute in a great measure of clothing, will very readily be perceived by all.

CLOTHING.

We will suppose the little stranger fairly introduced into the world, and ready for its first bath. The room should be of a moderate temperature, and the possibility of currents of air from doors, windows or cracks carefully guarded against. Drafts of air would be highly injurious, as well as the near vicinity of a large fire where the rays fall directly on the child. The temperature of the water should be about blood heat. Warmer than this would produce relaxation and consequent debility, colder, the animal heat would be rapidly withdrawn from the child at a time when its power of generating heat would be very limited. In washing the child, all that is generally necessary, is a soft sponge, by which the warm water can be thoroughly applied in a manner not to injure the delicate skin and the mucus or oily covering of the child effectually removed. Sometimes the peculiar substance with which the child is covered cannot be removed merely by soap-water; in these cases the parts may be smeared with fresh lard, butter or the yolk of an egg, and then washed off. The face should be washed first, and with a different sponge from the rest of the body, and great care taken to prevent any of the soap from getting into the eyes. By failing to observe these simple directions, an opthalmia of an exceedingly painful character is often induced.

While particular pains should be taken to have the child perfectly clean, it should not be forgotten that you are handling a delicate being, who is taking its first lesson in life. I have often seen nurses in the lower walks of life, and even where there was no excuse for their not knowing better, grasp the head firmly in one hand, with the other, armed with a rag, not of the softest quality, and plentifully covered with soap, scrub the little face with an energy and good will, which expended on pots and kettles would be highly meritorious, but which is not exactly the thing with the tender flesh of the young infant. If the child is very weak, it should not be still further fatigued by a long washing. In these cases, let the nurse make the child as clean as possible in a reasonable time, and leave the rest till the next washing. After the child has been washed and dried, the cord may be wrapped in a soft linen rag; over this a thin flannel bandage must be applied five or six inches in breadth, and long enough to go once or twice around the body. The object is partly warmth, and partly to prevent the bowels pressing out at the opening of the navel. In warm weather or where the skin is very sensitive, a linen or cotton bandage can be substituted. The bandage should not, as is often the case, be drawn too tightly, for this would prevent the proper action of the abdomen in respiration, and thereby produce much evil. The cord generally suppurates, and drops off in five or six days, and it is not necessary previous to that to change its dressing more than once or twice, if at all. As it regards the dress, the mother can consult the prevailing fashion, or her own taste, providing she also consults common sense, and while she uses light, soft, and warm clothing, such as will afford ample protection to the child, is careful to have it fit so as not to compress the body or prevent the utmost freedom of movement. The dress will of course vary somewhat according to the climate and season of the year. In the winter, or where the child is delicate, thin, soft flannel next the skin is generally preferable. The plan of rolling the child up in bandages like a mummy, thus preventing the expansion of the chest and abdomen, and the free motion of the limbs, has fortunately gone out of fashion. If flannel produces much perspiration and soreness, linen should be substituted. Whatever the clothing may be, it should be very frequently changed, and never put on until after it has been thoroughly aired and made comfortably warm. While the mother bears in mind the fact, that the supply of animal heat is the smallest in infancy, and therefore perceives the necessity of keeping her child sufficiently warm, she should not forget that too warm clothing, and too high a temperature in the room, are equally injurious as the other extreme.

As dressing is generally tiresome and irksome to the child, the garments should be made so as to be easily taken off or put on. Pins should be avoided wherever it is possible, and soft tapes, loops, or something of the kind substituted in their place. Unless great care is exercised, pins stick into the flesh, worry the child, and occasion, paroxysms of crying, often attributed to disease. The practice of leaving the upper portion of the chest and arms naked for the first five or six years cannot be too strongly condemned. The chest must be protected, or you will stand a pretty good chance of being called to watch with agonized emotions by the side of your child, suffering from croup, inflammation of the lungs, fevers, and those varied diseases which prevail to such an alarming extent at this period of life. Children who have their bosoms, arms, and legs covered for the first two years, are far less liable to colds, coughs, croups, inflammation of the lungs, and that long list of diseases which annually sweep off so many of the bright and beautiful little prattlers.

Formerly it was the pride of the mother, to see her child with a beautiful cap on its head, now, mothers generally prefer to see the little head without any covering, except what nature gradually provides it in the form of hair. And this is much the wisest plan. Caps after all, make them as beautiful as you choose, are a great nuisance, and often productive of much harm. By them the head is kept too warm, inducing alarming diseases of the brain ; and the tender scalp, constantly irritated, rendered much more liable to painful and fetid eruptions. The string also passing under the chin, often gives the poor thing the first sensation of hanging. Where the head is kept too warm, diseases of the brain, as a matter of course, are much more frequent. Pains should be taken to keep the temperature of the child as nearly alike at all times as possible. During the day the clothing may be very judicious, while at night the child may be almost buried in feathers and swelter under warm blankets. Considering, that two-thirds of the infant's life is spent in sleep, the danger of these sudden transitions from a high to a low temperature is very apparent.

In the course of a few months as the strength increases, a change of clothing becomes necessary, and the long dresses give place to those more suitable to increasing activity. The feet should now be protected by stockings, and whatever form of dress is adopted, the ridiculous fashion of leaving the legs, arms, and the upper portion of the chest naked, should never be indulged.

FOOD.

As we have before remarked, while the child is in the mother's womb, it has no need of appetite, as all its nutriment is imparted without any exertion on its part, through the circulation of the mother. When the connecting link, which for nine months has bound the child so closely to its mother, is severed, and the little being is ushered into the world, the various organs commence their proper functions, developing as a matter of course, *appetite*, and the first few days of a child is divided almost entirely between sleeping and gratifying its appetite. At this period it often is only aroused by hunger, and when this is appeased, drops to sleep.

Several years since, when engaged in the practice of my profession in a beautiful country village, I was called out late one evening by a Frenchman to see his little child, then about three days old. The father had called at my office several times during the evening before my return, and was then so much excited, that he could not give me any rational account of the difficulty until I reached the house, where I found the mother in tears, sobbing as if her heart would break, and insisting, in broken English, that "mine child shall die."

Her tears however were quickly changed to smiles, when I told her, that six months hence she would be delighted, if her child slept as quietly. There was nothing the matter. The child was merely obeying the first demands of its being. In the course of a few hours, as soon as the mother has obtained a little rest, it is always best to place the child by her side, and let it receive its first nourishment from her breast. The milk at this time, if there is any, is thin and watery, of a whey-like consistency, and does not gain its rich and creamy character, until the lapse of several days. In this we see another beautiful arrangement of nature. The milk is precisely of the character best adapted to the wants of the child. It acts gently on the bowels, causing the removal of the dark and slimy *meconium*, with which they are loaded at birth, and gradually, as it becomes richer in its properties, prepares the stomach for its reception. The mother's milk is of itself a laxative, and generally all the laxative the child requires. The habit of dosing the little being with castor-oil, catnip-tea, rheubarb and even calomel, cannot be too strongly condemned. Bear in mind the delicate organization, and remember that the organs are all new and unused, requiring the most delicate stimulus. However much the robust system may be abused, infancy will not be trifled with without showing the effects of it in cries, fretfulness, convulsions, colic, diarrhœa and often death. The bills of mortality show, that an enormous per-centage of death, nearly one-third, occurs before the age of three years. We are to look, as one frightful cause of this mortality, to the trifling with nature, and the kindly meant, though unwise intermeddling of friends and relatives. If, after the lapse of four or five hours there should be no movement from the bowels, and the child is evidently suffering from this cause, a small amount of tepid sugar and water, or molasses and water, will generally be all that is necessary to relieve the difficulty.

If those having the care of an infant would bear in mind the fact, that up to the moment of birth it has been nourished by the rich blood of the mother, they would be less anxious to crowd its delicate stomach with food of their own contriving, often to its injury. The cramps, colics, and cries of pain, which are so often heard in the nursery, are frequently the result of this forcing system. The cry of pain, which tortures the ear, is too often the voice of nature, protesting in the strongest terms against this abuse of her laws. An ordinary flow of milk is generally established in three or four days, and this gradually becoming rich and nourishing, as the wants of the child demand it, is with but few exceptions, all that it requires. If however during the first few days there is not a sufficient secretion of milk, its want may be supplied by a little tepid sugar and water, or weak milk and water. System and order are necessary in all things, and in nothing more than in the care of the infant. The practice is very common, whenever the child cries, to stop its mouth with the breast. This is often done fifty or a hundred times a day, and at night, the mother's sleep is broken every half hour by the cries of her child; thus both are deprived of their natural rest, the mother becomes a slave to her child, and the child develops as a reward a peevish and restless temper. This habit strongly reminds us of an anecdote of an old lady, who in the fullness of her kindness begged her guest to "eat, eat, eat till you split. I really wish you would."

The stomach of an infant, when a few days old, is very small, holding not much more than a tablespoonful; as the child increases in age, of course the stomach becomes larger, but this repeated filling it with food in too large quantities, leaves it no time for digestion, and produces flatulence, colic, diarrhœa, indigestion, and sometimes entails on the young being a lasting disease. Crying is not always an indication of hunger. The babe can tell its sufferings in no other way, and it just as often cries from repletion, as from lack of food. It cries when too warm or too cold, or whenever anything affects its delicate organization unpleasantly. Crying, however unpleasant it may be, is not unfrequently highly beneficial. The organs of respiration are developed and strengthened by the exercise. As we have already stated in speaking of the adult, the amount of food should be proportioned to the waste in the system. Crowding the stomach with food more than it can digest, whether in the adult or infant, leads to the most serious difficulties. During the first few weeks of infancy the child requires food oftener than when a few months old, but even then every three hours will as a general thing be all-sufficient, unless it should be demanded more frequently by those evident signs of hunger which no mother need mistake. If the breast is not offered on every occasion and for every cry, it will only be demanded at stated intervals. As the child advances in age, the length of time between the period of taking nourishment will of course be proportionally increased. At first the child will require nourishment three or four times in the course of the night, but after a short time once late in the evening and again early in the morning will be all that is necessary. The child may, in a warm room, be suffering from thirst, and a drink of water be all that is necessary to still its crying.

It is a curious fact, that great fatigue, strong mental emotion, fear, passion, or wild and excessive grief often produce a strong effect on the mother's milk. Hence she should by no means give the breast when suffering from great fatigue, or violent mental emotion. The case recorded of the German woman, is probably familiar to all. A soldier attacked her husband with a drawn sword. At first she was paralyzed with terror, but in a moment she sprang forward with fury, wrenched the sword from the soldier's hand, and parted the combatants. While in this strong state of excitement she took her child from the cradle and placed it to her breast. The doom of the little being, at the time perfectly healthy, was sealed, for in a few moments it was dead. Will those who will believe in nothing but tangible doses, tell us how much poison was contained in the mother's milk, and how the chemical change was produced, instantaneously, by the action of the mind?

> There are more things in heaven and earth,
> Than are dreamed of in your philosophy.

ARTIFICIAL FEEDING.

In all cases where the mother can nurse her child with safety, she should certainly do so, as the mortality among infants thus nourished is far less than among those who are "brought up by hand," as it is termed. At times, however, from a variety of causes, such as the non-secretion of the mother's milk, disease or death, it is necessary to administer food. In these cases a healthy wet-nurse should be obtained if possible, if not, the food should resemble that of the mother's milk as nearly as possible.

The following analysis of several kinds of milk may guide us in a proper selection.

CONSTITUENTS.	COW.	ASS.	WOMAN.	GOAT.	EWE.
Caseine	4.48	1.82	1.52	4.02	4.50
Butter	3.13	0.11	3.35	3.32	4.20
Sugar of milk	4.77	6.08	6.50	5.25	5.00
Various salts	0.60	0.34	0.45	0.58	0.68
Water	87.02	91.65	87.98	86.80	85.82
Total	100.00	100.00	100.00	100.00	100.00
Solid Substances	12.98	8.35	12.02	13.20	14.38

We perceive from this analysis, that woman's milk is the poorest of all, but that it contains most saccharine matter; next to this comes ass's milk. In choosing our substitute we should either prefer the one, which approaches nearest the natural food of the child, or endeavor to modify the difference, in what we do take. Thus, a large proportion of water and sugar should be added to cow's milk, a less amount of each to goat's milk, &c.

Cow's milk is generally used on account of its being more readily obtained than most of the other varieties. It should be obtained perfectly fresh, from one cow if possible, sweetened, diluted at first with two-thirds water, reducing the quantity of water after a week, or two, to one-half, and again in a short time to one-third, at which strength the child can be fed for four or five months, after which, if the it is active, the milk can be given undiluted.

The utmost attention should be paid not only to the temperature of the milk, but to cleanliness. The food should be as nearly as possible the temperature of the mother's milk, at 96° or 98°. The water should be heated and poured on the milk, and in no case should the food thus prepared be heated for use a second time.

A variety of sucking-bottles are used, fitted with an artificial nipple, pierced with small holes. The nipple can be made of sponge, covered with a rag, chamois leather, folds of linen and a variety of materials. The sucking-bottle should never be put aside without, together with the nipple, being thoroughly washed with hot water. This may seem an excess of care, but there is far less trouble in doing things properly than in listening to the cries of the child or in watching by its sick-bed.

After taking its food, the child naturally in the earlier periods of its life feels an inclination to sleep. In this it should be indulged, for if tossed about and purposely kept awake, it will almost surely suffer from indigestion. I have often seen the nurse, after having fed the child, place it on her knees and trot it with an energy as if its life depended on having the contents of its stomach well churned, and have heartily wished, that immediately after dinner she could be placed on some machine, where she might receive a practical lesson in the beauties of trotting.

Sometimes after the first month or two, milk seems to disagree with the child. In this case it may be mixed with well boiled arrow root, sago, farina, or well baked and toasted bread. A very excellent food is "bread jelly." A quantity of the soft part of a loaf is broken up, and boiling water being poured on it, it is covered and allowed to steep for some time; the water is then strained off completely, and fresh water added, and the whole placed on the fire and allowed to boil slowly for some time, until it becomes smooth; the water is then pressed out, and the bread on cooling forms a thick jelly, a portion of which is to be mixed with milk, or water and sugar, for use as it is wanted.

The steeping in hot water, and the subsequent boiling, removes all the noxious matters used in making the bread.

Arrow-root made with water alone, or with milk and sugar, is very good food; but as it is somewhat astringent, it is more particularly suited to cases where the bowels are relaxed. In such cases also, boiled milk, or boiled rice and milk, may be given. Pap or panada, and gruels made in the usual way, also form a very good variety of food.

Not unfrequently a change from its usual food to some of the above articles, produces a speedy change in the movements of the bowels. In poor and weak children, weak chicken tea, or beef tea, may be required.

WEANING.

The time of weaning, anticipated with so much dread by anxious mothers, must be governed by circumstances. Some women are not able to suckle but a few months, while others continue it for two or three years. I know a lady, now a venerable grandmother, who nursed a child, now a strong athletic man, until he was so large that he was able to stand by her side and nurse. When visitors were present, a little ashamed to indulge in his favorite practice before them, he would call his mother out of the room, as if he had something of importance to tell, when he would commence nursing.

As a general thing, the child should not be weaned earlier than nine months, or later than twelve months. By this time it will generally be provided with teeth, although sometimes they are not developed until the child is eighteen or twenty months of age. Should, however, there be a non-sufficiency of milk, or the health of the mother suffer, weaning can take place at any time. It should in no case be continued, when it is apparent that it is injurious to the mother. Weaning should not take place, if it can be avoided, when the infant is unwell, or when suffering severely from teething, or during the warm weather of summer. It is best, generally, that the weaning shall be gradual, accustoming the child, before it is entirely deprived of the breast, to be fed with the spoon.

After the child is weaned, its diet should still be of a fluid or soft character, gradually changing as the system requires. Milk, thickened with arrow-root, sago, farina, bread, gruel, crackers pulverized in warm water and slightly sweetened, will at first constitute its principal diet. Regularity now in administering its food, is of equal importance, as in the earlier or later periods of life, and the child should not be accustomed to be fed whenever it cries, or is uneasy, unless there are signs that the uneasiness or crying is caused by hunger. If the child is really hungry, it should be fed, but in those cases a piece of bread will not be rejected, as it probably will in case the appetite is artificial, and only for nice things.

CLEANLINESS, AIR, AND EXERCISE.

Every mother will perceive the necessity of perfect cleanliness. The clothes should be frequently changed, and the child be accustomed to a daily bath. The water should be during the first few days after birth about blood heat, gradually lowering the temperature as the child becomes stronger, until in the course of a few months, the water may be used nearly if not quite cold. A bath should be used in which the whole body may be immersed. After bathing, the body should be thoroughly dried, followed by gentle friction with the hand or a soft towel. Particular attention should be paid to the hair and scalp. At first it is of course washed all over every day, but after the child is a year old, once a week or fortnight will be sufficient, if it be well brushed night and morning.

The Nursery.—There is one important subject in the training of the child, of which I have not spoken, I mean, *the nursery*. A healthy location, pure air, and cleanliness are of course essential. A situation away from contamination, with a dry and pure air, should be selected.

It is very common in New-York, and in fact in all populous cities, to see in certain localities, a dozen families occupying one house. Each family sometimes composed of six or eight children, besides the parents, have at most but two rooms, and often only one. Here within these dark, damp walls, sometimes in basements, and sometimes in attics, where the cold wind and rain penetrates through every crack, they cook, and eat, and sleep, huddled together like swine.

No wonder that disease and crime revel here. No wonder that these localities swell that dark and filthy stream of licentiousness, whose turbid waters cast their stench over society; morally and physically poisoned, what could we expect. And here they live in the midst of filth, pinched with poverty, seeing their children growing up around them candidates for crime, when at a less expense than they are now under, they could have pleasant homes in some of the many quiet villages clustering around, and within a few moments ride of our great cities.

Even among those who are possessed of wealth, the most unpleasant and worst ventilated part of the house is not unfrequently taken as a nursery. The upper rooms, being more airy and dry than the lower, should as a general thing be selected. Those having a southern exposure would of course be preferable. A want of pure air and healthy food, is one of the principle causes of various diseases, as well as the development in infancy of that scourge of our race, Scrofula or Tuberculosis. Nothing should be permitted in the nursery which would have a tendency to vitiate the air, or interfere with a proper ventilation. While we take particular pains not to have the nursery at too high a temperature, we should be equally cautious to have an even and comfortable warmth at all times. Drafts of cold air should be avoided, and the so-called hot air stoves, standing like a mass of heated metal, exhausting the life of the air, and creating no current should never find their way into the nursery.

The temperature must be regulated according to the season, and should range somewhere between 60° and 70°. During winter, and a portion of spring and autumn, fire will be required during the day, but it is not necessary at night, unless in case of sickness. After dressing in the morning, the children should leave the room for an hour or two, during which time it should be thoroughly ventilated.

Children must, as a matter of course, spend hours and days alone with their nursery attendants, at a time when first impressions are stronger than at any other period of their lives. Great care then should be taken in the selection of the nurse. She should be orderly, cleanly, addicted to no vulgar habit, and of a mild and cheerful temper. I have already referred to this subject, in speaking of the moral training of children.

Exercise.—This is essential to the proper developement of the muscles, and the various organs of the body, but we should bear in mind the softness of the bones, and the weakness of the body in the early months of infancy. Exercise at this period should be mostly of the passive kind, as violent exercise, or carrying the child in an erect or sitting position would have a tendency to produce curvature of the spine and limbs. Respiration, crying, tossing about the limbs, produce at first nearly all the exercise required.

In summer weather the child can hardly be too much in the open air, and should be accustomed to it at longer or shorter intervals daily. In winter, more caution is necessary, but even then it may be taken out after the first or second month, in pleasant weather, for a short time. The indiscriminate exposure of children for the purpose of hardening them, is a barbarous practice. They should be warmly clothed, and not exposed to the weather when there is danger of being chilled. During the first four or five months, in taking exercise, the child should not be carried in a sitting position. The head is large and heavy, and for want of sufficient strength in the neck to keep it in an erect position, it falls from one side to the other, impeding respiration. The best way to carry young infants, is in an oblong basket, or on the arm of the nurse in a reclining position, so as to protect the body and head. It should never be lifted by the arms or guided by them, when it makes its first effort to walk, but one hand should be placed on each side of the chest, just below the arm-pits.

The cradle in which the child is rocked to sleep, or its cries stilled, is rapidly losing favor, and should be entirely banished from every household. Rocking, with the rapidity often practiced, undoubtedly induces sleep, but it is an apoplectic sleep, endangering the brain and the nervous system.

When a child is able to walk he will show his ability in a way which cannot be misunderstood, and then a little help, rather to enable him to balance than to support himself will be sufficient. Walking requires not merely physical strength, but the power of balancing, and we should be cautious about forcing the child to step alone, until the latter as well as the former has been in a measure acquired. The child itself decides on the different steps of its progress, and a little watchfulness on the part of the mother or nurse, will easily discover the indications. As the child increases in strength, air and exercise are even more indispensable; in fact, from two to ten, or twelve years of age, it cannot have too much fresh air, provided there is not an undue exposure. I have already referred to this part of the subject in speaking of the moral, physical, and intellectual training of children.

SELECTION OF A WET NURSE.

In the selection of a nurse, the physician should of course be consulted. She should be cheerful, amiable, orderly and cleanly; there should be no traces of hereditary or other disease; the skin should be sound, without eruption or trace of scrofulous disease; the mouth and teeth healthy; the breasts of moderate size and firm. It is desirable to choose a nurse whose child is about the age of the one she is about to suckle, although this is not always necessary. The milk should be thin, clear, of a bluish white color, limpid and sweet. The food should be plain but nourishing, with the addition sometimes at dinner of a moderate allowance of ale or porter. She should exercise daily in the open air; her digestion should be good, and her bowels regular.

2. DISEASES OF CHILDREN.

As we have glanced at the general treatment of the child during the first few years of its existence, we will now speak of some of the affections with which it is most liable to be troubled.

.APPARENT DEATH OF A NEW-BORN INFANT.

Where a new-born infant does not breathe for some minutes after delivery, steps should be promptly taken to resuscitate it. The back should be rubbed along the spinal processes, the limbs and chest should also be rubbed, gently but firmly, and the abdomen around the cord rubbed with brandy and water. If after the lapse of five or ten minutes there are no signs of life, the cord should be cut, and the child placed in a warm bath, at the same time squeezing the limbs and chest gently. Put about as much *Tartar Emetic* as will lie on a three cent piece into a tumbler half full of water, and put two or three drops of this mixture into the mouth. Sometimes it is possible to inflate the lungs by placing the mouth over the child's mouth, and gently breathing, at the same time closing the nostrils with the thumb and finger to prevent the air passing out. After the lungs are filled, the chest should be gently compressed so as to imitate as nearly as possible respiration. Infants have sometimes been restored after two or three hours of apparent death, so that efforts at resuscitation should not be given up too soon. Where there are unmistakable signs of the death of the child previous to delivery, it would of course be useless to make efforts at resuscitation.

SWELLING OR ELONGATION OF THE HEAD.

At birth, the bones of the cranium, where they unite with each other are more or less soft, so that there is frequently an elongation or swelling of the head, especially after difficult labor. The difficulty will usually disappear in two or three days. If the swelling should be extensive, however the head should be washed with cold water or bathed with a mixture composed of six drops of *Arnica*, to a tumbler half full of water.

COLD IN THE HEAD. SNUFFLES. CORYZA.

This is a very common affection among infants. The nose becomes obstructed, so as to render it necessary for them to breathe in a measure through the mouth, hence they are obliged, when nursing, to relinquish the nipple frequently, in order to get breath.

Nux-v. will frequently be all that is required, especially where there is obstruction of the nose with dryness. Three globules may be placed on the tongue, morning and night.

Sambucus may be given if after two doses of *Nux* no relief is obtained. Three globules may be taken once in four or six hours, until better, unless one of the following remedies is indicated.

Chamomilla, where the obstruction is attended with watery discharge from the nose. *Calcarea*, where *Chamomilla* has been ineffectual.

Stibium will be required, where together with the running at the nose, there is cough, rattling of mucus in the chest, &c.

Dose.—Same as *Sambucus*.

COLIC. CRYING, AND WAKEFULNESS OF INFANTS.

Where it is evident that the cries of a child proceed from pain, as they generally do, the cause should be ascertained. The dress should be carefully examined, to see that the flesh is not irritated by pins. If it is evident, that the pain proceeds from colic, a few doses of *Chamomilla* will generally be all that is necessary to produce relief, especially if there are griping pains, indicated by writhing of the body, and drawing up the legs, together with diarrhœa.

Belladonna or *Coffea* will be indicated where there is apparently no exciting cause, but the infant is peevish, wakeful and has prolonged fits of crying. *Ipecac.*, where the colic is attended with sickness of the stomach.

Dose.—Give every half hour or hour until relieved.

Rheum.—Screaming, restlessness, violent griping pains, and sour-smelling diarrhœic stools.

Nux-v. will be required, where the bowels are constipated, and where there is flatulent colic, accompanied by sudden fits of crying.

SWELLING OF THE BREASTS.

Shortly after birth the breasts of the infant are frequently found to be swollen. This swelling is not occasioned, as is sometimes supposed, by the presence of milk, and therefore squeezing the breast will not only be productive of no good, but a vast amount of harm. The swollen parts may be covered with a linen cloth dipped in sweet oil. If this produces no relief, the parts may be bathed in warm brandy and water, giving *Chamomilla* and *Belladonna* in alternation, three globules, six hours apart. If notwithstanding this treatment, the swelling still continues to increase, apply a bread and milk poultice, and if the gathering has opened, give three globules of *Mercury*, one evening and three of *Hepar-s.* the next.

INFLAMMATION OF THE EYES. PURULENT OPHTHALMIA.

This affection is very common among infants, setting in sometimes when only a few days old. It generally commences in the lids, but if neglected, soon extends to the eyeballs.

It may be occasioned by allowing soap or some of the substance which covers the child to get into the eye, at the first washing ; also by exposure to a strong light, a draft of air or the glare of a fire.

A little of the mother's milk should be dropped in the eye four or five times a day. Give also two globules of *Aconite* in alternation with the same amount of *Belladonna*, three or four hours apart.

If in the course of two or three days no improvement is perceptible, and there is great intolerance of light, redness, swelling and agglutination of the lids, give two globules of *Chamomilla*, once in four hours.

Mercury and *Pulsatilla* may be given in alternation, two globules three hours apart, if there are redness of the eyes and eyelids, small yellowish ulcers along the margin of the lid, with purulent discharge.

Euphrasia and *Rhus* may be alternated, two globules six

hours apart, if there should still remain accumulation of matter in the eyes, and great intolerance of light.

Sulphur and *Calcarea* may be alternated twenty-four hours apart, where the disease occurs in scrofulous children.

Continue to bathe the eyes with the mother's milk, or tepid milk and water.

EXCORIATION.

The utmost cleanliness is of course essential, to guard against this difficulty. Bathe the parts frequently with cold water; wipe dry with a soft cloth, and dust on a little fine wheaten starch, or apply a lotion composed of six drops of *Arnica* to a tea-cup of water.

If there is considerable redness and inflammation, give two globules of *Belladonna* every night.

If the child is very restless, and in fact, in most forms of excoriation, where it is not occasioned by abuse of *Chamomile-tea*, two globules of *Chamomilla* every night will usually produce relief.

Mercury will be required, where the excoriation is extensive and severe, two globules every night. If after several days the difficulty still continues, one of the following remedies may be given, *Sulphur*, *Sepia*, *Calcarea*, or *Carb.-v.*

JAUNDICE.

This trouble is frequently occasioned by the administration of cathartics shortly after birth, and also from cold. There is yellowness of the whites of the eyes, skin, and urine. The bowels are sometimes costive, at others loose.

Chamomilla and *Mercury* may be given in alternation, two globules of one, in the morning, and two of the other at night. If after four or five days there is no improvement, *Nux* may be given in the same way, or it may precede the others, where there is restlessness and constipation.

China will be required if the symptoms still continue after the administration of the other remedies.

THRUSH. SORE MOUTH. APHTHÆ.

This very common affection in infancy, is characterized by the appearance of small, round, white vesicles on the interior of the mouth and over the tongue, which, if not checked, run together, forming patches, producing a superficial ulceration of the mucous membrane of the mouth and throat. There is of course difficulty of nursing and swallowing, and generally, a deranged state of the stomach and bowels. Where the attack is severe and the ulceration extensive, there is more or less fever, pain, restlessness, &c.

There is another variety of Aphthæ, sometimes mistaken for *Thrush.*—It consists at first of small points or patches of curdy matter on the surface of the membrane, and generally easily wiped away with a cloth. In severe cases, blood may exude from the mucous membrane at these points.

CAUSES.—The prominent cause is a constitutional taint. It is also frequently produced by improper food in those who are fed with the bottle or spoon.

TREATMENT.—If the inflammation is not very severe, equal parts of borax and loaf sugar may be mixed dissolved in water and applied to the mouth three or four times a day; or *borax* and *honey* may be mixed and applied in the same way, or the mouth may be washed with a mixture made by dissolving a few grains of borax in a tea-cup of water.

Mercury should be given two globules twice a day, when the disease first makes its appearance, especially if there is salivation and ulceration. *Sulphur* should follow *Mercury* at the same intervals, if the latter fails to effect a cure in three or four days.

HEAT SPOTS. PRICKLY HEAT.

During the heat of summer and occasionally at other times, children are subject to an eruption of small vesicles about the size of a pin's head, filled with watery fluid. These sometimes break and form into thin scabs. They are attended with an itching burning heat and some fever. It is generally occasioned by warm rooms and too warm clothing.

Daily bathing and proper attention to dress are essential to a cure. If much fever and restlessness are present, two globules of *Aconite* may be given in alternation with the same amount of *Chamomilla*, four hours apart. If the eruption is extensive and attended with a burning itching, two globules of *Rhus* may be given morning and night, followed, if relief is not obtained in a few days, by *Arsenic* or *Sulphur*, two globules at night.

There is another form of eruption, called the "*Red Gum*," which consists of small red pimples, chiefly confined to the neck and arms, although sometimes extending over the body. The treatment is similar to that indicated above.

RETENTION OF URINE.

Retention of the urine frequently occurs in young infants, especially shortly after birth. A warm cloth may be placed over the region of the bladder, and two globules of *Aconite* given once in two hours ; if after two or three doses no relief is obtained, *Pulsatilla* may be administered in the same manner.

For other urinary difficulties, see affections of urinary organs, chapter IX.

CONSTIPATION.

Constipation in infants generally arises from an improper manner of living, either of the nurse or child. The bowels should be evacuated at least once a day, and if they are delayed longer than this, it will be necessary to assist nature. Frequently entire relief may be obtained by changing the food of the mother or nurse, but if remedies are necessary for the child, two globules of *Nux-v.*, *Bryonia*, *Opium* or *Sulphur* may be given morning and night, changing the remedy if it seems to have produced no effect in two or three days. Cathartics should never be used but when it is necessary to obtain a speedy movement from the bowels, it may be done by means of an injection, consisting of a small piece of soap, dissolved in a little tepid water.

DIARRHŒA.

Healthy infants usually have three or four, and sometimes five or six movements in a day; should the discharges become more frequent than this, be unnatural in color, and attended with more or less pain, one of the following remedies may be given:

Chamomilla, where the diarrhœa is of a greenish, watery, bilious, yellowish or frothy character, sometimes looking like beaten up eggs, and having an offensive smell; and where it is attended with colic, crying, and restlessness.

Rheum.—Sour smelling discharges; colic and straining before and after the discharges.

Ipecac.—If it arises from overloading the stomach or is accompanied with nausea and vomiting.

Belladonna.—Small and frequent evacuations; great restlessness, disposition to sleep, and frequent starts.

Dulcamara.—When the result of a cold.

When accompanied with considerable flatulence: *Nux-v.* or *Pulsatilla.*

When it occurs in the heat of the summer: *Ipecac*, *Nux-v.* or *Bryonia.*

Dose.—Two globules of the selected remedy once in two or three hours.

CONVULSIONS.

Convulsions may attack infants and children of all ages, and are almost always attended with more or less danger.

The causes are numerous. They may be the result of feebleness on the part of parents; marrying at too early or too advanced an age. Where the mother has been subject to a great shock, or fright, or strong mental emotion before the birth of her child, the child will be very liable to have convulsions soon after its birth. Protracted and difficult labor may also cause convulsions in the child.

They may also be occasioned by shame, anger, or fright; by tight bandaging, excessive mental emotion, a loud noise, sudden exposure to a bright light, hot, impure air, or severe cold. Want of proper ventilation is a fruitful cause of convulsions. During the first year of life they may be traced to the milk of the mother disagreeing with the infant. Cases are by no means rare where fright, passion, or suffering on the part of the mother gives rise to such a change in her milk as to produce convulsions, if the child is permitted to nurse, while the mother is under the influence of these causes. As the child grows older, they may be occasioned by dentition, suppressed eruption, a bruise on the head, &c. They also frequently set in, in connection with some serious disease, as inflammation of the brain, or tubercles on the brain, and in fact with nearly all the serious diseases to which a child is subject.

TREATMENT.—The appearance of the child during the spasm or convulsion is often so frightful as to alarm the friends to such a degree that they are entirely unfit for action. This is wrong, for we certainly can do no good by giving way to excitement, while if we control our own feelings, and are prompt and decided in our treatment, we may frequently be the means of saving the life of the child.

The child should immediately be placed in a warm bath and left there five or ten minutes, or until the severity of the paroxysm is broken. It should then be taken out and wrapped in a warm dry flannel. If the spasms still continue, or are only partially relieved, immerse the feet and legs in water as warm as it can be borne, at the same time pouring a stream of cold water on the head, from a distance of two or three feet. This process should be frequently repeated, if necessary.

The first inquiry should be, *the cause* of the convulsion. If the gums are red and swollen, and the attack evidently arises from dentition, with a sharp pen-knife they should be cut, applying the knife to the top of the gum and cutting down, until the teeth are reached. If occasioned by costiveness or irritating substance in the stomach or bowels, give immediately an injection of tepid water, sweetened with molasses.

Chamomilla is indicated particularly when the convulsions have been excited by teething, a chill or a fit of passion or vexation; there is restlessness, disposition to drowsiness when awake, moaning, loss of consciousness, twitches of the eyelids and muscles of the face, jerks and convulsions of the limbs, with clenched thumbs, rolling of the head from side to side.

Belladonna.—Particularly where connected with disturbance in the brain and derangement of the nervous system; there are sudden starts, dilated pupils, rigidity of different parts of the body, clenching of the hands, forehead and hands dry and burning.

Ignatia.—Especially during teething, and in pale and delicate infants, where the fit returns at regular hours, and is followed by fever and perspiration; convulsive starts, tremor of the whole body, attended with violent crying and agonizing shrieks; muscles of single limbs are convulsed.

Ipecac.—When occasioned by undigested food or an overloaded stomach; there is nausea, vomiting and diarrhœa; constant inclination to remain in a recumbent posture; convulsions are preceded or accompanied by spasmodic twitchings.

Nux-v.—When occasioned by a fit of anger, indigestion or constipation; there are convulsive jerkings of the limbs and tossings backward of the head.

Cina.—When the attacks are produced by worms.

Opium.—Where the fits are the result of a fright, and are accompanied with flushed face, snoring breathing, and at length entire insensibility.

Stramonium.—Where the attack is produced by sudden fright; the convulsions are sudden and violent; the attacks are renewed by luminous objects, such as a mirror or candle, and are sometimes accompanied with involuntary discharges of fæces and urine.

Hyosciamus.—Convulsions from fright. Twitching of the muscles of the face, foaming at the mouth, and great wildness.

Administration.—One drop of the tincture, or ten globules, may be mixed with a tumbler half full of water, and a teaspoonful, or a few drops, given at a dose; or three globules may be placed on the tongue. The remedy may be given during the paroxysm every ten or twelve minutes.

DENTITION. TEETHING.

The period of the first dentition is subject to many variations, but as a general thing it occurs between the seventh and the twentieth or the thirtieth month, although sometimes it is delayed much longer. The teeth* usually appear in each jaw in couples; thus, about the seventh month the two central incisors of the lower jaw appear; then in a short time those of the upper jaw, followed, after a short interval by the lower lateral incisors, and then by the upper lateral incisors. From the twelfth to the fourteenth month the first four molar teeth appear, and from the sixteenth to the twentieth, the lower and upper canine teeth; last of all the last four molars.

Notwithstanding the above sketch describes the usual process of teething, yet in very many cases there are deviations. Sometimes children are born with teeth, or they make their appearance shortly after birth. Thus Louis XIV. of France, Mirabeau, and Richard III. were born with teeth. Often the order of succession mentioned above is violated, the upper incisors making their appearance before the lower, the molars before the canine teeth, and so on; frequently also they do not appear in pairs, there being a difference of some months between the appearance of the first teeth.

But the first set of teeth are only temporary, being supplanted after a certain length of time by a permanent set. Up to the age of five, six, or seven years, the jaws of a child may be said to contain two sets of sockets, which are kept distinct by a bony lamina. But at length, while the process of growth and development of the jaw and the second set of teeth are going on, another commences, having reference to the first set. The root is gradually absorbed, so that after a time the tooth

* See plate 5, also page 42.

itself may easily be removed with the fingers. In its place the second or permanent tooth shortly makes its appearance.

The first two central incisors of the lower jaw usually fall away about the age of seven years, and are speedily followed by the permanent teeth. About a year is occupied in shedding the four central incisors, and another year in that of the four lateral incisors. The anterior bicuspid teeth of the lower, then those of the upper jaw are next shed, usually occupying about a year. The posterior bicuspids go next, then the canine teeth. At length, usually before the age of twelve or thirteen, the second set of twenty-eight teeth is completed. A few years now elapse, when, usually between the age of seventeen and twenty-one, four new molar teeth are put forth, called the wisdom teeth, completing the full number of thirty-two teeth in the mouth. Deviations from the ordinary rule, are as common with the second dentition as with the first.

Appearance of first teeth.—If the child is healthy, and the process of dentition favorable, the suffering is slight. For some time the gums are swollen; the child dribbles incessantly and thrusts its finger or any thing it can seize into its mouth. As the teeth advance the gums swell, and become tender, but with a feeling of tension and itching, which causes the child to wish to bite some hard substance. The gums are inflamed, and are hot to the finger; the child is fretful and uneasy. Dentition is usually more severe in winter than in summer.

In severe cases of dentition, the symptoms are much more violent; the mouth is hot, the gums swollen and so exceedingly sensitive, that the child does not wish them touched. There is fever, thirst, and sometimes convulsions.

Connected with teething there are many sympathetic affections. There may be either constipation, or diarrhœa, swelling and suppuration of the glands, eruptions on the head and other parts of the body, cough, and great irritability of the nervous system.

TREATMENT.—It is important that the bowels should be kept open and the head cool, as there is more or less determination of blood to the head. The child should be permitted to bite on some hard or elastic substance, such as, a crust of bread, a piece of silver, ivory, or india rubber. If the gums are hot, swollen, and painful, they may be bathed with cold water, and if they are evidently near the surface, and there is danger of convulsions, they may be cut with a knife, being careful to cut through the gums until the teeth are reached. This operation however is very seldom necessary.

*Aconite.**—Should there be much fever and restlessness. Three globules may be given once in three or four hours.

Belladonna will be indicated, if there is derangement of the nervous system, swollen and inflamed gums, flushed face, and indications that the brain is becoming involved. Also where there are convulsions generally followed by sleep; the child starts from sleep as if frightened; the pupils of the eyes are dilated; the body becomes stiff, and there is burning heat in the temples and hands.

DOSE.—The remedy is often required in alternation with *Aconite*, three globules three or four hours apart. When given alone, it may be taken once in three or four hours, except in cases of convulsions, when it should be given once in ten or fifteen minutes. See *Convulsions.*

Chamomilla is a prominent remedy in many of the difficulties connected with teething. It is particularly useful where the child is restless and uneasy at night, has spasmodic jerking and twitching of the limbs during sleep, starts from the slightest noise; hacking cough and oppression of the chest; also where there is diarrhœa with watery, slimy and greenish evacuations worse at night. See also *Diarrhœa.*

DOSE.—Three globules once in four or six hours.

Cina.—Dry cough, and disposition to rub the nose, and also grate the teeth during sleep, together with other symptoms of worms.

DOSE.—Two globules morning and night.

Coffea.—When the child is restless, nervous, and cannot sleep. Give the same as *Cina.*

---

* For further directions as to the administration of remedies, see page 10.

Ipecac., where there is nausea, vomiting, and diarrhœa. Give once in four or six hours.

Ignatia.—Convulsive jerkings of single limbs; heat followed by perspiration. Starting from sleep, with piercing cries. Give same as *Ipecac.* Consult *Convulsions.*

Calcarea should be given where the teeth are slow in making their appearance. Two globules may be taken every night.

Mercurius.—Diarrhœa with straining; profuse salivation and redness and soreness of the gums. Give two globules morning and night.

Nux-v. and *Bryonia* should be given, where there is obstinate constipation; three globules of one, one night, and the same quantity of the other the next. Follow in a week's time if necessary, by *Sulphur* in alternation with *Nux-v.* in the same manner.

Diet and Regimen.—If the child is nursing, the mother or nurse should pay particular attention to her own diet; if it has already been weaned, its diet should be simple, and unstimulating, avoiding those articles which have a tendency to derange the system. Cleanliness is of course essential as well as pure air. Daily bathing should be practiced, and the rooms kept thoroughly ventilated.

DROPSY OF THE BRAIN.

Hydrocephalus.

This disease, so full of danger to the child, has an acute and chronic form. We shall first notice the acute variety.

ACUTE HYDROCEPHALUS.

In one variety of the disease the child may exhibit for some time symptoms of deranged health, such as loss of appetite, wandering pains, deranged state of the bowels, headache, crick in the neck, and a growing weakness. Accompanying these symptoms there may be occasional chills, pale countenance, and disturbed temper. At length the child complains of headache, or if an infant, gives signs of it by putting its hands to its head, rolling it uneasily about. To this succeeds vomiting, the child becomes dull and heavy, complaining of weariness, and is sensitive to light and noise. Thus the disease may continue for several days, but by degrees febrile paroxysms are observed, the vomiting continues, the bowels are generally torpid, the urine scanty and frequently voided. The child gradually becomes dull and stupid. He becomes greatly emaciated, the pulse increases, decided symptoms of pressure on the brain are seen, in starting, screaming, and partial or complete convulsions, with insensibility, squinting, glazed eye, &c. This state may continue for two or three days, until at length it is terminated by a convulsion or coma.

Again, the disease may be sudden in its development, and marked by high fever. The child complains of severe pain in its head, or pressing it with its hands, and rolling it from side to side, indicates the locality of the suffering; or it may lie still, heavy, and dull, with an occasional cry of pain. The eyes are sometimes heavy, and have a muddy expression, but they are more frequently bright and restless, having a peculiar stare and moving quickly from one object to another. The child is generally wakeful, or sleeping restlessly, drowsy, but waking up suddenly, crying or screaming, as from fright. There is an entire loss of appetite, nausea, and vomiting.

Thus far the disease may have advanced with more or less rapidity, but at length the fever rapidly becomes intense, with occasional intermissions; there is great heat in the head, severe headache, delirium, and often loud outcries. The eyes are bright but sunken, the pupils contracted, and painfully sensitive to light, as the ears are to sound. The pulse varied, sometimes quick, at others irregular or intermitting. The vomiting usually continues, and the constipation increases.

As the disease advances, the symptoms gradually change from those of excitement to those consequent on effusion or pressure. The headache is less complained of, although the head is still rolled about uneasily; the delirium subsides or occurs occasionally; the sensibility of the eye is gradually lost, the pupil is generally dilated, and it is evident the patient can no longer see; the eye is rolled about, turned upward, or squinting takes place; the hearing, which may for a time have been acute, at length diminishes, until the infant seems unconscious of sound. The convulsions, which may have occurred at intervals from the commencement of the disease, now increase in frequency and sometimes in strength, or perhaps there may be convulsions of one side of the body and paralysis of the other.

About this time a new symptom is developed, the sharp piercing scream, which the child utters from time to time, which adds so much to the distress of the mother, but which is not in reality the result of pain. During the intervals of the convulsions, consciousness and sensibility diminish until they are finally lost. The child now lies quiet, occasionally moving the head or throwing about an arm or leg; the eyes are open or only half closed, and acquire a glazed appearance; the face is pallid, sometimes waxlike, without expression; sometimes sunken and anxious, as representing the last conscious feeling; the vomiting rarely continues; the bowels are sometimes evacuated unconsciously, but generally confined. The attack terminates by a convulsion or in coma.

The duration of this form of the disease varies from thirty-six hours to ten or twelve days.

Another variety of this disease has been called the "*water stroke.*" It consists of a sudden almost instantaneous effusion of fluid within the brain, and may occur either idiopathically, or as the result of obstructed secretion from some other organ, or as a secondary affection in the course of some other disease, as small-pox, measles, or other febrile eruptions, or on the sudden stoppage of diarrhœa, dysentery, or profuse perspiration. The child may go to bed apparently well, or suffering from some other disease, and in the morning it may be found dead. Or it may be attacked by a convulsion, followed by paralysis, or apparent apoplexy, with insensibility, stertorous breathing, dilated or contracted pupils, terminating in death after a few hours.

TREATMENT.—Medical aid should be obtained as soon as possible. The external application of cold is highly beneficial. The best way of applying it is by filling a bladder with pounded ice, and placing it on the head.

Aconite should be given in the commencement of the disease if the skin is hot and the pulse quick.

DOSE.—One drop, or six globules, in a tumbler half full of water, a tablespoonful once in three hours; or two globules on the tongue at the same intervals.

Belladonna.—Great heat and severe pain in the head; burying the head in the pillow or moving it from side to side; sensitiveness to light or noise; shooting or burning pains in the head, eyes red and sparkling, or with a wild expression; contraction or dilation of the pupils; violent delirium; drowsiness and stupor; loss of consciousness; frantic screams; low muttering; nausea, vomiting, and convulsions.

DOSE.—One drop, or six globules, in a tumbler half full of water, a teaspoonful at a dose. If in alternation with *Hyosciamus* or *Hellebore*, give one or two hours apart; if alone, give every one or two hours.

Hyosciamus.—Especially where there are violent convulsions; loss of consciousness; delirium; redness of the face with wild or fixed look; picking at the bed-clothes.

DOSE.—Same as *Belladonna.*

Strammonium.—The symptoms resemble those indicating *Belladonna* or *Hyosciamus*; the spasmodic or convulsive symptoms are more prominent.

Hellebore.—A highly important remedy in all well marked and severe cases. There is total loss of nervous control; the senses are generally obtuse, and the head feels stupefied; the look is fixed and vacant; the eyes turned upward and remain half open during sleep.

DOSE.—Same as *Belladonna.*

Opium.—Lethargic sleep, with snoring respiration; confusion or giddiness after waking. Give once in two or three hours.

Bryonia.—Constipation, yellow coated tongue; hurried,

laborious, and anxious respiration ; great thirst, delirium, sudden starts with cries.

Rhus.—In the low protracted form of the disease, and also where there is headache, giddiness, and heaviness of the head; aching, pressing pain in the back of the head with creeping sensation ; drowsiness, convulsive movement of the limbs, and great restlessness at night.

DOSE.—Same as *Belladonna*. Give once in two or three hours.

Arsenic.—Particularly in the chronic variety, where there is debility, weak and irregular pulse, and marked intermission in the disease.

Sulphur.—Particularly towards the termination of the disease ; also where the appropriate remedy seems to have lost effect, in which case two or three doses may be given, and then return again to the original remedy.

2. CHRONIC HYDROCEPHALUS.

This variety of the disease may be symptomatic of other diseases of the brain, as tubercles, &c. It is sometimes the sequel of the acute form, in which case the symptoms subside in a great degree, but do not entirely disappear. It frequently sets in without any acute form. There is headache, drowsiness, and unequal temper. The intellect is generally clouded, and all the organs of sense more or less affected. There is a peculiar look to the eyes, sometimes squinting, and the pupils sometimes dilated.

After effusion takes places, the intelligence is more or less affected, except in those cases, where the head rapidly enlarges, when for a time the intellect may be even brighter than usual. After a time the child retrogrades until it has the look of an idiot, forgetful, babbling words without meaning, until at last it sinks into indifference, stupor or coma. A striking feature of the disease is the enlargement of the head, which sometimes reaches an enormous size. The face after a time seems to shrink, presenting an old and withered look. The limbs are feeble and the walk uncertain. Very often the child is attacked by general or partial convulsions, followed by paralysis, which may effect nearly all the organs of the body. The pulse gradually becomes weak, the respiration after a time fails, and the appetite at length diminishes.

This disease may be developed during the progress of scarlatina, measles, small-pox, hooping cough, difficult dentition, &c.

TREATMENT.—We can only mention here some of the prominent remedies. Among them we may notice *Arsenic*, *Hellebore*, *Mercury*, *Sulphur*. For particular indications, see acute Hydrocephalus. The appropriate remedy should be administered two or three times a day.

INFANTILE REMITTENT FEVER.

This is a variety of fever, to which children from one to ten or twelve years of age are liable to be affected. It is characterized by one or more daily exacerbations and remissions, by pain in the belly and sometimes in the head, loss of appetite and by an unnatural state of the alvine discharges. It is very often, although erroneously, attributed to worms, and sometimes called "*worm fever*."

The affection usually comes on gradually, manifesting itself generally by irregularities in the bowels, which are usually costive. In the course of the day there are several slight accessions of fever, marked by drowsiness, in the intervals appearing well, though peevish. The appetite is variable, and the pulse ranges from 100 to 130. These symptoms may continue for 8 or 10 days, when a violent paroxysm sets in, preceded by chilliness and attended with vomiting, the pulse rises in frequency, the drowsiness is increased, and the cheeks are flushed. There is picking of the nose, lips, and angles of the eyes. Cough may also be present, also grinding of the teeth, and startings in sleep. Digestion is deranged, and food taken into the stomach is brought up some time after, or is evacuated from the bowels apparently undigested, and resembling a mass of putrid animal and vegetable matter subjected to heat and moisture; sometimes worms appear in the discharges. The breath is sickly, appetite is gone and delirium sometimes occurs for two or three days together. The causes of the disease may be traced in part to the use of improper food, neglect of the bowels, want of pure air, and cleanliness.

TREATMENT.—*Ipecac.* should commence the treatment, particularly if the attack has been occasioned by indigestible food or eating too fast. There is heat, thirst; extreme restlessness; perspiration at night, foul tongue, quick breathing, nausea and vomiting.

DOSE.—A powder, or three globules, on the tongue once in three or four hours.

Pulsatilla.—If *Ipecac* fail to produce relief after five or six doses, or there is fetid whitish or bilious diarrhœa, accompanied with griping and distension of the bowels.

DOSE.—One drop, or six globules, in a tumbler half full of water, once in three or four hours.

Nux-v.—Constipated bowels with frequent inclination to stool, or straining followed by watery motions, mixed with mucus or blood; peevish temper, loss of appetite, nausea, disgust at food, restlessness.

DOSE.—Same as *Ipecac.*

Chamomilla.—Lethargic sleep, or restless and agitated with frequent jerks and starts of the limbs; head hot and heavy, skin hot, pulse quick, thirst, nausea and bilious vomiting; constipation or diarrhœa with greenish evacuations.

DOSE.—Same as *Pulsatilla.*

Belladonna.—In alternation with *Chamomilla*, where there is considerable disturbance about the head; tenderness of the bowels to the slightest pressure.

DOSE.—Same as *Pulsatilla.*

Bryonia.—Constipation, sometimes alternating with diarrhœa, derangement of the stomach and painful state of the bowels; headache, thirst, and laborious respiration.

DOSE.—One drop, or six globules, in a tumbler half full of water, a teaspoonful once in four hours.

Mercury.—Tenderness of the bowels, cloudy or milk-like

urine; diarrhœa, with straining stools, mixed with slime or blood.

Dose.—Same as *Ipecac.*

Cina.—Picking at the nose and lips, starting and screaming during sleep, colic and diarrhœa.

Dose.—Same as *Bryonia.*

Sulphur.—After the employment of other remedies, to complete the cure.

Dose.—A powder morning and night.

Diet and Regimen.—Particular attention should be paid to the diet, which should be of a light farinaceous character, such as toast, gruels, &c., carefully avoiding the more solid articles of food, such as meat and fish.

INTESTINAL WORMS.

It is very common to refer those little ailments which children are so liable to have, and for which no cause can readily be found, to worms, when in reality worms have nothing to do with the difficulty. The presence of worms, is often looked upon as the cause of all the suffering. This is a mistake, for notwithstanding certain symptoms are coincident with their presence, yet these symptoms are usually a coincidence merely, or the result of an irritation, which gives rise to worms, or which disturbs them in their usual quiet. Worms often exist in the system, when no unpleasant symptoms are present. Worms may be developed in every part of the system, but they are more frequently found in the intestinal canal. Some of the prominent varieties we shall briefly notice.

a. Ascaris lumbricoides, usually occupy the small intestines, sometimes in great numbers, and occasionally accumulating in the form of a ball. They are usually from three to twelve inches long, occasionally find their way into the stomach, and may be discharged through the mouth or nostrils.

b. Tænia, or Tapeworm, is white, flat and very long, often twenty feet, and sometimes it is said even sixty or seventy feet in length. It is usually found in the small intestines, and is one of the worst variety of worms.

c. The long *thread worm* is usually found in the upper portion of the large intestines. It is from an inch to two inches in length, the anterior portion of the body being slender like a hair, and the rest much thicker.

d. Ascarides, or *pinworms*, are very small, white, and slender, and are found in large numbers in the large intestines, and especially in the rectum, from whence they may often be wiped away with a cloth.

Diagnosis.—Preceding and accompanying the appearance of worms, are derangements of the stomach and bowels. There may be disgust of food ; appetite sometimes nearly gone, at others voracious, or each alternately; hiccough, fetid breath, nausea and mucus or acid vomiting; belching of wind, umbilical colic, sometimes constipation, at others glairy or mucus diarrhœa.

To these symptoms are added puffiness of the face, emaciation and weakness, tickling cough, headache, agitation, sleeplessness, dilated pupils, itching and picking of the nose, grinding of the teeth, creeping of the skin, and some fever. There may be more or less pain about the bowels, and swelling of the abdomen, and the urine is generally yellowish, or whitish, like milk and water. There is also, sometimes, bleeding at the nose, and convulsions.

Some of the signs indicating the presence of *tapeworm*, are, sensation as if something were rising in the throat and falling back, or as if there were a lump in the side, making an undulatory motion.

The signs indicating *pin-worms* are, violent itching in the anus, difficulty in making water, and if in the female, often *leucorrhœa*.

Treatment.—This variety of disease occurs principally in infancy, and may give rise to an almost innumerable variety of symptoms. Particular attention should be directed to the general health. The food should be simple and easy of digestion, the whole body bathed every day, either with cold or tepid water, moderate exercise should be taken, and ill ventilated rooms and impure air carefully avoided.

Aconite is particularly indicated in the commencement, where febrile symptoms are present, with restlessness at night, and irritability of temper; and also where there is continued burning and itching at the anus.

Dose.—One drop, or six globules, in a tumbler half full of water, a teaspoonful during the presence of fever, once in three or four hours.

Ignatia may follow *Aconite* after the febrile symptoms have subsided, especially if there are spasmodic twitchings in the muscles of the anus, or intense itching in the anus, indicating the presence of pin-worms.

Dose.—Same as *Aconite*.

Cina.—Boring at the nose, irritable temper, fits of crying when touched, restlessness, a desire for things which are rejected when offered; paleness of the face, with livid circle around the eyes; constant craving for food; colic pains and hardness of the bowels, constipation or diarrhœic evacuations, great restlessness at night, tossing about, starting, talking or calling out suddenly during sleep; weakness of the limbs; occasional delirium; face at times pale and cold, at others red and hot; nausea and vomiting, prostration and occasionally convulsive movements in the limbs; itching in the anus, and crawling out of pin-worms; urine white and turbid, sometimes passing involuntarily.

Dose.—Same as *Aconite*. Give once in six or twelve hours.

Spigelia.—Especially where the symptoms recur at about the same time of the day; there may be colic, diarrhœa and craving for food, also fever.

Dose.—Where the symptoms are violent, the same as *Aconite*. In chronic cases every night.

Belladonna.—Great nervous excitement; delirium at night with starting during sleep, severe colic, headache and fever.

Dose.—Same as *Aconite*, with which, if much fever be present, it may be alternated.

Silicea may follow *Belladonna*, if the patient is of tuberculous habit, and that remedy fails to produce effect. It may also be given where the disease assumes a slow chronic form.

Dose.—A powder, or three globules, morning and night.

Mercury.—Diarrhœa, distension of the bowels, and increased secretion of saliva.

Dose.—A powder, or three globules, morning and night.

Nux-v.—Derangement of the stomach, with constipation, nausea, and painful sensibility of the stomach and bowels.

Dose.—Same as *Mercury.*

China.—Long continued diarrhœa, distension and painful sensation of the abdomen and stomach; debility, great nervous excitability with spasmodic twitching of the muscles.

Dose.—Three drops, in a tumbler half full of water, a teaspoonful morning and night.

Sulphur.—After the prominent symptoms have subsided, to complete the cure.

Dose.—A powder, or three globules, every night.

Diet and Regimen.—Fruits and vegetables should be prohibited, as well as pastry and sweetmeats. The diet should consist principally of meat broths, except in acute cases, when it should be the same as in fevers.

DIARRHŒA.

Summer Complaint.

Children are very liable to derangement of the stomach and bowels, especially during teething, and the warm weather of summer. Particular attention should be given to the food. Vegetables and uncooked fruit should be prohibited. Daily bathing, fresh air, and if residing in the city, a trip into the country are advisable.

Ipecac. should be given where there is nausea, vomiting, no appetite; fermented stools, mixed with mucus, sometimes tinged with blood; cutting pain in the bowels and sometimes straining.

Bryonia.—Especially during hot weather, and where there is thirst, putrid smell of the stools, and nausea after eating.

Chamomilla.—Where there is great restlessness, greenish

20*

diarrhœa, and more or less rumbling or cutting pain in the bowels.

Stibium.—Nausea, offensive stools, gagging and great prostration.

Dulcamara.—Diarrhœa, the result of cold.

Mercury.—Straining, like dysentery, with colic, and bloody or slimy discharges.

Sulphur.—In obstinate cases. Give a powder morning and evening.

For indications of other remedies, see *Cholera Infantum*.

DOSE.—One drop, or six globules, in a tumbler half full of water; in severe cases, a teaspoonful once in two or three hours; when the symptoms are less violent every four or six hours.

CHOLERA INFANTUM.

This disease is confined to infants, generally between the age of four and twenty months, and occurs mostly during the summer months.

The attack is sometimes preceded by diarrhœa, but in most cases the vomiting and purging commence together, and are attended with great prostration; sometimes there are premonitory symptoms, such as languor, fretfulness, loss of appetite, or craving for food. At first the discharge from the bowels usually consists of a turbid frothy fluid, mixed with portions of green bile, or of a nearly colorless water containing small flocculi of mucus, but after the disease is fully developed, it loses all trace of bilious matter. In some cases the disease proceeds with such violence as to terminate in death in a single day, but usually the vomiting and purging, though violent, are not so rapid as to prostrate the system immediately. Sometimes the vomiting after four or five hours, gradually ceases, while the diarrhœa goes on until it assumes a chronic character. In the early stage of the disease, there is a peculiarly distressing sensation in the stomach and bowels, and where the discharges are violent and frequent, there may be cramps or spasms in the muscles of the abdomen and extremities

If the disease continues even for a few days, rapid emaciation ensues, the countenance becomes pale and contracted, the eyes sunk, the nose sharp, and the lips thin, dry, and wrinkled. The thirst is great, but the cold water so much desired, is thrown up almost as soon as swallowed. At length, if the disease is not checked, the patient becomes somnolent, sleeps with its eyes half open, rolls its head about when awake, and at last sinks into insensibility and coma, and dies in convulsions, or under symptoms resembling acute hydrocephalus. If the disease is of long duration, the discharges at length become offensive and acrid, and food passes undigested through the bowels. Aphtha appears on the tongue, and inside of the cheeks, and the face has a bloated appearance.

TREATMENT.—The treatment should be prompt and active, as the delay of a few hours will often allow the disease to gain such headway as to bid defiance to all efforts at control.

Ipecac. should be given at the commencement of the disease in alternation with *Veratrum*. Its indications are nausea, vomiting; diarrhœa of fermented stools, or watery diarrhœa with white flocks; great thirst.

Veratrum is indicated by the great exhaustion, violent vomiting and diarrhœa; vomiting produced by the slightest movement, or even taking cold water for which there is great desire: sensitiveness over the pit of the stomach and sometimes cramps.

DOSE.—*Veratrum*, in alternation with *Ipecac.* or following that remedy, will usually be sufficient to arrest the violent symptoms. Mix two drops, or twelve globules, in a tumbler half full of water, and give a teaspoonful in alternation, ten or fifteen minutes apart, increasing the intervals as the symptoms abate.

Arsenic.—If there are cold extremities; nausea and vomiting; great prostration, thirst and offensive diarrhœa.

DOSE.—A powder, or three globules, once in two hours.

For other remedies indicated during the progress of the disease, see *Hydrocephalus*, page 440, also *Diarrhœa*, page 300 and 446.

Diet and Regimen.—The food should consist mostly of gruels. Cold water may be given a little at a time.

CROUP.

The approach of this terrible disease fills the mother's heart with alarm, for she has learned to dread its fearful ravages, and to rightly look upon it as the scourge of infancy. The ringing, brassy cough, which characterizes the disease, is so peculiar, that once heard it is never forgotten. It generally attacks children between the age of one and five years, although it sometimes occurs at a later period, or even when the child is not more than four or five months old. It consists of an inflammation of the mucous membrane of the larynx or windpipe, the inflamed surface secreting a kind of thick lymph, which narrows the passage for the admission of air, and at length a false membrane may be formed, which almost or entirely chokes up the passage, causing the child to die from suffocation. Our object in the treatment, is of course to remove this secretion, which is filling the windpipe and choking the child, by dissolving it, or causing it to be thrown up, at the same time breaking up the inflamed state of the organ, thereby checking its diseased secretions.

Diagnosis.—Preceding an attack of croup, there is generally more or less fever, cough, huskiness of voice, and other catarrhal symptoms. These symptoms may only last a few hours, and do not usually continue longer than twenty-four hours. These symptoms increase towards evening, or the attack may come on without any premonitory symptoms, the child suddenly awakes out of a sound sleep by a sensation of suffocation, with a hoarse, ringing cough, hurried respiration and great distress. The cough resembles slightly the crowing of a cock, or the bark of a dog; it has a peculiar ringing or brassy sound, like air passing through a brazen instrument. The paroxysms of coughing become more frequent and spasmodic, until breathing is almost suspended. It is with great difficulty the child can breathe, and its flushed face, sometimes bedewed with sweat, its clenched hands, arms tossing about, removing all covering from the chest, and its look of intense agony, show the violence of its struggles for breath. The pulse is quick, the skin hot, the face livid and swollen, the eyes injected and almost seeming to start from their sockets, the child restless, and tossing from side to side, in the vain hope of obtaining relief by a change of position.

There may be a partial remission of symptoms during the day, returning again at night with renewed violence. All the symptoms are now fearfully aggravated. The voice is whispering and almost suppressed, the respiration extremely difficult and accompanied with a hissing noise. The convulsive struggles for breath are fearful, the head is thrown back, the face livid, cold sweat-drops stand on the forehead, respiration becomes more and more difficult, until at length with signs of convulsive suffocation, or falling into a state of stupor, it dies. The mother who has watched with bitter agony the fearful struggles of her child, breathes a sigh of relief as the last breath is drawn, and as the look of anguish changes to the sweet calm of death, she knows that suffering is over, and her little one is at rest.

The above is a description of the more severe attacks of croup, but they are often of a lighter character. There is a kind of croupy cough, which is sometimes mistaken for croup, and unnecessarily alarms the friends, as it is unattended with immediate danger, but if not cured may end in inflammation of the lungs. In real croup, as we have before said, the child is almost always attacked at night, is aroused from its sleep by violent spasmodic cough, is restless, and shows unmistakable signs of suffering; in a few moments however, it may again drop to sleep. In croupy cough the breathing may be labored, and the voice husky, but the child shows no indication of suffering, and the cough seldom fairly arouses it from sleep. As we have before said, there may be a slight remission of symptoms during the day, but even in the milder forms of croup, care should be taken not to expose the patient for three or four days, as the attacks are liable to return.

TREATMENT.—If premonitory symptoms are present, such as slight fever, hoarse cough, &c., *Aconite* and *Spongia* should be alternated one hour apart. If however in the evening the symptoms assume the distinct form of croup, or the attack commences suddenly with the barking, ringing, or suffocative cough, about as much crude *Tartar Emetic* (*Stibium*) as can be placed on a three cent piece should be mixed with a tumbler half full of water, and a teaspoonful given in alternation with *Spongia* ten or fifteen minutes apart until relieved. A warm bath at the same time would be beneficial, or the application of cloths to the neck, wrung out in cold water and covered with dry flannel. After the violence of the paroxysm has subsided, and the cough is less ringing, but of a more moist or loose character, *Spongia* and *Hepar-s.* may be alternated one hour apart. If at night the violent paroxysm should return, the same treatment should be repeated.

Iodine is a valuable remedy in almost all stages of croup, and will often produce a decided effect, when other remedies fail. When the remedies enumerated above seem still indicated, but fail to produce the desired effect, one drop of the first dilution of *Iodine* may be mixed in a tumbler half full of water, and a teaspoonful given every half hour, until four or five doses have been taken.

At length the disease, if unchecked, becomes very violent, and there are plain indications of the formation of the false membrane. The countenance wears a look of intense agony, and the breathing and cough are almost suffocative. It is evident, that unless speedy relief is obtained, death will soon close the scene. *Bichromate of Potash* and *Bromine* are here the prominent remedies.

Caustic Ammonia. When the voice is deep and weak, speech fatiguing and interrupted, great secretion of mucus in the bronchia, violent cough, with copious expectoration especially after drinking; rattling, labored, or stertorous breathing; suffocative fits and spasms in the chest.

Bromine. Hoarse, wheezing and fatiguing cough, sometimes with sneezing and suffocative fits; respiration accompanied with mucus rattling; wheezing; breathing slow and suffocative, or hurried and superficial, labored, painful, oppressed; gasping for air, and strong indications of suffocation.

Bi-chromate of Potash. This is an invaluable remedy in cases of membranous croup. Hoarse, dry and crowing or whistling cough; respiration accompanied with a whistling sound; the nose filled with mucus; evident signs of pain about the throat; great restlessness of the child; cough gradually subsides, breathing becomes more and more difficult, and the spasmodic efforts for breath, the tossing about from side to side, the look of intense agony, the flushed face and starting eyes, the nose and sometimes the mouth filled with mucus, all give clear indication of the rapid formation of the false membrane, and unless relief be obtained, the certainty of speedy death.

Hepar-s. and *Spongia* will generally complete the cure, with the addition, perhaps, if much soreness is present, of Phosphorus.

Dose.—*Bichromate* should be given a powder of the first trituration once in fifteen or twenty minutes.

If *Bromine* is given, a drop should be put in a tumbler filled with water, and if the mixture seems too strong, a portion of it may be thrown away. The tumbler may be then filled up and a teaspoonful given once in twenty minutes or half an hour.

With the other remedies, where the amount of the dose has not already been given, two drops of the tincture should be mixed with a tumbler half full of water, and a teaspoonful given at a dose; or a powder taken dry on the tongue.

Diet and Regimen.—During the attack, the diet should consist of arrow root, or gruels, or perhaps milk and water. Cold water may also be taken, if much thirst is present.

HOOPING COUGH. PERTUSSIS.

This is an epidemic and contagious disease, mostly confined to early childhood, and seldom occurs but once in the same person. It is probably most easily communicated in the second stage. There are two distinct stages, the *catarrhal* and *spasmodic* stage.

The *first stage* commences with the symptoms of an ordinary catarrh or cold. There is watery discharge from the nose and eyes, sneezing, coughing, languor, restlessness, and febrile symptoms. Sometimes however the fever is severe and the cough very painful, at first dry, but afterward with profuse expectoration; and sometimes, but very rarely, the catarrhal symptoms are entirely wanting.

This stage may last only a few days, and rarely continues more than two weeks.

As the catarrhal symptoms subside, the *second* or the nervous, spasmodic, or convulsive stage commences, in which the characteristic symptoms of the disease present themselves. The cough occurs in paroxysms, is very violent, and consists of a series of forced and quick expirations in such quick successions, that the patient seems almost in danger of suffocation. The face and neck are swollen and livid, the eyes protruded and full of tears; at length one or two inspirations are made with similar violence, which produce that peculiar sound, compared to a *whoop*, from which the disease takes its name. The paroxysms, or a rapid succession of them, usually last from one to fifteen minutes, and generally terminate in a profuse expectoration of ropy mucus or vomiting. The child is conscious, when the attack is about to commence, and flies to some object for support, until it has subsided. The paroxysms may occur in rapid succession, not more than ten or fifteen minutes apart, or there may not be more than five or six during the twenty-four hours. As the disease declines, the paroxysms gradually decrease in frequency and violence, until they entirely cease. This second stage may last only two or three weeks, or it may continue five or six months.

The first stage of hooping cough is, as we have already seen, characterized by symptoms of an ordinary catarrh, and appearance and duration of the peculiar cough and *whoop* mark the period of the second stage. Simple hooping cough is seldom attended with danger, but when it becomes complicated with some other difficulty, the danger may be imminent. Let us briefly glance at some of these complications.

1. *Complicated with Bronchitis and Pneumonia.*—The presence of bronchitis or pneumonia may be indicated in the first stage by an incessant cough, painful and difficult breathing and high fever. In the second stage there will be a return of fever, which will continue during the intervals of the paroxysms of coughing and be accompanied with hurried and difficult respiration. The prominent symptoms indicating a complication of these affections, are a greater amount of fever than usual, and the respiration quick, hurried and difficult. The expectoration is also more difficult, the sputa being less profuse and of a puriform appearance. In violent cases the cough may lose entirely its spasmodic character, and exhibit only the cough of bronchitis or pneumonia.

2. *Complicated with Infantile Remittent.*—A disordered condition of the bowels may occur, marked by unhealthy discharges, loss of appetite and foul tongue. If these symptoms are allowed to continue for some time, the infantile remittent may make its appearance, sometimes commencing with a rigor, but usually coming on gradually. The paroxysms of coughing are more frequent, and the breathing quick, hurried and unequal. Fever has distinct remissions in the morning and increases toward evening.

3. *Complicated with congestion of the Brain, Convulsions or Hydrocephalus.*—These complications occur chiefly in infancy about the period of the first dentition, and may generally be anticipated before they are fully developed. We should fear their occurrence, where the cough is of great severity, and the face remains livid for a considerable length of time. The first symptoms may be sleepiness and heaviness after the fits of coughing, or spasmodic twitchings of the face or extremities, or perhaps the first indications that the brain is affected, may be coma or a fit of convulsions. These complications occurring at any time, are exceedingly dangerous, but more especially so during the period of the first dentition.

TREATMENT.—The treatment of the first stage should be the same as that indicated by an ordinary catarrh or cold.

Aconite may be given on the first appearance of the febrile symptoms.

Belladonna may be given, if the cough is worse at night, and if there is headache and sore throat. It is particularly useful both in the first and second stage, where symptoms of congestion to the head are present.

Dose.—One drop, or ten globules, in a tumbler half full of water, a teaspoonful once in two or three hours.

Stibium or *Ipecac.* will be indicated, particularly in the commencement of the disease, where there is sneezing, watery discharge from the eyes and nose, pain on the forehead over the eyes, dry, hard or suffocative cough.

Dose.—A powder once in two or three hours. If there is severe pain about the head, soreness of the throat, *Belladonna* may be given in alternation.

Dulcamara, where the attack has been brought on by cold, and is attended with hoarseness, the cough is loose, and the expectoration copious.

Dose.—One drop, or twelve globules, in a tumbler half full of water, a teaspoonful once in two or three hours.

Nux-v.—Dry cough accompanied with vomiting, agitation, and sometimes bleeding at the nose; especially where it is more violent after midnight.

Dose.—A powder, or three globules, once in three hours.

Mercurius.—Hoarseness, watery discharge from the nose, with soreness of the nostrils: dry, fatiguing cough, generally occurring in two successive fits, bleeding from the nose, and vomiting.

Dose.—A powder, or three globules, once in two hours.

Pulsatilla.—Loose cough with watery discharge from the eyes, thick discharge from the nose, hoarseness and inclination to vomit after coughing, occasional diarrhœa.

Dose.—Same as *Dulcamara.*

Chamomilla.—Paroxysms of coughing, exited by an irritation in the windpipe and upper part of the chest.

Dose.—Same as *Dulcamara.*

Bryonia or *Phosphorus.*—Either separately or in alternation, and sometimes also with *Ipecac.* or *Stibium* will be indicated, where there are symptoms of a complication of bronchitis or pneumonia.

DOSE.—They may be given once in two hours. After the disease passes into the second or spasmodic stage, the prominent remedies are *Hydrocianic-acid*, *Veratrum*, *Drosera*, and *Cuprum*.

Hydrocianic-acid.—Violent concussive cough, with rattling of mucus, suffocating respiration and sometimes, ejection of blood from the nose and mouth. Two drops of the first dilution in eight tablespoonfuls of water, a teaspoonful once in three hours.

Veratrum may be given if the violence of the paroxysms continues unabated, and especially if there is great weakness, fever, and cold perspiration, and also when during the paroxysms there are pains in the chest and abdomen, involuntary emission of urine, and vomiting.

Drosera.—Especially in violent cases, with loud and hoarse cough, and where there is no fever, or the febrile symptoms are strongly marked, with shuddering and heat, aggravation of symptoms during repose; and also where there is vomiting of food or slimy water.

DOSE.—One drop, or six globules, in a tumbler half full of water, a teaspoonful once in two or three hours. It may also be followed by *Veratrum*.

Cuprum.—When during the paroxysm there is rigidity of the body with suspended respiration, and loss of consciousness; vomiting after the paroxysm, and rattling of mucus in the chest, when not coughing.

DOSE.—A powder, or three globules, once in one, or two hours.

Carb.-v.—Particularly where the attack threatens to proceed into the second stage, or where from the first the cough is of a convulsive kind, appearing especially in the evening, attended with sore throat and shooting pain in the head and chest.

Cina is especially indicated, when, in addition to the usual characteristics of the disease, worm symptoms are present.

Iodine will be of benefit, where the cough is exited by a constant tickling in the bronchia, with excessive anguish before the fits, and undulating respiration during the attack.

Where there is danger of convulsions, or congestion to the brain, *Hellebore*, *Belladonna*, and *Hyosciamus* are the prominent remedies. Consult *Convulsions* and *Hydrocephalus.* Where there are symptoms of *Remittent fever*, consult Infantile Remittent. And should the disease become complicated with bronchitis or pneumonia. Consult Cough and also *Bronchitis* and *Pneumonia.*

General Directions.—The frequency of the repetition of the medicines must be guided in a measure by the severity of the symptoms. Where they are violent, the remedy may be given as heretofore directed, but in the decline of the disease, and where the attack is light, a dose morning, noon, and night will be sufficient.

Diet and Regimen.—The rooms should be freely ventilated, taking care, however, that the child does not take cold. After the severity of the symptoms are over, but the disease still continues for a long time, a change of air will often prove highly beneficial. If no fever is present, there need be no change of diet, but if more or less fever attends the disease, the diet should consist of arrow-root, gruels, &c.

ASTHMA OF CHILDREN.

Asthma of Millar.

This disease is sometimes called Spasmodic Croup or False Croup. It consist of spasms of the glottis and windpipe, and occurs during the night. It commences with a spasmodic inspiration, accompanied with a crowing noise ; if the fit continues, the face and extremities become purple, and there may be also spasmodic constriction of the muscles of the extremities.

Ipecac. should be given immediately, especially if the attack has been occasioned by indigestible food, and where there are spasmodic constriction and symptoms of suffocation, and rattling in the chest, with anxious respiration, cramps, or rigidity of the frame.

Dose.—One drop in a tumbler half full of water, a teaspoonful at a dose ; or a powder, or three globules on the tongue, given every ten or fifteen minutes.

Sambucus should follow or be alternated with *Ipecac.*, if there is ineffectual inclination to sleep, with oppressed respiration, and wheezing, convulsive efforts for breath, livid hue of the face and agonizing tossings.

Dose.—Same as *Ipecac.*

Arsenic may be given where there is great prostration of strength, anguish, and cold perspiration. If these remedies fail, *Cuprum* or *Belladonna* may be indicated.

VACCINATION.

This homœopathic preventative to small-pox has been the means of saving thousands from the ravages of one of the most loathsome plagues which ever desolated the earth. Formerly whole neighborhoods were depopulated by the small-pox, and its presence was sufficient to cause friends and neighbors to fly in terror from its poisonous breath. But now, protected by the homœopathic preventative of cow-pox, its presence creates but little terror, as we know that we possess a power to prevent its further progress. The best time to vaccinate is between the third month and the twelfth, although where the small-pox is present in the neighborhood, vaccination may take place at an earlier period. The best time is in the fall, spring or winter, as in the heat of summer the arm is liable to become very sore. Usually no treatment is required, as the pustule pursues a regular course, and at a certain time the scab drops off.

It is of vast importance, that the pus used in vaccination should be taken from the cow, or from a perfectly healthy child. Unless this precaution is adopted, disease may be transmitted through vaccination from one child to another.

PART THIRD.

EXTERNAL INJURIES. POISONS AND THEIR ANTIDOTES. REAL AND APPARENT DEATH. MATERIA MEDICA.

CHAPTER I.

EXTERNAL INJURIES.

Of the numerous accidents which are liable to happen every day, some are trifling in their character, and others, unless promptly relieved, capable of producing severe suffering and sometimes death. It is well to know what to do in these cases, until the aid of a physician can be obtained, if necessary, as from want of proper knowledge and in the excitement and confusion of the moment, steps are often taken productive of far more harm than good. We shall first notice

BURNS AND SCALDS.

These may be slight and unattended with danger, or they may involve a large surface and endanger life. For a superficial burn or scald, the part should be held as near the fire as possible ; this, although it may at first increase the pain, in a short time produces entire relief. Where the skin is destroyed, or where the burn is extensive, though not deep, *turpentine*, *alcohol*, *brandy* or *rum*, warmed, should be applied. The burn should be constantly moistened with the spirits as long as the pain is aggravated. In these cases also *raw cotton* if applied immediately, is beneficial.

In deep and severe burns, as well as those more superficial, *soap* is a very valuable remedy. Castile soap should be taken, scraped, and made into a salve with tepid water, and this spread on linen or muslin applied over the whole burn or scald. If blisters have formed, they should be punctured with a needle. The dressing may be changed if necessary once in twenty-four hours, being careful not to disturb the parts by washing them. The application should be continued, until the parts are well.

Another very excellent application, especially where the soap is too irritating, is a linament composed of equal parts of *sweet oil* and *lime-water*. It should be applied in the same way as the *soap*. Another application in extensive burns, is *wheat flour* dusted plentifully over the injured part. The parts should be kept covered with the flour, by new applications if necessary.

Urtica Urens, or the tincture of nettles, is a very valuable application for fresh burns. The tincture may be mixed with an equal amount of tepid water and the parts kept constantly moist by means of rags, wet with the mixture.

Six or eight drops of the tincture of *cantharides*, mixed with a tumbler half full of water, may also be used, applied in the same way as the *Urtica Urens*. For burns in the mouth and throat, caused by steam or hot food, a few drops of *spirits of soap*, or of *soap* dissolved in alcohol, taken once in fifteen or twenty minutes, will produce relief.

In dressing the burns, the blisters should be punctured, the old skin removed and the parts exposed to the action of the air as little as possible.

If much fever is present, *Aconite* may be given internally once in three or four hours. If the nervous system is highly excited, *Rhus* may be taken, and if head symptoms should be developed, *Belladonna*.

FROZEN LIMBS.

For the treatment in cases of frozen limbs, see "*chilblains*" and "*apparent death* from cold."

SPRAINS.

Apply cloths wet with cold water, or a mixture, composed of equal parts of *Arnica* and water. Keep the parts constantly wet. In persons on whom *Arnica* produces erysipelatous inflammation, or when the skin is broken and the part considerably bruised, *Calendula* may be applied. Where there are stiffness and lameness, particularly after a strain, *Bryonia* or *Rhus* may be taken internally a dose, three or four times a day. The treatment I have given for sprains, is also that, which will prove most beneficial for bruises.

CONCUSSIONS.

A heavy blow or a fall may so jar the system as to produce disturbance in the brain and nervous system, and through them affect other organs. In these cases the appropriate remedies are *Arnica* and *Belladonna*. *Arnica* should be given, where some part of the body may have been bruised by a fall or blow, and *Belladonna*, where there are indications of cerebral disturbance, such as convulsions, giddiness, or pain in the head, and stupor. A dose should be taken, where the symptoms are violent, every hour, increasing the intervals, as they subside to three or four hours.

DISLOCATIONS.

The severe pain and the appearance of the joint are sufficient indications of dislocation. To reduce the luxation without injury to the surrounding parts, a knowledge of the joint and the muscles is necessary, so that it is generally best, to obtain the assistance of a physician or surgeon. In the mean time external applications may be made of cold water or the tincture of *Arnica*.

FRACTURES.

There are several varieties of fractures. What is called a simple fracture, is a mere fracture of the bone, unattended by contusions. In a compound fracture there is an external wound or a protruded bone. The presence of fracture can very readily be detected by the peculiar crepitous or grating sound heard on moving the parts. There is also more or less pain and swelling present. In setting the bones the fractured parts are placed together, so that, when united, the limb shall be as nearly as possible as it was, before the bone was broken. While the union or knitting together of the bone is going on, the limb should be kept perfectly still, This is done by means of long splints and bandages, the bandages not applied very tightly, or they may prevent the free circulation of the blood. Both before and after the limb is set, if much swelling and heat are present, cold water or *Arnica* should be applied, the cloths which cover the part being kept constantly wet. Where there is much laceration of the parts, *Calendula* should be applied.

It would be impossible and in fact unnecessary, to go into the minutia of the treatment of fractures here, as every one will see the importance of calling in the aid of the experienced surgeon.

WOUNDS.

Simple incisive wounds will usually heal by the first intention, that is, the incised parts on being brought together unite directly without suppuration, without much if any functional disturbance; but punctured, lacerated, or gunshot wounds generally suppurate, new granulations forming, thus healing by the second intention, and when they are deep and extensive, give rise to considerable fever. Thus punctured wounds in any part of the body, sometimes made by the thrust of a sword, bayonet or knife, or in the foot by treading on a nail, are often exceedingly painful, and not unfrequently give rise to *lockjaw*. In gunshot and lacerated wounds the surrounding parts are often seriously injured, and the pain and fever which accompany them severe. In the punctured, lacerated or gunshot wound, and sometimes where the parts are very much contused, for want of proper reaction in the system, mortification may take place.

Our object of course in the treatment of all wounds is to heal them up quickly and prevent as much functional disturbance as possible. Incised wounds bleed freely, but lacerated or gunshot wounds seldom cause much hæmorrhage, even though large blood-vessels are injured.

In all wounds the parts should be carefully examined, to see that there are no foreign substances present, such as glass or dirt. The wound should be washed with cold water, and any foreign substance which is not removed by this process carefully extracted. Steps should be taken to control the hæmorrhage. This can often be done by pressing the parts together with the fingers, bathing them with cold water, with which may be mixed a little *Arnica* ; or *Kreasote* may be placed on the bleeding parts. If, however, one of the arteries is severed, which may be known by the bright red blood spouting out in jets at every pulsation of the heart, and the bleeding cannot be controlled in the way indicated above, the current should be shut off by compressing the artery above the wound. The location of the artery can generally be ascertained by pressing with the fingers on the inside of the limb, when the heat may be felt beneath the fingers. Over this spot place a piece of cork, or a pebble stone, binding around the limb over the cork or pebble a handkerchief. Now by introducing a small stick under the handkerchief, and twisting it round, a very good tourniquet is formed, the pebble or cork is pressed against the artery, compressing its walls and checking the current of blood. Where the wound is below the knee the above application should be made in the hollow on the inside of the leg and the bend of the knee, and where it occurs in the arm below the elbow, the compression should be at the elbow. Of course a surgeon should be obtained as speedily as possible. In the cut wound, as we have before said, if the parts are brought closely together and kept in that position they will heal in a short time. This may be done, where the wounds are deep and long, by taking two or three stitches with a needle and thread, thus drawing and holding the parts together. As a general thing however all that will be required, will be the application of adhesive plaster. This should be cut in long narrow strips, so as to extend well on either side ; these strips, first warmed by the fire, should pass directly over the wound from side to side, drawing the lips closely together. A small space may be left between each strip, where it crosses the wound, to permit the escape of pus, should suppuration take place. Externally the only application necessary will be *Arnica* or cold water.

In lacerated or contused wounds the parts may be closed in a similar manner, bathing the parts freely with *Calendula*, and afterward, if much heat and swelling is present, applying cold water. In deep wounds, particularly in punctured, or gunshot wounds, great care should be taken, that the healing process should commence at the bottom. If the edges are brought together the wound may heal on the surface, while no union has taken place below. To prevent this, lint should be introduced into the wound, keeping the upper portion open while the healing process is going on at the bottom. This lint should be removed daily, and the parts washed with tepid water.

If considerable fever should set it, *Aconite* should be given once in three or four hours. If the parts are swollen and exceedingly painful, *Belladonna* may be given at the same intervals. Where the suppuration seems unhealthy, a powder of *Hepar-s.* may be taken in the morning, and of *Silicea* at night.

POISONED WOUNDS.

Stings of insects, and bites of serpents.

The sting of the bee, mosquito and other insects is often attended with considerable swelling and pain. Where attacked by bees, the better plan is not to fight them with the hands, but to cover the face by lying on the ground, face downwards, and remaining perfectly quiet.

The sting of the bee, mosquito, spider, and most poisonous insects will be relieved by bathing the parts with spirits of *Ammonia*, or *Hartshorn*, or *black garden mould* may be placed over the swollen parts, renewing the application, when the pain increases. For the sting of the bee in the mouth or eye, *honey* may be applied.

Smoke, *tobacco smoke*, burning *brown sugar* on coals, will usually drive off mosquitoes. In addition to the remedies, mentioned above, the parts may be held near the fire.

Bites of poisonous serpents not unfrequently produce speedy death, and even where death is not the result, the victim always suffers intense pain. No time is to be lost, as the poison is speedily transmitted to other parts of the system.

Dry heat should be applied, by means of a coal of fire, a

hot iron, or even the stump of a segar. Great care should be taken that the heat should be steady and continuous. The heated substance should be held as near the wound as possible without burning it, and continued until a stretching or shivering sensation is experienced. Where no fire can be obtained, a band may by drawn tightly above the wound, or the poison may be sucked out. *Oil*, *soap*, or *saliva* may be applied around the wound. A little *salt and water*, *gunpowder* or *garlic* may be taken into the mouth from time to time. If there are severe shooting pains, nausea, *Arsenic* may be given once in fifteen or twenty minutes followed, if relief is not obtained by *Belladonna*.

CHAPTER II.

[POISONS AND THEIR ANTIDOTES.

It is an interesting fact, that if poisons are taken at first in minute quantities, the amount can bo gradually increased, until at length, after years, the system becomes so far accustomed to them, that they may be taken in enormous doses without producing their peculiar poisonous effects, although not without injurious results. During a certain period, in Grecian and Roman history, a knowledge of poisons was considered an essential feature in the education the nobility and diplomatists, and never was poisoning reduced to such a science as then. The apparently friendly grasp of the hand might communicate through the imperceptible prick of a signet ring, a poison so quick and subtle as speedily to destroy life ; and the lady reclining on her couch in her luxuriant boudoir might inhale in the rich perfume of flowers a poison which would infuse through the system a dreamy languor, but gradually lock up the senses in the sleep of death. So skilfully were the poisons prepared that they would leave no trace of their work, save death. Death was there, but the knife of the anatomist could not reveal the cause. Thus thousands perished in every grade of society, and the souls of kings and nobles were deeply stained with murder. To the criminal condemned to die was presented the poisoned chalice. Thus poison was compelled to do alike the work of justice and of vengeance.

It is narrated of one of the kings that to guard him against the effect of poisons, they were administered to him in small quantities in infancy, and as he advanced in years he almost daily used some kind of poison. But he at length experienced reverses and wished to end his life by suicide, but the unhappy monarch found that he was proof even against the most subtle poisons. To him they would not bring death.

But our object here is not to examine these subtle poisons, but to ascertain how fatal effects may be prevented, when some of the common poisons have been taken, either from accident or design.

Where poison has been taken into the stomach, we should endeavor to remove it if possible by means of vomiting or the stomach-pump. If this cannot be done we should administer some remedy, which will destroy or neutralize the action of the poison.

Vomiting can generally be produced by drinking a large quantity of tepid water, by introducing the finger into the throat, or tickling the throat with a feather; by placing snuff or mustard mixed with salt on the tongue, or by injecting, by means of a tobacco-pipe, tobacco-smoke into the anus. In some cases *Ipecac.*, *Tartar emetic*, or *Sulphate of Zinc* may be administered.

Guided by the effect which poisons are known to produce on the system, we may arrange them into three distinct classes.

1. *The Irritants*, or those which corrode or inflame the parts. These may act as escharotics, destroying the parts, or as violent irritants, producing inflammation, which will speedily end in mortification or gangrene. These include the mineral, animal, and a portion of the vegetable poisons.

2. *The Narcotics*, producing delirium or coma.

3. *The Narcotico-acrid*, producing sometimes an irritating, and sometimes a narcotic effect.

1. THE IRRITANTS.—*Iodine and Hydriodate of Potash.*—Where poisonous effects are produced by either of these drugs, *starch*, or *wheat flour* should be given mixed with water. After the poisonous effects have subsided the remaining symptoms may be removed by a few doses of *Hepar-s.*, or *Belladonna.*

Muriatic, Nitric, or Sulphuric acid.—If nothing else is at hand, drink freely of water, which will dilate the acid, and thus destroy its corrosive, but not its irritating properties. Give immediately, if possible, *carbonate of magnesia*, *chalk*, *limestone*, *old mortar*, or even *plaster* scraped from the wall; or *soap-suds*, or *wood-ashes* mixed with water. If these are not at hand, *Saleratus* or *Carbonate of Soda* may be given. For the after treatment, consult the chapter under which the affections caused by these poisons may be found.

Oxalic-acid.—The action of this poison is exceedingly rapid, and no time should be lost in administering *chalk*, or *Carbonate of Magnesia.* When these are not at hand, *Lime*, *Carbonate of Soda*, or *Saleratus* may be given.

Arsenic.—Vomiting should be induced if possible. *Soap-suds*, the *white of eggs* or, the *hydrated peroxide of iron*, should be given immediately, repeating the antidote after vomiting. The latter remedy has been found to act almost as a complete antidote, when taken in time.

Corrosive Sublimate.—This form of mercury acts as a most powerful poison, and from the fact that it is frequently used in household-duties, it is very often taken by mistake. The *whites of eggs* should be mixed with cold water, and given every two or three minutes, so long as the matter vomited contains a white opaque material admixed, but when the substance vomited becomes transparent, no more should be given, as it will not only be useless but may prove injurious. Where white of eggs can not be obtained, *soap and water*, mixed with *wheat flour*, should be given plentifully. Emetics should be avoided.

Copper.—Poisoning from the metal generally arises from allowing the *acetate of copper*, better known as *verdigris*, to form on cooking utensils. The white of eggs, or sugar, should be given, and vomiting induced. Carbonate of Soda should be administered without delay.

Lead.—Poisoning by lead is very common both from lead paint, and the use of water which has been in contact for some length of time with lead pipe. Cases of sickness are constantly occurring in this city, which might be traced to drinking water which had been for some time in contact with lead pipe, which is now so extensively used in connection with the croton-water. Where the smell of paint is very strong in a house, water should be kept standing in some part of the room. The decided poisonous effects which we wish to antidote, are generally obtained by taking, through mistake, *sugar of lead.* Vomiting should be induced immediately, and diluted *Sulphuric-acid* given. If this is not at hand give *Epsom-salts* or *Glauber-salts.*

Nitrate of Silver, Lunar Caustic.—Give common *salt* in water, afterward mucilaginous drinks.

Antimony.—Poisonous effects are sometimes produced by *Antimonial Wine*, or *Tartar emetic.* A decoction of *Nut-galls, Oak-bark, Strong Coffee*, or *Green Tea* should be given.

Tin.—Sour food allowed to remain for some time in tin-vessels, may occasion poisoning. Give the *white of eggs, sugar*, or *milk.*

Nitre. Saltpetre.—Produce vomiting by tepid water, afterwards give copious draughts of mucilaginous drinks, such as *gum-water, flaxseed-tea*, &c

Cantharides.—Spanish flies. The best antidotes, to be used both inwardly, and applied externally, are *white of eggs*, and tepid, slimy substances.

Shellfish.—Clams and muscles, as well as some other kinds of fish are sometimes poisonous. Encourage vomiting, and give *charcoal*, with *sugar and water*, or *strong coffee* without milk.

Animal matter rendered poisonous by putrefaction or disease. Give diluted *vinegar* or *lemon-juice*, and afterwards if necessary, strong black *coffee* without milk, or strong black *tea.*

2. Narcotics.—***Prussic-acid.***—This is often obtained from peach leaves and peach pits. It is an exceedingly powerful poison, and very rapid in its action. At first the patient may be permitted to smell a little *Sal Ammoniac*, or a few drops may be administered in water, or he may smell *Camphor* or *Vinegar.* As soon as strong coffee can be prepared, give it freely.

Opium.—This drug in its various form, either in the gum, in laudanum or morphine, is frequently resorted to for the purpose of committing suicide, and Laudanum is often administered in mistake for paragoric.

Vomiting should be produced as speedily as possible, and for this purpose as much *Tartar Emetic* as can be placed on a five cent piece should be dissolved in a tumbler half full of tepid water, and one-third of it given once in ten minutes, if the first has not operated; giving in the interval copious draughts of tepid water, or tepid sugar and water. Often, however, it is impossible to produce vomiting, and in these cases a stomach-pump should be used. After some of the poison has been evacuated from the stomach, strong coffee, vinegar, or lemon-juice should be given. Usually the patient has a strong desire to sleep; this should be prevented, for if he sleep, he may soon sleep in death.—He should be kept in motion, walked about in the open air, and cold water dashed on his face and head.

In poisoning from *Hyosciamus*, *Belladonna*, *Strammonium*, *Hemlock*, *Digitalis*, *Nicotine*, *Camphor*, *Strychnine*, *Lobelia*, *Spigelia*, *Bloodroot*, the treatment is similar to that indicated for *Opium*.

RECAPITULATION.

Strong black coffee is a very powerful remedy for a large variety of poisons; such as *Opium*, *Strychnine*, *Strammonium*, *Mushrooms*, *Prussic-acid*, *Belladonna*, and *Hemlock*; also in poisoning from *Antimony* and *Phosphorus*.

Camphor is a very valuable remedy in poisoning from corrosive vegetable substances.

Mucilaginous drinks are useful against *alkaline* substances.

Soap is suitable principally for metallic poisoning, especially *Arsenic* and *Lead*. It is also suitable for corrosive acids and plants, with corrosive sap. It is injurious in poisoning by alkaline substances.

Sugar against poisoning by metallic substances, and vegetables with corrosive juice. It should be given after the appropriate antidote.

Vinegar is useful against *alkaline* substances, but is injurious in poisoning by mineral acids, arsenic, vegetables with corrosive sap.

White of egg, mixed with a suitable portion of water, is a very prominent remedy against poisoning by *corrosive sublimate*, *verdigris*, *tin*, *lead*, *sulphuric-acid*, *Arsenic* and other metallic substances.

CHAPTER III.

REAL AND APPARENT DEATH.

In this chapter we shall glance briefly at the cause of death, the signs which denote its near approach, and its final presence; and lastly, we shall speak of *apparent death*, and its proper treatment.

1. ACTUAL DEATH.

The direct cause of death and how it is that when a certain portion of the mechanism of the system is deranged, the whole machine may cease its motion, is an interesting subject of inquiry.

In looking at the human system, we notice what ample provisions have been made for maintaining life. We have, first, the heart and the blood vessels, which connect with and are distributed to every part of the system. Next we have the lungs, and the case in which they are lodged. And lastly, the power which works and regulates the machine vested in the nervous system. The main organs of these systems, the heart, the lungs, the brain, are called vital organs, and if the functions of one are arrested, the other two speedily cease.

That the heart may force the blood from its chambers, a certain power of contraction is necessary, and also, the presence of a sufficient quantity of blood in the chambers of the heart to stimulate them to contract. If this stimulus is withheld, or is deficient, the heart will soon cease to beat.

Respiration is subservient to the circulation of the blood. The heart and the lungs respond to each other, the blood being sent from the right heart to the lungs to be arterialized when it is conveyed back to the heart, and is then distributed to every part of the system. But to carry on respiration two things are necessary; first, air to enter the lungs and depart at intervals, and second, the movements of the chest, to cause its entrance and exit. These movements, although they may be regulated by the will, are essentially involuntary. The acts of respiration depends on a certain condition of the medulla oblongata, and if this condition fails, there is no action of the chest, no expansion of the lungs, no inhalation of air, and consequently no chemical change in the blood. Respiration therefore is dependent directly on the nervous system, and the cases are by no means rare where the nervous system receives a heavy shock, that the chest is paralyzed, and the lungs rendered incapable of performing their duty, thus causing death.

In death by *ænemia* the supply of blood for the heart fails. The heart retains the power of contraction, but there is no blood to contract upon. We see a striking instance of this in sudden and profuse hæmorrhage. The countenance and lips become exceedingly pale, cold sweats cover the body, the pupils are dilated, the sight becomes dim, the pulse is weak and faint, and insensibility speedily follows. In connection with these symptoms there is often nausea, vomiting, excessive restlessness, and tossing of the limbs, delirium, and convulsions; breathing faint and gasping, and this struggling for breath so violent that the cold sweat stands in drops upon the forehead, gradually grows fainter and fainter until death closes the scene. We see a train of symptoms similar to the above in the soldier bleeding to death on the battle-field, in the mother *flooding* after childbirth, and in those cases where large blood vessels are wounded. In death by *œnemia* the cessation of the nervous functions is occasioned by the lack of blood which should pass to the brain. The effect of position illustrates this. Syncope will much more rapidly ensue on venesection, where the patient is in an upright posture than when he is reclining. Hence in case of syncope we place the head as low if not lower than the trunk of body, so that the blood may more readily pass to the brain.

Death by *asthenia* is directly the converse of the above. Here the *nervous* system is the part first affected, and through it the heart or lungs. The heart may be full of blood, yet its power of contraction is gone. Death by *asthenia* is sometimes produced by causes which act primarily through the nervous system, such as intense grief, joy, and terror. Death occurring from blows on the epigastrium, from concussion where the brain is jarred, and from electricity—are of this kind. The phenomena are different, when death by asthenia occurs more slowly, from disease, especially in malignant cholera, mortification, and acute inflammation of the peritoneum. In these cases the muscular debility is extreme, but the intellect is clear, and the hearing sometimes painfully acute. In lingering disorders where there is a long continued drain on the system, the cause of death is owing in part to both *anemia* and *asthenia*. Death from want of a proper arterialization of the blood may be caused by some impediment which prevents the introduction of air into the lungs, or by insensibility of the muscles required for breathing, caused by disease or injury of the brain and nervous system. In the latter case it is generally denominated *coma*, in the former it is termed *asphyxia*. The means by which air, or oxygen, which is its vital principle, is prevented from entering the lungs are various. Azotic, hydrogen, or carbonic acid gases, all incapable of maintaining life, may be ranked among its causes. The entrance of air to the lungs may be prevented by *submersion*, and to death from this cause we give the name of *drowning*; or by stoppage of the mouth and nostrils—*smothering*; by mechanical obstruction of the larynx and trachea from within as by food—*choking*; or from without as with a cord—*strangulation*; or by impeding the mechanical action necessary for the admission and expulsion of air. The mechanism of respiration consists in an elevation and depression of the ribs, performed partly by the action of the intercostal muscles, and partly by the descent and ascent of the diaphragm and the action of the abdominal muscles. If motion both of the diaphragm and ribs be at the same time stopped, the result is death by *asphyxia*. This happens with persons who in digging are buried, with the exception of their head, by a mass of earth. A cast was attempted to be taken in one entire piece, as an academic model, of the body of an athletic black man. As soon as the plaster began to set, he felt on a sudden, deprived of the power of respiration, and to add to his misfortune was cut off from the means of expressing his distress ; his situation was perceived just in time to save his life. The same immoveable state of the lung-case is sometimes produced in tetanus, or poisoning by strychnine, or from disease or injury of the spinal chord above the origin of the nerves that give off the phrenic nerve; by section of the phrenic and intercostal nerves, and by ruptures in the walls of the thorax, through which air is admitted to the lungs, also when the pleura become filled with liquid of any kind.

We can more readily watch the development of successive symptoms, which arise from the slight and insufficient admission of oxygen to the lungs, than where there is entire cessation of breathing. In the latter case fatal effects follow so speedily as to give us but little time for observation. The following external phenomena present themselves in cases of impeded respiration. The first sensation is one of distress about the region of the lungs, accompanied with violent struggles for breath, in which there is an involuntary effort to expand the chest by bringing into action the intercostal muscles, the diaphragm and all the muscles connected with breathing. These struggles become exceedingly violent and almost convulsive, and are accompanied with a sensation of extreme agony. This agony, however, is of short duration being speedily followed by a torpor, which gradually deprives the sufferer of all consciousness. The struggles, however, continue, assuming the form of convulsions both of the trunks and limbs, in which nature seems to be making giant efforts for freedom, and to burst the fetters which are every moment pressing stronger and stronger on the seat of life. During these struggles the lips and face become blue and livid ; the veins in the head swell until they stand out like chords ; the eyes become bloodshot, and seem as if starting from the head. At length the convulsions subside into a scarcely perceptible twitching of the limbs, and this soon ceases, and is followed by a fatal immobility. The muscles relax, and even the sphincter which retain their irritability to the last moment, give way. The pulse is still perceptible, and the heart flutters for a moment longer, contracting feebly and with quick vibrations. In a few moments this also stops, and the circulation ceases. Now is the time when life is almost extinct, the lamp has gone out, leaving but a faint spark, and unless immediate and the most energetic measures are resorted to, no human power can fan that spark into a flame, and bring back warmth and life to the cold and torpid body. When asphyxia is more gradually induced, the sufferings are more protracted. The painful sense of anxiety is accompanied with vertigo, humming in the ears, scintillations before the vision, and various phenomena. The extinction of irritability is gradual, and is not attended with epileptic convulsions. There is a greater discoloration of the body but less of face.

Asphyxia, causing sudden death, is not generally witnessed in disease, but more frequently occurs in accidents. In chronic as well as acute cases, there is oftentimes a tendency to asphyxia for some little time. In these cases we see a gasping for breath, energetic and violent action of the muscles, livid looks, blood-shot eyes, dilated pupils, an expression of extreme agony, cold sweat, frequently delirium and those various phenomena we observe in shorter cases, showing that the blood is imperfectly arterialized. Examination after death gives us the same condition of the heart and blood-vessels as in shorter cases.

Death by coma as well as asphyxia is very common. In the former case certain morbid states of the brain produce stupor, the respiration becomes slow, irregular and stertorous, the functions of the nerves which produce the movement of the throat fail, the chest ceases to expand, the blood is no longer secreted and death ensues. The difference between death by coma and asphyxia is this — in the former case sensibility ceases first, then the movement of the thorax, and consequently the action of the lungs; in the latter case the chemical function of the lungs cease first.

Signs indicating the approach of death. There is often near the termination of life a comparative pause in the progress of the disease, when the mind emerges from the clouds which have hung around it, and shines with its accustomed brightness, and all physical suffering seems to have subsided. This is sometimes called the "lightning" before death, and is frequently viewed by friends with joy, who think they see in that delusive calm — death's herald, a sign of returning health. The amendment is not real, unless the pulse has improved; the energies of life are otherwise worn out, and the lamp is only flashing up for a moment, before it goes out in darkness. When sensibility to outward impressions is lost, and the mind either delirious or darkened by the mists of death, scenes which have been strongly impressed on the mind, may reappear and again pass before mental vision.

Dr. Armstrong departed delivering medical precepts. Lord Tenterden, who passed straight from the judgment-seat to his death-bed, fancied himself still presiding at a trial, and expired with "Gentlemen of the jury, you will now consider of your verdict." Dr. Adam, the author of the Roman Antiquities, imagined himself in school, and uttering the then touching and expressive words — "But it grows dark — the boys may dismiss," instantly died. He mistook the darkness of death which was casting its film over his eyes, and the eternal rest on which he was entering, for the shades of evening and the welcome rest which they brought. Before the spirit of Napoleon, in his last moments was moving the mighty panorama of the past. He was again on the battle-field, at the bridge of Lodi, struggling by the Pyramids; the thunder of battle was in his ears, and as there passed before his eyes that mighty army he had so often led to victory "Tête d'armée" broke from his dying lips.

The symptoms indicating the near approach of death are not always the same. Some in their last moments toss the clothes from the chest, as if their weight was uncomfortable, and though the attendants anxious to carry out their own ideas of comfort, and not permit the dying to contract a cold, are resolute in replacing them, they are as often thrust back. The patient is often unconscious of his acts, yet they indicate that the weight of the clothes is insupportable, and it is only a mistaken kindness to replace them, when he is using his utmost efforts, to cast them aside. Too often are the dying surrounded by friends, who cluster around the bedside, forgetting, that to him every breath of air is a precious boon, and by their sobs and lamentations torture and agonize the soul in its last moments. The hearing is often painfully acute, even when the patient is supposed to be in a state of insensibility, and the frantic bursts of agony from weeping friends are often to the dying, although they may be unable to express it, the bitterest ingredient in their cup of death. Others pick the sheets or work them between their fingers. This may be to excite by friction the sense of touch or the restlessness produced by excited nerves. The functions of the eye become disordered, and black spots or motes and various illusions float before the vision, which the patient attempts to clutch with his hand, or brush away. Many, on beholding these symptoms, look upon them as an infallible sign of death, but in this they are sometimes mistaken.

The awful shadows of death, which hang around the dying, seem at times to give the soul a glimpse, before it leaves the body, into the spirit world. In this peculiar state, when the spirit, although not separated from the body, seems partly in another state of existence, there is an expression on the countenance, almost unearthly, and occasionally words and disjointed sentences, which show, if the spirit is not passing the threshold of another world, and has become conscious of some of its scenes, it is unconscious of anything in this. A scene, which occurred several years since, produced at the time a strong impression on my mind. A young lady, a devoted christian, accomplished and beautiful, and whose fondness for music amounted to a passion, was dying. She seemed entirely unconscious, her eyes closed, the limbs cold, the pulse imperceptible or faintly fluttering, the breathing so faint as scarcely to stir the down of a feather. Her friends were standing around in silent anguish, expecting every moment the lamp which was burning so feebly would go out. Suddenly her lips slightly parted and a strain of heavenly music was heard, at first faint and trembling and then swelling in volume and harmony, until it seemed gushing forth, wave on wave of liquid melody; no words could be distinguished; the strain was like nothing earthly, surpassing in sweetness anything to which I had supposed the voice was capable of giving utterance. The strain ceased and she was silent for perhaps half an hour, when it again burst forth, gradually swelling into a song of triumph. It seemed as if she had already crossed the threshold of the spirit land, caught the symphony of the skies, and was tuning her harp to the song of angels. After the strain had ceased, which lasted about five minutes, she remained in the same unconscious state for an hour, and then breathed her last.

When disease passes into dying, the symptoms assume a certain defined character, which generally tells the tale to every eye. The eyes half closed and turned upwards, sunk in their sockets, wear a glazed and filmy appearance. Cheeks and temple are generally sunken, the nose sharp, the lips and face sometimes pale, and wearing that ashy hue, which involuntarily reminds one of death, or livid with the dark blood which creeps sluggishly through the veins. The voice loses its familiar tones, and becomes faint or comes with a muffled sound. The cold of death seizes on the extremities and gradually creeps towards the centre of life; the breath is chill, cold and clammy sweat bedews the skin. The respiration whether faint and languid, or labored, grows slow and feeble. The breath comes with a gurgling sound, and the death rattle is heard at every expulsion of air. The lungs like the pulse are intermittent in their action, and the breathing is in broken gasps. The pulse is faint and intermittent, and the artery scarcely swells beneath the finger. The pulse ceases, trembles along the artery, and again ceases; the heart flutters, the chest faintly rises; it is the last effort of expiring vitality; again the pulse quivers beneath your finger — stops — and all is over. "Life's fitful dream is past." A finely moulded form is before you, but the spark of vitality has fled. Death has conquered, and his seal is on the cold pulseless form before you.

Signs of death. Shakespeare, whose active brain allowed nothing to escape him, must have watched by many a death-bed, as in the description which the Friar gives to Juliet of the effects of the draught which is to transform her into the temporary likeness of a corpse, he thus sums up the more obvious characteristics of death:

> "No pulse shall keep
> His natural progress, but surcease to beat;
> No warmth, no breath, shall testify thou livest:
> The roses on thy lips and cheeks shall fade
> To paly ashes; thine eye's windows fall,
> Like death when he shuts up the day of life;
> Each part, deprived of supple government,
> Shall stiff, and stark, and cold appear, like Death."

Respiration is a function essential to life, as without it, we know there can be no arterialization of the blood, and therefore no circulation. Sir B. Brodie says, the heart never continues to act more than five minutes after respiration entirely ceases. The cessation of this function then may be considered a sure indication of death. To ascertain with certainty whether it had entirely ceased, it was formerly the custom, and is to a certain extent among the masses at present, to place a feather or a mirror before the lips, and if the feather moved, or a mist stained the glass, they were convinced that life was not extinct. When Lear brings in Cordelia, dead, he exclaims:

> "Lend me a looking glass;
> If that her breath will mist or stain the stone,
> Why then she lives!"

and immediately adds, "*This feather moves: she lives!*"

Prince Henry also was equally mistaken in believing his father dead,

> "By these gates of breath
> There lies a downy feather, which stirs not:
> Did he suspire that light and weightless down
> Perforce must move!"

Neither of these tests can be relied on, as the down may be moved by some agitation of the surrounding air, and the mirror be covered, by some exhalation of the body, presenting the appearance of condensed vapor of the breath. Owing to extreme physical exhaustion, respiration may be so faint, that to the casual observer it appears to have entirely ceased. It is frequently the case, that the transition from life to death is so quiet and gentle, that the observer is not conscious of the change, until the drooping jaw and stiffening features tell that life is extinct.

Dr. Paris says, however slow and feeble respiration may become by disease, yet it must always be perceptible, provided the naked breast and belly be exposed; for when the intercostal muscles act, the ribs are elevated, and the sternum is pushed forward: when the diaphragm acts, the abdomen swells, now this can never escape the attentive eye; and by looking at the chest and belly, we shall form a safer conclusion, than by the popular methods which have been usually adopted." No perceptible motion of the heart or arteries may be perceived, and yet respiration not have entirely ceased.

The temperature of the body relied on by some, is by no means a correct guide. An icy skin, although sooner or later an unfailing accompaniment, is not of itself a sufficient evidence of death. The temperature of the body for hours after death will be owing in a great measure to age, the disease of which the person died, habits of body and the temperature of the room, in which it is placed. The bodies of young persons retain heat longer than those of old. In old age or slow and exhausting disease the bodies are frequently cold even before the breath has left the body, certainly in a very short time after. In most kinds of asphyxia, except drowning, the bodies grow cold very slowly, also in diseases which are very rapid in their progress. The change from warmth to cold will be slower where the body is well wrapped up, in summer than in winter, in still atmosphere than in currents of air. There are numerous cases, as in hysterics and various other forms of disease, where the coldness of the body is corpse-like, notwithstanding there are no immediate indications of death. The first apparent effect of death is relaxation of the muscles. The flesh is soft, the joints flexible, the lower jaw drops, and the limbs hang heavily. This is followed by contraction, in which the flesh is hard, the muscles rigid and the joints unbending. The rigidity commences in the trunk and neck; it then appears in the thoracic extremities, then in the lower, and in receding passes off in the same way. Its appearance is varied by age, the constitution of the person, and the form of disease. It appears on an average five or six hours after death, and ordinarily continues from sixteen to twenty-four hours. In those who die of lingering diseases, old age, and where life slowly ebbs away, it comes on more quickly, sometimes in half an hour, and remains but a short time, continuing longer, where it commences latest. In the strong and athletic, in most of those who die a speedy or violent death, the contraction is strong in a ratio with the development of the muscular system at death, is slow in advancing and slow in going off. In these cases it is often a day or two before it commences, and sometimes lasts a week. When contraction of the muscles commences, we know that life is extinct, as this phenomenon never occurs as long as the body retains the least particle of vitality. When this rigidity passes off, the body again becomes flexible, and this is another strong indication of death. Flexibility after rigidity is not to be mistaken for that which occurs before. So long as the limbs continue flexible before rigidity we may suppose there may be some remains of life.

After rigidity passes off, and not before, begins putrefaction. It generally commences in the belly, the skin of which turns a bluish green, gradually increasing to brown or black, and progressively spreads over the body. Myston regards this stiffness as a measure of resistance opposed by organic to chemical forces. "Life on the point of extinction seems to take refuge in the muscles, and there causes the spasms we speak of, and during their continuance is able to resist the operation of chemical forces." It will readily be perceived that the rigidity of the body is a point of great importance, and there is no necessity for the cadaverous stiffness to be mistaken for any other. In stiffness, occasioned by freezing where the body is not yet dead, not the muscles only but the entire body, belly, breasts, and skin are hard. This together with the crackling of the joints on forcible flexure, is a sufficiently marked point of distinction. Neither can the stiffness, which occurs in certain forms of disease, well be mistaken for that which takes place after death. In the former case it occurs while the body has a certain amount of heat, and precedes apparent death—in the latter, the body is comparatively cold, and there is a distinct interregnum after apparent death. In both cases there is great difficulty in moving the limb, but in the former when bent, if the force is removed, it flies back to its former position, while in the latter, it continues its bent form; and if death takes place in these convulsive diseases, the stiffness passes off, and is followed at the proper time by the rigidity of death, which runs its usual course. But a mark which cannot be mistaken *is the termination of cadaverous rigidity, in flexibility, which is a certain indication of dissolution.*

From what has been said, it will be seen that the detection of the presence of death is not generally a very difficult matter. Instances have undoubtedly occurred where persons have been buried alive; yet they were principally in days of ignorance and superstition, or during a period when some terrific pestilence was numbering its victims by hundreds or thousands; when the change from life to apparent death covered over but a few hours, and when a person was hurried, in the clothes in which he died, into his coffin and grave. At these times when the community and friends are panic-stricken, we may reasonably suppose that occasionally cases occurred, where apparent was mistaken for real death. There are but few cases in which a physician would have any difficulty in detecting the presence of death.

In opening graves for the purpose of removing the dead or for other causes, bodies have been found turned on their sides, the grave-clothes disarranged, and the flesh lacerated. Many a tender heart has been made sad, and many a bitter tear shed at these developments of life in the grave have been unfolded. These mysteries, however, are very easily explained, without torturing the heart with the idea that a friend has aroused from the stupor of apparent death to find himself in the grave, and there writhing and gnawing his flesh in the agony of despair, died. A gas sooner or later is developed in the decaying body, which by its mechanical force, mimics many of the movements of life. It twists about the body, blows out the skin until it rends, and sometimes bursts the coffin. This gas is so powerful in corpses which have been some time in the water, that M. Devergie, the physician to the Morgue in Paris, says, that unless secured to the table they are often heaved up and thrown to the ground. The food is sometimes forced from the mouth, and the blood from the nose, and even the pores in the skin. The bloody sweat which in days of superstition was supposed to appear on the murdered body in the presence of the assassin, must have been produced by the struggling gas forcing out the fluid.

Is dying painful? This question by the community at large has been answered in the affirmative. Thousands have looked forward with a thrill of fear to that period when the soul should make its final exit from the body; not in all cases, that they feared for the future, or that they had any very strong attachments for life, but it was the sepulchral chill of that breeze which swept over them from the land of shadows, that fearful death agony forcing the cold sweat from every pore in the body, that appalling struggle with a power, whose grasp is the freezing grasp of death, a struggle in which the silver cord drawn to its utmost tension, breaks, which made death appear so terrible. And yet death is not painful. It comes in truth like a welcome sleep to a weary traveller. When dying commences, pain ceases, and the change is like that produced in an atmosphere laden with the narcotic exhalations of poppies in which the senses, while a feeling almost of delight pervades the system, are gradually overpowered. As death creeps on, the strength declines, a torpor steals over the nervous system, and notwithstanding there may be physical indications of pain, such as contortions of the countenance, and spasms of the limbs, suffering does not in reality exist. A few years since I was standing by the side of a patient, whose case I had watched with unusual interest, and who had for several days been so near death, that every visit I made I trembled lest I should find her a corpse. Starting from a torpor in which she had been for some time, her breath came in hurried gasps, the countenance was distorted, the limbs convulsed, the body writhed, so that it was almost impossible to hold her in the bed. Her friends believing that she was dying, burst into tears, but were somewhat quieted when I told them there was no immediate danger. She has since told me that during this period she had no control over these convulsions, yet was entirely free from pain excepting that occasioned by the agony of her friends. She retained even after her recovery an almost vivid recollection of every thing which occurred during this period. We should suppose that the so-called agony could never be more formidable than where the brain is the last to yield, and the patient retains his consciousness to the last. Yet persons thus situated generally say there are few things in life less painful than the close. William Hunter said: "If I had strength enough to hold a pen I would write how easy and delightful it is to die." The observation very commonly is heard from lips soon to be cold in death. "If this be dying, it is a pleasant thing to die." "I thought that dying had been more difficult, said Louis XIV." In those who retain their consciousness to the last, an agreeable disappointment seems to pervade the minds of all. The stream instead of growing turbulent, loses itself in a gentle placid current.

There are but very few diseases more painful than asthma, before the sensibility is blunted and the strength enfeebled, and in this disease we should naturally suppose the patient would fight vehemently for life. Dr. Campbell, the well-known Scotch professor, had an attack which well nigh carried him off a few months before he finally succumbed to the disease. A cordial gave him speedy and unexpected relief, and his first words were those of astonishment at the sad countenances of his friends, because he said his own mind was in such a state at the crisis of the attack from the expectation of immediate dissolution, that there was no other way to describe his feelings than by saying he was in rapture. If physical agony had existed, it would not have been so entirely subdued by mental ecstacy.

Persons who have been rescued from drowning, have invariably said, that after the first struggle was over, the sensation was of the most pleasant character. A gentleman once stated to me who was rescued at the last moment, that as he sunk for the last time all consciousness of danger gave place to sensations of pleasure. At first he wondered whether his friends would be successful in rescuing him, hoping they would not, then as languor gradually crept over him, he watched the changes of light and shadow until complete insensibility took place. When being resuscitated, however, he suffered the most intense tortures ; as the machinery of the system resumed its play, every nerve was full of the most exquisite pain. The account given by a distinguished British naval officer of his own case is familiar to all. While in the water he said every event of his life flashed like lightning across his mind. There was also an absence of pain. Intense cold, instead of being attended after the first few moments with pain, brings on a stupor, which quickly passes into the sleep of death. In hanging, where the victim has been cut down at the last moment all agree, that the uneasiness is quite momentary, that a pleasurable feeling immediately succeeds, that colors of various hues start up before the sight, and that these having been gazed on for a trivial space, all is oblivion. As we have already said, unless the stage of agony is crossed at a stride, disease stupefies when it is about to kill. As the disease has been painful, so generally is dying entirely the reverse.

2. APPARENT DEATH.

Apparent death from drowning.

The symptoms met with in drowning are varied. Some, on being precipitated into the water, paralyzed by fear, or stunned by the fall, sink like lead and die without a struggle. Others, still possessed of their faculties, struggle to keep themselves on the surface, but as their strength fails, their motions are made at random, and they clutch at every thing within their reach. From the irregularity of their motions, they rise and sink several times. At every opportunity an attempt is made to obtain a breath of air, but usually water is introduced with it, which exciting a cough, is expelled from the trachea, the same effort also expelling the air which had been introduced. A fresh demand for air is thus created, and a hurried attempt made to gratify it, but the very eagerness defeats its own object, for water is again introduced. Unless the head is fully raised, some portion of the water passes into the stomach, but the larger portion, together with the air taken in, is expelled by the spasms of the glottis. In this continued struggle the blood rushes to the head, the brain becomes congested, and all effort for life ceases. The victim sinking for the last time, unable to obtain air, whereby respiration may be continued and the blood arterialized, the lungs become filled with venous blood, the strokes of the heart grow weaker and weaker, sensibility gradually departs, and the victim glides quietly and with a feeling of luxury creeping over him into the arms of death.

From what has been already said, it will very readily be seen, that drowning is simply a kind of suffocation, caused not by the presence of water in the lungs or stomach, for there is but very little there, but by the shutting out the atmospheric air from the air-passages of the lungs, thus preventing the oxygenation of blood, and thereby extinguishing the lamp of life.

Let us now inquire into the treatment to be pursued in resusitating persons taken from the water.

If there are no marks of violence sufficient to have caused death, and there is reason to believe the person was alive when immersed, or there is a possibility that life may not be quite extinct, the treatment should at once be judicious, active, and decided, yet there should be the utmost caution in avoiding every thing like rough usage. The mouth and nostrils should be cleaned. The wet clothes immediately stripped from the body, the body wiped dry, and immediately covered with warm dry clothes or blankets. The colder the weather, the more necessary it is that this should be done on the spot, unless there is some place very near at hand, where these matters can be more readily carried into execution. It cannot be too strongly impressed on the mind of those who are first on the ground, and generally non-professional men, to confine themselves rigidly to these plain and simple directions. By doing this they will have paved the way for the more active treatment, which is to follow.

An error in the first steps may prove fatal. There are hundreds lost in the confusion and want of order which prevails at first, that might have been saved, if the attendants would only bear in mind the fact, that every thing which is done, must be done at the right time, and in the right way.

In removing the body, care should be taken that it is not lifted by the shoulders and legs, so that the head would fall backward, or forward, for this would be highly injurious. It should be placed on a door-board, or in a cart, in a recumbent posture with the head and breast raised. On reaching its destination, the body should be placed on a table of convenient height, stripped and covered with warm blankets, the head and chest raised, and the mouth and nostrils kept free and open. Artificial respiration should now be commenced.

The tube of a common pair of bellows can be made, by the assistance of a strip of linen, riband, or tape, to fit accurately into one nostril, while the other is closed by the hand of an assistant, who at the same time closes the mouth. Another assistant (who ought to be placed on the opposite or left hand of the body) is with his right hand to press backwards, and draw gently downward toward the chest the upper end of the wind-pipe, that part which lies a little below the chin, and which from its prominence in men, is vulgarly called *Adam's apple ;* by doing this, the gullet or passage into the stomach will be completely stopped, whilst the wind-pipe will be rendered more open to let the air pass freely to the lungs. The left hand of the second assistant is to be spread lightly over the pit of the stomach, ready to compress the chest and expel the air again, as soon as the lungs have been moderately filled by the bellows ; the first assistant unstopping the mouth or nostril at the same time to let the air escape. The same operation is to be repeated in a regular and steady manner, either until natural respiration begins, or until this and the other measures recommended have been persisted in for three or four hours without any appearance of returning life, unless the stiffness of the limbs and other positive signs of death set in. In the absence of the bellows, until one can be procured, air can be blown into the lungs by applying the mouth of the operator to that of the patient, and expelled from the chest in the manner directed above. To imitate the natural movements in respiration the motions in artificial respiration should be about fifteen times in a minute. While the process of artificial respiration is going on, some of the assistants should be engaged in communicating continued heat to the body. Dry warm blankets, bags of warm grain, bottles of hot water, hot bricks, or blankets wrung out in hot water, are among the means to be used. Should the accident happen in the vicinity where warm water can be readily obtained, a warm bath, moderated to a heat not exceeding 100° would be highly advantageous. Bottles of hot water should be placed at the bottom of the feet, to the joints of the knees and under the arm pits. A bladder, filled with hot water, should be applied to the region of the stomach, and some warm substance, as a heated brick, wrapped in cloths, should be passed over the body, particularly along the back. The application of heat, however, should be gradual. Slight shocks of electricity or galvanism passed through the diaphragm and heart would probably be of advantage, as this agent possesses an immense power over the nervous system. The first evidences of returning life are slight convulsive twitchings in the muscles of respiration, producing gasping or sighing. Our efforts on the approach of these signs should be increased as the life of the patient is still comparatively in our hands and can only be saved by the greatest effort, as it takes some time before the blood can be arterialized, and the mechanism of the body resume its wonted motion; a little brandy may now from time be introduced in the stomach, and an enema of tepid water given. As the suspension of animation is devoid of pain and attended with a feeling of luxury, so is the return of life agonizing in the extreme, so much so, that the patient often instead of expressing gratitude, curses the officiousness of friends, who have made him suffer such torture.

Even when the breathing has become calm and the circulation apparently restored, there still remains a period of danger, and the patient for a few hours should be closely watched. The treatment we have detailed as necessary in drowning, would also be applicable in asphyxia from strangulation, or in fact from any cause, with those deviations which would naturally suggest themselves to the mind of every intelligent medical man.

Apparent Death from Hanging, Choking, or Smothering.

The treatment in apparent death from any of the above causes is similar to that indicated in apparent death from drowning.

Apparent Death from noxious Gases.

Deaths from *Carbonic-acid gas*, *Carburetted Hydrogen gas*, and other poisonous gases are very common. Carbonic-acid gas is often found in the bottom of wells, and in large vessels, where fermentation has been going on. The presence of the gas may readily be detected by lowering a candle; if it goes out, of course the air will not support life, while if it burns brightly, there is no danger. In burning charcoal, the carbon of the coal uniting with the oxygen of the air, forms carbonic-acid gas, and unless the room is freely ventilated, the air soon becomes incapaple of supporting life. Hence deaths often occur by burning a pan of charcoal in a tight room, the occupants unconscious of danger, having retired to rest. Death in this way is like the gliding into a dreamy and pleasant sleep.

The body should immediately be removed into a cool, fresh current of air. Cold water should be freely dashed on the neck, face, and breast, or if the body is cold, warmth should be applied. Artificial respiration and the application of galvanism may also be resorted to, as directed in drowning. After life has been restored, a drop of Opium may be mixed with a tumbler half full of water, and a teaspoonful given once in half an hour.

Apparent Death from Hunger.

The agony endured where life slowly ebbs away from starvation, is beyond description. Small injections of warm milk should be repeatedly given, and cloths wet with warm milk or brandy placed on the stomach. As signs of returning life manifest themselves, warm milk may be given drop by drop, gradually increased to a teaspoonful, followed after a short interval by a little beef tea, or a few drops of wine. After a little sleep solid food may be taken, and the patient permitted gradually to return to a full diet.

Apparent Death from Freezing.

In freezing, the first symptom of approaching danger is an intense and almost irresistible drowsiness. Notwithstanding the person knows that to sleep is to die, yet the desire to sleep is so strong that he often neglects to take the only precaution left him—exercise, but quietly lies down and dies.

Where a person is found in the stupor or apparent death,

caused by intense cold, he should be removed, not to a heated apartment, as we should thereby preclude all hope of restoring animation, but to a place of shelter, such as a barn or a room without a fire, where he can be protected from drafts of air. He should then, especially if there be stiffness or rigidity, be covered several inches with snow, leaving the nostrils free, or if snow cannot be obtained, he should be placed in a bath, the water being made as cold as possible by means of ice. After the stiffness is removed by this treatment, the clothes should gradually be removed, by cutting them off if necessary, and the body rubbed with snow until it becomes red, or if snow is not to be obtained, it should be wiped dry —placed in a room moderately warm—covered with flannel, and briskly rubbed with the hands of several persons at the same time. If notwithstanding the above treatment, no signs of life show themselves, an enema of Camphor and water may be given once in fifteen minutes; the rubbing being continued. As soon as symptoms of approaching life become apparent, a little strong black coffee without milk may be administered in an enema, and the patient also be permitted to swallow a little as soon as able. For the severe pains which are often felt after life is restored, a powder of *Carbo-veg.* should be given once in fifteen or twenty minutes, followed or alternated, if necessary, after five or six doses, with *Arsenic.* The patient should avoid for some time the heat of a fire, as it will produce intense pain, and have a tendency to cause serious derangement of the system.

Apparent Death by Lightning.

The body should be placed in the open air or an open room, and cold water freely dashed on the face, neck, and chest. If the body be cold, warmth or friction may be applied. Artificial respiration should also be practiced as recommended in drowning.

Some have recommended that the patient should be placed in a recumbent posture, and covered with newly excavated earth until signs of returning life are apparent. A powder of *Nux-v.* may be placed on the tongue, and repeated if necessary in fifteen or twenty minutes.

Apparent Death from a Fall.

The patient should be placed gently on a bed with the head elevated. A little *Arnica* mixed with water may be introduced into the mouth, and the body carefully examined to see if there are no fractures. If the pulse is full and slow the patient should be bled.

CHAPTER IV.

MATERIA MEDICA.

ACONITE.

Monk's Hood.

Inflammatory diseases and local congestions. The first stage of fevers and nearly all those diseases where there is a rapid increase of circulation, dry and hot skin. Also in spasmodic affections produced by fright.

General Symptoms.—Thirst with redness of the cheeks. Bruised sensation and great sensitiveness to the touch; congestion of blood to the head and other organs; uneasiness as from a chill or suppressed perspiration; shivering sensation, or feeling as if the blood were stagnant.

Skin.—Fever with dry and burning skin. Scarlatina. Measles, Small-Pox, and other eruptive diseases, attended with fever.

Sleep.—Drowsiness with dreams, or sleeplessness with great restlessness and tossing from side to side. Startings in sleep; nightly delirium.

Fever.—Shivering with dry burning heat of the skin; burning heat with dry hot skin and great thirst; rapid pulse, at times hard, at others wiry and intermittent.

Head.—Vertigo, particularly on raising the head. Piercing throbbing pain in the head, forehead, and temples, or fullness in the forehead, as if the brain would press out; pinching pain over the root of the nose, and bruised or tensive sensation; congestion to the head with heat of the face; pains increased by movement.

Eyes, Ears, and Nose.—Acute ophthalmia with great redness, heat, and shooting pain in the eyes. Roaring in the ears. Bleeding from the nose.

Teeth, Mouth, and Throat.—Toothache especially from a cold, with heat and throbbing pain in one side of the face. Rheumatic and congestive tooth and face-ache. Acute inflammation of the throat, with violent fever and difficulty in swallowing.

Stomach and Abdomen.—Inflammation of the stomach. Inflammation of the bowels and intestines, with burning lacerating pain; great sensitiveness of the abdomen and stomach to the touch.

Fæces and Urinary organs.—Frequent, scanty and loose stools with tenesmus; watery diarrhœa. Retention or incontinence of urine; high colored urine, with or without brick dust sediment.

Genital Organs.—Milk-fever, puerperal fever, derangement of the menses, especially when accompanied with fever.

Larynx.—Short, dry cough, as if from a tickling sensation in the larynx; spasmodic cough, or cough with bloody or mucus expectoration. Dry cough, with heat, thirst, and restlessness. First stage of hooping cough, &c.

Chest.—Anxious, quick, or labored breathing. Asthmatic suffering; aching pain in the chest. Pneumonia, pleurisy, and affections of the heart.

ALUMINA.

Pure Clay.

Affections of the mucous membrane, sometimes with ulceration; scrofulous affections. Congestions arising from suppression of hæmorrhoidal flux; constipation; spasmodic conditions, twitching of the limbs, &c.

Skin.—Corrosive itching, particularly in the evening; excoriations, humid scurf, and itching tetters.

Head.—Vertigo; heaviness or lacerating in the head; itching eruption on the scalp.

Eyes, Ears, and Nose.—Burning in the eyes; nightly agglutinations; humming, vibrations and other sounds in the ears; bleeding at the nose; stoppage of the nose, or nose painful, swollen or ulcerated; itching eruptions on the face.

Abdomen and Fæces.—Colic; inactivity and paralysis of the rectum; constipation, piles.

Sexual Organs.—Headache before, and pain during the menses; profuse leucorrhœa, sometimes with itching; toothache, and constipation during pregnancy.

AGARICUS.

Particularly indicated in derangements of the nervous system.

Skin.—Itching burning and redness as if frozen, and sometimes itching eruptions.

Mental emotions.—Great restlessness; uneasiness of mind, sometimes developed in insanity.

Head.—Vertigo or dullness in the head; pressive pain or drawing tearing pain, particularly above the root of the nose and on the top of the head; painful sensitiveness of the scalp; itching and redness of the face.

Eyes, ears and nose.—Burning sensation in the eyes, itching and tingling; indistinct sight, objects seen as if through turbid water, surrounded with mist and covered with a cobweb; itching and burning of the ears, and various sounds in the ears; itching and soreness of the nose, sometimes with discharge of blood.

ARNICA.

Leopard's Bane.

Rheumatic and arthritic pains; hot and shining swellings; lacerating and shooting pains; paralysis or convulsions; affections occasioned by sprains, bruises and falls; sores of bed-ridden persons.

Fever.—Intermittent fever; pain in the bones, accompanied by headache.

Head.—Concussion of the brain by a blow or fall; great heat in the head; lacerating or tearing pain in the head, particularly the forehead.

Fæces.—Constipation; blind-piles; white diarrhœa.

Larynx and chest.—Dry cough as from tickling in the throat; expectoration of blood; difficult breathing; aching and bruised-like sensation in the chest.

ARSENIC.

Arsenious Acid.

Rapid sinking of strength, great prostration and emaciation; spasms; convulsions and epileptic fits; diseases of the mucous membrane; dropsical complaints and scrofulous affections.

Burning, especially in the interior of the affected parts.

Skin.—Pustules, ulcers, and cancerous affections, accompanied with burning; fetid secretions and tendency to run into mortification, general dropsy.

Sleep.—Great weariness and restlessness, tossing about, or starting as if in affright; burning as if hot water were coursing through the veins.

Fever.—General coldness, with dryness of the skin or profuse sweat; intermittent fever, the stages flowing imperceptibly into each other, typhoid and putrid fever and other fevers, where there is rapid prostration, dry and burning skin.

Head and face.—Periodical headache, great weight in the head, humming in the ears; beating pain in the head; painful sensitiveness of the scalp; swelling in the head and face, and burning excoriating eruptions with fetid smell; sunken countenance or bloated and puffed face; cancerous affections of the face.

Eyes, ears and nose.—Burning sensation in the eyes, and redness and congestion; scrofulous, rheumatic and catarrhal ophthalmia; swelling of the lids, specks and ulcers on the cornea; roaring in the ears; burning in the nose, sometimes with excoriation or ulceration; dryness of the nose, or discharge of an acrid fluid; profuse acrid discharge from the nose with sneezing; stoppage.

Teeth, mouth and throat.—Fetid smell from the mouth, tongue and lips, covered with burning vesicles; burning in the throat.

Stomach and abdomen—Violent thirst, or absence of thirst; water brush; nausea and excessive vomiting, sometimes of a chronic character and attended with burning sensation and pain in the stomach; vomiting sometimes of blood or of a blackish substance; stomach painful to the touch, sometimes with burning and of a weight like a stone; great anguish in the stomach; cancer and inflammation of the stomach; dropsy of the abdomen; spasmodic pain in the bowels; burning in the abdomen or cold and chilly sensation; swelling of the abdomen, great anguish and sensitiveness of the touch.

Fæces.—Constipation; or diarrhœa attended with colic; vomiting; straining, the evacuations burning and fetid; bloody evacuations with vomiting and colic.

Genital organs.—Acrid and corrosive leucorrhæa, cancer of the uterus.

Larynx and chest.—Dryness and burning in the larynx; consumption of the trachea; cough dry, short and hacking; difficult expectoration sometimes of blood-streaked mucus, with burning in the whole body, or succeeded by nausea; suffocative cough, soreness and bruised sensation in the chest, oppressive and labored breathing, sometimes with debility; asthma; dropsy of the chest; short and anxious breathing.

AURUM.

Gold.

Particularly useful in affections of the nervous system; scrofulous or dropsical affections; complaints from the abuse of Mercury; severe nightly pain in the bones, sometimes with inflammation and ulceration; syphilitic and mercurial affections of the bones.

Skin.—Bony tumors on the head, arms and legs; dropsical swellings; scrofulous and mercurial glandular affections; eruptions, ulcers and cancerous affections.

Mental Emotions.—Fear; insanity; violent anger or dejected spirits and longing for death.

Head and Face.—Rush of blood to the head; tumult and roaring in the head, especially of nervous persons; eruptions on the face; swollen and ulcerated lips, especially of tuberculous persons.

Eyes, Ears and Nose.—Scrofulous affections of the eyes; incipient amaurosis; roaring in the ears; fetid discharge from the ears, hardness of hearing, and affections from abuse of Mercury; caries of the nose; swelling, ulceration and soreness of the nose.

Chest.—Palpitation of the heart; chronic affections of the heart.

BELLADONNA.

Deadly Night-shade.

Scarlatina. Rheumatic and erysipelatous inflammations; great derangement of the nervous system; congestion to the head; spasms; convulsions; neuralgia.

Skin.—Scarlet spots and scarlet redness, sometimes with hot swelling of the parts; erysipelatous and rheumatic inflammations, with red and hot swellings; boils and painful glandular swellings.

Sleep.—Drowsiness, stupor, or great sleeplessness and restlessness, screaming, moaning and starting in sleep, with anxious and frightful dreams; headache on waking.

Fever.—Chilliness from a current of air; violent burning heat, redness of the face, congestion to the head, and violent thirst; pulse strong and quick, or full and slow.

Mental Emotions.—Melancholy, nightly delirium; insanity with changeable feelings; at times merry and foolish, at others sad with weeping, at others violent rage, howling and screaming; illusion of the senses; conversing with absent friends or imaginary things.

Head.—Violent headache, especially in the forehead, so severe as to cause him to close the eyes, and increased by motion; headache above the orbits as if the brain were pressed out, violent pulsative and throbbing headache; lacerating and shooting pains in the head; fullness and heaviness of the head; congestion to the head.

Face.—Redness of the face, sometimes swollen; erysipelatous inflammation; violent neuralgia.

Eyes, Ears and Nose.—Great sensitiveness to light, run

ning at the eyes, and violent pain in the balls, severe pain in the orbit, as if the eyes would be forced out, spasms of the eyes ; staring, shining or glistening eyes ; amaurosis ; great dimness of sight, cloudiness of the head, sparks before the eyes. Lacerating stitching pain in the ear ; swelling of the parotid gland. Bleeding at the nose. Ulcers on the nostrils and the corners of the lips.

Mouth and Throat.—Locked jaw ; throbbing and ulcerative pain in the gums, violent and lacerative toothache, worse at night; rheumatic toothache, particularly during pregnancy; toothache with red, hot face, beating in the head; swelling and inflammation of the mouth and tongue; tremor of the tongue; roughness and soreness of the throat; sore throat with pain and swelling and difficult swallowing; inflammation of the tonsils, rawness of the throat; spasmodic constriction of the throat.

Stomach and Abdomen.—Loss of appetite, hiccough, spasms of the stomach, resembling a cramp; pain in the pit of the stomach, colic and shooting pain or cramp-like and constrictive pain in the bowels; great sensitiveness of the stomach and abdomen ; peritonitis.

Fæces and Urine.—Dysenteric or diarrhœic stool with straining; paralysis of the neck of the bladder; inflammation of the bladder and kidneys.

Genital organs.—Derangement of the womb, affecting the head and nervous system ; puerperal fever; spasms of parturient women; toothache and colic of parturient women, swelling and pain in the breast.

Larynx and chest.—Hoarseness, painfulness of the larynx when coughing ; dry night-cough ; hooping cough. Labored and difficult breathing; asthma ; stitches or shooting pains in the chest; spasms of the chest and throat, palpitation, and tremor of the heart.

Back and extremities.—Rheumatic or neuralgic pains; stiffness of the parts; glandular swellings ; erysipelatous inflammation.

BRYONIA ALBA.

White Bryony.

Inaction of the liver and bowels. Rheumatic and arthritic affections. Gastric and nervous affections.

Sleep.—Drowsiness during the day; inclination to sleep after a meal; sleep with twitchings in the face.

Fever.—Chilliness and creeping chills; pains in the bones, from cold. Intermittent fever; acute inflammatory fevers with irritation of the nervous system; gastric and bilious fevers; and for the fever preceding the eruption of small-pox, measles, &c.

Mental Emotions.—Lowness of spirits; irritable temper; delirious talk at night, with desire to escape.

Head.—Headache in the morning on opening the eyes; rush of blood to the head and throbbing pulsations; heaviness of the head; headache when stooping as if the brain would burst from the forehead; pain aggravated by movement.

Nose and Face.—Swelling of the nose with ulcerative pain when touched and ulcerations; dryness and obstruction of the nose; bleeding of the nose; pale or yellow face; bloatedness or swelling of the face; swollen or chapped lips.

Mouth and Throat.—Darting pain in the teeth; painful soreness and looseness of the teeth and pain when chewing; hoarseness and sore throat with difficult swallowing.

Stomach and Abdomen.—Loss of appetite or morbid hunger and frequently bitter, putrid, or sickly taste; eructations; nausea, particularly in the morning on waking; empty retching; vomiting, sometimes bitter or bloody, frequently after eating or drinking. Pressure in the stomach as of a stone, particularly after eating, contractive pain, or darting, shooting or painful soreness in the stomach; spasms of the stomach; inflammation of the liver and stomach; tension, burning and stinging in the region of the liver; colic; colic during pregnancy; dropsy of the abdomen; inaction of the bowels from sendentary habits.

Fæces and Urine.—Constipation; chronic constipation;

hard stool with protrusion of the rectum; diarrhœa with previous colic, also from cold, alternating with constipation and spasm of the stomach; hot and red urine.

Genital organs.—Suppression of the menses with bleeding at the nose; profuse menstruation of dark red blood; pain in the small of the back and headache; puerperal fever, swelling and hardness of the breasts; milk-fever with rheumatic pains.

Larynx and Chest.—Violent coryza without cough; violent cough with retching and sensation, as if the head and chest would fly in pieces; painful cough, the expectoration sometimes streaked with blood; acute and chronic bronchitis; difficult breathing; asthma; pleurisy; pneumonia; painful respiration and great pain in coughing; stitches in the chest, shooting pains in the chest; rheumatic affection of the muscles of the chest.

Back and Extremities.—Painful stiffness in the nape of the neck, on moving the head; soreness and stiffness of the muscles of the trunk; bruised sensation in the small of the back; lumbago; lacerating pain in the back. Lacerating pains in the arms and legs; shining, red, rheumatic swelling of the joints with lacerating and tension on moving the parts. Coxagra; limping, cutting pain in the hips, lameness and drawing pains in the legs.

CALCAREA CARBONICA.

Carbonate of Lime.

Tuberculous affections. Eruptive diseases. Ulcers. Affections of drunkards.

Skin.—Rough skin; nettle rash, going off in cool air; itching, vesicular eruption, herpes; readily ulcerated skin; warts; ulcers; polypus.

Mental Emotions.—Low-spirited; peevishness, sadness or ill-humor.

Head.—Dullness or dizziness in the head; stupefying, oppressive headache, violent throbbing headache as if the head would burst, hammering in the head, and seething of the blood; itching eruption on the scalp and face; falling out of the hair; glandular swellings.

Eyes, Ears, and Nose.—Swelling and redness of the eyelids, readily ulcerating and stuck together with matter; ulcers and spots on the cornea; amaurosis. Pulsations in the ears; purulent discharge; polypus; snapping, roaring, ringing and hammering in the ear. Sore and ulcerated nostrils; polypus and scrofulous swelling of the nose; stoppage of the nose or discharge of pus. Itching eruption on the face; swelling of the glands.

Mouth and Throat.—Throbbing or gnawing pain in the teeth; swelling and bleeding of the gums.

Stomach and Abdomen.—Waterbrash; nausea, and sour eructations; spasms in the stomach; swelling of the mesenteric glands.

Larynx and Chest.—Dry, spasmodic cough, particularly at night; palpitation of the heart, and excoriating pain in the chest.

Trunk and Limbs.—Swelling of the glands. Boils, corns, &c.

CAMPHOR.

First stage of influenza. Dizziness; loss of consciousness, and coldness of the body. Spasms; convulsions. Cholera. Epileptic spasms.

Skin.—Blue cold skin, with coldness of the body.

Sleep.—Sopor and delirium; headache.

Fever.—Chilliness and coldness of the body; heat with trembling.

Head.—Dizziness of the head; loss of memory; dull headache or violent throbbing pain in the head; inflammation of the brain; pale countenance; contortions of the muscles of the face.

Nose.—First stage of influenza; coryza.

Stomach and Abdomen.—Excessive thirst or absence of thirst; nausea; vomiting, cold sweats and dizziness; burning in the stomach; Asiatic cholera with cramps; abdominal spasms; bruised, pinching, or contractive pain in the abdomen.

Fæces.—Difficult movement or involuntary diarrhœa.

Larynx and Chest.—Roughness of the voice, with cough, occasioned by mucus in the air-passages; oppression of the chest; stitches in the chest after a cold.

Extremities.—Drawing cramp-like pain in the muscles.

CANNABIS.

Hemp.

Affections of the kidney and bladder. Rheumatic drawings in the bones. Complaints occasioned by fatigue.

Urinary Organs.—Chronic retention of urine; painful discharge of bloody urine; severe burning pain in the urethra during and after making water; inflammation of the urethra; discharge of mucus from the urethra; ulcerative pain in the kidneys.

Chest.—Chronic catarrh. Inflammation of the chest and heart.

CANTHARIS.

Spanish Fly.

Burning and itching in the skin. Rawness and soreness in the whole body; inflammation and gangrene of the parts; convulsions with distortion of the limbs.

Skin.—Erysipelatous inflammation with blisters.

Urinary and Genital Organs.—Inflammation and pain in the kidneys, burning pain in the bladder; paralysis of the neck of the bladder; violent cutting in the urethra; suppression or retention of urine; constant desire to urinate, the urine passing in drops, sometimes streaked with blood, attended with burning pain; tenesmus of the bladder, strangury or discharge of drops of blood; eneuresis; discharge of pus and yellowish fluid from the urethra; painful gonorrhœa; inflammation of the neck of the uterus and the ovaries.

CAPSICUM.

Cayenne Pepper.

Skin.—Burning itching over the whole body; shuddering and chilliness; intermittent fevers.

Head.—Beating throbbing headache, as if the head would burst.

Throat.—Soreness of the throat, and painful swallowing; smarting sensation in the throat, as if it had been gargled with red pepper.

Larynx and Chest.—Hoarseness, cough, difficult breathing and sticking and throbbing pain in the chest.

CARBO-VEGETABILIS.

Vegetable Charcoal.

Intermittent fever. Rheumatic drawing or bruised sensation in the limbs and joints. Attacks of weakness. Vertigo. General prostration.

Skin.—Nettle rash; chilblains; glandular and lymphatic swellings; herpes and itching eruptions; unhealthy ulcers, and fetid smell.

Sleep.—Drowsiness going off by motion; sleeplessness, pain in the head.

Fever.—Chilliness, beating in the temples, and lacerating in the bones and limbs; last stage of typhoid fever; collapse of pulse, morning or night sweats.

Head.—Heaviness in the head, beating or pulsating headache, congestion to the head.

Nose and Face.—Swelling and ulceration of the nose; bleeding at the nose, violent coryza or stoppage of the nose. Chapped lips; eruptions on the face.

Mouth and Throat.—Looseness and aching pain in the teeth; soreness of the gums. Rawness of the throat; sore throat after measles.

Stomach and Abdomen.—Loss of appetite; nausea; waterbrash; spasms in the stomach; pain in the liver as if bruised; stitches and lacerating pain in the liver; distension of the abdomen; aching and rumbling pain, with emission of flatulence.

Fæces and Urine.—Constipation; burning diarrhœa; or burning in the rectum after movement; bloody stool with tenesmus; piles; ascarides in the rectum.

Genital Organs.—During the menses, cutting pain in the abdomen and headache. Leucorrhœa.

Larynx and Chest.—Hoarseness; cough when taking the least cold; cough, sometimes dry and hard, sometimes accompanied with purulent expectoration and soreness in the chest; hooping cough and consumption; spasmodic cough.

Back and Extremities.—Bruised sensation in the back and limbs; rheumatic drawing or lacerating pain in the joints and muscles.

CAUSTICUM.

Arthritic pain in the limbs. Lacerating in the joints and bones; stiffness in the joints; bruised sensation or sticking pain in every part of the body. Epileptic fits. Paralysis, especially on one side.

Skin.—Itching of the body, sometimes with burning pimples, warts.

Sleep.—Great drowsiness, severe headache; general sweat with uneasy sleep.

Eyes, Ears and Nose.—Sensations of sand in the eyes; inflammation of the eyes, with burning and redness, especially in tuberculous individuals; dimness of sight, and sensations as of objects or fiery sparks flitting before the eyes. Running of the ear, roaring and buzzing in the ear, bleeding of the nose, and obstructions of the nose, sometimes with dry coryza.

Face, Mouth and Throat.—Pains in the lower jaw and in the face; itching of the face; burning ulcers of the lips; throbbing or lacerating toothache; painful sensitiveness, or looseness of the teeth, with sensation as if they were elongated; swelling and bleeding of the gums; paralysis of the tongue; hoarseness and phlegm in the throat; soreness of the throat and constant disposition to swallow.

Stomach and Abdomen.—Spasms of the stomach; griping and pressure in the stomach; dull, aching pain or pressure in the abdomen; bruised sensation and distension of the abdomen from flatulence.

Fæces.—Constipation; bloody stool with burning and soreness; itching of the anus; burning or cutting in the urethra on passing water; hæmorrhage from the urethra.

Larynx and Chest.—Burning and roughness in the throat, or hoarseness and roughness; loss of voice; catarrh with dryness; cough and rawness of the throat; short hacking cough and tickling in the throat, soreness of the throat, when coughing; spasmodic asthma; palpitation of the heart; constriction of the chest, and difficult breathing; shooting pains in the chest.

Back and Extremities.—Bruised sensation, lacerating or stiffness in the back, nape of the neck and extremities; violent itching and sometimes pimples; paralysis, numb sensation.

CHAMOMILLA.

Chamomile.

Bilious affections, also in children and persons of a nervous temperament. Toothache. Affections arising from grief or passion. Spasms, especially of children. Drawing lacerating pain in the bones. Paralysis of the parts.

Skin.—Rash of infants and nursing females; unhealthy skin. Erysipelas; great sensitiveness, especially to currents of air.

Sleep.—Drowsiness; sleeplessness or soporous condition; anguish during sleep, with sudden cries.

Fever.—Shuddering sensation; great sensitiveness to the cold air. Intermittent fever, with nightly exacerbations; nausea, vomiting; colic and diarrhœa; heat with shuddering, inflammatory and gastric fevers.

Moral symptoms.—Great restlessness; peevishness and weeping.

Head.—Oppressive heaviness, dizziness; throbbing headache; hysteric, nervous or catarrhal headache.

Eyes, Ears, and Nose.—Twitchings of the muscles of the eyes, and yellowness of the whites; drawing in the ears, and discharge from the ears; swelling of the parotid gland; bleeding from the nose.

Face, Mouth and Throat.—Redness and burning heat on the face, particularly of one cheek while the other is cold and pale; erysipelas and swelling of one side of the face; convulsive movement of the facial muscles; sore throat with swelling of the parotids; stinging and burning in the throat, extending to the mouth and stomach. Grumbling and drawing toothache, aggravated by warm drinks and sometimes accompanied by swelling of the glands and stomach; nightly toothache, especially in the warmth of bed; throbbing and jerking toothache.

Stomach and Abdomen.—Vomiting, sometimes sour preceded by nausea; acidity of the stomach; painful bloatedness and weight in the stomach as from a stone; spasms in the stomach, particularly after the use of coffee or after a meal; flatulent colic; tensive or compressive pain in the abdomen; abdominal spasms; sensitiveness of the abdomen to the touch.

Fæces and Genital Organs.—Undigested stools, hot diarrhœic stools, with putrid smell, smelling like rotten eggs; green or watery diarrhœa; nightly diarrhœa with colic; diarrhœa during dentition, from cold, anger or chagrin. Corrosive leucorrhœa; cutting colic before the monthly period; profuse menstruation, sometimes with labor like pains. Affections of females during and after pregnancy.

Larynx and Chest.—Wheezing, hoarseness, cough, and rattling of mucus in the throat. Catarrhal cough of children; stitches in the chest, and difficult breathing.

Back and Extremities.—Pain in the back, especially at night, nightly pain in the limbs, sometimes with paralytic weakness.

CHINA.

Peruvian Bark.

Weakness from loss of animal fluids. Intermittent and other miasmatic fevers; slow and chronic fevers. Inaction of the stomach, liver and bowels. Painful weariness in the limbs; debility with disposition to sweat; weakness with trembling; great sensitiveness to the touch.

Skin.—Yellow color of the skin; swelling of the limbs.

Sleep.—Unrefreshing sleep, with frightful dreams.

Fever.—Intermittent fever; shuddering and chilliness, followed by violent fever, hot and dry skin, and this by profuse perspiration. Acute fevers with profuse sweat. Hectic and putrid fevers; exhausting night-sweats and sweat easily excited.

Head.—Headache from suppressed coryza. Soreness or bruised sensation of the brain; aching and heaviness of the head; congestion of the head, with heat and fullness. Sensation, as if the brain were balancing to and fro; headache, aggravated by contact or currents of air.

Eyes, Ears and Nose.—Incipient amaurosis, dimness and weakness of sight, with sensation as of black motes floating before the eyes. Bleeding of the nose and mouth.

Face and Mouth.—Pale or yellow face. Neuralgia, excited by the slightest touch; throbbing toothache; painful swelling of the tongue.

Stomach and Abdomen.—Bitter taste of food; great languor and drowsiness, especially after eating; oppression of the stomach; nausea and vomiting; swelling and pain in the liver; colic with nausea or thirst; distension of the abdomen, flatulent colic or violent pinching, cutting colic; dropsical swellings, and asthmatic sufferings.

Fæces and Genital Organs.—Constipation and heat, and dizziness in the head; loose diarrhœic and sometimes undigested stools, exceedingly variable in their color. Suppression of the menses or profuse menses, with discharge of clots of black blood, sometimes with uterine spasms and colic. Leucorrhœa before the menses ; bloody leucorrhœa.

Larynx and Chest.—Suffocative or spasmodic cough, excited by laughing or movement. Hæmorrhage from the lungs. Oppression in the chest and soreness in the larynx when coughing, difficult breathing ; suffocative catarrh, and paralysis of the lungs in old people, stitches in the side ; congestion to the chest.

CINA.

Worm Seed.

Affections arising from worms. Bronchial catarrhs remaining after measles.

Sleep.—Restlessness with colic and anguish.

Nose and Face.—Picking at the nose ; stoppage of the nose ; paleness of the face, especially around the lips ; grinding of the teeth.

Stomach and Abdomen.—Variable appetite or excessive hunger ; vomiting of worms and bilious vomiting ; pinching and cutting pain in the abdomen, writhing in the abdomen.

Fæces.—Diarrhœic movements like pap ; itching in the anus ; discharge of worms. Turbid and milky urine ; wetting of the bed. Cough with loss of consciousness ; hoarse, hollow cough or dry and spasmodic. Hooping cough, preceded by rigidity of the bowels, especially in tuberculous children, and those affected with worms. Oppression of the chest.

Extremities.—Paralytic sensation in the back and extremities, contraction and twitching of the muscles.

COCCULUS.

Indian Cockel.

Derangement of digestive organs ; hysterical affections ; paralytic affections and convulsions connected with menstruation. Paralysis of one side. Symptoms are aggravated by drinking, eating, sleeping, talking, and by tobacco and coffee.

Head.—Dizziness as from intoxication, sometimes with

nausea; cloudiness of the head; aching pain in the forehead; lacerating and throbbing headache, as if the eyes would be torn out; sensation, as if the head were empty.

Stomach and Abdomen.—Nausea with tendency to faint; nausea and inclination to vomit, especially when riding in a carriage or on the water; vomiting with headache and bruised sensation of the bowels; griping or lacerating pain in the stomach; flatulent colic, especially at night; distension of the abdomen; lacerating, cutting pain in the bowels.

Genital Organs.—Nervous difficulties, attending menstruation; painful menstruation with scanty or copious discharge of coagulated blood. Leucorrhœa resembling serum or pus.

Chest.—Oppression of the chest as from a stone; hysteric or other spasms in the chest. Palpitation of the heart and rush of blood to the chest.

Back and Extremities.—Paralytic pain in the small of the back and sometimes in the extremities. Drawing lacerating pain in the joints; numb sensation. Hot swelling in the hands and knees.

COFFEA.

Affections of the nervous system.

Sleep.—Sleeplessness; drowsiness.

General Symptoms.—Headache as if the brain would be dashed in pieces; aching pain in the top of the head; headache in the morning and on stooping forward; darting in the teeth; toothache with restlessness and anguish; neuralgia; violent cutting, shooting or neuralgic pain in the bowels or extremities. Oppression of the chest. Convulsions with grinding of the teeth. Pains are generally worse in the open air.

COLCHICUM.

Meadow Saffron.

Rheumatic and arthritic affections. Fall dysentery and diarrhœa.

Skin.—General dropsy.

General Symptoms.—Swelling of the abdomen, and dropsy; colicky pains in the abdomen. Violent vomiting, with trembling and spasms, excited by every motion; disposition to diarrhœa; stools preceded by colic; bloody stools mixed with a skinny substance or a jelly like mucus; burning at the anus; constant desire to urinate, sometimes attended with pain and a burning sensation. Brown or black urine, sometimes however depositing a white sediment; difficulty of breathing, and lacerating cutting pains in the chest; dropsy of the chest and palpitation of the heart. Rheumatic and arthritic pains in the back and extremities; most of the pains are aggravated by mental exertion, and are worse from evening till morning.

COLOCYNTH.

Wild Cucumber.

Complaints arising from indignation or grief. Neuralgic affections and violent colic.

Head.—Pressing headache, most violent when stooping or lying on the back; headache confined to one side, increased by motion.

Eyes, Face and Teeth.—Burning cutting in the eyes with pain in the head; rheumatic ophthalmia; lacerating and tension, or burning and stinging in one side of the face, extending to the ear and head.

Stomach and Abdomen.—Nausea and vomiting, sometimes with diarrhœa; pain in the stomach after eating; squeezing or cramp like pain in the stomach; colic and diarrhœa after the least nourishment; violent griping colic; cutting pain in the bowels as from knives; bruised feeling in the bowels.

Fæces.—Diarrhœa with tenesmus; dysentery with griping cramp like pain in the bowels.

Back and Extremities.—Paralytic pain in the muscles; drawing or cutting pain.

CONIUM.

Hemlock.

Cancerous affections. Affections of old people. Tuberculous difficulties. Dropsy. Paralysis.

Skin.—Chronic eruption. Stinging and itching sensation, as from flea-bites ; fetid and bleeding ulcers with tendency to gangrene; swelling of the glands, particularly from contusion; cancerous ulcers.

Fever.—Catarrhal fever with sore throat and aching pain in the throat; slow fever with loss of appetite and night-sweat.

Head.—Stupefying semilateral headache, sometimes with nausea, and coming on in the morning when waking ; lacerating headache, especially in the forehead and back of the head. Dropsy of the brain. Vertigo, dizziness, and wheeling sensation in the head, especially on looking around; apoplexy and paralysis of old people.

Eyes, Ears and Nose.—Heat and redness of the eyes; inflamed eyelids with styes; weakness of sight; sensitiveness to the light; fiery sparks or dark points before the eyes ; tingling or roaring in the ears. Affections of the nose from abuse of Mercury.

Face and Mouth.—Cancerous ulcers of the face and lips ; itching and gnawing eruption. Neuralgia of the face ; drawing or darting pain in the teeth ; gums swollen and bleeding. Sore throat, with aching and pain on swallowing.

Stomach and Abdomen.—Eructations and waterbrash ; nausea and vomiting during pregnancy. Contractive, pinching or spasmodic pains in the stomach; swelling and hardness of the abdomen, with soreness. Colic.

Urinary and Genital Organs.—Pain in passing water. Diabetes. Weakness of the genital organs. Suppression of or feeble menses, accompanied with spasms or cutting pain ; smarting and excoriating leucorrhœa. Profuse lochia. Cancer of the womb and breast.

Larynx and Chest.—Catarrhal fever, with soreness of the

chest. Nightly cough; dry tickling or short and convulsive cough; hooping cough, with bloody expectoration. Cough during pregnancy, and also in scrofulous persons. Shortness of breath, particularly when taking exercise. Asthma; shooting pain in the chest. Palpitation of the heart.

CROCUS.

Saffron.

General Symptoms.—Restless sleep; staggering and giddiness on raising the head. Alternation of cheerful and sad humor; absence of mind. Bubbling sensation in the abdomen. Colic as if from a cold, or as if the menses would make their appearance. Profuse menses of black slimy blood. Hæmorrhage from the womb on slightest movement. Colic and dragging pain preceding the menses. Seething of the blood, as if the body were filled with moving things.

CUPRUM.

Copper.

Convulsions and spasmodic affections. Spasmodic asthma. Cholera. Hooping cough. Diarrhœa.

General Symptoms.—General convulsions and convulsive movement of the limbs. Epileptic convulsions; rigidity of the limbs and trunk. St. Vitus dance. Great weakness of the body. Paralysis and nervous affections.

Head.—Insanity. Painful, hollow sensation in the head; violent headache; bruised sensation of the brain.

Stomach.—Nausea; violent vomiting with nausea and diarrhœa; excessive vomiting with colic and diarrhœa; violent pains in the stomach and its vicinity; pressure in the pit of the stomach; violent spasms in the abdomen or cramp like pain, also in the upper and lower limbs; cutting and lacerating in the bowels.

Fæces.—Constipation; violent and profuse diarrhœa. Asiatic cholera.

Larynx and Chest.—Continued hoarseness. Short and dry cough like hooping cough; cough with almost suppressed breathing. Cough with expectoration of blood; spasmodic cough with rattling in the chest. Asthma.

Trunk and Extremities.—Twitching of the muscles and cramps in the arms and legs.

DIGITALIS.

Foxglove.

Painfulness of the whole body. Nervous affections. Convulsions. Serous apoplexy of old people.

Sleep.—Uneasy, unrefreshing sleep, or lethargy.

Head.—Dizziness and trembling. Violent lancinating headache; semi-lateral headache, sudden cracking in the head.

Eyes and Ears.—Throbbing pain in the orbits; redness of the eyes with stinging pain; swelling of the lids. Ophthalmia, particularly in tuberculous or rheumatic individuals. Amaurosis; illusions of sight. Hissing before the ears.

Stomach and Abdomen.—Nausea and vomiting; weakness of the stomach, particularly after eating; pressure, lancinating or burning in the stomach. Dropsy in the bowels.

Chest.—Painful asthma; excoriating pain in the chest, especially on coughing. Derangement of the circulation, indicated by the beats of the heart.

DROSERA.

Sun Dew.

Rapid emaciation. Bruised sensation of the limbs. Hooping cough. Epileptic paroxysms, with subsequent sleep and discharge of blood.

Fever.—Chilliness and shuddering. Intermittent fever; night-sweats; fever with headache and spasmodic cough.

Head.—Dizziness in the open air. Headache on stooping; beating and hammering in the forehead.

Eyes and Ears.—Weakness of the eyes with the appearance of gauze and of vibrations before them. Inflammation of the ear.

Larynx and Chest.—Tickling sensation of the throat, producing a hacking cough. Pain in the stomach and region of the liver. Nightly cough ; cough with vomiting ; cough with expectoration of blood ; chronic catarrh ; hacking cough ; dry spasmodic cough with gagging ; hooping cough, sometimes with hæmorrhage from the mouth and nose ; wheezing breathing, and suffocation.

DULCAMARA.

Bitter-Sweet.

Affections in consequence of cold. Eruptions.

Skin.—Itching and stinging eruptions of white blotches. Herpetic crusts over the body.

Head.—Stupefying headache. Congestion of the head. Headache aggravated by exercise and conversation.

Face.—Warts and scurfy eruptions on the face.

Stomach and Abdomen.—Nausea. Pressure or aching in the stomach ; colic as if from cold, or as if diarrhœa would come on.

Fæces.—Diarrhœa from cold, and accompanied with colic, particularly in the summer with nocturnal watery evacuations ; slimy white or mucous diarrhœa ; chronic, bloody diarrhœa.

EUPHRASIA.

Eye Bright.

Affections of the eyes.

Eyes.—Smarting or stinging in the eyes with redness. Inflammation, ulceration and swelling of the margin of the eyelids. Eruption around the eyes ; sensitiveness to light. Rheumatic ophthalmia.

Nose.—Soreness of the nose. Profuse bleeding at the nose ; profuse fluent coryza, with sneezing, discharge of mucus and smarting tears in the eyes.

FERRUM.

Aceticum. Acetate of Iron.

Great weakness. Emaciation and languor. Hæmorrhage. Congestion of blood and chronic diarrhœa.

Fever.—Want of animal heat, shuddering and exhausting sweats. Intermittent fever.

Head.—Dizziness, with reeling sensation and heaviness. Rush of blood to the head ; hammering and throbbing headache.

Face.—Livid or jaundiced complexion, puffiness of the face.

Fæces.—Chronic diarrhœa, frequent stools with burning, itching or gnawing in the rectum, and sometimes with discharge of ascarides.

Genital organs.—Nocturnal emissions. Delay of the menses. Miscarriage. Whitish leucorrhœa, smarting and corroding.

Larynx and Chest.—Spasmodic cough. Cough sometimes with bloody expectoration, also of bloody phlegm. Asthma.

GRAPHITIS.

Black Lead.

Various forms of eruptions. Tuberculous affections.

Skin.—Dryness of the skin. Itching pimples ; spots like flea bites ; unhealthy skin, every little itching producing suppuration ; thickness of the nails ; boils. Herpetic and other eruptions.

Head.—Itching of the scalp. Humid and scabby eruptions on the head ; burning on the top of the head, headache especially in the morning on waking.

Eyes.—Redness of the eyes. Painful inflammation of the lids ; profuse secretion of tears ; intolerance of light.

Ears.—Eruptions around and in the ears ; ulcerative pain in the ears ; bloody discharge, or discharge of pus in the ear ; roaring in the ear.

Nose.—Soreness and swelling of the nose ; scabs and dry soreness in the nose ; sore, cracked and ulcerated nostrils. Bleeding at the nose.

Face and Teeth.—Erysipelas. Incipient paralysis. Ulcerated corners of the mouth, and eruptions on the face; swellings of the glands and of the gums, stinging toothache, especially at night, with heat in the face.

Stomach.—Weakness of digestion. Nausea and vomiting.

Fæces.—Constipation. Hæmorrhoidal tumors.

Genital organs.—Itching and smarting eruptions on the labia. Soreness between limbs; itching in the genital organs. Derangement of the menses, generally delayed and insufficient.

Back and Extremities.—Pain and stiffness in the nape of the neck and back. Eruptions. Arthritic nodosities on the fingers. Soreness between the thighs. Ulcers and Herpes on different parts of the extremities.

HELLEBORUS NIGER.

Black Hellebore.

Dropsical affections; affections of the head and nervous system.

Skin.—Rash; watery swelling of the skin; general dropsy especially after suppressed eruptions.

Head.—Inflammation of the brain; hydrocephalus; dullness of the head and heaviness; painful stupefaction of the head; violent headache with heaviness.

Face.—Œdematous swelling of the face and lips.

HEPAR SULPHURIS.

Sulphuret of Lime.

Skin and glandular affections. Affections from the abuse of Mercury. Croup and other inflammatory coughs. Chronic coughs.

Skin.—Chapped skin. Unhealthy skin; injuries produce suppuration. Nettle rash.

Fever.—Burning feverish heat, red face, violent headache during the night; profuse sweat.

Head.—Headache when shaking the head; aching in the

forehead, like a boil as if bruised; headache in the night or in the morning on waking. Blotches and humid eruptions on the scalp; falling off of hair. Boring pain at the root of the nose.

Eyes.—Erysipelatous swelling of the eyes with soreness and bruised pain in the limbs. Redness, inflammation and swelling of the eyelids, sometimes with styes and ulcerated edges. Specks and ulcers of the cornea, dimness of sight.

Ears.—Scurfs in and behind the ears; itching; inflammation of the ears and discharge of pus; hardness of hearing.

Nose.—Itching of the nose and formation of scurfs and scabs. Coryza. Inflammatory swelling of the nose, bleeding at the nose.

Face.—Erysipelatous swelling of the checks. Pain of the bones of the face, when touching them. Pimples on the face of young people; swelling of the lips. Ulcers or itching pimples on the chin and around the mouth. Swelling of the gums, looseness of the teeth and jerking toothache.

Stomach and Abdomen.—Frequent attacks of nausea with coldness and paleness; swelling and suppuration of the inguinal glands.

Fæces.—Diarrhœa with colic and tenesmus; dysenteric diarrhœa; bloody or clay colored stools, soreness of the rectum.

Urine.—Wetting the bed at night, irritation of the urethra and discharge of mucus.

Genital organs.—Weakness of the genital organs. Leucorrhœa with smarting.

Throat.—Sensation as of swelling of the throat on swallowing, rawness, roughness or scraping sensation in the throat; stitches or stinging in the throat, as if caused by a splinter, especially on taking a deep inspiration or turning the head; swelling of the tonsils.

Larynx.—Seated pain in the larynx; hoarseness; deep, dry and violent cough, especially in the evening, frequently brought on by exposing any part of the body to the cold;

violent cough, affecting the head and followed by sneezing or creeping.

Chest.—Hoarse, frequent and wheezing breathing, danger of suffocation when lying down. Spasmodic constriction of the chest.

Back and Extremities.—Weakness in the whole spine, bruised or drawing sensation in the small of the back. Ulceration and suppuration of the axillary glands; bruised sensation in the arms. Nettle rash and swelling on the hands, fingers and joints. Panaris. Swelling of the knees. Cracks and ulcerations of the feet and toes.

HYOSCIAMUS.

Henbane.

Convulsions; spasmodic affections and other derangements of the nervous system; sleeplessness, hydrocephalus and other affections of the brain.

Skin.—Creeping and itching sensation in the skin, redness of the skin and rash from abuse of *Belladonna.*

Sleep.—Drowsiness; sleeplessness, sometimes with convulsions and concussions, as if occasioned by fright; grasping at flocks; frightful dreams, moaning, grinding of the teeth, and starting from sleep.

Fever.—Burning heat of the blood.

Moral Symptoms.—Fearfulness, violent delirium, stupefaction, loss of sense, alternations of ease and rage, screaming and sleeplessness.

Head.—Delirium with muttering, or great excitability; mental derangement of drunkards. Dizziness; inflammation of the brain; hydrocephalus; stupefying headache, especially in the forehead; undulating sensation in the brain, and headache with unnatural heat.

Eyes.—Illusions of sight, staring and distorted eyes; eyes red and sparkling; twitching of the lids, sometimes with swelling. Nocturnal blindness and spasmodic closing of the lids.

***Mouth and Throat.*—Lacerating toothache with congestion**

of blood to the head, sensation as if the teeth were elongated, burning and dryness of the tongue and lips ; partial or entire paralysis of the tongue and throat ; burning and dryness in the throat with difficulty in swallowing.

Genital Organs.—Profuse menstruation of bright, red blood. Puerperal fever.

Larynx and Chest.—Dry spasmodic cough, particularly at night, as if occasioned by tickling in the throat, especially when lying down, and attended with redness of the face. Difficulty of breathing ; spasms of the chest.

IGNATIA.

Hysteric affections, also convulsive or spasmodic disorders, especially when occasioned by fright or grief. Nervous affections of infants. Great excitability of the nervous system ; pain from the least touch.

Skin.—Itching of the skin and great sensitiveness to a draft of air.

Sleep.—Restless sleep with sudden starting, unpleasant dreams, waking with spasmodic yawning.

Head.—Headache, increased by stooping, and relieved by lying on the back ; aching and cramp like headache over the root of the nose, or as if something hard were pressed on the brain, recurring in paroxysms ; headache as if a nail were driven into the head.

Eyes.—Sensation in the eyes as of sand with inflammation ; sensitiveness to light. Scrofulous ophthalmia ; convulsive movements of the eyes and eyelids ; convulsive face ; convulsive twitchings and distortions of the muscles.

Throat.—Stitches from the throat to the ear ; difficulty of swallowing or sensation, as if the food passed over a lump ; pain in the throat and in the submaxillary glands.

Stomach and Abdomen.—Hiccough after eating or drinking ; perodical pains in the stomach, disturbing rest ; sensation in the stomach as if from fasting ; periodical abdominal spasms, especially in hysteric individuals ; flatulent colci, particularly at night.

Fæces.—Diarrhœic stools with colic and rumbling in the abdomen; constipation from cold; itching and soreness of the rectum.

Genital Organs.—Derangement of the nervous system, during the menses, the blood being black, and generally coagulated.

Larynx and Chest.—Chronic nightly cough; concussive, spasmodic cough, especially on waking; oppression of the chest. Palpitation of the heart, especially at night with stitches.

IMPONDERABILIA.

Electricity. Galvanism. Magnetism.

In the above group we include electricity, however excited, whether by the galvanic or magnetic battery, or animal magnetism.

This agent produces a powerful effect in paralysis, and other affections produced by derangements of the nervous system, in rheumatic and arthritic affections, especially of the chronic form, contraction of the muscles and stiffness of the joints. It is also invaluable in asphyxia and apparent death, and in general inaction of the whole system. The application of this powerful agent requires much care and correct judgment. The electric current should be light at first, gradually increasing as circumstances indicate. The poles of the battery should be so applied, that a continuous current should be sent through the length of the muscles and along the course of the nerves. Every person possesses a certain amount of animal magnetism, although some possess it to a much greater degree than others. Where there is great nervous excitability, pain, and sleeplessness, a few magnetic passes will often produce immediate relief. The will of the operator should be strongly concentrated on the patient. The hand should be gently moved over the parts, making the passes downward; or the hands may be pressed gently on the parts for a moment, removed and applied again.

When the magnetic effect has been too powerful, it may be relieved by reversing the passes.

IPECACUANHA.

Coughs, fevers, and affections produced by a derangement of the stomach and bowels ; gastric and bilious fevers, intermittent fever, &c.

Fever.—Shuddering and yawning and great sensitiveness to cold and heat ; external coldness and internal heat. Intermittent fever with an absence of the sweating stage.

Head.—Headache as if the brain and skull were bruised; aching pain in the head, especially over the eyes ; headache with sickness of the stomach.

Nose.—Coryza with stoppage of the nose, and pain in the forehead, frequent sneezing.

Stomach.—Nausea and effort to vomit and vomiting; vomiting of mucus and various other substances; vomiting with diarrhœa. Colic of children; flatulent colic ; griping and pinching in the bowels.

Fæces.—Diarrhœic, fermented stools; diarrhœa with nausea and vomiting; dysenteric stools, sometimes of bloody mucus and with tenesmus.

Genital Organs.—Profuse menstrual discharge of bright, red and coagulated blood.

Larynx and Chest.—Rattling in the bronchial tubes, suffocative cough ; cough without eruption, in the cold air, excited by a tickling in the throat or deep inspiration, and sometimes accompanied with nausea and headache ; ordinary catarrhal cough.

Chest.—Asthma; palpitation of the heart and oppression of the chest.

IODINE.

Scrofulous affections ; abdominal phthisis.

Skin.—Rough, dry skin, and unhealthy eruptions, especially in tuberculous persons. Glandular swellings and indurations ; night-sweat.

Eyes and ears.—Sore and inflamed eyes; hardness of hearing.

Abdomen.—Pinching and aching colic; swelling of the inguinal glands.

Genital Organs.—Corroding leucorrhœa; delaying of the menstrual functions.

Larynx and Chest.—Pain in the larynx; inflammation of the trachea; hoarseness in the morning; dry, short cough, especially in the morning, sometimes with stitches in the chest, and bloody expectoration. Great difficulty in breathing; violent pulsations in the chest; sore pain in the chest.

Back and Limbs.—Rheumatic pain and swelling in the limbs and joints; glandular swellings. Dropsical or inflammatory swelling of the knee.

KALI CARBONICUM.

Carbonate of Potash.

Chronic and protracted disorders attended with debility; dropsical accumulations; hectic, consumptive and low nervous fevers; derangement of menstruation in feeble constitutions; abscesses; chronic inflammation of the eyes and ears; glandular affections and affections of the liver and stomach.

Skin.—Dryness of the skin; burning itching of the whole body; scaly or red spots. Herpes. Old warts. Abdominal and general dropsy.

Sleep.—Drowsiness in the day time; restless nights, and sleep full of fanciful dreams; starting when asleep, congestion of blood and gnashing of teeth. Nightmare. Excessive pain in the body at night, like strokes of a hammer.

Fever.—Night sweat; shuddering and internal chilliness, sometimes with thirst or internal heat.

Head.—Weak memory and sometimes loss of consciousness; dullness and stupid feeling in the head as if from intoxication; dizziness as from walking. Headache when riding in a carriage, or when sneezing or coughing; aching pain sometimes in the whole head, the eyes, forehead or back of the head, aggravated by contact, sometimes accompanied with nausea, and frequently going off in the open air; seething of the blood through the head. Stitches and throbbing pain through the forehead and sides of the head, frequently intermitting. Liability of the head to take cold, with headache and toothache. Scurf on the head, with itching pimples.

Eyes.—Soreness and burning in the eyes with feeling as of sand. Lids stuck together with matter in the morning; swelling and inflammation of the lids; sensitive to light, colors and sparks before the eyes, black points, spots and gauze before the eyes or in the open air.

Ears.—Severe pain in the ears; itching, swelling and suppuration in the ear with discharge of matter; swelling of the parotid gland. Partial deafness with various noises in the ears.

Nose and Face.—Pimples on the nose, sore, scurfy, or ulcerated nostrils; bleeding of the nose; obstructions of the nose. Old eruptions, warts, ulcers, and burning itching of the face.

Mouth and Throat.—Toothache when eating, and touched by either cold or warm substances. Inflammation of the gums and looseness of the teeth. Swelling of the tongue, and painful vesicles in the inner mouth. Sore pain in the throat or scraping sensation, especially when swallowing food.

Stomach.—Drowsiness during and after a meal, and sense of fullness in the stomach; acidity in the stomach and sour eructations; nausea sometimes with faintness, or as if the stomach were empty, or deranged; pressure; spasmodic, cutting, sore or throbbing pain in the stomach, which is also painful to the touch. Pressure, stitches, burning pain in the region of the liver.

Abdomen.—Distension of the abdomen; colic with eructations; inactivity, coldness or uneasiness in the abdomen; flatulent colic; abdominal dropsy.

Fæces.—Burning at the anus after stool, itching of the anus. Large painful varices.

Urinary and Genital Organs—Long continued, contusive

pain in the region of the kidneys, especially in the afternoon when sitting. Frequent desire to urinate ; turbid urine, sometimes with brick dust sediment and burning in the urethra. Swelling of the testes. Soreness, burning and itching about the female genitals. Menstrual blood, acrid, having a bad pungent smell. Suppression of the menses, with dropsy, leucorrhœa.

Larynx and Chest.—Hoarseness and night cough, and short, hacking or spasmodic cough, sometimes causing vomiting. Oppressed and difficult breathing. Asthma, spasms and lacerating or cutting pain in the chest.

Back and Extremities.—Violent pain in the back and extremities, sometimes stiffness, paralytic sensation or a bruised pain. Dropsical swelling, pimples and excoriation, swelling of the glands. Stitches or pressure in the region of the kidneys, pulsative or throbbing sensation.

KALI BICHROMICUM.

Bichromate of Potash.

In addition to many of the symptoms indicated in the previous remedy, the most important indications for the selection of this drug, are to be found in connection with the respiratory organs.

Larynx and Chest.—Old coughs, obstinate colds and coughs, and derangements which threaten to terminate in consumption. Asthmatic affections. Dropsy of the chest. Cough with slate colored sputa. Aching pain as of ulceration in the larynx. Wheezing cough. Stuffing cough as if the air passages were clogged with mucus ; danger of suffocation. This is an invaluable remedy in membranous croup. For particular indications see that disease.

KREASOTE.

This remedy is particularly useful in old ulcers and cancerous affections, especially of the stomach. Hemorrhage also in chronic leucorrhœa ; bleeding from the womb ; profuse menses with discharges of dark or badly smelling blood.

LACHESIS.

Poison of the Lance-headed Viper.

Particularly against the effects of intoxication or the abuse of Mercury; also in severe and protracted fevers and nervous disorders. Erysipelas; and various diseases where there is a sinking of the vital powers, and where there is a tendency to suppuration or mortification.

General Symptoms.—Great weakness of the body; paralysis. Hemiphlegia. Convulsions with rigidity of the limbs.

Skin.—Erysipelas, particularly where there is a tendency to suppuration, gangrenous blisters; ulcers with fetid discharge.

Moral Emotions.—Melancholy during pregnancy. Insanity with a tendency towards suspicion or malice.

Head.—Fullness and dullness of the head, weakness of the memory and great difficulty in thinking. Affections of drunkards. Dizziness, particularly on closing the eyes. Apoplectic fits with distortion of the facial muscles and sometimes hemiphlegia. Acute dropsy of the brain; daily headache with languor, drowsiness and loss of appetite; headache from the heat of the sun; headache after a cold and also daily in the morning, sometimes with nausea and vomiting; undulating pulsative beating in the head, sometimes with twinkling before the eyes.

Eyes, Ears and Nose.—Inflammation of the eyes and lids, ulcers on the cornea. Soreness and scurfs on the ears, scurfs and soreness of the nose, with discharge of yellow matter and blood.

Mouth and Throat.—Lockjaw. Toothache with swelling of the teeth and gums. Salivation. Paralysis of the tongue after apoplexy. Difficulty of speech. Soreness, swelling or gangrene of the tongue. Sore and burning pain in the throat with scarlet redness, ulceration and great difficulty in swallowing.

Stomach and Abdomen.—Nausea and vomiting, sometimes in paroxysms and accompanied with diarrhœa, and especially of drunkards and pregnant females. Swelling and indurations of the glands. Hard and distended abdomen. Inflammation and abscess of the liver.

Fæces.—Chronic constipation or alternate constipation and diarrhœa.

Larynx and Chest.—Swelling and pain in the larynx. The symptoms are generally worse at night, cough occasioned by ulcers in the throat. Cough with bloody or purulent expectorations. Shortness of breath, pains as from soreness in the chest. Pneumonia. Affections of the heart.

LYCOPODIUM.

Wolfsfoot.

Skin.—Itching. Herpetic spots; humid suppurating herpes. Fistulous, mercurial and carious ulcers. Boils returning periodically. Chilblains. Glandular swellings. Arthritic nodes.

Head.—Rush of blood to the head in the morning on waking. Rheumatic headache; headache from chagrin. Eruptions on the head, swelling of the glands, sometimes suppurating.

Eyes, Ears and Nose.—Vertical half-sightedness; excessive sensitiveness of hearing and sight; drawing in the teeth and swelling and ulceration of the gums. Chronic sore throat. Ulcers of the tonsils.

Stomach and Abdomen.—Pain in the stomach after a meal or on taking a slight cold, with sensitiveness to the touch; distended abdomen; glandular swellings in the groins, and grumbling and gurgling in the bowels.

Fæces.—Chronic costiveness and constipation, sometimes with tenesmus.

Larynx and Chest.—Cough, particularly at night, sometimes with bloody or purulent expectoration; shortness of breath from the slightest motion. Palpitation of the heart.

Back and Extremities.—Swelling of the glands. Rheumatic pains in the muscles, and aching redness and lacerating pains in the joints.

MERCURIUS.

Under this head we shall include the indications for the various forms of Mercury, as the symptoms indicating the use of this drug, will generally be relieved by either, *Mercurius Solubilis*, *Mercurius Corrosivus*, or *Mercurius Vivus*.—The former, however, is better indicated in sore throat, glandular swellings, and suppuration. The *Corrosivus* in dysenteric affections, and the *Vivus* in the general derangements, which seem to indicate the use of Mercury.

General Indications.—Swelling, inflammation and suppuration of the glands. Scrofulous, catarrhal, rheumatic or syphilitic ophthalmia. Rheumatic or arthritic pains in the joints and limbs, especially at night; aching in the bones. Rheumatic headache, toothache, and neuralgia; emaciation; profuse perspiration at night, especially in slow fevers.

Skin.—Glandular swellings with beating, stinging and suppuration; swelling and caries of the bones. Carious ulcers; spreading ulcers, either healthy or malignant; syphilitic ulcers. Itching eruption with burning; eruptions readily bleeding.

Fever.—Copious sweat, night and day.

Head.—Nightly headache. Catarrhal and rheumatic headache. Pain of the skull bone; swelling of the head, the scalp sensitive to the touch. Itching and humid eruption on the scalp.

Eyes.—Inflammation with itching and burning of the eyes; ophthalmia; swelling, redness and ulceration of the margin of the eyelid; scurfs around the eyes and ulcers in the cornea.

Ears.—Swelling of the parotid gland; soreness and excoriation in the ear, sometimes with discharge of pus.

Nose.—Swelling and ulceration of the nose; coryza, sneezing.

Face.—Yellow scurf on the face. Swelling of the face with toothache. Cracks of the lips and ulcers on the corners of the mouth.

Mouth and Throat.—Looseness of the teeth and swelling of the gums ; gums recede from the teeth and are sometimes ulcerated or bleeding ; violent toothache, particularly at night ; pain in decayed teeth with swelling in the face ; also swelling in the submaxillary glands, with stinging and throbbing. Salivation. Fetid smell from the mouth ; swelling of the mouth ; apthæ ; ulcers and sores in the mouth. Stinging pains in the throat, especially when swallowing ; sore throat with difficult swallowing ; elongation and swelling of the uvula. Inflammatory swelling and ulceration of the tonsils ; syphilitic ulcers in the throat, the soreness frequently extends to the ears and the glands of the throat and neck ; the pains are usually aggravated by empty deglutition, at night, in the cool air, or when speaking.

Stomach.—Empty eructations ; headache and nausea. Painfulness in the pit of the stomach, sometimes with burning or ulcerative pain, weight in the stomach, especially after a meal. Swelling, hardness and ulcerative pain in the region of the liver.

Abdomen.—Colic from cold with diarrhœa, passing off in a recumbent posture ; soreness and distension of the abdomen, syphilitic and scrofulous swellings of the inguinal glands, sometimes with suppuration.

Fæces.—Constant desire for stool with straining, tenesmus and a very slight discharge, which may be either of blood or bloody mucus, or present the appearance of the scrapings of the intestines. Bloody stools with painful acrid sensation at the anus. Stools preceded or accompanied with nausea, chilliness and anguish ; stools like chopped eggs. Green, slimy, putrid, acid, or bilious stools.

Larynx.—Catarrh with shivering cough, dread of the open air ; hoarseness and loss of voice. Violent racking or spasmodic cough, with violent pain in the head, shortness of breath on going up-stairs, when walking or after a meal. Pain in the side at every inspiration.

Back and Extremities.—Swelling of the glands, lacerating pain in the bones and joints, especially at night.

MOSCHUS.

Musk.

An invaluable remedy in the various forms of nervous affections; hysteric spasms, &c.

MURIATIC ACID.

This is a very valuable remedy in the last stage of typhoid or putrid fevers, where there is sliding down in the bed, black and swollen lips.

NATRUM MURIATICUM.

Effects produced by the loss of animal fluids, scrofulous paralytic, and hysteric affections; great liability to take cold. Intermittent fevers.

Fever.—Chilliness and want of animal heat. Intermittent fever with yellow or livid complexion; pain in the bones; headache, debility, and loss of appetite; fever, generally coming on towards morning. Intermittent fevers from abuse of Cinchona. Typhoid fevers with debility; dryness of the tongue and great thirst; profuse sweat.

Head.—Oppressive or stupefying headache, especially in the morning. Congestion of the head. Scurf and itching eruption on the head.

Eyes, Ears and Nose.—Inflammation of the eyes with excoriating pain and discharge of acrid tears. Dim-sightedness and incipient amaurosis, sensations of gauze-black points or flushes of light before the eyes. Coryza with sneezing and obstruction of the nose.

Face.—Aching in the bones of the face, lips dry, cracked, and smarting with ulcers in the corners of the mouth and in the throat. Swelling of the submaxillary glands. Toothache on drawing in air, after a meal or at night; sometimes with swelling of the cheeks and gums; ulcers on the gums, salivation; burning vesicles on the tongue.

Fæces.—Burning and painful varices in the anus. Constipation. Hæmorrhoidal tumors; watery diarrhœa.

Genital Organs.—Leucorrhœa sometimes acrid and corrosive.

Larynx and Chest.—Cough from tickling in the throat, particularly when walking or taking a deep breath; cough in the morning and after going to bed, with violent pain in the forehead; soreness of the chest, and wheezing breathing. Palpitation of the heart, irregular beats of the heart.

NITRIC-ACID.

This is an invaluable remedy in affections from the abuse of Mercury. Syphilitic and sycotic, and also in rheumatic difficulties. There are lacerating and drawing pain in the whole body, and in the bones, easily taking cold, emaciation; pains are usually worse towards evening.

Head.—Congestion of blood to the head; heaviness and dullness of the head; lacerating and shooting pain in the head; pain as if the head were surrounded by a tight bandage.

Eyes.—Inflammation of the eyes, from abuse of Mercury or from syphilis; swelling and ulceration of the lids; dimness or loss of sight.

Ears.—Glandular swellings behind the ears, and ulcerations in the ears; soreness and scurf in the nostrils; yellow fetid discharge from the nose, coryza and swelling of the nose, dry cough and headache.

Face.—Pain in the bones of the face. Neuralgic pain in the face; lips are chapped and ulcerated; pain and swelling of the submaxillary glands.

Mouth and Throat.—Pain in the teeth, in the evening or when chewing; sometimes with the sensation as if they were spongy or elongated; bleeding of the gums; salivation; sore throat, ulcers of the mouth and throat, especially from abuse of Mercury, with stinging pain, and sensation on swallowing, as if the throat were raw and ulcerated.

Fæces.—Constipation and difficult stool; bloody dysenteric stool with tenesmus, fever, and headache. Itching and burning of the anus.

Genital Organs.—Ulcers on the penis. Leucorrhœa, greenish, fetid or flesh colored.

Larynx and Chest.—Barking cough, especially in the evening; ulcerative phthisis, cough with purulent or bloody expectoration; palpitation of the heart, and want of breath after the slightest exercise.

Arms and Legs.—Copper colored eruption; swelling and inflammation of the axillary glands; pain in the bones.

NUX-VOMICA.

Bilious affections. Derangement of the stomach and bowels. Paralytic or spasmodic affection; affections from the abuse of ardent spirits, sedentary habits and various forms of dissipation, derangement during pregnancy, and complaints arising from chagrin or anger.

Sleep.—Great drowsiness after a meal and in the daytime; light sleep with starting and frequent waking; anxious and frightful dreams.

Head.—Muttering delirium; illusions of fancy and frightful visions; stupefaction and loss of consciousness, confusion and dizzy sensation as from intoxication. Apoplexy with soporous condition and paralysis of the limbs. Headache from taking wine or coffee, when coughing or stooping, aggravated by mental exertion. Headache from constipation and sedentary habits. Headache with nausea and vomiting. Hemicrania as if a nail were pressing in the brain. Congestion of blood to the head, with pain in the forehead and dizziness.

Nose.—Dry coryza of infants; stoppage of the nose, particularly of one side.

Mouth and Throat.—Constant toothache in the open air, aggravated by fatiguing the head, toothache brought on by cold water. Putrid and painful swelling and bleeding of the gums; fetid smell from the mouth; difficult speech; inflammatory swelling, aphthæ, and fetid ulcers in the mouth and fauces; swelling of the uvula; bitter taste in the mouth.

Stomach.—Frequent hiccough and belching of wind, sour or bitter eructations; nausea or vomiting early in the morning or after a meal. Vomiting during pregnancy. Pressure in the stomach as from a stone, the exterior painful to the touch; fullness in the stomach, especially after a meal. Cramplike pains in the stomach. Swelling and throbbing pain in the region of the liver.

Abdomen.—Colic during pregnancy. Colic during cold, as if diarrhœa would set in, from suppression of the hæmorrhoidal flux. Periodical colic. Hysteric spasm. Contractive colic with griping and clutching sensation. Flatulent colic.

Fæces.—Constipation sometimes with pain in the head, frequent urging to stool, with tenesmus and cutting pain in the bowels; small mucous stools with urging and tenesmus. Dysenteric or diarrhœic stools of a bloody, mucous or watery character, accompanied with pain in the bowels. Hæmorrhoids with burning and pricking in the rectum.

Urine.—Ineffectual desire to urinate with a partial or entire paralysis of the neck of the bladder.

Genital Organs.—Menses are accompanied with abdominal spasms and labor-like pain; congestion of blood to the uterus.

Larynx.—Constrictive spasms of the larynx. Cough on moving or after a meal, most violent in the morning, dry, fatiguing or spasmodic cough, with pain in the head, and sore pain in the throat as from excoriation.

Chest.—Asthma. Anxious oppression of the chest, and suffocative fits after midnight; spasms of the chest; congestion of blood to the chest. Rheumatism of the muscles of the chest.

Back and Extremities.—Bruised pain in the back and loins; increased by motion, contact or pressure; numbness and paralytic sensation in the limbs and side. Rheumatic and arthritic drawing and shooting pains and stiffness.

OPIUM.

Generally useful only in recent cases; insensibility of the nervous system and want of reaction against medicines; derangements of drunkards; ailments of old people; bad effects from fright, fear, or sudden joy; convulsions and spasmodic motions; apoplexy; congestion to the head; great torpor of the intestinal canal, and inaction of the whole system; delirium tremens.

Sleep.—Snoring sleep; lethargy; great drowsiness, sometimes with inability to sleep.

Fever.—Pulse generally slow, although sometimes quick and violent, with headache and flushed face; heavy sleep with snoring.

Mental Symptoms.—Great anguish; stupefaction and sometimes complete loss of consciousness; visions; frightful fancies; furious delirium; delirium tremens.

Head.—Painful headache, increased by moving the eyes; heaviness and congestion of blood to the head.

Fæces.—Constipation from torpor of the intestinal canal, especially after chronic diarrhœa, abuse of cathartics, and also from want of exercise. Involuntary stools.

Chest.—Snoring breathing; oppressed and difficult respiration.

PETROLEUM.

Stone-oil, Naphta.

Scrofulous affections; gastric difficulties; sea-sickness; affections of the skin, &c.

Skin.—Painful sensitiveness of the skin; unhealthy skin, slight wounds, readily suppurating; chapped lips; chapped hands and excoriations.

Head.—Heaviness, throbbing, or ulcerative pain in the head; scurf and pimples on the scalp, with itching.

Gastric Symptoms.—Sea-sickness, also nausea, produced by riding in a carriage; waterbrash.

Chest.—Hoarseness; dry cough with stinging under the sternum; stitches in the chest.

PHOSPHORUS.

Tuberculous affections; catarrhal difficulties; weakness from loss of animal fluids; want of vital reaction; chronic diarrhœa; affections of the throat and chest.

Skin.—Small boils; round herpetic spots over the body; lymphatic abscesses with hectic fever.

Sleep.—Restless, unrefreshing sleep with frightful dreams; stupefying slumber in the morning.

Fever.—Hectic fever with dry heat, especially towards evening; night sweats; fever, commencing or attended with chilliness.

Head.—Various kinds of dizziness; sometimes accompanied with nausea, or violent headache; chronic dizziness. Dull, stupefying headache; sometimes accompanied with numbness. Bruised pain in the brain. Congestion of blood to the head.

Eyes.—Inflammation and redness of the eyes; swelling of the eyelids with agglutination in the morning. Scrofulous or arthritic ophthalmia; blackness or black spots before the eyes. Amaurosis.

Mouth and Throat.—Toothache with swelling of the face, also from the least cold; sore pain in the teeth on pressing them together. Inflammation and ulcers on the gums.

Stomach.—Violent eructations, or vomiting of bitter or sour substances; sour regurgitation of food; cramps and griping pain, and contraction in the region of the stomach; the stomach painful to the touch; burning and inflammation in the stomach.

Abdomen.—Spasmodic or cutting colic; sore pain in the whole abdomen; flatulent colic.

Fæces.—Paralysis of the intestinal canal; chronic diarrhœa; typhoid diarrhœa.

Larynx and Chest.—Violent catarrh; with hoarseness; hoarseness, sometimes with loss of voice; cough with rawness, hoarseness, sore and excoriating pain in the chest; cough with purulent or bloody expectoration. Difficulty of breathing; tension and tightness of the chest; rush of blood to the chest; palpitation of the heart. Phosphorus is an invaluable remedy in chest difficulties, especially where there is soreness in the chest, long continued cough and danger of of tubercular development.

Back and Extremities.—Stiffness in the nape of the neck, and paralytic weakness in the small of the back and extremities with tremor; drawing pain and arthritic stiffness of the joints; swelling of the feet.

PHOSPHORIC-ACID.

Debility from loss of animal fluids; bad effects of onanism; difficulties arising from rapid growth, grief, chagrin or care; great prostration, and nervous weakness; chronic diarrhœa.

Skin.—Itching and ulcerative pimples over the body.

Fever.—Attended with great prostration, profuse sweat, &c.

Genital Organs.—Frequent nocturnal emissions; voluptuous dreams; yellowish leucorrhœa with itching. Painful constriction of the bladder, and sometimes a free discharge of a milky or fetid urine, depositing a white sediment.

Larynx and Chest.—Violent hoarseness; constant cough, sometimes with pain in the abdomen, headache, or vomiting; breathing heavy and oppressed; shortness of breath; palpitation of the heart.

PLATINA.

Neuralgia; affections of females, particularly in nervous and hysteric individuals; spasmodic affections; derangement of the menstrual functions; affections caused by anger or chagrin. The symptoms are generally relieved by motion.

Head.—Derangement after fright or chagrin; cramp like pressing in the temples; roaring in the head.

Teeth.—Creeping and numbness in the face; lock-jaw; throbbing digging in the teeth.

Fæces.—Obstinate constipation, especially when travelling, or produced by lead poisoning.

Genital Organs.—Painful pressing towards the genital organs; profuse menstruation, attended with cutting or cramp-like pain, headache, and anguish; metrorrhagia of thick deep colored blood; leucorrhœa like the white of an egg.

Back and Extremities.—Aching pain in the small of the back; weakness and numbness in the extremities.

PULSATILLA.

Pasque-flower.

Especially adapted to female derangements, or to persons of gentle disposition, who easily laugh or weep, with disposition to catarrh or leucorrhœa, and of lympathic constitutions, chronic difficulties arising from abuse of sulphur water, quinine, chamomile, mercury; also in derangements of the stomach, produced by the use of greasy food, such as fat pork, fat pastry, &c. Bad effects from fright or shame. Rheumatic or arthritic affections; nervous difficulties, &c.

Skin.—Measles and their secondary ailments; itching eruptions and ulcers; chilblains with swelling and heat.

Sleep.—Restless sleep, full of anxious and frightful dreams.

Fever.—Intermittent fever, thirst only during the hot stage. Acute fevers.

Head.—Dizziness as if intoxicated, especially in the eveing, after dinner, or when sitting. Heaviness of the head on stooping. Headache on moving the eyes; hemicrania, sometimes with vomiting; aching pain on stooping; lacerating or beating headache; headache as from overloading the stomach, or from intoxication.

Eyes.—Pressure in the eyes as from sand with inflammation and corrosive tears; swelling of the lids; stye; dimness of sight.

Ears.—Inflammation of the ear; starting and stinging pain in the ear; swelling in and below the ear. Noise in the ear as of water or a cracking sound.

Mouth.—Rheumatic toothache; toothache during pregnancy, from a cold, accompanied with pain in the ear; drawing, gnawing toothache, coming on when eating or taking any thing warm into the mouth.

Stomach.—Nausea with disposition to vomit; vomiting; sour or bitter eructations; waterbrush; vomiting after a meal; pain in the stomach during an inspiration and on pressure; lacerating and cutting pain; nausea after eating fat food.

Abdomen.—Abdominal spasms, particularly in pregnant females; colic aggravated by motion; flatulent colic and painful sensitiveness of the bowels.

Fæces.—Constipation; watery diarrhœa, or consisting of a mucous, green, or slimy substance, generally preceded by rumbling and cutting pain; dysenteric diarrhœa, and diarrhœa after measles; blind and bleeding hæmorrhoids.

Genital Organs.—Incontinence of urine; drawing or tensive pain from the abdomen through the spermatic cord into the testicles. Uterine spasms, resembling labor pains; derangement and irregularity of the menses, attended with severe pain, colic, nausea, vomiting and headache. Metrorrhagia; discharge of thick, dark clotty menstrual blood, or else pale and watery; thin, acrid, or thick milky leuchorrhœa.

Larynx.—Catarrhal huskiness of the chest; dry night cough, relieved on sitting up, but aggravated on lying down; cough with bitter, yellow or bloody expectoration, attended with pain in the chest, and sometimes vomiting.

Chest.—Difficulty of breathing, especially at night in bed, and in cold air; congestion of blood to the chest; constrictive sensation and sticking pain in the chest, especially at night.

Back and Extremities.—Swelling and rheumatic pains in the nape of the neck, also in the back and extremities; drawing and jerking pain, or trembling in the limbs; swelling of the knee with pain.

RHEUM,

Rhubarb.

Particularly in diarrhœas in children; the stools are sour smelling, and are generally preceded and accompanied by cutting pain; frequent urging to stool, increased on moving about.

RHUS TOXICODENDRON.

Poison Oak.

This is an invaluable remedy in rheumatic and arthritic affections, vesicular erysipelas, excitability and derangement of the nervous system; bruised sensation or bad consequences from a sprain or bruise; semilateral complaints and partial or entire paralysis, or stiffness of portions of the body. The pain is worse at night in bed and also in cold or damp weather.

Skin.—Itching of the body; erysipelatous inflammation with small vesicles, sometimes burning; burning itching eruption; glandular swellings; red shining swellings.

Sleep.—Sleeplessness, or great restlessness at night, with tossing about, and sometimes delirium; frightful dreams.

Fever.—Low fevers with delirium; bruised or aching pain throughout the body, sometimes with rash, dizziness of the head and inclination to vomit.

Head.—Dizziness or aching pain in the head on rising or after a meal; heaviness of the head; reeling or wavering sensation in the brain at every step; itching eruption on the scalp, soon forming a scab.

Eyes.—Sore pain in the eyes; swelling of the lids; rheumatic ophthalmia.

Ears.—Swelling and inflammation of the parotid, especially after fever.

Face.—Erysipelatous inflammation of the face, attended with aching, stinging or burning pain; vesicular erysipelas; chronic eruptions, sometimes suppurating and forming scabs; swelling of the face.

Larynx and Chest.—Short, anxious and painful cough, excited by tickling, and sometimes expectoration of bright red blood; oppression of the chest and sticking pain when sneezing or drawing a long breath.

Back.—Aching or bruised sensation in the small of the

back, stiff and painful during motion; creeping coldness in the back; rheumatic stiffness in the neck and shoulders, sometimes with a sprained sensation.

Extremities.—Erysipelatous swelling; bruised, aching, boring, lacerating rheumatic pain; stiffness and partial paralysis of the limbs; warts.

SABINA.

Rheumatic or neuralgic pains, especially in females; partial suppression of urine with difficulty in passing water. Profuse menstruation; hæmorrhage from the uterus at the time of the menses, also after parturition or miscarriage.

SAMBUCUS.

Elder.

Violent dyspnœa; suffocative paroxysms of asthma; cough, especially at night, with rattling of mucus; suffocative paroxysms of cough; dry heat over the body, with dread of uncovering.

SANGUINARIA.

Blood Root.

Rheumatic pains; swelling of the extremities. Pain in the head in spots, sometimes with nausea and vomiting. Chronic dryness in the throat and sometimes loss of voice; violent tormenting cough with pain in the chest. Asthma. Pneumonia; burning, pressing or sticking pain in the chest with cough.

SECALE.

Ergot.

Long continued stupor; lethargic sleep; restless night sleep with dreams. Constant retching and vomiting and pressure in the stomach. Diarrhœa, sometimes involuntary, with great prostration; diarrhœa after cholera. Cholera-like paroxysms; the eye-balls are sunken and surrounded by a blue margin; there is nausea and vomiting, profuse evacuations from the bowels, cramps in the calves, hollow voice, great prostration and almost imperceptible pulse. Congestion of blood to the uterus ; metrorrhagia.

This remedy is most useful in a certain stage of cholera, the diarrhœa of the old, and metrorrhagia of delicate women.

SEPIA.

Cuttle Fish.

Particularly useful in female affections. The pains are relieved by the application of warmth, and usually disappear during violent exercise.

Skin.—Glandular and lympathic swellings ; dry and itch-like eruption; itching of the whole body, ringworm ; scurfy and humid eruption.

Head.—Intense headache in the morning, sometimes with nausea ; rush of blood to the head, beating headache in the evening and at every motion ; headache as if the eyes would fall out or the head burst. Itching and eruption on the scalp.

Eyes, Ears and Nose.—Inflammation of the eyes and lids with pain in the head. Eruption and discharge of pus from the ear; roaring and whizzing in the ear. Ulcerated, scabby and swollen nostril ; obstruction of the nose ; bleeding at the nose. Eruption and yellow spots on the face.

Teeth.—Toothache of pregnant females ; painful swelling of the gums.

Stomach.—Nausea and vomiting during pregnancy ; cramp in the stomach and abdomen, and pressive pain after a meal. Aching in the region of the liver.

Abdomen.—Weight and distension of the abdomen and frequent attacks of colic, especially in the morning and after exercise ; sometimes with nausea.

Fæces.—Constipation. Exhausting diarrhœa ; hæmorrhoids ; pain in the rectum.

Urine.—Turbid and fetid urine, with white or brick dust sediment.

Genital Organs.—Itching and soreness of the parts ; prolapsus uteri and bearing-down pain. Acrid leucorrhœa, with itching and excoriation. Affections during pregnancy; toothache, nausea, vomiting, &c.

Larynx.—Hoarseness and dry cough, sometimes with saltish, purulent or bloody expectoration.

Chest.—Difficulty of breathing and pressure in the chest; seething of blood and congestion to the chest; rawness in the chest, pain from motion, or on breathing or coughing; palpitation of the heart.

Back.—Pain or weariness in the small of the back; stiffness of the neck; eruption on the neck and back.

Extremities.—Paralytic sensation in the arms; bruised pain in the limbs. Itching and scurfy eruptions, sometimes ulcerating.

SILICEA.

Chronic affections from abuse of Mercury; rachitis; scrofulous affections; affections of the bones, eruptive diseases, &c.

Skin.—Itching sensation over the whole body. Carbuncles, boils; swelling and suppuration of the glands; dry eruption or having an ulcerative tendency.

Eyes.—Inflammation of the eyes and redness and ulceration of the lids; ulcers on the cornea; paroxysms of blindness; specks or dark spots before the eyes, cataract and amaurosis.

Ears.—Beating in the ears; scurf behind the ears; swelling of the parotid gland, with pain.

Nose.—Ulcers or scabs in the nose; frequent sneezing; chronic obstruction, coryza and catarrh.

Face.—Chapped skin; ulcers and eruptions on the lip; cancer.

Mouth and Throat.—Caries and swelling of the jaw; sore gums and ulceration at the root of the teeth; toothache, especially when eating warm food, or when cold air gets into the mouth. Sore throat with stinging pain, when swallowing.

Stomach.—Nausea and vomiting, after heating exercise, taking a drink, and from various other causes; sour eructations; acidity of the stomach. Painfulness of the pit of the stomach to pressure and sensation of a load there.

Abdomen.—Colic with constipation; inflammation of the inguinal glands; constipation.

Genital Organs.—Milky leucorrhæa; inflammation and suppuration of the nipples.

Larynx and Chest.—Suffocative night cough; dry fatiguing cough; continued cough with bloody or purulent expectoration; shortness of breath.

Back and Extremities.—Curvature of the spine; stiff back; glandular swellings and suppuration; ulcers; softening and caries of the bones.

SPIGELIA.

Pink Root.

Neuralgic affection; diseases of the heart; affections caused by worms.

Head.—Periodical headache; pain in the head when shaking it; sensation as if the brain were loose, when walking; pain worse in the open air.

Eyes, Ears and Nose.—Aching and pressive pain in the eyes, as if the eye-balls were too large; inflammation and redness of the eyes. Arthritic and rheumatic ophthalmia; great sensitiveness to light. Pain and stoppage of the ears; periodical deafness; itching and stoppage of the nose; eruption around the nose.

Face.—Pale, disfigured face; typical nervous prosopalgia. Prosopalgia on one side of the face, with anguish about the heart; violent pains in the face, not allowing the least contact or motion with shining swelling.

Teeth.—Toothache with prosopalgia; darting pain through all the teeth, aggravated by cold water or air.

Stomach.—Great sensitiveness of the pit of thc stomach; loss of appetite or canine hunger.

Stool.—Pinching stitching in the bowels; discharge of worms; crawling and itching in the anus.

Chest.—Shortness of breath, particularly in talking or from exercise. Sudden suffocative attacks with palpitation of the heart. Constriction of the chest with anguish; strong and violent beating of the heart, so that it is perceptible to sight and hearing, attended with anguish and oppression of the chest, and increased on sitting down or bending forward.

SPONGIA.

Sponge.

Larynx.—Hoarseness, cough and coryza; hollow cough with expectoration; difficult respiration, as if the throat were closed with a plug, with pain in the throat and chest on coughing; barking, dry or whistling cough, worse towards evening.

Chest.—Asthma; breathing hurried and panting, or slow and deep; stitching pain in the muscles of the chest and back.

STRAMONIUM.

Thorn-apple.

Spasms, convulsions, twitching of the muscles and great derangement of the nervous system. The convulsions and delirium are particularly excited by contact.

Sleep.—Deep sleep with snoring breathing; restless sleep, interrupted by screams and moaning.

Moral Symptoms.—Melancholy, or convulsions of rage and ungovernable fury. Talkative delirium or frightful fancies.

Head.—Stupidity, stupefaction or dullness of the head; headache with obscuration of sight and hardness of hearing; convulsions of the head and arms.

Eyes.—Dilation of the pupil; sparkling, glistening or staring eyes; illusions of sight.

Mouth.—Constant muttering; paralysis of the organs of speech; spasmodic hiccough.

SULPHUR.

Skin.—Sulphur is an important remedy in the various forms of skin difficulties. Nettle rash with fever; burning and itching eruption; dry and scaly eruptions; scabies; herpetic eruptions; swelling and suppuration of glands; ulcers, chilblains, affections of the bones, &c.

Head.—Nightly headache; rush of blood to the head.

Eyes.—Weakness of sight; purulent discharge from the eyes; inflammation of the eyes with burning or bruised pain; inflammation, swelling and ulceration of the lids.

Ears.—Drawing and lacerating in the ears. Itching and eruption of the ears. Whizzing, humming and roaring in the head.

Nose.—Inflammation and swelling of the nose; ulcers in the nose; violent coryza; obstruction of the nose.

Face.—Swelling and redness of the face; chapped lips; glandular swelling. Eruptions on the face.

Teeth.—Toothache from cold air, also aggravated by warmth; sensation of looseness and elongation of the teeth; swelling of the gums with throbbing pain. Aphtha in the mouth; mercurial affections of the mouth.

Stomach.—Sour eructations and vomiting; pressure in the stomach; cramp like pain in the stomach.

Abdomen.—Painful sensitiveness of the abdomen, as if the parts were raw; colic after eating or drinking; spasmodic contractive colic, relieved sitting bent.

Fæces.—Constipation, sometimes with piles; hard, knotty, insufficient stools.

Genital Organs.—Itching and excoriation of the parts; burning and painful leucorrhœa; violent and long continued leucorrhœa.

Larynx.—Rough throat and loss of voice; chronic hooping cough; headache or vomiting when coughing; loose or dry cough with soreness in the chest. Chronic cough.

Chest.—Rattling in the chest; nightly suffocative fit; stitches or contractive pain in the chest; palpitation of the heart; rush of blood to the chest.

Back and Extremities.—Curvature of the spine; pain in the small of the back when rising. Drawing and lacerating pain in the limbs; heaviness and weakness of the limbs; trembling of the hands; rheumatic pain in the limbs.

STIBIUM.

Tartar Emetic.

This is an important remedy in the first stage of influenza; dry cough, and affections of the chest, also in bilious affections; small-pox. Asphyxia of new-born infants.

Skin.—Itching suppurative rash. Pustular eruptions on the whole body. Malignant pustules. The pustular stage of varioloid and small-pox; gangrenous ulcers.

Fever.—Chilliness with flushes of heat; great restlessness, heat, thirst and headache, especially over the eyes. Profuse sweat.

Head.—Dizziness. Violent headache; fullness, dullness and stupefaction of the head; stupefying headache with pressure over the eyes.

Stomach.—Nausea, vomiting and diarrhœa; nausea and dispostion to vomit. Putrid eructations; ineffectual retching and violent spasmodic vomiting; violent oppression of the stomach.

Abdomen.—Lacerating, violent cutting and pinching in the abdomen.

Larynx.—Rattling of mucus; cough and sneezing; dry, hard, whistling and barking cough; suffocative, spasmodic cough.

Chest.—Difficulty of breathing, especially at night. Palpitation of the heart and oppression of the chest.

THUJA.

Tree of Life.

Rheumatic and arthritic affections; syphilitic and sycotic affections; warty excrescences. Ulcers in the throat. Aching pain in the bones and in the head. Rheumatic pains. Ulcers produced by syphilis.

VERATRUM ALBUM.
White Hellebore.

Cholera; cramps in the limbs and bowels; great weakness and convulsions; paralytic pain in the limbs.

Skin.—Cutaneous eruptions resembling itch, dry with nightly itching.

Fever.—Coldness of the whole body; cold sweat; collapsed or almost imperceptible pulse.

Head.—Headache with nausea, vomiting and paleness of the face; intermittent, beating headache; headache when stooping or walking.

Face.—Cold, disfigured face, with pointed nose and sunken checks; pale or red face; black and parched lips.

Teeth.—Toothache and headache; toothache with nausea, vomiting and coldness of the limbs.

Gastric Symptoms.—Nausea and vomiting with great thirst; violent excessive vomiting, renewed by the least motion, or by swallowing the least liquid; black vomit. Asiatic cholera.

Abdomen and Stomach.—Burning sensation in the stomach; anguish, violent pressure and cramp-like pain in the stomach. Painful sensitiveness of the abdomen to pressure; cramps and violent cutting pain in the bowels, as if cut with knives.

Fæces.—Chronic constipation. Greenish, watery, flocculent diarrhœa; brownish or blackish diarrhœa; nocturnal diarrhœa; great weakness after stool.

Larynx and Chest.—Violent suffocating or dry and hacking cough with vomiting; cough resembling hooping cough, with vomiting; hoarse, dry cough at night. Palpitation of the of the heart; difficult breathing.

Extremities.—Paralytic and bruised pain in the extremities; coldness of the arms and legs, and violent cramps in the calves.

EUPATORIUM.

Bone-Set.

This is an important remedy in those forms of intermittent fever, when there is but little or no sweat, during any period of the disease.

Fever.—Pain in the bones and head, with soreness of the flesh; weakness and prostration; chilliness with trembling and nausea; absence of sweat.

Head.—Throbbing headache, sometimes with sick stomach in the morning on waking; soreness on the top and back part of the head.

Stomach and Abdomen.—Want of appetite; bilious vomiting with trembling and prostration.

Larynx and Chest.—Nocturnal loose cough, or cough with flushed face and tearful eyes; cough following and preceding measles, and also from suppressed intermittent fever.

APIS MEL.

Poison of the Honey Bee.

This remedy has been found highly efficacious in dropsical affections, nettle rash and erysipelas. When the skin is affected, there ts a burning heat of the skin and stinging sensation like the sting of bees.

Ii is also useful in derangements of the urinary organs, when the urine is scanty and its emission attended with scalding burning sensation.

It has been given with decided benefit in abdominal dropsy.

GLOSSARY OF MEDICAL TERMS.

Abortus. Miscarriage; abortion.

Abrasion. Excoriation.

Abscess. A collection of pus seated in any particular organ or tissue.

Absorbents. In anatomy this term is applied to small, delicate, transparent vessels which take up and convey any substances from the surface of the body, or from any cavity, into the blood.

Acetum. Vinegar.

Adhesion. In surgery, the reunion of parts that have been divided, by means of a special kind of inflammation denominated the *adhesive*.

Adhesive Inflammation. The process by which wounds are united. It is often synonymous with *union by the first intention*.

Adypsia. The absence of natural thirst.

Agglutination. Adhesion.

Alkali. A substance which unites with acids in the definite proportions, so as to neutralize their properties more or less perfectly, and to form salts. It changes vegetable blues to green.

Alkaloids. Substances having some of the properties of *alkalis*.

Allopathy. A term used by homœopathic writers to designate the old practice of medicine in contradistinction to their own, now generally employed by both parties; literally implies curing one disease by another, or a medicine which produces a dissimilar one.

Amenorrhœa. Absence or stoppage of the menstrual flux.

Anasarca. Dropsy of the cellular tissue, or membrane, immediately under the skin.

Anchylosis. Stiffening of a joint, either from deposit of ossific or bone-forming matter, or contraction of the muscles or ligaments; adhesion of the articulating surfaces.

Angina. Sore throat. The term is also applied to diseases with difficult respiration.

Angina Membranacea. Croup.

Angina Parotidea. Mumps.

Angina Pharyngia. Inflammation of the membrane which forms the pharynx.

Anorexia. Want of appetite.

Anthrax. Carbuncle.

Anus. The inferior opening of the rectum.

Aphonia. Loss of voice.

Apoplexia. Apoplexy; a loss of voluntary motion and consciousness. See *Diagnosis* under this head.

Apyrexia. The intervals between febrile paroxysms.

Arthritis. Gout.

Ascaris, pl. Ascarides. Thread-worms.

Ascites. General dropsy.

Asphyxia. Apparent death.

Asthenic. Low; applied to disease; literally want of strength.

Astringents. Medicaments used in the old practice to contract the animal fibre.

Atony. A want of tone or energy in the muscular power.

Atrophy. A morbid state of the digestive system, in which the food taken into the stomach fails to afford sufficient nourishment. A wasting of the whole, or of individual parts of the body.

Auscultation. The detection of symptoms by the ear in disease.

Biliary. Connected with the secretion of bile.

Blepharitis. Inflammation of the eyelids.

Borborygmus. Rumbling in the intestines, caused by flatus or wind.

Bronchia; Bronchi. The tubes into which the trachea or windpipe divides.

Bronchitis. Inflammation of the ramifications of the windpipe.

Bulimy; Bulimia. Canine, or excessive hunger.

Cadaverous. Resembling a corpse.

Cæcum. The blind gut; so called from its being perforated at one end only.

Canthus. The angle of the eye.

Carcinoma. Cancer, adj. *Carcinomatous.*

Cardialgia. Spasm of the stomach.

Carditis. Inflammation of the heart.

Caries. Ulceration of the bones.

Carphologia. Picking at the bed-clothes.

Cartilage. Gristle.

Catamenia. The menstrual flux.

Catarrh. Cold; used also to express inflammation of the mucous membrane.

Catarrhal Ophthalmia. Simple inflammation of the conjunctiva.

Cathartic. Purgative.

Cellular Tissue. The fine net-like membrane enveloping or connecting most of the structures of the human body.

Cephalalgia. Headache.

Cephalic. Pertaining to the head.

Cerebral. Appertaining to the brain.

Cervical. Belonging to the neck.

Cessatio Mensium. Discontinuance of the menstrual flux.

Chlorosis. Green sickness.

Chronic. Long continued, in contradistinction to acute.

Cicatrix, plur. *Cicatrices.* A scar, left after the healing of a wound, &c.

Clavi Pedis. Corns.

Clonic Spasm. A spasm which is not of long duration. It is opposed to *tonic* spasm, which see.

Coagula. Clots of blood.

Coagulable Lymph. The term given to the fluid which is slowly effused into wounds, and afterwards forms the uniting medium or cicatrice.

Colic. Griping in the intestines.

Collapse. Failing of vitality.

Colliquative. Excessive discharge of any secretion.

Coma. Drowsiness.

Coma Somnolentium. Drowsiness, with relapse on being roused.

Comatose. Drowsy.

Compress. Soft lint, linen, &c. folded together so as to form a pad, for the purpose of being placed, and secured by means of a bandage, on parts which require pressure.

Congestio ad Caput. Determination of blood to the head.

Congestio ad Pectus. Determination of blood to the chest.

Congestion. Overfullness of the blood-vessels of some particular organ.

Conglobate Glands. Glands of a globular form, composed of a texture of lymphatic vessels. They have no excretory duct.

Conjunctiva. The membrane lining the eyelids, and extending over the forepart of the eyeballs.

Contagion. Propagation of a disease by contact.

Cornea. The anterior transparent portion of the eye. It is of a horny consistence.

Coryza. Cold in the head.

Coxagra. Inflammation of the hipjoint. Literally, seizure or pain in the.

Coxalgia. Literally pain in the hip; inflammation of the hip-joint.

Cranium. The skull.

Crepitation. Grating sensation, or noise, such as is caused by pressing the finger upon a part affected with emphysema; by the ends of fractured bone when moved; or by certain salts during calcination.

Crepitant Rhonchus, or Rale. The fine crackling noise heard in consequence of the passage of air through a viscid fluid. It is heard in the first stage of inflammation of the lungs.

Crepitus. Crackling or grating.

Cutaneous. Appertaining to the skin.

Cuticle. The outer or scarf skin.

Cystitis. Inflammation of the bladder.

Deglutition. The act of swallowing.

Delirium. Derangement of the brain, raving.

Depletion. Abstraction of the fluids; generally applied to venesection.

Desiccation. A drying up.

Desquamation. Falling off of the epidermis in form of scales.

Diagnosis. Distinction of maladies.

Diarrhœa. Looseness of the bowels.

Diarrhœa Neonatorum. The same as the above, in infants.

Diathesis. Constitutional tendency.

Dietetic. Relating to diet.

Diplopia. Affection of the eyes, in which objects appear double or increased in number.

Diuretic. Medicines which increase the secretion of urine.

Dorsal. Appertaining to the back.

Drastic. Powerful purgatives.

Duodenum. The first intestine after the stomach, so called from its length; the twelve-inch gut.

Dyscrasia. A morbid condition of the system; adj. *Dyscrastic.*

Dysecoia. Deafness.

Dysmenorrhœa. Painful menstruation.

Dyspepsia. Indigestion; literally difficulty of appetite.

Dyspnœa. Difficulty of respiration. Shortness of breath.

Dysuria. Difficulty in passing urine.

Effusion. A pouring out or escape of lymph or other secretion.

Emaciation. A falling off in the flesh.
Emetic. Provoking vomiting.
Encephalitis. Inflammation of the brain and membranes.
Endemic. Peculiar to a particular locality.
Enema. A clyster.
Engorgement. Swelling up of.
Enteralgia. Colic.
Enteritis. Inflammation of the intestines.
Ephemeral. Of a day's duration.
Epidemic. Diseases arising from general causes.
Epigastrium. The region of the stomach.
Epilepsy. Epilepsia. Falling sickness.
Epistaxis. Bleeding from the nose.
Epithelium. The cuticle.
Erysipelas. St. Anthony's fire. Rose. A disease of the skin.
Erysipelas Phlegmonodes. Phlegmonous erysipelas.
Erysipelas Œdematodes. Œdematous erysipelas.
Erysipelas Erraticum. Wandering erysipelas.
Erysipelas Gangrenosum. Gangrenous erysipelas.
Erysipelas Neonatorum. Induration of the cellular tissue in infants.
Exacerbation. Aggravation of fever, &c.
Exanthema, plur. *Exanthemata.* Eruption terminating in exfoliation.
Expectoration. Discharge of any matter; phlegm; pus from the chest.
Exudation. Discharge of fluid from the skin, &c.

Fæces. Alvine excrement.
Fascia. In anatomy, the tendinous expansion of muscles which bind parts together are called *fasciæ.*
Fauces. The throat.
Febris, plur. Febres. Fever.
Febris Nervosa. Nervous fever, or typhus.
Femur. The bone of the thigh.
Fetor. Stench.
Fistula. An obstinate tube-like sore, with a narrow orifice; adj. *Fistulous.*
Fistula Lachrymalis. An ulcerated opening in the lachrymal sac.
Flatus. Wind in the intestines. Flatulency.
Fœtus. The infant in the womb.
Fomentation. The application of flannel wet with warm water.
Functional Diseases. Those in which there is supposed to be only derangement of action.
Furunculus. A boil.
Furunculus Malignans. Carbuncle.

Gangrene. Incipient mortification; adj. *Gangrenous.*
Gastralgia. Pain in the stomach.
Gastric. Belonging to the stomach.
Gastritis. Inflammation of the stomach.
Gastrodynia. Vide *Cardialgia.*
Gestation. Pregnancy.
Gland. A small body met with in many parts of the body, and consisting of various tissues, blood-vessels, nerves, &c.
Glossitis. Inflammation of the tongue.
Glottis. Opening of the windpipe. The superior opening of the larynx.
Granulation. See *Incarnation.*

HÆMATEMESIS. Vomiting of blood.

HÆMOPTYSIS. Discharge of blood from the lungs. Spitting of blood.

HÆMORRHAGE. Discharge of blood.

HÆMORRHOIDS. Piles.

HECTIC FEVER. Habitual or protracted fever.

HELMINTHIASIS. Worm disease.

HEMIPHLEGIA. Paralysis of one side of the body longitudinally.

HEPATITIS. Inflammation of the liver.

HEPATIZATION. Structural derangement of the lungs, the result of inflammation; changing them into a substance resembling the liver, hence its name.

HERNIA. Rupture.

HERNIA CONGENITA. Congenital hernia. Literally, hernia from birth.

HERPES. A species of eruption.

HERPES CIRCINNATUS. Ringworm.

HORDEOLUM. Stye.

HYDROCEPHALUS. Water in the head.

HYDROPHOBIA SYMPTOMATICA— Symptoms resembling those arising from hydrophobic virus, appearing during the course of other diseases.

HYPERTROPHY, A morbid increase of any organ, arising from excessive nutrition.

HYPOCRATIC. Sunken and corpse-like.

HYPOCHONDRIUM. Region of the abdomen, contained under the cartilage of the false ribs.

HYPOCHONDRIASIS. Spleen disease; great depression of spirits, with general functional derangement; adj. *Hypochondriacal.*

HYPOGASTRIUM. The lower anterior portion of the abdomen.

HYSTERIA. Nervous affection; almost peculiar to females.

ICHOR. A thin watery discharge secreted from wounds, ulcers, &c.; adj. *Ichorous.*

ICTERUS. Jaundice.

ICTERUS NEONATERUM. Jaundice of infants.

IDIOPATHIC. Original, or primary disease.

IDIOSYNCRASY. Individual pecularity.

ILIUM. The haunch-bone. It, together with the pubis, sacrum, and ischium, contributes to form the pelvis.

ILEUS MISERERE. A form of colic, a twisting pain in the region of the navel.

INCARCERATED. Strangulated or constricted; a term applied to rupture.

INCARNATION. The process by which abscesses or ulcers are healed; this takes place by means of little grain like fleshy bodies, denominated granulations, which form on the surface of ulcers or suppurating wounds, &c., and serve the double purpose of filling up the cavities and bringing closely together and uniting their sides.

INCUBUS. The nightmare.

INFECTION. Propagation of disease by effluvia.

INFILTRATION. Diffusion of fluids into the cellular tissue.

INGESTA. Food; aliment.

INSPISSATED. Thickened.

INTEGUMENTS. The coverings of any part of the body. The skin with the adherent fat and cellular membrane form the common integuments.

ISCHIAS. Pain in the hip.

ISCHIUM. Hip-bone.

ISCHURIA. Suppression of urine.

LACHRYMATION. Tear shedding.

LACTATION. Suckling; also the process of the secretion of milk.

LARYNGEAL. Belonging to the larynx.

LARYNGISMUS STRIDULUS. Asthma of Millar.

LARYNGITIS. Inflammation of the larynx.

LARYNX. Upper part of the windpipe.

LESIONS. Injuries inflicted by violence, &c.

LESION, ORGANIC. Structural derangement, or injury.

LEUCO-PHLEGMATIC. Torpid or sluggish; mostly applied to a temperament characterized by want of tension of fibre; with light hair, and general inertness of the physical and mental powers.

LEUCORRHŒA. Female sexual weakness; vulg. *Whites*.

LOCHIA. Discharge from the womb after delivery.

LUMBAGO. Rheumatism in the loins.

LUMBAR. Appertaining to the loins.

LUMBRICUS, plur. *Lumbrici*. The round or long worm.

LUXATION. Dislocation.

LYMPH. A colourless liquid, circulating in the lymphatics.

LYMPHATIC. As applied to temperament; same as Leuco-phlegmatic.

LYMPHATICS. Absorbent vessels with glands and valves distributed over the body.

LYMPHATIC GLANDS. See CONGLOBATE GLANDS.

MAMMA. The breast in the female; adj. *Mammillary*.

MANIA. Insanity; madness.

MARASMUS. A wasting away of the body.

MECONIUM. The excrementitious matter discharged from the intestines of a newly-born infant.

MEGRIM. A pain affecting only one side of the head.

MEIBOMIAN GLANDS. Small glands within the inner membrane of the eyelids.

MENORRHAGIA. Excessive discharge of blood from the uterus.

MENSTRUAL FLUX. The monthly period.

MENINGITIS SPINALIS. Inflammation of the spinal membranes.

METASTASIS. The passing of a disease from one part to another.

METRORRHAGIA. Discharge of blood from the womb.

MIASM, or *Miasma* (*Marsh*). Peculiar effluvia or emanations from swampy grounds.

MICTURITION. Urination.

MILIARIA. Eruptions of minute transparent vesicles of the size of millet seeds; miliary eruption.

MILIARIA PURPURA. Scarlet-rash.

MORBUS COXARIUS. Disease of the hip; hip-disease.

MUCOUS MEMBRANE. The membrane which lines the sides of cavities which communicate with the external air, such as that which lines the mouth, stomach, &c.

MUCUS. One of the primary animal fluids; secretion from the nostrils.

MYELITIS. Inflammation of the spinal marrow.

Myopia. Short sight; near-sightedness.

Narcotic. Having the property of inducing sleep.
Nasal. Belonging to the nose.
Nasal Cartilages. The cartilages of the nose.
Nates. The buttocks.
Nephritis. Inflammation of the kidneys.
Neuralgia. Pain in a nerve.
Neuralgia Facialis. Face-ache.
Nodosities. Swellings; nodes, a swelling of the bone or thickening of the periosteum.
Notalgia. Pains in the loins.

Obesity. Corpulency.
Odontalgia. Tooth-ache.
Œdema. Swelling; dropsical swelling; adj. *Œdematous.*
Olfaction. The act of smelling.
Omentum. The caul. The viscus consists of folds of the peritoneum connected together by cellular tissue; it is attached to the stomach, lying on the anterior surface of the bowels.
Ophthalmia. By this term is now usually understood simple inflammation of the *conjunctiva.* (Catarrhal Ophthalmia.)
Ophthalmitis. Inflammation of the entire ball of the eye.
Orchitis. Swelling of the testicle.
Organic Disease. In pathalogy, diseases in which there is derangement or alteration of structure are termed organic.
Os Uteri. The mouth or opening of the womb.
Otalgia. Ear-ache.
Otitis. Inflammation of the ear.

25

Otorrhœa. A discharge, or running from the ear.
Ozæna. An ulcer situated in the nose. See *Ozæna.*

Palpebræ. The eyelids.
Palpitatis Cordis. Palpitation of the heart.
Panaris. Whitlow; panaritium; paronychia.
Pancreas. A gland situated transversely behind the stomach.
Paralysis. Palsy.
Paralysis Paraplegica. Paralysis affecting one half of the body transversely.
Parenchyma. The connecting medium of the substance of the lungs.
Parotitis. Inflammation of the parotid gland; the *mumps.*
Paroxysm. A periodical fit of a disease.
Parturition. The act of bringing forth.
Pathogenetic. The producing or creating of abnormal phenomena.
Pathognomonic. Characteristic of and peculiar to any disease.
Pathology. The investigation of the nature of disease.
Pectoral. Appertaining to the chest.
Pectus. The chest.
Pediculi. Lice.
Pelvis. The basin-shaped cavity below the abdomen, containing the bladder and rectum; and womb in woman.
Percussion. The act of striking upon the chest, &c. in order to elicit sounds to ascertain the state of the subjacent parts.
Perinæum. The space between the anus and the external sexual organs.

PERIOSTEUM. The membrane which envelopes the bones.

PERITONÆUM. The serous membrane which lines the cavity of the abdomen, and envelopes the viscera contained therein.

PERITONITIS. Inflammation of the peritoneum.

PERNIONES. Chilblains.

PERTUSSIS. Hooping-cough.

PETECHIÆ. Spots of a red or purple hue, resembling a flea-bite.

PHAGEDENIC. A term applied to any sores which eat away the parts as it were.

PHARYNX. The throat, or upper part of the gullet.

PHASES. Appearances,or changes exhibited by any body, or by *disease.*

PHLEGMATIC. Vide *Leuco-phlegmatic.*

PHLEGMON. An inflammation of that nature which is otherwise termed *healthy inflammation.*

PHRENITIS. Inflammation of the brain.

PHTHISIS. Pulmonalis). Consumption, abscess of the lungs.

PHYSIOLOGY. The branch of medicine which treats of the functions of the human body.

PLETHORA. An excessive fullness of the blood-vessels.

PLEURA. The serous membrane which lines the cavity of the thorax or chest.

PLEURITIS, or PLEURISY. Inflammation of the pleura.

PLEURODYNIA. Pain or stitch in the side.

PNEUMONIA, PNEUMONITIS, PERIPNEUMONIA. Inflammation of the parenchyma of the lung.

POLYPUS. A tumor most frequently met with in the nose, uterus or vagina.

PORRIGO SCUTULATA. Ringworm of the scalp.

PORRIGO CERVALIS. Milk-crust; milk-scab.

POSTERIOR NARES. The posterior nostrils which open into the fauces.

PRÆCORDIAL REGION. The fore-part of the chest.

PRIMÆ VIÆ. The stomach, and intestinal tube. (The first passages.)

PROGNOSIS. The faculty of predicting what will take place in diseases.

PROLAPSUS ANI. Protrusion of the intestines.

PROPHYLAXIS, plur. *Prophylaxes.* Means or remedies used as preservatives against disease.

PROSOPALGIA. Face-ache.

PRURIGO. Itching of the skin.

PSOAS MUSCLES. The names of two muscles situate in the loins.

PSOITIS. Inflammation of the psoas muscle.

PRESBYOPIA. Obscure sight.

PTYALISM. Salivation.

PUBIS. The pubic or share bone.

PUERPERAL FEVER. Appertaining to childbed.

PURIFORM. Pus-like, resembling pus.

PURULENT. Of the character of pus.

PUS. Matter. A whitish, bland, cream-like fluid, found in abscesses, or on the surface of sores.

PUSTULE.—An elevation of the scarf-skin, containing pus or lymph, and having an inflamed base.

PYROSIS. Haartburn, Waterbrash.

QUINSY. Inflammatory sore throat.

QUOTIDIAN. Intermittent, about

twenty-four hours intervening between the attacks.

RABIES. Madness arising from the bite of a rabid animal, generally applied to the disease showing itself in the brute creation.
RACHITIS. The rickets.
RALE, RATTLES. Sound in the chest, &c. on auscultation, &c.
RANULA. A tumor under the tongue.
RAUCITAS. Hoarseness.
RECTUM. The last of the large intestines, terminating in the anus.
REMITTENT. A term applied to fevers with marked remissions, and generally subsequent exacerbation. The yellow fever of tropical countries.
REPERCUSSED. Driven in.
RESOLUTION. A termination of inflammatory affections without abscess, mortification, &c. The term is also applied to the dispersion of swellings, indurations, &c.
RHEUMATIC OPHTHALMIA. Inflammation of the tunica albuginea, and of the sclerotica.
RIGORS. Coldness, attended more or less by shivering.
ROSE. A term applied to erysipelas, from its color.
RUBEOLA. Measles.

SACRUM. The bone which forms the base of the vertebral column.
SALIVA. The fluid secreted by the salivary glands into the cavity of the mouth.
SATURNINE. Preparations containing lead.
SANGUINEOUS. Consisting of blood.
SANIES. A thin greenish discharge of fetid matter, from sores, fistulæ, &c.
SCABIES. PSORA. Itch.
SCAPULA. The shoulder-blade.
SCIATICA. A rheumatic affection of the hip-joint.
SCIRRHUS. Indolent, glandular tumor, generally preceding cancer in an ulcerated form.
SCLEROTICA. The hard membrane of the eye ; it is situated immediately under the conjunctiva.
SCORBUTUS. Scurvy.
SCROFULOUS OPHTHALMIA. Inflammation of the conjunctiva, with slight redness, but great intolerance of light, and the formation of pimples, or small pustules.
SECRETORY VESSELS, or ORGANS. Parts of the animal economy, which separate or secrete the various fluids of the body.
SEMI-LATERAL. Limited to one side.
SEQUELA, plur. *Sequelæ*.
SINUS. A cavity or depression.
SLOUGH. The part that separates from a foul ulcer.
SOLIDIFICATION. Vide *Hepatization*.
SOMNOLENCE. Disposition to sleep.
SORDES. The viscid, fetid, brownish, red-colored matter discharged from ulcers. The matter which forms round the teeth in fever, &c. has likewise received this appellation.
SPECIFIC. A remedy possessing a peculiar curative action in certain diseases.
SPLENITIS. Inflammation of the spleen.
SPUTA. Expectoration of different kinds.
ST. ANTHONY'S FIRE. Erysipelas.

STERTOROUS. Snoring.

STOMACACE. Canker, or scurvy of the mouth.

STRABISMUS. Squinting.

STRANGURY. Painful discharge of urine.

STERNUM. The breast-bone.

STETHOSCOPE. An instrument to assist the ear in examining the morbid sounds of the chest.

STRICTURE. A constriction of a tube or duct of some part of the body.

STRUMA. SCROFULA. The king's evil; adj. *Strumous.*

STYE. An inflammatory small tumor on the eyelid.

SUB-MAXILLARY. Under the jaw.

SUB-MAXILLARY GLANDS. Glands on the inner side of the lower jaw.

SUB-MUCOUS TISSUE. Placed under the mucous membrane.

SUPPURATION. The morbid action by which pus is deposited, in inflammatory tumor, &c.

SUBSULTUS TENDINUM. Twitchings; sudden starts of the tendons; weak convulsive movements which are often too feeble to elevate the limb itself, but sufficiently strong to be readily seen or felt in the muscles and their tendons. They are most frequently met with in states of extreme debility, particularly in low, nervous, or typhoid fevers, and are, in such cases, usually to be dreaded as progostications of approaching dissolution.

SYNCOPE. Fainting or swooning.

SYNOCHIA. Continued inflammatory fever.

SYNOVIA. A peculiar, unctuous fluid secreted within the joints, which it lubricates, and thereby serves to facilitate their motions.

SYNOVIAL MEMBRANE. The membrane which lines the cavities of the joints, and secretes the synovia.

TABES MESENTERICA. A disease of a set of glands situated in the abdomen.

TÆNIA. Tape-worm.

TARTAR. A concretion encrusting the teeth.

TEMPORAL. Appertaining to the temples.

TENDON. The white and shining extremity of a muscle.

TENESMUS. Painful and constant urging to alvine evacuations, without a discharge.

TETANUS, adj. *Tetanic.* A spasmodic rigidity of the parts affected.

THERAPEUTICS. That branch of medicine which describes the action of the different means employed for the curing of diseases, and of the application of those means.

THORAX. The chest, or that part of the body situated between the neck and the abdomen.

THRUSH. Numerous small white vesicles in the mouth. See Thrush.

TIC DOULOUREUX. Face-ache.

TINEA ANNULARIS. TINEA CAPITIS. Ringworm of the scalp.

TINEA FACIEI. Milk-crust; milk-scab.

TONIC. Medicines which are said to increase the tone of the muscular fibre when debilitated and relaxed.

TONSILS. The oblong, sub-oval glands placed between the arches of the palate.

Tonsillitis. Inflammation of the tonsils.
Topical. Remedies applied to a particular part.
Tourniquet. An instrument for stopping the flow of blood until some more permanent method of arresting the hæmorrhage has been adopted, or until some operation has been performed.
Trachea. The windpipe.
Tracheotomy. An operation by opening the windpipe.
Traumatic. Appertaining to wounds; arising from wounds.
Tremor. Trembling.
Trephine. A surgical instrument used for sawing a circular portion of bone out of the cranium.
Trismus. Lock-jaw.
Trituration. The reduction of a substance to minute division, by means of long-continued rubbing.
Tubercle. A small, round, eruptive swelling, anatomically speaking. In pathology, the name is applied to a peculiar morbid product occurring in various organs or textures, in the form of small, round, isolated masses of a dull whitish yellow, or yellowish gray colour, opaque, unorganized, and varying in shape and consistence according to their stage of development and the texture of part in which they are engendered.
Tumefaction. Swelling.
Tumefied. Swollen.
Tumid. Vide *Tumefied.*
Tussis Convulsiva. Hooping-cough.
Typhoid. Applied to diseases of a low character.

Umbilical Cord. The navel string.
Umbilicus. The navel.
Urethra. The urinary canal.
Urticaria. Nettle-rash.
Uterus. The womb.

Varicella. Pimples, quickly forming pustules, seldom passing into suppuration, but bursting at the point and drying into scabs. Chicken-pock.
Variola. Smallpox.
Variola Spuria. (*Varicella.*) Chicken-pock.
Varix, plur. *Varices.* Swelling or enlargement of the veins.
Venesection. The abstraction of blood by opening a vein.
Vesiccations. An eruptive elevation of the cuticle, containing a clear serous fluid.
Vertigo. Giddiness, with a sensation as if falling.
Vesicle. A small bladder-like eruption; an elevation of the cuticle containing a transparent watery fluid.
Vicarious. Acting as a substitute.
Virus. Contagion or poison.
Viscid. Glutinous and gelatinous.
Viscus, plur. *Viscera.* Any organ of the system. A bowl.
Vomica. An abscess of the lungs.

Whitlow. A collection of pus in the finger.

Zona. Shingles.

INDEX.

www.ingramcontent.com/pod-product-compliance
Lightning Source LLC
LaVergne TN
LVHW021105110826
845150LV00001B/177

9781425565251